Visual Basic .NET

Professional Projects

Visual
Basic .NET
Professional Projects

Kuljit Kaur
Pooja Bembey

WITH

NIIT

Premier
Press

ISBN: 1-931841-29-2

Library of Congress Catalog Card Number: 2001097575

Printed in the United States of America

02 03 04 05 06 RI 10 9 8 7 6 5 4 3 2 1

Publisher:
Stacy L. Hiquet

Marketing Manager:
Heather Buzzingham

Managing Editor:
Sandy Doell

Editorial Assistant:
Margaret Bauer

Book Production Services:
Argosy

Cover Design:
Mike Tanamachi

About NIIT

NIIT is a global IT solutions corporation with a presence in 38 countries. With its unique business model and technology-creation capabilities, NIIT delivers software and learning solutions to more than 1,000 clients across the world.

The success of NIIT's training solutions lies in its unique approach to education. NIIT's Knowledge Solutions Business conceives, researches, and develops all of its course material. A rigorous instructional design methodology is followed to create engaging and compelling course content.

NIIT trains over 200,000 executives and learners each year in information technology areas using stand-up training, video-aided instruction, computer-based training (CBT), and Internet-based training (IBT). NIIT has been featured in the Guinness Book of World Records for the largest number of learners trained in one year!

NIIT has developed over 10,000 hours of instructor-led training (ILT) and over 3,000 hours of Internet-based training and computer-based training. IDC ranked NIIT among the Top 15 IT training providers globally for the year 2000. Through the innovative use of training methods and its commitment to research and development, NIIT has been in the forefront of computer education and training for the past 20 years.

Quality has been the prime focus at NIIT. Most of the processes are ISO-9001 certified. It was the 12th company in the world to be assessed at Level 5 of SEI-CMM. NIIT's Content (Learning Material) Development facility is the first in the world to be assessed at this highest maturity level. NIIT has strategic partnerships with companies such as Computer Associates, IBM, Microsoft, Oracle, and Sun Microsystems.

About the Authors

Kuljit Kaur is an MCSD who has worked with NIIT since 1998 as a technical trainer, technical writer, instructional designer, and an ID reviewer. She has two years of experience in teaching various career programs at NIIT's Career Education Group division. Kuljit has taught various technical subject areas, including Networking Essentials, SQL Server 6.5, Microsoft Windows NT Server 4.0, Windows 95, Windows 98, Microsoft Office 97 and 2000, Microsoft Visual Basic 6.0, Microsoft Visual C++ 4.0, Windows 32 API programming, HTML, Microsoft Visual Java, Unix, C, and C++. She has also set up and managed labs for students, and in addition has administered Novell 3.11 and UNIX (SCO)-based networks.

Kuljit has worked extensively as an instructional designer and as a developer with NIIT's Knowledge Solutions Business division to develop and review instructor-led training (ILT) products for various software and technologies. These include Microsoft Office 2000, Microsoft Office XP, Macromedia Flash 5, Macromedia Dreamweaver 3.0 and 4.0, Authorware, Macromedia Fireworks 3 and 4, Web Site Design, Netscape Communicator 6, and VBA. She has worked on projects for various U.S.-based clients on these technologies.

Pooja Bembey works as an instructional designer in the Knowledge Solutions Business (KSB) division of NIIT. In this position, Pooja designs, develops, tests, and implements instructor-led, Web-based, and classroom-based training material. Pooja's responsibilities include training development executives, project management, instructional review, technical review, and ensuring compliance to ISO and SEICMM standards.

Contents at a Glance

Contents

Introduction

Goal of the Book

This book provides a hands-on approach to learning Visual Basic.NET, one of the most popular and easy-to-learn language provided by the .NET framework. The book is aimed at readers with programming knowledge of earlier versions of Visual Basic. These readers are assumed to be experienced application developers who have knowledge of developing applications using any of the earlier versions of Visual Basic.

The book starts with a few overview chapters that cover the key concepts of Visual Basic.NET. These chapters act as an information store for readers and provide a concrete idea about the concepts. After that follows a chapter on how to migrate existing Visual Basic applications to the .NET platform. A major part of the book revolves around professional projects that are based on real-life situations. They follow a simple-to-complex approach to cover specific subject areas and to guide the readers in implementing their learning in practical scenarios. The projects range from a simple project to create a Windows application using ADO.NET as the data access model to a complex project to create a Web application using a Web service. In addition, there are projects that will introduce how to create a Word-to-XML converter application and how to create a mobile Web application. These projects help readers accomplish their goals by understanding the practical and real-life application of Visual Basic.NET.

In addition to the overview chapters and the professional projects, this book also includes another section, the appendixes. This section acts as a quick reference to some of the additional concepts that will help readers learn know more about .NET framework.

How to Use this Book

This book has been organized to facilitate a better grasp of content covered in the book. The various conventions used in the book are as follows:

- ◆ **Analysis.** This book incorporates an analysis of code, explaining line by line what it did and why.
- ◆ **Tips.** Tips have been used to provide special advice or unusual shortcuts with the product.

◆ **Notes.** Notes give additional information that might be of interest to the reader but is not essential to performing the task at hand.

◆ **Cautions.** Cautions are used to warn users of possible disastrous results if they perform a task incorrectly.

◆ **New-term definitions.** All new terms have been italicized and then defined as a part of the text.

PART I

Introducing
Visual Basic .NET

Chapter 1

.NET Overview

The .NET framework is the latest platform from Microsoft, and it provides a multilanguage environment that enables you to develop, deploy, and run Web-based applications and services. It provides a new level of interoperability that enables you to reuse components created in other languages. It also provides new and advanced features such as garbage collection and enhanced security. This chapter examines the components of the .NET framework.

Components of the .NET Framework

The .NET framework is composed of classes and services that form a layer between applications and the operating system. It consists of the following two main components:

- ◆ Common language runtime (CLR)
- ◆ .NET framework class library

The next sections look at these two components in detail.

Common Language Runtime

The CLR is the runtime environment of the .NET framework. CLR provides a common set of services—such as exception handling, security, and debugging—to languages that are CLR compatible. All programming languages in Visual Studio.NET, such as Visual Basic.NET and Visual C#.NET, support the CLR.

During the execution of a program, the CLR controls the interaction of code with the operating system. Code that is executed by the CLR is known as *managed code*. In contrast, code that is not executed by the CLR is known as *unmanaged code*. Managed code "cooperates" with the CLR by providing metadata to the CLR. The CLR, in turn, provides services, such as garbage collection and memory management, to the code. Unlike managed code, unmanaged code can bypass the .NET Framework API and make direct calls to the operating system.

During compilation, the CLR converts code into Microsoft Intermediate Language (MSIL). *MSIL* is a set of instructions that are CPU independent. MSIL includes instructions for loading, storing, initializing, and calling methods. It also contains instructions about arithmetic and logical operations and exception handling. When any code is compiled in addition to MSIL, metadata is created and stored with the compiled code. Metadata contains information about the members, types, and references in the code. The CLR uses metadata to locate and load classes, generate native code, provide security, and execute code. Thus, after code is compiled, the compiled file contains MSIL and metadata. The compiled file containing MSIL and metadata is known as a *portable executable* (PE) file. Before code is executed, however, the MSIL in the PE file is converted to *native code*. The just-in-time (JIT) compiler of the CLR uses the metadata and converts MSIL into native code. Unlike MSIL, native code is CPU dependent. Therefore, the CLR provides various JIT compilers, and each works on a different architecture. This implies that, depending on the JIT compiler used to compile MSIL, the same MSIL can be executed on different architectures.

While managing code, the CLR also performs various tasks such as managing memory, security, and threads and verifying and compiling code. For example, when an application is running, the CLR allocates memory, manages threads and processes, and enforces the security policy.

The CLR defines the *common type system* (CTS), which is a standard type system used by all languages that support the CLR. The CTS lists the types supported by the CLR, and they include the following:

- Classes
- Interfaces
- Value types
- Delegates

The use of the CTS ensures that data types, such as Integer, String, and Long, have the same implementation across CLR-compatible languages. This implies that you can pass a variable from a class created in a CLR-compatible language to another class regardless of the programming language used because data types have the same implementation across languages.

Now that you've looked at the features of the CLR, you'll look at the features of the .NET framework class library.

.NET Framework Class Library

The .NET framework class library includes multiple reusable, object-oriented, and extensible classes. It is integrated with the CLR and is common to all programming languages in Visual Studio.NET.

The .NET framework class library provides a common set of classes across programming languages. While developing applications, you can use these classes to create new classes. You can use the classes in the .NET framework class library to develop applications and implement cross-language inheritance.

The classes in the .NET framework class library are organized hierarchically. In the .NET framework class library, the System namespace is at the top of the hierarchy and contains all other classes. On a broad level, the System namespace contains classes that enable you to perform the following tasks:

◆ Converting data types

◆ Manipulating parameters

◆ Invoking local and remote programs

◆ Managing the application environment

You will learn more about using namespaces later in this chapter. Table 1-1 describes some of the namespaces in the .NET framework class library.

Table 1-1 Namespaces in the .NET Framework Class Library

Namespace	Contains Classes That Enable You To
Microsoft.Csharp	Compile and generate code in Visual C#.NET
Microsoft.Jscript	Compile and generate code in JScript
Microsoft.VisualBasic	Compile and generate code in Visual Basic.NET
Microsoft.Win32	Manipulate the system registry and manage operating system events
System	Manage exceptions and define data types, events and event handlers, interfaces, and attributes

The System namespace contains various other namespaces, such as System.Xml, System.Web, System.Text, and System.Security.

Now that you know the basic structure of the .NET framework, you will take a look at its features.

.NET Framework Features

The .NET framework provides the basic functionality that can be used across languages. For example, the .NET framework provides Windows forms and Web forms. You can use Windows forms to create Windows applications in any .NET language. Similarly, using any language that supports the .NET framework, you can access Web forms and create Web applications.

The .NET framework provides an integrated debugger. You can use the integrated debugger to debug the code written for the .NET framework regardless of the programming language used to write the code. For example, you can use the debugger to debug an application that was written in Visual Basic.NET and that includes components created in Visual C#.NET. In addition, in the .NET framework, you can also debug a program while it is running. To do so, you attach the debugger to the running program. The debugger also enables you to perform remote debugging.

The .NET framework introduces the concept of assemblies. An *assembly* is a collection of one or more classes that can be used by multiple applications. You can use assemblies to build applications. The applications you create are made up of one or more assemblies. Assemblies, which are self-describing components, simplify the deployment of applications. In the .NET framework, you don't need to register assemblies in the system registry. You can store assemblies in a directory on your computer. In addition, assemblies enable you to solve version-control problems. Assemblies provide an infrastructure that enables you to enforce versioning rules. As mentioned earlier, you don't need to register assemblies. However, if multiple applications need to access an assembly, you must add the assembly to the global assembly cache (GAC). The GAC stores the assemblies that are shared among applications running on a computer. You can install and remove assemblies from the GAC. You can use the Global Assembly Cache tool to install and remove assemblies. You can also view the contents of an assembly by using the Global Assembly Cache tool.

The .NET framework also introduces a new security mechanism for applications by providing code-access security (CAS) and role-based security. CAS enables you to specify permissions for code. CAS settings determine the actions that the code can or cannot perform. By specifying CAS, you ensure that the code is not misused. Role-based security ensures that unauthorized users cannot access applications. Using role-based security, you can specify permissions for a user, also known as the *principal*. The .NET framework validates the individual and group permissions of the principal. Role-based security enables you to specify generic, Windows, and custom principals for applications. In addition, you can define new principals for an application by using role-based security. Although you can use role-based security on both the client side and the server side, it is most suitable for applications in which processing occurs on the server side, such as ASP.NET Web applications.

Now that you've looked at the .NET framework and its features, you will look at the features of Visual Studio.NET.

Introduction to Visual Studio .NET

Visual Studio.NET, which is the latest version of Visual Studio, is based on the .NET framework. Visual Studio.NET provides languages and tools that enable you to build Web-based, desktop, and mobile applications. You can also create Web services in Visual Studio.NET.

Visual Studio.NET includes the following programming languages:

- ◆ Visual Basic.NET
- ◆ Visual C++.NET
- ◆ Visual C#.NET

It also provides additional technologies, such as ASP.NET, that enable you to develop and deploy applications. In addition, Visual Studio.NET includes the MSDN library that contains documentation on various development tools and applications.

Using the integrated development environment (IDE) of Visual Studio.NET, you can create applications in the various .NET languages. The IDE of Visual Studio.NET enables you to share tools and create applications in multiple languages.

Visual Studio.NET includes various enhancements over earlier versions of Visual Studio. The following sections describe the enhancements in Visual Studio.NET.

Visual Basic .NET

Visual Basic.NET is the latest version of Visual Basic, and it includes many new features. Unlike Visual Basic 6.0, Visual Basic.NET is an object-oriented language. To elaborate, Visual Basic.NET supports the abstraction, encapsulation, inheritance, and polymorphism features. You will learn more about these features in Chapter 2. The earlier versions of Visual Basic, versions 4 through 6, supported interfaces but not implementation inheritance. Visual Basic.NET supports implementation inheritance as well as interfaces. You will learn about implementation inheritance later in this chapter. Another new feature is overloading. You will learn about overloading in the Chapter 7, "Procedures and Functions." In addition, Visual Basic.NET supports multithreading, which enables you to create multithreaded and scalable applications. Visual Basic.NET is also compliant with the common language specification (CLS) and supports structured exception handling.

Visual C# .NET

Visual Studio.NET provides a new language, Visual C#.NET, which is an object-oriented language based on the C and C++ languages. Using Visual C#.NET, you can create applications for the .NET framework. As mentioned earlier, Visual C#.NET supports the CLR, therefore, any code written in Visual C#.NET is managed code. The IDE provides various templates, designers, and wizards to help you create applications in Visual C#.NET.

Visual C++ .NET

Visual C++.NET is an enhanced version of Visual C++. Visual C++.NET includes features such as support for managed extensions and attributes.

THE COMMON LANGUAGE SPECIFICATION (CLS)

The CLS is a set of rules and constructs that are supported by the CLR. Visual Basic.NET is a CLS-compliant language. Any objects, classes, or components that you create in Visual Basic.NET can be used in any other CLS-compliant language. In addition, you can use objects, classes, and components created in other CLS-compliant languages in Visual Basic.NET. The use of the CLS ensures complete interoperability among applications, regardless of the language used to create the application. Therefore, while working in Visual Basic.NET, you can derive a class based on a class written in Visual C#.NET, and the data types and variables of the derived class will be compatible with those of the base class.

Managed extensions include a set of language extensions for C++ to enable you to create applications for the .NET framework. Using managed extensions, you can easily convert existing components to components that are compatible with the .NET framework. Therefore, with the help of managed extensions, you can reuse existing code and thus save both time and effort. In addition, by using managed extensions, you can combine both unmanaged and managed C++ code in an application.

Visual C++.NET also supports attributes, which enable you to extend the functionality of the language and to simplify the creation of COM components. You can apply attributes to classes, data members, or member functions.

Web Forms

Visual Studio.NET introduces Web forms, which are based on Microsoft ASP.NET technology. Web forms are used to create Web pages. In Visual Studio.NET, you can drag controls to the designer and then add code to create Web pages. A Web forms page can open in any Web browser. The controls in a Web forms page are based on server-side logic.

Windows Forms

Windows forms provide a platform for developing Windows applications based on the .NET framework. Windows forms include a set of object-oriented and extensible classes that enable you to implement visual inheritance. *Visual inheritance* enables you to inherit a form from an existing form. Using these classes, you can develop Windows applications by creating a form based on an existing form. When you create forms based on existing forms, you can reuse code and thus enhance productivity. Typically, Windows forms are used to create user interfaces for a multitier application.

EXTENSIBLE MARKUP LANGUAGE (XML)

XML is a markup language based on Standard Generalized Markup Language (SGML), which is a standard for all markup languages. XML is a subset of SGML. XML enables you to define the structure of data by using markup tags. In addition, you can also define new tags using XML.

The World Wide Web Consortium (W3C) has defined XML standards to ensure that structured data is uniform and independent of applications.

Web Services

Web services are applications that exchange data by using eXtensible Markup Language (XML). Web services can also receive requests over HTTP. Web services are not a part of any specific component technology. Therefore, any language or operating system can use Web Services. You can use Visual Basic.NET, Visual C#.NET, or ATL Server to create Web services.

XML Support

Visual Studio.NET includes support for XML. It also provides XML Designer, which enables you to create and edit XML documents and create XML schemas.

Introduction to Visual Basic .NET

Visual Basic.NET is modeled on the .NET framework. Therefore, along with the features of earlier versions of Visual Basic, Visual Basic.NET also inherits various features of the .NET framework. In this section, you will look at some of the new features in Visual Basic.NET that were unavailable in earlier versions of Visual Basic.

As previously mentioned, Visual Basic.NET supports *implementation inheritance* in contrast to the earlier versions of Visual Basic that supported *interface inheritance*. In other words, with earlier versions of Visual Basic, you can only implement interfaces. When you implement an interface in Visual Basic 6.0, you need to implement all the methods of the interface. Additionally, you need to rewrite the code each time you implement the interface. On the other hand, Visual Basic.NET supports implementation inheritance. This implies that, while creating applications in Visual Basic.NET, you can derive a class from another class, known as the base class. The derived class inherits all the methods and properties of the base class. In the derived class, you can either use the existing code of the base class or override the existing code. Therefore, with the help of implementation inheritance, code can be reused. Although a class in Visual Basic.NET can implement multiple interfaces, it can inherit from only one class.

Visual Basic.NET provides constructors and destructors. *Constructors* are used to initialize objects. In contrast, *destructors* are used to release the memory and resources used by destroyed objects. In Visual Basic.NET, the Sub New procedure replaces the Class_Initialize event. Unlike the Class_Initialize event available in earlier versions of Visual Basic, the Sub New procedure is executed when an object of the class is created. In addition, you cannot call the Sub New procedure. The Sub New procedure is the first procedure to be executed in a class. In Visual Basic.NET, the Sub Finalize procedure is available instead of the Class_Terminate event. The Sub Finalize procedure is used to complete the tasks that must be performed when an object is destroyed. The Sub Finalize procedure is called automatically when an object is destroyed.

Garbage collection is another new feature in Visual Basic.NET. The .NET framework monitors allocated resources such as objects and variables. In addition, the .NET framework automatically releases memory for reuse by destroying objects that are no longer in use. In Visual Basic 6.0, if you set an object to `Nothing`, the object is destroyed. In contrast, when an object is set to `Nothing` in Visual Basic.NET, it still occupies memory and uses other resources. However, the object is marked for garbage collection. Similarly, when an object is not referenced for a long period of time, it is marked for garbage collection. In Visual Basic.NET, the garbage collector checks for the objects that are not currently in use by applications. When the garbage collector comes across an object that is marked for garbage collection, it releases the memory occupied by the object. The garbage collector automatically handles the memory allocated to managed resources. However, you need to manage the memory allocated to unmanaged resources.

In the .NET framework, you can use the `GC` class, the `Sub Finalize` procedure, and the `IDisposable` interface to perform garbage collection operations for unmanaged resources. The `GC` class is present in the `System` namespace. It provides various methods that enable you to control the system garbage collector. The `Sub Finalize` procedure, which is a member of the `Object` class, acts as the destructor in the .NET framework. You can override the `Sub Finalize` procedure in your applications. However, the `Sub Finalize` procedure is not executed when your application is executed. The `GC` class calls the `Sub Finalize` procedure to release memory occupied by a destroyed object. Thus, implementing the `Sub Finalize` procedure is an implicit way of managing resources. However, the .NET framework also provides an explicit way of managing resources in the form of the `IDisposable` interface. The `IDisposable` interface includes the `Dispose` method. After implementing the `IDisposable` interface, you can override the `Dispose` method in your applications. In the `Dispose` method, you can release resources and close database connections.

Unlike earlier versions of Visual Basic, Visual Basic.NET supports overloading. *Overloading* enables you to define multiple procedures with the same name, where each procedure has a different set of arguments. In addition to procedures, you can also use overloading for constructors and properties in a class. You need to use the `Overloads` keyword for overloading procedures. Consider a scenario in which you need to create a procedure that displays the address of an employee. You should be able to view the address of the employee based on either the employee name or the employee code. In such a situation, you can use an overloaded procedure. You will create two procedures. Each procedure will have the same name but different arguments. The first procedure will take the employee name as the argument, and the second takes the employee code as the argument.

As mentioned earlier in this chapter, the .NET framework class library is organized into namespaces. A namespace is a collection of classes. Namespaces are used to logically group classes within an assembly. These namespaces are available in all the .NET languages, including Visual Basic.NET.

In Visual Basic.NET, you must use the `Imports` statement to access the classes in namespaces. For example, to use the button control defined in the `System.Windows.Forms` namespace, you must include the following statement at the beginning of your program:

```
Imports System.Windows.Forms
```

After adding the `Imports` statement, you can use the following code to create a new button:

```
Dim MyButton as Button
```

If you do not include the `Imports` statement in the program, however, you would need to use the full reference path of the class to create a button. If you didn't include the `Imports` statement, you would use the following code to create a button:

```
Dim MyButton as System.Windows.Forms.Button
```

In addition to using the namespaces available in Visual Basic.NET, you can also create your own namespaces. The next chapter will describe how to create a namespace.

As previously mentioned, Visual Basic.NET supports multithreading. An application that supports multithreading can handle multiple tasks simultaneously. You can use multithreading to decrease the time taken by an application to respond to user interaction. To do this, you must ensure that a separate thread in the application handles user interaction.

Visual Basic.NET supports structured exception handling, which enables you to detect and remove errors at runtime. In Visual Basic.NET, you need to use `Try…Catch…Finally` statements to create exception handlers. Using `Try…Catch…Finally` statements, you can create robust and effective exception handlers to improve the performance of your application. You will learn more about `Try…Catch…Finally` statements in Chapter 11, "Working with ADO.NET."

Now that you've looked at the new features of Visual Basic.NET, the next section explains the differences between Visual Basic 6.0 and Visual Basic.NET.

Differences Between Visual Basic 6.0 and Visual Basic .NET

Although there are numerous differences between Visual Basic 6.0 and Visual Basic.NET, Table 1-2 briefly describes some of them.

Table 1-2 Differences Between Visual Basic 6.0 and Visual Basic.NET

Feature	Visual Basic 6.0	Visual Basic.NET
Line control	Available	Not available
OLE container control	Available	Not available
Shape controls	Available	Not available
Dynamic data exchange (DDE) support	Available	Not available
Data access objects (DAO) data binding	Supported	Not supported
Remote data objects (RDO) data binding	Supported	Not supported
Option base statement	Available	Not available
Fixed-length strings	Supported	Not supported
Fixed-size arrays	Supported	Not supported
Use of the `ReDim` statement	Array declaration	Array resizing
Universal data type	`Variant`	`Object`
Currency data type	Supported	Not supported
Data type to store date values	`Double`	`DateTime`
`DefType` statements	Supported	Not supported
`Eqv` operator	Supported	Not supported
`Imp` operator	Supported	Not supported

Feature	Visual Basic 6.0	Visual Basic.NET
Default properties for objects	Supported	Not supported
Declaring structures	`Type….End Type`	`Structure….End Structure`
Scope of a variable declared in a block	Procedure scope	Block scope of code within a procedure
Values for optional arguments	Not required	Required
Declaring procedures as static	Supported	Not supported
`GoSub` statement	Available	Not available
Default mechanism for passing arguments	`ByRef`	`ByVal`
Syntax of `While` loop	`While….Wend`	`While….End While`
`Null` keyword	Supported	Not supported
`Empty` keyword	Supported	Not supported
`IsEmpty` function	Supported	Not supported
`Option Private Module` statement	Supported	Not supported
`Class_Initialize` event	Supported	Not supported
`Class_Terminate` event	Supported	Not supported

In addition to the differences mentioned above, Visual Basic.NET does not support various applications supported by Visual Basic 6.0. For example, Visual Basic.NET does not support ActiveX documents. Additionally, Visual Basic.NET does not support DHTML applications and Web classes that Visual Basic 6.0 supports. Visual Basic.NET is also incompatible with Windows common controls and the data-bound grid controls available in Visual Basic 6.0.

There are various changes related to syntax in Visual Basic.NET. The syntax differences related to variables, operators, arrays, collections, procedures, functions, and various constructs are discussed in the remaining chapters of this part of the book.

Summary

In this chapter, you learned that the .NET framework provides a multilanguage environment that enables you to develop, deploy, and run Web-based applications and services. You also learned that the CLR is a runtime environment in Visual Basic.NET. In addition, you learned that the .NET framework class library includes multiple reusable, object-oriented, and extensible classes. You also looked at the features of the .NET framework. You learned about the enhancements and new features in Visual Studio.NET and, in particular, Visual Basic.NET. Finally, you learned about the differences between Visual Basic 6.0 and Visual Basic.NET.

Chapter 2

Object-Oriented
Features in Visual
Basic .NET

In Chapter 1, ".NET Overview," you looked at the differences between Visual Basic 6.0 and Visual Basic.NET. This chapter describes the object-oriented features of Visual Basic.NET. Unlike earlier versions of Visual Basic, Visual Basic.NET supports all the features of an object-oriented programming language.

First you will take a look at the various features of an object-oriented programming language, and then you will learn how Visual Basic.NET implements these features.

Object-Oriented Features

Objects serve as the building blocks in an object-oriented programming language. An object has a unique identity and displays unique behavior. An example of an object from the world around us is a car, a ball, or a clock. In a programming language, an *object* is defined as an instance of a class. All applications created in an object-oriented programming language are made up of objects.

A programming language qualifies as an object-oriented programming language if it supports the following features:

- Abstraction
- Encapsulation
- Inheritance
- Polymorphism

The following sections look at these features in detail.

Abstraction

When buying a refrigerator, you are interested in its size, durability, and features. As a consumer, you are not interested in the machinery within the refrigerator. You will focus only on the essential aspects of the refrigerator and will ignore the nonessential aspects. This is known as *abstraction*. In a programming language, abstraction enables you to focus on the essential aspects of an object and ignore the nonessential aspects.

Like other object-oriented programming languages, Visual Basic.NET also provides abstraction through classes and objects. A *class* defines the attributes and behaviors shared by similar objects. An *object* is an instance of a class. Each object has a set of characteristics or attributes that are the *properties* of the object. In addition, each object can perform a set of actions. These actions are known as *methods*. Visual Basic.NET enables you to specify the properties and methods for objects while creating classes. As a developer, you use abstraction to reduce the complexity of an object by exposing only the essential properties and methods of the object. In addition, abstraction enables you to generalize an object as a data type. You can generalize objects as data types by declaring classes.

You will learn about creating classes, properties, and methods later in this chapter.

Encapsulation

Encapsulation is also known as information hiding. It refers to hiding the nonessential details of an object. For example, when you switch on a refrigerator, the refrigerator starts functioning. You cannot view the internal processes of the refrigerator. In other words, the functioning of the refrigerator is hidden or encapsulated.

Encapsulation is a method of implementing abstraction. As discussed in the preceding section, abstraction refers to concentrating on the essential details of an object and ignoring the nonessential ones. This is achieved by encapsulation.

Encapsulation hides the internal implementation of the classes from the user. In other words, encapsulation means displaying only the properties and methods of an object. It enables developers to hide the complexity of an object and use different implementations of the same object.

Inheritance

As discussed in Chapter 1, earlier versions of Visual Basic supported interface inheritance but not implementation inheritance. However, Visual Basic.NET supports both.

Implementation inheritance means deriving a class from an existing class. The derived class is known as the *subclass*, and the class from which it is derived is known as the *base class*.

> **NOTE**
>
> All classes that you create in Visual Basic.NET are derived from the Object class, which is a part of the System namespace.

The subclass inherits the properties and methods of the base class. In addition, you can add methods and properties to the subclass to extend the functionality of the base class. In the derived class, you can also override the methods of the base class. You will learn more about overriding methods later in this chapter.

Inheritance enables you to create hierarchies of objects. For example, consider a class named animals. The mammals class is derived from the animals class, and the cats class is derived from the mammals class. Therefore, the hierarchy of the classes in this case is as shown in Figure 2-1.

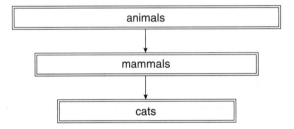

FIGURE 2-1 *A sample hierarchy of classes*

In the preceding example, the cats class inherits the properties and methods of the mammals class, which in turn inherits all the properties and methods of the animals class. Therefore, the cats class inherits the properties and methods of both the mammals class and the animals class.

By default, all the classes you create in Visual Basic.NET can be inherited. Inheritance enables you to reuse code and create complex objects from simpler ones. To elaborate, after creating a class in Visual Basic.NET, you can use it as a base class to create derived classes.

Visual Basic.NET provides multiple keywords that enable you to implement inheritance. You will learn about these keywords later in this chapter.

Polymorphism

Polymorphism refers to the capability of an object to exist in different forms. To understand this better, go back to the refrigerator example.

To purchase a refrigerator, you either contact a dealer or call the manufacturing company. When you contact a dealer, the dealer takes the order and then contacts the company. When you contact the company, however, the company contacts the dealers in your region and makes arrangements to deliver the refrigerator. In this case, the dealer and the company are two different classes. Each class, the dealer and the company, responds differently to the same order. This is known as polymorphism in object-oriented programming.

Polymorphism enables you to use the same method to perform different tasks. To elaborate, you can change the implementation of a base class method in the derived classes. Therefore, when you derive two classes from a base class, you can create a method with the same name in both classes. However, the method in each derived class performs different tasks. You select the method to be invoked based on the task you need to perform. The implementation of polymorphism in Visual Basic.NET is explained later in this chapter.

You've now learned about abstraction, encapsulation, inheritance, and polymorphism. Next, you need to understand the implementation of each of these in Visual Basic.NET.

Implementation of Object-Oriented Features in Visual Basic .NET

As previously discussed, abstraction is implemented by using classes. A class defines the attributes and behaviors shared by similar objects.

To create a class in earlier versions of Visual Basic, you had to define the class in a file with a .CLS extension. In contrast, Visual Basic.NET enables you to define classes within code. Take a look at the following syntax for creating a class:

```
[AccessModifier][Keyword] Class ClassName [Implements InterfaceName]


'Declare properties and methods
End Class
```

In the preceding syntax:

◆ `AccessModifier` defines the accessibility of the class, which can be `Pub-lic`, `Private`, `Protected`, `Friend`, or `Protected Friend`. Table 2-1 explains the access modifiers available in Visual Basic.NET.

◆ `Keyword` specifies whether derived classes can inherit the class. This can either be `NotInheritable` or `MustInherit`.

◆ `Class` marks the beginning of a class.

◆ `ClassName` is the name of the class.

◆ `Implements` specifies that the class implements interfaces.

◆ `InterfaceName` represents the names of interfaces. A class can implement one or more interfaces.

◆ `End Class` marks the end of the declaration of a class.

Within the `Class` and `End Class` statements, you declare the variables, properties, events, and methods of a class.

> **NOTE**
>
> An *event* is a message sent by an object to the operating system to indicate an action to which a program might need to respond. Typically, events are generated due to user interactions such as button clicks and mouse movements.

You will learn more about creating properties and methods later in this chapter.

Consider the following example that declares the `Communication` class:

```
Public Class Communication

'Declare properties and methods
End Class
```

In the preceding example, note that the `Public` access modifier is used before the `Class` statement. When declaring classes in Visual Basic.NET, you can use various access modifiers. Table 2-1 describes the access modifiers available in Visual Basic.NET.

Table 2-1 Access Modifiers Available in Visual Basic.NET

Access Modifier	Used With	Specifies That
Public	A module, class, or structure	Elements are accessible from the same project, from other projects, or from assemblies built from the project.
Private	A module, class, or structure	Elements are accessible from the same module, class, or structure.
Protected	Classes and class members	Elements are accessible within the same class or from a derived class.
Friend	A module, class, or structure	Elements are accessible within the same project but not from outside the project.
Protected Friend	Classes and class members	Elements are accessible within the same project and from derived classes.

As mentioned in the preceding table, in addition to classes, you can use access modifiers when declaring modules and structures. A *module* is a loadable unit in which you can define classes, properties, and methods. A module is always included in an assembly. A *structure* is used to create a user-defined data type. You declare variables and methods in a structure. In addition, you use access modifiers when defining class members. Class members include the procedures, fields, and methods defined in a class.

You can use access modifiers to implement abstraction and encapsulation. For example, to enable other classes to access the properties and methods defined in a class, you need to use the Public access modifier when declaring the properties and methods. Similarly, to ensure that other classes *cannot* access the members defined in a class, you use the Private access modifier. Therefore, access modifiers enable you to implement abstraction and encapsulation.

As previously discussed, Visual Basic.NET also supports inheritance. Inheritance enables you to create multiple derived classes from a base class. You can use the Inherits statement to derive a class from another class. The syntax for using the Inherits statement is as follows:

```
Public Class ThisClass
        Inherits OtherClass
        'Property and method declarations
```

```
        'Other code
End Class
```

In the preceding example, `ThisClass` is the derived class, and `OtherClass` is the base class. Therefore, `ThisClass` inherits all the properties and methods of `Other-Class`. Additionally, you can extend the functionality of the `OtherClass` class in `ThisClass` by overriding the methods of `OtherClass`.

In addition to the `Inherits` statement, Visual Basic.NET provides various other keywords that enable you to implement inheritance. Table 2-2 describes the keywords used to implement inheritance in Visual Basic.NET.

Table 2-2 Keywords Used to Implement Inheritance

Keyword	Used With	Used To
Inherits	Classes	Inherit all nonprivate members of the specified class.
MustInherit	Classes	Specify that the class can be used only as a base class.
NotInheritable	Classes	Specify that the class cannot be used as a base class.
Overridable	Procedures	Specify that the procedure can be overridden in the derived classes.
NotOverridable	Procedures	Indicate that the procedure cannot be overridden in the derived classes.
MustOverride	Procedures	Specify that the procedure must be overridden in all the derived classes.
Overrides	Procedures	Indicate that the procedure overrides a procedure of the base class.
MyBase	Code	Invoke code written in the base class from the derived class.
MyClass	Code	Invoke code written in a class from within the class.
Protected	Procedures, fields	Specify that the procedures and fields can be accessed within the class in which they are created and also from the derived classes.

In addition to classes, you can use these keywords while declaring procedures and fields. A *procedure* is a set of statements that performs a specific task. A *field* is a variable declared in a class that is accessible from other classes. You will learn more about procedures and fields later in this chapter.

Next you will look at an example to understand inheritance in Visual Basic.NET.

```
Public MustInherit Class Communication
                Public MustOverride Function Send() As Boolean
End Class


Public Class Email
                Inherits Communication
                Overrides Function Send() As Boolean


'Add code specific to this class here
                                Send =True
                End Function
End Class


Public Class Fax
                Inherits Communication
                Overrides Function Send() As Boolean


'Add code specific to this class here
                                Send =True
                End Function
End Class
```

In the preceding example, the `Email` and `Fax` classes are derived from the `Communication` base class. The `Communication` class provides basic functionality to the derived classes. Notice that the `Email` and `Fax` classes override the `Send` method of the `Communication` class to extend the functionality of the `Communication` class.

As previously discussed, Visual Basic.NET also supports polymorphism. In Visual Basic.NET, polymorphism enables you to vary the implementation of an `Overridable` method. Alternatively, the implementation of a `NotOverridable` method is the same whether you invoke it from the class in which it was declared or from a derived class. To elaborate, when you override a method of a base class, it can perform different actions based on the object that invokes the method. The following code explains polymorphism by using the `Communication` class example discussed earlier:

```
Public Module MyMod
    Public MustInherit Class Communication
        Public Sub New()
            MyBase.New()
            MsgBox("Constructor of Communication class", MsgBoxStyle.OKOnly)
        End Sub
        Public MustOverride Function Send() As Boolean

'Code specific to the Communication class
    End Class


Public Class Email
        Inherits Communication
        Public Sub New()
            MyBase.New()
            MsgBox("Constructor of Email class", MsgBoxStyle.OKOnly)
        End Sub
        Overrides Function Send() As Boolean
            MsgBox("Send function of Email class", MsgBoxStyle.OKOnly)

'Code specific to the Email class
            Send = True
        End Function
    End Class


Public Class Fax
        Inherits Communication
        Public Sub New()
            MyBase.New()
            MsgBox("Constructor of Fax class", MsgBoxStyle.OKOnly)
        End Sub
        Overrides Function Send() As Boolean
            MsgBox("Send function of Fax class", MsgBoxStyle.OKOnly)

'Code specific to the Fax class
            Send = True
        End Function
    End Class
```

In the preceding code, the Communication, Email, and Fax classes are declared in the MyMod module. Notice that the classes in this example contain the Sub New procedure. You will learn more about the Sub New procedure later in this chapter. You can access methods of both the Email and Fax classes with an object of the Communication class because the Email and Fax classes are derived from the Communication class. Take a look at the following example:

```
Private Sub Button1_Click(ByVal sender As System.Object, ByVal e As System.EventArgs)
Handles Button1.Click
          Dim int1 As Integer
          Dim communicate As Communication
          int1 = InputBox("Enter 1 to send an e-mail message and 2 to send a fax
message.")
          Select Case (int1)
              Case "1"
                    communicate = New Email()
                    communicate.Send()
              Case "2"
                    communicate = New Fax()
                    communicate.Send()
          End Select
End Sub
```

The procedure in the preceding example in an event-handling procedure. You will learn about creating event-handling procedures in Chapter 7, "Procedures and Functions." The preceding code provides the user with a choice of sending either an e-mail message or a fax message. The communicate object of the Communication class is used to call the Send method of the Email and Fax classes. However, in the application, the Send method that is called depends on the choice of the user. Therefore, in this case, late binding is used.

To understand late binding, you need to first understand binding. During compilation, the compiler associates each method with a class by identifying the type of object used to invoke the method. This process of associating a method to an object is called *binding*.

In the preceding example, you need to call the Send method based on the choice entered by the user. Therefore, the objects are created dynamically, and the type of the object is not known at the time of compilation. In such cases, binding is performed not at compile time, but at runtime. This is known as *late binding*. Late binding increases the flexibility of a program by allowing the appropriate method to be invoked, depending on the context. In Visual Basic.NET, you can use late binding only for `Public` members of a class.

Visual Basic.NET also enables you to use interfaces to implement polymorphism. An *interface* defines a set of properties and methods that classes can implement. Interfaces are used when classes have only a few common properties and methods. In other words, if classes do not have many common properties and methods, you can implement interfaces instead of deriving the classes from a base class. For example, the `MusicSystem` and `Guitar` classes do not have many common properties and methods. Therefore, the `MusicSystem` class can implement the `ElectricityRun` and `PlayMusic` interfaces. Similarly, the `Guitar` class can implement the `PlayMusic` and `ManuallyOperated` interfaces.

Interfaces do not include implementation code. Therefore, each time you implement an interface, you need to add implementation code for the properties and methods of the interface. This enables the implementation of the methods in each class to be different.

In addition, a class can implement multiple interfaces but inherit only one base class. You cannot use late binding for interface members. Conversely, interfaces use early binding. In *early binding*, a function is bound to the calls at compile time. In cases of early binding, when the program is executed, the calls are already bound to the appropriate functions.

After defining a class, you can create objects of the class to access the properties and methods of the class. Consider an example that creates an object of the `Communication` class. You can use either of the following statements to create an object of the `Communication` class:

```
Dim MyObject as New Communication
```

or

```
Dim MyObject as Communication = New Communication
```

Now that you've looked at how abstraction, encapsulation, inheritance, and polymorphism are implemented in Visual Basic.NET, the next section describes how to create constructors, destructors, fields, and properties in a class.

Declaring Class Members

You declare class members within a class. As previously mentioned, class members include variables, properties, fields, and methods. In this section, you will learn how to create the following:

◆ Constructors

◆ Destructors

◆ Methods

◆ Fields

◆ Properties

Constructors

As discussed in Chapter 1, constructors are used to initialize objects. In Visual Basic.NET, the Sub New procedure acts as a constructor.

The Sub New procedure is executed when an object of the class is created. You can use the Sub New procedure to perform essential tasks before using an object of the class. For example, you can connect to databases and initialize variables in the Sub New procedure.

All classes in Visual Basic.NET are derived from the Object class. Therefore, when creating a class, you need to call the constructor of the Object class. To do this, you must include the MyBase.New statement as the first line in the constructor of your class. As previously mentioned, the MyBase keyword is used to invoke code written in a base class from a derived class. After the MyBase.New statement, you can add code to initialize objects and variables that you create. Consider the following example:

```
Public Class MyNewClass
        Public Sub New()
            MyBase.New()


'Code for Initializing objects and variables
        End Sub


'Other class members
End Class
```

You can call a constructor only from within the constructor of either the same class or a derived class. In derived classes, the first line in the constructor calls the constructor of the base class to initialize the inherited objects. After calling the constructor of the base class, you can add code to initialize the objects and variables created in the derived class.

In Visual Basic.NET, constructors can also take arguments. In other words, you can create parameterized constructors in Visual Basic.NET. Consider the following example:

```
Public Sub New(Optional ByVal iempcode As Integer = 0)
```

The preceding example defines a parameterized constructor for the `Employee` class. The constructor accepts the employee code, a unique identification number assigned to each employee, as an argument. Therefore, each time you create an object of the `Employee` class, you can assign a unique identification number to the employee. If you do not provide an identification number to the employee when creating the employee object, a default value of 0 is assigned.

You can use either of the following statements to create an object of the `Employee` class:

```
Dim Emp1 As New Employee(1001)
```

or

```
Dim Emp2 As Employee = New Employee(1001)
```

Constructors are optional procedures. You can also create classes without constructors. However, it is recommended that you initialize objects created in a class by using a constructor.

Now that you know how to create constructors in Visual Basic.NET, you will take a look at how to declare destructors in Visual Basic.NET.

Destructors

Visual Basic.NET also provides the `Sub Finalize` procedure, which acts as a destructor. The function of a destructor is opposite that of a constructor. A destructor releases the memory and resources used by a destroyed object. The `Sub Finalize` procedure is a protected method of the `Object` class. You can override the Sub Finalize procedure in the classes you create. Take a look at the following example:

```
Protected Overrides Sub Finalize()
        MyBase.Finalize()
                                                              'Add
code here
End Sub
```

In the preceding example, notice that the Overrides keyword is used. This is because the Sub Finalize procedure is a method of the Object class. In addition, the MyBase keyword is used to access the Sub Finalize method of the Object class.

Although you might override the Sub Finalize procedure in your application, the Sub Finalize procedure is not called when your application is executed. This is because the .NET framework controls the execution of the Sub Finalize procedure. The .NET framework calls the Sub Finalize procedure when an object is destroyed to release the memory and resources used by the object. Therefore, garbage collection in the .NET framework is performed automatically. This implies that you do not need to perform additional tasks in the .NET framework to ensure that unused resources and memory are released. However, because the .NET framework calls the Sub Finalize procedure, the time lag between object destruction and memory release is not defined.

In addition to the Sub Finalize procedure, the .NET framework provides the IDisposable interface to help you manage resources. You can implement the IDisposable interface to manage resources such as window handles and database connections in your applications. The IDisposable interface includes the Dispose method. Unlike the Sub Finalize procedure, you can explicitly call the Dispose method. In the Dispose method, you can add code to release resources and perform tasks such as closing database connections.

The Sub Finalize procedure acts as a backup to the Dispose method. You define the Sub Finalize procedure to ensure that the garbage collector performs clean-up operations for the objects you create if the Dispose method is not called.

Now that you've learned how to use the Dispose method and the Sub Finalize procedure to release resources in Visual Basic.NET, the next section explains how to create methods within classes in Visual Basic.NET.

Methods

In addition to constructors and destructors, you can define other methods in a class. The methods in a class comprise the public `Sub` or `Function` procedures declared in the class.

As previously mentioned, a procedure is a set of statements that performs a specific task. After grouping the statements in a procedure, you can call the procedure from anywhere in the application. When a procedure completes execution, it returns control to the calling code. Visual Basic.NET enables you to define `Sub`, `Function`, and `Property` procedures. (`Property` procedures are discussed in the "Fields and Properties" section of this chapter.)

- ◆ `Sub` *procedures.* `Sub` procedures cannot return any values. You use the `Sub` and `End Sub` statements to define a `Sub` procedure. When a `Sub` procedure is called, all the statements within the procedure are executed, starting from the first until an `End Sub`, `Exit Sub`, or `Return` statement is encountered. Typically, `Sub` procedures are used to define event-handling procedures. Event-handling procedures are discussed in detail in Chapter 7.

- ◆ `Function` *procedures.* Unlike `Sub` procedures, `Function` procedures return values to calling code. You use the `Function` and `End Function` statements to define a `Function` procedure. Similar to a `Sub` procedure, a `Function` procedure executes starting from the first executable statement until an `End Function`, `Exit Function`, or `Return` statement is encountered.

Both `Function` and `Sub` procedures can take arguments. Calling code can pass arguments—such as constants, variables, or expressions—to `Sub` and `Function` procedures.

You can also overload methods in Visual Basic.NET. In other words, you can create multiple methods with the same name but with different types or numbers of parameters. You can override a method of a base class by declaring a method with the same name and the same number of arguments in the derived class. In the derived class, you need to use the `Overrides` keyword to override the base class method. In the base class, however, the method should be defined as an `Overridable` method.

In addition to procedures, you can define fields and properties in a class. The next section describes fields and properties.

Fields and Properties

As previously mentioned, fields are variables declared in a class that are accessible from other classes. You can declare fields by using a single declaration statement.

You declare fields within classes. Consider the following example, which shows how to declare a field named `MyField` in the `MyClass1` class:

```
Public Class MyClass1
        Public MyField As Integer                        'Declaring a field


'Other declarations and code
End Class
```

You can manipulate the `MyField` field by using an object of `MyClass1`. Take a look at the following example:

```
Dim MyObject As New MyClass1()
MyObject.MyField = 6
```

In the preceding example, `MyObject` is an object of the `MyClass1` class. Notice that the `MyObject` object is used to assign a value to the `MyField` field defined in the `MyClass1` class.

Properties define the attributes of an object. To create a property, you need to declare `Property` procedures.

To define a property, you need to use the `Property` and `End Property` statements. Within the `Property` and `End Property` statements, you declare `Property` procedures. When the value of a property is set or accessed, `Property` procedures are executed. `Property` procedures enable you to manipulate the properties defined in modules, classes, or structures. Typically, you declare two `Property` procedures for each property, `Get` and `Set`. You use the `Get` and `End Get` statements to define a `Get Property` procedure. The `Get Property` procedure returns the value of a property. To elaborate, the `Get Property` procedure is called when you retrieve the value of a property. Similarly, you use the `Set` and `End Set` statements to define a `Set Property` procedure. However, unlike the `Get Property` procedure, the `Set Property` procedure is used to set the value of a property to a specified value. In other words, the `Set Property` procedure is called when you assign a value to a property. Consider the following example:

```
Private PropValue As Integer = 0
Public Property MyProperty() As Integer
```

```
        Get

'Add code
            Return PropValue                                  'Where
PropValue is the property's value
        End Get
        Set(ByVal value As Integer)

'Add code
            PropValue = value                                 'Where
PropValue is the new value to be assigned
        End Set
End Property
```

In the preceding example, the Get Property procedure returns the value of the MyProperty property. In addition, the Set Property procedure assigns the value in the PropValue variable to the MyProperty property. You can use the following statement to assign a value to the MyProperty property:

```
MyProperty = MyValue
```

In the preceding example, the value in the variable MyValue is assigned to the MyProperty property.

To retrieve the value of the MyProperty property, you can use the following statement:

```
MyNum = MyProperty
```

In the preceding code, the value of the MyProperty property is assigned to the MyValue variable.

In the earlier example, the Public access modifier was also used when declaring the property. When defining a property, you can use the Public, Private, Protected, Friend, or Protected Friend access modifier. The default value for the access modifier in the case of properties is Public.

By default, a property has both read and write attributes. However, in Visual Basic.NET, you can also define a read-only or write-only property by using the ReadOnly or WriteOnly keyword. To define a read-only or write-only property, you need to include the ReadOnly or WriteOnly keyword before the access modifier while declaring the property. As previously mentioned, Property procedures are defined in pairs by using both the Get and Set keywords. However, in the case of a read-only property, you need to define only the Get Property procedure. Alternatively, in the case of a write-only property, you need to define only the Set Property procedure.

In Visual Basic.NET, you can also define default properties in a class by using the Default keyword. Default properties must accept parameters. In Visual Basic .NET, you can assign values to and retrieve values of default properties without specifying the property name.

> ### NOTE
>
> As in Sub and Function procedures, you can also pass arguments to properties.

Now that you've looked at declaring properties and fields, the next section describes how you can declare namespaces.

Declaring Namespaces

As discussed in Chapter 1, Visual Basic.NET provides namespaces. Namespaces are used to organize the objects defined in an assembly. In addition, namespaces enable you to organize objects hierarchically. A hierarchical structure groups similar objects, simplifying access. For example, you need to define objects, methods, and properties for a grocery store. To do so, you create the GroceryStore namespace. Within the GroceryStore namespace, you can create subnamespaces, such as Inedible and Edible, to organize the goods sold at the grocery store. Now, under the Edible namespace, you can create the Vegetables and Drinks namespaces. Therefore, to determine the vegetables available in the store, you can use the classes and methods defined in the GroceryStore.Edible.Vegetables namespace. As is evident in this example, you can use namespaces to group classes logically.

In Visual Basic.NET, you can declare multiple namespaces either in a program or across programs. In addition, the classes defined within a namespace should have unique names. In other words, you cannot create two classes with the same name in a namespace. However, classes can have the same name across namespaces.

Each project you create in Visual Basic.NET contains a namespace by default. This namespace is assigned the same name as the project. For example, if you define an object in a project named `MyProject`, the executable file (which is MyProject.exe in this case) will contain a namespace named `MyProject`.

As mentioned in Chapter 1, you can also create your own namespaces. You need to use the `Namespace` and `End Namespace` statements to declare a namespace. Take a look at the following example:

```
Namespace MyNamespace
        Public Class MyOwnClass1


'Code for the MyOwnClass1
        End Class
        Public Class MyOwnClass2


'Code for the MyOwnClass2
        End Class
End Namespace
```

In the preceding example, note that the declaration does not include an access modifier. This is because namespaces are always `Public`. Typically, you define classes in a namespace. In addition to classes, you can define structures and interfaces in namespaces. The classes, structures, and interfaces in a namespace can have either `Public` or `Friend` access.

Visual Basic.NET also enables you to create nested namespaces. The following code explains how to create nested namespaces using the grocery store example previously discussed:

```
Namespace GroceryStore
        Namespace Edible
                Public Class Vegetables


'Code for the class
                End Class
                Public Class Drinks
```

```
'Code for the class
                      End Class
          End Namespace
          Namespace Inedible
                    Public Class Cosmetics


'Code for the class
                      End Class
                    Public Class Toiletries


'Code for the class
                      End Class
          End Namespace
End Namespace
```

The `Edible` namespace declared in the example can also be declared in the following manner:

```
Namespace GroceryStore.Edible
                    Public Class Vegetables


'Code for the class
                      End Class
                    Public Class Drinks


'Code for the class
                      End Class
End Namespace
```

In the preceding example, the name of the `Edible` subnamespace follows the name of the `GroceryStore` namespace. This implies that the `Edible` subnamespace is qualified. You can also use qualified names when declaring namespaces. Qualified names prevent naming conflicts. In addition, you use qualified names to access the objects defined in a namespace. However, remembering the complete names of namespaces can be very difficult. Visual Basic.NET provides an easy way out. As explained in Chapter 1, you can to use the `Imports` statement to access the classes in namespaces. When you add the `Imports` statement to your application, you do not need to use the qualified name for the imported namespace.

Summary

In this chapter, you learned about inheritance, abstraction, encapsulation, and polymorphism and how they are implemented in Visual Basic.NET. In addition, you learned to declare constructors and destructors when creating classes in Visual Basic.NET. The chapter also described how to declare methods, fields, and properties. Finally, you learned how to declare namespaces.

Chapter 3

In the preceding chapter, you learned about the features of Visual Basic.NET. In this chapter, you will learn about the Visual Studio.NET integrated development environment (IDE), which enables you to develop applications based on the .NET framework. The Visual Studio.NET IDE is common to all of the .NET languages, and this means you can use the same set of tools and windows across languages.

Figure 3-1 displays the Visual Studio.NET IDE.

FIGURE 3-1 *The opening screen of Visual Studio.NET*

As shown in the Figure 3-1, the Visual Studio.NET IDE displays various windows and tools. The following section describes these.

Windows and Tools in the Visual Studio .NET IDE

The following sections describe the features and functions of the following windows and tools:

- ◆ The menu bar
- ◆ Toolbars
- ◆ The Start page
- ◆ Solution Explorer
- ◆ Class View
- ◆ Dynamic Help
- ◆ The Toolbox
- ◆ Server Explorer

The Menu Bar

The menu bar in the Visual Studio.NET IDE displays the File, Edit, View, Tools, Window, and Help menus by default. These menus include commands that enable you to perform various tasks such as opening, saving, editing, and formatting files. In addition to the menus available by default on the menu bar, the IDE also displays menus that are relevant to the task you are currently performing. For example, when you open a project in Code Editor, the menu bar displays the Project, Build, and Debug menus in addition to the default menus. Similarly, when you open a project in Windows Forms Designer, the Data and Format menus also appear on the menu bar.

> **NOTE**
>
> Visual Studio.NET provides you with various designers—such as Windows Forms Designer, Web Forms Designer, XML Designer, and Component Designer—that help you design applications quickly and easily.

The following sections take a more detailed look at some of the commonly used menus in Visual Studio.NET.

The File Menu

Visual Studio.NET provides solutions and projects to help you organize and manage your applications. A solution can contain multiple projects, files, and items, such as references, data connections, and folders. Similarly, a project can contain multiple files and items that are associated with the project. The items in a solution are independent of the projects in the solution. However, the items in a project include references to libraries, data connections, and folders for the project.

The File menu provides commands to open, close, and save projects, files, and solutions. The File menu also provides commands to add items such as forms, controls, modules, and classes to projects and solutions.

The Edit Menu

You can use the commands in the Edit menu to cut, copy, or delete the selected text or component. You can use the Paste command in this menu to insert the copied text or component at the required location. This menu also provides the Undo and Redo commands, which enable you to reverse or repeat the last action, respectively.

The View Menu

The View menu provides commands to access the various windows and tools available in Visual Studio.NET. Using the View menu, you can open the Solution Explorer, Class View, Server Explorer, Resource View, and Properties windows. Additionally, the View menu also provides commands to open the Toolbox, Web browser, and other windows such as the Command window and Task List. You will learn more about these windows later in this chapter.

The Project Menu

The Project menu provides commands to add components to projects. Using the Project menu, you can add components such as forms, modules, classes, and controls to your projects.

The Build Menu

As the name suggests, this menu provides commands to build your projects. This menu also provides the Configuration Manager command. When you click on the

Configuration Manager command, the Configuration Manager dialog box displays. Using the Configuration Manager dialog box, you can create and modify build configurations for solutions and projects.

The Debug Menu

The Debug menu provides commands to locate and correct errors in your applications. Some of the commands in the Debug menu are as follows:

◆ *Start*, *Step Into*, and *Step Over*. You can use these commands to start debugging your applications.

◆ *Processes*. Selecting this command displays the Processes dialog box. You can use the Processes dialog box to view and manipulate the processes running on your computer.

◆ *Exceptions*. When you select the Exceptions command, the Exceptions dialog box displays. In the Exceptions dialog box, you can specify the manner in which the debugger should handle exceptions or the categories of exceptions. An exception is a problem or an error that causes the processor to stop the current process and handle the error.

◆ *New Breakpoint*. You can select this command to open the New Breakpoint dialog box. In the New Breakpoint dialog box, you can add breakpoints in the code. When Visual Studio.NET encounters a *breakpoint* in a program, it suspends the execution of the program.

The Format Menu

As the name suggests, the Format menu provides commands to format controls while working in a designer. Some of the commands on the Format menu are as follows:

◆ Align
◆ Center in Form
◆ Horizontal Spacing
◆ Vertical Spacing

When you select any of the preceding commands, the submenu associated with the command displays. The commands in the various submenus help align and organize controls in the designer.

The Tools Menu

The Tools menu provides commands such as Debug Processes, Customize Toolbox, Add-in Manager, Customize, and Options. When you select one of the following commands, a corresponding dialog box displays.

◆ *Debug Processes* displays the Processes dialog box.

◆ *Customize Toolbox* displays the Customize Toolbox dialog box. In this dialog box, you can specify the Component Object Model (COM) and .NET framework components to be displayed in the Toolbox.

◆ *Add-in Manager* displays the Add-in Manager dialog box, which lists all the add-ins available in the Visual Studio.NET IDE. Using this dialog box, you can add or remove add-ins from the IDE.

◆ *Customize* displays the Customize dialog box. You can use the Customize dialog box to create your own toolbars, to add or remove buttons from the existing toolbars, and to modify the appearance of the toolbars.

◆ *Options* displays the Options dialog box. In the Options dialog box, you can modify the settings for the IDE.

The Window Menu

As the name suggests, the Window menu provides commands to work with the windows in the IDE. Some of the commands on the Window menu are as follows:

◆ *New Window.* You can use this command to create a new window. For example, when working in Code Editor, you can select the New Window command to open another Code Editor window.

◆ *Split.* You can use this command to divide a window into two sections. You can view either different files or the same file in the two sections simultaneously.

◆ *Dockable*, *Hide*, and *Floating*. These commands help you organize and manage the windows in the IDE.

◆ *New Vertical Tab Group* and *New Horizontal Tab Group*. These commands enable you to create tab groups to organize the windows in the IDE. You can group windows into either vertical or horizontal tab groups.

◆ *Close All Documents.* This command enables you to close all open documents.

The Help Menu

Some of the commands of the Help menu are as follows:

♦ *Dynamic Help.* This command enables you to open the Dynamic Help window. You will learn about the Dynamic Help window later in this chapter.

♦ *Contents.* When you select the Contents command, the Contents window displays. Using the Contents window, you can browse the table of contents of the MSDN library.

♦ *Index.* The Index window displays when you select the Index command. You can use the Index window to find information about a specific topic in the MSDN library.

♦ *Search.* When you select the Search command, the Search window opens. Using the Search window, you can search for information in the MSDN library.

♦ *Previous Topic* and *Next Topic.* These commands enable you to navigate through the MSDN library.

Toolbars

The Visual Studio.NET IDE provides various toolbars such as Text Editor, Build, and Debug. However, only the Standard and Web toolbars are displayed by default.

The toolbars displayed in the IDE depend on the designer, tool, or window you are using. In other words, the Visual Studio.NET IDE displays toolbars that are relevant to the task you are performing. Table 3-1 describes some of the toolbars available in the Visual Studio.NET IDE.

Table 3-1 Toolbars Available in Visual Studio.NET

Toolbar	Provides Commands To
Build	Build applications
Crystal Reports—Insert	Open the Insert Summary, Insert Group, Insert Subreport, Insert Chart, and Insert Picture dialog boxes

continues

Table 3-1 (continued)

Toolbar	Provides Commands To
Crystal Reports—Main	Perform basic formatting operations such as justifying text, applying fonts, and accessing dialog boxes such as Select Expert and Object Properties
Data Design	Generate datasets and preview data
Database Diagram	Work with database objects
Debug	Start and stop the debugging of applications
Debug Location	View the program, thread, and stack frame of an error encountered while debugging a program
Design	Work with controls in Web Forms Designer
Formatting	Format text
Full Screen	Work in the full-screen mode
HTML Editor	Format, validate, and work with HTML documents
Image Editor	Create and manipulate images
Layout	Modify the layout of controls in the designer
Source Control	Maintain different versions of your applications
Standard	Work with solutions, projects, and files and open windows such as Solution Explorer and Class View
Style Sheet	Format and view style sheets
Table	Work with the tables in a database
Text Editor	Work in Code Editor
Web	Browse for Web pages
XML Data	Create schemas
XML Schema	Preview datasets and edit keys and relations

The Start Page

The Start page provides a centralized location for you to begin work in Visual Studio.NET. The Start page appears when you start Visual Studio.NET. You can also open the Start page by selecting the Show Start Page command from the Help menu. The Start page is the default home page for the Web browser in Visual Studio.NET.

The Start page provides various links that enable you to work quickly and efficiently in Visual Studio.NET. The following links are available on the Start page:

◆ *Get Started* enables you to create new projects and open existing projects.

◆ *What's New* provides information about Visual Studio.NET products and resources. When you click on this link, a list of links related to Visual Studio.NET products and resources is displayed. You can also use this link to check for Visual Studio.NET updates. In addition, you can view information about a specific topic by selecting an appropriate option from the Filter list box.

◆ *Online Community* displays a list of links to Web sites and newsgroups. This link enables you to exchange information with other developers using Visual Studio.NET.

◆ *Headlines* provides links to news and technical articles available on the Microsoft Developer Network (MSDN) Web site. To access information about a specific topic, you can select an option from the Filter list box.

◆ *Search Online* helps you search for information about a topic on the MSDN Web site. You can use the Advanced button on this page to specify the scope and criteria for the search.

◆ *Downloads* enable you to download tools and service packs for Visual Studio.NET. In addition, you can also download code samples and updated products from the Internet.

◆ *Web Hosting* enables you to access the Visual Studio.NET Web hosting portal. This portal was formed as a result of Microsoft's collaboration with several companies. You can use this portal to access and host Web applications and Web services developed using Visual Studio.NET.

◆ *My Profile* helps customize the Visual Studio.NET IDE. Using this link, you can specify your profile by selecting an option from the listed developer profiles. In addition, you can specify the settings for the Help filter. You can also specify settings for the scheme of the keyboard and the layout of different windows. In the At Startup list box, you can specify the actions to be performed when Visual Studio.NET starts.

Solution Explorer

The Solution Explorer window provides a hierarchical view of your solutions, projects, and files. You can open the Solution Explorer window by selecting the Solution Explorer command from the View menu.

When you open a solution, the Solution Explorer window lists the various projects, files, and references present in the solution, as shown in Figure 3-2.

FIGURE 3-2 *The Solution Explorer window*

The Solution Explorer window simplifies file management by enabling you to view and manipulate solutions, projects, and files. When you double-click on a file in the Solution Explorer window, the file opens in the editor or tool associated with the file. Using the Solution Explorer window, you can also work on multiple files. For example, you can select multiple files and open them for editing.

In addition to the files associated with solutions and projects, the Solution Explorer window enables you to work with files that are not a part of any solution or project. These files are known as *miscellaneous files*.

Using the Solution Explorer window, you can open and manage files and add and remove items. When you right-click on a selected item in the Solution Explorer window, a context menu displays. You can use the commands in the context menu to perform various operations such as copying, cutting, deleting, or renaming the selected item. Additionally, you can also perform tasks such as disassociating an item from a project by selecting the Exclude from Project command. However, the options in the context menu vary based on the object selected in the Solution Explorer window. For example, the commands that appear in the context menu when you select a form are different than the commands that appear when you select the References folder for a project. The References folder for a project includes references to libraries, namespaces, and data connections.

The Solution Explorer window displays a toolbar. Similar to the commands in the context menu, the buttons on the toolbar also vary depending on the item selected in the Solution Explorer window. For example, when you select a form in the Solution Explorer window, the View Code and View Designer buttons appear on the toolbar. When you select an assembly in the Solution Explorer window, however, the View Designer button does not display. In addition to the View Designer and View Code buttons, the toolbar displays other buttons such as the Show All Files and Properties buttons. When you select multiple files in the Solution Explorer window, the toolbar displays only the buttons that are common to the selected files.

Class View

The Class View window provides a hierarchical view of solutions and projects. To open the Class View window, select the Class View tab in the Visual Studio.NET IDE. Refer to Figure 3-1 to see where the Class View tab is located in the Visual Studio.NET IDE. Alternatively, you can also open the Class View window by selecting the Class View command from the View menu.

As previously mentioned, a solution includes one or more projects. Each project within a solution can include components such as namespaces, classes, interfaces, forms, functions, and variables. In the Class View window, the components are organized based on the project in which they are contained. The Class View window provides a structured view of code to help you understand how components are organized within a project. In addition, the Class View window provides a logical view of components with regard to projects. A logical view helps you understand the inter-relationships between components and projects. Figure 3-3 shows the Class View window.

In the Class View window, each type of component is represented by an icon. In other words, different icons are used to represent different types of components such as namespaces, classes, and interfaces.

Using the Class View window, you can navigate through projects in a solution. The Class View window also enables you to view the various classes, methods, properties, and interfaces defined within a project.

FIGURE 3-3 *The Class View window*

Using this window, you can also view the properties or code for a component. For example, to view the code associated with a method, right-click on the method name in the Class View window and select the Browse Definition command from the context menu. This displays the corresponding code for the selected method.

The Class View window also contains a toolbar. This toolbar displays two buttons, Sort By and New Folder. When you select the Sort By button, a drop-down list displays. The options in the Sort By drop-down list are as follows:

◆ *Sort Alphabetically* organizes the components in ascending order of their names.

◆ *Sort By Type* groups the components within a project based on the type of the component. For example, when you select the Sort By Type option, all classes are listed together. Similarly, all interfaces are listed together and so on. The components within each project are grouped based on an order, but you cannot change this order.

◆ *Sort By Access* lists the components based on their access type, such as `Public`, `Protected`, or `Private`.

◆ *Group By Type* organizes the components within each project based on the type of component. Unlike the Sort By Type option, however, the Group By Type option groups similar components in a virtual folder. In addition, as with the Sort By Type option, you cannot modify the order in which the components are displayed.

The New Folder button on the toolbar enables you to create virtual folders. You can create virtual folders to group commonly used components. Therefore, virtual folders provide quick access to components.

Dynamic Help

At times, you might need to know how to perform a particular task. In Visual Studio.NET, the Dynamic Help window provides access to information relevant to the current selection or task. When you open the Visual Studio.NET IDE, the Dynamic Help window displays. You can also open the Dynamic Help window by selecting the Dynamic Help command from the Help menu.

The Dynamic Help window displays links related to the current window or the current task. For example, when you are working in the Class View window, the Dynamic Help window displays information about the Class View window. Similarly, if you select a button control while working in the designer, the Dynamic Help window displays information related to the `Button` class, as displayed in Figure 3-4.

FIGURE 3-4 *The Dynamic Help window*

Therefore, the information displayed in the Dynamic Help window depends on the selection in the IDE.

The Dynamic Help window displays information from the Microsoft Developer Network (MSDN) library. In other words, information from the MSDN library is filtered based on the current selection or the cursor placement and then is displayed in the Dynamic Help window. If the MSDN library does not contain any information related to the current selection, the Dynamic Help window displays a message stating that "No links are available for the current selection."

The information displayed in the Dynamic Help window is organized into categories. By default, the Dynamic Help window includes the Help, Samples, and Getting Started categories. However, you can also customize the Dynamic Help window by using the Options dialog box. To open the Options dialog box, select the Options command from the Tools menu. To edit settings for the Dynamic Help window, select the Dynamic Help option in the Environment folder. After you select the Dynamic Help option, you can specify the categories to be displayed in the Dynamic Help window. You can also specify the sequence in which the categories should be displayed. In addition, you can specify the type of information—such as articles, procedures, and samples—that needs to be displayed in the Dynamic Help window. Under Show links for, you can select an option to specify the filter for the Dynamic Help window.

The Dynamic Help window also contains a toolbar. This toolbar displays the Contents, Index, and Search buttons, which help you browse the MSDN library.

The Toolbox

As the name suggests, the Toolbox contains various tools available in Visual Studio.NET. To open the Toolbox, you can click on the Toolbox tab displayed in the left margin of the IDE. (Refer to Figure 3-1 to see where the Toolbox tab is located in the Visual Studio.NET IDE.) Alternatively, you can open the Toolbox by selecting the Toolbox command from the View menu.

By default, the Toolbox displays only the General and Clipboard Ring tabs. However, the Toolbox displays additional tools on various tabs depending on the currently open designer or editor. To view all the tabs in the Toolbar, you can right-click on the Toolbox and select the Show All Tabs option from the context menu.

The following are some of the tabs available in the Toolbox:

◆ *General tab*

By default, the General tab displays only the Pointer control. However, you can also add controls, such as custom controls, to the General tab. *Custom controls* are controls defined by users or third-party vendors.

Figure 3-5 displays the General tab.

◆ *Clipboard Ring tab*

Similar to the General tab, the Clipboard Ring tab displays the Pointer control by default. In addition to the Pointer control, the Clipboard Ring tab displays the last 12 items added to the clipboard. The *clipboard* is a memory cache maintained by the Microsoft Windows operating system. Each time you perform a cut or copy operation, the selected item is

FIGURE 3-5 *The General tab*

placed on the clipboard. You use the Paste command to retrieve the copied item from the clipboard. When working in Code Editor in Visual Studio.NET, you can press Ctrl + Shift + V to select an item from the clipboard.

Figure 3-6 displays the Clipboard Ring tab.

FIGURE 3-6 *The Clipboard Ring tab*

◆ *Crystal Reports tab*

The Crystal Reports tab appears in the Toolbox when you are working in Crystal Report Designer. This tab displays components—such as text objects, line objects, and box objects—that you can use in Crystal Reports.

Figure 3-7 displays the Crystal Reports tab.

FIGURE 3-7 *The Crystal Reports tab*

◆ *Data tab*

The Toolbox displays the Data tab when you create a project that has an associated designer. The Data tab provides data objects—such as datasets and dataviews—that you can include in Visual Basic.NET and Visual C#.NET forms and components. For example, you can insert a DataView control in your form to sort and filter data retrieved from a table.

Figure 3-8 displays the Data tab.

FIGURE 3-8 *The Data tab*

◆ *XML Schema tab*

The XML Schema tab appears when you are working on ADO.NET datasets and XML schemas. Therefore, this tab displays controls that you can add to XML schemas and ADO.NET datasets.

Figure 3-9 displays the XML Schema tab.

FIGURE 3-9 *The XML Schema tab*

◆ *Web Forms tab*

The Web Forms tab displays Web controls and validation controls that you can add to Web forms. The controls displayed on the Web Forms tab can work within the ASP.NET framework only. Using validation controls, you can validate user input for any Web control or HTML control on the Web Forms page.

Figure 3-10 displays the Web Forms tab.

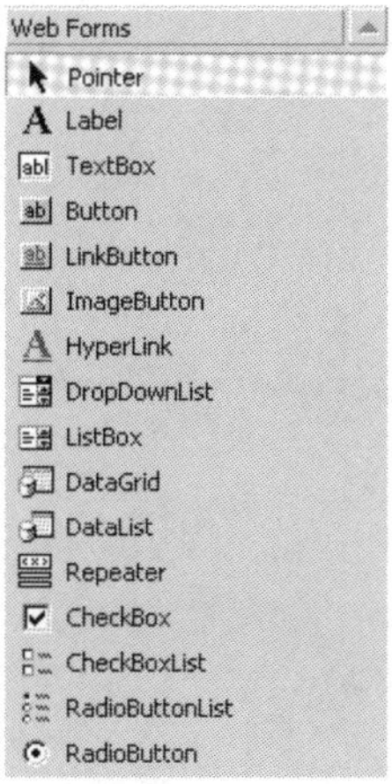

FIGURE 3-10 *The Web Forms tab*

◆ *Components tab*

The Components tab displays components—such as an EventLog and MessageQueue—that you can add to Visual Basic.NET and Visual C#.NET projects. You can also add user-defined components to this tab.

Figure 3-11 displays the Components tab.

FIGURE 3-11 *The Components tab*

◆ *Windows Forms tab*

The Windows Forms tab appears in the Toolbox when you open a Windows application. The Windows Forms tab displays controls and dialog boxes that you can use in Windows applications.

Figure 3-12 displays the Windows Forms tab.

◆ *HTML tab*

The HTML tab appears in the Toolbox when you open any document in HTML Designer. This tab provides controls—such as labels, buttons, and text fields—that you can use to create Web pages and Web forms.

Figure 3-13 displays the HTML tab.

You can also customize the Toolbox by adding tabs and tools. To customize the Toolbox, use the Customize Toolbox dialog box. You can open the Customize Toolbox dialog box by selecting the Customize Toolbox command from the Tools menu.

FIGURE 3-12 *The Windows Forms tab*

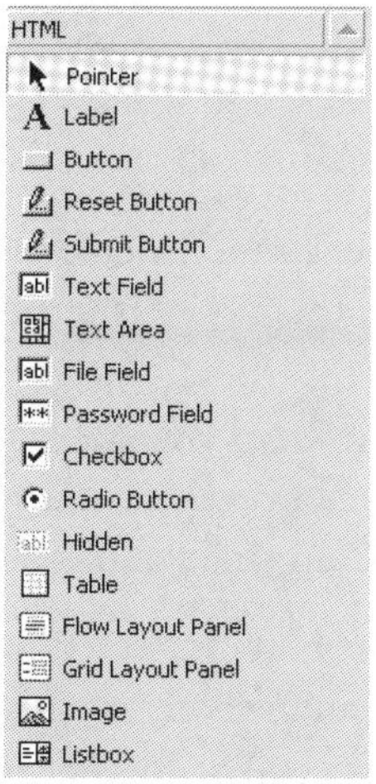

FIGURE 3-13 *The HTML tab*

Server Explorer

The Server Explorer window enables you to manage servers in Visual Studio.NET. You can open the Server Explorer window by selecting the Server Explorer tab, which is displayed in the left margin of the IDE. Alternatively, you can open the Server Explorer window by selecting the Server Explorer command from the View menu.

Using this window, you can create database connections. A *database connection* is a link to a database. You can also log on to a server and access the databases available on the server by using the Server Explorer window.

The Server Explorer window displays two nodes, Data Connections and Servers, as shown in Figure 3-14.

FIGURE 3-14 *The Server Explorer window*

The Data Connections node lists the various database connections you have added to the server. In addition to database connections, this node lists the database objects—such as tables, views, stored procedures, and functions—for each database. Using the Server Explorer window, you can also manipulate database objects. For example, you can add a table to a database. However, to manipulate database objects, you must have the required permissions on the database.

The Servers node lists the various servers to which your machine is connected. Using the Server Explorer window, you can connect to any server to which you have network access. This node also displays system resources—such as event logs and messaging queues—that are available on the servers to which your computer is connected.

Using the Server Explorer window, you can add database connections and data components to your projects. You can drag the required component or service from the Server Explorer window to your project to include a reference to the component or service. For example, when you select a service and drag it to the designer, a ServiceController component that interacts with the service is created.

In addition to services and database connections, the Server Explorer window also enables you to add event logs, message queues, and performance counters to your project.

The Server Explorer window also displays a toolbar that provides buttons for commonly used commands. You can use the buttons on the toolbar to perform tasks such as connecting to databases and servers.

Now that you've learned about the various tools available in the Visual Studio.NET IDE, the following section describes the other windows available in Visual Studio.NET.

Other Windows in Visual Studio .NET

In addition to the windows you learned about in the preceding sections, Visual Studio.NET also provides other windows that are not displayed when you open the Visual Studio.NET IDE. However, you can access these windows when creating projects in the IDE.

In this section, you will learn about the following windows:

♦ Properties

♦ Task List

♦ Command

You will now take a look at each of these windows.

The Properties Window

As the name suggests, the Properties window displays the properties of a component. You can open the Properties window by selecting the Properties Window command from the View menu. When you select a component or object in the Solution Explorer window or designer, the properties associated with the selected component are displayed in the Properties window. Using the Properties window, you can view and edit the properties of a file, folder, project, or solution. You can also use this window to modify the properties of the components of projects and solutions.

The Properties window also enables you to edit the properties of the controls you add to forms. For example, to view and modify the properties of a button control, open the designer and select the button control. When you select the button control, the properties associated with the button control are displayed in the Properties window, as shown in Figure 3-15. In the Properties window, you can edit the properties associated with the button control.

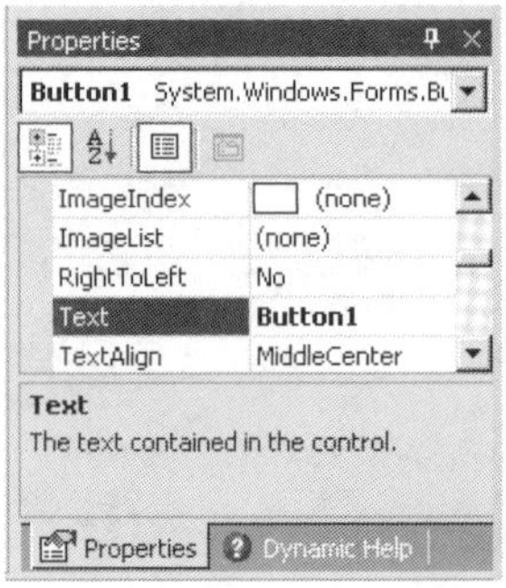

FIGURE 3-15 *The Properties window*

The properties displayed in the Properties window are different for different controls. In other words, the properties available for a button control differ from the properties available for a label control. Note that some properties in the Properties window appear in gray. These are read-only properties.

The Properties window also displays a toolbar that contains various buttons such as Categorized, Alphabetic, and Property Pages. Some of the buttons available on the toolbar are explained in the following list:

◆ *Categorized* enables you to group the properties for a control into categories. For example, when you select a button control and click the Categorized button on the toolbar, the properties for the button control are grouped into categories such as Appearance, Behavior, Data, and Layout. Similarly, when you select a form in the Solution Explorer window and click the Categorized button on the toolbar, the form properties are grouped into Advanced and Misc. categories.

◆ *Alphabetic* helps arrange the properties for a control alphabetically.

◆ *Property Pages* displays the Property Pages dialog box for the selected component. You can use the Property Pages dialog box to view and edit properties related to the configuration of the project.

The Task List

The Task List window displays error messages and warnings when you compile your applications. You can double-click on an error message in the Task List window to view the part of the code in which the error was encountered.

To open the Task List window, select the Other Windows command from the View menu. From the Other Windows submenu, select the Task List command to open the Task List.

Figure 3-16 displays the Task List window. Note that the Task List window displays error messages, warnings, and tasks.

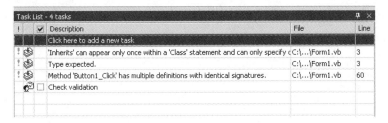

FIGURE 3-16 *The Task List window*

In addition to displaying error messages and warnings, the Task List window enables you to add comments to your code. You can add comments to code for future reference. When other developers need to work on your project, they can use comments to understand the structure of the code in your application.

The Command Window

You can use the Command window to execute the commands available in Visual Studio.NET. To open the Command window, select the Other Windows command from the View menu. From the Other Windows submenu, select the Command Window command to open the Command window.

The Command window has two modes, Command and Immediate. In the Command mode, you can execute Visual Studio.NET commands such as Print, Open, Save, SaveAs, and SaveAll.

The Command window is displayed in Figure 3-17.

In the Immediate mode, you can debug applications. The Immediate mode also enables you to evaluate expressions.

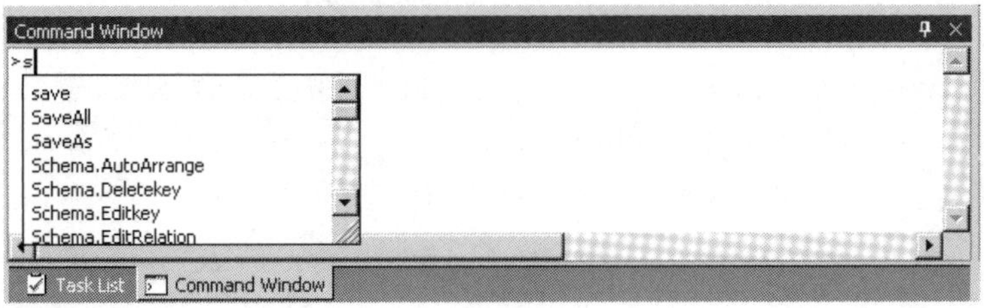

FIGURE 3-17 *The Command window*

Summary

In this chapter, you learned about the components of the Visual Studio.NET IDE, such as the menus and toolbars available. You also learned about the features and functions of the various windows and tools in the IDE.

Chapter 4

In the preceding chapter, you were introduced to the Visual Basic.NET IDE. This chapter will familiarize you with how variables and operators are used in Visual Basic.NET.

Using Variables

Most applications deal with different types of data, such as text or numeric. An application needs to store this data for later use and for performing certain operations on the data, such as calculating totals. To store data, a programming language uses variables. A *variable* is a temporary memory location. Like all programming languages, Visual Basic.NET also uses variables to store data. A variable has a name (a word to refer to it) and a data type (which determines what kind of data it can hold).

Visual Basic.NET provides various data types that help you store different kinds of data. The following section discusses these data types.

Data Types

A *data type* refers to the kind of data a variable can hold. Some of the data types that Visual Basic.NET provides are Integer, Long, String, and Byte. A more thorough list of data types can be found in Table 4-1.

Table 4-1 The Data Types in Visual Basic.NET

Data Type	Description
Integer	Stores numeric data. Integer data is stored as a 32-bit (4-byte) number.
Long	Stores numeric data that can exceed the range supported by the Integer data type. Long data is stored as a 64-bit (8-byte) number.
Short	Stores a smaller range of numeric data (between −32,678 and 32,767). Short data is stored as a signed 16-bit (2-byte) number.
Byte	Stores binary data. Can also store ASCII character values in the numeric form.

Data Type	Description
Double	Stores large floating-point numbers. `Double` data is stored as an IEEE 64-bit (8-byte) floating-point number.
Single	Stores single-precision floating-point values. `Single` data is stored as an IEEE 32-bit (4-byte) floating-point number.
Decimal	Stores very large floating-point values. `Decimal` data is stored as a 128-bit (16-byte) signed integer to the power of 10.
Boolean	Stores data that can have only two values: True or False. `Boolean` data is stored as a 16-bit (2-byte) number.
Char	Stores a single character. `Char` data is stored as a 16-bit (2-byte) unsigned number.
DateTime	Stores date and time. `DateTime` data is stored as IEEE 64-bit (8-byte) long integers.
String	Stores alphanumeric data (that is, data containing numbers as well as text).
Object	Stores data of any type, such as `Integer`, `Boolean`, `String`, or `Long`.

Some changes to the data types in Visual Basic.NET (as compared to earlier versions of Visual Basic) are worth mentioning here:

◆ In Visual Basic 6.0, the `Variant` data type is used to store data of any type. In Visual Basic.NET, the `Object` data type does this job.

◆ In Visual Basic 6.0, a date is stored in the `Double` data type. In Visual Basic.NET, the `DateTime` data type stores data in the date and time format.

◆ Visual Basic.NET doesn't support the `Currency` data type. Instead, the `Decimal` data type does the same job (that is, it stores currency values).

Now that you've had a look at the various data types, you'll see how variables are declared in Visual Basic.NET.

Variable Declarations

Declaring a variable means telling a program about it in advance. To declare a variable, use the `Dim` statement. The syntax for declaring a variable is as follows:

```
Dim VariableName [As Type]
```

The optional As Type clause in the Dim statement defines the data type or object type of the variable you are declaring. Consider the following two statements:

```
Dim NumVar As Integer
Dim StrVar As String
```

The first statement declares an Integer variable with the name NumVar, and the second one declares a String variable with the name StrVar.

You can also declare variables by using identifier type characters. These characters specify the data type of a variable. For example, consider the following statement:

```
Dim StrVar$
```

In this statement, $ is the identifier type character for a String variable. Table 4-2 lists the various identifier type characters that can be used in Visual Basic.NET.

Table 4-2 The Identifier Type Characters in Visual Basic.NET

Data Type	Identifier Type Character
Integer	%
Long	&
Single	!
Double	#
Decimal	@
String	$

Before discussing the various variable declarations possible in Visual Basic.NET, it is a good idea to have a look at some of the ground rules for naming a variable. Although it is not necessary to follow a naming convention when naming variables, following one does make coding easy for the developers and for people who want to understand the code.

A variable name . . .

◆ Must begin with a letter.

◆ Can't contain a period or an identifier type character.

◆ Must not exceed 255 characters.

◆ Must be unique within the same scope. (A *scope* defines the range from which a variable can be accessed, such as a procedure, a form, or a module.)

NOTE

A *module* is a collection of procedures, and a *procedure* is a set of statements used to perform some specific task. You will learn about procedures, forms, and modules in later chapters.

Now that you've had a look at how to declare a variable, it is time to discuss how to initialize variables. You'll also take a look at some related keywords in Visual Basic.NET.

Variable Initialization

By default, a variable contains a value when it is declared. For example, an `Integer` variable contains 0, and a `Boolean` variable stores False by default.

You can initialize a variable to set a start value. The following code explains this:

```
Dim NumVar As Integer
NumVar = 20
```

The first statement declares an `Integer` variable `NumVar`, and the second one initializes it with the value `20`. Earlier versions of Visual Basic did not allow the initialization of variables in the same line as their declarations. At last, Visual Basic.NET now allows this. This means you can now write the following:

```
Dim NumVar As Integer = 20
```

The New Keyword

As you know, you use the `Dim` statement to declare or create variables. However, the variables are actually created when you use them in code or initialize them. You can use the `New` keyword to actually create a variable the moment you declare it. Consider the following code statements:

```
Dim NumVar As Integer
NumVar = New Integer()
```

or

```
Dim NumVar As Integer = New Integer()
```

or

```
Dim NumVar As New Integer()
```

Each of the preceding statements creates an Integer variable with the name NumVar.

The Nothing *Keyword*

Visual Basic.NET provides you with the Nothing keyword if you want to dissociate a variable from its data type. For example, if you assign Nothing to an Integer variable, the variable no longer contains the value it was holding and instead contains default value of its data type. To understand this better, here's an example:

```
Dim Ctr As Integer=10
Ctr=Nothing
```

After the execution of the first statement, Ctr contains the value 10. After the execution of the second statement, it contains Nothing. This means it now contains the value 0, which is the default value for an Integer variable.

The Null *Keyword*

As you know, in Visual Basic 6.0, the Null keyword is used to indicate that the variable contains no valid data, and the IsNull function is used to test for Null. In Visual Basic.NET, Null is still a reserved keyword, but it has no syntactical value, and the IsNull function is not supported. Visual Basic.6.0 supports Null propagation. This means that if you use Null in an expression, the result is also Null. Visual Basic.NET doesn't support this Null propagation.

When upgrading your Visual Basic 6.0 application to Visual Basic.NET, Null is converted to DBNull and IsNull to IsDBNull. There is a slight difference in the behavior of DBNull as compared to Null. The difference is that Null can be used in functions and assignments and DBNull cannot.

> **NOTE**
>
> You will learn about functions in Chapter 7, "Procedures and Functions."

Implicit and Explicit Declarations

Visual Basic.NET allows you to declare variables implicitly as well as explicitly. *Implicit declaration* means using a variable without declaring it. For example, consider the following statement:

```
NumVar = 2 * 5
```

In this statement, NumVar is a variable that stores the product of 2 and 5. In such a situation, Visual Basic.NET creates the variable automatically and also stores the result, 10, in it. However, this might lead to undesirable program results. For example, if you misspell the name of an implicitly declared variable at some other point in the program, the program will not give errors, but the result will be incorrect. To prevent this, you should declare variables explicitly.

The Option Explicit statement ensures that variables are declared before being used. The syntax is as follows:

```
Option Explicit [On ¦ Off]
```

On is used for explicit declarations, and Off is for implicit declaration. By default, Option Explicit is On.

Variable Scope

The *scope* of a variable determines its accessibility—that is, which part of the program or application can use it. For example, a variable can be used only within a particular block of code or in the entire program. Based on its accessibility, a variable can be called a *local* or *module-level* variable.

A variable that is declared inside a procedure can be accessed only within that procedure. Such a variable is referred to as a local variable. Sometimes you need to use a variable throughout an application or across modules within an application. Such variables are referred to as module-level variables. These variables are declared in the declaration section of the module. Module-level variables are further classified as *private* or *public*.

Private variables can be used only within the module in which they are declared. These can be declared only at the module level. The following statements declare a private variable:

```
Private Dim NumVar As Integer
```

or

```
Private NumVar As Integer
```

Public variables can be used across modules. These can also be declared at the module level. The following statements declare a public variable:

```
Public Dim NumVar As Integer
```

or

```
Public NumVar As Integer
```

Type Conversions

Consider an application in which you use three text boxes to accept three numbers from the user. The application needs to calculate and display the result. However, when you try to store the input numbers in some `Integer` variables, Visual Basic.NET flashes an error message saying that implicit conversion from `String` to `Integer` is not allowed. The same code in Visual Basic 6.0 would have worked fine. This is because Visual Basic 6.0 automatically does some data-type conversions—such as from `String` to `Number` and vice versa—depending on the data stored in a variable. This process of converting from one data type to another is referred to as *type conversion*. Visual Basic.NET does not do this automatically. Instead, you have to use some predefined functions provided by Visual Basic.NET, such as `CInt` and `CStr`, to achieve the same result. `CInt` and `CStr` convert the supplied data to `Integer` and `String`, respectively.

Visual Basic.NET provides two types of conversions, widening and narrowing:

◆ *Widening* conversions do not result in data loss and are always successful. For example, data conversion from `Short` to `Integer`.

◆ *Narrowing* conversions might result in data loss and might or might not be successful. For example, data conversion from Integer to Short.

The functions used for type conversions are also referred to as *cast operators*, and the conversions that involve these cast operators are called *explicit* conversions. The type conversions that do not involve cast operators are referred to as *implicit* conversions. Both of the conversion types supported by Visual Basic.NET, widening and narrowing, can be explicit and implicit.

The Option Strict statement performs type conversions successfully. The syntax for this statement is as follows:

```
Option Strict [ On ¦ Off ]
```

If you set Option Strict as On, the data type of variables is checked before conversion. If it is set as Off, implicit type conversion can happen. By default, this is set as On.

NOTE

When Option Strict is set as On, you need to declare variables explicitly.

Thus far, you have looked at data types and some associated concepts. Now, you will go a step further and see whether Visual Basic.NET supports constants.

Constants

Consider a situation in which you need to use a particular value throughout an application. For example, you need an application that calculates and displays the percentage of scores obtained by each candidate in an examination. For such a calculation, the application needs to use the maximum score in a number of places. In such a scenario, instead of repeating the value each time, you can use constants. A *constant* is a variable whose value remains the same during the execution of a program.

Consider the following statements:

```
Const MaxScore As Integer = 100
```

or

```
Const MaxScore = 100
```

Each of the preceding statements declares a constant with the name `MaxScore` and initializes it with the value `100`.

The processing of constants is faster than variables, and if there is any change in value, you just need to change the value at the point of declaring the constant.

Now that you understand variables and related concepts, the next logical step is to discuss how to perform various operations on these variables.

Using Operators

An *operator* is a unit of code that performs an operation on one or more variables or elements. An operator can be used to perform arithmetic, concatenation, comparison, or logical operations.

Visual Basic.NET supports the following operators:

◆ *Arithmetic operators* for mathematical calculations

◆ *Assignment operators* for assignment operations

◆ *Comparison operators* for comparisons

◆ *Logical/bitwise operators* for logical operations

◆ *Concatenation operators* for combining strings

Next, you will take a look at arithmetic, assignment, comparison, and logical/bitwise operators in more detail.

Arithmetic Operators

As explained in the preceding section, arithmetic operators are used to perform mathematical calculations. The arithmetic operators available in Visual Basic.NET are discussed in the following sections.

The ^ Operator

The ^ operator is used to raise a specified number to the power of another number. The syntax for the ^ operator is as follows:

```
Number ^ Exponent
```

In the syntax, both `Number` and `Exponent` denote numeric expressions. When you use the ^ operator, the resultant value is `Number` raised to the power of the `Exponent`.

The ^ operator supports only the `Double` data type. If the numbers supplied to the ^ operator are of any other data type, they are converted to `Double`. Consider the following examples:

```
Dim MyNum As Double
MyNum = 2 ^ 2
                                                'Returns a value of 4

MyNum = (-5) ^ 3
                                                'Returns a value of -125

MyNum = (-5) ^ 4
                                                'Returns a value of -625
```

The * Operator

The * operator is used to multiply two numbers. The syntax for the * operator is as follows:

```
Number1 * Number2
```

In the syntax, `Number1` and `Number2` are numeric expressions. When you use the * operator, the result is the product of `Number1` and `Number2`.

The * operator supports the following data types:

◆ `Byte`

◆ `Short`

◆ `Integer`

◆ `Long`

◆ `Single`

◆ `Double`

◆ `Decimal`

Take a look at the following examples:

```
Dim MyNum As Double
MyNum = 2 * 2
```

```
                                                           'Returns a value of 4
MyNum = 459.35 * 334.903
                                                           'Returns a value of
153836.315
```

The / Operator

The / operator divides two numbers and returns the result as a floating-point number. The syntax for the / operator is as follows:

```
Number1 / Number2
```

In the syntax, Number1 and Number2 are numeric expressions. The / operator returns the quotient of Number1 divided by Number2 as a floating-point number.

The / operator supports the following data types:

◆ Byte

◆ Short

◆ Integer

◆ Long

◆ Single

◆ Double

◆ Decimal

The following examples use the / operator to divide two numbers:

```
Dim MyNum As Double
MyNum = 10 / 4
                                                           'Returns a value
of 2.5
MyNum = 10 / 3
                                                           'Returns a
value of 3.333333
```

The \ Operator

The \ operator divides two numbers and returns the result as an integer. The syntax for the \ operator is as follows:

```
Number1 \ Number2
```

In the syntax, `Number1` and `Number2` represent two integers. When you use the \
operator to divide two numbers, the result is the integer quotient of `Number1` and
`Number2`. When dividing `Number1` by `Number2`, the remainder (if any) is ignored.

The following data types are supported by the \ operator:

- ◆ `Byte`
- ◆ `Short`
- ◆ `Integer`
- ◆ `Long`

Take a look at the following examples to understand how the \ operator works.
The result is an integer representing the integer quotient of the two operands.

```
Dim MyNum As Integer
MyNum = 11 \ 4
                                                      'Returns 2

MyNum = 9 \ 3
                                                      'Returns 3

MyNum = 100 \ 3
                                                      'Returns 33

MyNum = 67 \ -3
                                                      'Returns -22
```

Notice that in each of the preceding examples, the remainder is ignored.

The Mod Operator

The `Mod` operator divides two numbers and returns the remainder. The syntax for
the `Mod` operator is as follows:

```
Number1 Mod Number2
```

In the syntax, `Number1` and `Number2` represent any two numbers. When you use
the `Mod` operator, it returns the remainder left after dividing `Number1` by `Number2`.

The Mod operator supports the following data types:

◆ Byte

◆ Short

◆ Integer

◆ Long

◆ Single

◆ Double

◆ Decimal

Let's look at a few examples in which the Mod operator is used.

```
Dim MyRem As Double
MyRem = 6 Mod 2
                                            'Returns 0

MyRem = 7 Mod 3
                                            'Returns 1

MyRem = 12 Mod 4.3
                                            'Returns 3.4

MyRem = 47.9 Mod 9.35
                                            'Returns 1.15
```

Note that if you use a floating-point number with the Mod operator, the remainder is also a floating-point number.

The + Operator

The + operator is used to add two numbers or to concatenate two strings. The syntax for the + operator is as follows:

```
Expression1+ Expression2
```

In the syntax, Expression1 and Expression2 can either be numbers or strings. When you use the + operator with numbers, the result is the sum of Expression1 and Expression2. If Expression1 and Expression2 are strings, the result is a concatenated string. When you use the + operator, however, both Expression1 and Expression2 should be of the same type.

The + operator supports the following data types:

- Byte
- Short
- Integer
- Long
- Single
- Double
- Decimal
- String

Consider the following examples:

```
Dim MyNum As Integer
Dim StrVar As String
MyNum = 2 + 5
                                            'Returns 7

MyNum = 569.08 + 24889
                                            'Returns 25458.08

StrVar = "Visual Basic" + ".NET"
                                            'Returns Visual Basic.NET
```

The – Operator

The - operator is used to calculate the difference between two numbers. The syntax for the - operator is as follows:

```
Number1 - Number2
```

In the syntax, `Number1` and `Number2` are two numbers.

The - operator supports the following data types:

- Byte
- Short
- Integer
- Long
- Single
- Double
- Decimal

Consider the following examples:

```
Dim MyDiff As Double

MyDiff = 7 - 2
                                              'Returns 5

MyDiff = 470.35 - 247.72
                                              'Returns 222.63
```

Assignment Operators

As previously mentioned, assignment operators are used for assignment operations. In other words, they are used to assign values or expressions to variables or properties. The most commonly used assignment operator is =. Additionally, Visual Basic.NET now supports assignment operators such as +=, -=, *=, /=, \=, &=, and ^=. The following sections explain these operators.

The += Operator

The += (addition assignment) operator is a combination of two operators, + and =. Therefore, it performs these two operations (addition and assignment) using a single += operator. In other words, the += operator adds the expression to the variable and also assigns the result value to the variable in one shot. The syntax for += is as follows:

```
Variable+=Expression
```

In the preceding syntax, `Variable` is any numeric or string variable, and `Expression` is any numeric or string expression. Consider the following example that uses numeric variables:

```
Dim NumVar As Integer=10
                                        'NumVar contains 10

NumVar += 50
                                        'NumVar now contains 60
```

Consider another example that uses the += operator:

```
Dim NumVar1 As Integer=20
Dim NumVar2 As Integer=30
NumVar1+=NumVar2
```

```
                                    'NumVar1 now contains 50 and NumVar2
still contains 30
```

Now consider the following code that uses the += operator with string values:

```
Dim StrVar As String="String"
StrVar+="Result"
                                    'StrVar now contains the value String
Result
```

The –= Operator

The –= (subtraction assignment) operator is a combination of the - and = operators. Therefore, it performs these two operations (subtraction and assignment) using a single –= operator. In other words, the –= operator subtracts the value and also assigns the result to the variable in one shot. The syntax for –= is as follows:

```
Variable-=Expression
```

In the preceding syntax, `Variable` is any numeric variable, and an `Expression` is any numeric expression. Consider the following example, which uses the –= operator:

```
Dim NumVar As Integer=100
                                    'NumVar contains 100
NumVar -= 60
                                    'NumVar now contains 40
```

Consider another example:

```
Dim NumVar1 As Integer=50
Dim NumVar2 As Integer=30
NumVar1-=NumVar2
                                    'NumVar1 now contains 20 and NumVar2
still contains 30
```

The *= Operator

The *= (multiplication assignment) operator is a combination of the * and = operators. Therefore, it performs these two operations (subtraction and assignment) using a single *= operator. In other words, the *= operator subtracts the expression from the variable and also assigns the result to the variable in one step. The syntax for *= is as follows:

```
Variable*=Expression
```

In the preceding syntax, Variable is any numeric variable, and Expression is any numeric expression. Consider the following example, which uses the *= operator:

```
Dim NumVar As Integer=10
                                        'NumVar contains 10

NumVar *= 4
                                        'NumVar now contains 40
```

Consider another example:

```
Dim NumVar1 As Integer=10
Dim NumVar2 As Integer=2
NumVar1*=NumVar2
                                        'NumVar1 now contains 20 and NumVar2

still contains 2
```

The /= Operator

The /= (division assignment) operator is a combination of the / and = operators. Therefore, it performs these two operations (division and assignment) using a single /= operator. In other words, the /= operator divides the variable by the expression and also assigns the result to the variable. The syntax for /= is as follows:

```
Variable/=Expression
```

In the preceding syntax, Variable is any numeric variable, and Expression is any numeric expression. Consider the following example, which uses the /= operator:

```
Dim NumVar As Double=10.4
                                        'NumVar contains 10.4

NumVar /= 2
                                        'NumVar now contains 5.2
```

Consider another example:

```
Dim NumVar1 As Integer=50
Dim NumVar2 As Integer=10
NumVar1/=NumVar2
                                        'NumVar1 now contains 5 and

NumVar2 still contains 10
```

The \= Operator

The \= (integer division assignment) operator is a combination of the \ and = operators. Therefore, it performs these two operations (integer division and assignment) using a single \= operator. In other words, the \= operator divides the variable by the expression and also assigns the integer result to the variable. The syntax for \= is as follows:

```
Variable\=Expression
```

In the preceding syntax, Variable is any numeric variable, and an Expression is any numeric expression. Consider the following example, which uses the \= operator:

```
Dim NumVar As Double=10.4
                                        'NumVar contains 10.4
NumVar \= 2
                                        'NumVar now contains 5
```

Consider another example:

```
Dim NumVar1 As Integer=50
Dim NumVar2 As Integer=10
NumVar1\=NumVar2
                                        'NumVar1 now contains 5 and NumVar2 still
contains 10
```

The &= Operator

The &= (concatenate assignment) operator is a combination of the & and = operators. Therefore, the &= operator concatenates the string variable and the string expression and also assigns the concatenated string to the string variable. The syntax for &= is as follows:

```
Variable&=Expression
```

In the preceding syntax, Variable is any string variable, and an Expression is any string expression. Consider the following example, which uses the &= operator:

```
Dim StrVar As String="My string"
                                        'NumVar contains My string
NumVar &= " is concatenated."
                                        'NumVar now contains My string is
concatenated.
```

Consider another example:

```
Dim StrVar1 As String="My string"
Dim StrVar2 As String=" is concatenated."
StrVar1&=StrVar2
                                'StrVar1 now contains My string is con-
catenated and StrVar2 still contains My string
```

The ^= Operator

The ^= operator is used to raise a variable to the power of an expression and also to assign the result to the variable. The syntax for the ^= operator is as follows:

```
Number ^= Exponent
```

In this syntax, both Number and Exponent denote numeric expressions. When you use the ^= operator, first Number is raised to the power of Exponent, and then the result is assigned back to Number.

Consider the following example:

```
Dim NumVar As Double = 3
NumVar ^= 2
                                'NumVar now contains 9
```

Comparison Operators

As the name suggests, you use comparison operators to compare expressions. In Visual Basic.NET, you can use the following operators to compare expressions:

◆ The relational operators
◆ The Is operator
◆ The Like operator

The Relational Operators

You use relational operators to compare any two expressions. When you use a relational operator, the result is a Boolean value. The syntax for using relational operators is as follows:

```
Result = Expression1 ComOperator Expression2
```

In the syntax, `Result` is a `Boolean` value representing the result of the comparison, `ComOperator` represents the relational operator, and `Expression1` and `Expression2` represent expressions that are being compared.

The various relational operators available in Visual Basic.NET are listed in Table 4-3. Table 4-3 also explains the conditions that determine the value of `Result`.

Table 4-3 The Relational Operators in Visual Basic.NET

Operator	Result Is True If	Result Is False If
< (less than)	Expression1 < Expression2	Expression1 >= Expression2
<= (less than or equal to)	Expression1 <= Expression2	Expression1 > Expression2
> (greater than)	Expression1 > Expression2	Expression1 <= Expression2
>= (greater than or equal to)	Expression1 >= Expression2	Expression1 < Expression2
= (equal to)	Expression1 = Expression2	Expression1 <> Expression2
<> (not equal to)	Expression1 <> Expression2	Expression1 = Expression2

When you use the relational operators to compare strings, the result is calculated on the basis of the alphabetical sort order of the strings. When comparing strings, you need to enclose the string expressions in quotes.

Here are a few examples to help you understand the use of relational operators:

```
Dim MyResult As Boolean
MyResult = 56 < 35
                                        'Returns False

MyResult = 3 <> 9
                                        'Returns True

MyResult = "6" > "333"
                                        'Returns True
```

The Is Operator

In Visual Basic.NET, the `Is` operator is used to compare two object references. The syntax for the `Is` operator is as follows:

```
Result = Object1 Is Object2
```

In the syntax, `Result` is a `Boolean` value representing the result of the comparison, and `Object1` and `Object2` represent objects being compared. The `Is` operator determines whether both `Object1` and `Object2` refer to the same object. However, the `Is` operator does not compare the values of `Object1` and `Object2`. The value of `Result` is `True` if `Object1` and `Object2` refer to the same object; otherwise, `Result` is `False`.

Here are a few examples in which the `Is` operator is used:

```
Dim Object1, Object2 As New Object
Dim MyObjectA, MyObjectB, MyObjectC As Object
Dim MyResult As Boolean
MyObjectA = Object1
MyObjectB = Object2
MyObjectC = Object2
MyResult = MyObjectA Is MyObjectB

'Returns False
MyResult = MyObjectB Is MyObjectC

'Returns True
MyResult = MyObjectA Is MyObjectC

'Returns False
```

The Like Operator

In Visual Basic.NET, the `Like` operator is used to compare strings. The syntax for the `Like` operator is as follows:

```
Result = String Like Pattern
```

In the syntax, `Result` is a `Boolean` value that represents the result of the comparison, `String` represents a string expression, and `Pattern` also represents a string expression. When using the `Like` operator, you can also use wildcards to specify a `Pattern`. Table 4-4 shows the various characters allowed in `Pattern` and provides a description.

Table 4-4 The Characters Allowed in *Pattern* in the *Like* Operator

Character in `Pattern`	Matches
?	Any one character
*	Zero or more characters
#	Any single digit (0–9)
[list]	Any one character in the specified list
[!list]	Any one character other than the characters in list

When you use the `Like` operator, `Result` is `True` if `String` matches `Pattern`. In addition, if both `String` and `Pattern` are empty strings, `Result` is `True`. If `String` does not match `Pattern`, `Result` is `False`. Also, if either `String` or `Pattern` is an empty string, `Result` is `False`.

Consider the following examples:

```
Dim MyValue As Boolean
MyValue = "A" Like "A"
                                                'Returns True

MyValue = "A" Like "a"
                                                'Returns False

MyValue = "C" Like "[A-F]"
                                                'Returns True

MyValue = "H" Like "[A-F]"
                                                'Returns False

MyValue = "D" Like "[!A-F]"
                                                'Returns False

MyValue = "zxyz" Like "z*z"
                                                'Returns True

MyValue = "GFdAT13h4g" Like "GF?A*"
                                                'Returns True
```

Logical/Bitwise Operators

As previously mentioned, logical operators enable you to perform logical operations. Visual Basic.NET provides the following logical operators:

- ◆ And operator
- ◆ Not operator

- ◆ `Or` operator
- ◆ `Xor` operator
- ◆ `AndAlso` operator
- ◆ `OrElse` operator

You might be familiar with the first four operators because they are available in previous versions of Visual Basic. The `AndAlso` and `OrElse` operators are additional operators provided by Visual Basic.NET.

The following sections look at each of the logical operators in detail.

The And *Operator*

The `And` operator is used to perform logical operations on `Boolean` expressions. You can also use the `And` operator to perform bitwise operations on numeric expressions. The syntax for the `And` operator is as follows:

```
Result = Expression1 And Expression2
```

In the syntax, `Result`, `Expression1`, and `Expression2` are either `Boolean` values or numeric expressions.

When using `Boolean` expressions with the `And` operator, if both `Expression1` and `Expression2` evaluate to `True`, then `Result` is `True`. If either of the `Boolean` expressions evaluate to `False`, `Result` is `False`. If both `Expression1` and `Expression2` evaluate to `False`, `Result` is `False`.

When using the `And` operator with numeric expressions, the `And` operator performs a bitwise comparison of identically positioned bits in two numeric expressions. Based on the comparison, the `And` operator sets the value of `Result`. The calculation of `Result` in a bitwise comparison is explained in Table 4-5.

Table 4-5 The Calculation of *Result* in a Bitwise Comparison by Using the *And* Operator

If Bit in Expression1 Is	And Bit in Expression2 Is	Result Is
0	0	0
0	1	0
1	0	0
1	1	1

Consider the following examples:

```
Dim X As Integer = 8
Dim Y As Integer = 7
Dim Z As Integer = 5
Dim MyResult As Boolean
MyResult = X > Y And Y > Z
                                            'Returns True
MyResult = Y > X And Y > Z
                                            'Returns False
```

This following examples explain using the And operator for performing bitwise comparison:

```
Dim A As Integer = 10
Dim B As Integer = 8
Dim C As Integer = 6
Dim MyResult As Integer
MyResult = (A And B)
                                            'Returns 8
MyResult = (A And C)
                                            'Returns 2
MyResult = (B And C)
                                            'Returns 0
```

The Not *Operator*

The Not operator is used to perform logical operations on Boolean expressions and bitwise operations on numeric expressions. The syntax for the Not operator is as follows:

```
Result = Not Expression
```

In the syntax, both Result and Expression are either Boolean values or numeric expressions.

When using Boolean values with the Not operator, if Expression is True, then Result is False. If Expression is False, Result is True.

When using numeric expressions with the Not operator, if the bit in Expression is 0, then the bit in Result is 1. If the bit in Expression is 1, the bit in Result is 0.

The following examples use the Not operator to perform bitwise operations on numeric expressions:

```
Dim X As Integer = 8
Dim Y As Integer = 7
Dim MyResult As Boolean
MyResult = Not(X > Y)
                                                'Returns False

MyResult = Not(Y > X)
                                                'Returns True

Dim A As Integer = 10
Dim B As Integer = 8
Dim MyCheck As Integer
MyCheck = (Not A)
                                                'Returns -11

MyCheck = (Not B)
                                                'Returns -9
```

The Or Operator

The Or operator is used to perform logical and bitwise operations on Boolean and numeric expressions, respectively. The syntax for the Or operator is as follows:

```
Result = Expression1 Or Expression2
```

In the syntax, Result, Expression1, and Expression2 are either Boolean values or numeric expressions.

When using Boolean expressions with the Or operator, if either Expression1 or Expression2 evaluates to True, then Result is True. If both Expression1 and Expression2 evaluate to True, Result is True. If both Expression1 and Expression2 evaluate to False, Result is False.

When using the Or operator with numeric expressions, the Or operator works in the same manner as the And operator. It performs a bitwise comparison of identically positioned bits in two numeric expressions. Based on the comparison, the Or operator sets the value of Result. The calculation of Result in a bitwise comparison is explained in Table 4-6.

Table 4-6 The Calculation of *Result* in a Bitwise Comparison by Using the *Or* Operator

If Bit in Expression1 Is	And Bit in Expression2 Is	Result Is
0	0	0
0	1	1
1	0	1
1	1	1

Consider the following examples:

```
Dim A As Integer = 9
Dim B As Integer = 8
Dim C As Integer = 7
Dim MyCheck As Boolean
MyCheck = A > B Or B > C
                                        'Returns True
MyCheck = B > A Or B > C
                                        'Returns True
MyCheck = B > A Or C > B
                                        'Returns False
```

The following example uses the Or operator to perform bitwise operations on numeric expressions:

```
Dim A As Integer = 5
Dim B As Integer = 6
Dim C As Integer = 7
Dim MyCheck As Integer
MyCheck = (A Or B)
                                        'Returns 7
MyCheck = (A Or C)
                                        'Returns 7
MyCheck = (B Or C)
                                        'Returns 7
```

The Xor *Operator*

You can use the Xor operator to perform logical exclusion operations on two Boolean expressions. In addition, the Xor operator is also used to perform bitwise exclusion operations on two numeric expressions. The syntax for the Xor operator is as follows:

```
Result = Expression1 Xor Expression2
```

In the syntax, Result, Expression1, and Expression2 are either Boolean values or numeric expressions.

When using Boolean expressions with the Xor operator, if either Expression1 or Expression2 evaluates to True, then Result is True. If both Expression1 and Expression2 evaluate to True, Result is False. If both Expression1 and Expression2 evaluate to False, Result is False.

When using the Xor operator with numeric expressions, the Xor operator works as a bitwise operator. In other words, it performs a bitwise comparison of expressions. Based on the comparison, the Xor operator sets the value of Result. The calculation of Result in a bitwise comparison is explained in Table 4-7.

Table 4-7 The Calculation of *Result* in a Bitwise Comparison by Using the *Xor* Operator

If Bit in Expression1 Is	And Bit in Expression2 Is	Result Is
0	0	0
0	1	1
1	0	1
1	1	0

The following examples use the Xor operator to perform bitwise operations on numeric expressions:

```
Dim A As Integer = 10
Dim B As Integer = 5
Dim C As Integer = 2
Dim MyCheck As Boolean
MyCheck = A > B Xor B > C
```

```
                                                          'Returns
False
MyCheck = B > A Xor B > C
                                                          'Returns
True
MyCheck = B > A Xor C > B
                                                          'Returns
False

Dim A As Integer = 10
Dim B As Integer = 5
Dim C As Integer = 2
Dim MyCheck As Integer
MyCheck = (A Xor B)
                                                          'Returns 15
MyCheck = (A Xor C)
                                                          'Returns 8
MyCheck = (B Xor C)
                                                          'Returns 7
```

The AndAlso *Operator*

As previously mentioned, the AndAlso operator is new to the Visual Basic.NET language. This operator was not available in previous versions of Visual Basic. The AndAlso operator is used to perform logical operations on expressions. The syntax for the AndAlso operator is as follows:

```
Result = Expression1 AndAlso Expression2
```

In the syntax, Result, Expression1, and Expression2 are all Boolean expressions. The AndAlso operator works like the And operator, but it is smarter.

When using Boolean expressions with the AndAlso operator, the operator first checks the value of Expression1. If Expression1 evaluates to True, the AndAlso operator checks the value of Expression2. It sets the value of Result based on the value of Expression2. If Expression2 evaluates to True, Result is True; otherwise, Result is False. However, if Expression1 evaluates to False, the AndAlso operator does not check the value of Expression2 and sets the value of Result to False.

Take a look at the following example:

```
Dim A As Integer = 15
Dim B As Integer = 10
Dim C As Integer = 5
Dim MyResult As Boolean
MyResult = A > B AndAlso B > C
                                                              'Returns
True
MyResult = B > A AndAlso B > C
                                                              'Returns
False
MyResult = A > B AndAlso C > B
                                                              'Returns
False
```

In this example, the second expression of the second statement is not evaluated because the first expression evaluates to False. On the other hand, the second expression of the third statement is evaluated because the first expression evaluates to True.

The OrElse Operator

Like the AndAlso operator, the OrElse operator is also a new addition to the Visual Basic language. This operator is available only in Visual Basic.NET. The OrElse operator is used to perform logical operations on Boolean expressions. The syntax for the OrElse operator is as follows:

```
Result = Expression1 OrElse Expression2
```

In the syntax, Result, Expression1, and Expression2 are Boolean expressions.

Just as the AndAlso operator is a smarter version of And, the OrElse operator is a smarter version of the Or operator.

When using Boolean expressions with the OrElse operator, the operator first checks the value of Expression1. If Expression1 evaluates to True, the OrElse operator does not check the value of Expression2 and sets the value of Result to True. However, if Expression1 evaluates to False, the OrElse operator checks the value of Expression2. It sets the value of Result based on the value of Expression2. If Expression2 evaluates to True, Result is True; otherwise, Result is False.

Take a look at the following example to understand how the OrElse operator works:

```
Dim A As Integer = 15
Dim B As Integer = 10
Dim C As Integer = 5
Dim MyResult As Boolean
MyResult = A > B OrElse B > C
                                                          'Returns
True
MyResult = B > A OrElse B > C
                                                          'Returns
True
MyResult = B > A OrElse C > B
                                                          'Returns
False
```

In this example, the second expression of the first statement is not evaluated because the first expression evaluates to True. On the other hand, in the second and third statements, the second expression is evaluated because the first expression evaluates to False.

Summary

A variable is a memory location in which to store data. Visual Basic.NET provides various data types to store different kinds of data. You need to declare a variable before you can use it, and the Dim statement is used to declare a variable. Visual Basic.NET now allows initialization of the variable in the same line where it is declared. Declaration can be explicit or implicit. The scope of the variable refers to its accessibility and can be public or private. Visual Basic.NET allows type conversions and constants. You can use many operators in Visual Basic.NET to perform operations on variables. These can be classified as arithmetic operators (for mathematical calculations), assignment operators (for assignment operations), comparison operators (for comparisons), logical/bitwise operators (for logical operations), and concatenation operators (for combining strings). The AndAlso and OrElse operators are additional logical operators provided by Visual Basic.NET.

Chapter 5

In the preceding chapter, you learned to use variables and operators in Visual Basic.NET. In this chapter, you will take a look at the various types of arrays and collections supported by Visual Basic.NET.

Arrays

You already know that you use variables to store data. There might be situations in which you need to work with multiple variables that store similar information. For example, consider a scenario in which you need to store the names of 50 students. To do so, you can declare 50 variables. However, declaring 50 variables is a tedious and time-consuming task. Alternatively, you can declare an array.

An *array* is a collection of variables of the same data type. All the variables in an array have the same name. These variables are called *array elements*. Each variable in an array is referred to by an *index number*, which is its position in the array. Therefore, the index number is what distinguishes one array element from another. For example, you can declare an array that contains 50 variables of the String data type to store the names of 50 students. When you declare an array, you create and initialize all variables at once. For example, when you declare an Integer array, all the elements are initialized to 0. It is easier to manipulate an array and its elements as compared to multiple variables. For example, you can use the various loop structures that Visual Basic.NET provides to manipulate arrays. You will learn more about how to manipulate arrays later in this chapter.

All arrays that you create in Visual Basic.NET are derived from the Array class of the System namespace. This implies that you can use the methods and properties of System.Array type to manipulate arrays.

Now that you've had an overview of arrays, you'll take a look at how to declare arrays.

Declaring Arrays

Just like a variable, before you can use an array in a program, you need to declare the array. When you declare an array, you specify the name of the array, its data type, and the number of variables it contains. In Visual Basic.NET, you declare arrays in the same manner as you declare variables, by using the `Dim`, `Public`, or `Private` statements. The syntax for declaring an array is as follows:

```
Dim ArrayName (NumElements) [As DataType]
```

In the preceding syntax:

◆ `ArrayName` is the name of the array.

◆ `NumElements` is the number of elements the array can contain.

◆ `DataType` is the data type of the elements and is optional.

When declaring arrays, include parentheses after the array name to indicate that it is an array and not a variable. To understand this better, consider the following code statement:

```
Dim IntArray(10) As Integer
```

The preceding statement declares an `Integer` array by the name `IntArray` that can contain 11 elements. You might be wondering why it can contain 11 elements and not 10 as stated in the code. Well, the answer is that the arrays are zero based. This means, for the preceding statement, the index number is between 0 and 10, which adds up to 11. The preceding statement is actually a short form of the following statement:

```
Dim IntArray () As Integer = New Integer(10) {}
```

Now you will take a look at some differences between Visual Basic.NET and earlier versions of Visual Basic in terms of arrays. In Visual Basic 6.0, the default starting index of an array is 0. You can change the starting index to 1 using the `Option Base` statement. In addition, you can also change the starting index for individual array declarations. If the default starting index is 0, the number of elements in the array is equal to the number specified during declaration plus one. However, in Visual Basic.NET, the starting index for every array is 0, and you cannot change it. This means that Visual Basic.NET does not support the `Option Base` statement. This allows interoperability with arrays of other programming languages, as most programming languages support zero-based arrays.

In an array, each element of an array is initialized as if it were a separate variable. However, if you do not initialize an array, Visual Basic.NET initializes each array element to the default value of the array's data type.

The following code explains how to declare and initialize an array:

```
Dim BooksArray(3) As String
BooksArray(0) = "VB.NET"
BooksArray(1) = "ADO.NET"
BooksArray(2) = "VC++.NET"
BooksArray(3) = "ASP.NET"
```

In the preceding code, BooksArray is an array that can contain four String-type elements. VB.NET is stored at index 0 of the BooksArray array. ADO.NET is stored at index 1, VC++.NET at index 2, and ASP.NET at index 3. Here, 0 is the starting index, or the *lower bound*, of the array. The lower bound is fixed for all the arrays. The end index, or the *upper bound*, is 3 and can differ from one array to another.

Visual Basic.NET provides a new syntax that you can use to declare and initialize an array in a single line. The following example shows how to declare an array by using a single line of code:

```
Dim BooksArray() As String = {"VB.NET", "ADO.NET", "VC++.NET", "ASP.NET"}
```

To retrieve the values stored at a particular index position, you need to specify the index number along with the array name. For example, consider the following statements:

```
Dim StrVar As String
StrVar = BooksArray(2)
```

After the execution of the preceding statements, the StrVar String variable contains the value VC++.NET, which is stored at index position 2 in BooksArray.

Now that you've learned to create and initialize one-dimensional arrays, you'll learn about multidimensional arrays.

Multidimensional Arrays

In the preceding sections, you looked at one-dimensional arrays. To understand multidimensional arrays, you will take the same book array example further. Now you need to store book names as well as their prices. For this, you can create one array for storing the book names and another for the prices. This might not be a very good idea, however, because you need to declare two arrays and also remember their names to refer to them. A good alternative would be to create an array having two dimensions and store data at one place.

A *multidimensional* array is an array with more than one dimension. Although Visual Basic.NET supports up to 32 dimensions in an array, in most cases, you would generally use two- or three-dimensional arrays. The following statement declares a two-dimensional array with 5 rows and 10 columns.

```
Dim BooksArray (5,10) As String
```

In the preceding statement, BooksArray is the name of the String array that can contain 66 elements. Why 66? Well, because 66 is the product of 6 (one plus the size of the first dimension) and 11 (one plus the size of the second dimension) and therefore is the maximum number of elements that BooksArray can contain.

The following statement declares a three-dimensional array:

```
Dim BooksArray (4,9,4) As String
```

Again, follow the same calculation you used to arrive at 66 in the case of the two-dimensional array from the earlier code statement. Here, the total number of elements that the array can contain is 250. Here, 250 is the product of 5 (one plus the size of the first dimension), 10 (one plus the size of the second dimension), and 5 (one plus the size of the third dimension).

Now, this question arises: How do you initialize a multidimensional array? Consider the following statements:

```
Dim BooksArray(5,1) As String
BooksArray(0,0) = "VB.NET"
..................................'Stores the value VB.NET at the index position (0,0)
BooksArray(0,1) = "$1250"
.................................. 'Stores the value $1250 at the index position (0,1) i.e 0th row and
1st column
BooksArray(1,0) = "ADO.NET"
.................................. 'Stores the value ADO.NET at (1,0) i.e. 1st row and 0th column
```

As you can see in the preceding statements, you need to refer to individual elements in a multidimensional array by their row and column numbers. In this example, the index value ranges from 0 through 5 for a row and from 0 through 1 for a column.

You can process a multidimensional array effectively by using For loops. Consider the following code:

```
Dim StrArray(2, 2) As String
Dim Counter1, Counter2 As Integer
For Counter1 = 0 To 2
    For Counter2 = 0 To 2
                    StrArray(Counter1, Counter2) = CStr(Counter1) + "," +
CStr(Counter2)
      Next
Next
```

In the preceding code, the first statement declares a String array called StrArray that has two rows and two columns. The second statement declares two Integer variables, Counter1 and Counter2, for processing the For loops. The statements from the third statement onward execute the For loops and initialize every element of the StrArray array to a String that varies from 0,0 through 2,2, depending on its location (row, column) in the array. In other words, the values assigned are as follows:

```
StrArray(0,0)=0,0
StrArray(0,1)=0,1
...
StrArray(2,2)=2,2
```

You will learn about the For loops in Chapter 6, "Conditional Logic."

NOTE

CStr is a type conversion function that converts the data passed as a parameter to the String data type. In the preceding code, because this function takes an Integer variable as a parameter, it converts the Integer data to String. You need to use this function because Visual Basic.NET doesn't allow implicit conversion of Integer data to String.

In this section, you learned to specify the size of an array at the time of declaring the array. Next you will look at how to create arrays with varying sizes in Visual Basic.NET.

Dynamic Arrays

You might need an application in which you are not aware of the total number of elements to be stored in an array. For example, you might need an array to store the names of items bought by a customer. You cannot specify a size for this array because you don't know how many items a customer will buy. For such an application, you can use a *dynamic* array. The size of a dynamic array can change during the execution of the program. Consider the following statement:

```
Dim ItemNames() As String
```

The preceding statement declares an array named `ItemNames` that is of type `String`. Note that the number of elements in the array is not specified.

Now that you know how to create dynamic arrays, you will look at how to resize a dynamic array to suit your program's requirements.

The ReDim *Statement*

You use the `ReDim` statement to resize an array. Before you can resize an array, you must first declare the array. To resize the array you declared earlier, you can use the following statement:

```
ReDim ItemNames (25)
```

The preceding statement resizes the `ItemNames` array to store 26 elements.

You can also resize multidimensional arrays, but you cannot change the number of dimensions and the data type of an array. Consider the following statements:

```
Dim BooksArray(2,3) As String
ReDim BooksArray (4,5)
```

In the preceding code, the first statement declares a two-dimensional array, `BooksArray`, with two rows and three columns. You can store 12 elements in this array. The second statement resizes the same array to store 30 elements. The first dimension is changed from 2 to 4 rows and the second one from 3 to 5.

When you use the `ReDim` statement, an array loses all its existing data, and the elements of the new array are initialized with the default value of their data type. To prevent data loss due to the resizing of an array, you can use the `Preserve` keyword. The following section explains this keyword.

The Preserve *Keyword*

As the name suggests, the `Preserve` keyword helps you preserve the existing data in an array. Consider the following statement:

```
ReDim Preserve BooksArray(25)
```

The preceding statement resizes the `BooksArray` array and also preserves its existing data.

You can also use the `Preserve` keyword for multidimensional arrays. However, only the last dimension of a multidimensional array can be modified. To understand this better, consider the following example:

```
Dim BooksArray(5,5) As String
```

You can resize the preceding `BooksArray` in the following manner:

```
ReDim Preserve BooksArray(10,10)
```

After the execution of the preceding statement, Visual Basic.NET flashes an error message because you are trying to resize both dimensions while preserving the existing data. However, you can use the following statement:

```
ReDim Preserve BooksArray(5,10)
```

The preceding statement resizes the last dimension of the array (from 5 to 10) and also preserves its existing data. The following code illustrates the use of the `ReDim` statement and the `Preserve` keyword:

```
Dim BooksArray() As String = {"VB.NET"}
..............................................'Declare and initialize the array
'Displaying the content of the array
MessageBox.Show(BooksArray(0))
..............................................'Displays VB.NET
'Specifying the size of the array
ReDim BooksArray(1)
..............................................'Resizes the array to store two elements
'Displaying the content of the array
MessageBox.Show(BooksArray(0))
..............................................'Displays a blank dialog box
'Initializing the array
BooksArray(0) = "VB.NET"
```

```
BooksArray(1) = "ADO.NET"
'Displaying the contents of array
MessageBox.Show(BooksArray (0))
...............................................'Displays VB.NET
MessageBox.Show(BooksArray (1))
...............................................'Displays ADO.NET
'Modifying the size of array using Preserve
ReDim Preserve BooksArray (2)
'Displaying the contents
MessageBox.Show(BooksArray (0))
...............................................'Displays VB.NET
MessageBox.Show(BooksArray (1))
...............................................'Displays ADO.NET
'Adding more contents
BooksArray (2) = "ASP.NET"
'Displaying the new content
MessageBox.Show(BooksArray (2))
............................................... 'Displays ASP.NET
```

In the preceding example, BooksArray is an array of the String type. Initially, BooksArray contains the value VB.NET. The array is then resized using the ReDim statement. All the contents of the array are lost. Then the values of VB.NET and ADO.NET are stored in the array. Now the size of the array is further increased. However, this time the Preserve keyword is used along with the ReDim statement. As a result, the initial contents are retained.

The Erase *Statement*

When you no longer need an array in your program, it is a good practice to release the memory assigned to it. For releasing memory assigned to an array, you can use the Erase statement. Here's how you can release the memory assigned to the BooksArray array:

```
Erase BooksArray
```

You can also specify multiple names in a single Erase statement as shown in the following:

```
Erase BooksArray, ItemNames, ItemPrice
```

The preceding statement erases the memory assigned to all of the three arrays: `BooksArray`, `ItemNames`, and `ItemPrice`.

As you already know, Visual Basic.NET provides the `System.Array` class for working with arrays. This class provides various methods you can use to manipulate arrays easily. The next section discusses these methods.

The Array Class Methods

Some of the commonly used methods of the `System.Array` class are discussed in the following sections.

The GetUpperBound *Method*

The `GetUpperBound` method takes the dimension of an array as a parameter and returns the upper bound of the specified dimension. The syntax for this method is as follows:

```
ArrayName.GetUpperBound(Dimension)
```

In the preceding syntax:

- ◆ `ArrayName` refers to the name of the array whose upper bound you want to find.
- ◆ `Dimension` refers to the dimension number for which you want to find the upper bound. You use 0 for the first dimension, 1 for the second dimension, and so on.

Consider the following example:

```
Dim BooksArray(10,20,30) As String
Dim BoundVar As Integer
BoundVar = BooksArray.GetUpperBound(0)
                                                    'Returns 10
BoundVar = BooksArray.GetUpperBound(2)
                                                    'Returns 30
```

The GetLowerBound *Method*

The `GetLowerBound` method takes the dimension of an array as a parameter and returns the lower bound of the specified dimension. However, this method will always return 0 because the lower bound for all the dimensions is 0. The syntax for this method is as follows:

```
ArrayName.GetLowerBound (Dimension)
```

In the preceding syntax:

◆ `ArrayName` refers to the name of the array whose lower bound you want to find.

◆ `Dimension` refers to the dimension number for which you want to find the lower bound.

Consider the following example:

```
Dim BooksArray(10,20,30) As String
Dim BoundVar As Integer
BoundVar = BooksArray.GetLowerBound(0)

'Returns 0
BoundVar = BooksArray. GetLowerBound (2)

'Returns 0
```

The GetLength Method

The `GetLength` method takes the dimension of an array and returns the number of elements in the specified dimension. The syntax is as follows:

```
ArrayName.GetLength(Dimension)
```

In the preceding syntax:

◆ `ArrayName` refers to the name of the array whose length you want to find.

◆ `Dimension` refers to the dimension number whose length you want to find.

Consider the following example:

```
Dim BooksArray(10,20,30) As String
Dim BoundVar As Integer
BoundVar = BooksArray.GetLength(0)
```

```
'Returns 11
BoundVar = BooksArray. GetLength(2)


'Returns 31
```

The SetValue *Method*

The SetValue method sets a value for the specified array element. It takes two parameters: the value that needs to be set and the index number of the element whose value you want to set. The syntax for this method for a one-dimensional array is as follows:

```
ArrayName.SetValue(Value, Pos)
```

In the preceding syntax:

- ◆ ArrayName refers to the name of the array.
- ◆ Value refers to the value you want to set for the specified index number.
- ◆ Pos refers to the index number of the element whose value you want to set.

The syntax for this method for a two-dimensional array is as follows:

```
ArrayName.SetValue(Value, Pos1, Pos2)
```

In the preceding syntax:

- ◆ ArrayName refers to the name of the array.
- ◆ Value refers to the value you want to set for the specified index number.
- ◆ Pos1 and Pos2 refer to the row number and column number of the array element whose value you want to set.

For a three-dimensional array, the syntax is as follows:

```
ArrayName.SetValue(Value, Pos1, Pos2, Pos3)
```

In the preceding syntax:

- ◆ ArrayName refers to the name of the three-dimensional array.
- ◆ Value refers to the value you want to set for the specified index number.
- ◆ Pos1, Pos2, and Pos3 refer to the first, second, and third dimension index for the array element whose value you want to set.

For a multidimensional array, the syntax is as follows:

```
ArrayName.SetValue(Value, Pos())
```

In the preceding syntax:

◆ `ArrayName` refers to the name of the array.

◆ `Value` refers to the value you want to store or set for the specified index number.

◆ `Pos()` refers to the one-dimensional array that stores the index numbers at which the value needs to be set.

Consider the following example to understand this better:

```
Dim BooksArray(5,5) As String
'Store VB.NET at index number 0,0
BooksArray.SetValue("VB.NET",0,0)
'Store ADO.NET at index number 0,1
BooksArray.SetValue("ADO.NET",0,1)
```

Arrays of Arrays

Until now, you've looked at the various types of arrays that are possible in Visual Basic.NET. Now you will learn about something called an *array of arrays*. As the name suggests, it is actually an array containing arrays. To create an array of arrays, you need to declare an array of the type `Object`. This way, you can store different types of data in an array. The following code explains this:

```
'Declare an Integer array
Dim ItemPrice(2) As Integer
'Declare a String array
Dim ItemNames(2) As String
'Initialize arrays
ItemPrice(0) = 30
ItemPrice(1) = 50
ItemNames(0) = "VB.NET"
ItemNames(1) = "ADO.NET"
'Declare Object array
Dim BooksDetails(2) As Object
'Initialize Object array
BooksDetails(0) = ItemNames
BooksDetails(1) = ItemPrice
'Displaying the values stored in Object array
```

```
MessageBox.Show(BooksDetails(0)(0))
                                                    'Displays VB.NET as
the first index 0 refers to the array ItemNames and
                                                    'the second index 0
refers to the first element in the array ItemNames
MessageBox.Show(BooksDetails(1)(0))
                                                    'Displays 30 as the
first index 1 refers to the array ItemPrice and the
                                                    'second index 0
refers to the first element in the array ItemPrice
```

The preceding code will give an error if the `Option Strict` is set to `On`. The reason for the error is that the Visual Basic compiler does not allow late binding when the `Option Strict` is set to `On`. As you already know, that late binding is the runtime binding of objects with their classes. The concept of late binding was covered in detail in Chapter 2, "Object-Oriented Features in Visual Basic.NET."

Some differences between Visual Basic 6.0 and Visual Basic.NET in terms of arrays are worth mentioning here. In Visual Basic 6.0, you can initialize an array with controls. In Visual Basic.NET, you cannot store controls as array elements. However, in Visual Basic.NET, you can place controls into arrays and various types of collections by using code.

In the preceding sections, you looked at various types of arrays. Now, you will look at a related concept called collections.

Collections

Generally speaking, just like an array is a group of variables, a *collection* is a group of related objects. Mostly, you use a collection to work with related objects, but collections can be used to work with any data type.

Visual Basic.NET uses many types of collections to organize and manipulate objects in an efficient way. For example, a `Controls` collection stores all the controls on a form. Similarly, a `Forms` collection contains all the forms in a Visual Basic.NET project. A collection provides an efficient way to keep track of the objects your application needs to create and destroy during runtime. Here's an example: In your application, you need to take input from the user in four text boxes and then validate whether the user has entered data in all of them. One way to do this is to write code to check for each of the text boxes separately. Another way (and an easier one) is to check using the `Controls` collection. As discussed earlier, every form has a `Controls` collection that represents all the controls (such as text boxes, command buttons, and labels) present on the form. Using this `Controls` collection, you can easily do the input validation check. Consider the following code:

```
Dim ConObject As Control
.........................'Declares an instance of the Control class
For Each ConObject In Controls
.........................'Starts the For Each loop to process each control in the Controls
.........................'collection
        If TypeOf(ConObject) Is TextBox Then
.........................'Checks for the type of control using the TypeOf…Is operator
            If ConObject.Text = "" Then
.........................Checks if the TextBox control is empty using the Text property
                MessageBox.Show(ConObject.Name + " Cannot be left blank.")
.........................'Displays a message box containing the control name and the text
.........................'"cannot be left blank"
            End If
        End If

Next
```

In the preceding code, first an instance of the `Control` class `ConObject` is created. In the `For Each` loop that follows, each control in the `Controls` collection is processed one after the other. In the following `If` statement, a check is made for the type of control. If it is a `TextBox`, the following `If` statement checks for the text in that text box using the `Text` property. If the text box is empty, a message box appears that displays the text box name and the message.

You will learn about the `For Each` loop in Chapter 6.

NOTE

Control is a class provided by Visual Basic.NET. It is the base class for all the controls, and it is included in the `System.Windows.Forms` namespace.

The `TypeOf…Is` operator is used to check for the type of an object. It returns True if the object is of the specified type or is derived from a specific type.

Now that you've had an overview of collections, you will learn how to create your own collections.

Creating Collections

In addition to the various standard collections available in Visual Basic, you can also create your own. For this, Visual Basic.NET provides the `Collection` class. The syntax to create your own collection is as follows:

```
Dim CollectionName As New Collection()
```

In the preceding syntax, `CollectionName` is the name of the collection you want to create. The `New` keyword in the declaration statement indicates that an instance of the `Collection` class is created.

After you create your own collection, you can manipulate it in the same way you would manipulate the standard collections provided by Visual Basic.NET. However, there are differences between the two. Consider the following example:

```
Dim CollObject As New Collection()
CollObject = Controls
```

The second statement in the preceding code initializes the collection object `CollObject` with the `Controls` collection. However, this statement generates an error message. You might be wondering why this is so. This is because the `Controls` collection and the `Collection` class object are not interchangeable because both are of different types with different usage. Moreover, they don't have the same methods and don't use the same kinds of index values.

You will now learn about the starting index of a collection.

Zero-Based and One-Based Collections

A collection can be zero-based or one-based, depending on its starting index. This means, for the zero-based collection, that the starting index is 0, and for the one-based collection, it is 1. The `Controls` collection is zero-based, and an instance of the `Collection` class is one-based. For a zero-based collection, the index number ranges from 0 to one less than the total number of items in the collection. For a one-based collection, the index number ranges from 1 to the total number of items in the collection.

The following section describes how a collection is different from an array.

Arrays vs. Collections

As you know, most applications need to manage groups of related objects. For example, a sales application needs to store and group data about the items available and about customers and suppliers. You can either create arrays of objects or create collections.

Arrays are relatively inflexible structures. This means that, if you want to change the size of the array at runtime, you need to use the ReDim statement to redeclare it. All the elements of the array should be of the same type. You can sequentially process elements in an array and also have empty elements in between. For all these reasons, arrays are useful for creating and working with a fixed number of groups of objects. Collections, on the other hand, provide a more flexible way of working with groups of objects. Because a collection is an object of a class, you need to declare a new collection object before you can add items to that collection. Another advantage of using collections is that the items in a collection can grow or shrink dynamically as and when the program demands it.

Most of the collections provided by Visual Basic.NET (and the one you created) allow you to add and remove items. But some collections like CheckedList-Box.CheckedItems do not provide methods to add and remove items. The next section looks at how to add items in a collection.

Adding Items in a Collection

First of all, you need to create an object of the Collection class before you can create a collection of objects. Consider the following example:

```
Dim CollObject As New Collection()
```

In the preceding example, CollObject is the name of the new collection you are creating. The next step is to use the Add method to add members to your collection. The syntax for the Add method is as follows:

```
CollectionName.Add (Object, [Key], [Before], [After])
```

In the preceding syntax:

- ◆ CollectionName is the name of the new collection you are creating.
- ◆ Object is the object to be added to the collection. It can be of any data type.

- Key is a numeric or string key that uniquely identifies the object or item being added, and it is optional. If you do not specify this key, an index number is automatically assigned to the item being added. For the first item, it is 1; for the second item, it is 2; and so on.

- Before is the expression that is the unique identifier for the item before which you want to add the new item. It is an optional argument and can be a numeric or string expression. If it is specified as a numeric expression, it should be between 1 and the maximum number of items in the collection. If specified as a string expression, it should be the unique string identifier of the item before which you want to add the new item.

- After is the expression that is the unique identifier for the item after which you want to add the new item. It is an optional argument and can be numeric or string expression. If it is specified as a numeric expression, it should be between 1 and the maximum number of items in the collection. If specified as a string expression, it should be the unique string identifier of the item before which you want to add the new item.

You cannot specify the Before and After arguments together. In other words, if Before is specified, After cannot be specified and vice versa.

Consider the following example:

```
CollObject.Add("VB.NET")
.........................'Adds the VB.NET string to the CollObject collection
```

Consider the following code:

```
CollObject.Add("VB.NET","VB")
.........................'Adds the VB.NET string to the CollObject collection and VB is the
.........................'String that uniquely identifies this item in the collection
CollObject.Add("ADO.NET", "ADO")
.........................'Adds the ADO.NET string to the CollObject collection and ADO is the
.........................'string that uniquely identifies this item in the collection. Now,
there
.........................'are two items in the collection, VB.NET and ADO.NET.
CollObject.Add("ASP.NET", "ASP",2)
```

After the execution of the preceding third statement, the ASP.NET string is added to the CollObject collection, and ASP is the string that uniquely identifies this item in the collection. Notice the third argument. This specifies that this item is to be added before the second item in the collection. After this statement, the sequence of items in the CollObject collection is VB.NET, ASP.NET, and ADO.NET. The same statement can also be written as follows:

```
CollObject.Add("ASP.NET", "ASP", "ADO")
```

Here, the string identifier for the second item is used instead of the index number 2.

Consider the following statement:

```
CollObject.Add("VC++.NET","VC",,"ASP")
```

After the execution of the preceding statement, the VC++.NET string is added to the CollObject collection, and VC is the string that uniquely identifies this item in the collection. Note that the third argument in this method is not specified. Instead, the fourth argument is specified, and it indicates that this item needs to be added after the item with ASP as the string identifier. After this statement, the sequence of the items in the CollObject collection is VB.NET, ASP.NET, VC++.NET, and ADO.NET. The same statement can also be written using the index number instead of the string identifier, as follows:

```
CollObject.Add("VC++.NET","VC",,2)
```

Removing Items from a Collection

The method to remove items from a collection is Remove. The syntax is as follows:

```
CollectionName.Remove(Key)
```

In the preceding syntax, CollectionName is the name of the collection, and Key is the unique numeric or string identifier for the item you want to remove. If you are using the numeric key, the value can be between 1 and the maximum number of items in the collection.

Consider the following example:

```
CollObject.Remove(1)
....................'Removes first item from the collection
CollObject.Remove("ASP")
....................'Removes the item that has ASP as the unique String identifier
```

The items in a collection object automatically update their numeric index number as and when you add and remove items from the collection object.

Retrieving Items from a Collection

The `Item` property is used to retrieve a particular item from a collection object. The syntax is as follows:

```
CollectionName.Item(Key)
```

In the preceding syntax, `CollectionName` is the name of the collection, and `Key` is the unique identifier (string or numeric expression) for the item you want to retrieve.

`Item` is the default property for a collection object. Therefore, you need not specify the property name while using this property. Consider the following syntax:

```
CollectionName(Key)
```

Consider the following example:

```
Dim StrVar As String
StrVar = CollObject.Item(2)
                                      'Returns the item at the index position 2
StrVar = CollObject.Item("ASP")
                                      'Returns the item that has the ASP String identifier
```

To retrieve all the items from a collection, you can use the `For Each…Next` loop. Consider the following code example that displays all the items of a collection object in a message box one by one:

```
Dim StrVar As String
For Each StrVar in CollObject
        MessageBox.Show(StrVar)
Next
```

You will learn about the `For Each…Next` loop in Chapter 7, "Procedures and Functions."

Counting Items in a Collection

To count the total number of items in a collection, you can use the `Count` property. The syntax is as follows:

```
CollectionName.Count()
```

In the preceding syntax, CollectionName is the name of the collection whose total number of items you want to know. Consider the following example, assuming that there are three items in the CollObject collection:

```
Dim BoundVar As Integer
BoundVar = CollObject.Count()
                                'Returns 3
```

Summary

In this chapter, you learned about arrays. You also learned about one- and multi-dimensional arrays. Then you learned about some commonly used methods provided by the System.Array class for manipulating arrays. You also learned about collections and how to create them. Finally, you learned how to add and remove items from a collection.

Chapter 6

In the preceding chapter, you learned to work with arrays and collections. Now, you will learn about the heart of any programming language, conditional logic. Most applications carry out a set of tasks such as accepting data from a user, validating the data, and performing operations based on the data. To be able to perform these tasks, your program consists of a set of statements that contain the logic required to perform these tasks. There might be situations, however, when the user does not enter the correct data, leading to erroneous or unpredictable results. In addition, there might be situations when you need to execute a set of statements only if a condition is `True`. For example, you might want to allow a user to use an application only if the password entered by the user is correct. So, your program should be able to handle such situations and adjust accordingly. To counter such situations, Visual Basic.NET provides decision structures—such as `If…Then…Else` and `Select…Case` statements—that enable your program to execute conditionally. In addition, various loop structures are available in Visual Basic.NET—such as `Do…Loop`, `While…End While`, and `For…Next` statements—to perform a set of statements repeatedly depending on a condition. This chapter explains the syntax and implementation of the decision structures as well as the loop structures.

Decision Structures

As the name suggests, decision structures enable your program to make decisions. In other words, the decision structures enable your program to execute a set of statements based on the result of a condition. In your program, this condition might depend on user input or the value of a particular variable. For example, you need a program that takes input from the user. The program processes certain statements based on the user input. If the information is incorrect or incomplete, the program can display an error message, inform the user, or close the program, depending on the action you specify. This is where the decision structures come into the picture. Two commonly used decision structures provided by Visual Basic.NET are `If…Then…Else` and `Select…Case` statements. The next sections take a look at these statements.

The *If...Then...Else* Statement

You use the `If...Then...Else` statement to execute one or more statements based on a condition. This condition is a `Boolean` expression that can either return `True` or `False`. The following is the syntax for the `If...Then...Else` statement:

```
If Condition Then
    Statement(s)
[Else
    Statement(s)]
End If
```

In the preceding syntax, `Condition` is the expression that is evaluated. If this expression returns `True`, the statements following `Then` are executed. If this expression returns `False`, the statements following `Else` are executed. Note that `Else` is an optional statement and can be skipped. The `End If` statement marks the end of an `If...Then...Else` statement.

Take an example of a sales application to understand this better. The sales application needs to calculate the credit points to be offered to the customers based on the number of items bought by them. The customers can then use these credit points to utilize the special schemes offered by the company. Upon buying more than 20 items, a customer is awarded 25 points. Otherwise, 10 credit points are awarded to the remaining customers. To implement this logic, consider the following code:

```
If QtyOrdered > 20 Then CreditPoints = 25 Else CreditPoints = 10
```

The preceding statement is an example of a single-line form of an `If...Then...Else` statement. Here, the `CreditPoints` variable is assigned a value of `25` if the value of the `QtyOrdered` variable is greater than `20`. Otherwise, the `CreditPoints` variable is assigned a value of `10`. Note that you can omit the `End If` statement if the code is written in a single line. You can also write multiple statements in the single-line form of the `If...Then...Else` statement. In that case, you need to separate the statements by a colon (:) while still having the complete statement on the same line. The syntax for such a statement is as follows:

```
If Condition Then Statement:[Statement]:[Statement]
```

The following is an example of multiple statements in the single-line form of the `If...Then...Else` statement:

```
If QtyOrdered> 20 Then CreditPoints = 25 : MessageBox.Show ( "Credit points
offered: " & CreditPoints)
```

In the preceding example, the value of the variable QtyOrdered is checked. If the value is greater than 20, the CreditPoints variable is assigned a value of 25, and a message box appears displaying the text "Credit points offered:" along with the value of the variable CreditPoints. However, it is good practice to write such statements in multiple lines because writing all of the statements in a single line can affect the code's readability. So, you can also write the preceding code in the following manner:

```
If QtyOrdered>20 Then
            CreditPoints=25
Else
            CreditPoints=10
End If
MessageBox.Show ( "Credit points offered: " & CreditPoints)
```

At times, you might need to check the expression result more than once. Taking the same example further, now you need to offer 15 credit points to those customers who buy more than 10 items. This is in addition to the credit-point conditions mentioned earlier. In such a situation, the code written earlier will not work because now you have three conditions instead of two. These conditions are as follows:

Number of Items Bought	Credit Points Offered
Less than or equal to 10	10
More than 10 and less than 20	15
More than or equal to 20	25

For these conditions, you can use the ElseIf statement. The following is the syntax for the ElseIf statement:

```
If Condition1 Then
            Statement1(s)
[ElseIf Condition2 Then
            Statement2(s)]
End If
```

In the preceding syntax, first Condition1 is evaluated. If the Condition1 is True, Statement1(s) is executed. If Condition1 is False, the control moves to the ElseIf statement and Condition2 is evaluated. If Condition2 is True, Statement2(s) is executed. If Condition2 is also False, however, statements following Else are executed. The following is the code that implements this logic for the sales application with three conditions:

```
If QtyOrdered>20 Then
        CreditPoints=25
ElseIf QtyOrdered>10 And QtyOrdered<=20 Then
        CreditPoints=15
Else
        CreditPoints=10
End If
```

In the preceding code, the value of the variable QtyOrdered is checked more than once, and accordingly, the variable CreditPoints is assigned a value.

You can also use one If…Then…Else statement within another If…Then…Else statement. Such types of statements are called *nested* statements. You can nest If…Then…Else statements to as many levels as you require. However, you need to have a separate End If for each If…Then…Else statement.

Consider the following example:

```
If QtyOrdered > 20 Then
     CreditPoints = 25
ElseIf QtyOrdered > 10 Then
        'Nested If…Then…Else statement
        If QtyOrdered <= 20 Then
           CreditPoints = 15
        End If
Else
        CreditPoints = 10
End If
```

In the preceding example, one If…Then…Else statement is nested inside another. This code also does the same job as the code mentioned earlier.

Another decision-making structure is the Select…Case statement that helps you add decision-making capability to your program. The next section looks at that statement.

The *Select…Case* Statement

Just like an If…Then…Else statement, the Select…Case statement also enables you to execute a set of statements based on the result of an expression. However, there are differences between the two statements. The If and ElseIf statements evaluate different expressions in each statement, whereas the Select…Case statement evaluates only one expression. The Select…Case statement then uses the resultant expression to execute different sets of statements. Another difference is that the expression used in the Select…Case statement does not return a Boolean value.

The Select…Case statement is preferred when you need to use multiple conditions because it makes code easy to read and understand. The following is the syntax for the Select…Case statement:

```
Select Case Expression
      Case ValueList
            Statement(s)
     [Case Else
            Statement(s)]
End Select
```

In the preceding syntax, Expression is evaluated, and the result is compared against the constants and expressions mentioned in the ValueList of each of the Case statements. If the result of the expression matches any constants or expressions mentioned in the ValueList of the Case statement, statements following that Case statement are executed. If the result of the expression does not match any of the Case constants or expressions mentioned in the ValueList, statements following Case Else are executed. End Select marks the end of a Select…Case statement.

Consider the following example that accepts a number from the user and displays the weekday depending on the number entered. If the number entered is not in the range of 1 to 7, a message box appears informing that an incorrect number has been entered.

```
Select Case WeekNumber
```

```
        Case 1
                MessageBox.Show("Monday")
        Case 2
                MessageBox.Show("Tuesday")
        Case 3
                MessageBox.Show("Wednesday")
        Case 4
                MessageBox.Show("Thursday")
        Case 5
                MessageBox.Show("Friday")
        Case 6
                MessageBox.Show("Saturday")
        Case 7
                MessageBox.Show("Sunday")
        Case Else
                MessageBox.Show("Number not in the range…")
End Select
```

You will learn about the `MessageBox.Show` method in Chapter 7, "Procedures and Functions."

The credit-points example discussed in the `If…Then…Else` section can be rewritten using the `Select…Case` statement. It would be impractical, however, to write `Case` statements for each and every value of the quantity ordered. However, you can specify a conditional expression. To do so, you can use the `Is` keyword as follows:

```
Select Case QtyOrdered
    Case Is < 10
        CreditPoints = 10
    Case Is > 20
        CreditPoints = 25
    Case Is <= 20
        CreditPoints = 15
    Case Else
        MessageBox.Show("No credit points available.")
End Select
```

In the preceding code, the first statement evaluates the value in the variable Qty-Ordered and compares the value against the expression mentioned in the Case statements. If any of the expressions evaluate to True, the CreditPoints variable is assigned a value. If none of them returns True, the statement following Case Else is executed, and a message box appears informing that there are no credit points available.

The same can also be written using the To keyword as follows:

```
Select Case QtyOrdered
    Case 1 To 10
        CreditPoints = 10
    Case 11 to 20
        CreditPoints = 15
    Case Is > 20
        CreditPoints = 25
    Case Else
        MessageBox.Show("No credit points available")
End Select
```

There might be situations in which you need to execute the same set of statements for more than one value of the Case expression. In such a situation, you can specify multiple values or ranges in a single Case statement. Consider the following example in which you check whether the number entered (between 1 and 10) by the user is even or odd.

```
Select Case Number
    Case 2, 4, 6, 8,10
        MessageBox.Show("Even number")
    Case 1,3,5,7,9
        MessageBox.Show("Odd number")
    Case Else
        MessageBox.Show("Number out of range..")
End Select
```

In the preceding example, the value of the variable Number is evaluated. If the value is 2, 4, 6, 8 or 10, the statement following the first Case statement is executed. If the value is 1, 3, 5, 7, or 9, the statement following the second Case statement is executed. If the variable Number contains any value other than the values mentioned, the statement following Case Else is executed.

Now you will look at the various loop structures available in Visual Basic.NET.

Loop Structures

Sometimes the user might input incorrect values, and then you might need to repeat the same set of statements until the user enters the correct value or quits. Consider an application that accepts a logon name and a password from the user. If the user enters an incorrect value(s), the application should prompt the user to enter the values again. This process needs to be repeated until the values entered by the user are correct. In such a situation, you can use the looping structures provided by Visual Basic.NET. The following sections take a look at various looping structures such as While...End While, Do...Loop, For...Next, and For Each...Next statements.

The *While...End While* Statement

The While...End While statement is used to specify that a set of statements should repeat as long as the condition specified is True. The syntax is as follows:

```
While Condition
        Statement(s)
        [Exit While]
End While
```

In the preceding syntax, Condition is an expression that is evaluated at the beginning of the loop, and it can be True or False. If the Condition is True, the set of statements following Condition is executed. End While marks the end of a While loop. The Exit While statement is optional and is used to exit from a While....End While loop.

Consider the following example:

```
Dim Counter As Integer=1
While Counter <= 5
    MessageBox.Show("Value is: " & Counter)
    Counter =Counter + 1
End While
```

In the preceding example, `Counter` is an `Integer` variable that is initialized with 1. The `While…End While` loop executes until the value of `Counter` is less than or equal to 5. This means that the statements within the `While…End While` statements are repeated five times.

The *Do…Loop* Statement

In your application, you might need to execute a set of statements repeatedly based on a condition. Using the `Do…Loop` statement, you can repeat a set of statements while a given condition is either `True` or `False`.

The `Do…Loop` statements evaluate a condition to determine whether to continue the execution or not. Two types of `Do…Loop` statements are available in Visual Basic.NET—one that checks for a condition before executing the loop and the other that checks for a condition after the statements have executed at least once.

The syntax for the first type of `Do…Loop` statement, which checks for a condition before executing the loop, is as follows:

```
Do While¦Until Condition
        Statement(s)
        [Exit Do]
Loop
```

In the preceding syntax:

 ◆ The `While` keyword repeats the statements while the `Condition` is `True`. The `Until` keyword repeats the statements while the `Condition` is `False`. You can use one of these keywords at a time.

 ◆ The `Exit Do` statement is used to exit a `Do…Loop` statement.

The code mentioned earlier in the `While…End While` section can be written using the `Do…Loop` statement in the following manner:

```
Dim Counter As Integer = 1
Do While Counter <= 5
        MessageBox.Show("Value is :" & Counter)
        Counter=Counter + 1
Loop
```

In the preceding example, the Do...Loop statement displays the value stored in the variable Counter. This loop is repeated five times because the condition specified is while the Counter is less than or equal to 5.

The syntax for the second type of Do...Loop statement, which checks for a condition after the statements have executed once, is as follows:

```
Do
        Statement(s)
        [Exit Do]
Loop While¦Until Condition
```

The example mentioned in the first type of Do...Loop statement can be written as follows:

```
Dim Counter As Integer = 1
Do
      MessageBox.Show("Value is: " & Counter)
      Counter=Counter + 1
Loop While Counter<=5
```

In the preceding example, the statements following the Do statement execute once, and then the value of Counter is checked. This loop is also repeated five times.

However, a word of caution here: Sometimes your application might run into an infinite or endless loop. This might happen because you did not specify the condition correctly or because the value of the counter variable is not incremented or decremented as required. Consider the following example:

```
Dim Counter As Integer = 1
Do While Counter<=5
          MessageBox.Show("Value is: " & Counter)
          Counter = Counter -1
Loop
```

The preceding code runs into an infinite loop because the value of Counter gets decremented every time the loop runs and is never incremented. In other words, the value of the Counter variable is always less than 5, and this makes the loop run an infinite number of times. In such a situation, you need to close the Visual Basic.NET application. This will result in the loss of all unsaved information.

Therefore, it is a good programming practice to carefully examine the code involving loops before executing the code.

The following code illustrates the use of the Do…Loop statement for checking the password entered by a user:

```
Dim Pass As String
        Dim Counter As Integer = 1
        Do
                Pass = InputBox("Enter password:")
                                                        'Prompts the user for
the password in an input box
                If Pass = "mypass" Then
                                                        'Compares the password
entered by the user with the correct password
                        MsgBox("Welcome")
                        Exit Do
                                                        'Exits from the loop
                Else
                        MsgBox("Incorrect password")
                        Counter = Counter + 1
                                                        'Increments the value
of the counter variable
                End If
        Loop While Counter <= 5
'Checking for the value of Counter. A value more than five means the user is
through with the maximum
'possible chances to enter the password but has failed to provide the correct pass-
word.
        If Counter > 5 Then
                MsgBox("Unauthorized user….")
        End If
```

The *For…Next* Statement

You can use the For…Next statements to repeat a set of statements a specific number of times. The syntax for the For…Next statement is as follows:

```
For Counter = <Startvalue> To <Endvalue> [Stepvalue]
                Statement(s)
                [Exit For]
Next [Counter]
```

In the preceding syntax:

◆ `Counter` is any numeric variable.

◆ `Startvalue` is the initial value of `Counter`, and `Endvalue` is the final or end value of `Counter`.

◆ `Stepvalue` is the numeric value by which `Counter` needs to be incremented. The `Stepvalue` can be either a positive or negative value and is optional. If no value is specified, the default value is 1.

◆ `Statement(s)` are the set of statements executed for the specified number of times.

◆ The `Next` statement marks the end of a `For...Next` loop. When this statement is encountered, the `Stepvalue` is added to `Counter`, and the loop executes.

TIP

It is a good programming practice to mention the name of the counter or numeric variable in the `Next` statement.

Consider the example mentioned earlier in the `Do...Loop` statement to display the value of the counter variable. Here's how to write using the `For...Next` loop:

```
Dim Counter As Integer
For Counter = 1 to 5
        MessageBox.Show("Value is:" & Counter)
Next Counter
```

In the preceding example, the `For...Next` loop executes five times, and the step value is 1. Consider the following example with a different step value:

```
Dim Counter As Integer
For Counter = 1 to 10 Step 2
```

```
            MessageBox.Show("Value is: " & Counter)
Next Counter
```

In the preceding example, the For…Next loop executes five times, and the step value is 2. The values displayed are 1, 3, 5, 7, and 9.

Consider the following example with a negative step value:

```
Dim Counter As Integer
For Counter = 10 to 1 Step -2
            MessageBox.Show("Value is:" & Counter)
Next Counter
```

In the preceding example, the For…Next loop executes five times, and the step value is −2. The values displayed are 10, 8, 6, 4, and 2.

You can also nest one For…Next statement inside another For…Next statement. The only point to keep in mind is to use a unique counter variable for each For….Next loop. In addition, remember to specify the Next statement for each loop.

The following is an example of how to use two nested For…Next statements:

```
Dim Counter1, Counter2 As Integer
For Counter1=1 To 5
            For Counter2=1 To 5
                                    'Some code statements using Counter1 and Counter2
            Next Counter2
Next Counter1
```

The *For Each…Next* Statement

The For Each…Next statement is used to execute a set of statements for each element in an array or a collection. Arrays and collections were covered in detail in Chapter 5, "Arrays and Collections."

The syntax for the For Each….Next statement is as follows:

```
For Each Item in List
        Statement(s)
        [Exit For]
Next [Item]
```

In the preceding syntax:

◆ Item is the variable to refer to the elements in an array or a collection.

◆ List is the array or the collection object.

Consider the following example:

```
Dim BooksArray() As String = {"VB.NET", "ADO.NET","VC++.NET","ASP.NET"}
Dim BookName As String
For Each BookName in BooksArray
        MessageBox.Show(BookName)
                                'Displays each element from BooksArray
Next
```

The preceding code can also be written as follows:

```
Dim BookName As String
For Each BookName in {"VB.NET", "ADO.NET","VC++.NET","ASP.NET"}
        MessageBox.Show(BookName)
                                'Displays each element from the list mentioned in the
For Each statement
Next
```

Consider the following code to check whether the data has been entered in each of the text boxes, as discussed in Chapter 5. The following code example uses the Controls collection to check text box controls on a form.

```
Dim ConObject As Control
........................................'Declares an instance of the Control class
For Each ConObject In Controls
........................................'Starts the For Each loop to process each control in the Controls
........................................'collection
        If TypeOf(ConObject) Is TextBox Then
........................................'Checks for the type of control using the TypeOf...Is operator
            If ConObject.Text = "" Then
........................................'Checks for the blankness of the TextBox control
                    MessageBox.Show(ConObject.Name + " Cannot be left blank.")
........................................'Displays a message box containing the control name and the text
........................................'"Cannot be left blank"
            End If
        End If
Next
```

In the preceding code, first an instance of the Control class ConObject is created. In the For Each loop that follows, each control in the Controls collection is processed one after the other. In the following If statement, the type of the control is checked. If the control is a TextBox, the following If statement checks for the text in that text box by using the Text property. If the text box is empty, a message box appears displaying both the text box name and the message.

> **NOTE**
>
> Control is a class provided by Visual Basic.NET. It is the base class for all the controls and is included in the System.Windows.Forms namespace.
>
> The TypeOf...Is operator is used to check the type of an object. It returns True if the object is of the specified type or is derived from a specific type.

Summary

In this chapter, you learned to implement conditional logic in your program by using various conditions and loop structures provided by Visual Basic.NET. You learned the syntax and implementation of various condition structures such as If...Then...Else and Select...Case statements. In addition, you also learned various loop structures—such as Do...Loop, While...End While, For...Next, and For Each...Next statements—to execute a set of statements repeatedly depending on a condition.

Chapter 7

Procedures and Functions

In Chapter 6, "Conditional Logic," you learned how to implement conditional logic in your program. Now you will go a step further and see how to reuse code in your program using procedures. In this chapter, you will learn to create and use various types of procedures. You will also learn about the various built-in functions provided by Visual Basic.NET that help you add interactivity to your programs and develop your programs easily and quickly.

Procedures

Consider a scenario in which you need to perform a task repeatedly, such as generating invoices for customers based on the unit price and number of items bought. In such a case, instead of writing the statements repeatedly, you can group them in a procedure. A *procedure* is a set of statements grouped together to perform a specific task. Procedures enable you to organize your applications by letting you chunk and group the program code logically.

After you group the statements in a procedure, you can call the procedure from anywhere in the application. Calling a procedure means executing a statement that further instructs the compiler to execute the procedure. After the code in the procedure is executed, the control returns to the statement following the statement that called the procedure. The statement that calls a procedure is known as a *calling statement*. The calling statement includes the name of the procedure. This statement can also include the data values needed by the procedure for performing the specified task. These data values are referred to as *arguments* or *parameters*. Taking the example of invoice generation further, you can create a procedure that takes the unit price and the number of items bought by a customer as data values and calculates the total invoice amount. To call this procedure, the calling statement must supply the unit price and the number of items. In this case, the unit price and the number of items are the parameters or arguments for the procedure.

Now you will learn about some of the advantages that procedures offer. The first and foremost advantage is the reusability of code. In other words, you create a procedure once and use it whenever required. If you have to change any statement, you just need to change it at a single place. As previously mentioned, procedures enable you to chunk and group your application code logically. This is especially useful in cases of large and complex applications. Using procedures in such applications can help you easily debug and maintain the code. In addition, you can trace errors in a procedure far easier than having to go through the entire application code.

Now that you've had an overview of procedures, let's look at the scope or accessibility of procedures in an application. Just like variables and classes, procedures also have a scope. A procedure is declared in a class or a module. So, a procedure can be called from the same class or module within which it is created, and this depends on the access modifiers you use while declaring procedures. Table 7-1 lists these access modifiers.

Table 7-1 Access Modifiers For Procedures

Access Modifier	Can Be Called From
Public	Any class or module in the application
Private	The same class or module in which it is declared
Protected	The same class or module in which it is declared and also from the derived classes
Friend	Any class or module that contains its declaration, and also any class in the same namespace

The procedures in Visual Basic.NET can be classified on the basis of their functionality, as follows:

- ◆ Sub procedures perform specific tasks.
- ◆ Function procedures perform specific tasks and return a value to the calling statement.
- ◆ Property procedures assign or access a value from an object.
- ◆ Event-Handling procedures perform specific tasks when a particular event occurs.

The following sections explain these procedures in detail.

Sub Procedures

As previously mentioned, Sub procedures are procedures that perform specific tasks but do not return values to the calling code. You can declare a Sub procedure in modules, classes, or structures. The syntax for declaring a Sub procedure is as follows:

```
[AccessModifier] Sub ProcName [(ArgumentList)]
                    'Code statements

End Sub
```

In the preceding syntax:

◆ AccessModifier defines the accessibility of a Sub procedure. You can specify any of the values listed in Table 7-1. It is optional, and if omitted, the default value for the access modifier is Public.

◆ The Sub statement marks the beginning of a Sub procedure.

◆ ProcName is the name of a Sub procedure.

◆ ArgumentList represents the list of arguments associated with a Sub procedure. Calling code can pass arguments—such as constants, variables, or expressions—to Sub procedures. ArgumentList is optional, and if omitted, you still need to include an empty set of parentheses.

◆ The End Sub statement marks the end of a Sub procedure.

As discussed in the "Methods" section of Chapter 2, "Object-Oriented Features in Visual Basic.NET," when a Sub procedure is called, all the statements within the procedure are executed. The execution of a Sub procedure starts from the first statement within the procedure and continues until an End Sub, an Exit Sub, or a Return statement is encountered.

Here's an example to help you understand Sub procedures. The following procedure is used to calculate invoices for customers based on the unit price of the item and the number of items bought by a customer:

```
Public Sub CalculateInvoice(NumItems As Integer, UnitPrice As Integer)
        Dim InvoiceAmount As Integer
        InvoiceAmount = NumItems * UnitPrice
        Msgbox(InvoiceAmount)
End Sub
```

In the preceding example, `CalculateInvoice` is the name of a procedure that takes two parameters, `NumItems` and `UnitPrice`. This procedure displays the calculated invoice amount in a message box. `CStr` is a conversion function and is discussed later in this chapter.

You can also use the condition and loop structures (discussed in Chapter 6) in procedures. For example, you might encounter a situation in which a customer is offered credit points based on the amount of the invoice. To accomplish this, you can modify the `CalculateInvoice` procedure to offer credit points. Take a look at the following code:

```
Public Sub CalculateInvoice(NumItems As Integer, UnitPrice As Integer)
        Dim InvoiceAmount As Integer
        Dim CreditPoints As Integer
        InvoiceAmount = NumItems * UnitPrice
        If InvoiceAmount >= 1000 And InvoiceAmount <= 2000 Then
            CreditPoints=25
        ElseIf InvoiceAmount >= 2001 Then
            CreditPoints=10
        End If
        MsgBox("Credit Points offered: " & CStr(CreditPoints))
        MsgBox("Invoice amount is: " & CStr(InvoiceAmount))
End Sub
```

In the preceding example, an `If…Then…Else` statement is used to check the value of the `InvoiceAmount` variable. The credit points to be offered are based on the value of this variable. Then the values of the `CreditPoints` and `InvoiceAmount` variables are displayed in a message box.

After you create a procedure, you can call it using the `Call` statement. However, you can also invoke a `Sub` procedure without using the `Call` statement. To call the `CalculateInvoice` procedure, you can use either of the following statements:

```
Call CalculateInvoice(2, 900)
```

or

```
CalculateInvoice(2, 900)
```

Each of the preceding statements passes two arguments, `2` and `900`, to the `CalculateInvoice` `Sub` procedure. You will learn more about arguments later in this chapter.

> **TIP**
>
> It is possible to write code for more than one logical task within a procedure. However, you cannot use such a procedure across projects or applications. This is because each project or application might have different requirements, and a procedure performing more than one logical task might not meet those requirements. Therefore, you must code your procedure in such a way that it performs only one logical task.

Before discussing `Function` procedures, take a look at the `Sub Main` procedure that Visual Basic.NET provides. This procedure is the starting point of a console application (a command-line application) and is the first `Sub` procedure executed when you run an application. The syntax for the `Sub Main` procedure is as follows:

```
Sub Main()
              'Code statements
End Sub
```

In the `Sub Main` procedure, you can add code that you want to execute first when an application starts. For example, you can include code to connect to a database or initialize variables.

The following section discusses another type of procedure, the `Function` procedure.

Function Procedures

Unlike `Sub` procedures, `Function` procedures (or just functions) can return values to the calling statement. Similar to a `Sub` procedure, a `Function` procedure also starts executing from the first statement within the procedure until an `End Function`, an `Exit Function`, or a `Return` statement is encountered. The syntax for declaring a `Function` procedure is as follows:

```
[AccessModifier] Function FunName [(ArgumentList)] As DataType
      'Statements
End Function
```

In the preceding syntax:

◆ `AccessModifier` defines the accessibility of a `Function` procedure. You can specify any of the values mentioned in Table 7-1. It is optional, and if omitted, the default value for the access modifier is `Public`, as is the case for a `Sub` procedure.

◆ The `Function` statement marks the beginning of a `Function` procedure.

◆ `FunName` is the name of a `Function` procedure.

◆ `ArgumentList` is the list of arguments associated with a `Function` procedure. As with `Sub` procedures, the calling code can also pass arguments to `Function` procedures.

◆ `DataType` defines the data type of the return value of a `Function` procedure.

◆ The `End Function` statement marks the end of a `Function` procedure.

You can declare `Function` procedures in a module, class, or structure. To return a value from a `Function` procedure, you can use the `Return` statement or assign the return value to the name of the `Function` procedure. To understand this better, consider the following code that uses the name of the `Function` procedure to return a value:

```
Public Function CalculateInvoice(NumItems As Integer, UnitPrice As Integer) As Integer
                'Calculate invoice amount and assign it to the Function procedure
name
                CalculateInvoice=NumItems*UnitPrice
End Function
```

The program control returns to the statement following the calling statement only when an `End Function`, an `Exit Function`, or a `Return` statement is executed. Consider the following example, which uses the `Return` statement to return the calculated invoice amount:

```
Public Function CalculateInvoice (NumItems As Integer, UnitPrice As Integer) As
Integer
        Dim InvoiceAmount As Integer
        InvoiceAmount=NumItems*UnitPrice
        Return InvoiceAmount
                            'Returns the calculated invoice amount
End Function
```

Consider the credit points example discussed in the preceding section. The following code creates a Function procedure to calculate invoice amounts for customers based on the unit price and the number of items bought. In addition, if the invoice amount is more than a specified value, a customer is offered credit points.

```
Public Function CalculateInvoice (NumItems As Integer, UnitPrice As Integer) As
Integer
        Dim InvoiceAmount As Integer
        Dim CreditPoints As Integer
        InvoiceAmount = NumItems * UnitPrice
        If InvoiceAmount >= 1000 And InvoiceAmount <= 2000 Then
            CreditPoints=10
        ElseIf InvoiceAmount >= 2001 Then
            CreditPoints=25
        End If
        MsgBox ("Credit Points offered:" & CStr(CreditPoints))
        Return InvoiceAmount
End Function
```

In the preceding code, the CalculateInvoice Function procedure returns a value of the Integer type to the calling code. You can use the following statements to call the CalculateInvoice Function procedure and display the value returned by it:

```
Dim InvoiceValue As Integer
InvoiceValue = CalculateInvoice(3, 1000)
MsgBox("Invoice amount is: " & CStr(InvoiceValue))
```

The preceding code displays the value of the invoice amount. Note that the Call statement is not used. You can use the Call statement to call Function procedures, but the return value of a Function procedure is ignored if you use the Call statement to invoke the procedure. Typically, the value returned by a Function procedure is used for further processing in the program.

You can also call a Function procedure within an expression. For example, consider the following code:

```
If (InvoiceValue=CalculateInvoice(3,1000))>2000 Then
            CreditPoints=25
End If
```

In the preceding code, the `CalculateInvoice` function returns the calculated invoice amount. This invoice amount is then assigned to the `InvoiceValue` variable. The `If...Then...Else` statement checks the value of the `InvoiceValue` variable, and then a value is assigned to the `CreditPoints` variable.

Although `Function` procedures return a value, it is up to you to use the value further in the program. If you do not use the return value, all the statements in the function are performed or executed, but the return value is ignored.

The next section discusses another type of procedure, the `Event-Handling` procedure.

Event-Handling Procedures

As the name suggests, an `Event-Handling` procedure, or an *event handler*, is executed when an event is generated, such as a button click, a mouse move, or a key press. The object that generates the event is known as an *event sender* or an *event source*. For example, when you click on a button, the `Click` event is generated, and the button you clicked on is the event sender.

The syntax for an `Event-Handling` procedure is the same as for a `Sub` procedure. You must ensure that the name of an `Event-Handling` procedure reflects the name of the event as well as the name of the event sender. `Event-Handling` procedures are always `Private`. The following is the syntax for an `Event-Handling` procedure:

```
Private Sub EventSender_EventName ([ArgumentList])
                'Code statements
End Sub
```

In the preceding syntax, `EventSender_EventName` is a standard naming convention used for `Event-Handling` procedures. In other words, the name of an `Event-Handling` procedure includes the name of the event sender, an underscore, and then the name of the event. For example, if the event sender is a button named `GenerateID` and the event name is `Click`, the `Event-Handling` procedure would be named as `GenerateID_Click`.

In Visual Basic.NET, each form and control has a predefined set of events that you can code. In other words, you get the start and end statements for an `Event-Handling` procedure, and you just need to write the remaining procedure statements. For example, to code the `Click` event of a button, you need to add your code statements between the following two statements that are generated automatically by Visual Basic.NET:

```
Private Sub Button1_Click(ByVal sender As System.Object, ByVal e As System.EventArgs)
Handles Button1.Click
                    'Code statements to handle the Click event
End Sub
```

> **CAUTION**
>
> If you change the name of a control after writing the code for any of its `Event-Handling` procedures, you need to change the name of the event handler so that it matches the new name.

In addition to the various predefined events for controls, Visual Basic.NET enables you to declare events in classes and write event handlers for them. The following section describes the various statements you need to use to attach an event to an object.

First of all, you need to see how to declare an event in a class. You can declare an event in the `Declarations` section of a class. The following is an example of declaring an event:

```
Public Event MyEvent (Argument1 As Integer, Argument2 As Integer)
```

In the preceding example:

◆ `MyEvent` is the name of an event.

◆ `Argument1` and `Argument2` are the arguments for the event.

By default, events are `Public`. Declaring an event in a class means an object of that class can raise the event.

After creating an event, you can associate the event with either the class-level or module-level objects. In other words, you need to declare class- or module-level objects that can raise events. To accomplish this, you need to use the `WithEvents` statement while declaring the object that is going to raise the event. The following is the syntax for the `WithEvents` statement:

```
Public WithEvents ObjectName As ClassName
```

In the preceding statement, ObjectName refers to the object of the ClassName class. This statement specifies that ObjectName is name of the object that will raise an event. For example, to handle the events for EventObject of EventClass, you need to add the following code to the Declarations section of EventClass:

```
Public WithEvents EventObject As New EventClass
```

The next step is coding the event handler for the declared event. As previously mentioned, Event-Handling procedures are coded using the Sub and End Sub statements, just like Sub procedures. To code the event handler, use the Handles clause. The syntax for this clause is as follows:

```
 [AccessModifier] Sub ObjectName_EventName([ArgumentList]) Handles
ObjectName.EventName
                        'Code for handling event
End Sub
```

In the preceding syntax:

- ◆ AccessModifier defines the accessibility of an event handler.
- ◆ The Sub statement indicates that the procedure is a Sub procedure.
- ◆ ObjectName_EventName represents the name of the event handler. The names of event handlers are based on a specific convention, as previously mentioned.
- ◆ ArgumentList represents the list of arguments associated with the event handler.
- ◆ The Handles clause is used to associate events with event handlers. In the preceding syntax, the Handles clause associates the ObjectName_EventName procedure with the EventName event of the ObjectName object.
- ◆ The End Sub statement marks the end of a Sub procedure (here, an Event-Handling procedure).

When you use the WithEvents statement and the Handles clause, Event-Handling procedures are bound to the associated events at compile time. However, you can also dynamically associate events with one or more Event-Handling procedures at runtime by using the AddHandler and RemoveHandler statements.

Now, after declaring an event and its associated Event-Handling procedure, the next logical step is to discuss how to raise a declared event. For raising an event, you use the RaiseEvent statement. The following is the syntax for the RaiseEvent statement:

```
RaiseEvent EventName()
```

In the preceding syntax, EventName is the name of the declared event.

The following section discusses another type of procedure, the Property procedure.

Property Procedures

As discussed in the "Fields and Properties" section of Chapter 2, Property procedures enable you to manipulate properties defined in a class, module, or structure. Property procedures are defined in pairs by using the Get and Set keywords. As the name suggests, Get is used to get or access the value of a property of an object, whereas Set is used to assign a value to the property of an object.

For more details about Property procedures, refer to the "Fields and Properties" section in Chapter 2. As discussed in the preceding sections, procedures of all types can take parameters or arguments. The next section takes a look at them as well.

Arguments

As previously discussed, procedures can accept variables, constants, or expressions as arguments. Therefore, each time you call a procedure that accepts arguments, you need to pass arguments to the procedure. With each call to a procedure, the result can differ depending on the data values passed as arguments. You can pass arguments to procedures either by value or by reference. The following sections discuss these argument-passing mechanisms.

Passing Arguments by Value

When you pass an argument variable by value, a copy of the original variable is created. Therefore, the procedure cannot modify the contents of the original variable. Passing arguments by value is the default argument-passing mechanism, and you use the ByVal keyword to specify that an argument should be passed by value.

Consider the following procedure, which takes one Integer variable as an argument and adds 20 to this argument:

```
Public Sub AddNumber(ByVal Number As Integer)
        Number = Number + 20
        MsgBox("The number is: " + CStr(Number))
End Sub
```

Next, you will see how to call this AddNumber procedure by passing the argument value. Assume the value entered is 50.

```
Dim InputNum As Integer
InputNum = InputBox("Enter number:")
MsgBox("The entered number is: " + CStr(InputNum))


'Displays 50
AddNumber (InputNum)


'AddNumber procedure is called


'Displays 70
'Control returns to the calling code
MsgBox("The original number is: " + CStr(InputNum))


'Displays 50
```

Note in the preceding example that the original number is not affected because the number is passed by value. In other words, a copy of the InputNum variable is passed as an argument, and 20 is added to the value of this copy. Therefore, the original variable remains unaffected. Now that you know how to pass arguments by value, the next section explains passing arguments by reference.

Passing Arguments by Reference

When you pass a variable by reference, a reference to the original variable is passed to the procedure. Therefore, the procedure can modify the contents of the variable. You use the ByRef keyword to specify that an argument be passed by reference. The following example modifies the previous procedure to accept arguments by reference:

```
Public Sub AddNumber(ByRef Number As Integer)
        Number = Number + 20
        MsgBox("The number is : " + CStr(Number))
End Sub
```

Assume that you call the `AddNumber` procedure and assume the value entered is 50.

```
Dim InputNum As Integer
InputNum = InputBox("Enter number:")
MsgBox("The entered number is: " + CStr(InputNum) )


'Displays 50


'Displays 70
AddNumber(InputNum)


'AddNumber procedure is called


'Displays 70
'Control returns to the calling code
MsgBox("The original number is: " + CStr(InputNum) )


'Displays 70
```

Note in the preceding example that the original number is also modified because the argument is passed by reference and 20 is added to the value of the original variable.

Another way to classify the argument-passing mechanisms is by position and by name. In other words, you can pass arguments by position (in which you use the order specified in the procedure declaration), or you can pass arguments by name (in which you use the argument name irrespective of the position). To understand this better, consider the following procedure that takes three arguments:

```
Public Sub SupplierDetails(ByVal Id As String, ByVal Name As String, ByVal Address
As String)
        'Code statements
End Sub
```

You can pass arguments to this procedure in either of the following manners:

```
SupplierDetails("001", "Jon", "ABCD")
                        'Passing arguments by position
```

or

```
SupplierDetails(Id="001", Address="ABCD", Name="John")
                        'Passing arguments by name
```

You can also choose to pass arguments by both position and name. Consider the following example:

```
SupplierDetails(Id="001","Jon", Address="ABCD")
```

Passing arguments by name is very useful when there is more than one optional argument for a procedure. (Optional arguments are discussed in the following section.) In other words, you don't have to mention the commas, which are required to specify the missing positional arguments. Another advantage is that it's easier to keep track of which arguments are passed and which are skipped.

Now that you're familiar with the various argument-passing mechanisms, take a look at two more concepts related to arguments: optional arguments and parameter arrays.

Optional Arguments

As the name suggests, arguments that are optional or that can be omitted are known as *optional* arguments. When creating procedures, you can also specify any argument as an optional argument. When you call a procedure, you can choose whether or not to specify a value for an optional argument.

Consider a procedure that accepts supplier details such as the supplier code, name, address, state, phone number, and fax number. Each supplier might not have a fax number. Therefore, you can specify the fax number argument as an optional argument. Similarly, you can also specify the state and phone number arguments as optional.

You use the Optional keyword to specify an argument as an optional argument. In addition, during procedure declaration, you must specify a default value for each optional argument. The default value should be a constant. In addition, you cannot specify any nonoptional arguments after an optional argument when declaring a procedure. In other words, optional arguments should be the last arguments specified for a procedure. Consider the following example:

```
Sub SupplierDetails(Id As String, Name As String, Address As String, Optional State As
String = "California")
                                'Code statements
End Sub
```

In the preceding example, the `SupplierDetails` procedure accepts four arguments: `Id`, `Name`, `Address`, and `State`. Note that the `State` argument is an optional argument that has a default value as `California`. When calling the `SupplierDetails` procedure, you might or might not specify the value of the `State` argument. You can use either of the following statements to call the `SupplierDetails` procedure:

```
SupplierDetails ("001", "Karen Brown","ab/d, xyz street", "New Jersey")
```

or

```
SupplierDetails ("002", "David Bacon","12/ze, pqrs street")
```

In the preceding code, the value for the `State` argument is not provided in the second statement. Therefore, the `State` argument takes the default value `California`.

Parameter arrays are discussed in the following section.

Parameter Arrays

You might come across a situation in which you need to create a procedure that can accept an indefinite number of arguments. Consider a procedure that accepts supplier details such as ID, name, and items supplied. In this case, the number of items supplied by each supplier will vary, so you can use a parameter array. A *parameter array* enables a procedure to accept an array of values. When declaring a parameter array, you don't need to specify the number of elements in the array.

In Visual Basic.NET, you use the `ParamArray` keyword to declare a parameter array. Consider the following example:

```
Sub SupplierDetails(ByVal Id As String, ByVal Name As String, ByVal ParamArray
Items() As String)
                        'Code statements
End Sub
```

Here, the `SupplierDetails` procedure accepts the ID, name, and items provided by a supplier. Because a supplier can provide multiple items, a parameter array,

Items, is used to pass the details of the items provided by a supplier. You can call the SupplierDetails procedure by using the following statement:

SupplierDetails ("008", "IDG Inc.","Toothpaste", "Toothbrush")

In this example, the SupplierDetails procedure is called with four arguments: the ID, the name, and the two items provided by the supplier.

You can declare only one parameter array in a procedure, and the parameter array should be passed by value. In addition, for a procedure declaration, there should be no arguments following the parameter array. In other words, the parameter array should be the last argument in a procedure declaration. By default, the parameter array is optional. Additionally, a procedure that includes a parameter array cannot include any optional arguments. The statements in a procedure with a parameter array should treat the parameter array as a one-dimensional array when manipulating the values stored in it.

When specifying a value for the parameter array, you can specify any of the following values:

◆ An array with the same data type as the parameter array.

◆ Any number of arguments, which are separated by commas.

◆ An empty array is passed if the parameter array is skipped.

The next section discusses overloading procedures.

Overloading Procedures

As the name suggests, *overloading* a procedure means having multiple versions of it. In other words, it refers to procedures that have the same name but different signatures. Here, *signature* refers to the type, number, and order of arguments for a procedure. To understand this better, consider an application that accepts student details. A student can be identified uniquely by ID, name, or both. You can create three different procedures to accept these student details separately. However, it is difficult to give an appropriate name to each of the procedures and then is even more difficult to memorize these names. Instead, you can overload one procedure. In other words, you can create multiple procedures having the same name but different signatures. You use the Overloads keyword to overload a procedure.

For the student details example discussed in the preceding paragraph, consider the following code statements:

```
Overloads Sub StudentDetails (ByVal StudId As Integer, ParamArray Scores() As
Integer)
                'Code statements
End Sub
```

In the preceding statement, the `StudentDetails` procedure accepts two arguments, `StudId` and `Scores`. Now, consider the following statement:

```
Overloads Sub StudentDetails (ByVal StudName As String, ParamArray Scores() As
Integer)
                'Some code statements
End Sub
```

In the preceding statement, the `StudentDetails` procedure accepts two arguments, `StudName` and `Scores`.

When overloading a procedure, consider the following rules:

◆ The versions of an overloaded procedure should have different signatures, which does not mean different return types only.

◆ It is possible to overload a `Function` procedure with a `Sub` procedure or vice versa. However, they must have different signatures.

A procedure with an optional parameter(s) is an example of an overloaded procedure because it can be used in two forms: one with its optional parameter(s) and another one without it. A procedure with a `ParamArray` argument is also another implicit form of overloaded procedure. This is because a procedure with the `ParamArray` argument differs in the number of arguments passed and, therefore, is overloaded.

Now that you've learned about the various types of procedures and argument-passing mechanisms, the following section discusses the built-in functions that Visual Basic.NET provides.

Built-in Functions

Visual Basic.NET provides various built-in functions that you can use in your applications. Some of these include `MsgBox`, `InputBox`, `CStr`, `DateDiff`, and

StrComp. These built-in functions are defined in the Microsoft.VisualBasic namespace. Depending on the tasks performed by the various built-in functions, you can classify these functions as follows:

◆ Application-enhancement functions to enhance your programs. For example, MsgBox and InputBox functions.

◆ String functions to manipulate strings. For example, StrComp, Len, and Trim.

◆ Date functions to manipulate date and time values. For example, DateDiff, Now, and Month.

◆ Conversion functions to convert from one data type to another. For example, CStr, CDate, and Val.

The following sections discuss these functions in detail.

Application-Enhancement Functions

As the name suggests, you can use these functions to enhance your applications by adding interactivity. This interactivity can be in the form of accepting data from the user or displaying some message to the user. Two commonly used functions are MsgBox and InputBox. The MsgBox function is used to display a customized message, and the InputBox function is used to accept input from a user. Visual Basic.NET also provides the MessageBox class, which enables you to display a message to the user. The following sections describe these functions.

The MsgBox *Function*

You must have seen message boxes that display error messages or provide tips and warnings. In some cases, message boxes also display the result of an operation. This section discusses how you can display your own message box.

The MsgBox function is used to display information in a message box. The syntax for this function is as follows:

```
RetValue=MsgBox( Message, [, Buttons][, Title])
```

In the preceding syntax:

◆ RetValue is an Integer value that traps the value of the button clicked by the user. As previously mentioned, the return value of a function can be ignored; therefore, it is up to you to trap it or not.

◆ Message is the prompt or message to be displayed. The number of characters in a message cannot exceed 1,024.

◆ Buttons is the numeric expression that is the sum of the values that specify the number and type of buttons, the icon to be displayed, the default buttons, and the modality of the message box. A modal message box is one that doesn't allow you to work with the rest of the application while the message box is displayed. The Buttons argument is optional, and if not specified, the default value is 0.

◆ Title is the string value that appears as a title in the title bar of the message box. It is optional, and if not specified, the application name appears as the title of the message box.

Consider the following example:

```
MsgBox("My message")
                                                    'Displays a message box
with default values
```

In the preceding statement, you don't need the return value of the message box. Therefore, you don't need to store it in a variable. Figure 7-1 displays this message box. Note that this message box has just an OK button, and the title of the message box displays the name of the application.

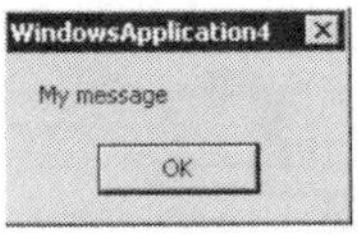

FIGURE 7-1 *A message box with default values*

Visual Basic.NET provides two enumerations (lists of constants) that you can use for a message box. These enumerations contain certain members that, in turn, are associated with some numeric values. The first enumeration is the MsgBoxStyle enumeration, and it is used to specify buttons, icons, and the modality of the message box. The second enumeration is the MsgBoxResult enumeration that is used to check the button clicked by the user. The following sections discuss these enumerations in detail.

The *MsgBoxStyle* Enumeration

As the name suggests, the MsgBoxStyle enumeration is used to specify the style of the message box. The style of a message box includes the buttons and icons to be displayed in the message box and also the modality of the message box. The Msg-BoxStyle enumeration contains members such as OKOnly and OKCancel, and these members represent the OK button and the OK and Cancel button, respectively. There is a numeric value associated with each one of these members. For example, 0 is the value for OKOnly, and 1 is the value for OKCancel.

Consider the following statement:

```
MsgBox("My message", MsgBoxStyle.OKOnly, "Sample")
```

The preceding statement displays the message My message. The title bar of the message box displays the text Sample. This message box contains an OK button along with your message. Figure 7-2 displays this message box.

FIGURE 7-2 *A message box with a customized title*

The preceding statement can also be written as follows:

```
MsgBox("My message", 0, "Sample")
```

Note in the preceding statement that the numeric value 0 refers to the Msg-BoxStyle enumeration. This statement also displays a message box containing the OK button along with the message.

Next consider the following statement:

```
MsgBox("My message", MsgBoxStyle.OKCancel + MsgBoxStyle.Critical, "Sample")
```

The preceding statement displays the message My message. The title bar of the message box displays the text Sample. This message box contains the OK and Cancel buttons and also a critical warning icon. Figure 7-3 displays this message box.

FIGURE 7-3 *A message box with OK and Cancel buttons*

Table 7-2 lists the MsgBoxStyle enumeration members and their values.

Table 7-2 The *MsgBoxStyle* Enumeration Members

Member	Value	Description
OKOnly	0	Displays the OK button
OKCancel	1	Displays OK and Cancel buttons
AbortRetryIgnore	2	Displays Abort, Retry, and Ignore buttons
YesNoCancel	3	Displays Yes, No, and Cancel buttons
YesNo	4	Displays Yes and No buttons
RetryCancel	5	Displays Retry and Cancel buttons
Critical	16	Displays the Critical message icon
Question	32	Displays the Warning query icon
Exclamation	48	Displays the Warning message icon
Information	64	Displays the Information message icon
DefaultButton1	0	Selects the first button by default
DefaultButton2	256	Selects the second button by default
DefaultButton3	512	Selects the third button by default
ApplicationModal	0	Specifies that the message box is application modal, which means the user first needs to respond to the message box before continuing to work in the current application
SystemModal	4096	Specifies that the message box is system modal, which means the user first needs to respond to the message box before continuing working with any application
MsgBoxSetForeground	65536	Specifies that the message box window is the foreground window
MsgBoxRight	524288	Right-aligns the message box text

The next section describes the MsgBoxResult enumeration.

The *MsgBoxResult* Enumeration

When you click on any of the buttons in a message box, a value is returned. You can use this value to find out which button is clicked. Visual Basic.NET provides the MsgBoxResult enumeration, which you can use to trap the result of a message box. In other words, you can find out which button is clicked. Some of the commonly used MsgBoxResult enumeration members are OK, Cancel, Yes, No, and Abort.

Table 7-3 lists the MsgBoxResult enumeration members and their values.

Table 7-3 The *MsgBoxResult* Enumeration Members

Member	Value
OK	1
Cancel	2
Abort	3
Retry	4
Ignore	5
Yes	6
No	7

Consider the following code, which illustrates the use of the MsgBoxStyle and MsgBoxResult enumerations.

```
Dim Var As Integer
Var = MsgBox("My message", MsgBoxStyle.AbortRetryIgnore + MsgBoxStyle.Critical + _

MsgBoxStyle.DefaultButton2, "Sample")
If Var = MsgBoxResult.Abort Then
        MsgBox("You clicked the Abort button.")
ElseIf Var = MsgBoxResult.Retry Then
        MsgBox("You clicked the Retry button.")
Else
        MsgBox("You clicked the Ignore button.")
End If
```

In the preceding code, the second statement displays a message box with three buttons: Abort, Retry, and Ignore. The return value of the message box is trapped in the variable `Var`. The next statements check for the value of the variable `Var` using the If...Then...Else statement. An appropriate message is displayed, depending on the button clicked by the user. Figure 7-4 displays the message box you'll get after the execution of the second statement in the preceding code.

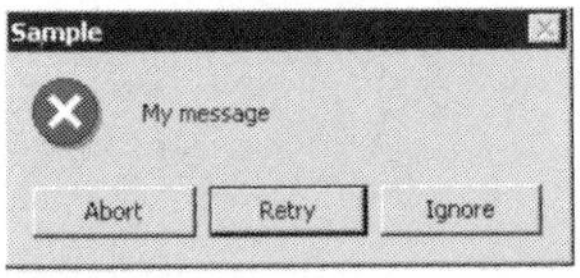

FIGURE 7-4 *A message box with three buttons*

Figure 7-5 displays the message box you'll get if you click on the Retry button in the message box shown in Figure 7-4.

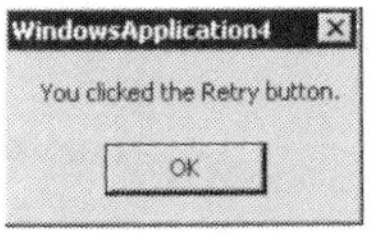

FIGURE 7-5 *A message box displaying the result message*

The If...Then...Else statement is discussed in Chapter 6. The following section discusses another application-enhancement function, the InputBox function.

The InputBox Function

As the name suggests, the InputBox function is used to accept input from the user. The syntax is as follows:

```
InputBox(Prompt, [Title],[Default],[X],[Y])
```

In the preceding syntax:

◆ `Prompt` is the prompt or message to be displayed. If the message is more than one line, you can use the carriage return character (Chr(13)) and the linefeed characters (Chr(10)) to separate the lines.

◆ `Title` is the text to be displayed in the title bar of the input box. It is optional, and if omitted, the name of the application appears in the title bar.

◆ `Default` is the default value or response to be displayed in the text box of the input box. It is optional, and if omitted, an empty text box appears.

◆ `X` is the horizontal distance between the left edge of the input box and the left edge of the screen and x-coordinate value specified in twips (1/20th of a point). A twip is 1/1440th of an inch or 1/567th of a centimeter. It is optional, and if omitted, the input box displays at the horizontal center of the screen.

◆ `Y` is the vertical distance between the top edge of the input box and the top edge of the screen and y-coordinate value specified in twips. It is optional, and if omitted, the input box displays at a position that is approximately one-third the distance from the lower edge of the screen.

The `InputBox` function returns a string containing the value entered by the user. Consider the following statement:

```
Dim InputValue As String
InputValue =InputBox("Enter a value:","Sample","Try", 100,100)
```

In the preceding example, the application prompts the user for a value. The input box displays the text `Sample` in the title bar, and `Try` is the default value displayed in the text box. Figure 7-6 displays the input box that will be displayed when the preceding statement is executed.

FIGURE 7-6 *An input box with a default response*

Consider the following code:

```
Dim InputValue As String
InputValue =InputBox("Enter a value:", "Sample",,100,100)
```

In the preceding example, the application prompts the user for a value. The input box displays the text Sample in the title bar and an empty text box. Figure 7-7 displays this input box. Note that the default value is not specified. However, the corresponding delimiter (,) is specified.

FIGURE 7-7 *An input box with no default response*

As previously mentioned, the input box returns a string value. How then do you accept other types of data such as Integer, Single, or Double? For accepting other types of data, you can use the type-conversion functions. These type-conversion functions convert the accepted data to the required type. Type-conversion functions are discussed later in this chapter.

Consider the following code:

```
Dim StrVar As String
Dim NumVar As Integer
StrVar =InputBox("Enter a number:", "Sample")
                                            'Accepts a string value in
StrVar
NumVar =CInt(StrVar)
                                            'Converts the string value to
integer using the CInt function
```

The preceding code accepts a number from the user and converts the accepted value to Integer using the CInt function.

The following section discusses the MessageBox class that has been included in Visual Basic.NET.

The MessageBox *Class*

You can display messages—which can contain text, buttons, and symbols—using the MessageBox class. This class is contained in the System.Windows.Forms namespace and provides various methods such as Show, ToString, and Equals. However, the most common method is the Show method. As the name suggests, the Show method is used to display a message box. This method has been overloaded in the class. This means that many forms are available in the class for this method. This section examines one of the most commonly used forms of this method and explains how to use it.

The syntax for the Show method is as follows:

```
MessageBox.Show([Window], Message, [Title], [Buttons], [Icon],
[DefaultButton],[Options])
```

In the preceding syntax:

- ◆ Window refers to the window in front of which the message box will appear. It is an optional argument.

- ◆ Message is the message to be displayed.

- ◆ Title is the text to be displayed in the title bar of the message box and is optional.

- ◆ Buttons specifies the buttons to be displayed in the message box and is optional. For this, you can use the MessageBoxButtons enumeration that Visual Basic.NET provides.

- ◆ Icon specifies the icons to be displayed in the message box and is optional. You can use the MessageBoxIcon enumeration for the icons.

- ◆ DefaultButton specifies the default button for the message box and is optional. For this, you can use the MessageBoxDefaultButton enumeration.

- ◆ Options specifies the various display and association options for the message box and is optional. For this, you can use the MessageBoxOptions enumeration.

Consider the following statement:

```
MessageBox.Show("My message","Sample")
```

The preceding statement displays a message box that contains the message My message and the text Sample in the title bar of the message box.

The *MessageBoxButtons* Enumeration

The MessageBoxButtons enumeration contains the members you can use to specify the buttons in a message box. Some of these members are OK, OKCancel, YesNo, and YesNoCancel. Consider the following statement:

```
MessageBox.Show("My message","Sample",MessageBoxButtons.OKCancel)
```

The preceding statement displays a message box with OK and Cancel buttons. Table 7-4 lists the various constants contained in the MessageBoxButtons enumeration.

Table 7-4 The *MessageBoxButtons* Enumeration Members

Member	Displays
OK	The OK button
OKCancel	The OK and Cancel buttons
AbortRetryIgnore	The Abort, Retry, and Ignore buttons
YesNo	The Yes and No buttons
YesNoCancel	The Yes, No, and Cancel buttons
RetryCancel	The Retry and Cancel buttons

The *MessageBoxIcon* Enumeration

Visual Basic.NET provides the MessageBoxIcon enumeration, which you can use to specify the icons to be displayed in the message box. Some of the commonly used members of this enumeration are Information, Error, and Exclamation. For example, consider the following code statement:

```
MessageBox.Show("My message","Sample",MessageBoxButtons.YesNo,
MessageBoxIcon.Question)
```

The preceding statement displays a message box with a Question icon and two buttons, Yes and No. Table 7-5 explains the MessageBoxIcon enumeration members you can use.

Table 7-5 The *MessageBoxIcon* Enumeration Members

Member	Displays An Icon Containing
Question	A question in a circle
Error	A white X in a circle with a red background
Asterisk	A lowercase i in a callout with a white background
Information	A lowercase i in a callout with a white background
Exclamation	An exclamation mark in a triangle with a yellow background
Stop	A white X in a circle with a red background

The *MessageBoxDefaultButton* Enumeration

The MessageBoxDefaultButton enumeration contains members you can use to specify the default button in a message box. Some of the commonly used MessageBoxDefaultButton enumeration members are Button1, Button2, and Button3. The Button1 constant specifies the first button as the default button. Similarly, Button2 and Button3 specify the second button and third button (respectively) as the default button in a message box. For example, consider the following statement:

```
MessageBox.Show("My message","Sample",MessageBoxButtons.YesNoCancel, _

MessageBoxIcon.Information, MessageBoxDefaultButton.Button3)
```

The preceding code statement displays a message box with the third button, Cancel, as the default button.

The *MessageBoxOptions* Enumeration

The MessageBoxOptions enumeration contains members you can use to specify options for a message box. Two of the commonly used MessageBoxOptions enumeration members are RightAlign and RtlReading. RightAlign right-aligns the text, and RtlReading sets the reading order for the message box from right to left. For example, consider the following statement:

```
MessageBox.Show("My message","Sample",MessageBoxButtons.YesNoCancel, _
        MessageBoxIcon.Information, MessageBoxDefaultButton.Button3,
MessageBoxOptions.RightAlign))
```

The preceding code statement displays a message box with right-aligned text and the third button as the default button. Figure 7-8 displays this message box.

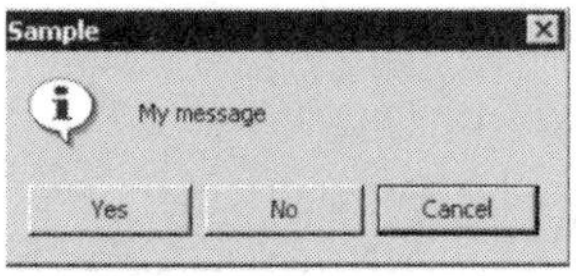

FIGURE 7-8 *A message box with the third button as the default button*

Next you will look at the various string functions that Visual Basic.NET provides.

The String Functions

String functions are used to manipulate strings, and Visual Basic.NET provides a lot of them. For example, the `Len` function is used to calculate the number of characters in a string, and it returns an `Integer` value. Consider the following statement:

```
Dim Length As Integer
Length=Len("Sample")
                                            'Returns 6
```

Some of the other commonly used string functions are `StrComp`, `StrConv`, `StrReverse`, `InStr`, `Mid`, `LCase`, `UCase`, `Trim`, `LTrim`, and `RTrim`. The following sections take a look at these functions.

Comparing Strings

The `StrComp` function is used to compare two strings. Two types of comparison are possible in Visual Basic.NET—textual and binary. Textual comparison depends on your computer system's settings. Binary comparison is based on the internal binary representations of characters. You can specify the comparison type at the module level of a project. To set the comparison type, you can use the `Option Compare` statement. The syntax for this statement is as follows:

```
Option Compare <ComparisonType>
```

In the preceding syntax, ComparisonType refers to the default comparison type for a project. It can be specified as Binary or Text. If omitted, Binary is the default comparison type.

The syntax for the StrComp function is as follows:

```
StrComp(String1, String2 [,CompareType])
```

In the preceding syntax:

- ◆ String1 and String2 are the strings to be compared.
- ◆ CompareType is comparison type and is optional. It can take the value CompareMethod.Text or CompareMethod.Binary. If omitted, the comparison type is the one specified in the Option Compare statement.

The StrComp function returns a numeric value that determines the result of the string comparison. Table 7-6 lists various return values along with their descriptions, assuming that String1 and String2 are the two strings being compared.

Table 7-6 Return Values for the *StrComp* Function

Return Value	Description
1	String1 is greater than String2.
0	String1 is equal to String2.
-1	String1 is less than String2.
NULL	String1 or String2 is NULL.

The following is a code example that uses the StrComp function:

```
Dim NumVar As Integer
Dim StrVar1,StrVar2 As String
StrVar1="SAMPLE"
StrVar2="sample"
NumVar=StrComp(StrVar1,StrVar2,CompareMethod.Text)

'Returns 0
NumVar=StrComp(StrVar1,StrVar2,CompareMethod.Binary)

'Returns -1
```

```
NumVar=StrComp(StrVar2,StrVar1,CompareMethod.Text)
```

```
'Returns 0
NumVar=StrComp(StrVar2,StrVar1,CompareMethod.Binary)
```

```
'Returns 1
```

Reversing Strings

You can use the StrReverse function to reverse a string. The following is the syntax for this function:

```
StrReverse(String)
```

In the preceding syntax, String is the string to be reversed. The StrReverse function returns the specified string with its characters reversed. Consider the following statement:

```
Dim StrVar As String
StrVar=StrReverse("My string")
                                              'Returns gnirts yM
```

Searching for a String Within Another String

You can use the InStr function to search for a string within another string. The syntax for the InStr function is as follows:

```
InStr([Start],String1,String2[,CompareType])
```

In the preceding syntax:

- ◆ Start is a numeric expression that indicates the starting index for the search. If omitted, the search starts from the first character.
- ◆ String1 is the string in which you want to search.
- ◆ String2 is the string to be searched.
- ◆ CompareType specifies the comparison type. It can be specified as Binary or Text and is optional. If omitted, the default comparison type is the one specified in the Option Compare statement.

Table 7-7 lists the various return values for the InStr function, assuming that String2 needs to be searched in String1.

Table 7-7 The Return Values for the *InStr* Function

Return Value	Description
0	String2 is not found, String1 is zero length, or Start is greater than the length of String2.
1	String2 is NULL.
Null	String1 is NULL.
Position	String2 is found within String1.
Start	String2 is zero length.

Consider the following code example:

```
Dim NumVar As String
NumVar=InStr("This is my sample string","sample", CompareMethod.Text)


'Returns 12
NumVar=InStr(15,"This is my sample string","sample", CompareMethod.Text)


'Returns 0
NumVar=InStr("This is my sample string", "", CompareMethod.Text)


'Returns 1
```

Extracting a Part of a String

You can use the Mid function to extract a specific number of characters from a string. The syntax for the Mid function is as follows:

```
Mid(String, Start [,Length])
```

In the preceding syntax:

◆ String is the string from which you want to extract characters.

◆ Start is the starting index in the String from which you want to start extracting.

◆ Length is the number of characters to be extracted and is optional. If not specified, the characters are extracted up to the last character in the String.

Consider the following example:

```
Dim StrVar As String
StrVar=Mid("This is my sample string",12)
                                                    'Returns

sample string
StrVar=Mid("This is my sample string",12,6)
                                                    'Returns

sample
```

Changing the Case of a String

You can use the LCase and UCase functions to change the case of a string. The LCase function converts all the uppercase characters to lowercase, and the UCase function converts all the lowercase characters to uppercase.

The syntax for the LCase function is as follows:

```
LCase(String)
```

In the preceding syntax, String is any string expression in which all the uppercase characters needs to be converted to lowercase.

The syntax for the UCase function is as follows:

```
UCase(String)
```

In the preceding syntax, String is any string expression in which all the lowercase characters needs to be converted to uppercase.

Consider the following code that uses the LCase and UCase functions:

```
Dim StrVar As String
StrVar=LCase("Sample string")
                                                    'Returns sample

string
StrVar=UCase("Sample string")
                                                    'Returns SAMPLE

STRING
```

Removing Spaces from a String

Visual Basic.NET provides three functions—LTrim, RTrim, and Trim—that you can use to remove extra spaces from a string.

- ◆ The LTrim function removes all the leading spaces (or the spaces to the left of a string).

- ◆ The RTrim function removes all the trailing spaces (or the spaces to the right of a string).

- ◆ The Trim function removes both leading and trailing spaces from a string.

```
Dim StrVar1,StrVar2 As String
StrVar1="----Sample----"
                                        'Assume each - represents a space
StrVar2=LTrim(StrVar1)
                                        'Returns Sample----
StrVar2=RTrim(StrVar1)
                                        'Returns ----Sample
StrVar2=Trim(StrVar1)
                                        'Returns Sample
```

Now that you've learned about various string-manipulation functions, you will take a look at the various date functions that Visual Basic.NET provides.

Date Functions

The date functions enable you to manipulate date and time values. You can modify, calculate, and extract the date and time parts from a Date variable using the date functions. Some commonly used date functions are Now, DateAdd, DateDiff, and DatePart. Table 7-8 lists some of the date functions. Here, datetime is the date value passed as an argument to a date function.

Table 7-8 Date Functions

Function	Syntax	Returns
Now	Now()	The current date and time
Day	Day(datetime)	A whole number between 1 and 31 that represents the day of a month
Month	Month(datetime)	A number between 1 and 12 that represents the month
Year	Year(datetime)	A number between 1 and 9999 that represents the year
Second	Second(datetime)	A number between 1 and 59 that represents the second
Minute	Minute(datetime)	A number between 1 and 59 that represents the minute
Hour	Hour(datetime)	A number between 0 and 23 that represents the hour of the day

In addition to the functions listed in the preceding table, Visual Basic.NET provides some functions that you can use to extract a part of the date, calculate the difference between two dates, and add a time interval to a date. The following sections describe these functions.

The DatePart Function

You can use the DatePart function to extract a specific part or component—such as the month, quarter, or day—from a date. The syntax for the DatePart function is as follows:

```
DatePart(Interval, Date)
```

In the preceding syntax:

◆ Interval is a string expression that refers to the type of interval. Some examples are DateInterval.Hour, DateInterval.Second, and DateInterval.Year. For specifying the Interval, you can use the DateInterval enumeration provided by Visual Basic.NET. Table 7-9 lists the DateIn-

terval enumeration members along with their string equivalent values
and the return value.

◆ Date is the date value whose date part you want to extract.

Table 7-9 The *DateInterval* Enumeration Members

Member	String Value	Extracts
DateInterval.Second	s	Second
DateInterval.Minute	m	Minute
DateInterval.Hour	h	Hour
DateInterval.Day	d	Day of month (1 to 31)
DateInterval.DayOfYear	y	Day of year (1 to 366)
DateInterval.Weekday	w	Day of week (1 to 7)
DateInterval.WeekOfYear	ww	Week of year (1 to 53)
DateInterval.Year	yyyy	Year

Consider the following code:

```
Dim DateVar As Date = Now()
                                        'Declares a date variable and ini-
tializes it with the current date
Dim NumVar As Integer
NumVar=DatePart(DateInterval.Weekday, DateVar)
                                        'Returns the week day
number of the current date
NumVar=DatePart("m", DateVar)
                                        'Returns the month num-
ber of the current date
```

The DateAdd *Function*

The DateAdd function is used to add a specified time interval to a date value. This
function returns a date value. The syntax for this function is as follows:

```
DateAdd(Interval, Number, Date)
```

In the preceding syntax:

- ◆ Interval is a string expression that specifies the time interval you want to add. You can use the DateInterval enumeration as specified in Table 7-9.

- ◆ Number is the number of intervals to be added. For example, if the Interval is specified as DateInterval.Year and the Number is 7, the interval that needs to be added to the specified date is 7 years. The Number value can be either positive or negative. A positive value returns a date after the specified date, and a negative value returns a date earlier than the specified date.

- ◆ Date is the date value to which you want to add the specified time interval.

Consider the following code statements:

```
Dim DateVar1 As Date = Now()
                                        'Declares a date variable and ini-
tializes it with the current date
Dim DateVar2 As Date
                                        'Declares another date variable to
store the result
DateVar2=DateAdd(DateInterval.Month, 5, DateVar1)
                                        'Returns the date after adding 5
months to the current date
DateVar2=DateAdd(DateInterval.Year, 10, DateVar1)
                                        'Returns the date after adding 10
years to the current date
```

The DateDiff Function

The DateDiff function is used to calculate the time interval between two dates. This function returns a Long value. The syntax for the DateDiff function is as follows:

```
DateDiff(Interval, Date1, Date2)
```

In the preceding syntax:

◆ `Interval` is a string expression that indicates the interval type in which you want the difference to be shown. You can use the `DateInterval` enumeration members mentioned in Table 7-9.

◆ `Date1` and `Date2` are the dates whose difference you want to calculate. The value of `Date1` is subtracted from `Date2`.

Consider the following example to calculate the time difference between the current date and a date that is accepted from the user:

```
Dim DateVar1 As Date = Now()
Dim DateVar2 As Date
Dim NumVar As Integer
DateVar2=InputBox("Enter a date:")
                                        'The conversion function is not
required as the DateDiff function can take string
                                        'value as an argument
NumVar= DateDiff("d",DateVar2, DateVar1)
                                        'Returns the difference in  num-
ber of days
                                        'between the current date and the
date entered by the user
NumVar=DateDiff("yyyy",DateVar2,DateVar1)
                                        'Returns the difference in  num-
ber of years
                                        'between the current date and the
date entered by the user
```

Type-Conversion Functions

As discussed in the "Type Conversions" section in Chapter 4, "Variables and Operators," you can convert one data type to another. For such conversions, Visual Basic.NET provides various type-conversion functions. These conversion functions takes strings or numeric data or expressions as arguments and return the converted value in the required data type. Table 7-10 lists some of the commonly used type-conversion functions.

Table 7-10 Type-Conversion Functions

Function	Converts the Given Expression To	Example
CInt	Integer format	Dim Var As Integer Var=CInt("123.45") 'Returns 123
CStr	String format	Dim Var As String Var=CStr(123.45) 'Returns 123.45
CBool	Boolean format	Dim Var As Boolean Var=CBool(12<45) 'Returns True
CByte	Byte format	Dim Var As Byte Var=CByte("123.67") 'Returns 124
CChar	Char format	Dim Var As Char Var=CChar("abcd") 'Returns a
CDate	Date format	Dim Var As Date Var=CDate("12/12/01") 'Returns 12/12/2001
CDbl	Double format	Dim Var As Double Var=CDbl("123.4567") 'Returns 123.4567
CDec	Decimal format	Dim Var As Decimal Var=CDec("123.456") 'Returns 123.456
CLng	Long format	Dim Var As Long Var=CLng("123.45") 'Returns 123
CObj	Object format	Dim Var As Object Var=CObj("123.45") 'Returns 123

Function	Converts the Given Expression To	Example

CShort	Short format	```Dim Var As Short```
		```Var=CShort("123.45")```
		    ```'Returns 123```

CSng	Single format	```Dim Var As Single```
		```Var=CSng("123.45")```
		    ```'Returns 123.45```

CType is another function that converts one data type value to another. The CType function has the following syntax:

```
CType(Expression, DataType)
```

In the preceding syntax:

◆ Expression is the data to be converted.

◆ DataType is the name of the data type, class, or structure to which the data needs to be converted.

The CType function returns a value of the type specified in the DataType argument of the function.

Consider the following example:

```
Dim Var As Object
                              'Declares an  object type variable
to store any data of any type
Var=CType("123.45", Integer)
                              'Returns an Integer value 123
Var=CType("123.708", Long)
                              'Returns a Long value 124
```

Summary

In this chapter, you learned how to reuse code in your program by using procedures. You also learned how to create and use different types of procedures. You also learned about the various built-in functions provided by Visual Basic.NET that help you add interactivity to your programs and develop your programs easily and quickly.

PART II

Professional Project 1

Project 1

Project 1 Overview

In this project, you will learn to upgrade an existing Visual Basic 6.0 application to Visual Basic.NET by using the Visual Basic Upgrade Wizard. You will also learn about the considerations to take into account before upgrading an application to Visual Basic.NET.

This project uses a sample application—PrjLenConversion—to help you understand how to upgrade a Visual Basic 6.0 project to Visual Basic.NET. The PrjLenConversion application enables you to convert lengths from one unit to another. You will use the Visual Basic Upgrade Wizard to upgrade the PrjLenConversion application. After you upgrade the application, you will learn about the changes made to the code in the project by the wizard. You will learn about the following changes:

◆ General changes

◆ Changes in the declaration of event-handling procedures

◆ Changes in manipulating controls

◆ Changes in data types

◆ Changes in the Msgbox function

In addition to preceding changes, this project will also explain how the Visual Basic Upgrade Wizard manages changes made to the following:

◆ Arrays

◆ Property procedures

◆ Late-bound objects

Chapter 8

**Upgrading Visual
Basic 6.0 Projects
to Visual Basic
.NET**

In the preceding chapters, you learned about the features available in Visual Basic.NET. You also learned about the differences between Visual Basic and Visual Basic.NET. In this chapter, you will learn how to upgrade an existing project created in Visual Basic 6.0 to Visual Basic.NET.

Now that you've learned about the features of Visual Basic.NET and their advantages, you might want to upgrade the projects you previously created in Visual Basic 6.0 to Visual Basic.NET. By doing so, your projects can benefit from the various new and enhanced features that the .NET framework provides. Visual Basic.NET provides tools that enable you to upgrade projects created in Visual Basic 6.0.

Before you upgrade an existing project, however, you must consider a few things. As discussed in Chapter 1, ".NET Overview," Visual Basic.NET does not support many features supported by Visual Basic 6.0. The following are a few of the features not supported by Visual Basic.NET:

- ◆ Object linking and embedding (OLE) container control
- ◆ Dynamic data exchange (DDE)
- ◆ Web classes
- ◆ DHTML applications
- ◆ ActiveX documents

Therefore, if your existing project uses any of these features, you must modify your project before you can upgrade it. However, the number of changes that you need to make to a project depends on various factors such as the size and type of the project. For example, Visual Basic.NET does not provide enhancements for all of the features of Visual Basic 6.0, such as DHTML applications. Therefore, a lot of rework might be required to upgrade a Visual Basic 6.0 project that uses DHTML applications. It is a good idea to first estimate the amount of rework required to upgrade the project. You can choose not to upgrade the DHTML application, as it can interoperate with Visual Basic.NET Web applications.

Visual Basic.NET provides a Visual Basic Upgrade Wizard that enables you to upgrade projects created in Visual Basic 6.0 to Visual Basic.NET. You will learn more about the Visual Basic Upgrade Wizard in subsequent sections of this chapter. The upgrade process involves either one or two steps, depending on the type of project you are upgrading. The first step involves using the Visual Basic Upgrade Wizard to upgrade the Visual Basic 6.0 project to a Visual Basic.NET project. The second step, if required, involves modifying a few sections of the code.

The following sections provide an example to help you understand how to upgrade a Visual Basic 6.0 project to Visual Basic.NET.

PrjLenConversion—A Visual Basic 6.0 Project

In this section, you will learn about the PrjLenConversion project that enables you to convert lengths from one unit to another. For example, you can convert length in miles to other units of measure such as yards, feet, or inches.

The interface of the PrjLenConversion project is displayed in Figure 8-1.

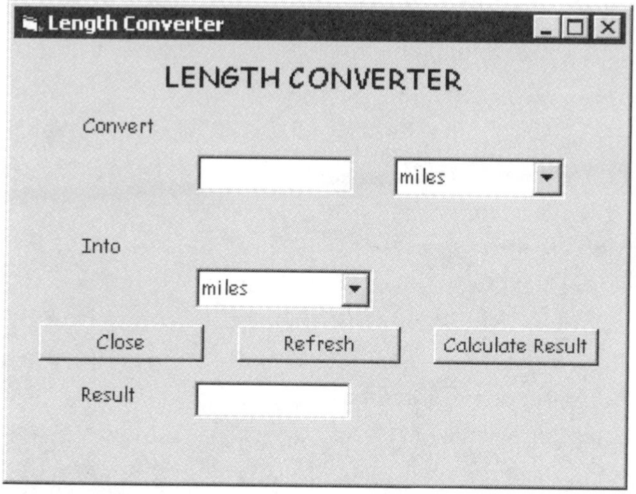

FIGURE 8-1 *The interface of the PrjLenConversion project*

To convert a length, enter the number in the text box in the Convert section and select the unit you need to convert from the drop-down list next to the text box. Then, in the Into section, select the unit into which the length should be converted. Then click on the Calculate Result button to display the result in the

Result section. To exit the project, click on the Close button. The Refresh button enables you reset the controls in the project.

Listing 8-1 contains the code for the PrjLenConversion project.

Listing 8-1 The PrjLenConversion Project

```vb
Dim InputNum As Long
Dim OutputNum As Long
Dim InputUnit As String
Dim OutputUnit As String
'Declaration of variables
Private Sub CmdCalculate_Click()
'Event handler for the Calculate button
        If TxtInput.Text = "" Or Not IsNumeric(TxtInput.Text) Then
'Validation for the text box
                MsgBox "Please enter a numeric value", vbOKOnly, "Value
Required"
                TxtInput.Text = ""
                TxtInput.SetFocus
                Exit Sub
        End If
        InputNum = TxtInput.Text
        InputUnit = CmbInputUnit.Text
'Picking up values from the combo box
        OutputUnit = CmbOutputUnit.Text
        If InputUnit = "miles" Then
'Calculating the result based on the
                                                'value entered in
the text box and the selections in the combo boxes
                Select Case OutputUnit
                        Case "miles"
                                OutputNum = InputNum
                        Case "feet"
                                OutputNum = 5280 * InputNum
                        Case "yards"
                                OutputNum = 1760 * InputNum
                        Case "inches"
```

```
                                        OutputNum = 63360 * InputNum
                End Select
        ElseIf InputUnit = "feet" Then
                Select Case OutputUnit
                        Case "miles"
                                OutputNum = 0.000189 * InputNum
                        Case "feet"
                                OutputNum = InputNum
                        Case "yards"
                                OutputNum = 0.333333 * InputNum
                        Case "inches"
                                OutputNum = 12 * InputNum
                End Select
        ElseIf InputUnit = "yards" Then
                Select Case OutputUnit
                        Case "miles"
                                OutputNum = 0.000568 * InputNum
                        Case "feet"
                                OutputNum = 3 * InputNum
                        Case "yards"
                                OutputNum = InputNum
                        Case "inches"
                                OutputNum = 36 * InputNum
                End Select
        ElseIf InputUnit = "inches" Then
                Select Case OutputUnit
                        Case "miles"
                                OutputNum = 0.000016 * InputNum
                        Case "feet"
                                OutputNum = 0.083333 * InputNum
                        Case "yards"
                                OutputNum = 0.027778 * InputNum
                        Case "inches"
                                OutputNum = InputNum
                End Select
        End If
        TxtOutput.Text = OutputNum
'Displaying the result
```

```
        LblResult.Caption = OutputUnit
End Sub
Private Sub CmdRefresh_Click()
'Event handler for the Refresh button
        CmbInputUnit.ListIndex = 0
'Reinitializing the controls
        CmbOutputUnit.ListIndex = 0
        LblResult.Caption = ""
        TxtOutput.Text = ""
        TxtInput.Text = ""
        InputNum = 0
        OutputNum = 0
End Sub
Private Sub CmdClose_Click()
'Event handler for the Close button
        Unload Me
'Closing the form
End Sub
Private Sub Form_Initialize()
        CmbInputUnit.AddItem ("miles")
'Adding items to the combo boxes
        CmbInputUnit.AddItem ("feet")
        CmbInputUnit.AddItem ("yards")
        CmbInputUnit.AddItem ("inches")
        CmbInputUnit.ListIndex = 0
        CmbOutputUnit.AddItem ("miles")
        CmbOutputUnit.AddItem ("feet")
        CmbOutputUnit.AddItem ("yards")
        CmbOutputUnit.AddItem ("inches")
        CmbOutputUnit.ListIndex = 0
End Sub
```

The PrjLenConversion project was created in Visual Basic 6.0. Now let's upgrade this project from Visual Basic 6.0 to Visual Basic.NET by using Visual Basic Upgrade Wizard. First, however, let's take a look at the wizard.

The Visual Basic Upgrade Wizard

Visual Basic.NET provides Visual Basic Upgrade Wizard to help you upgrade projects created in Visual Basic 6.0. To upgrade a project, open the project in Visual Basic.NET. When you open a Visual Basic 6.0 project in Visual Basic.NET, the Visual Basic Upgrade Wizard displays. This is because Visual Basic.NET automatically detects whether the project you are opening was created in Visual Basic 6.0 and therefore needs to be upgraded.

When you upgrade a project using the Visual Basic Upgrade Wizard, the existing project remains unmodified. Instead, the Visual Basic Upgrade Wizard creates a new Visual Basic.NET project with the modified code. In addition, the wizard copies each file from the existing project to the new project and modifies the code in the new project according to the Visual Basic.NET syntax. Also, the forms and controls in the existing Visual Basic 6.0 project are replaced with corresponding Visual Basic.NET forms and controls.

After the upgrade process is complete, the Visual Basic Upgrade Wizard creates an upgrade report. The upgrade report lists the project files and other information about the upgraded project, such as the location of the new project files. This upgrade report also lists the issues encountered by the Visual Basic Upgrade Wizard. As previously mentioned, in certain cases, due to the differences between Visual Basic 6.0 and Visual Basic.NET, the Visual Basic Upgrade Wizard cannot upgrade the entire project. As a result, you might need to modify the existing project to complete the upgrade process. Before you can execute an upgraded project, you must fix the issues listed in the upgrade report.

You need to perform the following steps to upgrade a Visual Basic 6.0 project to Visual Basic.NET:

1. Open the Visual Basic 6.0 project in Visual Basic.NET. When you open the project in Visual Basic.NET, the Visual Basic Upgrade Wizard displays.

2. Click on the Next button on the first page of the Visual Basic Upgrade Wizard, as shown in Figure 8-2. The second page of the wizard then appears.

FIGURE 8-2 *The first page of the Visual Basic Upgrade Wizard*

On the second page of the wizard, specify whether you want to upgrade the project as an EXE project or a DLL project. The options available in the Visual Basic Upgrade Wizard differ depending on the type of project you are upgrading. For example, when you upgrade an ActiveX EXE or ActiveX Document EXE project created in Visual Basic 6.0, you can upgrade it to either an EXE or a DLL file. In contrast, when you upgrade any other type of project to Visual Basic.NET, the type of project to which you can upgrade is already selected. Note in Figure 8-3 that the EXE option is selected.

3. Click the Next button to display the third page of the Visual Basic Upgrade Wizard, shown in Figure 8-4.

On the third page of the wizard, specify the location where you want to save the Visual Basic.NET project. The Visual Basic Upgrade Wizard creates a new folder to store the upgraded project. The wizard creates the folder in the same folder where the Visual Basic 6.0 project is stored and names it *<projectname>*.NET, where *projectname* represents the name of the Visual Basic 6.0 project. You can use the Browse button to specify a different location for the Visual Basic.NET project.

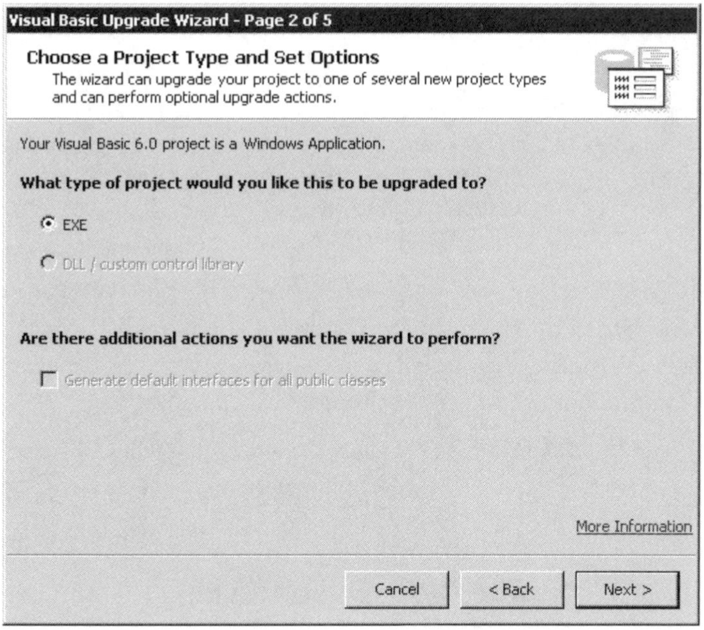

Visual Basic Upgrade Wizard - Page 2 of 5

Choose a Project Type and Set Options
The wizard can upgrade your project to one of several new project types and can perform optional upgrade actions.

Your Visual Basic 6.0 project is a Windows Application.

What type of project would you like this to be upgraded to?

   ⦿ EXE

   ○ DLL / custom control library

Are there additional actions you want the wizard to perform?

   ☐ Generate default interfaces for all public classes

More Information

Cancel   < Back   Next >

FIGURE 8-3 *The second page of the Visual Basic Upgrade Wizard*

Visual Basic Upgrade Wizard - Page 3 of 5

Specify a Location for Your New Project
The wizard will place your new project files in a new folder.

Where do you want your new project created?

D:\VB Projects\PrjLenConverter\PrjLengthConverter.NET   Browse...

The project will be created as: D:\VB Projects\PrjLenConverter\PrjLengthConverter.NET\prjLenConversion.vbproj

Cancel   < Back   Next >

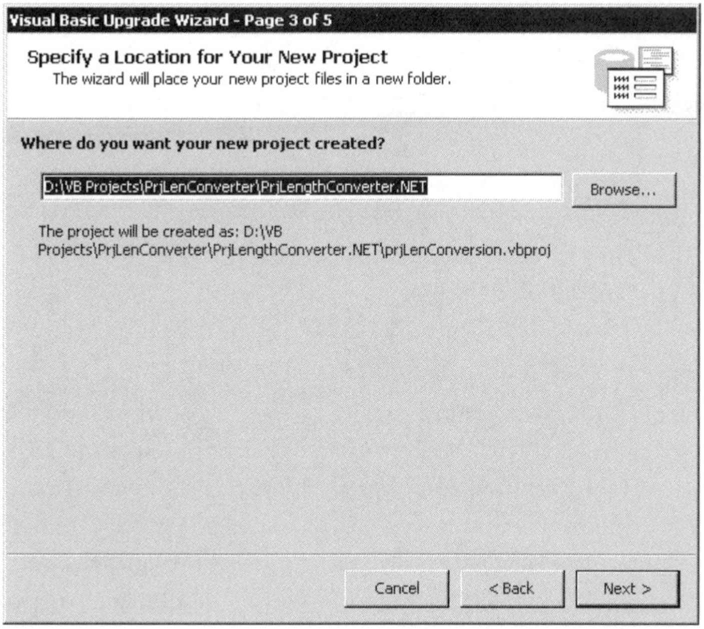

FIGURE 8-4 *The third page of the Visual Basic Upgrade Wizard*

NOTE

If a folder that contains files is specified as the destination folder for the Visual Basic.NET project, the Visual Basic Upgrade Wizard displays a message box stating that the existing files in the folder will be deleted. You can click on the OK button in the message box to delete the existing files in the folder.

---

4. Click on the Next button on the third page of the wizard. A message box appears, prompting you to confirm the creation of the folder in which the upgraded project will be stored.

5. Click on the OK button in the message box to continue. The fourth page of the Visual Basic Upgrade Wizard displays, as shown in Figure 8-5.

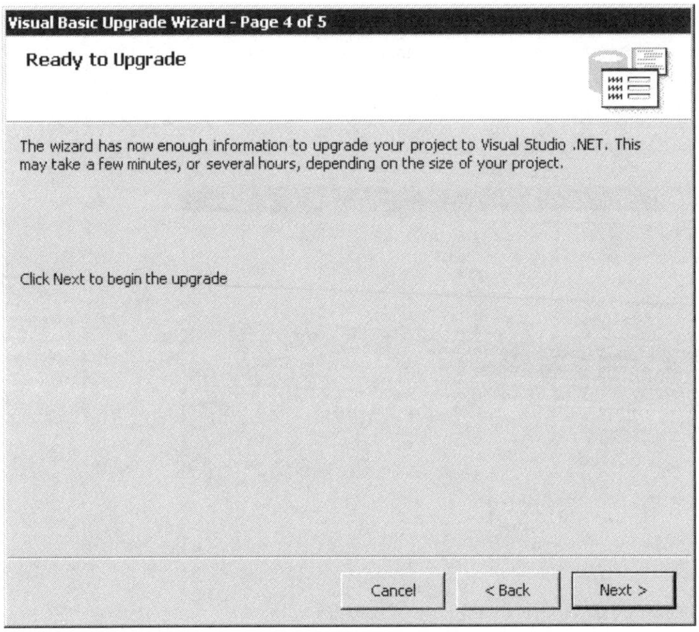

Visual Basic Upgrade Wizard - Page 4 of 5

Ready to Upgrade

The wizard has now enough information to upgrade your project to Visual Studio .NET. This may take a few minutes, or several hours, depending on the size of your project.

Click Next to begin the upgrade

[Cancel] [< Back] [Next >]

FIGURE 8-5 *The fourth page of the Visual Basic Upgrade Wizard*

6. Click on the Next button on the fourth page of the Visual Basic Upgrade Wizard to start the upgrade process. The fifth page of the wizard displays, as shown in Figure 8-6.

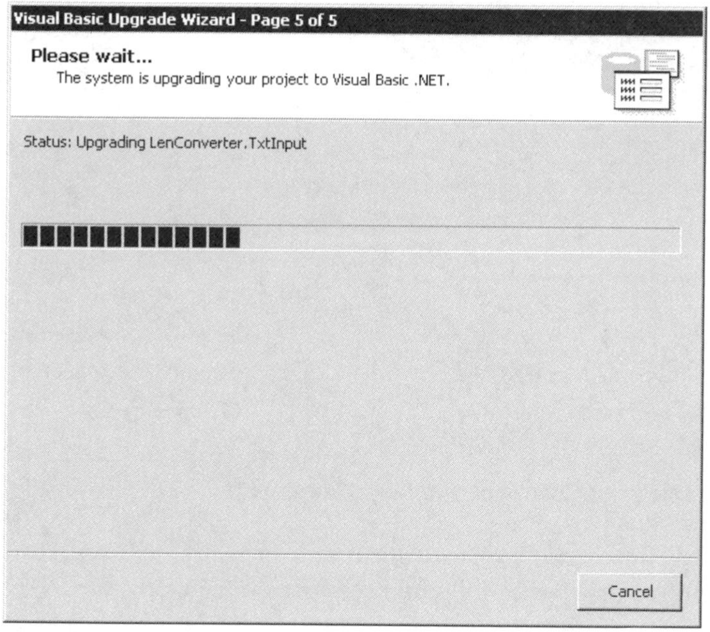

Visual Basic Upgrade Wizard - Page 5 of 5

Please wait...

The system is upgrading your project to Visual Basic .NET.

Status: Upgrading LenConverter.TxtInput

Cancel

FIGURE 8-6 *The fifth page of the Visual Basic Upgrade Wizard*

The fifth page of the wizard displays the progress of the upgrade. After the upgrade process is complete, you can view the new project in the Solution Explorer window, as shown in Figure 8-7.

FIGURE 8-7 *The Solution Explorer window*

Note that the Solution Explorer window also displays the _Upgrade-Report.htm file, which is the upgrade report. Double-click on the _UpgradeReport.htm file in the Solution Explorer window to view the upgrade report. Figure 8-8 displays the upgrade report for the upgraded PrjLenConversion project.

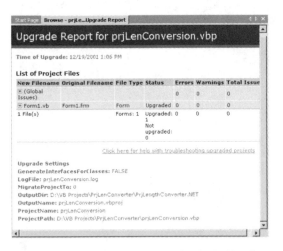

FIGURE 8-8 *The upgrade report for the PrjLenConversion project*

As is evident from the upgrade report shown in Figure 8-8, the PrjLenConversion project was upgraded successfully, and the Visual Basic Upgrade Wizard did not encounter any issues during the upgrade process.

Next you'll take a look at the changes made by the Visual Basic Upgrade Wizard to the upgraded project.

Changes in the Upgraded Project

To view changes made to the upgraded project, you need to view its code. To view the code, double-click the Form1.vb file in the Solution Explorer window. The form displays in the designer. Select Code from the View menu to view the code associated with the form. Listing 8-2 contains the code for the upgraded project.

Listing 8-2 The PrjLenConversion.NET Project

```
Option Strict Off
Option Explicit On
Friend Class LenConverter
'Added by the Visual Basic Upgrade Wizard
        Inherits System.Windows.Forms.Form
Windows Form Designer generated code
Upgrade Support
```

```
'Added by the Visual Basic Upgrade Wizard
        Dim InputNum As Integer
        Dim OutputNum As Integer
        Dim InputUnit As String
        Dim OutputUnit As String
'Declaration of variables
        Private Sub CmdCalculate_Click(ByVal eventSender As System.Object, ByVal
eventArgs As System.EventArgs) Handles CmdCalculate.Click
'Event handler for the Calculate button
            If TxtInput.Text = "" Or Not IsNumeric(TxtInput.Text) Then
'Validation for the text box
                MsgBox("Please enter a numeric value",
MsgBoxStyle.OKOnly, "Value Required")
                TxtInput.Text = ""
                TxtInput.Focus()
                Exit Sub
            End If
            InputNum = CInt(TxtInput.Text)
            InputUnit = CmbInputUnit.Text
'Picking up values from the combo box
            OutputUnit = CmbOutputUnit.Text
            If InputUnit = "miles" Then                      'Calculating
the result based on the value entered in the text box and the selections in the
combo boxes
                Select Case OutputUnit
                    Case "miles"
                        OutputNum = InputNum
                    Case "feet"
                        OutputNum = 5280 * InputNum
                    Case "yards"
                        OutputNum = 1760 * InputNum
                    Case "inches"
                        OutputNum = 63360 * InputNum
                End Select
            ElseIf InputUnit = "feet" Then
                Select Case OutputUnit
                    Case "miles"
```

```
                                      OutputNum = 0.000189 *
InputNum
                          Case "feet"
                                      OutputNum = InputNum
                          Case "yards"
                                      OutputNum = 0.333333 *
InputNum
                          Case "inches"
                                      OutputNum = 12 * InputNum
                End Select
        ElseIf InputUnit = "yards" Then
                Select Case OutputUnit
                          Case "miles"
                                      OutputNum = 0.000568 *
InputNum
                          Case "feet"
                                      OutputNum = 3 * InputNum
                          Case "yards"
                                      OutputNum = InputNum
                          Case "inches"
                                      OutputNum = 36 * InputNum
                End Select
        ElseIf InputUnit = "inches" Then
                Select Case OutputUnit
                          Case "miles"
                                      OutputNum = 0.000016 *
InputNum
                          Case "feet"
                                      OutputNum = 0.083333 *
InputNum
                          Case "yards"
                                      OutputNum = 0.027778 *
InputNum
                          Case "inches"
                                      OutputNum = InputNum
                End Select
        End If
        TxtOutput.Text = CStr(OutputNum)
```

```
'Displaying the result
                    LblResult.Text = OutputUnit
        End Sub
        Private Sub CmdRefresh_Click(ByVal eventSender As System.Object, ByVal
eventArgs As System.EventArgs) Handles CmdRefresh.Click
'Event handler for the Refresh button
                    CmbInputUnit.SelectedIndex = 0
'Reinitializing the controls
                    CmbOutputUnit.SelectedIndex = 0
                    LblResult.Text = " "
                    TxtOutput.Text = " "
                    TxtInput.Text = " "
                    InputNum = 0
                    OutputNum = 0
        End Sub


        Private Sub CmdClose_Click(ByVal eventSender As System.Object, ByVal
eventArgs As System.EventArgs) Handles CmdClose.Click
'Event handler for the Close button
                    Me.Close()
'Closing the form
        End Sub
'UPGRADE_NOTE: Form_Initialize was upgraded to Form_Initialize_Renamed.
        Private Sub Form_Initialize_Renamed()
                    CmbInputUnit.Items.Add(("miles"))
'Adding items to the combo boxes
                    CmbInputUnit.Items.Add(("feet"))
                    CmbInputUnit.Items.Add(("yards"))
                    CmbInputUnit.Items.Add(("inches"))
                    CmbInputUnit.SelectedIndex = 0
                    CmbOutputUnit.Items.Add(("miles"))
                    CmbOutputUnit.Items.Add(("feet"))
                    CmbOutputUnit.Items.Add(("yards"))
                    CmbOutputUnit.Items.Add(("inches"))
                    CmbOutputUnit.SelectedIndex = 0
        End Sub
End Class
```

The following sections describe the changes made by the Visual Basic Upgrade Wizard to the PrjLenConversion project.

General Changes

Note that the Visual Basic Upgrade Wizard adds the following two lines at the top of the code:

```
Option Strict Off
Option Explicit On
```

The first statement in the code enables the code to perform implicit data-type conversions. Implicit conversions may, however, result in loss of data when you convert a data type of a higher capacity to a data type of a lower capacity. For example, data may be lost when you convert a value of the Integer data type to the Short data type. In Visual Basic.NET, you can restrict implicit data-type conversions by using the Option Strict statement. When Option Strict is enabled (that is, set to On), you cannot perform any conversions that might result in data loss. By default, Option Strict is set to Off.

The second statement in the code ensures that you cannot use any undeclared variables in the code. The Option Explicit statement is used to ensure explicit declaration of all the variables used in a project. When the Option Explicit statement is set to On, you need to declare all variables that are used in the code.

As discussed in Chapter 2, "Object-Oriented Features in Visual Basic.NET," Visual Basic.NET, unlike Visual Basic 6.0, supports classes. When you upgrade a Visual Basic 6.0 project, the Visual Basic Upgrade Wizard also creates classes. Notice that the Visual Basic Upgrade Wizard includes the entire code in the following statements:

```
Friend Class LenConverter
        Inherits System.Windows.Forms.Form
                                'Code statements
End Class
```

Thus, the wizard declares the LenConverter class, which is derived from the System.Windows.Forms.Form class. All the variables and methods of the PrjLenConversion project are, as a result, part of the LenConverter class. Note that the LenConverter class is declared with the Friend access modifier. This implies that the LenConverter class is accessible only within the upgraded project.

In addition to the preceding changes, notice that the code window displays two additional nodes: Windows Form Designer generated code and Upgrade Support. These nodes are added during the upgrade process. The Windows Form Designer generated code node contains the Sub New and Dispose methods. This node also contains the code for the form and the controls on the form. In addition, it specifies the size, location, and other properties (such as font and name) for controls. The Upgrade Support node contains the code statements to complete the class definition for the upgraded project.

Changes in the Declaration of Event-Handling Procedures

Note that the Visual Basic Upgrade Wizard also changes the syntax for event-handling procedures.

In Visual Basic 6.0, you would use the following syntax to declare an event handler for the Click event of the Close button.

```
Private Sub CmdClose_Click()
                              'Code statements
End Sub
```

In contrast, you need to use the following statements to define the same event-handling procedure in Visual Basic.NET:

```
Private Sub CmdClose_Click(ByVal eventSender As System.Object, ByVal eventArgs As
System.EventArgs) Handles CmdClose.Click
                              'Code statements
End Sub
```

You can refer to Chapter 7, "Procedures and Functions," to revise the concepts related to event-handling procedures. Also note that the Form_Initialize procedure in a Visual Basic 6.0 project is changed to Form_Initialize_Renamed.

Changes in Manipulating Controls

The methods used to manipulate controls—such as combo boxes, text boxes, and labels—in Visual Basic 6.0 and Visual Basic.NET are also different.

Take a look at the following two statements that are part of a Visual Basic 6.0 project:

```
CmbInputUnit.AddItem ("inches")                        'In Visual Basic 6.0
CmbInputUnit.ListIndex = 0
```

In the first statement, the `AddItem` method adds the `inches` item to the `CmbInputUnit` combo box. In the second statement, the `ListIndex` method is used to specify the item at index position zero as the currently selected item.

Now take a look at the same code in Visual Basic.NET:

```
CmbInputUnit.Items.Add(("inches"))                     'In Visual Basic.NET
CmbInputUnit.SelectedIndex = 0
```

In the first statement, note that the name of the combo box is followed by the `Items` property, which in turn is followed by the `Add` method. The `Items` property returns an object representing a member of the `CmbInputUnit` combo box. The `Add` method adds the `inches` item to the `CmbInputUnit` combo box at the position returned by the `Items` property.

In the second statement, the `SelectedIndex` property sets the item at the specified index as the currently selected item.

Similar to combo boxes, the methods used with text boxes and labels have also changed. Consider the following examples.

In a Visual Basic 6.0 project, you would use the following statement to set the focus to the `TxtInput` text box:

```
TxtInput.SetFocus
```

In a Visual Basic.NET project, however, the following statement is used to set the focus to the `TxtInput` text box:

```
TxtInput.Focus()
```

Thus, the `SetFocus` method in Visual Basic 6.0 is replaced with the `Focus` method in Visual Basic.NET.

Similarly, the property used to specify the caption of a label control is also different in Visual Basic 6.0 and Visual Basic.NET. Consider the following example:

```
LblResult.Caption = OutputUnit                         'In Visual Basic 6.0
LblResult.Text = OutputUnit                            'In Visual Basic.NET
```

Changes in Data Types

Note the change in the variable declaration statements in the upgraded project. First look at how variables are declared in the PrjLenConversion project:

```
Dim InputNum As Long
Dim OutputNum As Long
```

The same statements are represented in the following manner in the upgraded project:

```
Dim InputNum As Integer
Dim OutputNum As Integer
```

It is evident from the comparison that the Visual Basic Upgrade Wizard changes the data type of the variables from Long to Integer. This is because the numeric data types in Visual Basic 6.0 and Visual Basic.NET are different.

In Visual Basic 6.0:

◆ A variable of the Integer data type is stored as a 16-bit (2-byte) number.

◆ A variable of the Long data type is stored as a 32-bit (4-byte) number.

In contrast, Visual Basic.NET offers three numeric data types. In Visual Basic.NET:

◆ A variable of the Short data type is stored as a 16-bit (2-byte) number.

◆ A variable of the Integer data type is stored as a 32-bit (4-byte) number.

◆ A variable of the Long data type is stored as a 64-bit (8-byte) number.

Therefore, when you upgrade a Visual Basic 6.0 project, the Visual Basic Upgrade Wizard converts all variables of the Long data type to the Integer data type.

Changes in the *MsgBox* Function

In the PrjLenConversion project, you used the following statement to display a message box:

```
MsgBox "Please enter a numeric value", vbOKOnly, "Value Required"
```

In the preceding statement:

◆ The first argument represents the message to be displayed.

◆ The second value is the constant used to specify the buttons to be displayed in the message box.

◆ The third argument specifies the title of the message box.

Now take a look at how the `MsgBox` function has changed in the upgraded project:

```
MsgBox("Please enter a numeric value", MsgBoxStyle.OKOnly, "Value Required")
```

Note the difference in the second argument. As discussed in Chapter 7, the second argument in the `MsgBox` function specifies the buttons to be displayed in the message box. In Visual Basic.NET, you can use members of the `MsgBoxStyle` enumeration to specify values for the second argument. The `MsgBoxStyle` enumeration includes members such as `OKOnly`, `OKCancel`, `YesNoCancel`, and `YesNo`. You can refer to Chapter 7 to revise the concepts related to the `MsgBox` function.

Now that you've looked at the changes made by the Visual Basic Upgrade Wizard to the project during the upgrade process, the following sections look at some other changes that the Visual Basic Upgrade Wizard makes to code while upgrading projects.

Other Modifications

In addition to the changes discussed in the preceding sections, the Visual Basic Upgrade Wizard makes various other changes to code during the upgrade process. In this section, you will learn how the Visual Basic Upgrade Wizard handles the following while upgrading projects:

◆ Arrays

◆ `Property` procedures

◆ Late-bound objects

Arrays

Unlike in Visual Basic 6.0, in Visual Basic.NET, you cannot specify the lower bound for an array. In Visual Basic 6.0, the default lower bound for an array is 0, but you can change this by using the `Option Base` statement. In contrast, Visual

Basic.NET does not support the Option Base statement. Therefore, you cannot modify the lower bound for an array in Visual Basic.NET.

Consider the following statement that is part of a project in Visual Basic 6.0:

```
Dim MyArray(11 To 22) As String
```

When you upgrade the Visual Basic 6.0 project containing the preceding code statement to Visual Basic.NET, the Visual Basic Upgrade Wizard successfully upgrades the project. However, the upgrade report for the project generated by the wizard displays the following run-time warning:

"Lower bound of array MyArray was changed from 11 to 0."

Now look at the same statement in the upgraded project. Because the wizard changes the lower bound of the array, the array declaration in the Visual Basic.NET project changes as shown in the following statement:

```
Dim MyArray(22) As String
```

Note that the size of MyArray has increased. Thus, when you upgrade a project to Visual Basic.NET, if the lower bound of an array in the Visual Basic 6.0 project is greater than 0, the size of the array changes.

If the code in your project relies on the array size, you might need to modify the code. For example, consider a situation in which you are assigning the values of MyArray1 to MyArray2 in a project. MyArray1 has a lower bound greater than 0, and MyArray2 has a lower bound of 0. After you upgrade the project, you will need to modify the code because the size of MyArray1 will change.

Property Procedures

The syntax to define properties in Visual Basic 6.0 and Visual Basic.NET is different. In Visual Basic 6.0, you use the Property Get and Property Let statements to define properties. In contrast, Visual Basic.NET does not support the Property Let statement.

Consider the following code declared in a Visual Basic 6.0 project:

```
Dim MyProp As Integer
Public Property Get MyProperty() As Integer
        MyProperty = MyProp
End Property
```

```
Public Property Let MyProperty(ByVal MyValue As Integer)
        MyProp = MyValue
End Property
```

When you upgrade the project, the Visual Basic Upgrade Wizard modifies the code. The modified code is as follows:

```
Dim MyProp As Short
Public Property MyProperty() As Short
        Get
                MyProperty = MyProp
        End Get
        Set(ByVal Value As Short)
                MyProp = Value
        End Set
End Property
```

While upgrading the project, the Visual Basic Upgrade Wizard changes the `Property Let` procedure to a `Property Set` procedure.

Late-Bound Objects

Like Visual Basic 6.0, Visual Basic.NET supports late-bound objects. When you upgrade your projects to Visual Basic.NET, however, late-bound objects can introduce problems. When upgrading a project, the Visual Basic Upgrade Wizard might not be able to resolve or convert the properties of a late-bound object. This is because Visual Basic Upgrade Wizard cannot determine the type of a late-bound object.

Let's look at an example to understand this. Consider the following code that is part of a Visual Basic 6.0 project. The following code is executed when you click on the button Command1:

```
Private Sub Command1_Click()
        Dim MyInt As Integer
        Dim MyObject As Object
        MyInt = InputBox("Enter 1 to change the caption of the first label and 2
to change the caption of the second label.")
        Select Case (MyInt)
                Case "1"
                        Set MyObject = Label1
```

```
                                 MyObject.Caption = "My First Label"
                 Case "2"

                                 Set MyObject = Label2
                                 MyObject.Caption = "My Second Label"
            End Select
End Sub
```

When you upgrade the project to Visual Basic.NET, the upgrade report displays the following warning:

> "Couldn't resolve default property of object MyObject.Caption."

Because late binding is used to change the captions of labels, the Visual Basic Upgrade Wizard cannot identify the type of the MyObject object. Therefore, the wizard generates a run-time warning.

In Visual Basic 6.0, you set the caption of a label control by using the Caption property of the label. In Visual Basic.NET, however, the Caption property is replaced with the Text property. The following is the upgraded code for the Click event of the Command1 button.

```
Private Sub Command1_Click(ByVal eventSender As System.Object, ByVal eventArgs As
System.EventArgs) Handles Command1.Click
            Dim MyInt As Short
            Dim MyObject As Object
            MyInt = CShort(InputBox("Enter 1 to change the caption of the text box
and 2 to change the caption of the command button."))
            Select Case (MyInt)
                    Case CInt("1")
                                MyObject = Label1
'UPGRADE_WARNING: Couldn't resolve default property of object MyObject.Caption.
                                MyObject.Caption = "My First Label"
                    Case CInt("2")
                                MyObject = Label2
'UPGRADE_WARNING: Couldn't resolve default property of object MyObject.Caption.
                                MyObject.Caption = "My Second Label"
            End Select
End Sub
```

In the preceding code, note that the wizard has added warnings stating that it cannot resolve the default property of MyObject. To ensure that the preceding code runs smoothly, you need to modify the upgraded code.

Alternatively, if you modify the code in the Visual Basic 6.0 project using early binding, the Visual Basic Upgrade Wizard will not generate any warnings. In such cases, you do not need to make any modifications to the code.

Summary

In this chapter, you learned about upgrading Visual Basic 6.0 projects to Visual Basic.NET. You also learned about the considerations to take into account before upgrading a project to Visual Basic.NET. In addition, you learned to upgrade an existing project to Visual Basic.NET by using the Visual Basic Upgrade Wizard. Next, you upgraded a sample project, PrjLenConversion, to Visual Basic.NET and learned about the changes made to the code in the project by the wizard. Finally, you learned how the Visual Basic Upgrade Wizard handles the changes made to arrays, Property procedures, and late-bound objects while upgrading projects.

PART III

Professional Project 2

Project 2

**Project
Development
Using ADO.NET**

Project 2 Overview

In this project, you will learn to create the MyMovies application for a fictitious video company that sells movie videos. The MyMovies application is designed for the customers and administrators of the various stores.

Customers visiting the MyMovies stores can use this application to perform the following tasks:

◆ To browse the database to obtain information related to movies

◆ To search for specific information by using the various criterions

◆ To purchase the movies

The database administrator can use this application to perform the following tasks:

◆ To add records to the tables in the database

◆ To update the tables in the database

◆ To generate reports

The MyMovies application is a Windows application developed by using Visual Basic.NET and ADO.NET. This application stores all client- and movie-specific details in a Microsoft SQL 2000 database. The key concepts used to create the MyMovies application are as follows:

◆ Visual Basic.NET

◆ Working with the Windows forms

◆ Error handling

◆ Connecting to a database using ADO.NET

◆ Retrieving data using ADO.NET and Writing data using ADO.NET

You will also learn to write the code for the various forms in the application to add functionality to the application.

Chapter 9

In the preceding chapter, you learned how to upgrade an existing Visual Basic project to Visual Basic.NET. Starting with this chapter, you will create your own projects in Visual Basic.NET. Before actually creating a project, however, you first need to take a look at the case study for the project you are going to create. This chapter describes the MyMovies Video Kiosk case study as well as its design.

MyMovies Video Kiosk: The Present Scenario

MyMovies is a video company based in New Jersey. The company sells movie videos and also provides information about the movies. The company owns a chain of stores in various cities across the United States. MyMovies enjoyed its monopoly in the video-selling market until few months back. Let's take a look at the company's existing system to identify reasons why the company is losing its market share in the movie video market.

Each MyMovies store provides information about movies in catalogs, and customers go through the catalogs to find movies of interest. After selecting a movie, a customer can buy the movie in the DVD, CD, or LCD format. When the sale of videos began to decline, the management of the company assigned a team to conduct a market survey to find out why. The team suggested that, in this time of automation, the old manual system of paper catalogs has become obsolete and slow, and at times, this leads to a disappointed customer. Hence, the solution for this problem lies in automating the existing system.

MyMovies Video Kiosk: The Solution

As mentioned in the preceding section, the solution is to automate the existing system. In other words, any customer walking into the store should be able to use a computer running an application that provides all the information related to a movie, such as the name of the movie, its cast, and the director's name. Using this information, the customer can then decide whether or not to buy the movie.

In addition, customers should be able to search for a movie based on some criteria, such as its name, director, or cast. Customers should also be able to view details about a specific movie, actor, or director. This information is stored in a Microsoft SQL 2000 database. What is required is a front-end desktop application to provide a simple and interactive interface. The following section describes a typical project cycle for developing an application.

Project Life Cycle

The development of a project actually starts when there is a need to develop or significantly change an existing system. In the case of MyMovies, there is a need to regain the company's lost monopoly in the video market. In other words, they need to change their existing old-age system of catalogs.

The development life cycle of a project involves three phases:

- Project initiation
- Project execution
- Project deployment

In the *project initiation* phase, a comprehensive project plan is prepared. This plan lists the tasks to be performed during the life cycle of the project. It also identifies the team members and assigns responsibilities to them based on their skills.

In the *project execution* phase, the team develops the required application. Because this is the most elaborate phase in terms of project cost and time, this phase can be further divided into the following stages:

- Requirements analysis
- High-level design
- Low-level design
- Construction
- Integration and testing
- User acceptance test

These stages are discussed in the following sections. First, however, I'll discuss the final phase in a project life cycle, the *project deployment* phase. As the name suggests, during this phase, the application is deployed at the client location. In addition, support is provided to the client for a particular period of time to take care of any bugs that might occur in the application after deployment.

Before proceeding any further, let's take a look at each of the stages in the project execution phase.

Requirements Analysis

As the name suggests, during the *requirements analysis* stage, the team analyzes the various requirements that need to be fulfilled by the video kiosk application. For this, the team working on the video kiosk application studies various existing automated video kiosk applications at the numerous video kiosks that have opened recently in various cities around the country. In addition, the team also interviews various customers who use these automated video kiosks. As a result, the following requirements are identified for the video kiosk application being created. The application should:

- Be easy to use in terms of navigation and should provide enough tips as well.
- Be simple, fast, and interactive.
- Provide a feature to search for a particular movie based on a criterion, such as a movie, director, or actor's name.
- Provide enough information about a movie to attract a customer to buy it.

After analyzing these requirements, the MyMovies team decided to make the following two modules for the video kiosk application:

- Customer module
- Administration module

The customers at the video kiosk will use the Customer module to browse the Movies database for the required information. They also will be able to search for specific information using the various criteria and will be able to purchase videos. The system administrators of MyMovies will use the Administration module to maintain the database and keep it updated.

The following requirements will be addressed by the Customer module:

- Provide an easy method for browsing the movie information.
- Offer an option to search based on various criteria.

◆ Provide a registration form that accepts information about a customer, such as his or her name, address, and e-mail address.

The following requirements will be addressed by the Administration module:

◆ Provide a simple and easy method for maintaining and updating the various tables in the Movies database

◆ Generate reports showing collated data, such as daily sales, movies in demand, and details of regular customers

High-Level Design

In the *high-level design* phase, the team decides on the functionality of the system. In addition, the various data input and output formats are finalized, and the operating requirements are identified. Approval is requested from the client regarding the functional specifications documentation of the proposed interfaces for the application. The design of the next phase is based on this design.

Figure 9-1 displays the Main screen for the customers. This screen provides options for registered customers as well as new customers.

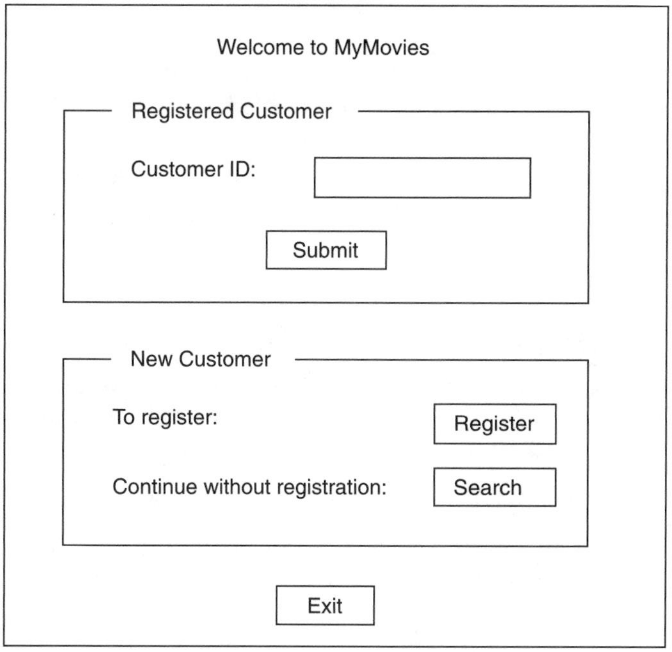

FIGURE 9-1 *The Main screen for the Customer module*

A registered customer needs to enter his or her Customer ID in a text box and then click on the Submit button. This will take the customer to the Search screen, shown in Figure 9-2.

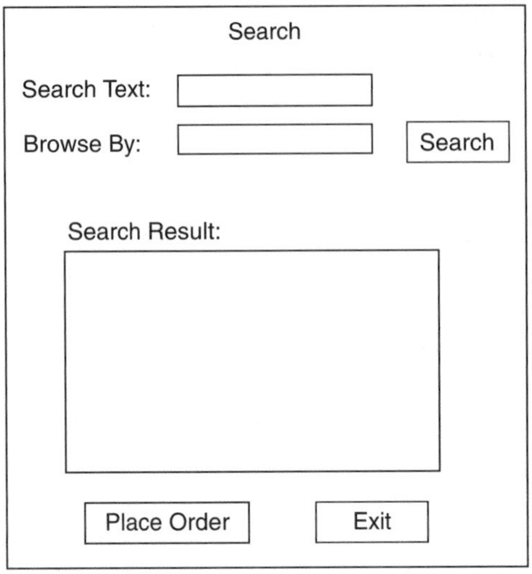

FIGURE 9-2 *The Search screen*

Using the Search screen, customers can search for movies of their choice and then select movies to buy. This screen has a text box in which customers can enter the text they want to search for, and they also can select a category from the Browse By drop-down list. Clicking the Search button displays the results in the Search Result section. The customers can select the movies of their choice and click on the Place Order button. This displays the Place Order screen, shown in Figure 9-3.

The Place Order screen displays the movies selected by the customer as well as the total amount payable for the order being placed. This screen also displays the credit card details for the customer. The customer needs to click the Place Order button to place the order, and the corresponding database tables also get updated. If a customer is not registered, clicking the Place Order button displays the Registration screen, as shown in Figure 9-4.

The Registration screen also appears if the customer clicks the Register button shown in the Main screen (refer to Figure 9-1).

For the Administration module, there will be a main form containing two menu options, Operations and Generate Reports. The Operations menu option is for

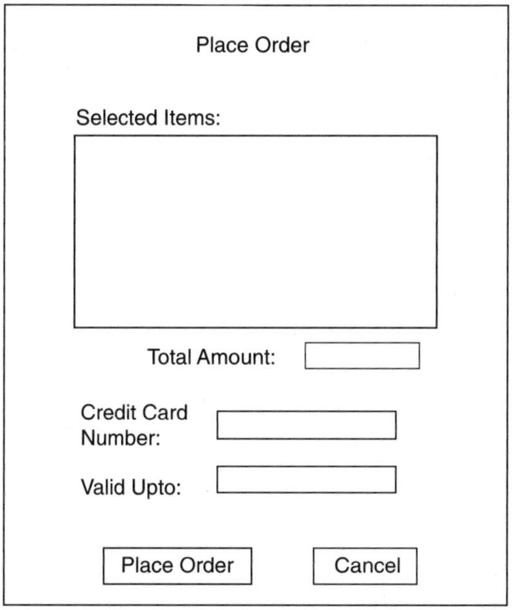

FIGURE 9-3 *The Place Order screen*

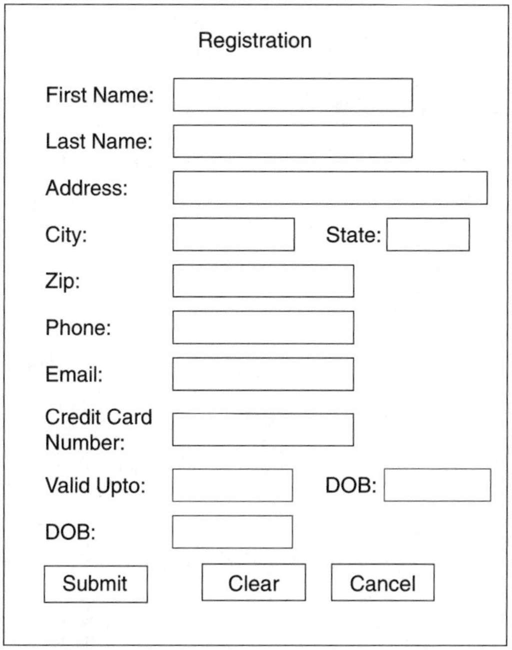

FIGURE 9-4 *The Registration screen*

the various database maintenance operations, and it further contains two suboptions, Insert and Update/Delete. The Insert option enables the administrator to insert data into the database tables. The Update/Delete option enables the administrator to update and delete records from the tables in the database. Figure 9-5 displays the Insert Movie Info screen for the Administration module. The other screens for adding data will also be similar, containing the corresponding fields of each table in the Movies database.

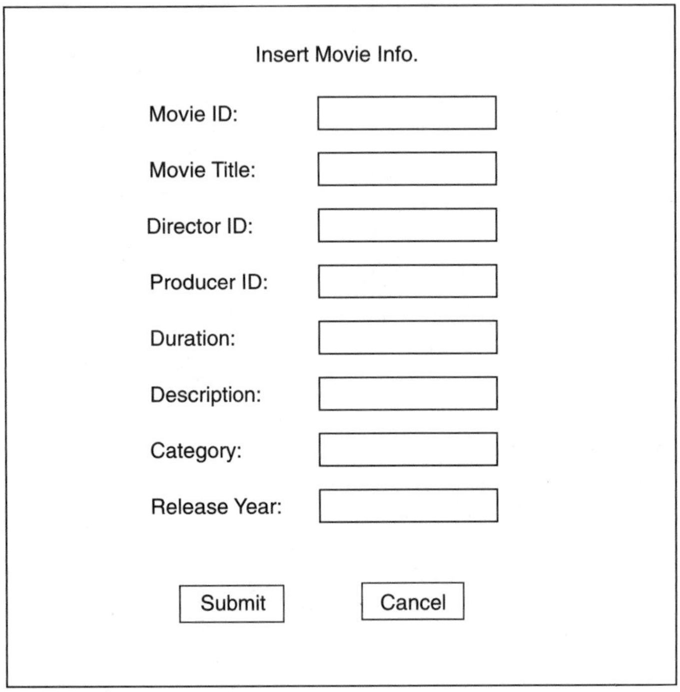

FIGURE 9-5 *The Insert Movie Info screen*

Figure 9-6 displays the Update/Delete screen, which is common for all the tables in the database. In this screen, the Search In drop-down list displays the various tables in the database, and the Search By drop-down list displays the various search criteria that can be used. Clicking on the Search button displays the results in the Search Results section, from which the administrator can select the data that needs to be updated or deleted. Then, after making modifications to the required data, the administrator can click the Update button to send the changes to the database. Clicking the Delete button deletes the record from the table.

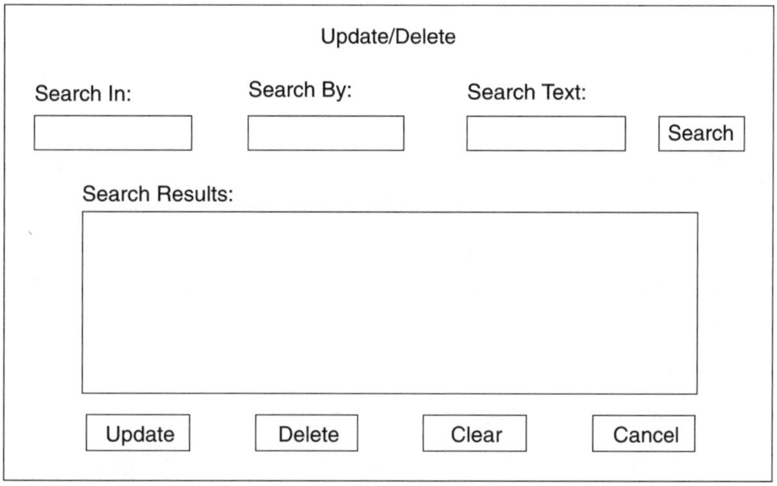

```
                              Update/Delete

Search In:          Search By:          Search Text:
┌─────────────┐     ┌─────────────┐     ┌─────────────┐  ┌─────────┐
│             │     │             │     │             │  │ Search  │
└─────────────┘     └─────────────┘     └─────────────┘  └─────────┘

   Search Results:
   ┌───────────────────────────────────────────────────────┐
   │                                                         │
   │                                                         │
   │                                                         │
   │                                                         │
   │                                                         │
   │                                                         │
   └───────────────────────────────────────────────────────┘

   ┌───────────┐   ┌───────────┐   ┌───────────┐   ┌───────────┐
   │  Update   │   │  Delete   │   │  Clear    │   │  Cancel   │
   └───────────┘   └───────────┘   └───────────┘   └───────────┘
```

FIGURE 9-6 *The Update/Delete screen*

As previously mentioned, the Administration module contains a Generate Reports menu, which provides three options:

- ◆ *Daily Sales.* Displays the daily sales for the store. The report displays the video ID, movie ID, and total amount of each purchase.

- ◆ *Movies in Demand.* Displays the details of movies that are in maximum demand.

- ◆ *Customer Details.* Displays the details of customers who frequently visit the store.

Low-Level Design

During the *low-level design* phase, a detailed design of the various software modules is prepared using the high-level design. The team decides on various standards, such as naming conventions for variables, controls, and forms for a project. All these specifications are documented so that consistency can be maintained among the various modules for an application. The MyMovies team also has documented the various standards to be followed while constructing this project.

Construction

During the *construction* phase, various components of the application are coded. The various specifications identified during the low-level design phase are used to accomplish this. In the case of MyMovies, the Customer and Administration modules are coded.

Integration and Testing

In the *testing* phase, various tests and validations are carried out on the various modules, and their integration functionality is checked. In the case of MyMovies, all the forms required for each of the modules (Customer and Administration) are integrated and tested.

User Acceptance Test

In the *acceptance* phase, various tests are carried out based on the predefined acceptance criteria provided by the client. In addition, system support is provided to troubleshoot any issues or bugs identified at this phase. In the case of MyMovies, a few users can be asked to use the application and provide feedback.

The Database Schema

As previously mentioned, the MyMovies video store is using an existing Microsoft SQL 2000 database. Figure 9-7 shows the database schema for this Movies database.

Figure 9-7 displays the database schema for the Movies database. This includes the following eight tables:

- ◆ *Actor.* Contains actor details such as actor ID, first name, last name, and date of birth
- ◆ *Movie.* Contains movie details such as movie ID, title, release year, and category
- ◆ *Director.* Contains director details such as director ID, first name, last name, and date of birth
- ◆ *Producer.* Contains producer details such as producer ID and name
- ◆ *ActorMovie.* Contains actor details such as actor ID, movie ID, and role
- ◆ *Video.* Contains video details such as video ID, movie ID, format, and price

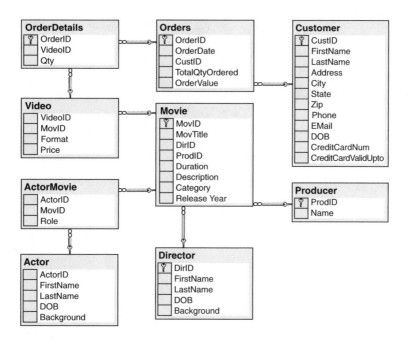

FIGURE 9-7 *The schema for the Movies database*

◆ *Orders.* Contains order details such as order ID, order date, customer ID, video ID, and order value

◆ *Customer.* Contains customer details such as customer ID, first name, last name, date of birth, and credit card details

◆ *OrderDetails.* Contains video order details, such as order ID, video ID, and quantity ordered

Summary

In this chapter, you learned about the MyMovies video company that is still using the age-old system of paper catalogs, which has resulted in a decline in sales for the company. You then looked at the proposed solution for this problem—automation. Then you looked at the various requirements for this solution and were introduced to the various screens required for the application. Finally, you were introduced to the database schema for the Microsoft SQL 2000 database that the company is presently using.

In the next chapter, you will learn to create the user interface for the Customer module.

Chapter 10

Using ADO.NET

So far in this project, you have learned about the video kiosk application. This chapter provides an overview of the technology you'll use to connect to the SQL database—ADO.NET.

Visual Studio.NET provides ActiveX Data Objects for the .NET framework (ADO.NET). ADO.NET is an enhanced version of ActiveX Data Objects (ADO).

ADO

ADO, a technology developed by Microsoft, is based on the Component Object Model (COM). Unlike other data access technologies, such as Data Access Objects (DAO) and Remote Data Objects (RDO), ADO enables you to access data from nonrelational databases. Using ADO, you can work with connected and disconnected architectures.

With the introduction of the .NET framework, Microsoft has redesigned ADO to create ADO.NET. This is because the .NET framework has brought with it a new programming model that supports disconnected data architecture. In disconnected data architecture, an application does not remain connected to a data source throughout a series of transactions. Instead, the application connects to a data source as and when required. Data access technologies—such as Data Access Object (DAO) and Remote Data Objects (RDO)—do not support disconnected data architecture. However, you can work with distributed Web applications by using ADO with Remote Data Services (RDS).

ADO.NET includes various enhancements over the existing data access technologies. In other words, ADO.NET resolves the limitations of earlier data access technologies. Unlike DAO and RDO, ADO.NET supports disconnected data architecture. ADO.NET includes a set of classes that enable to you create distributed Web applications. Using ADO.NET, you can also create distributed multitier and data-sharing applications.

In this chapter, you will learn about the features and functions of ADO.NET. This chapter also covers the architecture and components of ADO.NET. The following section discusses the features of ADO.NET.

Features of ADO.NET

Because ADO.NET is an enhanced version of ADO, it provides features that earlier data access technologies were lacking. Take a look at the features of ADO.NET:

◆ *It uses disconnected data architecture.* In disconnected data architecture, an application connects to the data source only to access or update data. This means that after the application connects to the data source and retrieves the required data, the connection is terminated. To update the data source, the application again connects to it. Therefore, the application connects to the data source only to save or retrieve records. In addition, the use of disconnected data architecture ensures optimum utilization of system resources because ADO.NET does not retain database locks or active connections for extended time periods.

◆ *It provides datasets.* Similar to the record set available in ADO, ADO.NET provides a dataset. Unlike a record set, however, a dataset is a virtual database. This is because, unlike in connected data architecture, in disconnected data architecture an application cannot access the data source after processing each record. Because the application cannot access the data source repeatedly, after the data is retrieved, it needs to be stored somewhere. This is where the dataset is useful. The dataset is used to store data retrieved from the data source. It can contain one or more tables. In addition to tables, a dataset can also store additional information about relationships and constraints between tables in a dataset. Therefore, disconnected data architecture is implemented by using datasets.

◆ *It supports eXtensible Markup Language (XML).* ADO.NET uses XML to transfer data from the data source to the dataset and from the dataset to other components. Applications created in ADO.NET are interoperable with other applications. This is because any application or component that understands XML can access data from an ADO.NET application.

The following section describes the benefits of using ADO.NET.

Benefits of ADO.NET

As compared to other data access technologies, ADO.NET provides multiple benefits. The following sections discuss the benefits provided by ADO.NET.

Scalability

Disconnected data architecture enables applications to service more users efficiently as compared to connected data architecture. This is because, in disconnected data architecture, the connection with a data source is terminated as soon as data is retrieved from the data source, leaving the data source available for other users. In other words, applications created in ADO.NET can effectively manage multiple users. Therefore, ADO.NET makes applications scalable.

Performance

In ADO, COM marshalling is used to transfer data between applications. This mode of data transfer requires that the data types used in an application be converted to a data type supported by COM. Unlike ADO, ADO.NET uses XML to transfer data between applications. In ADO.NET, no conversion of data types is required. Therefore, ADO.NET applications provide better performance as compared to ADO applications.

Programmability

ADO.NET enables quick and easy programming with a minimum of errors. ADO.NET also enables you to use typed programming, which makes the code more readable. Typed programming also makes it easier to write code. Furthermore, it checks for errors at compile time, which increases the safety of the code. For example, if you misspell the name of the TxtActor text box as TxActor, the misspelled word is highlighted. When you move the cursor to the misspelled word, an error message displays stating that the control TxActor is not declared. Therefore, unlike untyped programming, typed programming generates errors at compile time.

Interoperability

As previously mentioned, ADO.NET supports XML to transfer data. Any application that interprets XML can exchange data with an ADO.NET application. Therefore, applications created in ADO.NET are interoperable with other applications.

Maintainability

Using ADO.NET, you can create applications that are logically divided into layers. For example, you can create an application with separate layers for the user interface, business logic, and data access. Dividing an application into logical layers simplifies the maintenance of the application. In addition, you can add layers to an ADO.NET application as and when required. For example, consider a scenario in which you need to make changes to an existing application to improve its performance. The application was created in ADO.NET. To solve this problem, you can either modify an existing layer or add a layer to the application to improve its performance.

The following section describes the components of ADO.NET.

Components of ADO.NET

ADO.NET enables you to create distributed multitier and data-sharing applications by allowing you to access data from a relational database, an XML source, or another application. To enable you to access and manage data, ADO.NET provides two components:

◆ .NET data provider
◆ Dataset

The .NET data provider is used to access data, and the dataset is used to manipulate data. Figure 10-1 illustrates the components of ADO.NET. The subsequent sections describe the components of ADO.NET.

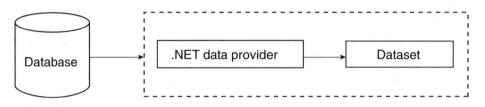

FIGURE 10-1 *Components of ADO.NET*

.NET Data Provider

The .NET data provider links an application to a data source and enables the application to access data from it. Using the .NET data provider, you can perform the following tasks:

◆ Connect to a data source

◆ Execute commands

◆ Retrieve results

Using ADO.NET, you can access and manage data from different data sources. To enable you to access and manipulate different data sources, ADO.NET provides different types of .NET data providers. You will learn more about the types of .NET data providers later in this chapter.

To enable an application to communicate with a data source, the .NET data provider uses four objects. These objects are known as the *.NET data provider objects*, and they are discussed in the next section.

The .NET Data Provider Objects

As previously mentioned, the .NET data provider enables you to connect to a data source, execute commands, and retrieve the results of the commands. To enable you to perform these tasks, the .NET data provider uses .NET data provider objects. The .NET data provider objects are as follows:

◆ The Connection object

◆ The Command object

◆ The DataReader object

◆ The DataAdapter object

The *Connection* Object

The Connection object of ADO.NET is similar to the Connection object of ADO. Using the Connection object, you can establish a connection to a data source. You can also manage a connection using the Connection object.

To establish a connection, use the Open method of the Connection object. The Open method accepts the data source name, user ID, and password as parameters to establish a connection. After you retrieve the required data from the data source, you need to close the connection. To do so, you can use either the Close or Dispose method of the Connection object.

The *Command* Object

After you connect to a data source, you must use the Command object to execute commands—such as SQL queries or stored procedures—and return results from the data source.

Before you can execute a command, however, you must specify the type of command for the Command object. To specify the command type, you must specify the CommandType property of the Command object. For example, to execute a stored procedure, you must set the CommandType property of the Command object to Stored-Procedure. When you set the CommandType property to StoredProcedure, in addition to specifying the CommandType property, you must specify the name of the stored procedure by using the CommandText property.

The *DataReader* Object

After you execute a command, you need to retrieve the data returned by the command. To do so, you can use the DataReader object. The DataReader object is similar to a read- and forward-only cursor. To elaborate, the DataReader object retrieves a read-only stream of data from the data source in a sequential manner.

The DataReader object also helps reduce system overhead and increase application performance. This is because the DataReader object does not cache the entire result set into the system memory. Instead, the DataReader object retrieves only one row at a time.

The *DataAdapter* Object

As previously mentioned, ADO.NET uses disconnected data architecture. Disconnected data architecture is implemented in an application by using datasets. A dataset is a virtual database that stores the data retrieved from any data source. ADO.NET provides the DataAdapter object to help you manipulate datasets.

The DataAdapter object acts as a link between the dataset and the data source. It enables you to transfer data from the dataset to the data source and vice versa. To enable you to access and manipulate data, the DataAdapter object provides multiple properties. Table 10-1 lists the commonly used properties of the DataAdapter object.

Table 10-1 Properties of the *DataAdapter* Object

Property	Enables You To ...
SelectCommand	Select records from a data source
InsertCommand	Insert records into a data source
UpdateCommand	Update records in a data source
DeleteCommand	Delete records from a data source

Figure 10-2 illustrates the interaction between the .NET data provider objects.

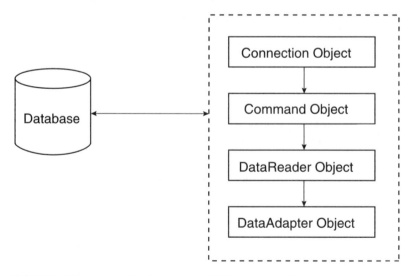

FIGURE 10-2 *Interaction between the .NET data provider objects*

As previously mentioned, ADO.NET provides different types of .NET data providers that enable you to access data from different data sources. The following sections describe the types of .NET data providers.

Types of .NET Data Providers

ADO.NET enables you to access data from a relational database, an XML source, or another application by providing different types of .NET data providers. ADO.NET provides the following .NET data providers:

- ◆ OLE DB .NET data provider
- ◆ SQL Server .NET data provider

As previously discussed, to enable an application to communicate with a data source, the .NET data provider uses the `Connection`, `Command`, `DataReader`, and `DataAdapter` objects. The OLE DB and SQL Server .NET data providers also provide these objects.

The following sections describe the SQL Server .NET data provider and the OLE DB .NET data provider.

The SQL Server .NET Data Provider

The SQL Server .NET data provider enables you to access data from any SQL Server 7.0 or higher database. The SQL Server .NET data provider uses the Tabular Data System (TDS) protocol to connect to Microsoft SQL Server databases. Using the TDS protocol, the SQL Server .NET data provider can connect directly to a SQL Server.

Using the SQL Server .NET data provider, you can access data from Microsoft SQL Server 7.0 or later. To access data from previous versions of Microsoft SQL Server, you need to use the OLE DB .NET data provider.

The classes associated with the SQL Server .NET data provider are stored in the `System.Data.SqlClient` namespace. Therefore, to implement the SQL Server .NET data provider in your application, you need to import the `System.Data.SqlClient` namespace. You can use the following statement to import this namespace:

```
Imports System.Data.SqlClient
```

The System.Data.SqlClient namespace includes other namespaces and classes related to the SQL Server .NET data provider. Table 10-2 describes some of the classes in the System.Data.SqlClient namespace.

Table 10-2 Classes in the *System.Data.SqlClient* Namespace

Class	Description
SqlConnection	Represents a connection to a database
SqlCommand	Represents a Transact-SQL statement or stored procedure that can be executed on a database
SqlDataReader	Represents a forward-only object used to read a stream of data from the database
SqlDataAdapter	Represents the data commands and database connection used by the application to transfer data from a database to a dataset and vice versa
SqlException	Represents the exception thrown when the database returns an error or warning
SqlError	Used to create objects that can store error- or warning-related information returned by the database

The OLE DB .NET Data Provider

As the name suggests, the OLE DB .NET data provider enables you to access data from OLE DB–compliant data sources such as Oracle and SQL Server 6.0 or earlier. Unlike the SQL Server .NET data provider, the OLE DB .NET data provider cannot connect to the data source directly. Instead, the OLE DB .NET data provider uses the following components to access the data source:

◆ OLE DB service component

◆ OLE DB provider

To enable you to access data from OLE DB–compliant data sources, the OLE DB .NET data provider interacts with an OLE DB service component that provides pooling and transaction services. The OLE DB service component, in turn, communicates with an OLE DB provider.

Figure 10-3 illustrates the relationship between the OLE DB .NET data provider, the OLE DB service component, and the OLE DB provider.

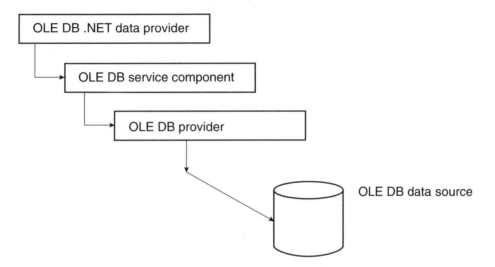

FIGURE 10-3 *The relationship between the OLE DB .NET data provider, the OLE DB service component, and the OLE DB provider*

The OLE DB .NET data provider can work with the following OLE DB providers:

◆ SQL OLE DB provider (SQLOLEDB)
◆ Oracle OLE DB provider (MSDAORA)
◆ Jet OLE DB provider (Microsoft.Jet.OLEDB.4.0)

> **NOTE**
>
> The OLE DB .NET data provider does not support MSDASQL, the OLE DB provider for open database connectivity (ODBC). In addition, the OLE DB .NET data provider does not support OLE DB version 2.5 interfaces.

The classes related to the OLE DB .NET data provider are stored in the `System.Data.OleDb` namespace. To implement the OLE DB .NET data provider in your application, you need to import the `System.Data.OleDb` namespace to your application by using the following statement:

```
Imports System.Data.OleDb
```

Similar to the `System.Data.SqlClient` namespace, the `System.Data.OleDb` namespace includes other namespaces and classes associated with the OLE DB .NET data provider. Some of the commonly used classes in the `System.Data.OleDb` namespace are as follows:

- ◆ `OleDbConnection`
- ◆ `OleDbCommand`
- ◆ `OleDbDataReader`
- ◆ `OleDbDataAdapter`
- ◆ `OleDbException`
- ◆ `OleDbError`

Note that the classes in the `System.Data.OleDb` namespace are similar to those in the `System.Data.SqlClient` namespace. The classes in the `System.Data.OleDb` namespace perform the same function as their counterparts in the `System.Data.SqlClient` namespace.

Now that you've looked at the .NET data provider, I'll discuss the dataset.

Dataset

After you connect to a data source, execute commands, and retrieve the results using the .NET data provider, you need to store the retrieved data. This is where the dataset comes into the picture.

As previously mentioned, data retrieved from a data source can be stored in a dataset, which is a virtual database. In other words, datasets enable you to work with data independent of the data source. In addition, datasets enable you to use disconnected data architecture in your applications.

In addition, unlike the `DataReader` object that stores only one row at a time, the dataset enables you to store multiple tables. Consider a scenario in which you need to retrieve data from multiple data sources. In this case, using the `DataReader` object would mean reading one row of data into memory and combining data from multiple data sources. In contrast, the dataset retrieves the required data from the data source and stores it in memory. Now you can perform data-manipulation operations on the dataset. Therefore, unlike the `DataReader` object, which is suitable in scenarios in which you need to retrieve data from a single data source, datasets are suitable in scenarios in which you need to retrieve data from multiple data sources.

The namespaces and classes associated with datasets are stored in the `System.Data` namespace. The `DataSet` class in the `System.Data` namespace represents a dataset.

Now that you have learned about the classes associated with .NET data providers and the dataset, look at the following example to understand how you can use these classes in your applications. Assume that the `System.Data.SqlClient` namespace is imported in the application.

```
        Dim SqlConn As New SqlConnection()
                                'Declares SqlConn as an object of the
SqlConnection class
        Dim MyDataset As New DataSet()
                                'Declares MyDataset as an object of the
DataSet class
        Try
                SqlConn.ConnectionString = "Data Source=localhost;USER
ID=sa;pwd=;Initial Catalog=Pubs"
                                'Specifies the connection string for
connecting to the data source
                SqlConn.Open()
                                'Uses the open command to open the con-
nection
                Dim MySqlDataAdapter As New SqlDataAdapter("select * from
authors", SqlConn)
                                'Specifies the query to select records
from the authors table
                MySqlDataAdapter.Fill(MyDataset)
                                'Populates the MyDataset dataset with
the records
        Catch MyException As Exception
                                'Declare MyException as an object of
the Exception class
                MsgBox(MyException.ToString, "Error")
                                'Displays the error message if an
exception occurs
```

```
End Try
SqlConn.Close()
                                'Used to close the connection
```

A dataset stores data in a format similar to a relational database. Just as a relational database contains tables, a dataset can also contain tables. To elaborate, a DataSet object consists of one or more DataTable objects. In addition to DataTable objects, a DataSet object can contain various other objects. Table 10-3 describes the classes associated with a DataSet object.

Table 10-3 Classes Associated with a *Dataset* Object

Class	Description
DataTable	Represents a table in a DataSet object
DataRow	Represents a row of data in a DataTable object
DataColumn	Represents a column schema in a DataTable object
DataRelation	Represents the relationship between two DataTable objects
Constraint	Represents a constraint that can be enforced on one or more DataColumn objects

In addition to the classes mentioned in Table 10-3, a DataSet object is associated with the following objects:

◆ DataTableCollection

The DataTableCollection object associated with a DataSet object stores the DataTable objects in the DataSet object. You can use the DataTable-Collection object to manipulate the tables in the DataSet object. You can use the Add and Remove methods of the DataTableCollection class to add and remove tables from a dataset. You can also remove all the DataTable objects stored in a DataTableCollection object by using the Clear method. In addition, you can determine whether a table exists in a DataTableCollection object by using the Contains method.

◆ DataRowCollection

As previously mentioned, a DataTable object is identical to a table in a relational database because it is also composed of rows and columns. Each DataTable object has a DataRowCollection object associated with it. The `DataRowCollection` object associated with a `DataTable` object stores all the rows for the `DataTable` object. The `DataRowCollection` object consists of multiple `DataRow` objects, and each `DataRow` object represents a row in the table. Therefore, the `DataRowCollection` contains the actual data for a table. You can use the `Add` and `Remove` methods of the `DataRowCollection` class to insert and delete `DataRow` objects.

◆ `DataColumnCollection`

In addition to the `DataRowCollection` object, a `DataColumnCollection` object also is attached to each `DataTable` object. Just as the `DataRow-Collection` object is made up of multiple `DataRow` objects, the `Data ColumnCollection` object is made up of multiple `DataColumn` objects. However, unlike the `DataRowCollection` object that stores the actual data of a table, the `DataColumnCollection` object defines the schema of the table. In addition, the `DataColumnCollection` object also determines the type of data each `DataColumn` object can store. You can use the `Add` and `Remove` methods of the `DataColumnCollection` class to insert and delete `DataColumn` objects from a `DataColumnCollection` object. In addition, the `DataColumnCollection` class provides the `Contains` method, which enables you to check whether a column exists in the `DataColumn-Collection` object.

◆ `DataRelationCollection`

Similar to a relational database, a `DataSet` object can also store information about the relationships between `DataTable` objects. The `Data-RelationCollection` object stores the relations between columns of `DataTable` objects in a `DataSet` object. The relations between columns of `DataTable` objects are stored as objects of the `DataRelation` class in the `DataRelationCollection` object. To access the `DataRelationCollection` object for a `DataSet` object, you need to use the `Relations` property of the `DataSet` object. In addition, you can use the `Add`, `Remove`, and `Clear` methods to manipulate `DataRelation` objects in a `DataRelation-Collection` object.

◆ `ConstraintCollection`

All the constraints on data in a table are stored in the `Constraint Collection` object associated with the `DataTable` object. You can access the `ConstraintCollection` object of a table by using the `Constraints` property of the `DataTable` object. The `ConstraintCollection` object consists of UniqueConstraint and ForeignKeyConstraint objects. The UniqueConstraint and ForeignKeyConstraint objects ensure the integrity of data.

Figure 10-4 illustrates the relationship between the components of a dataset and a table.

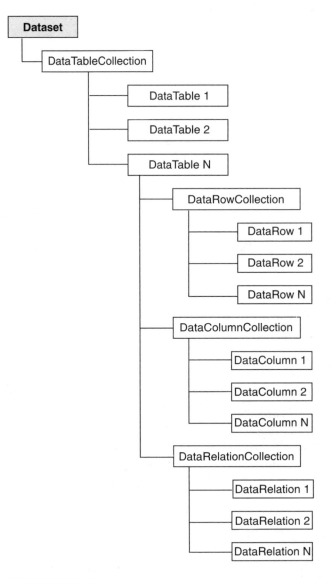

FIGURE 10-4 *The components of a dataset*

Summary

In this chapter, you learned about the features of ADO.NET. You also learned about the benefits offered by ADO.NET as compared to other data access technologies. You then learned about the components of ADO.NET. This chapter described the .NET data provider objects and the types of .NET data providers. You also learned about the features and components of a dataset.

Chapter 11

In the preceding chapters, you learned how to create the video kiosk application. When executing an application, however, you might encounter some errors. Consider a situation in which you've coded a complete application and it is running fine on your computer. Your project leader is ready to walk through the application, but some unexpected error messages crop up, and to your horror, the system running the application crashes. At that point, you realize you have not handled the unexpected errors that resulted in this crashing. This chapter provides insight into the error-handling mechanisms you can use to save your application from such errors.

In this chapter, you will learn about the types of errors that can occur when you debug an application. You also will learn about structured and unstructured error handling. Furthermore, you will learn about the debugging tools available in Visual Basic.NET. To start with, let's take a look at the types of errors you might encounter when executing an application.

Types of Errors

In this section, you will learn about errors that can slip into your code when compiling. Even though you might write an assumingly error-free code, there are chances that your error-free program might throw some obnoxious errors during execution. The types of errors you might encounter while executing an application can be classified as follows:

◆ Syntax errors
◆ Runtime errors
◆ Logic errors

The following sections describe these errors in greater detail.

Syntax Errors

A *syntax error* is the most common type of error. It occurs when you write code in a manner that's not allowed by the rules of the programming language. Syntax errors typically are caught by the complier or an interpreter. When the complier or interpreter encounters a syntax error, an error message informing you of the problem is displayed. Visual Basic.NET enables you to fix such errors when you type the code. For example, when you mistype or misspell a word, a wavy red line appears under the misspelled word. The wavy red line acts as a visual clue to indicate that something's amiss. In addition, if you mistype a keyword, omit necessary punctuation, or use a `Next` statement without a corresponding `For` statement at design time, Visual Basic.NET detects these errors when you compile the application. Therefore, syntax errors are also known as *compile errors*. Let's consider an example. Assume you have the following statement in your code:

```
Left
```

Although `Left` is a valid keyword (as in the preceding example), without an object, the `Left` keyword does not meet the syntactical requirements for the keyword. The correct syntax for this keyword is `<Object>.Left`, where `<Object>` represents the name of an object.

Runtime Errors

Runtime errors are the errors that occur when the code is executed. These errors might occur because you forgot to initialize a variable or assign memory to an object. For example, a runtime error is generated when you divide any variable or number by zero. Consider the following statement:

```
Speed = Miles / Hours
```

If the variable `Hours` contains `zero`, the division is an invalid operation even though the statement is syntactically correct. In addition, when you try to execute this code, Visual Basic.NET generates an error message.

Semantic/Logic Errors

You might encounter a situation in which the syntax you have used in the code is correct but the program does not deliver the required output. This can occur due to semantic errors in the code. Semantic errors occur when the meaning of the code does not match the intended meaning.

Compilers or interpreters cannot catch semantic errors. This is because compilers and interpreters deal with the structure of the code, not the meaning of the code.

Semantic errors can cause your program to terminate abnormally. Before termination, the program might or might not display an error message. In addition, semantic errors can cause your program to crash or hang.

At times, a program might continue to run even with semantic errors. However, the internal state of the program will not be the intended one. When a program generates an undesired output, such errors are defined as *logic errors*. For example, if you forget to add a statement to increment the counter variable while working with loops in a program, no errors are generated. However, when you execute the program, it goes into an infinite loop. You can detect logic errors by testing your program manually or automatically and verifying that the output is the required one.

To enable you to deal with errors, Visual Basic.NET provides the Exception class. The next section describes the Exception class in detail.

The Exception *Class*

As the name suggests, the Exception class in Visual Basic.NET represents errors or exceptions that might occur during application execution. Any abnormal condition encountered by an application during execution is known as an *exception*. The condition might occur due to an incorrect data type specified by a user or errors in programming logic. For example, if your application tries to access a nonexistent member of an array, the application throws an exception. If the exception is not caught, your application can terminate abnormally.

The System namespace includes the Exception class, which acts as the parent class for handling all types of exceptions. This Exception class provides multiple properties that enable you to identify the location where the exception occurred, the exception type, and the reason for the exception. You will learn how to use these properties later in this chapter. Table 11-1 describes the properties of the Exception class.

Table 11-1 Properties of the *Exception* Class

Property	Function
HelpLink	Provides detailed information in the form of a uniform resource locator (URL) or uniform resource name (URN)

Property	Function
InnerException	Provides a method to embed exceptions within exceptions, thus enabling developers to include the original exception with any additional exception that they throw
Message	Provides a localized description of the exception that has occurred
StackTrace	Provides a complete trace of the call stack, including the line number and source-code filename

The Exception class acts as a base class. In other words, multiple classes are derived from the Exception class. Figure 11-1 displays the hierarchy of the exception classes.

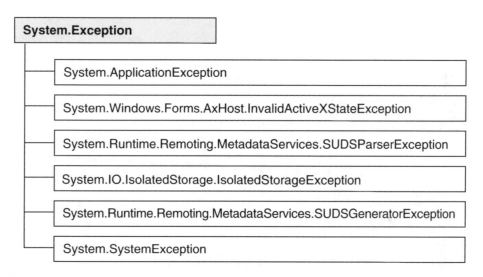

FIGURE 11-1 *The hierarchy of the exception classes*

Visual Basic.NET provides these classes to enable you to work with exceptions. In most cases, you would use the exception classes available in Visual Basic.NET. However, Visual Basic.NET enables you to define your own exception classes. When you define a new exception class, it is recommended that you derive the class from the ApplicationException class instead of the Exception class. In addition, the name of user-defined exception classes should end with the word "exception." Consider the following example:

```
Imports System
Namespace Exp
        Public Class MyException Inherits ApplicationException
                Public Sub New()
                        MyBase.New()
                End Sub
                Public Sub New(ByVal message As String)
                        MyBase.New(message)
                End Sub
                Public Sub New(ByVal message As String, ByVal exp As
Exception)
                        MyBase.New(message, exp)
                End Sub
        End Class
End Namespace
```

After you define your own exception class, you can throw exceptions of your exception class by using the Throw statement. You will learn more about the Throw statement later in this chapter.

As previously mentioned, handling exceptions prevents your applications from terminating abruptly. Unlike Visual Basic 6.0, which supports only unstructured exception handling, Visual Basic.NET supports both structured and unstructured exception handling. The following sections describe each of these exception-handling techniques.

Structured Error Handling

Structured error handling is an object-oriented approach to handling exceptions. This is because when an exception is encountered, the actual exception information is stored in an object. Visual Basic.NET allows structured error handling, which helps you create programs with robust error handlers. This involves designing code in such a way that the code can detect the errors during execution of the program and respond accordingly.

You can implement structured exception handling in Visual Basic.NET by using the Try...Catch...Finally statement, which checks for errors. By using this statement, you can separate the program code and the exception-handling code into

`Try` and `Catch` blocks, respectively. Program code that can generate an error is written within a `Try` statement, and this set of statements is known as a `Try` block. Similarly, code that handles exceptions thrown by a `Try` block is placed within a `Catch` statement, and this set of code is known as a `Catch` block.

▲ TIP

When using the `Try…Catch…Finally` statement, you should put the code that can generate an error within the `Try` block. In addition, you should try to place all the `Catch` blocks at one location. When you place all the `Catch` blocks together, make sure you order the `Catch` blocks in a specific-to-generic sequence. In other words, you must place the `Catch` blocks that trap exceptions of the classes derived from the `Exception` class before the `Catch` blocks that trap exceptions of the `Exception` class itself. For example, a `Catch` block that handles an exception of the `ApplicationException` class should be placed before a `Catch` block that handles an exception of the `Exception` class.

Let's take a look how the `Try…Catch…Finally` statement works in an application. The following syntax demonstrates the use of the `Try…Catch…Finally` statement:

```
Try
        'Code that could cause an exception
Catch MyException As SomeSortofException
        'Code that will execute if the exception is encountered
Finally
        'Code that will always execute
End Try
```

In the preceding syntax, the `Try` block contains statements that can throw an exception. Code enclosed within a `Try` block is executed until an exception occurs. If an exception occurs in the code in the `Try` block, control moves to the `Catch` block. However, the type of exception encountered determines the `Catch` block to which the control moves. In other words, the `Catch` block executed depends on the type of exception encountered in the `Try` block.

Next, the `Catch` block traps the exception and applies exception-handling logic. You can include multiple `Catch` blocks in a `Try…Catch…Finally` statement, where each `Catch` block traps an error of a different type. A `Try…Catch…Finally` statement must have at least one `Catch` block.

The `Finally` block is executed regardless of the result of the code in the `Try...Catch` blocks. Therefore, you can include code that needs to be executed whether the `Try` block threw an exception in the `Finally` block or not. Typically, the `Finally` block is used to handle cleanup code. For example, you can perform operations such as closing files and database connections within the `Finally` block.

As the name suggests, the `Exit Try` statement is used to quit a `Try` block. This statement is similar to the `Exit For` or `Exit Do` statements used with the `For` and `Do` loops, respectively.

TIP

When coding, you should use the `Try...Catch...Finally` statement judiciously. You should avoid using it in situations in which you can check for errors programmatically. Consider a scenario in which you need to close a connection with a data source. To do so, you can use the following code snippet.

```
Try
        SqlConnection1.Close()
Catch MySqlException as SqlException
                                        'Error-handling
code
End Try
```

Alternatively, you can use this code snippet to close the connection:

```
If SqlConnection1.State <> ConnectionState.Closed Then
        SqlConnection1.Close()
End If
```

The method you use to close the connection will depend on the frequency of the error's occurrence. In addition, when deciding the method to use, you should keep the criticality of the error in mind. Typically, the `Try...Catch...Finally` statement is used with code in which there is a lesser possibility of encountering errors.

Now that you know about structured exception handling, take a look at this example:

```
        Dim MyConn As String
        Dim MyDataSet As DataSet
        Dim MyDataAdapter As SqlDataAdapter
        Dim MyAuthorId As String
'Declares variables
        MyConn = "data source=localhost;user id=sa;pwd=;initial catalog=pubs"
'Establishes the connection to the data source
        Try
                MyDataSet = New DataSet()
                MyDataAdapter = New SqlDataAdapter("select * from authors
where Au_id = 'A0001'", MyConn)
                MyDataAdapter.Fill(MyDataSet)
'Populates the MyDataSet object with the results returned by the MyDataAdapter
object
                MyAuthorId = MyDataSet.Tables(0).Rows(0).Item(0)
'Assigns the value of the Author ID stored in the dataset to the MyAuthorId string
        Catch MySqlException As SqlException
'Traps any database exception
                MsgBox("Message:" & MySqlException.Message & vbNewLine &
"Source: " & MySqlException.Source & vbNewLine & "Error Number:" &
MySqlException.Number)
'Displays the values stored in the Message, Source, and Number properties of the
MySqlException object
        Catch MyIndexException As IndexOutOfRangeException
'Traps the error raised if no data is found in the dataset
                MsgBox(MyIndexException.Message & "¦¦" &
MyIndexException.Source & "¦¦" & MyIndexException.HelpLink)
'Displays the values stored in the Message, Source, and Number properties of the
MyIndexException object
        Catch MyOtherException As Exception
'Traps any other exception
                MsgBox(MyOtherException.Message.ToString)
'Displays the value stored in the Message property of the MyOtherException object
        Finally
                MyDataSet.Dispose()
'Releases the resources used by the MyDataSet object
                MyDataAdapter.Dispose()
'Releases the resources used by the MyDataAdapter object
        End Try
```

In addition to the Try…Catch…Finally statement, Visual Basic.NET provides the Throw statement. There might be a situation in which you need to generate an exception. For example, to where should control of the program pass when a condition that is not valid is detected? In such situations, you can use the Throw statement. The syntax of the Throw statement is as follows:

```
Throw ExceptionObject
```

In the preceding syntax, ExceptionObject is a mandatory parameter for the Throw statement. The ExceptionObject parameter is an object of a class inherited from the Exception class. Consider the following example:

```
Throw New Exception("This is to throw an exception.")
```

As previously mentioned, you can also throw exceptions of user-defined exception classes. To throw an exception of the MyException class, you can use either of the following statements:

```
Throw New MyException()
Throw New MyException("This is an exception of a user-defined exception class.")
```

To use any of the preceding statements in your application, however, you need to import the namespace in which the MyException class is defined.

In the next section, you'll learn about unstructured exception handling.

Unstructured Error Handling

Unstructured exception handling involves the use of the On Error statement. When an exception is raised in a program, control of the program moves to the argument specified in the On Error statement. You use an On Error statement at the beginning of a set of statements, such as a procedure. There are four forms of the On Error statement:

- ◆ On Error GoTo <*Line*> statement
- ◆ On Error Resume Next statement
- ◆ On Error GoTo 0 statement
- ◆ On Error GoTo -1 statement

The subsequent sections describe each form of the On Error statement.

On Error GoTo <Line> Statement

You use the On Error GoTo <Line> statement to specify the error-handling code, where the <Line> parameter indicates the starting of the error-handling code. When an error is encountered in code that follows an On Error GoTo <Line> statement, control moves to the line number specified as the <Line> parameter. Therefore, when you use the On Error GoTo <Line> statement, you must place the error-handling code after the line that you specify as an argument.

When a runtime error is encountered, control moves to the line specified as the <Line> argument. In other words, the error handler is activated. Consider the following example:

```
Sub CheckSub
        On Error GoTo MyHandler
                                    'Code that may or may not have errors
Exit Sub
MyHandler:
                                    'Code that handles errors
            Resume
End Sub
```

In the preceding example, the name of the error handler is MyHandler. If any code in the CheckSub procedure generates an error, the code following the MyHandler label is immediately executed.

Also note that the Resume statement is used in the preceding code. The Resume statement passes control back to the line of code where the error occurred. Therefore, in this example, the Resume statement returns control back to the CheckSub procedure.

When you use the Resume statement in an error handler, you must include the Exit Sub statement before the error handler. If you do not use the Exit Sub statement, the error handler will also be executed again. If the error-handling code is executed repeatedly, the procedure will not generate the required results. To prevent the repeated execution of the error handler, you need to use the Exit Sub statement. The Exit Sub statement exits the procedure before the error-handling code is executed.

On Error Resume Next Statement

As the name suggests, you use the On Error Resume Next statement to specify that, when an error is encountered, control should move to the statement following the one in which the error was encountered. By using the On Error Resume Next statement, you can handle errors where they occur rather than transferring control to any other location in the program.

CAUTION

To be able to identify errors in code, make sure the On Error Resume Next statement is disabled when you debug code.

As previously mentioned, you can also use the Resume statement independently. When you use the Resume statement outside the On Error statement, Visual Basic.NET returns control to the statement where the error occurred. Typically, after the error handler corrects the error, the Resume statement is used to transfer control to the statement where the error occurred.

In addition to the Resume statement, Visual Basic.NET provides the Resume Next statement. The Resume Next statement moves control to the line following the line where the error was encountered. Typically, the Resume Next statement is used to ignore the error. You can use the Resume Next statement when you know that the encountered error does not change the expected results of your application.

Visual Basic.NET provides another variation of the Resume statement—the Resume Line statement. The Resume Line statement is similar to the On Error GoTo *<Line>* statement. Unlike the On Error GoTo *<Line>* statement, however, you can use the Resume Line statement only in an error handler.

On Error GoTo 0 Statement

There might be situation in which you do not want any error handler to be executed. In such situations, you can use the On Error GoTo 0 statement. The On Error GoTo 0 statement is used to disable all error handlers in the current procedure. If you do not use the On Error GoTo 0 statement, the error handlers in the current procedure are disabled when the procedure completes execution.

On Error GoTo –1 Statement

The On Error GoTo -1 statement is used to disable exception handlers in the current procedure. In addition, as with the On Error GoTo 0 statement, it is not mandatory to use the On Error GoTo -1 statement. This is because the exception handlers in the current procedure are automatically disabled when the procedure ends.

The following is the syntax for unstructured exception handling:

```
Sub ErrorCheck()
        On Error GoTo ErrHandler

                                        'Code that might generate an
error
        Exit Sub
        ErrHandler:

                                        'Code that handles the error
        Resume
End Sub
```

In this section, you learned about unstructured exception handling and how it is implemented in Visual Basic.NET. By using structured and unstructured exception handling, you can handle the errors that occur when a program is executed. However, just handling the errors is not enough. You need to locate the errors and remove them. To help you to locate and remove errors, Visual Studio.NET provides various debugging tools. The next section describes how you can use these debugging tools in Visual Basic.NET.

Debugging Tools

Visual Basic.NET cannot diagnose or fix errors for you, but it does provide debugging tools. Debugging tools enable you to perform the following tasks:

◆ Diagnose and resolve logic and runtime errors

◆ Observe the behavior of code that has no errors

To elaborate, debugging tools enable you to analyze how execution flows from one part of the procedure to another. In addition, you can check how variables and property settings change as statements are executed.

In this section, you will learn about the various debugging tools available in Visual Basic.NET. Some of the commonly used debugging tools are as follows:

◆ Breakpoints

◆ The Watch window

◆ The QuickWatch dialog box

◆ The Autos window

◆ The Locals window

◆ The Call Stack window

You will learn more about the aforementioned debugging tools in the remainder of this chapter.

You can access and use most debugging tools in Visual Basic.NET only when your program is in break mode. In Visual Basic.NET, when the execution of a program halts due to an error, the program is said to be in break mode. A program can enter break mode automatically when it encounters one of the following:

◆ An error

◆ The Stop statement

◆ A breakpoint

You can use the Stop statement in code to stop the execution of an application. You will learn about breakpoints in the next section.

Breakpoints

When Visual Basic.NET encounters a breakpoint in a program, it suspends the execution of the program. A *breakpoint* is defined as a location in a program where execution is halted and the application enters break mode. When an application is in break mode, you can examine the status of the program, the contents of variables, and so on. In other words, because the execution of the application is suspended, you can examine the state of the application.

The steps for inserting a breakpoint in your application are as follows:

1. Position the cursor on the line of code where you want to insert break-point.

2. Select the New Breakpoint command from Debug menu.

◆ **TIP**

Alternatively, you can click on the left margin of Code Editor to insert a breakpoint.

The New Breakpoint dialog box appears, as shown in Figure 11-2. The New Breakpoint dialog box enables you to add breakpoints to your application.

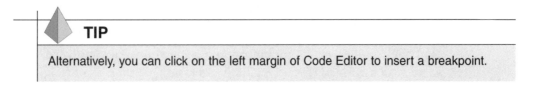

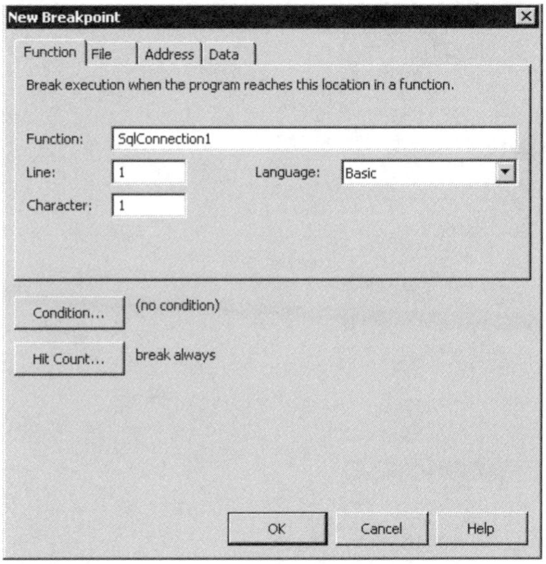

FIGURE 11-2 *The New Breakpoint dialog box*

As shown in Figure 11-2, the New Breakpoint dialog box contains four tabs. Each of the tabs enables you to add a breakpoint of a specific type. The tabs in the New Breakpoint dialog box are as follows:

◆ *Function.* This tab enables you to set a breakpoint in a function. You can set a function breakpoint either at the beginning of a function or at a certain position from the beginning.

- *File.* You can use this tab to set a breakpoint on a location in a file.
- *Address.* This tab enables you to set a breakpoint at a memory location.
- *Data.* You can use this tab to set a breakpoint on a variable.

Note that the four tabs in the New Breakpoint dialog box share a common set of buttons, Condition and Hit Count.

When you click on the Hit Count button, the Breakpoint Hit Count dialog box displays. Typically, the execution of an application stops as soon as a breakpoint is encountered. In Visual Basic.NET, however, you can specify a breakpoint's hit count, which is the number of times the breakpoint is hit before the execution of an application halts. You can specify a hit count in the Breakpoint Hit Count dialog box, which is shown in Figure 11-3.

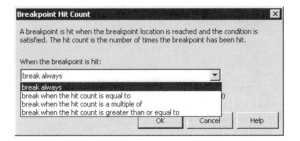

FIGURE 11-3 *The Breakpoint Hit Count dialog box*

When you select an option from the When the breakpoint is hit list box, a text box appears next to the list box, as shown in Figure 11-4.

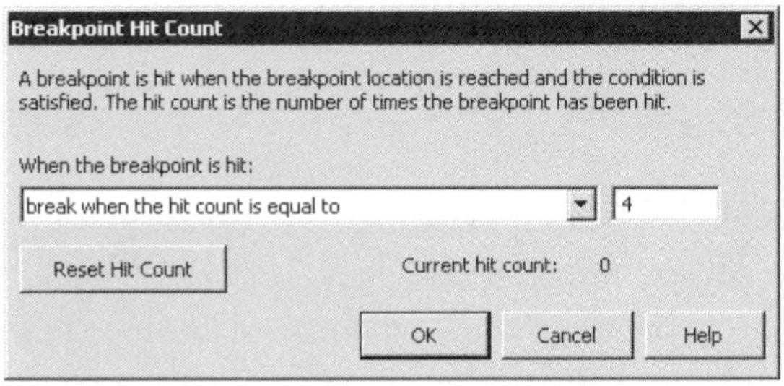

FIGURE 11-4 *The text box in the Breakpoint Hit Count dialog box*

In this text box, you can specify the condition based on which the execution of the application should be stopped.

In addition to the Hit Count button, the New Breakpoint dialog box displays the Condition button. You can click on the Condition button to specify the condition based on which the program will either execute or enter break mode. As with the hit count, each condition is also associated with a breakpoint. The condition you specify is evaluated when the breakpoint is hit. If the condition is met, the execution of the program stops; otherwise, it continues. For example, consider a scenario in which you specify the condition as Month>12. In this case, the program will stop executing when the value of the Month variable is greater than 12.

The steps to specify a condition are as follows:

1. Click on the Condition button in the New Breakpoint dialog box. The Breakpoint Condition dialog box displays, as shown in Figure 11-5.

2. Specify an expression in the text box.

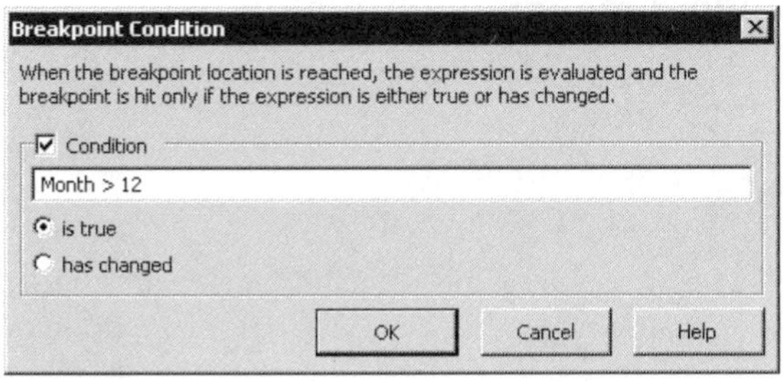

FIGURE 11-5 *The Breakpoint Condition dialog box*

3. Click on OK to close the Breakpoint Condition dialog box.

After you add a breakpoint to code, a dark brown bullet appears next to the line of code representing the breakpoint, as shown in Figure 11-6.

Visual Studio.NET provides the Breakpoints window that enables you to edit and manage breakpoints in your applications. In addition, you can use the Breakpoints window to view all the breakpoints in your application. By using the Breakpoints window, you can also remove breakpoints and change the properties of breakpoints.

Alternatively, you can modify a breakpoint by using the context menu. When you right-click on a breakpoint symbol, the context menu displays multiple options such as Add Task List Shortcut, Disable Breakpoint, and Remove Breakpoint.

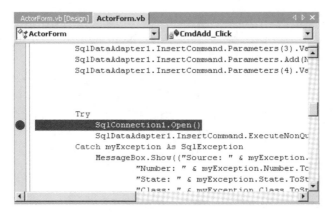

FIGURE 11-6 *A new breakpoint added to code*

After you add a breakpoint, you can run the application to check the output when the application encounters the breakpoint. When the application encounters a breakpoint, the execution halts and the application is said to be in break mode.

The Watch Window

The Watch window enables you to check the values of variables and expressions in your program. By using the Watch window, you can also modify the value of a variable. You cannot, however, use this window to edit the values of constant variables.

Consider a scenario in which you are creating a calculator application. This application relies heavily on the values of variables and expressions. To check and correct expressions for errors, instead of browsing through the entire code, you can use the Watch window. You can open the Watch window only when your program is in break mode. To do so, select the Windows command from the Debug menu. From the Windows submenu, you need to select the Watch command. The Watch submenu displays. Select the Watch 1, Watch 2, Watch 3, or Watch 4 option from the Watch submenu.

When you select an option from the Watch submenu, a new Watch window displays. The caption of the displayed window corresponds to the selected option. For example, when you select the Watch 1 option, the window that is displayed has Watch 1 as the caption.

Let's look at an example to understand the use of the Watch window. The following code snippet is executed when you click on the Button1 control in an application:

```
Dim MyArray(5) As Integer
        Dim MyInt As Integer
        For MyInt = 1 To 5
            MyArray(MyInt) = MyInt + 2
        Next
Dim Num1, Num2 As Integer
        For Num2 = 1 To 5
            Num1 = Num1 + MyArray(Num2)
        Next
```

As previously mentioned, you can use the Watch window to check the values of variables. The following steps describe how you can use this window to check the value of the Num1 variable.

1. Before you can use the Watch window, you need to insert a breakpoint into the code. To insert a breakpoint, click on the left margin in Code Editor, as shown in Figure 11-7.

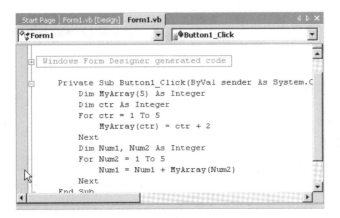

FIGURE 11-7 *Inserting a breakpoint*

After you insert a breakpoint, a dark brown bullet appears next to the line of code, which also is highlighted in dark brown (see Figure 11-8).

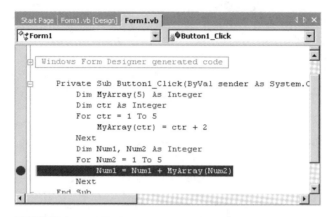

FIGURE 11-8 *The breakpoint inserted in the code*

2. Execute the application and click on Button1. Note that the application enters break mode. In addition, the line at which the breakpoint is set is highlighted in yellow, as shown in Figure 11-9.

FIGURE 11-9 *The line highlighted in yellow*

3. Select the Windows command from the Debug menu to open the Windows submenu. From the Windows submenu, select the Watch command. Note that the Watch submenu displays. Select the Watch 1 command from the Watch submenu. The Watch 1 window displays, as shown in Figure 11-10.

As shown in Figure 11-10, the Watch 1 window contains the following columns:

◆ *Name.* Displays the name of the variables

◆ *Value.* Displays the current value of a variable or expression

◆ *Type.* Displays the data type of the variable or expression

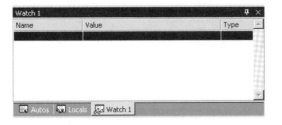

FIGURE 11-10 *The Watch 1 window*

4. To add the Num1 variable to the Watch 1 window, right-click on the Num1 variable in Code Editor and select the Add Watch option from the context menu. The Num1 variable is added to the Watch 1 window, as shown in Figure 11-11.

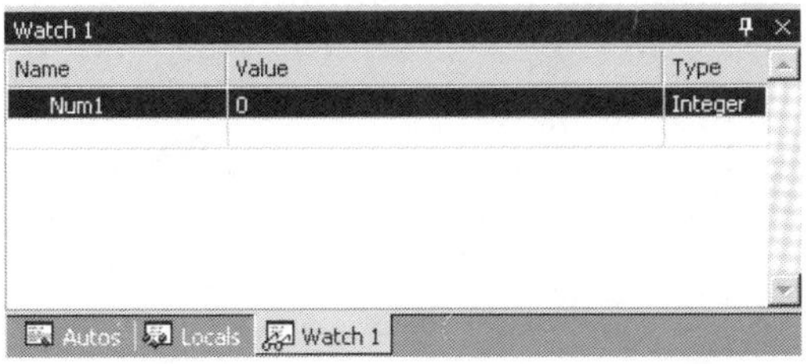

FIGURE 11-11 *The* Num1 *variable added to the Watch 1 window*

5. Select the Continue command from the Debug menu. Note that the value of the Num1 variable is displayed in the Watch 1 window. Now you can monitor the value of the Num1 variable by using the Watch 1 window.

Using the Watch window, you can also modify the values of variables. To modify the value of the Num1 variable, select the Num1 entry in the Watch 1 window and change the value of the variable.

When you stop debugging the application, the Watch 1 window closes.

The QuickWatch Dialog Box

In addition to the Watch window, Visual Studio.NET provides the QuickWatch dialog box to enable you to view the values of variables or expressions. Although the QuickWatch dialog box performs the same function as the Watch window, it is useful when you need to perform scratch calculations. In addition, using the QuickWatch dialog box ensures that you do not unnecessarily clutter the Watch window.

Like the Watch window, the QuickWatch dialog box is also available only when your application is in break mode. However, unlike the Watch window, the QuickWatch dialog box is resizable.

NOTE

Visual Studio.NET also provides DataTips. When you place the cursor over the variable, the value of the variable is displayed in a small box. This small box is known as a DataTip.

As with the Watch window, you can open the QuickWatch dialog box only when the application is in break mode. You can open the QuickWatch dialog box by selecting the QuickWatch command from the Debug menu. Alternatively, you can right-click on a variable name in Code Editor and select the QuickWatch command from the context menu. This method automatically places the variable in the QuickWatch dialog box.

Figure 11-12 displays the QuickWatch dialog box.

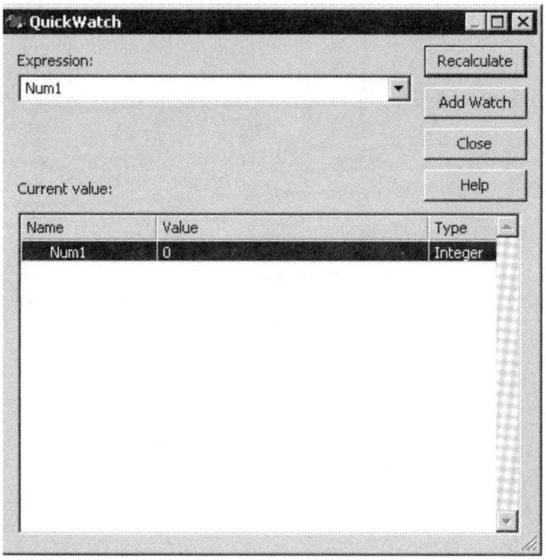

FIGURE 11-12 *The QuickWatch dialog box*

The Autos Window

Visual Studio.NET provides the Autos window to enable you to edit the value of a variable. The Autos window displays the variables used in the currently executing statement. In addition, it also displays the variables used in three statements above and below the currently executing statement. The Autos window derives its name from the fact that the debugger automatically identifies the variables to be displayed.

As with the QuickWatch dialog box, you can open the Autos window only when the application is in break mode. You can open the Autos window by using the following steps:

1. Select the Windows command from the Debug menu. The Windows submenu displays.

2. Select the Autos command from the Windows submenu.

Figure 11-13 displays the Autos window.

Autos		
Name	Value	Type
⊟ MyArray	{Length=6}	Integer()
(0)	0	Integer
(1)	3	Integer
(2)	4	Integer
(3)	5	Integer
(4)	6	Integer
(5)	7	Integer
Num1	0	Integer
Num2	1	Integer

FIGURE 11-13 *The Autos window*

As shown in Figure 11-13, the Autos window displays three columns: Name, Value, and Type. To modify the value of a variable, double-click on the value to be changed in the Value column, type the new value, and press the Enter key.

The Locals Window

The Locals window displays all the variables local to the currently executing location. For example, during the execution of a procedure, the Locals window displays the variables local to the procedure. Using the Locals window, you can also edit the values of variables.

You can open the Locals window only when the application is in break mode. You can open the Locals window by using the following steps:

1. Select the Windows command from the Debug menu. The Windows submenu displays.

2. Select the Locals command from the Windows submenu.

Figure 11-14 displays the Locals window.

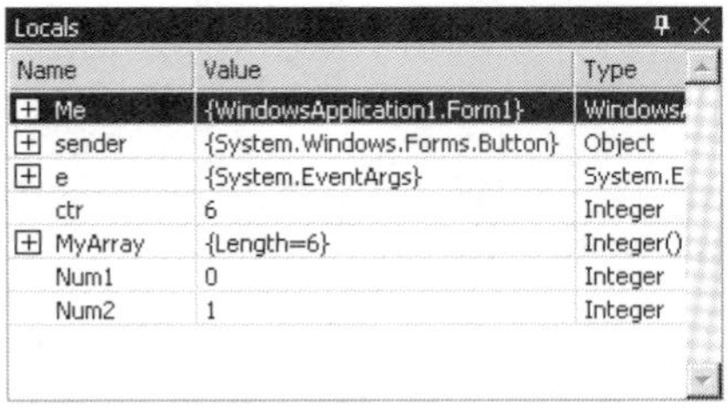

Locals			
Name	Value	Type	
⊞ Me	{WindowsApplication1.Form1}	Windows/	
⊞ sender	{System.Windows.Forms.Button}	Object	
⊞ e	{System.EventArgs}	System.E	
ctr	6	Integer	
⊞ MyArray	{Length=6}	Integer()	
Num1	0	Integer	
Num2	1	Integer	

FIGURE 11-14 *The Locals window*

As with the Autos window, the Locals window displays three columns: Name, Value, and Type.

The Call Stack Window

You can use the Call Stack window to view the names of active procedure calls. Procedures that are currently loaded in memory are known as *active procedures*. Using the Call Stack window, you can view and check the sequence in which the various procedures in a program are executed.

You can open the Call Stack window only when your application is in break mode. You can open this window by using the following steps:

1. Select the Windows command from the Debug menu to open the Windows submenu.

2. Select the Call Stack command from the Windows submenu.

Figure 11-15 displays the Call Stack window.

As shown in Figure 11-15, the Call Stack window displays two columns: Name and Language.

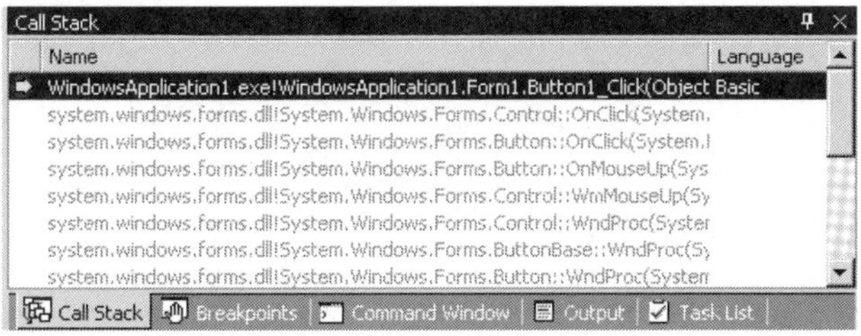

FIGURE 11-15 *The Call Stack window*

Summary

In this chapter, you learned about the types of errors that can occur when you debug an application. You also learned about structured exception handling and the `Try…Catch…Finally` statement. This chapter also described unstructured exception handling and the various forms of the `On Error` statement. Finally, you learned about the various debugging tools available in Visual Basic.NET, such as breakpoints, the Watch window, the QuickWatch dialog box, and the Autos window.

Chapter 12

In Chapter 9, "Project Case Study—Creating a Video Kiosk," you learned about the MyMovies video kiosk application. In the rest of this part, you will learn how to create this application. As discussed in Chapter 9, the video kiosk application is divided into two modules—Customer module and Administration module.

In this chapter, you will learn to create the user interface of the Customer module, and you will create the forms you need for this module. In addition, you will learn about the controls you need to add to each form and the properties of these controls.

As discussed in Chapter 9, the Customer module of the video kiosk application consists of the following forms:

◆ The Main form
◆ The Search form
◆ The Place Order form
◆ The Registration form

The following sections describe each of these forms in detail. To start with, take a look at how to design the Main form of the Customer module.

The Main Form

As the name suggests, the Main form is the first form a customer will see in the Customer module. The Main form is the central location from which customers can browse for and place orders for movies. In addition, the Main form enables a customer to register with the MyMovies kiosk and obtain a customer ID. Figure 12-1 shows the Main form.

Before adding controls, you need to specify some properties for the Main form. The properties you need to assign to the Main form are as follows:

Property	Value
Name	FrmMain
Text	MyMovies World
Size	320, 368
WindowState	Normal

FIGURE 12-1 *The interface of the Main form*

The Customer module enables a customer to browse for movies regardless of whether he or she is a registered user. As shown in Figure 12-1, the Main form contains two group boxes, Registered Customer and New Customer.

If customers are registered users, they can use the controls in the Registered Customer group box. Customers can enter their customer identification number in the Customer ID text box and click on the Submit button. When a customer clicks on the Submit button, the Search form displays. The Search form enables a customer to search for movies.

If a customer is not a registered user, he or she can use the controls in the New Customer group box. In this group box, the customer can click on either the Register button or the Search button. If the customer clicks on the Register button, the Registration form displays. The customer can use the Registration form to register and obtain a customer identification number. Alternatively, the customer can click on the Search button to search for movies. You'll learn more about the Registration and Search forms later in this chapter.

Table 12-1 lists the properties of the Registered Customer and New Customer group boxes.

Table 12-1 Properties Assigned to Group Boxes

Control	Property	Value
Group box 1	Name	GrbRegisteredCustomer
Group box 1	Text	Registered Customer
Group box 1	Visible	True
Group box 2	Name	GrbNewCustomer
Group box 2	Text	New Customer
Group box 2	Visible	True

In addition to group boxes, the Main form contains four labels. Table 12-2 lists the properties of the labels.

Table 12-2 Properties Assigned to Labels

Control	Property	Value
Label 1	Name	LblWelcome
Label 1	Text	Welcome to My Movies
Label 1	Visible	True
Label 2	Name	LblCustomerID
Label 2	Text	Customer ID:
Label 2	Visible	True
Label 3	Name	LblToRegister
Label 3	Text	To register:
Label 3	Visible	True
Label 4	Name	LblWithoutReg

Control	Property	Value
Label 4	Text	Continue without registration:
Label 4	Visible	True

The LblWelcome label is the caption on the Main form that displays the welcome message. The Registered Customer group box contains the LblCustomerID label. The New Customer group box contains the LblToRegister and LblWithoutReg labels. Note that the font settings for the LblWelcome label differ from the font settings for the other labels. The font settings you need to specify for the LblWelcome label are as follows:

Property	Value
Name	Comic Sans MS
Size	14.25
Unit	Point
Bold	True
ForeColor	Desktop

In addition to the LblCustomerID label, the Registered Customer group box contains a text box. The Name property of the text box is set to TxtCustomerID, and the Visible property is set to True.

The Main form also displays four buttons, one of which is placed in the Registered Customer group box, two are placed in the New Customer group box, and one is placed on the form. Table 12-3 describes the properties for the four buttons on the Main form.

Table 12-3 Properties Assigned to Buttons

Control	Property	Value
Button 1	Name	CmdRegCustomer
Button 1	Text	Submit
Button 1	Visible	True

continues

Table 12-3 *(continued)*

Control	Property	Value
Button 2	Name	CmdRegister
Button 2	Text	Register
Button 2	Visible	True
Button 3	Name	CmdSearch
Button 3	Text	Search
Button 3	Visible	True
Button 4	Name	CmdExit
Button 4	Text	Exit
Button 4	Visible	True

As the name suggests, customers can use the Exit button to close the application. When a customer enters a valid customer identification number in the Customer ID text box and clicks on the Submit button, the Search form displays. The Search form also displays when a customer clicks on the Search button in the New Customer group box. The next section describes the Search form.

The Search Form

As the name suggests, the Search form of the Customer module enables customers to search for movies. Figure 12-2 shows the Search form.

To start with, take a look at the properties of the Search form. The properties you need to assign to the Search form are as follows:

Property	Value
Name	FrmSearch
Text	Search
Size	384, 336
WindowState	Normal

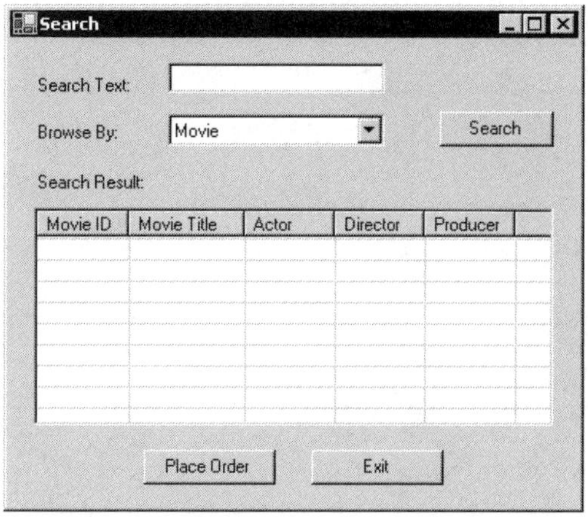

FIGURE 12-2 *The interface of the Search form*

As shown in Figure 12-2, the Search form contains three labels. Table 12-4 lists the properties of these labels.

Table 12-4 Properties Assigned to Labels

Control	Property	Value
Label 1	Name	LblSearchText
Label 1	Text	Search Text:
Label 1	Visible	True
Label 2	Name	LblBrowseBy
Label 2	Text	Browse By:
Label 2	Visible	True
Label 3	Name	LblSearchResult
Label 3	Text	Search Result:
Label 3	Visible	True

The Search form also contains a text box and a combo box. Table 12-5 lists the properties of these boxes.

Table 12-5 Properties Assigned to the Text Box and Combo Box

Control	Property	Value
Text box	Name	TxtSearch
Text box	Visible	True
Combo box	Name	CmbBrowseBy
Combo box	Visible	True
Combo box	DropDownStyle	DropDownList

In addition to these properties, you need to specify the Items property for the combo box. When you select the Items property, an ellipsis button appears next to the (Collection) value, as shown in Figure 12-3. You need to click on the ellipsis button to add items to the Browse By combo box.

FIGURE 12-3 *The* Items *property of the combo box*

When you click on the ellipsis button, the String Collection Editor dialog box displays. You can add items to the combo box by using this dialog box. Figure 12-4 shows the String Collection Editor dialog box.

In addition to the text box and combo box, the Search form also contains a list view control. The properties you need to specify for the list view control are as follows:

Property	Value
Name	LvwSearchResult
View	Details

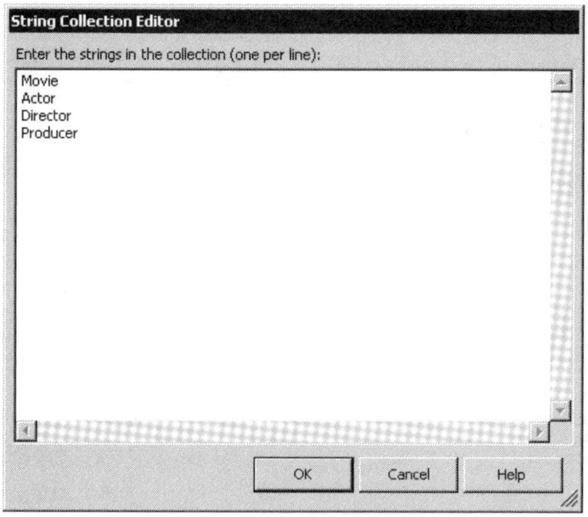

FIGURE 12-4 *The String Collection Editor dialog box*

Property	Value
FullRowSelect	True
GridLines	True

In addition to these properties, you also need to specify the Columns property for the list view control. The Columns property enables you to specify column headers for the list view control. When you select the Columns property, an ellipsis button appears next to the (Collection) value, as shown in Figure 12-5.

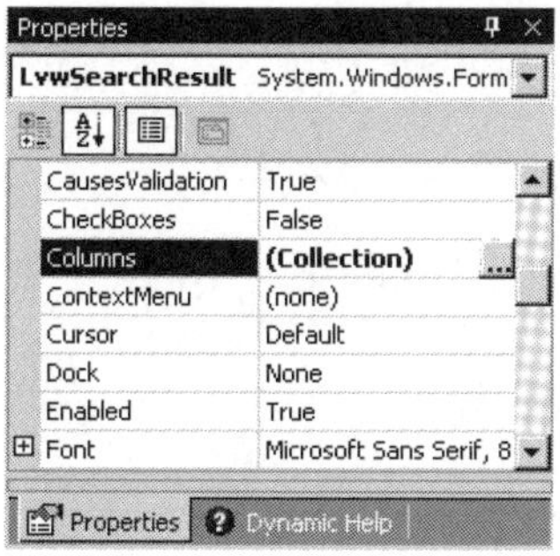

FIGURE 12-5 *The* Columns *property of the list view control*

When you click on the ellipsis button, the ColumnHeader Collection Editor dialog box appears, as shown in Figure 12-6.

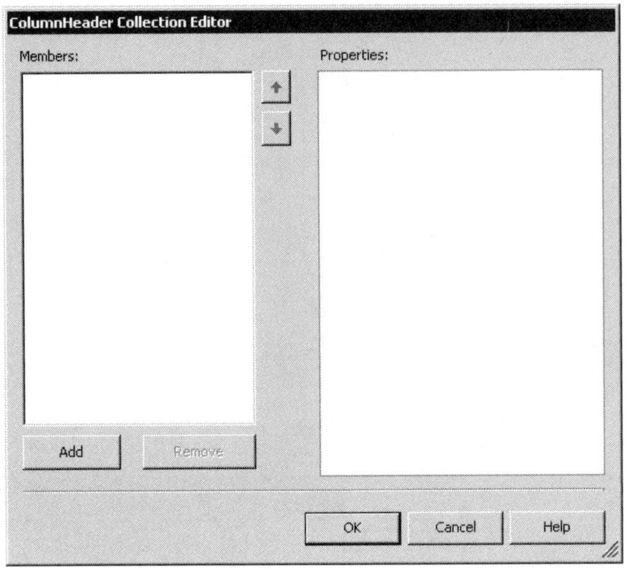

FIGURE 12-6 *The ColumnHeader Collection Editor dialog box*

Using the ColumnHeader Collection Editor dialog box, you can specify the columns for the list view control. To add a column to the list view control, click on the Add button in the ColumnHeader Collection Editor dialog box. When you click on the Add button, a column header object is added to the Members pane, as shown in Figure 12-7.

Note that the properties for the selected column appear in the right pane of the ColumnHeader Collection Editor dialog box. To edit the column name, you need to modify the Text property of the column header, as shown in Figure 12-8.

In the ColumnHeader Collection Editor dialog box, you need to add five columns and modify the Text property for each column. The properties you need to specify for the column headers are shown on page 274.

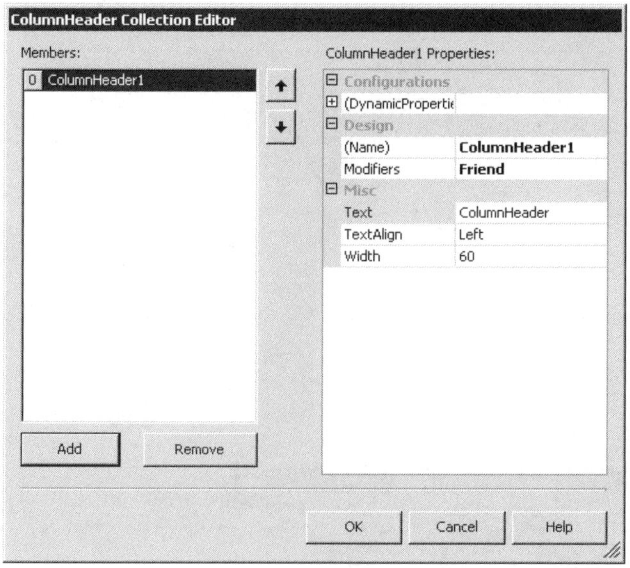

FIGURE 12-7 *The column added to the list view control*

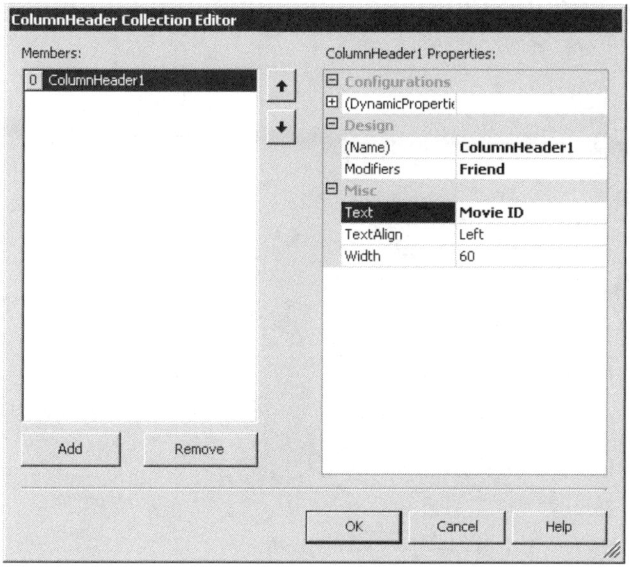

FIGURE 12-8 *Modifying the* Text *property for the ColumnHeader*

Name of Column Header	Value of Text Property
ColumnHeader1	Movie ID
ColumnHeader2	Movie Title
ColumnHeader3	Actor
ColumnHeader4	Director
ColumnHeader5	Producer

Figure 12-9 shows the ColumnHeader Collection Editor dialog box with all the columns.

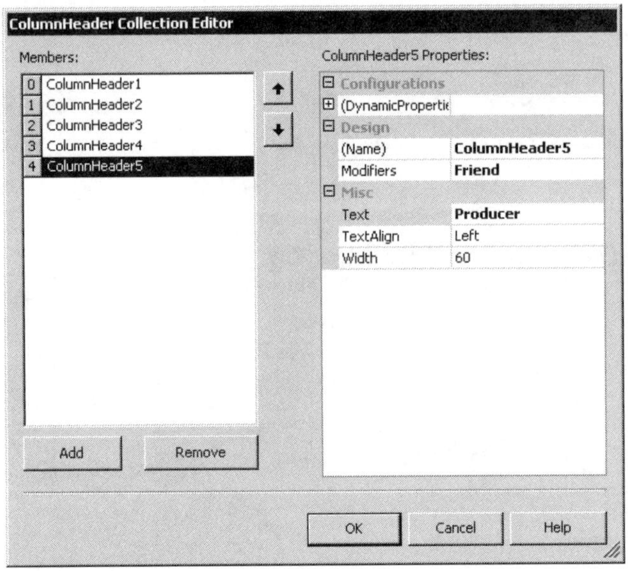

FIGURE 12-9 *The dialog box with all the columns*

After you add the columns to the list view control, you need to click on the OK button in the ColumnHeader Collection Editor dialog box. The Search form displays the columns you added to the dialog box. Figure 12-10 shows the Search form.

The Search form contains three buttons. Table 12-6 lists the properties assigned to the buttons on the Search form.

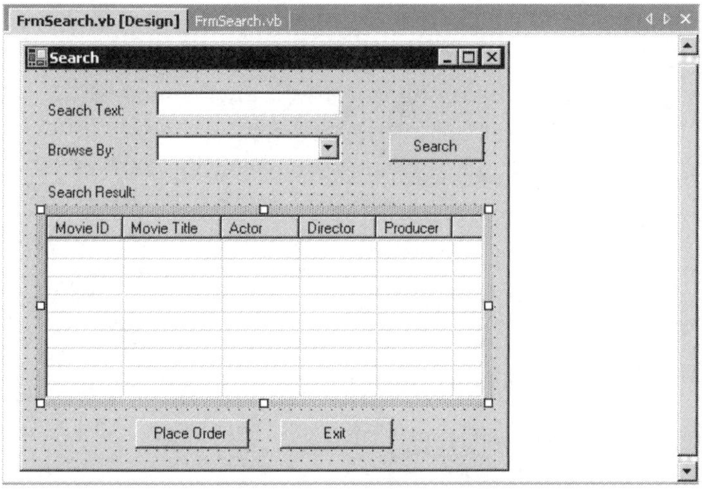

FIGURE 12-10 *The Search form after adding columns to the list view control*

Table 12-6 Properties Assigned to Buttons

Control	Property	Value
Button 1	Name	CmdSearch
Button 1	Text	Search
Button 1	Visible	True
Button 2	Name	CmdPlaceOrder
Button 2	Text	Place Order
Button 2	Visible	True
Button 3	Name	CmdExit
Button 3	Text	Exit
Button 3	Visible	True

As the name suggests, the Exit button enables customers to close the Search form. Alternatively, customers can use the Search button to browse the Movies database. To search for a movie, a customer needs to perform the following steps:

1. Type the text to search for in the Search Text text box. This text could be the name of an actor, director, producer, or movie.

2. Select a category from the Browse By combo box. The selection in this combo box determines the table to be searched. For example, if a customer selects the Actor option in the Browse By combo box, the text is searched for in the Actor table in the database.

3. Click on the Search button.

When a customer clicks on the Search button, results are displayed in the list view control. These results are based on the selection and the text entered in the text box. For example, if a customer enters "Harrison" in the text box, selects Actor from the Browse By combo box, and clicks on the Search button, the Search form appears as shown in Figure 12-11.

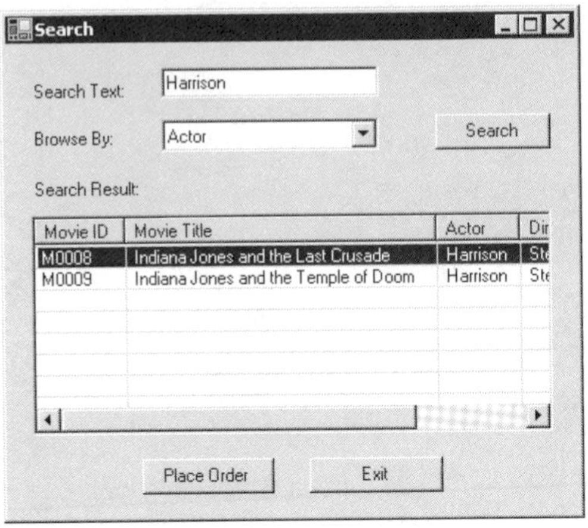

FIGURE 12-11 *The Search form with the results*

After the list view control displays the search results, a customer can choose to purchase a movie. To place an order for a movie, the customer needs to select the movie from the list view control and click on the Place Order button.

To place an order, a customer needs to be registered. So, depending on whether the customer specified a customer ID in the Main form, the Registration form or the Place Order form displays.

If the customer specified a customer identification number in the Main form, the Place Order form displays when the customer clicks on the Place Order button. In addition, the Place Order form displays the details of the selected movies. You will learn more about the Place Order form later in this chapter.

If the customer did not specify a customer identification number in the Main form, the Registration form displays when the customer clicks on the Place Order button. The next section describes the Registration form.

The Registration Form

As the name suggests, the Registration form enables customers to register. Figure 12-12 shows the Registration form.

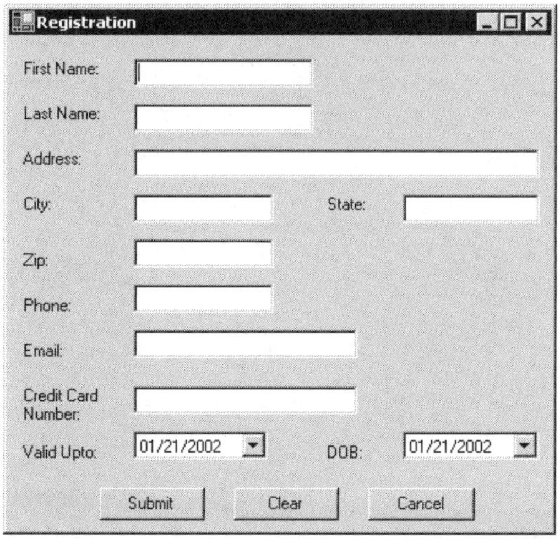

FIGURE 12-12 *The Registration form*

The Registration form appears when a customer clicks on the Register button in the Main form. The Registration form also appears when a customer does not specify an identification number in the Main form and then clicks on the Place Order button in the Search form.

The properties you need to assign to the Registration form are as follows:

Property	Value
Name	FrmRegistration
Text	Registration
Size	392, 376
WindowState	Normal

As shown in Figure 12-12, the Registration form contains multiple text boxes and labels. Table 12-7 lists the properties assigned to the labels on the Registration form.

Table 12-7 Properties Assigned to Labels

Control	Property	Value
Label 1	Name	LblFName
Label 1	Text	First Name:
Label 1	Visible	True
Label 2	Name	LblLName
Label 2	Text	Last Name:
Label 2	Visible	True
Label 3	Name	LblAddress
Label 3	Text	Address:
Label 3	Visible	True
Label 4	Name	LblCity
Label 4	Text	City:
Label 4	Visible	True
Label 5	Name	LblState
Label 5	Text	State:
Label 5	Visible	True
Label 6	Name	LblZip
Label 6	Text	Zip:
Label 6	Visible	True
Label 7	Name	LblPhone
Label 7	Text	Phone:
Label 7	Visible	True
Label 8	Name	LblEmail
Label 8	Text	Email:

Control	Property	Value
Label 8	Visible	True
Label 9	Name	LblCCNumber
Label 9	Text	Credit Card Number:
Label 9	Visible	True
Label 10	Name	LblValidUpto
Label 10	Text	Valid Upto:
Label 10	Visible	True
Label 11	Name	LblDOB
Label 11	Text	DOB:
Label 11	Visible	True

Table 12-8 lists the properties assigned to the text boxes on the Registration form.

Table 12-8 Properties Assigned to Text Boxes

Control	Property	Value
Text box 1	Name	TxtFName
Text box 1	Visible	True
Text box 2	Name	TxtLName
Text box 2	Visible	True
Text box 3	Name	TxtAddress
Text box 3	Visible	True
Text box 4	Name	TxtCity
Text box 4	Visible	True
Text box 5	Name	TxtState
Text box 5	Visible	True
Text box 6	Name	TxtZip
Text box 6	Visible	True

continues

Table 12-8 *(continued)*

Control	Property	Value
Text box 7	Name	TxtPhone
Text box 7	Visible	True
Text box 8	Name	TxtEmail
Text box 8	Visible	True
Text box 9	Name	TxtCCNumber
Text box 9	Visible	True

In addition to labels and text boxes, the Registration form contains two date time picker controls. One is associated with the Valid Upto label, and the other is associated with the DOB label. The Name property of the date time picker control associated with the Valid Upto label is set to DtpCCValidUpto. The Name property of the date time picker control associated with the DOB label is set to DtpDOB.

The Registration form also contains three buttons. Table 12-9 lists the properties of the buttons on the Registration form.

Table 12-9 Properties Assigned to Buttons

Control	Property	Value
Button 1	Name	CmdSubmitReg
Button 1	Text	Submit
Button 1	Visible	True
Button 2	Name	CmdClear
Button 2	Text	Clear
Button 2	Visible	True
Button 3	Name	CmdCancel
Button 3	Text	Cancel
Button 3	Visible	True

Customers can use the Submit button to update the database with the information entered in the Registration form. The Clear button enables customers to clear the controls on the Registration form. Customers can use the Cancel button to close the Registration form.

The Place Order Form

As previously mentioned, the Place Order form enables customers to place orders for movies. When a customer selects a movie in the Search form and clicks on the Place Order button, the Place Order form displays. Figure 12-13 shows the Place Order form.

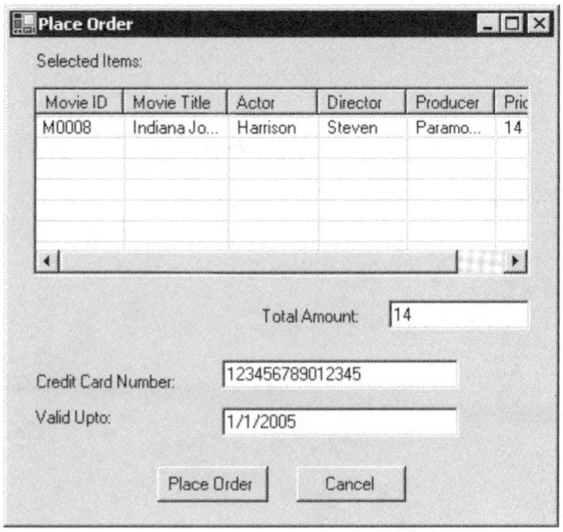

FIGURE 12-13 *The Place Order form*

To start with, take a look at the properties you need to assign to the Place Order form. They are as follows:

Property	Value
Name	FrmOrder
Text	Place Order
Size	376, 352
WindowState	Normal

As shown in Figure 12-13, the Place Order form contains four labels. Table 12-10 lists the properties assigned to the labels on the form.

Table 12-10 Properties Assigned to Labels

Control	Property	Value
Label 1	Name	LblSelectedItems
Label 1	Text	Selected Items:
Label 1	Visible	True
Label 2	Name	LblTotalAmount
Label 2	Text	Total Amount:
Label 2	Visible	True
Label 3	Name	LblCCNumber
Label 3	Text	Credit Card Number:
Label 3	Visible	True
Label 4	Name	LblValidUpto
Label 4	Text	Valid Upto:
Label 4	Visible	True

The Place Order form also contains a list view control. The properties you need to assign to the list view control are as follows:

Property	Value
Name	LvwItemsOrdered
View	Details
FullRowSelect	True
GridLines	True

In addition to these properties, you also need to specify column headers for the list view control by using the Columns property.

The properties you need to specify for the column headers are as follows:

Name of Column Header	Value of Text Property
ColumnHeader1	Movie ID
ColumnHeader2	Movie Title
ColumnHeader3	Actor
ColumnHeader4	Director
ColumnHeader5	Producer
ColumnHeader6	Price

After you specify the values for the Columns property, the ColumnHeader Collection Editor dialog box appears, as shown in Figure 12-14.

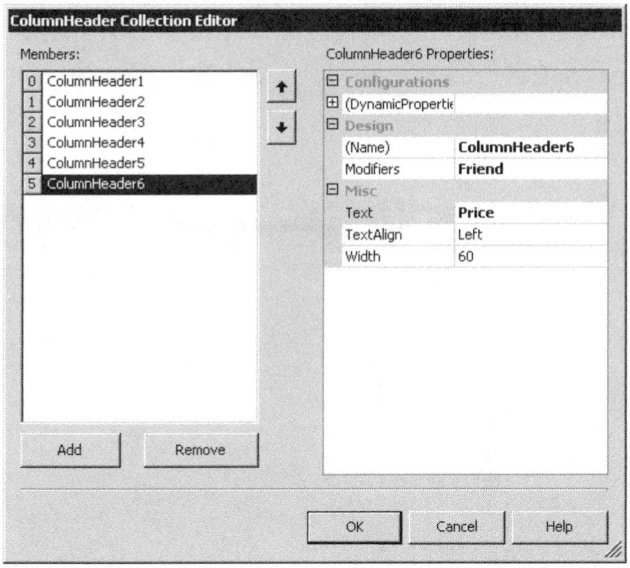

FIGURE 12-14 *The ColumnHeader Collection Editor dialog box*

After you specify the values for the Columns property for the list view control, the Place Order form appears, as shown in Figure 12-15.

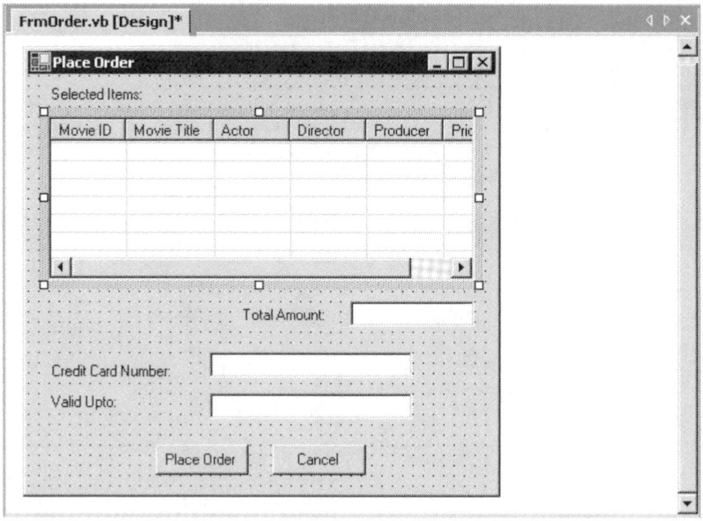

FIGURE 12-15 *The list view control in the Place Order form*

In addition to the list view control, the Place Order form contains three text boxes. Table 12-11 lists the properties assigned to the text boxes in the Place Order form.

Table 12-11 Properties Assigned to Text Boxes

Control	Property	Value
Text box 1	Name	TxtTotalAmount
Text box 1	Visible	True
Text box 2	Name	TxtCCNumber
Text box 2	Visible	True
Text box 3	Name	TxtValidUpto
Text box 3	Visible	True

In addition to text boxes, the Place Order form also contains two buttons, Place Order and Cancel. The properties of these buttons are listed in Table 12-12.

Table 12-12 Properties Assigned to Buttons

Control	Property	Value
Button 1	Name	CmdPlaceOrderFinal
Button 1	Text	Place Order
Button 1	Visible	True
Button 2	Name	CmdCancel
Button 2	Text	Cancel
Button 2	Visible	True

To order the selected movie(s), a customer needs to click on the Place Order button in the Place Order form. To close the Place Order form, a customer can click on the Cancel button.

Summary

In this chapter, you learned to create the forms for the Customer module of the video kiosk application. You learned to create the Main, Search, Registration, and Place Order forms. This chapter also described the properties you need to assign to the various controls on the forms. The next four chapters will discuss the functionality you need to add to the Customer module.

Chapter 13

Adding Functionality to the Main Form

n Chapter 12, "Designing the User Interface of the Customer Module," you learned to create the user interface for the Customer module of the video kiosk application. In these next few chapters, you will add functionality to forms in the Customer module.

As previously discussed, the Customer module consists of the following forms:

◆ The Main form
◆ The Search form
◆ The Place Order form
◆ The Registration form

In this chapter, you will learn to write code to add functionality to the Main form of the Customer module. To review, take a look at the Main form in Figure 13-1.

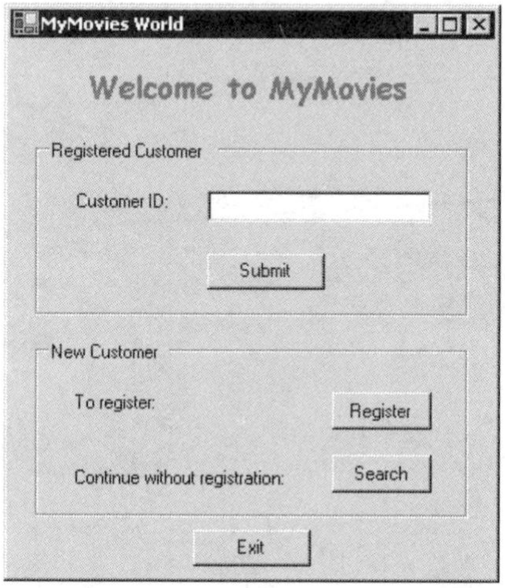

FIGURE 13-1 *The interface of the Main form*

To enable the Main form to connect to the Movies database, you need to use the SQL Server .NET data provider. To use the classes associated with the SQL Server .NET data provider, you must import the `System.Data.SqlClient` namespace. You can include the following statement in the Main form to import the `System.Data.SqlClient` namespace:

```
Imports System.Data.SqlClient
'Imports classes used by the SQL Server .NET data provider.
```

In addition to the preceding statement, you need to include the following statements in the Main form:

```
Imports System
Imports System.Data
'Includes the classes that make up the ADO.NET architecture
Imports System.String
'Includes the classes that enable you to work with strings
Imports System.Collections
'Includes the collection classes
Imports System.Data.SqlTypes
'Includes the classes for native data types within SQL Server
Imports App1.Module1
'Includes the StrConnectionString, which is used to initialize the connection
object
```

In addition, to connect to the Movies database from the Main form, you need to use an object of the `SqlConnection` class. To transfer data from the Main form to a dataset and vice versa, you need to use an object of the `SqlDataAdapter` class. You also need to declare the following variables in the Main form:

```
Public Shared ObjSearch As FrmSearch
'Declares ObjSearch as an object of the FrmSearch class
Public Shared ObjRegistration As FrmRegistration
'Declares ObjRegistration as an object of the FrmRegistration class
```

Before you write code, take a look at the flow of the functions in the Main form. As depicted in Figure 13-2, the Main form consists of the following functions:

- ◆ CmdRegCustomer_Click
- ◆ IsCustomerIDValid
- ◆ CmdRegister_Click
- ◆ CmdSearch_Click
- ◆ CmdExit_Click

The following sections describe the code for these functions.

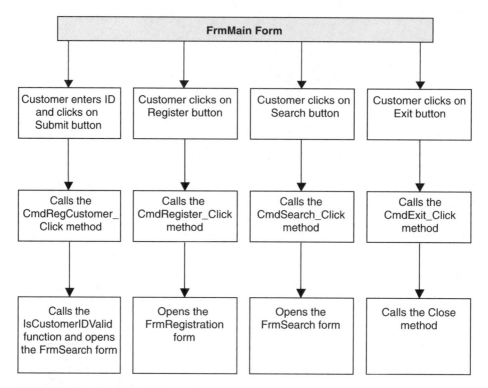

FIGURE 13-2 *The flow of the functions in the Main form*

The CmdRegCustomer_Click Function

The CmdRegCustomer_Click function is executed when a customer clicks on the Submit button the Main form.

The CmdRegCustomer_Click function checks to see whether the value entered in the Customer ID text box is numeric. Next, the function calls the IsCustomerID-Valid function to see if the customer ID entered by the customer is valid. You will learn about the IsCustomerIDValid function in the next section. After the IsCustomerIDValid function validates the ID entered by the customer, the ID is passed to the SetRegistrationID function of the FrmSearch class. Next, the Search form is displayed.

Take a look at the code for the CmdRegCustomer_Click function:

```
Private Sub CmdRegCustomerSubmit_Click(ByVal sender As System.Object, ByVal e As
System.EventArgs) Handles CmdRegCustomer.Click
```

```
            If TxtCustomerID.Text.Trim = "" Then
'Checks if user has not entered the customer ID
            MessageBox.Show("Please enter your ID.")
        Else


            ObjSearch = New FrmSearch()
'Creates an object of the FrmSearch class
            If (IsNumeric(TxtCustomerID.Text)) Then
'Checks if the ID entered by the customer is a number
                If (IsCustomerIDValid(TxtCustomerID.Text)) Then
'Passes the ID entered by the customer to the IsCustomerIDValid function
                    ObjSearch.SetRegistrationID(TxtCustomerID.Text)
'Passes the ID entered by the customer to the SetRegistrationID function of the
FrmSearch class
                    ObjSearch.Show()
'Displays the Search form
                Else
                    MessageBox.Show("Invalid CustomerID")
'Displays a message if customer ID is not found in the database
                End If
            Else
                MessageBox.Show("Invalid CustomerID")
'Displays a message if the ID entered by the customer is not numeric
            End If
        End If
    End Sub
```

The IsCustomerIDValid *Function*

The IsCustomerIDValid function validates the customer ID entered by the customer. To do so, the IsCustomerIDValid function takes the customer ID entered by the user as a parameter. The IsCustomerIDValid function contains statements to connect to the Movies database and check whether the ID entered by the customer exists in the Customer table. This function returns a value of True if the ID entered by the user exists in the database and returns False if the ID does not exist in the database.

The code for this function is as follows:

```
Private Function IsCustomerIDValid(ByVal custID As String) As Boolean
        Dim StrRowCount As String
        Dim StrQuery As String
'Declares variables
        Dim SqlConnection1 As New SqlConnection(StrConnectionString)
'Declares the connection object
        StrQuery = "SELECT COUNT(CustID) FROM Customer WHERE CustID ='" & custID
& "'"
'Specifies the query
        SqlConnection1.Open()
'Establishes a connection with the database
        Dim SelectCmd As New SqlCommand(StrQuery, SqlConnection1)
'Executes the query
        StrRowCount = SelectCmd.ExecuteScalar()
'Stores the first column of the first row in the results returned by the query in
the StrRowCount variable
        SqlConnection1.Close()
'Closes the SqlConnection1 object
        SqlConnection1.Dispose()
'Releases the resources used by the SqlConnection1 object
        SelectCmd.Dispose()
'Releases the resources used by the SelectCmd object


        If (CInt(StrRowCount) > 0) Then
                IsCustomerIDValid = True
'Returns True if the customer ID exists in the dataset
        Else
                IsCustomerIDValid = False
'Returns False if the customer ID does not exist in the dataset
        End If
End Function
```

The CmdRegister_Click *Function*

As discussed in the preceding chapter, a customer can click on the Register button to obtain a customer ID. The CmdRegister_Click function is executed when the customer clicks on the Register button in the Main form.

The code for the CmdRegister_Click function is as follows:

```
Private Sub CmdRegister_Click(ByVal sender As System.Object, ByVal e As
System.EventArgs) Handles CmdRegister.Click
        ObjRegistration = New FrmRegistration()
'Declares ObjRegistration as an object of the FrmRegistration class
        ObjRegistration.Show()
'Displays the Registration form
End Sub
```

When the customer clicks on the Register button, the Registration form opens.

The CmdSearch_Click *Function*

The Customer module enables registered and unregistered customers to browse the Movies database. To browse the Movies database, a registered customer needs to click on the Submit button after entering his or her customer ID. An unregistered customer can click on the Search button to browse the Movies database. The CmdSearch_Click function is executed when a customer clicks on the Search button in the Main form.

The code of the CmdSearch_Click function is as follows:

```
Private Sub CmdSearch_Click(ByVal sender As System.Object, ByVal e As
System.EventArgs) Handles CmdSearch.Click
        ObjSearch = New FrmSearch()
'Declares ObjSearch as an object of the FrmSearch class
        ObjSearch.Show()
'Displays the Search form
End Sub
```

When the customer clicks on the Search button, the Search form opens.

The CmdExit_Click *Function*

The CmdExit_Click function is executed when a customer clicks on the Exit button in the Main form.

The code for the CmdExit_Click function is as follows:

```
Private Sub CmdExit_Click(ByVal sender As System.Object, ByVal e As
System.EventArgs) Handles CmdExit.Click
        Me.Close()
'Closes the current form, which is the Main form
End Sub
```

A customer can click on the Exit button to close the Customer module.

Complete Code for the Main Form

In the preceding sections, you looked at the code associated with the events and functions in the Main form. Listing 13-1 lists the complete code for the Main form.

Listing 13-1 The Code for the Main Form

```
Imports System
Imports System.Data
Imports System.String
Imports System.Collections
Imports System.Data.SqlClient
Imports System.Data.SqlTypes
Imports App1.Module1


Public Class FrmMain
        Inherits System.Windows.Forms.Form

        Public Shared ObjSearch As FrmSearch
        Public Shared ObjRegistration As FrmRegistration


Windows Form Designer generated code
```

'Contains the code that specifies the size, location, and other properties, such as font and name, for the controls on the form.

```
        Private Sub CmdRegCustomerSubmit_Click(ByVal sender As System.Object, ByVal e As System.EventArgs) Handles CmdRegCustomer.Click
                If TxtCustomerID.Text.Trim = "" Then
                        MessageBox.Show("Please enter your ID.")
                Else
                        ObjSearch = New FrmSearch()
                                If (IsNumeric(TxtCustomerID.Text)) Then
                                        If
(IsCustomerIDValid(TxtCustomerID.Text)) Then

ObjSearch.SetRegistrationID(TxtCustomerID.Text)
                                                ObjSearch.Show()
                                        Else
                                        MessageBox.Show
("Invalid CustomerID")
                                        End If
                                Else
                                MessageBox.Show("Invalid
CustomerID")
                                End If
                        End If
                End If
        End Sub

        Private Function IsCustomerIDValid(ByVal custID As String) As Boolean
                Dim StrQuery As String
                Dim StrRowCount As String
                Dim SqlConnection1 As New SqlConnection(StrConnectionString)

                StrQuery = "SELECT COUNT(CustID) FROM Customer WHERE CustID ='" &
custID & "'"

                SqlConnection1.Open()
                Dim SelectCmd As New SqlCommand(StrQuery, SqlConnection1)
                StrRowCount = SelectCmd.ExecuteScalar()
```

```
                    SqlConnection1.Close()
                    SqlConnection1.Dispose()
                    SelectCmd.Dispose()


                    If (CInt(StrRowCount) > 0) Then
                                IsCustomerIDValid = True
                    Else
                                IsCustomerIDValid = False
                    End If
              End Function

              Private Sub CmdRegister_Click(ByVal sender As System.Object, ByVal e As
        System.EventArgs) Handles CmdRegister.Click
                    ObjRegistration = New FrmRegistration()
                    ObjRegistration.Show()
              End Sub

              Private Sub CmdSearch_Click(ByVal sender As System.Object, ByVal e As
        System.EventArgs) Handles CmdSearch.Click
                    ObjSearch = New FrmSearch()
                    ObjSearch.Show()
              End Sub

              Private Sub CmdExit_Click(ByVal sender As System.Object, ByVal e As
        System.EventArgs) Handles CmdExit.Click
                    Me.Close()
              End Sub
        End Class
```

Summary

In this chapter, you learned to add functionality to the Main form. You also learned about the functions you need to create in the Main form. This chapter also described the events you need to trap to add functionality to the Main form. Finally, you looked at the complete code for the Main form.

Chapter 14

*Adding
Functionality to
the Search Form*

In the preceding chapter, you learned to add functionality to the Main form. In this chapter, you will learn to add functionality to the Search form of the Customer module.

First let's review what the Search form looks like (see Figure 14-1).

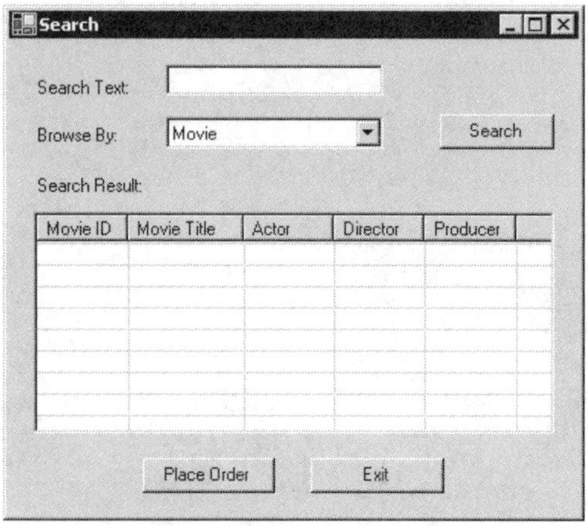

FIGURE 14-1 *The interface of the Search form*

The Search form enables customers to search the Movies database. To connect to the database from the Search form, you need to use the SQL Server .NET data provider. To use the SQL Server .NET data provider, you need to import the classes stored in the `System.Data.SqlClient` namespace. You can import the `System.Data.SqlClient` namespace by including the following statement in the Search form:

```
Imports System.Data.SqlClient

'Imports classes used by the SQL Server .NET data provider
```

In addition to the preceding statement, you need to include the following statements in the Search form:

```
Imports System.Data
'Includes the classes that make up the ADO.NET architecture
Imports System.String
'Includes the classes that enable you to work with strings
Imports System.Collections
'Includes the collection classes
Imports System.Data.SqlTypes
'Includes the classes for native data types within SQL Server
```

You also need to declare the following variables in the Search form:

```
Public Shared ObjPlaceOrder As FrmOrder
'Declares ObjPlaceOrder as an object of the FrmOrder class
Public Shared ObjRegistration As FrmRegistration
'Declares ObjRegistration as an object of the FrmRegistration class
Public Shared ArrayMovieID() As String = New String(10) {}
'Declares a string array
Private Shared StrRegistrationID As String
'Declares a string, which stores the customer ID
```

Before you write code, take a look at the flow of the functions in the Search form. Figure 14-2 depicts this flow.

As depicted in Figure 14-2, the Search form consists of the following functions:

- ◆ FrmSearch_Load
- ◆ CmdSearch_Click
- ◆ SetRegistrationID
- ◆ CmdPlaceOrder_Click
- ◆ CmdExit_Click

The following sections describe the code for these functions.

The FrmSearch_Load Function

As the name suggests, the FrmSearch_Load function is executed before an instance of the FrmSearch form displays. In the Search form, the FrmSearch_Load function performs the following tasks:

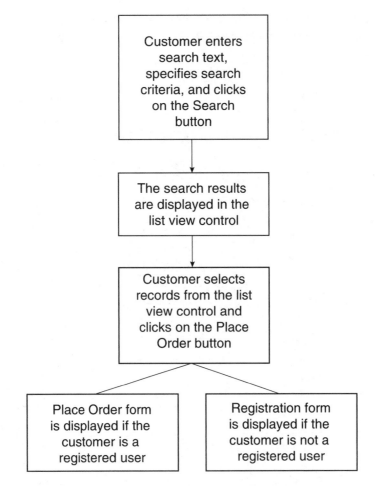

FIGURE 14-2 *The flow of functions in the Search form*

◆ It specifies that Movie is displayed in the Browse By combo box when the Search form loads.

◆ It disables the Place Order button.

Therefore, when the customer opens the Search form, the Movie option is selected in the Browse By combo box, and the Place Order button is disabled. The code for the FrmSearch_Load function is as follows:

```
Private Sub FrmSearch_Load(ByVal sender As System.Object, ByVal e As
System.EventArgs) Handles MyBase.Load
        CmbBrowseBy.SelectedIndex = 0
```

```
'Specifies Movie as the default option in the Browse By combo box
        CmdPlaceOrder.Enabled = False
'Disables the Place Order button
    End Sub
```

The CmdSearch_Click Function

The CmdSearch_Click function is executed when the customer clicks on the Search button.

When the CmdSearch_Click function is executed, it first checks to see whether the customer entered any text in the Search text box. If the Search text box is blank, a message box asks the customer to enter text in the Search text box. Next, based on the value specified in the Browse By combo box and the text entered in the Search text box, a query is created. Then the query is executed, and results are stored in a dataset. Finally, the results, if any, are displayed in the list view control. In addition, the Place Order button is enabled. If the query returns no records and the dataset is empty, a message stating this is displayed.

The code for the CmdSearch_Click function is as follows:

```
Private Sub CmdSearch_Click(ByVal sender As System.Object, ByVal e As
System.EventArgs) Handles CmdSearch.Click
        Dim DsDataSet As DataSet
        Dim DrRowPicker As DataRow
        Dim StrBrowseBy As String
        Dim StrQuery As String
        Dim Result As Integer
        Dim StrMessage As String
        Dim BSearchStrEmpty As Boolean
        Dim SqlConnection1 As New SqlConnection(StrConnectionString)
        Dim SqlDataAdapter1 As New SqlDataAdapter()
        Dim SqlSelectCommand1 As New SqlCommand()
'Declares variables

        BSearchStrEmpty = False
'Assigns a value of False to the BSearchStrEmpty variable

        If TxtSearch.Text.Trim = "" Then
```

```
'Checks if the Search text box is empty
                    BSearchStrEmpty = True
'Assigns True to the BSearchStrEmpty variable
          End If


          StrBrowseBy = CmbBrowseBy.Text
'Stores the option selected by the customer in the Browse By combo box in the
StrBrowseBy string
          If (Compare(StrBrowseBy, "Movie", True) = 0) Then
'Checks if the customer has selected the Movie option in the Browse By combo box
                    Result = 0
'Assigns a value of 0 to the Result flag
                    StrQuery = "SELECT DISTINCT a.MovID, b.ActorID, c.DirID, d.ProdID,
a.MovTitle, b.FirstName AS Actor, c.FirstName AS Director, d.name AS Producer FROM
movie a, actor b, director c, producer d, actormovie e WHERE a.MovID = e.MovID AND
e.ActorID = b.ActorID AND a.DirID = c.DirID AND a.ProdID = d.ProdID "
                    If Not BSearchStrEmpty Then
                         StrQuery += " AND a.MovTitle LIKE '" &
TxtSearch.Text & "%'"
'Specifies the query to search for the text entered in the Search Text text box in
the Movie Title field of the Movie table. If a match is found, the Movie ID, Actor,
Director, and Producer associated with the Movie are displayed in the list view
control. If the customer has not entered any text in the Search Text text box, all
records from the Movie table are displayed.
                    End If
          ElseIf (Compare(StrBrowseBy, "Actor", True) = 0) Then
'Checks if the customer has selected the Actor option in the Browse By combo box
                    Result = 1
'Assigns a value of 1 to the Result flag
                    StrQuery = "SELECT DISTINCT a.MovID, b.ActorID, c.DirID, d.ProdID,
a.MovTitle, b.FirstName AS Actor, c.FirstName AS Director, d.name AS Producer FROM
movie a, actor b, director c, producer d, actormovie e WHERE a.MovID = e.MovID AND
e.ActorID = b.ActorID AND a.DirID = c.DirID AND a.ProdID = d.ProdID "
                    If Not BSearchStrEmpty Then
                         StrQuery += "AND (b.FirstName LIKE '" & TxtSearch.Text
& "%' OR b.LastName LIKE '" & TxtSearch.Text & "%') "
'Specifies the query to search for the text entered in the Search Text text box in
the First Name and Last Name fields of the Actor table. If a match is found, the
```

Movie ID, Actor, Director, and Producer associated with the Movie are displayed in the list view control. If the customer has not entered any text in the Search Text text box, all records from the Actor table are displayed.

```
                    End If
                    ElseIf (Compare(StrBrowseBy, "Director", True) = 0) Then
'Checks if the customer has selected the Director option in the Browse By combo box
                    Result = 2
'Assigns a value of 2 to the Result flag
                        StrQuery = "SELECT DISTINCT a.MovID, b.ActorID,
c.DirID, d.ProdID, a.MovTitle, b.FirstName AS Actor, c.FirstName AS Director,
d.name AS Producer FROM movie a, actor b, director c, producer d, actormovie e
WHERE a.MovID = e.MovID AND e.ActorID = b.ActorID AND a.DirID = c.DirID AND
a.ProdID = d.ProdID "
                    If Not BSearchStrEmpty Then
                        StrQuery += "AND (b.FirstName LIKE '" &
TxtSearch.Text & "%' OR b.LastName LIKE '" & TxtSearch.Text & "%') "
```

'Specifies the query to search for the text entered in the Search Text text box in the First Name and Last Name fields of the Director table. If a match is found, the Movie ID, Actor, Director, and Producer associated with the Movie are displayed in the list view control. . If the customer has not entered any text in the Search Text text box, all records from the Director table are displayed.

```
                    End If
                    ElseIf (Compare(StrBrowseBy, "Producer", True) = 0) Then
'Checks if the customer has selected the Producer option in the Browse By combo box
                    Result = 3
'Assigns a value of 3 to the Result flag
                        StrQuery = "SELECT DISTINCT a.MovID, b.ActorID,
c.DirID, d.ProdID, a.MovTitle, b.FirstName AS Actor, c.FirstName AS Director,
d.name AS Producer FROM movie a, actor b, director c, producer d, actormovie e
WHERE a.MovID = e.MovID AND e.ActorID = b.ActorID AND a.DirID = c.DirID AND
a.ProdID = d.ProdID "
                    If Not BSearchStrEmpty Then
                        StrQuery += " AND d.Name LIKE '" & TxtSearch.Text
& "%'"
```

'Specifies the query to search for the text entered in the Search Text text box in the Name field of the Producer table. If a match is found, the Movie ID, Actor, Director, and Producer associated with the Movie are displayed in the list view control. If the customer has not entered any text in the Search Text text box, all

```
records from the Producer table are displayed.
                          End If
            Else
                    Result = -1
'Assigns a value of -1 to the Result flag
                    StrQuery = ""
'Assigns a space to the StrQuery variables
          End If


          DsDataSet = New DataSet()
'Creates the dataset
          SqlDataAdapter1.SelectCommand = SqlSelectCommand1
          SqlDataAdapter1.SelectCommand.CommandText = StrQuery
'Executes the query
          SqlDataAdapter1.SelectCommand.Connection = SqlConnection1
          SqlDataAdapter1.Fill(DsDataSet, "SearchResult")
'Populates the SearchResult table in the DsDataSet dataset with the query results


          LvwSearchResult.Items.Clear()
'Clears the list view control
          Dim IntRowCount As Integer
'Declares IntRowCount as a Integer variable
          IntRowCount = 0
'Assigns a value of 0 to the IntRowCount variable


          For Each DrRowPicker In DsDataSet.Tables("SearchResult").Rows
                  Dim StrSearchRow As String() = {DrRowPicker(0), DrRowPicker(4),
DrRowPicker(5), DrRowPicker(6), DrRowPicker(7)}
'Picks up the values of the Movie ID, Movie Title, First Name of Actor, First Name
of Director, and Producer name for each record in the dataset and adds it to the
StrSearchRow array
                  LvwSearchResult.Items.Add(New ListViewItem(StrSearchRow))
'Displays each member of the StrSearchRow array in the list view control
                  IntRowCount += 1
'Increments the IntRowCount variable by 1
          Next


          Dim IntRes As Integer
```

```
        IntRes = CInt(Result)
'Assigns the value stored in the Result flag to the IntRes variable


        If (IntRowCount = 0) Then
                CmdPlaceOrder.Enabled = False
'Disables the Place Order button if the dataset is empty
        Else
                CmdPlaceOrder.Enabled = True
'Enables the Place Order button if the dataset contains records
        End If


        If IntRowCount = 0 Then
'Checks if the table in the dataset contains no records
                If (IntRes = 0) Then
'Checks if the customer had selected the Movie option in the Browse By combo box
                        MessageBox.Show("Couldn't find this movie.")
                ElseIf (IntRes = 1) Then
'Checks if the customer had selected the Actor option in the Browse By combo box
                        MessageBox.Show("Couldn't find any movie of this
actor.")
                ElseIf (IntRes = 2) Then
'Checks if the customer had selected the Director option in the Browse By combo box
                        MessageBox.Show("Couldn't find any movie of this
director.")
                ElseIf (IntRes = 3) Then
'Checks if the customer had selected the Producer option in the Browse By combo box
                        MessageBox.Show("Couldn't find any movie of this
producer.")
                End If
        End If


        SqlConnection1.Close()
'Closes the SqlConnection1 object
        SqlConnection1.Dispose()
'Releases the resources used by the SqlConnection1 object
        SqlSelectCommand1.Dispose()
'Releases the resources used by the SqlSelectCommand1 object
        SqlDataAdapter1.Dispose()
```

```
'Closes the SqlDataAdapter1 object
End Sub
```

The SetRegistrationID *Function*

As discussed in the preceding chapter, when the customer enters his or her customer ID in the Main form and clicks on the Submit button, the ID entered by the customer is validated. In addition, after the ID is validated, the Main form passes the ID to the `SetRegistrationID` function of the `FrmSearch` class. Therefore, the `SetRegistrationID` function accepts a string as a parameter.

The code for the `SetRegistrationID` function is as follows:

```
Public Sub SetRegistrationID(ByVal RegID As String)
'Takes the ID entered by the customer as a parameter and stores it in the RegID
variable
        StrRegistrationID = RegID
'Assigns the value in the RegID variable to the StrRegistrationID variable
End Sub
```

The CmdPlaceOrder_Click *Function*

As previously discussed, a customer can select a record from the list view control in the Search form and click on the Place Order button to place an order for the movie. The `CmdPlaceOrder_Click` function executes when the customer selects a record from the list view control and clicks on the Place Order button.

When the `CmdPlaceOrder_Click` function executes, it first checks to see if the customer has selected any records from the list view control. If the customer has not selected any movies from the list view control, a message box prompts the customer to select a record. If the customer selects a movie from the list view control and clicks on the Place Order button, either the Registration form or the Place Order form displays. The form displayed depends on the whether the customer specified a customer ID in the Main form. If the customer is a registered user and specified his or her customer ID in the Main form, then the Place Order form displays when the customer clicks on the Place Order button. If the customer did not specify a customer ID in the Main form, the Registration form displays when the customer clicks on the Place Order button.

The code of the CmdPlaceOrder_Click function is as follows:

```
Private Sub CmdPlaceOrder_Click(ByVal sender As System.Object, ByVal e As
System.EventArgs) Handles CmdPlaceOrder.Click
        Dim LstViewCollection As ListView.SelectedListViewItemCollection
'Declares LstViewCollection as an object of the SelectedListViewItemCollection
class. The SelectedListViewItemCollection class represents the collection of
selected items in a list view control.
        LstViewCollection = New
ListView.SelectedListViewItemCollection(LvwSearchResult)
'Stores the selected item in the list view control in the LstViewCollection object
        Dim IntTotalSelectedCount As Integer
        IntTotalSelectedCount = LstViewCollection.Count()
'Stores the number of items in the LstViewCollection object in the
IntTotalSelectedCount variable
        If (IntTotalSelectedCount < 1) Then
'Checks if the LstViewCollection object contains any items
            MessageBox.Show("You have not selected any movie. Please select
movies from the list and then click on the ""Place Order"" button")
'Displays a message informing the customer to select records from the list view
control
            Return
        End If


        If (StrRegistrationID = "") Then
'Checks if the StrRegistrationID variable is blank, which implies that the customer
is not a registered user
            MessageBox.Show("You need to register before placing any order.")
            ObjRegistration = New FrmRegistration()
'Creates an object of the FrmRegistration class
            ObjRegistration.BlnFromSearchButton = True
'Assigns a value of True to the BlnFromSearchButton variable
            ObjRegistration.Show()
'Opens the Registration form
        Else
'Executed if the StrRegistrationID variable stores a customer ID, which implies
that the customer is a registered user
```

```
                    ObjPlaceOrder = New FrmOrder()
'Creates an object of the FrmOrder class
                        ObjPlaceOrder.SetRegistrationID(StrRegistrationID)
'Invokes the SetRegistrationID function of the FrmOrder class and passes the cus-
tomer Id as a parameter

                    Dim IntCounter As Integer
                    For IntCounter = 0 To IntTotalSelectedCount - 1
                            ArrayMovieID(IntCounter) =
LstViewCollection.Item(IntCounter).Text
'Stores the Movie Id associated with each item in the LstViewCollection object in
the ArrayMovieID array
                    Next

                    ObjPlaceOrder.SetSelectedMovies(ArrayMovieID,
IntTotalSelectedCount)
'Invokes the SetSelectedMovies function of the FrmOrder class. The
SetSelectedMovies function takes the array containing the Movie IDs of the selected
records and the number of selected records as parameters.
                    ObjPlaceOrder.Show()
'Displays the Place Order form
        End If
End Sub
```

The CmdExit_Click *Function*

The CmdExit_Click function executes when a customer clicks on the Exit button
in the Search form. A customer can click on the Exit button to close the Search
form.

The code for the CmdExit_Click function is as follows:

```
Private Sub CmdExit_Click(ByVal sender As System.Object, ByVal e As
System.EventArgs) Handles CmdExit.Click
        Me.Close()
'Closes the Search form
    End Sub
```

Complete Code for the Search Form

In the preceding sections, you looked at the code for the functions in the Search form. Listing 14-1 lists the complete code for the Search form.

Listing 14-1 The Code for the Search Form

```vbnet
Imports System.Data
Imports System.String
Imports System.Collections
Imports System.Data.SqlClient
Imports System.Data.SqlTypes


Public Class FrmSearch
        Inherits System.Windows.Forms.Form

        Public Shared ObjPlaceOrder As FrmOrder
        Public Shared ObjRegistration As FrmRegistration
        Public Shared ArrayMovieID() As String = New String(10) {}
        Private Shared StrRegistrationID As String

Windows Form Designer generated code
'Contains the code that specifies the size, location, and other properties, such as
font and name, for the controls on the form.

        Private Sub CmdExit_Click(ByVal sender As System.Object, ByVal e As
System.EventArgs) Handles CmdExit.Click
                Me.Close()
        End Sub


        Private Sub CmdPlaceOrder_Click(ByVal sender As System.Object, ByVal e As
System.EventArgs) Handles CmdPlaceOrder.Click
                Dim LstViewCollection As ListView.SelectedListViewItemCollection
                LstViewCollection = New
ListView.SelectedListViewItemCollection(LvwSearchResult)
                Dim IntTotalSelectedCount As Integer
```

```
IntTotalSelectedCount = LstViewCollection.Count()
If (IntTotalSelectedCount < 1) Then
        MessageBox.Show("You have not selected any movie.
Please select movies from the list and then click on the ""Place Order"" button")
        Return
End If


If (StrRegistrationID = "") Then
        MessageBox.Show("You need to register before placing
any order.")
        ObjRegistration = New FrmRegistration()
        ObjRegistration.BlnFromSearchButton = True
        ObjRegistration.Show()
Else
        ObjPlaceOrder = New FrmOrder()
        ObjPlaceOrder.SetRegistrationID(StrRegistrationID)
        Dim IntCounter As Integer
        For IntCounter = 0 To IntTotalSelectedCount - 1
                ArrayMovieID(IntCounter) =
LstViewCollection.Item(IntCounter).Text
        Next
        ObjPlaceOrder.SetSelectedMovies(ArrayMovieID,
IntTotalSelectedCount)
        ObjPlaceOrder.Show()
End If
End Sub


Private Sub CmdSearch_Click(ByVal sender As System.Object, ByVal e As
System.EventArgs) Handles CmdSearch.Click
        Dim DsDataSet As DataSet
        Dim DrRowPicker As DataRow
        Dim StrBrowseBy As String
        Dim StrQuery As String
        Dim Result As Integer
        Dim StrMessage As String
        Dim BSearchStrEmpty As Boolean
        Dim SqlConnection1 As New SqlConnection(StrConnectionString)
        Dim SqlDataAdapter1 As New SqlDataAdapter()
```

```
Dim SqlSelectCommand1 As New SqlCommand()

BSearchStrEmpty = False
If TxtSearch.Text.Trim = "" Then
            BSearchStrEmpty = True
End If


StrBrowseBy = CmbBrowseBy.Text
If (Compare(StrBrowseBy, "Movie", True) = 0) Then
Result = 0
StrQuery = "SELECT DISTINCT a.MovID, b.ActorID, c.DirID,
d.ProdID, a.MovTitle, b.FirstName AS Actor, c.FirstName AS Director, d.name AS
Producer FROM movie a, actor b, director c, producer d, actormovie e WHERE a.MovID
= e.MovID AND e.ActorID = b.ActorID AND a.DirID = c.DirID AND a.ProdID = d.ProdID "
            If Not BSearchStrEmpty Then
                        StrQuery += " AND a.MovTitle LIKE '" & TxtSearch.Text
& "%'"
            End If
            ElseIf (Compare(StrBrowseBy, "Actor", True) = 0) Then
                        Result = 1
                        StrQuery = "SELECT DISTINCT a.MovID, b.ActorID,
c.DirID, d.ProdID, a.MovTitle, b.FirstName AS Actor, c.FirstName AS Director,
d.name AS Producer FROM movie a, actor b, director c, producer d, actormovie e
WHERE a.MovID = e.MovID AND e.ActorID = b.ActorID AND a.DirID = c.DirID AND
a.ProdID = d.ProdID "
                        If Not BSearchStrEmpty Then
                                    StrQuery += "AND (b.FirstName LIKE '" & TxtSearch.Text
& "%' OR b.LastName LIKE '" & TxtSearch.Text & "%') "
                        End If
                        ElseIf (Compare(StrBrowseBy, "Director", True) = 0) Then
                                    Result = 2
                                    StrQuery = "SELECT DISTINCT a.MovID, b.ActorID,
c.DirID, d.ProdID, a.MovTitle, b.FirstName AS Actor, c.FirstName AS Director,
d.name AS Producer FROM movie a, actor b, director c, producer d, actormovie e
WHERE a.MovID = e.MovID AND e.ActorID = b.ActorID AND a.DirID = c.DirID AND
a.ProdID = d.ProdID "
                                    If Not BSearchStrEmpty Then
                                                StrQuery += "AND (b.FirstName LIKE '" &
```

```
TxtSearch.Text & "%' OR b.LastName LIKE '" & TxtSearch.Text & "%') "
                End If
            ElseIf (Compare(StrBrowseBy, "Producer", True) = 0) Then
                    Result = 3
                    StrQuery = "SELECT DISTINCT a.MovID, b.ActorID,
c.DirID, d.ProdID, a.MovTitle, b.FirstName AS Actor, c.FirstName AS Director,
d.name AS Producer FROM movie a, actor b, director c, producer d, actormovie e
WHERE a.MovID = e.MovID AND e.ActorID = b.ActorID AND a.DirID = c.DirID AND
a.ProdID = d.ProdID "
                If Not BSearchStrEmpty Then
                        StrQuery += " AND d.Name LIKE '" & TxtSearch.Text
& "%'"
                End If
            Else
                    Result = -1
                    StrQuery = ""
            End If


            DsDataSet = New DataSet()
            SqlDataAdapter1.SelectCommand = SqlSelectCommand1
            SqlDataAdapter1.SelectCommand.CommandText = StrQuery
            SqlDataAdapter1.SelectCommand.Connection = SqlConnection1
            SqlDataAdapter1.Fill(DsDataSet, "SearchResult")


            LvwSearchResult.Items.Clear()


            Dim IntRowCount As Integer
            IntRowCount = 0


            For Each DrRowPicker In DsDataSet.Tables("SearchResult").Rows
                    Dim StrSearchRow As String() = {DrRowPicker(0),
DrRowPicker(4), DrRowPicker(5), DrRowPicker(6), DrRowPicker(7)}
                    LvwSearchResult.Items.Add(New
ListViewItem(StrSearchRow))
                    IntRowCount += 1
            Next


            Dim IntRes As Integer
```

```
                        IntRes = CInt(Result)


                        If (IntRowCount = 0) Then
                                CmdPlaceOrder.Enabled = False
                        Else
                                CmdPlaceOrder.Enabled = True
                        End If


                        If IntRowCount = 0 Then
                                If (IntRes = 0) Then
                                        MessageBox.Show("Couldn't find this movie.")
                                ElseIf (IntRes = 1) Then
                                        MessageBox.Show("Couldn't find any movie of
this actor.")
                                ElseIf (IntRes = 2) Then
                                        MessageBox.Show("Couldn't find any movie of
this director.")
                                ElseIf (IntRes = 3) Then
                                        MessageBox.Show("Couldn't find any movie of
this producer.")
                                End If
                        End If


                        SqlConnection1.Close()
                        SqlConnection1.Dispose()
                        SqlSelectCommand1.Dispose()
                        SqlDataAdapter1.Dispose()
                End Sub


                Private Sub FrmSearch_Load(ByVal sender As System.Object, ByVal e As
System.EventArgs) Handles MyBase.Load
                        CmbBrowseBy.SelectedIndex = 0
                        CmdPlaceOrder.Enabled = False
                End Sub


                Public Sub SetRegistrationID(ByVal RegID As String)
                        StrRegistrationID = RegID
```

```
              End Sub

End Class
```

Summary

In this chapter, you learned to add functionality to the Search form. This chapter also described the functions you need to create in the Search form. Finally, you looked at the complete code for the Search form.

Chapter 15

*Adding
Functionality to
the Registration
Form*

In the preceding chapter, you learned to add functionality to the Search form. In this chapter, you will learn to add functionality to the Registration form of the Customer module.

Before you learn to add functionality to the form, let's review what it looks like (see Figure 15-1).

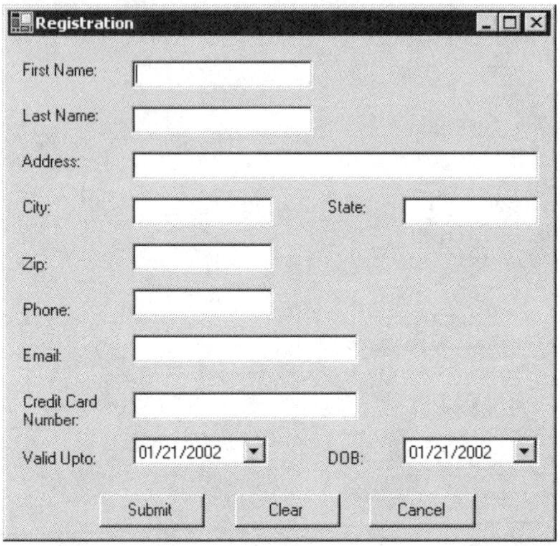

FIGURE 15-1 *The interface of the Registration form*

You learned to create the interface of the Registration form in Chapter 12, "Designing the User Interface of the Customer Module." Before you can add functionality to this form, you need to import the System.Data.SqlClient namespace. To import the namespace, you need to add the following statement to the Registration form:

```
Imports System.Data.SqlClient
'Imports classes used by the SQL Server .NET data provider
```

In addition to the preceding statement, you need to include the following statements in the Registration form:

```
Imports System.Data
'Includes the classes that make up the ADO.NET architecture
```

```
Imports System.Data.SqlTypes
'Includes the classes for native data types within SQL Server
```

In addition to including namespaces, you also need to declare the following variables in the Registration form:

```
Public Shared BlnFromSearchButton As Boolean
'Declares a Boolean variable to checks if the customer is a registered user
Public Shared ObjSearch As FrmSearch
'Declares an object of the FrmSearch class
```

The Registration form consists of the following functions:

- FrmRegistration_Load
- CmdSubmitReg_Click
- CmdClear_Click
- Empty_Controls
- CmdCancel_Click

The following sections describe the code you need to add to each of these functions.

The FrmRegistration_Load *Function*

The FrmRegistration_Load function executes before an instance of the FrmRegistration class displays. The code for the FrmRegistration_Load function is as follows:

```
Private Sub FrmRegistration_Load(ByVal sender As System.Object, ByVal e As
System.EventArgs) Handles MyBase.Load
        DtpDOB.Format = DateTimePickerFormat.Custom
'Specifies that the DtpDOB date time picker control displays the date-time value in
a customized format
        DtpDOB.CustomFormat = "MM/dd/yyyy"
'Sets the format for the DtpDOB date time picker control to MM/dd/yyyy
        DtpCCValidUpto.Format = DateTimePickerFormat.Custom
'Specifies that the DtpCCValidUpto date time picker control displays the date-time
value in a customized format
        DtpCCValidUpto.CustomFormat = "MM/dd/yyyy"
```

```
'Sets the format for the DtpCCValidUpto date time picker control to MM/dd/yyyy
End Sub
```

The `FrmRegistration_Load` function specifies the format in which date-time values are displayed in the two date time picker controls in the Registration form. This function specifies `MM/dd/yyyy` as the format for the `DtpDOB` and `DtpCC-ValidUpto` controls.

The CmdSubmitReg_Click Function

When the customer enters information in the Registration form and clicks on the Submit button, the `CmdSubmitReg_Click` function executes. The `CmdSubmit-Reg_Click` function checks and validates the data entered by the customer in the Registration form. If the customer has not specified any information, a message box stating this displays. If the customer has entered the required data, the data specified by the customer is added to the Customers table, and the customer is assigned a customer ID. Finally, the Registration form closes and the Search form displays.

The code for the `CmdSubmitReg_Click` function of the `FrmRegistration` class is as follows:

```
Private Sub CmdSubmitReg_Click(ByVal sender As System.Object, ByVal e As
System.EventArgs) Handles CmdSubmitReg.Click
        Dim StrQuery As String
        Dim SqlConnection1 As New SqlConnection(StrConnectionString)
        Dim SqlDataAdapter1 As New SqlDataAdapter()
'Declares variables

        If (TxtFName.Text.Trim = "") Then
'Checks if the customer has not entered the first name
                MessageBox.Show("Please enter the First name.", "Message Box",
MessageBoxButtons.OK)
'Displays a message asking the customer to enter the first name
                TxtFName.Focus()
'Sets the focus on the First Name text box
                Return
        End If
```

```
        If (TxtLName.Text.Trim = "") Then
'Checks if the customer has not entered the last name
                    MessageBox.Show("Please enter the Last name.", "Message Box",
MessageBoxButtons.OK)
'Displays a message asking the customer to enter the last name
                    TxtLName.Focus()
'Sets the focus on the Last Name text box
                    Return
        End If


        If (TxtAddress.Text.Trim = "") Then
'Checks if the customer has not entered the address
                    MessageBox.Show("Please enter the Address.", "Message Box",
MessageBoxButtons.OK)
'Displays a message asking the customer to enter the address
                    TxtAddress.Focus()
'Sets the focus on the Address text box
                    Return
        End If


        If (TxtCCNumber.Text.Trim = "") Then
'Checks if the customer has not entered the credit card number
                    MessageBox.Show("Please enter the Credit card number.", "Message
Box", MessageBoxButtons.OK)
'Displays a message asking the customer to enter the credit card number
                    TxtCCNumber.Focus()
'Sets the focus on the Credit Card Number text box
                    Return
        ElseIf (TxtCCNumber.Text.Trim.Length <> 16) Then
'Checks if the credit card number entered by the customer is not equal to 16 digits
                    MessageBox.Show("Invalid Credit card number. Please enter your
credit card number again.", "Message Box", MessageBoxButtons.OK)
'Displays a message asking the customer to enter a valid credit card number
                    TxtCCNumber.Focus()
'Sets the focus on the Credit Card Number text box
                    Return
        End If
```

```
        If (CDate(DtpCCValidUpto.Text) < Now()) Then
'Checks if the date entered by the customer is less than the current date
                MessageBox.Show("Invalid date.")
'Displays a message asking the customer to enter a valid date
                DtpCCValidUpto.Focus()
'Sets the focus on the Valid Upto date time picker control
            Return
        End If


        StrQuery = "INSERT INTO customer (FirstName, LastName, Address, City,
State, Zip, Phone, EMail, DOB, CreditCardNum, CreditCardValidUpto) VALUES (@FirstName,
" & _
        "@LastName, @Address, @City, @State, @Zip, @Phone, @EMail, @DOB,
@CreditCardNum, " & _
        "@CreditCardValidUpto)"
'Specifies the query to insert the details entered by the customer to the Customer
table
'Note that named parameter variables (variables prefixed with the @ symbol) are used
to assign values to the fields in the table


        Dim CmdString As New SqlCommand(StrQuery, SqlConnection1)
'Declares CmdString as an object of the SqlCommand object


        SqlDataAdapter1.InsertCommand = CmdString
'Specifies the query stored in the CmdString variable as the query to be executed
        SqlDataAdapter1.InsertCommand.Parameters.Add(New SqlParameter
("@FirstName", System.Data.SqlDbType.VarChar, 50, "FirstName"))
        SqlDataAdapter1.InsertCommand.Parameters(0).Value = TxtFName.Text
        SqlDataAdapter1.InsertCommand.Parameters.Add(New SqlParameter
("@LastName", System.Data.SqlDbType.VarChar, 50, "LastName"))
        SqlDataAdapter1.InsertCommand.Parameters(1).Value = TxtLName.Text
        SqlDataAdapter1.InsertCommand.Parameters.Add(New SqlParameter("@Address",
System.Data.SqlDbType.VarChar, 25, "Address"))
        SqlDataAdapter1.InsertCommand.Parameters(2).Value = TxtAddress.Text
        SqlDataAdapter1.InsertCommand.Parameters.Add(New SqlParameter("@City",
System.Data.SqlDbType.VarChar, 25, "City"))
        SqlDataAdapter1.InsertCommand.Parameters(3).Value = TxtCity.Text
        SqlDataAdapter1.InsertCommand.Parameters.Add(New SqlParameter("@State",
```

```
System.Data.SqlDbType.VarChar, 15, "State"))
        SqlDataAdapter1.InsertCommand.Parameters(4).Value = TxtState.Text
        SqlDataAdapter1.InsertCommand.Parameters.Add(New SqlParameter("@Zip",
System.Data.SqlDbType.VarChar, 7, "Zip"))
        SqlDataAdapter1.InsertCommand.Parameters(5).Value = TxtZip.Text
        SqlDataAdapter1.InsertCommand.Parameters.Add(New SqlParameter("@Phone",
System.Data.SqlDbType.VarChar, 10, "Phone"))
        SqlDataAdapter1.InsertCommand.Parameters(6).Value = TxtPhone.Text
        SqlDataAdapter1.InsertCommand.Parameters.Add(New SqlParameter("@EMail",
System.Data.SqlDbType.VarChar, 50, "EMail"))
        SqlDataAdapter1.InsertCommand.Parameters(7).Value = TxtEmail.Text
        SqlDataAdapter1.InsertCommand.Parameters.Add(New SqlParameter("@DOB",
System.Data.SqlDbType.DateTime, 8, "DOB"))
        SqlDataAdapter1.InsertCommand.Parameters(8).Value = DtpDOB.Text
        SqlDataAdapter1.InsertCommand.Parameters.Add(New
SqlParameter("@CreditCardNum", System.Data.SqlDbType.VarChar, 16, "CreditCardNum"))
        SqlDataAdapter1.InsertCommand.Parameters(9).Value = TxtCCNumber.Text
        SqlDataAdapter1.InsertCommand.Parameters.Add(New
SqlParameter("@CreditCardValidUpto", System.Data.SqlDbType.DateTime, 8,
"CreditCardValidUpto"))
        SqlDataAdapter1.InsertCommand.Parameters(10).Value = DtpCCValidUpto.Text
'Associates the named parameter variables with the fields in the table
'Assigns the value specified by the customer in the controls to the named parameter
variables


        Dim LCustID As Long
        Try
                SqlConnection1.Open()
'Establishes a connection
                SqlDataAdapter1.InsertCommand.ExecuteNonQuery()
'Executes the query
                CmdString.CommandText = "SELECT MAX(CustID) from Customer"
'Specifies the query to be executed
                LCustID = CmdString.ExecuteScalar
'Stores the first column of the first row of the results returned by the query in
the LCustID variable
                Dim Strmsg As String
                Strmsg = CStr(LCustID)
```

```
'Converts the Customer ID stored in the LCustID variable into the string data type
and stores it in the Strmsg variable
                        MessageBox.Show("Customer's registration ID is: " & Strmsg,
"Message Box", MessageBoxButtons.OK, MessageBoxIcon.Information)
'Displays a message informing the customer of the ID assigned to the customer
        Catch MyException As SqlException
                        MessageBox.Show(("Source: " & MyException.Source &
ControlChars.Cr & _
                            "Number: " & MyException.Number.ToString() &
ControlChars.Cr & _
                            "State: " & MyException.State.ToString() &
ControlChars.Cr & _
                            "Class: " & MyException.Class.ToString() &
ControlChars.Cr & _
                            "Server: " & MyException.Server & ControlChars.Cr & _
                            "Message: " & MyException.Message & ControlChars.Cr & _
                            "Procedure: " & MyException.Procedure & ControlChars.Cr
& _
                            "Line: " & MyException.LineNumber.ToString()))

                    CmdString.Dispose()
'Releases the resources used by the CmdString object in case an exception occurs
                    SqlConnection1.Close()
'Closes the SqlConnection1 object in case an exception occurs
                    SqlConnection1. Dispose ()
'Releases the resources used by the SqlConnection1 object in case an exception
occurs
                    SqlDataAdapter1.Dispose()
'Releases the resources used by the SqlDataAdapter1 object in case an exception
occurs
                    Return
        End Try

        MessageBox.Show("The record has been added.", "Record added",
MessageBoxButtons.OK, MessageBoxIcon.Information)
```

```
'Displays a message informing the customer that the record has been added

        ObjSearch = New FrmSearch()
'Creates a new instance of the Search form
        ObjSearch.SetRegistrationID(CStr(LCustID))
'Opens the Search form and passes the ID of the customer to the SetRegistrationID
function

        CmdString.Dispose()
'Releases the resources used by the CmdString object
        SqlConnection1.Close()
'Closes the SqlConnection1 object
        SqlDataAdapter1.Dispose()
'Closes the SqlDataAdapter1 object
        Me.Close()
'Closes the Registration form
End Sub
```

The CmdClear_Click Function

The CmdClear_Click function executes when the customer clicks on the Clear button in the Registration form. The code for the CmdClear_Click function is as follows:

```
Private Sub CmdClear_Click(ByVal sender As System.Object, ByVal e As System.EventArgs)
Handles CmdClear.Click
        Empty_Controls()
'Calls the Empty_Controls function
End Sub
```

When a customer clicks on the Clear button, the Empty_Controls function is invoked. You will learn about the Empty_Controls function in the next section.

The Empty_Controls Function

As the name suggests, the Empty_Controls function clears the controls in the Registration form.

The code of the Empty_Controls function is given below.

```
Private Sub Empty_Controls()
        TxtFName.Text = ""
'Clears the First Name text box
        TxtFName.Focus()
'Sets the focus on the First Name text box
        TxtLName.Text = ""
'Clears the Last Name text box
        TxtAddress.Text = ""
'Clears the Address text box
        TxtCity.Text = ""
'Clears the City text box
        TxtState.Text = ""
'Clears the State text box
        TxtZip.Text = ""
'Clears the Zip text box
        TxtPhone.Text = ""
'Clears the Phone text box
        TxtEmail.Text = ""
'Clears the EMail text box
        TxtCCNumber.Text = ""
'Clears the Credit Card Number text box
        DtpCCValidUpto.Text = ""
'Clears the Valid Upto date time picker control
        DtpDOB.Text = ""
'Clears the DOB date time picker control
End Sub
```

In addition to clearing all the controls in the Registration form, the Empty_ Controls function sets the focus on the First Name text box.

The CmdCancel_Click Function

The CmdCancel_Click function executes when a customer clicks on the Cancel button in the Registration form. The code for the CmdCancel_Click function is as follows:

```
Private Sub CmdCancel_Click(ByVal sender As System.Object, ByVal e As
System.EventArgs) Handles CmdCancel.Click
        Me.Close()
'Closes the Registration form
End Sub
```

A customer can click on the Cancel button to close the Registration form.

Complete Code for the Registration Form

In the preceding sections, you looked at code for the functions in the Registration form. Listing 15-1 lists the complete code for the Registration form.

Listing 15-1 The Code for the Registration Form

```
Imports System.Data
Imports System.Data.SqlClient
Imports System.Data.SqlTypes


Public Class FrmRegistration
        Inherits System.Windows.Forms.Form


        Public Shared BlnFromSearchButton As Boolean
        Public Shared ObjSearch As FrmSearch
Windows Form Designer generated code
'Contains the code that specifies the size, location, and other properties, such as
font and name, for the controls on the form.
        Private Sub CmdSubmitReg_Click(ByVal sender As System.Object, ByVal e As
System.EventArgs) Handles CmdSubmitReg.Click
                Dim StrQuery As String
                Dim SqlConnection1 As New SqlConnection(StrConnectionString)
                Dim SqlDataAdapter1 As New SqlDataAdapter()
                If (TxtFName.Text.Trim = "") Then
                        MessageBox.Show("Please enter the First name.",
"Message Box", MessageBoxButtons.OK)
                        TxtFName.Focus()
```

```
                              Return
                End If
                If (TxtLName.Text.Trim = "") Then
                              MessageBox.Show("Please enter the Last name.",
"Message Box", MessageBoxButtons.OK)
                              TxtLName.Focus()
                              Return
                End If
                If (TxtAddress.Text.Trim = "") Then
                              MessageBox.Show("Please enter the Address.",
"Message Box", MessageBoxButtons.OK)
                              TxtAddress.Focus()
                              Return
                End If
                If (TxtCCNumber.Text.Trim = "") Then
                              MessageBox.Show("Please enter the Credit card
number.", "Message Box", MessageBoxButtons.OK)
                              TxtCCNumber.Focus()
                              Return
                ElseIf (TxtCCNumber.Text.Trim.Length <> 16) Then
                              MessageBox.Show("Invalid Credit card number. Please
enter your credit card number again.", "Message Box", MessageBoxButtons.OK)
                              TxtCCNumber.Focus()
                              Return
                End If
                If (CDate(DtpCCValidUpto.Text) < Now()) Then
                              MessageBox.Show("Invalid date.") ', "Message Box",
MessageBoxButtons.OK)
                              DtpCCValidUpto.Focus()
                              Return
                End If


                StrQuery = "INSERT INTO customer (FirstName, LastName, Address,
City, State, Zip, Phone, EMail, DOB, CreditCardNum, CreditCardValidUpto) VALUES
(@FirstName, " & _
                "@LastName, @Address, @City, @State, @Zip, @Phone, @EMail, @DOB,
@CreditCardNum, " & _
```

```
                    "@CreditCardValidUpto)"

                    Dim CmdString As New SqlCommand(StrQuery, SqlConnection1)

                    SqlDataAdapter1.InsertCommand = CmdString
                    SqlDataAdapter1.InsertCommand.Parameters.Add(New
SqlParameter("@FirstName", System.Data.SqlDbType.VarChar, 50, "FirstName"))
                    SqlDataAdapter1.InsertCommand.Parameters(0).Value = TxtFName.Text
                    SqlDataAdapter1.InsertCommand.Parameters.Add(New
SqlParameter("@LastName", System.Data.SqlDbType.VarChar, 50, "LastName"))
                    SqlDataAdapter1.InsertCommand.Parameters(1).Value = TxtLName.Text
                    SqlDataAdapter1.InsertCommand.Parameters.Add(New
SqlParameter("@Address", System.Data.SqlDbType.VarChar, 25, "Address"))
                    SqlDataAdapter1.InsertCommand.Parameters(2).Value = TxtAddress.Text
                    SqlDataAdapter1.InsertCommand.Parameters.Add(New
SqlParameter("@City", System.Data.SqlDbType.VarChar, 25, "City"))
                    SqlDataAdapter1.InsertCommand.Parameters(3).Value = TxtCity.Text
                    SqlDataAdapter1.InsertCommand.Parameters.Add(New
SqlParameter("@State", System.Data.SqlDbType.VarChar, 15, "State"))
                    SqlDataAdapter1.InsertCommand.Parameters(4).Value = TxtState.Text
                    SqlDataAdapter1.InsertCommand.Parameters.Add(New
SqlParameter("@Zip", System.Data.SqlDbType.VarChar, 7, "Zip"))
                    SqlDataAdapter1.InsertCommand.Parameters(5).Value = TxtZip.Text
                    SqlDataAdapter1.InsertCommand.Parameters.Add(New
SqlParameter("@Phone", System.Data.SqlDbType.VarChar, 10, "Phone"))
                    SqlDataAdapter1.InsertCommand.Parameters(6).Value = TxtPhone.Text
                    SqlDataAdapter1.InsertCommand.Parameters.Add(New
SqlParameter("@EMail", System.Data.SqlDbType.VarChar, 50, "EMail"))
                    SqlDataAdapter1.InsertCommand.Parameters(7).Value = TxtEmail.Text
                    SqlDataAdapter1.InsertCommand.Parameters.Add(New
SqlParameter("@DOB", System.Data.SqlDbType.DateTime, 8, "DOB"))
                    SqlDataAdapter1.InsertCommand.Parameters(8).Value = DtpDOB.Text
                    SqlDataAdapter1.InsertCommand.Parameters.Add(New
SqlParameter("@CreditCardNum", System.Data.SqlDbType.VarChar, 16, "CreditCardNum"))
                    SqlDataAdapter1.InsertCommand.Parameters(9).Value =
TxtCCNumber.Text
                    SqlDataAdapter1.InsertCommand.Parameters.Add(New
```

```
SqlParameter("@CreditCardValidUpto", System.Data.SqlDbType.DateTime, 8,
"CreditCardValidUpto"))
                        SqlDataAdapter1.InsertCommand.Parameters(10).Value =
DtpCCValidUpto.Text

                Dim LCustID As Long
                Try
                        SqlConnection1.Open()
                        SqlDataAdapter1.InsertCommand.ExecuteNonQuery()
                        CmdString.CommandText = "SELECT MAX(CustID) from
Customer"

                        LCustID = CmdString.ExecuteScalar
                        Dim Strmsg As String
                        Strmsg = CStr(LCustID)
                        MessageBox.Show("Customer's registration ID is: " &
Strmsg, "Message Box", MessageBoxButtons.OK, MessageBoxIcon.Information)

                Catch MyException As SqlException
                        MessageBox.Show(("Source: " & MyException.Source &
ControlChars.Cr & _
                                "Number: " & MyException.Number.ToString()
& ControlChars.Cr & _
                                "State: " & MyException.State.ToString() &
ControlChars.Cr & _
                                "Class: " & MyException.Class.ToString() &
ControlChars.Cr & _
                                 "Server: " & MyException.Server &
ControlChars.Cr & _
                                 "Message: " & MyException.Message &
ControlChars.Cr & _
                                "Procedure: " & MyException.Procedure &
ControlChars.Cr & _
                                "Line: " &
MyException.LineNumber.ToString()))

                        CmdString.Dispose()
                        SqlConnection1.Close()
```

```
                            SqlConnection1.Dispose()
                            SqlDataAdapter1.Dispose()
                            Return
                End Try

                            MessageBox.Show("The record has been added.", "Record added",
MessageBoxButtons.OK, MessageBoxIcon.Information)

                            ObjSearch = New FrmSearch()
                            ObjSearch.SetRegistrationID(CStr(LCustID))

                            CmdString.Dispose()
                            SqlConnection1.Close()
                            SqlDataAdapter1.Dispose()
                            Me.Close()
                End Sub


                Private Sub CmdClear_Click(ByVal sender As System.Object, ByVal e As
System.EventArgs) Handles CmdClear.Click
                            Empty_Controls()
                End Sub


                Private Sub CmdCancel_Click(ByVal sender As System.Object, ByVal e As
System.EventArgs) Handles CmdCancel.Click
                            Me.Close()
                End Sub
                Private Sub Empty_Controls()
                            TxtFName.Text = ""
                            TxtFName.Focus() 'Set focus on first control
                            TxtLName.Text = ""
                            TxtAddress.Text = ""
                            TxtCity.Text = ""
                            TxtState.Text = ""
                            TxtZip.Text = ""
                            TxtPhone.Text = ""
                            TxtEmail.Text = ""
                            TxtCCNumber.Text = ""
                            DtpCCValidUpto.Text = ""
```

```
                    DtpDOB.Text = ""
        End Sub

        Private Sub FrmRegistration_Load(ByVal sender As System.Object, ByVal e As
System.EventArgs) Handles MyBase.Load
                    DtpDOB.Format = DateTimePickerFormat.Custom
                    DtpDOB.CustomFormat = "MM/dd/yyyy"
                    DtpCCValidUpto.Format = DateTimePickerFormat.Custom
                    DtpCCValidUpto.CustomFormat = "MM/dd/yyyy"
        End Sub
End Class
```

Summary

In this chapter, you learned to add functionality to the Registration form. You also learned about the functions you need to create in the Registration form. Finally, you looked at the complete code for the Registration form.

Chapter 16

**Adding
Functionality to
the Place Order
Form**

In the preceding chapter, you learned to add functionality to the Registration form of the Customer module. In this chapter, you will learn to add functionality to the Place Order form.

To start with, let's review what the Place Order form looks like (see Figure 16-1).

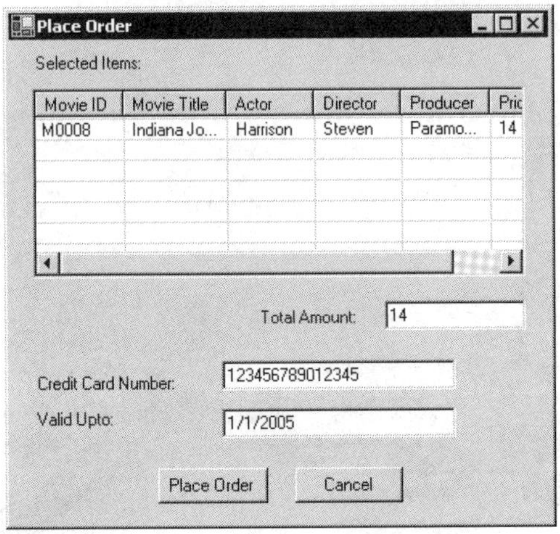

FIGURE 16-1 *The interface of the Place Order form*

You already know how to create the interface of the Place Order form. To add functionality to this form, you need to add a data adapter object to it.

The steps to add a SqlDataAdapter object to the Place Order form are as follows:

1. Select and drag the SqlDataAdapter control from the Data tab of the Toolbox to the form. When you do so, the SqlDataAdapter1 object is added to the form, and the first screen of the Data Adapter Configuration Wizard displays. Figure 16-2 shows the first screen of the Data Adapter Configuration Wizard.

2. Click on the Next button in this first screen to continue. The second screen of the Data Adapter Configuration Wizard displays. Figure 16-3 shows this second screen.

FIGURE 16-2 *The first screen of the Data Adapter Configuration Wizard*

FIGURE 16-3 *The second screen of the Data Adapter Configuration Wizard*

In the second screen, you can specify the connection that the data adapter should use. You can either create a new connection or select an existing one from the drop-down list.

To create a new connection, you need to click on the New Connection button. When you click on this button, the Data Link Properties dialog box displays. This dialog box contains four tabs—Provider, Connection, Advanced, and All. You need to specify the name of the server and database in the Connection tab. In this tab, you also need to specify the username and password. The Provider tab enables you to edit the provider to be used. After you specify the settings, you can click on the Test Connection button to check the settings. If the settings are correct and the connection is established, a message box appears confirming this.

3. Click on the Next button in the second screen of the Data Adapter Configuration Wizard. The third screen of the wizard displays. Figure 16-4 shows the third screen of the Data Adapter Configuration Wizard.

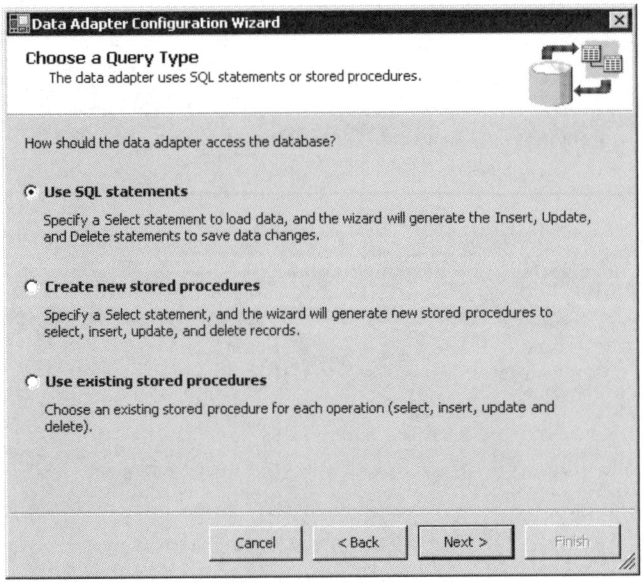

FIGURE 16-4 *The third screen of the Data Adapter Configuration Wizard*

In the third screen of the wizard, you can specify whether the data adapter should use SQL statements or stored procedures to access the database.

4. Select the Use SQL statements option in the third screen of the wizard and click on the Next button. The screen that displays next depends on the option you selected. When you select the Use SQL statements option, the screen shown in Figure 16-5 displays. This screen enables you to specify the SQL Select statement to be used.

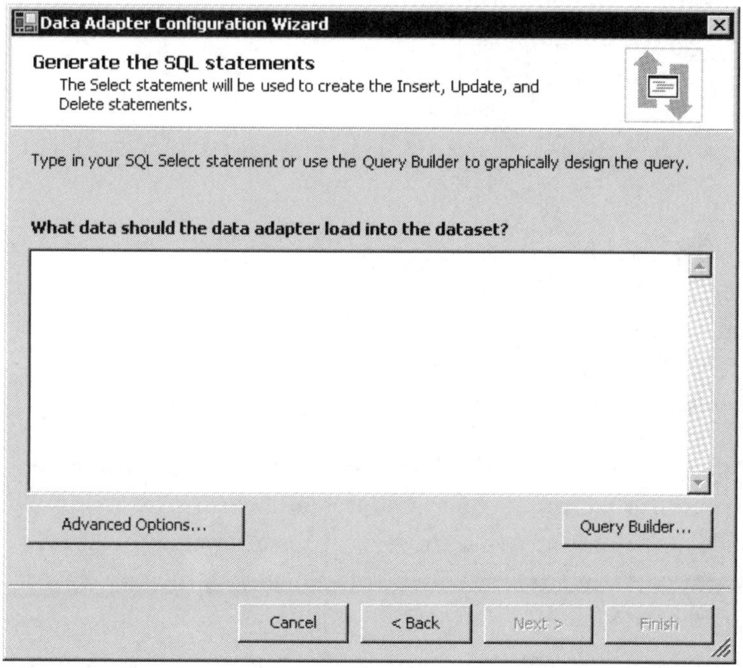

FIGURE 16-5 *The screen to specify the SQL statement when the Use SQL statements option is selected*

In this screen, you can either type a SQL Select statement or use the Query Builder to create a query. You can click on the Query Builder button to use this feature. You can also set advanced options to specify how the wizard should create the Insert, Update, and Delete commands for the data adapter. To specify these advanced options, you need to click on the Advanced Options button.

5. Click on the Next button to open the last screen of the wizard. This screen provides a list of the tasks that the wizard has performed, as shown in Figure 16-6.

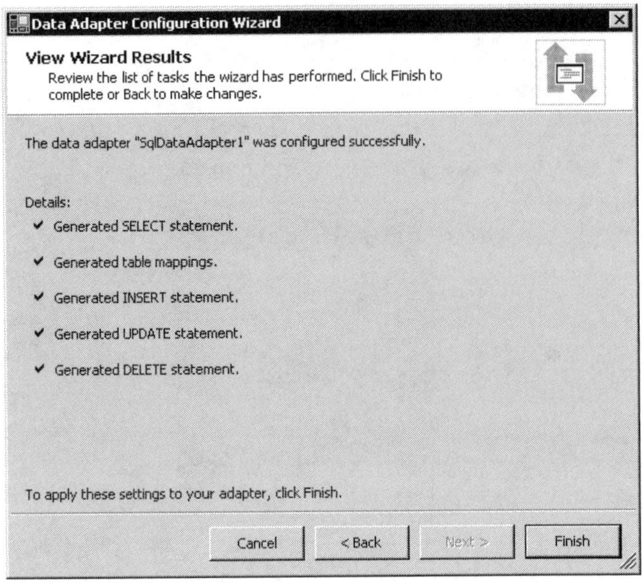

FIGURE 16-6 *The last screen of the Data Adapter Configuration Wizard*

As shown in Figure 16-6, the last screen of the wizard informs you that the wizard has successful configured the `SqlDataAdapter1` object. The last screen also indicates that the wizard has generated the `Select`, `Insert`, `Update`, and `Delete` statements along with the table mappings for the data adapter.

6. Click on the Finish button in the last screen to complete the process of configuring the data adapter. When you click on this button, the selected settings are applied to the data adapter. Note that an object of the `SqlConnection` class also appears on the Place Order form.

After you add the data adapter object to the Place Order form, the form appears as shown in Figure 16-7.

To use the data adapter and connection object, you need to import the `System.Data.SqlClient` namespace by adding the following statement to the Place Order form:

```
Imports System.Data.SqlClient

'Imports classes used by the SQL Server .NET data provider
```

In addition to the preceding statement, you need to include the following statements in the Place Order form:

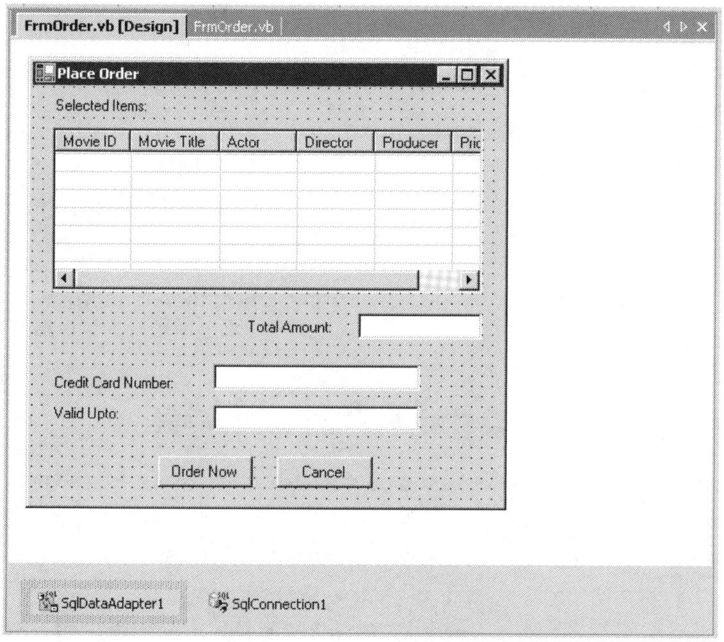

FIGURE 16-7 *The Place Order form after adding the data adapter*

```
Imports System
Imports System.Data
'Includes the classes that make up the ADO.NET architecture
Imports System.String
'Includes the classes that enable you to work with strings
Imports System.Collections
'Includes the collection classes
Imports System.Data.SqlTypes
'Includes the classes for native data types within SQL Server
```

You also need to declare the following global variables in the Place Order form:

```
Private Shared IntSelectedCount As Integer
'Used to store the number of selected records
Private StrRegistrationID As String
'Used to store the customer ID
Private Shared ArraySelectedMovieID() As String = New String(10) {}
'Used to store the Movie IDs of the selected records
```

The Place Order form consists of the following functions:

◆ SetRegistrationID

◆ SetSelectedMovies

◆ FrmOrder_Load

◆ CmdOrderNow_Click

◆ GetAutoGeneratedOrderID

◆ CmdCancel_Click

The following sections describe the code associated with these functions.

The **SetRegistrationID** *Function*

As discussed in previous chapters, when a customer enters his or her customer ID in the Main form and clicks on the Submit button, the ID entered by the customer is validated. In addition, after the ID is validated, the Main form passes the ID to the SetRegistrationID function of the FrmSearch class. When the customer selects movies in the Search form and clicks on the Place Order button, the SetRegistrationID function of the FrmOrder class is called.

The code for the SetRegistrationID function is as follows:

```
Public Sub SetRegistrationID(ByVal RegID As String)
'Takes the ID entered by the customer as a parameter
        StrRegistrationID = RegID
'Assigns the value in the RegID variable to the StrRegistrationID variable
End Sub
```

The SetRegistrationID function accepts the customer ID of the customer as a parameter. The customer ID is then stored in the StrRegistrationID variable.

The **SetSelectedMovies** *Function*

When the customer selects one or more movies in the Search form and clicks on the Place Order button, the SetSelectedMovies function is called. The CmdPlaceOrder_Click function of the FrmSearch class invokes the SetSelected Movies function of the FrmOrder class.

The code for the SetSelectedMovies function of the FrmOrder class is as follows:

```
Public Sub SetSelectedMovies(ByVal ArrayMovieID() As String, ByVal
IntTotalSelectedCount As Integer)
        Dim i As Integer
        IntSelectedCount = IntTotalSelectedCount
        For i = 0 To IntTotalSelectedCount - 1
                ArraySelectedMovieID(i) = ArrayMovieID(i)
        Next i
End Sub
```

As shown in preceding code, the SetSelectedMovies function takes two parameters. The first parameter, ArrayMovieID, stores the movie IDs associated with the records selected by the customer. The second parameter, IntTotalSelectedCount, stores the number of records selected by the customer.

The SetSelectedMovies function stores the movie IDs of the selected records and the number of selected records in the ArraySelectedMovieID array and the IntSelectedCount variable, respectively. The ArraySelectedMovieID array and IntSelectedCount variable are global variables accessed in the FrmOrder_Load function.

The FrmOrder_Load *Function*

The FrmOrder_Load function executes when the Place Order form loads. The code for the FrmOrder_Load function is as follows:

```
Private Sub FrmOrder_Load(ByVal sender As System.Object, ByVal e As
System.EventArgs) Handles MyBase.Load
        Dim DsDataSet As DataSet
        Dim DrRowPicker As DataRow
        Dim DrRowPicker2 As DataRow
        Dim StrConnectionString As String
        Dim StrBrowseBy As String
        Dim StrQuery As String
        Dim Result As Integer
        Dim StrMessage As String
        Dim SelectCmd As New SqlCommand()
'Declares variables
```

```
        If IntSelectedCount < 1 Then
'Checks if the customer has not selected any items
            Me.Close()
'Closes the Place Order form
        End If


        Dim i As Integer
        Dim StrTemp As String
        For i = 0 To IntSelectedCount - 1
            StrTemp += "'"
'Adds a single quotation mark
            StrTemp += ArraySelectedMovieID(i)
'Stores the ID of the selected movies in the StrTemp string
            StrTemp += "'"
'Adds another single quotation mark
            If i < IntSelectedCount - 1 Then
                StrTemp += ","
'Adds a comma to separate the movie IDs in the StrTemp string
            End If
        Next i


        StrQuery = "SELECT DISTINCT a.MovID, a.MovTitle, b.FirstName AS Actor,
c.FirstName AS Director, d.name AS Producer, f.Price as Price FROM movie a, actor b,
director c, producer d, actormovie e, video f WHERE a.MovID = e.MovID AND e.ActorID =
b.ActorID AND a.DirID = c.DirID AND a.ProdID = d.ProdID AND a.MovID = f.MovID AND
a.Movid in (" & StrTemp & ")"
'Specifies the query to search for the Movie ID, Movie Title, Actor, Director,
Producer, and Price associated with the movies selected by the customer
        DsDataSet = New DataSet()
'Creates a dataset


        SqlDataAdapter1.SelectCommand = SelectCmd
        SqlDataAdapter1.SelectCommand.Connection = SqlConnection1
'Associates the SqlDataAdapter1 object with the SqlConnection1 object
        SqlDataAdapter1.SelectCommand.CommandText = StrQuery
'Specifies the query stored in the StrQuery variable as the query to be executed
        SqlDataAdapter1.Fill(DsDataSet, "SearchResult2")
'Populates the SearchResult2 table in the DsDataSet dataset with the query results
```

```
            LvwItemsOrdered.Items.Clear()
'Clears the list view control before displaying the result


            Dim DblTotalCost As Double
            For Each DrRowPicker In DsDataSet.Tables("SearchResult2").Rows
                    Dim StrSearchRow As String() = {DrRowPicker(0), DrRowPicker(1),
DrRowPicker(2), DrRowPicker(3), DrRowPicker(4), DrRowPicker(5)}
'Picks up the values of the Movie ID, Movie Title, First Name of Actor, First Name
of Director, Producer name, and Price for each record in the dataset and adds it to
the StrSearchRow array
                    LvwItemsOrdered.Items.Add(New ListViewItem(StrSearchRow))
'Displays each member of the StrSearchRow array in the list view control
                    DblTotalCost += CDbl(DrRowPicker(5))
'Adds the price of each movie to the DblTotalCost variable to calculate the total
cost for the movies
            Next


            TxtTotalAmount.Text = DblTotalCost
'Displays the total cost of the movies in the Total Amount text box


            StrQuery = "SELECT CreditCardNum, CreditCardValidUpto FROM customer WHERE
CustID = '" & StrRegistrationID & "'"
'Specifies the query to retrieve the credit card number and the validity of the
credit card for the customer
            SqlDataAdapter1.SelectCommand.CommandText = StrQuery
'Specifies the query stored in the StrQuery variable as the query to be executed
            SqlDataAdapter1.Fill(DsDataSet, "CreditCardInfo")
'Populates the CreditCardInfo table in the dataset with the query results
            For Each DrRowPicker2 In DsDataSet.Tables("CreditCardInfo").Rows
                    TxtCCNumber.Text = DrRowPicker2(0)
'Displays the credit card number in the Credit Card Number text box
                    TxtValidUpto.Text = DrRowPicker2(1) 'Card Validity
'Displays the validity of the credit card in the Valid upto text box
            Next


            SqlConnection1.Close()
'Closes the SqlConnection1 object
            SqlDataAdapter1.Dispose()
```

```
'Closes the SqlDataAdapter1 object
End Sub
```

In the Place Order form, the `FrmOrder_Load` function performs the following tasks:

- ◆ It populates the list view control with the details of the movies selected by the customer.
- ◆ It displays the credit card information for the customer.

Therefore, when the customer opens the Place Order form, the list view control displays the details of the movies selected by the customer in the Search form. In addition, the credit card information for the customer is displayed.

The CmdOrderNow_Click *Function*

When a customer selects one or more records from the list view control in the Search form and clicks on the Place Order button, the Place Order form displays. The Place Order form displays the details of the movies selected by the customer. It also displays the customer's credit card details. To place an order for the movies displayed in the list view control, the customer clicks on the Order Now button. The `CmdOrderNow_Click` function executes when the customer clicks on the Order Now button.

The code of the `CmdOrderNow_Click` function is as follows:

```
Private Sub CmdOrderNow_Click(ByVal sender As System.Object, ByVal e As
System.EventArgs) Handles CmdOrderNow.Click
        Dim StrQuery As String
        Dim StrOrderID As String
        Dim StrTemp As String
        Dim IntOrderID As Integer
'Declares variables

        StrOrderID = GetAutoGeneratedOrderID()
'Calls the GetAutoGeneratedOrderID function and stores the maximum Order ID
returned by the GetAutoGeneratedOrderID function in the StrOrderID variable
        StrOrderID = StrOrderID.Substring(1, 4)
'Retrieves the integer part of the order ID
        IntOrderID = CInt(StrOrderID) + 1
```

```
'Increments the Order ID by 1 and stores it in the IntOrderID variable
        StrTemp = CStr(IntOrderID)
'Converts the value in the IntOrderID variable to the string data type and stores
the value in the StrTemp variable
        StrOrderID = "'"
'Adds a single quotation mark
        StrOrderID += "0"
'Stores 0 as the first character in the StrOrderID string
        If StrTemp.Length = 1 Then
                        StrOrderID += "000"
                ElseIf StrTemp.Length = 2 Then
                        StrOrderID += "00"
                ElseIf StrTemp.Length = 3 Then
                        StrOrderID += "0"
'Adds 000,00, or 0 to the StrOrderID string based on the length of the StrTemp
variable
        End If
        StrOrderID += StrTemp
'Concatenates the StrTemp to the StrOrderID string
        StrOrderID += "'"
'Adds another single quotation mark

        Dim i As Integer
        StrTemp = ""
'Reinitializes the StrTemp string
        For i = 0 To IntSelectedCount - 1
                StrTemp += "'"
'Adds a single quotation mark
                StrTemp += ArraySelectedMovieID(i)
'Stores the IDs of the selected movies in the StrTemp string
                StrTemp += "'"
'Adds another single quotation mark
                If i < IntSelectedCount - 1 Then
                        StrTemp += ","
'Adds a comma to separate the movie IDs in the StrTemp string
                End If
        Next i
```

```
        Dim StrSelectString As String
        StrSelectString = "SELECT MAX(VideoID), COUNT(MovID) from Video WHERE MovID
IN (" & StrTemp & ") GROUP BY MovID"
'Returns the Video IDs for the selected Movie IDs


        Dim DsDataSet As DataSet
        DsDataSet = New DataSet()
'Creates the dataset object
        Dim SelectCmd As New SqlCommand(StrSelectString, SqlConnection1)
        Try
                SqlDataAdapter1.SelectCommand = SelectCmd
                SqlConnection1.Open()
'Establishes the connection
                SqlDataAdapter1.Fill(DsDataSet, "VideoInfo")
'Populates the VideoInfo tables in the DsDataSet dataset with the query results
                Catch MyException As SqlException
                MessageBox.Show(("Source: " & MyException.Source &
ControlChars.Cr & _
                        "Number: " & MyException.Number.ToString() &
ControlChars.Cr & _
                        "State: " & MyException.State.ToString() &
ControlChars.Cr & _
                        "Class: " & MyException.Class.ToString() &
ControlChars.Cr & _
                        "Server: " & MyException.Server & ControlChars.Cr & _
                        "Message: " & MyException.Message & ControlChars.Cr
& _
                        "Procedure: " & MyException.Procedure &
ControlChars.Cr & _
                        "Line: " & MyException.LineNumber.ToString()))
'Displays an error message showing the details of the error

                SqlConnection1.Close()
'Closes the SqlConnection1 object
                SelectCmd.Dispose()
'Releases the resources used by the SelectCmd object
                SqlDataAdapter1.Dispose()
```

```
'Closes the SqlDataAdapter1 object
                        Return
            End Try

            Dim DrRowPicker As DataRow
            Dim StrVideoList As String
            Dim StrMovieCount As String
            Dim NTotalCount, NCount As Integer
'Declares variables

            NCount = 0
'Initializes the NCount variable to zero
            NTotalCount = DsDataSet.Tables("VideoInfo").Rows.Count()
'Stores the number of rows in the VideoInfo table in the NTotalCount variable

            Dim ArrayVideoList() As String = New String(10) {}
'Declares the ArrayVideoList array
            For Each DrRowPicker In DsDataSet.Tables("VideoInfo").Rows
                    StrVideoList += "'"
'Adds a single quotation mark
                    StrVideoList += DrRowPicker(0)
'Stores the Video IDs from the dataset in the StrVideoList string
                    StrVideoList += "'"
'Adds another single quotation mark
                    ArrayVideoList(NCount) = StrVideoList
'Stores the value in the StrVideoList string in the ArrayVideoList array
                    NCount += 1
'Increments the NCount variable by 1
                    StrMovieCount = DrRowPicker(1)
'Stores the movie count in the StrMovieCount variable
            Next

            Dim StrTotalOrderValue As String
            StrQuery = "SELECT SUM(Price) FROM Video WHERE VideoID IN (" &
StrVideoList & ")"
'Specifies the query to calculate the total price of the movies ordered by the cus-
tomer
            SqlDataAdapter1.SelectCommand.CommandText = StrQuery
```

```
'Specifies the query stored in the StrQuery variable as the query to be executed
        SqlDataAdapter1.Fill(DsDataSet, "OrderValue")
'Populates the OrderValue table in the DsDataSet dataset with the query results
        StrTotalOrderValue = DsDataSet.Tables("OrderValue").Rows(0).Item(0)
'Stores the first column of the first row in the results returned by the query in
the StrTotalOrderValue variable


        Dim StrTotalQty As String
        StrQuery = "SELECT COUNT(VideoID) FROM Video WHERE VideoID IN (" &
StrVideoList & ")"
'Specifies the query to calculate the number of items ordered by the customer
        SqlDataAdapter1.SelectCommand.CommandText = StrQuery
'Specifies the query stored in the StrQuery variable as the query to be executed
        SqlDataAdapter1.Fill(DsDataSet, "TotalQty")
'Populates the TotalQty table in the DsDataSet dataset with the query results
        StrTotalQty = DsDataSet.Tables("TotalQty").Rows(0).Item(0)
'Stores the first column of the first row in the results returned by the query in
the StrTotalQty variable


        Dim StrVideoID As String
        Dim j As Integer
        Dim IntQtyOrdered As Integer
        Dim StrTemp1 As String
'Declares variables


        StrQuery = "INSERT INTO Orders (OrderID, OrderDate, CustID,
TotalQtyOrdered, OrderValue) VALUES (" & StrOrderID & ", @OrderDate, @CustID," &
StrTotalQty & "," & StrTotalOrderValue & "); SELECT OrderID, OrderDate, CustID,
OrderValue FROM Orders WHERE OrderID = " & StrOrderID
'Specifies the query to insert data into the Orders table
        Dim InsertCmd As New SqlCommand(StrQuery, SqlConnection1)
'Creates the InsertCmd object of the SqlCommand class
        SqlDataAdapter1.InsertCommand = InsertCmd
'Specifies the query stored in the InsertCmd variable as the query to be executed
        SqlDataAdapter1.InsertCommand.Parameters.Add(New SqlParameter
("@OrderDate", System.Data.SqlDbType.DateTime, 8, "OrderDate"))
'Associates the @OrderDate parameter with the OrderDate field in the table
        SqlDataAdapter1.InsertCommand.Parameters(0).Value = Now()
```

```
'Assigns the system date to the @OrderDate parameter
        SqlDataAdapter1.InsertCommand.Parameters.Add(New SqlParameter("@CustID",
System.Data.SqlDbType.SmallInt, 2, "CustID"))
'Associates the @CustID parameter with the CustID field in the table
        SqlDataAdapter1.InsertCommand.Parameters(1).Value = StrRegistrationID
'Assigns the value stored in the StrRegistrationID to the @CustID parameter
        SqlDataAdapter1.InsertCommand.Parameters.Add(New SqlParameter
("@OrderValue", System.Data.SqlDbType.Money, 8, "OrderValue"))
'Associates the @OrderValue parameter with the OrderValue field in the table
        SqlDataAdapter1.InsertCommand.Parameters(2).Value =
CDbl(TxtTotalAmount.Text)
'Assigns the value in the Total Amount text box to the @OrderValue parameter


        Try
                SqlDataAdapter1.InsertCommand.ExecuteNonQuery()
'Executing the query


                For j = 0 To NCount - 1
                        StrVideoID = ArrayVideoList(j)
'Picks up a Video ID from the ArrayVideoList array
                        IntQtyOrdered = CInt(StrMovieCount)
'Stores the movie count in the IntQtyOrdered variable
                        SqlDataAdapter1.InsertCommand.CommandText = "INSERT
INTO OrderDetail (OrderID, VideoID, Qty) VALUES (" & StrOrderID & "," & StrVideoID
& ", 1)"
'Specifies the query to insert a record in the OrderDetail table
                        SqlDataAdapter1.InsertCommand.ExecuteNonQuery()
'Executes the query
                Next j


                Catch MyException As SqlException
                MessageBox.Show(("Source: " & MyException.Source & ControlChars.Cr
& _
                        "Number: " & MyException.Number.ToString() &
ControlChars.Cr & _
                        "State: " & MyException.State.ToString() &
ControlChars.Cr & _
```

```
                                    "Class: " & MyException.Class.ToString() &
ControlChars.Cr & _
                                    "Server: " & MyException.Server & ControlChars.Cr &
_
                                    "Message: " & MyException.Message & ControlChars.Cr
& _
                                    "Procedure: " & MyException.Procedure & ControlChars.Cr
& _
                                    "Line: " & MyException.LineNumber.ToString()))

                        SqlConnection1.Close()
'Closes the SqlConnection1 object
                        SqlDataAdapter1.Dispose()
'Closes the SqlDataAdapter1 object
                        Return
            End Try


            SqlConnection1.Close()
'Closes the SqlConnection1 object
            SelectCmd.Dispose()
'Releases the resources used by the SelectCmd object
            SqlDataAdapter1.Dispose()
'Closes the SqlDataAdapter1 object
            Me.Close()


            MessageBox.Show("You will receive your order within 5 business days.
Thank you for shopping with us.", "Order Message", MessageBoxButtons.OK)
'Displays the thank you message
End Sub
```

When the CmdPlaceOrder_Click function executes, it first calls the GetAuto-GeneratedOrderID function of the FrmOrder class. The GetAutoGeneratedOrderID function returns the order ID. The function then updates the Orders table based on the movies selected by the customer. Finally, the function also updates the OrderDetail table.

The **GetAutoGeneratedOrderID** *Function*

As the name suggests, the GetAutoGeneratedOrderID function generates the order ID for each order. The code of the GetAutoGeneratedOrderID function is as follows:

```
Private Function GetAutoGeneratedOrderID() As String
        Dim StrSelectString As String
        StrSelectString = "SELECT MAX(OrderID) FROM Orders"
'Specifies the query to return the maximum value in the Order ID field from the
Orders table

        Dim SelectCmd As New SqlCommand(StrSelectString, SqlConnection1)
'Creates SelectCmd as an object of the SqlCommand class
        Dim DsDataSet As DataSet
        DsDataSet = New DataSet()

        Try
                SqlDataAdapter1.SelectCommand = SelectCmd
'Specifies the SelectCmd query as the query to be executed
                SqlConnection1.Open()
'Establishes the connection with the database
                SqlDataAdapter1.Fill(DsDataSet, "OrderID")
'Populates the OrderID table in the DsDataSet dataset with the query results
        Catch MyException As SqlException
                MessageBox.Show(("Source: " & MyException.Source &
ControlChars.Cr & _
                        "Number: " & MyException.Number.ToString() &
ControlChars.Cr & _
                        "State: " & MyException.State.ToString() &
ControlChars.Cr & _
                        "Class: " & MyException.Class.ToString() &
ControlChars.Cr & _
                        "Server: " & MyException.Server & ControlChars.Cr & _
                        "Message: " & MyException.Message & ControlChars.Cr & _
```

```
                                      "Procedure: " & MyException.Procedure &
       ControlChars.Cr & _
                                      "Line: " & MyException.LineNumber.ToString()))


                          SqlConnection1.Close()
       'Closes the SqlConnection1 object
                          SelectCmd.Dispose()
       'Releases the resources used by the SelectCmd object
                          SqlDataAdapter1.Dispose()
       'Closes the SqlDataAdapter1 object
                      Return ""
              End Try


              Dim DrRowPicker As DataRow
              Dim StrOrderID As String
              For Each DrRowPicker In DsDataSet.Tables("OrderID").Rows
                      If DrRowPicker.IsNull(0) Then
                              StrOrderID = "00001"
       'Assigns a value of 00001 to the StrOrderID variable if the Order ID field in the
       dataset is empty
                      Else
                              StrOrderID = DrRowPicker(0)
       'Stores the value in the Order ID field in the dataset in the StrOrderID variable
                      End If
              Next


              SqlConnection1.Close()
       'Closes the SqlConnection1 object
              SqlDataAdapter1.Dispose()
       'Closes the SqlDataAdapter1 object
              GetAutoGeneratedOrderID = StrOrderID
       'Specifies the value stored in the StrOrderID variable as the return value for the
       function
       End Function
```

When the `GetAutoGeneratedOrderID` function executes, it retrieves the maximum value of the Order ID field from the database and returns this value. However, if the Order ID field does not contain any values, the Order ID field is initialized.

The CmdCancel_Click *Function*

The CmdCancel_Click function executes when a customer clicks on the Cancel button in the Place Order form. The code for the CmdCancel_Click function is as follows:

```
Private Sub CmdCancel_Click(ByVal sender As System.Object, ByVal e As
System.EventArgs) Handles CmdCancel.Click
        Me.Close()
'Closes the Place Order form
End Sub
```

A customer can click on the Cancel button to close the Place Order form.

Complete Code for the Place Order Form

In the preceding sections, you looked at the code for the functions in the Place Order form. Listing 16-1 lists the complete code for the Place Order form.

Listing 16-1 The Code for the Place Order Form

```
Imports System
Imports System.Data
Imports System.String
Imports System.Collections
Imports System.Data.SqlClient
Imports System.Data.SqlTypes


Public Class FrmOrder
        Inherits System.Windows.Forms.Form

        Private Shared IntSelectedCount As Integer
        Private StrRegistrationID As String
        Private Shared ArraySelectedMovieID() As String = New String(10) {}


Windows Form Designer generated code
```

```
'Contains the code that specifies the size, location, and other properties, such as
font and name, for the controls on the form.


        Public Sub SetSelectedMovies(ByVal ArrayMovieID() As String, ByVal
IntTotalSelectedCount As Integer)
                Dim i As Integer
                IntSelectedCount = IntTotalSelectedCount
                For i = 0 To IntTotalSelectedCount - 1
                        ArraySelectedMovieID(i) = ArrayMovieID(i)
                Next i
        End Sub


        Public Sub SetRegistrationID(ByVal RegID As String)
                StrRegistrationID = RegID
        End Sub


        Private Function GetAutoGeneratedOrderID() As String
                Dim StrSelectString As String
                StrSelectString = "SELECT MAX(OrderID) FROM Orders"

                Dim SelectCmd As New SqlCommand(StrSelectString,
SqlConnection1)


                Dim DsDataSet As DataSet
                DsDataSet = New DataSet()


                Try
                        SqlDataAdapter1.SelectCommand = SelectCmd
                        SqlConnection1.Open()
                        SqlDataAdapter1.Fill(DsDataSet, "OrderID")
                Catch MyException As SqlException
                        MessageBox.Show(("Source: " & MyException.Source &
ControlChars.Cr & _
                                        "Number: " & MyException.Number.ToString()
& ControlChars.Cr & _
                                        "State: " & MyException.State.ToString() &
ControlChars.Cr & _
```

```
                                        "Class: " & MyException.Class.ToString() &
ControlChars.Cr & _
                                        "Server: " & MyException.Server &
ControlChars.Cr & _
                                        "Message: " & MyException.Message &
ControlChars.Cr & _
                                        "Procedure: " & MyException.Procedure &
ControlChars.Cr & _
                                        "Line: " &
MyException.LineNumber.ToString()))

                        SqlConnection1.Close()
                        SelectCmd.Dispose()
                        SqlDataAdapter1.Dispose()
                        Return ""
                End Try

                Dim DrRowPicker As DataRow
                Dim StrOrderID As String
                For Each DrRowPicker In DsDataSet.Tables("OrderID").Rows
                        If DrRowPicker.IsNull(0) Then
                                StrOrderID = "00001"
                        Else
                                StrOrderID = DrRowPicker(0)
                        End If
                Next

                SqlConnection1.Close()
                SqlDataAdapter1.Dispose()
                GetAutoGeneratedOrderID = StrOrderID
        End Function

        Private Sub FrmOrder_Load(ByVal sender As System.Object, ByVal e As
System.EventArgs) Handles MyBase.Load
                Dim DsDataSet As DataSet
                Dim DrRowPicker As DataRow
                Dim DrRowPicker2 As DataRow
                Dim StrConnectionString As String
```

```
                    Dim StrBrowseBy As String
                    Dim StrQuery As String
                    Dim Result As Integer
                    Dim StrMessage As String
                    Dim SelectCmd As New SqlCommand()

                    If IntSelectedCount < 1 Then
                            Me.Close()
                    End If

                    Dim i As Integer
                    Dim StrTemp As String
                    For i = 0 To IntSelectedCount - 1
                            StrTemp += "'"
                            StrTemp += ArraySelectedMovieID(i)
                            StrTemp += "'"
                            If i < IntSelectedCount - 1 Then
                                    StrTemp += ","
                            End If
                    Next i

            StrQuery = "SELECT DISTINCT a.MovID, a.MovTitle, b.FirstName
AS Actor, c.FirstName AS Director, d.name AS Producer, f.Price as Price FROM movie
a, actor b, director c, producer d, actormovie e, video f WHERE a.MovID = e.MovID
AND e.ActorID = b.ActorID AND a.DirID = c.DirID AND a.ProdID = d.ProdID AND a.MovID
= f.MovID AND a.Movid in (" & StrTemp & ")"

            DsDataSet = New DataSet()

            SqlDataAdapter1.SelectCommand = SelectCmd
            SqlDataAdapter1.SelectCommand.Connection = SqlConnection1
            SqlDataAdapter1.SelectCommand.CommandText = StrQuery
            SqlDataAdapter1.Fill(DsDataSet, "SearchResult2")

            LvwItemsOrdered.Items.Clear()

            Dim DblTotalCost As Double
            For Each DrRowPicker In DsDataSet.Tables("SearchResult2").Rows
```

```vb
                                Dim StrSearchRow As String() = {DrRowPicker(0),
DrRowPicker(1), DrRowPicker(2), DrRowPicker(3), DrRowPicker(4), DrRowPicker(5)}
                                LvwItemsOrdered.Items.Add(New
ListViewItem(StrSearchRow))
                                DblTotalCost += CDbl(DrRowPicker(5))
            Next

            TxtTotalAmount.Text = DblTotalCost

            StrQuery = "SELECT CreditCardNum, CreditCardValidUpto FROM
customer WHERE CustID = '" & StrRegistrationID & "'"
            SqlDataAdapter1.SelectCommand.CommandText = StrQuery
            SqlDataAdapter1.Fill(DsDataSet, "CreditCardInfo")
            For Each DrRowPicker2 In DsDataSet.Tables("CreditCardInfo").Rows
                        TxtCCNumber.Text = DrRowPicker2(0)
                        TxtValidUpto.Text = DrRowPicker2(1)
            Next

            SqlConnection1.Close()
            SqlDataAdapter1.Dispose()
        End Sub

        Private Sub CmdOrderNow_Click(ByVal sender As System.Object, ByVal e As
System.EventArgs) Handles CmdOrderNow.Click
            Dim StrQuery As String
            Dim StrOrderID As String
            Dim StrTemp As String
            Dim IntOrderID As Integer

            StrOrderID = GetAutoGeneratedOrderID()
            StrOrderID = StrOrderID.Substring(1, 4)
            IntOrderID = CInt(StrOrderID) + 1
            StrTemp = CStr(IntOrderID)
            StrOrderID = ""
            StrOrderID += "O"
            If StrTemp.Length = 1 Then
                        StrOrderID += "000"
```

```
ElseIf StrTemp.Length = 2 Then
        StrOrderID += "00"
ElseIf StrTemp.Length = 3 Then
        StrOrderID += "0"
End If
StrOrderID += StrTemp
StrOrderID += "'"

Dim i As Integer
StrTemp = ""
For i = 0 To IntSelectedCount - 1
        StrTemp += "'"
        StrTemp += ArraySelectedMovieID(i)
        StrTemp += "'"
        If i < IntSelectedCount - 1 Then
                StrTemp += ","
        End If
Next i

Dim StrSelectString As String
StrSelectString = "SELECT MAX(VideoID), COUNT(MovID) from Video
WHERE MovID IN (" & StrTemp & ") GROUP BY MovID"

Dim DsDataSet As DataSet
DsDataSet = New DataSet()

Dim SelectCmd As New SqlCommand(StrSelectString,
SqlConnection1)

Try
        SqlDataAdapter1.SelectCommand = SelectCmd
        SqlConnection1.Open()
        SqlDataAdapter1.Fill(DsDataSet, "VideoInfo")
        Catch MyException As SqlException
        MessageBox.Show(("Source: " & myException.Source &
ControlChars.Cr & _
                "Number: " & MyException.Number.ToString()
& ControlChars.Cr & _
```

```
                                            "State: " & MyException.State.ToString() &
ControlChars.Cr & _

                                            "Class: " & MyException.Class.ToString() &
ControlChars.Cr & _

                                             "Server: " & MyException.Server &
ControlChars.Cr & _

                                             "Message: " & MyException.Message &
ControlChars.Cr & _

                                             "Procedure: " & MyException.Procedure &
ControlChars.Cr & _

                                             "Line: " &
MyException.LineNumber.ToString()))

                        SqlConnection1.Close()
                        SelectCmd.Dispose()
                        SqlDataAdapter1.Dispose()
                        Return
            End Try


            Dim DrRowPicker As DataRow
            Dim StrVideoList As String
            Dim StrMovieCount As String
            Dim NTotalCount, NCount As Integer
            NCount = 0
            NTotalCount = DsDataSet.Tables("VideoInfo").Rows.Count()
            Dim ArrayVideoList() As String = New String(10) {}
            For Each DrRowPicker In DsDataSet.Tables("VideoInfo").Rows
                    StrVideoList += "'"
                    StrVideoList += DrRowPicker(0)
                    StrVideoList += "'"
                    ArrayVideoList(NCount) = StrVideoList
                    NCount += 1
                    StrMovieCount = DrRowPicker(1)
            Next


            Dim StrTotalOrderValue As String
            StrQuery = "SELECT SUM(Price) FROM Video WHERE VideoID IN (" &
StrVideoList & ")"
```

```
              SqlDataAdapter1.SelectCommand.CommandText = StrQuery
              SqlDataAdapter1.Fill(DsDataSet, "OrderValue")
              StrTotalOrderValue =
DsDataSet.Tables("OrderValue").Rows(0).Item(0)


              Dim StrTotalQty As String
              StrQuery = "SELECT COUNT(VideoID) FROM Video WHERE VideoID IN
(" & StrVideoList & ")"
              SqlDataAdapter1.SelectCommand.CommandText = StrQuery
              SqlDataAdapter1.Fill(DsDataSet, "TotalQty")
              StrTotalQty = DsDataSet.Tables("TotalQty").Rows(0).Item(0)


              Dim StrVideoID As String
              Dim j As Integer
              Dim IntQtyOrdered As Integer
              Dim StrTemp1 As String


              StrQuery = "INSERT INTO Orders (OrderID, OrderDate, CustID,
TotalQtyOrdered, OrderValue) VALUES (" & StrOrderID & ", @OrderDate, @CustID," &
StrTotalQty & "," & StrTotalOrderValue & "); SELECT OrderID, OrderDate, CustID,
OrderValue FROM Orders WHERE OrderID = " & StrOrderID


              Dim InsertCmd As New SqlCommand(StrQuery, SqlConnection1)
              SqlDataAdapter1.InsertCommand = InsertCmd
              SqlDataAdapter1.InsertCommand.Parameters.Add(New
SqlParameter("@OrderDate", System.Data.SqlDbType.DateTime, 8, "OrderDate"))
              SqlDataAdapter1.InsertCommand.Parameters(0).Value = Now()
              SqlDataAdapter1.InsertCommand.Parameters.Add(New
SqlParameter("@CustID", System.Data.SqlDbType.SmallInt, 2, "CustID"))
              SqlDataAdapter1.InsertCommand.Parameters(1).Value =
StrRegistrationID
              SqlDataAdapter1.InsertCommand.Parameters.Add(New
SqlParameter("@OrderValue", System.Data.SqlDbType.Money, 8, "OrderValue"))
              SqlDataAdapter1.InsertCommand.Parameters(2).Value =
CDbl(TxtTotalAmount.Text)


              Try
                     SqlDataAdapter1.InsertCommand.ExecuteNonQuery()
```

```
                             For j = 0 To NCount - 1
                                      StrVideoID = ArrayVideoList(j)
                                      IntQtyOrdered = CInt(StrMovieCount)

SqlDataAdapter1.InsertCommand.CommandText = "INSERT INTO OrderDetail (OrderID,
VideoID, Qty) VALUES (" & StrOrderID & "," & StrVideoID & ", 1)"


SqlDataAdapter1.InsertCommand.ExecuteNonQuery()
                             Next j
                             Catch MyException As SqlException
                             MessageBox.Show(("Source: " & MyException.Source &
ControlChars.Cr & _

                                      "Number: " & MyException.Number.ToString()
& ControlChars.Cr & _

                                      "State: " & MyException.State.ToString() &
ControlChars.Cr & _

                                      "Class: " & MyException.Class.ToString() &
ControlChars.Cr & _

                                       "Server: " & MyException.Server &
ControlChars.Cr & _

                                       "Message: " & MyException.Message &
ControlChars.Cr & _

                                       "Procedure: " & MyException.Procedure &
ControlChars.Cr & _

                                       "Line: " &
MyException.LineNumber.ToString()))


                             SqlConnection1.Close()
                             SqlDataAdapter1.Dispose()
                             Return
                 End Try

                 SqlConnection1.Close()
                 SelectCmd.Dispose()
                 SqlDataAdapter1.Dispose()
                 Me.Close()
```

```
            MessageBox.Show("You will receive your order within 5 business
days. Thank you for shopping with us.", "Order Message", MessageBoxButtons.OK)
          End Sub

          Private Sub CmdCancel_Click(ByVal sender As System.Object, ByVal e As
System.EventArgs) Handles CmdCancel.Click
                Me.Close()
          End Sub
End Class
```

Summary

In this chapter, you learned to add functionality to the Place Order form. This chapter also described the functions you need to create in the Place Order form. Finally, you looked at the complete code for the Place Order form.

Chapter 17

In the preceding chapters, you learned to add functionality to the forms in the Customer module of the video kiosk application. In this chapter, you will learn to create the user interface of the Administration module and will learn about the forms you need to create for this module. You will also learn about the properties and controls associated with each form.

As previously discussed, the Administration module of the video kiosk application is designed to help the administrator manage the database. Using the Administration module, the administrator can add, modify, and delete records from the tables in the Movies database. In addition, the administrator can generate reports by using the Administration module.

The Administration module of the video kiosk application consists of the following forms:

◆ The Main form
◆ The Insert Actor form
◆ The Insert Director form
◆ The Insert Producer form
◆ The Insert Video form
◆ The Insert Movie form
◆ The Insert Customer form
◆ The Update/Delete form
◆ The Reports form

The following sections describe each of these forms in detail. First take a look at the Main form of the Administration module.

The Main Form

As the name suggests, the Main form is the startup form of the Administration module. The Main form is also the central location from which the administrator can perform the following tasks:

◆ Maintain and update the tables in the database

◆ Generate reports

Figure 17-1 shows the Main form.

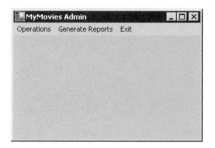

FIGURE 17-1   *The interface of the Main form*

The properties you need to assign to the Main form are as follows:

Property	Value
Name	FrmMainAdmin
Text	MyMovies Admin
Size	300, 208
WindowState	Normal

As shown in Figure 17-1, the Main form contains a menu bar. The menu bar in the Main form displays the Operations, Generate Reports, and Exit menus. The rest of this section describes the menus in the Main form.

The Operations menu provides commands that enable the administrator to add, modify, and delete records from the tables in the database. Figure 17-2 shows the commands in the Operations menu.

As shown in Figure 17-2, the Operations menu contains two commands, Insert and Update/Delete. Also note that a submenu is associated with the Insert command. When the administrator selects a command from the Insert submenu, the form associated with the selected command displays. For example, if the administrator selects the Actor command from the Insert submenu, the Insert Actor form appears. Similarly, if the administrator selects the Movie command from the

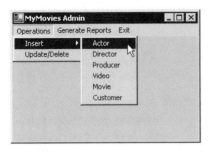

FIGURE 17-2 *The commands in the Operations menu*

Insert submenu, the Insert Movie form displays. Therefore, the commands in the Insert menu enable the administrator to add records to the various tables in the database. The administrator can use the Update/Delete command to update or delete records from tables in the database. You will learn about the various Insert forms later in this chapter.

The menu bar in the Main form also displays the Generate Reports menu. Figure 17-3 shows the commands available in the Generate Reports menu.

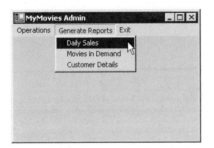

FIGURE 17-3 *The commands in the Generate Reports menu*

The commands in the Generate Reports menu enable the administrator to create reports. Using these commands, the administrator can create reports related to daily sales, the most requested movies, and customer details.

The Main form also displays the Exit menu. The administrator can select the Exit menu to close the Administration module.

Now that you know about the commands in the various menus in the Main form, you'll learn how to create the menu. To do this, you need to drag the MainMenu control from the Windows Form tab of the Toolbox to the form. After you add the MainMenu control to the Main form, the form appears as shown in Figure 17-4.

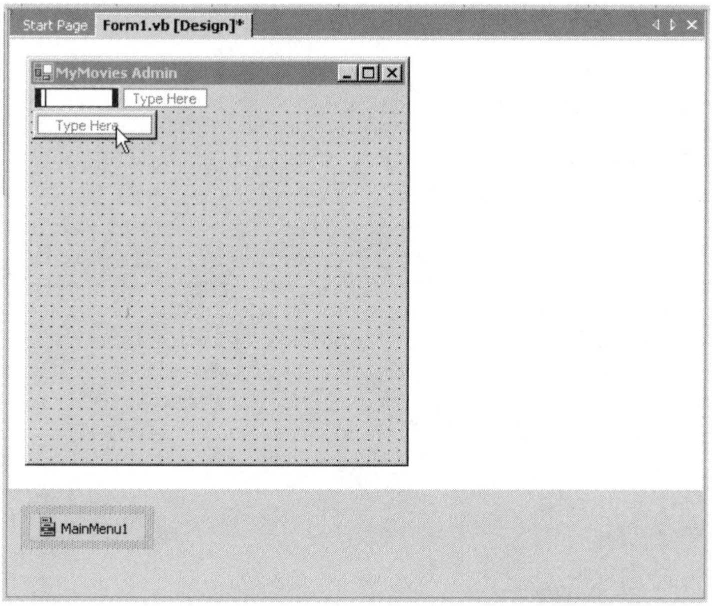

FIGURE 17-4 *The Main form with the MainMenu control*

You do not need to change any properties for the MainMenu control.

As shown in Figure 17-4, when you add a MainMenu control to a form, a menu bar appears on the form. When you click on the menu bar, a box with the message "Type Here" displays. To specify the menus and menu items, you need to type the names of the menus and menu items in the appropriate box. For example, to create the Operations menu, you need to type "Operations" in the first Type Here box. Then, to add the Insert menu item to the Operations menu, you need to type "Insert" in the Type Here box below the Operations menu. Next type "Update/Delete" in the box below the Insert menu item to add the Update/Delete menu item to the Operations menu, as shown in Figure 17-5.

Table 17-1 lists the properties you need to assign to the menus in the MainMenu control.

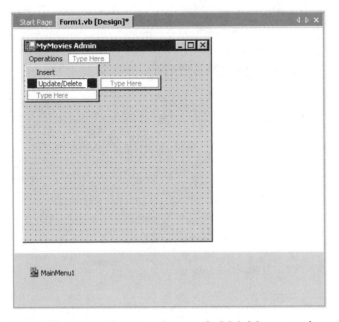

FIGURE 17-5 *Adding menu items to the MainMenu control*

Table 17-1 Properties Assigned to Menus

Menu	Property	Value
Menu 1	Name	MmnuOperations
Menu 1	Text	Operations
Menu 2	Name	MmnuReports
Menu 2	Text	Generate Reports
Menu 3	Name	MmnuExit
Menu 3	Text	Exit

Table 17-2 lists the properties you need to assign to the menu items in the menus in the Main form.

Table 17-2 Properties Assigned to Menu Items

Menu Item	Name of Container Menu	Property	Value
Menu item 1	MmnuOperations	Name	MitmInsert
Menu item 1	MmnuOperations	Text	Insert

Menu Item	Name of Container Menu	Property	Value
Menu item 2	MmnuOperations	Name	MitmUpdateDelete
Menu item 2	MmnuOperations	Text	Update/Delete
Menu item 3	MmnuReports	Name	MitmDailySales
Menu item 3	MmnuReports	Text	Daily Sales
Menu item 4	MmnuReports	Name	MitmMoviesInDemand
Menu item 4	MmnuReports	Text	Movies in Demand
Menu item 5	MmnuReports	Name	MitmCustDetails
Menu item 5	MmnuReports	Text	Customer Details

As shown in Figure 17-2, the Insert menu contains a submenu. Table 17-3 lists the properties you need to assign to the menu items in the MitmInsert submenu.

Table 17-3 Properties Assigned to the Menu Items in the MitmInsert Submenu

Form	Property	Value
Menu item 1	Name	MitmActor
Menu item 1	Text	Actor
Menu item 2	Name	MitmDirector
Menu item 2	Text	Director
Menu item 3	Name	MitmProducer
Menu item 3	Text	Producer
Menu item 4	Name	MitmVideo
Menu item 4	Text	Video
Menu item 5	Name	MitmMovie
Menu item 5	Text	Movie
Menu item 6	Name	MitmCustomer
Menu item 6	Text	Customer

After you create the menu, the Main form appears as shown in Figure 17-6.

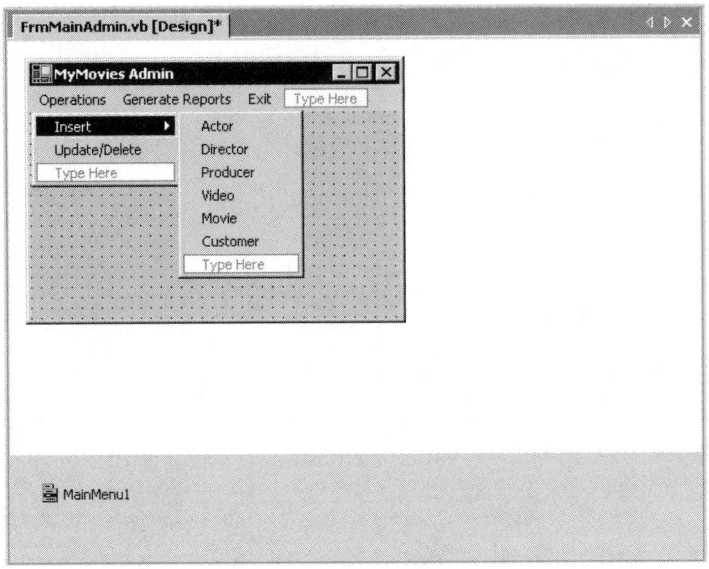

FIGURE 17-6 *The menu control added to the Main form*

Next you will learn to create the other forms. The next section describes the Insert Actor form.

The Insert Actor Form

As previously mentioned, the Insert Actor form enables the administrator to add records to the Actor table. The Insert Actor form displays when the administrator selects the Actor command from the Insert submenu in the Main form.

Figure 17-7 shows the Insert Actor form.

The properties you need to assign to the Insert Actor form are as follows:

Property	Value
Name	FrmInsertActor
Text	Insert Actor Info
Size	240, 240
WindowState	Normal

FIGURE 17-7 *The Insert Actor form*

As shown in Figure 17-7, the Insert Actor form contains five labels. Table 17-4 lists the properties you need to assign to the labels in the Insert Actor form.

Table 17-4 Properties Assigned to Labels

Control	Property	Value
Label 1	Name	LblActorID
Label 1	Text	Actor ID:
Label 1	Visible	True
Label 2	Name	LblFName
Label 2	Text	First Name:
Label 2	Visible	True
Label 3	Name	LblLName
Label 3	Text	Last Name:
Label 3	Visible	True
Label 4	Name	LblDOB
Label 4	Text	DOB:
Label 4	Visible	True
Label 5	Name	LblBackground
Label 5	Text	Background:
Label 5	Visible	True

The Insert Actor form also contains text boxes. Table 17-5 lists the properties you need to assign to these text boxes.

Table 17-5 Properties Assigned to Text Boxes

Control	Property	Value
Text box 1	Name	TxtActorID
Text box 1	Visible	True
Text box 2	Name	TxtFName
Text box 2	Visible	True
Text box 3	Name	TxtLName
Text box 3	Visible	True
Text box 4	Name	TxtBackground
Text box 4	Visible	True

In addition to text boxes, the Insert Actor form contains a date time picker control, which is associated with the Lb1DOB label. The Name property of the date time picker control is set to DtpDOB.

The Insert Actor form also contains two buttons. Table 17-6 lists the properties you need to assign to these buttons.

Table 17-6 Properties Assigned to Buttons

Control	Property	Value
Button 1	Name	CmdSubmit
Button 1	Text	Submit
Button 1	Visible	True
Button 2	Name	CmdCancel
Button 2	Text	Cancel
Button 2	Visible	True

The Insert Director Form

As the name suggests, the Insert Director form enables the administrator to add records to the Director table. The Insert Director form displays when the administrator selects the Director command from the Insert submenu.

Figure 17-8 shows the Insert Director form.

FIGURE 17-8 *The Insert Director form*

The properties you need to assign to the Insert Director form are as follows:

Property	Value
Name	FrmInsertDirector
Text	Insert Director Info
Size	240, 240
WindowState	Normal

As shown in Figure 17-8, the Insert Director form contains five labels. Table 17-7 lists the properties you need to assign to the labels in the Insert Director form.

Table 17-7 Properties Assigned to Labels

Control	Property	Value
Label 1	Name	LblDirectorID
Label 1	Text	Director ID:

continues

Table 17-7 *(continued)*

Control	Property	Value
Label 1	Visible	True
Label 2	Name	LblFName
Label 2	Text	First Name:
Label 2	Visible	True
Label 3	Name	LblLName
Label 3	Text	Last Name:
Label 3	Visible	True
Label 4	Name	LblDOB
Label 4	Text	DOB:
Label 4	Visible	True
Label 5	Name	LblBackground
Label 5	Text	Background:
Label 5	Visible	True

The Insert Director form also contains four text boxes. The properties you need to assign to the four text boxes are listed in Table 17-8.

Table 17-8 Properties Assigned to Text Boxes

Control	Property	Value
Text box 1	Name	TxtDirectorID
Text box 1	Visible	True
Text box 2	Name	TxtFName
Text box 2	Visible	True
Text box 3	Name	TxtLName
Text box 3	Visible	True
Text box 4	Name	TxtBackground
Text box 4	Visible	True

Note that a date time picker control is associated with the DOB text box in the Insert Director form. You need to set the Name property of this date time picker control to DtpDOB.

The Insert Director form also contains two buttons. Table 17-9 lists the properties you need to assign to these buttons.

Table 17-9 Properties Assigned to Buttons

Control	Property	Value
Button 1	Name	CmdSubmit
Button 1	Text	Submit
Button 1	Visible	True
Button 2	Name	CmdCancel
Button 2	Text	Cancel
Button 2	Visible	True

You will learn to create the Insert Producer form in the next section.

The Insert Producer Form

As the name suggests, the Insert Producer form enables the administrator to add records to the Producer table. The Insert Producer form displays when the administrator selects the Producer command from the Insert submenu.

Figure 17-9 shows the Insert Producer form.

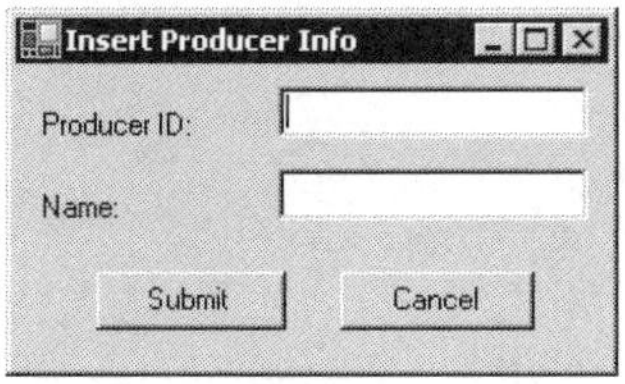

FIGURE 17-9 *The Insert Producer form*

The properties you need to assign to the Insert Producer form are as follows:

Property	Value
Name	FrmInsertProducer
Text	Insert Producer Info
Size	240, 144
WindowState	Normal

As shown in Figure 17-9, the Insert Director form contains two labels and two text boxes. Table 17-10 lists the properties you need to assign to the labels.

Table 17-10 Properties Assigned to Labels

Control	Property	Value
Label 1	Name	LblProducerID
Label 1	Text	Producer ID:
Label 1	Visible	True
Label 2	Name	LblName
Label 2	Text	Name:
Label 2	Visible	True

The properties you need to assign to the text boxes in the Insert Director form are listed in Table 17-11.

Table 17-11 Properties Assigned to Text Boxes

Control	Property	Value
Text box 1	Name	TxtProducerID
Text box 1	Visible	True
Text box 2	Name	TxtName
Text box 2	Visible	True

In addition to the labels and text boxes, the Insert Producer form contains two buttons. Table 17-12 lists the properties you need to assign to these buttons.

Table 17-12 Properties Assigned to Buttons

Control	Property	Value
Button 1	Name	CmdSubmit
Button 1	Text	Submit
Button 1	Visible	True
Button 2	Name	CmdCancel
Button 2	Text	Cancel
Button 2	Visible	True

You will learn to create the Insert Video form in the next section.

The Insert Video Form

The Insert Video form enables the administrator to add records to the Video table. The Insert Video form displays when the administrator selects the Video command from the Insert submenu.

Figure 17-10 shows the Insert Video form.

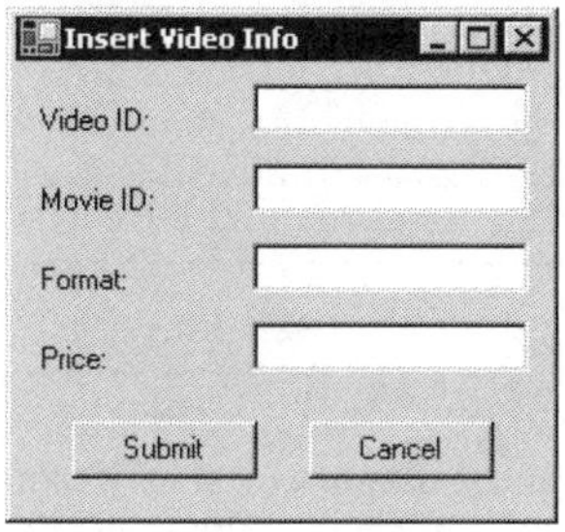

FIGURE 17-10 *The Insert Video form*

The properties you need to assign to the Insert Video form are as follows:

Property	Value
Name	FrmInsertVideo
Text	Insert Video Info
Size	224, 208
WindowState	Normal

As shown in Figure 17-10, the Insert Video form contains four labels. Table 17-13 lists the properties you need to assign to these labels.

Table 17-13 Properties Assigned to Labels

Control	Property	Value
Label 1	Name	LblVideoID
Label 1	Text	Video ID:
Label 1	Visible	True
Label 2	Name	LblMovieID
Label 2	Text	Movie ID:
Label 2	Visible	True
Label 3	Name	LblFormat
Label 3	Text	Format:
Label 3	Visible	True
Label 4	Name	LblPrice
Label 4	Text	Price:
Label 4	Visible	True

In addition to the labels, the Insert Video form contains four text boxes. The properties you need to assign to the four text boxes are listed in Table 17-14.

Table 17-14 Properties Assigned to Text Boxes

Control	Property	Value
Text box 1	Name	TxtVideoID
Text box 1	Visible	True
Text box 2	Name	TxtMovieID
Text box 2	Visible	True
Text box 3	Name	TxtFormat
Text box 3	Visible	True
Text box 4	Name	TxtPrice
Text box 4	Visible	True

Table 17-15 lists the properties you need to assign to the two buttons on the Insert Video form.

Table 17-15 Properties Assigned to Buttons

Control	Property	Value
Button 1	Name	CmdSubmit
Button 1	Text	Submit
Button 1	Visible	True
Button 2	Name	CmdCancel
Button 2	Text	Cancel
Button 2	Visible	True

In the next section, you will learn to create the Insert Movie form.

The Insert Movie Form

The administrator can use the Insert Movie form to add records to the Movie table. The Insert Movie form (see Figure 17-11) displays when the administrator selects the Movie command from the Insert submenu.

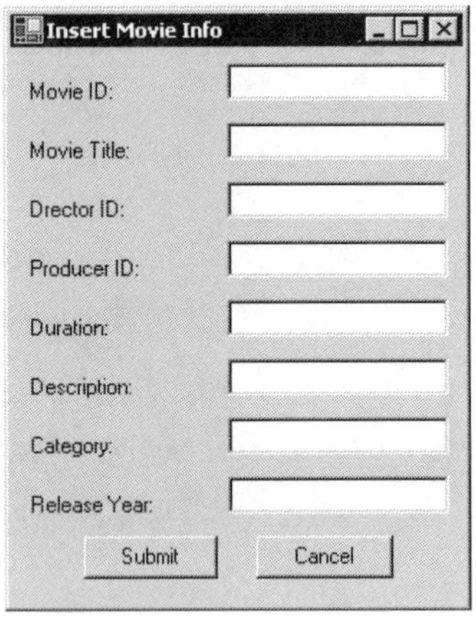

FIGURE 17-11 *The Insert Movie form*

Before adding controls to the Insert Movie form, you need to specify the properties for the form.

The properties you need to assign to the Insert Movie form are as follows:

Property	Value
Name	FrmInsertMovie
Text	Insert Movie Info
Size	256, 328
WindowState	Normal

After you set the properties for the form, you need to add controls to the form. As shown above in Figure 17-11, the Insert Movie form contains eight labels. Table 17-16 lists the properties you need to assign to these labels.

Table 17-16 Properties Assigned to Labels

Control	Property	Value
Label 1	Name	LblMovieID
Label 1	Text	Movie ID:
Label 1	Visible	True

Control	Property	Value
Label 2	Name	LblMovieTitle
Label 2	Text	Movie Title:
Label 2	Visible	True
Label 3	Name	LblDirectorID
Label 3	Text	Director ID:
Label 3	Visible	True
Label 4	Name	LblProducerID
Label 4	Text	Producer ID:
Label 4	Visible	True
Label 5	Name	LblDuration
Label 5	Text	Duration:
Label 5	Visible	True
Label 6	Name	LblDescription
Label 6	Text	Description:
Label 6	Visible	True
Label 7	Name	LblCategory
Label 7	Text	Category:
Label 7	Visible	True
Label 8	Name	LblRelYear
Label 8	Text	Release Year:
Label 8	Visible	True

In addition to labels, you also need to add text boxes to the Insert Movie form. The properties you need to assign to the text boxes in the Insert Movie form are listed in Table 17-17.

Table 17-17 Properties Assigned to Text Boxes

Control	Property	Value
Text box 1	Name	TxtMovieID
Text box 1	Visible	True
Text box 2	Name	TxtMovieTitle
Text box 2	Visible	True
Text box 3	Name	TxtDirectorID
Text box 3	Visible	True
Text box 4	Name	TxtProducerID
Text box 4	Visible	True
Text box 5	Name	TxtDuration
Text box 5	Visible	True
Text box 6	Name	TxtDescription
Text box 6	Visible	True
Text box 7	Name	TxtCategory
Text box 7	Visible	True
Text box 8	Name	TxtRelYear
Text box 8	Visible	True

In addition to the labels and text boxes, the Insert Movie form also contains buttons. Table 17-18 lists the properties you need to assign to the two buttons on the Insert Video form.

Table 17-18 Properties Assigned to Buttons

Control	Property	Value
Button 1	Name	CmdSubmit
Button 1	Text	Submit
Button 1	Visible	True

Control	Property	Value
Button 2	Name	CmdCancel
Button 2	Text	Cancel
Button 2	Visible	True

The next section describes the interface of the Insert Customer form.

The Insert Customer Form

As the name suggests, the Insert Customer form enables the administrator to add records to the Customer table. The Insert Customer form displays when the administrator selects the Customer command from the Insert submenu.

Figure 17-12 shows the Insert Customer form.

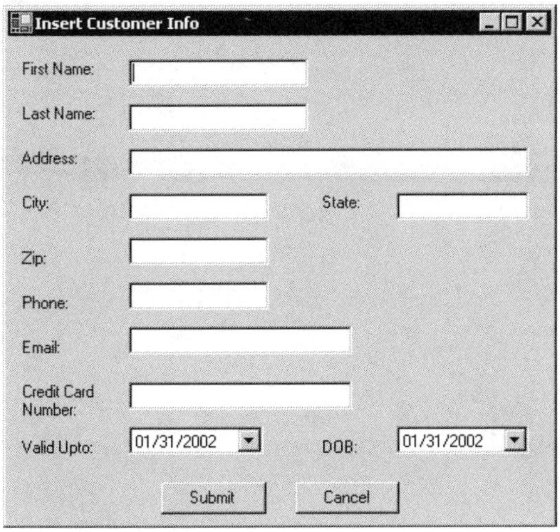

FIGURE 17-12 *The Insert Customer form*

To start with, you need to assign properties to the Insert Customer form. The properties you need to assign are as follows:

Property	Value
Name	FrmInsertCustomer
Text	Insert Customer Info
Size	400, 376
WindowState Normal	

As shown in Figure 17-12, the Insert Customer form contains multiple text boxes and labels. Table 17-19 lists the properties you need to assign to the labels on the Insert Customer form.

Table 17-19 Properties Assigned to Labels

Control	Property	Value
Label 1	Name	LblFName
Label 1	Text	First Name:
Label 1	Visible	True
Label 2	Name	LblLName
Label 2	Text	Last Name:
Label 2	Visible	True
Label 3	Name	LblAddress
Label 3	Text	Address:
Label 3	Visible	True
Label 4	Name	LblCity
Label 4	Text	City:
Label 4	Visible	True
Label 5	Name	LblState
Label 5	Text	State:
Label 5	Visible	True
Label 6	Name	LblZip
Label 6	Text	Zip:

Control	Property	Value
Label 6	Visible	True
Label 7	Name	LblPhone
Label 7	Text	Phone:
Label 7	Visible	True
Label 8	Name	LblEmail
Label 8	Text	Email:
Label 8	Visible	True
Label 9	Name	LblCCNumber
Label 9	Text	Credit Card Number:
Label 9	Visible	True
Label 10	Name	LblValidUpto
Label 10	Text	Valid Upto:
Label 10	Visible	True
Label 11	Name	LblDOB
Label 11	Text	DOB:
Label 11	Visible	True

The Insert Customer form also contains text boxes. Table 17-20 lists the properties you need to assign to the text boxes on the Insert Customer form.

Table 17-20 Properties Assigned to Text Boxes

Control	Property	Value
Text box 1	Name	TxtFName
Text box 1	Visible	True
Text box 2	Name	TxtLName
Text box 2	Visible	True
Text box 3	Name	TxtAddress

continues

Table 17-20 *(continued)*

Control	Property	Value
Text box 3	Visible	True
Text box 4	Name	TxtCity
Text box 4	Visible	True
Text box 5	Name	TxtState
Text box 5	Visible	True
Text box 6	Name	TxtZip
Text box 6	Visible	True
Text box 7	Name	TxtPhone
Text box 7	Visible	True
Text box 8	Name	TxtEmail
Text box 8	Visible	True
Text box 9	Name	TxtCCNumber
Text box 9	Visible	True

In addition to text boxes, the Insert Customer form contains two date time picker controls. One is associated with the Valid Upto label, and the other is associated with the DOB label. The Name property of the date time picker control associated with the Valid Upto label is set to DtpCCValidUpto. The Name property of the date time picker control associated with the DOB label is set to DtpDOB.

The Insert Customer form also contains two buttons. Table 17-21 lists the properties you need to assign to these buttons.

Table 17-21 Properties Assigned to Buttons

Control	Property	Value
Button 1	Name	CmdSubmitReg
Button 1	Text	Submit
Button 1	Visible	True
Button 2	Name	CmdCancel

Control	Property	Value
Button 2	Text	Cancel
Button 2	Visible	True

Now that you have learned to design the forms to add records to the various tables, the next section describes the Update/Delete form.

The Update/Delete Form

In addition to adding records, the Administration module enables the administrator to edit the records in the various tables. The Administration module provides the Update/Delete form to enable the administrator to modify and delete the records in the tables. The Update/Delete form displays when the administrator selects the Update/Delete command from the Operations menu. Figure 17-13 shows the Update/Delete form.

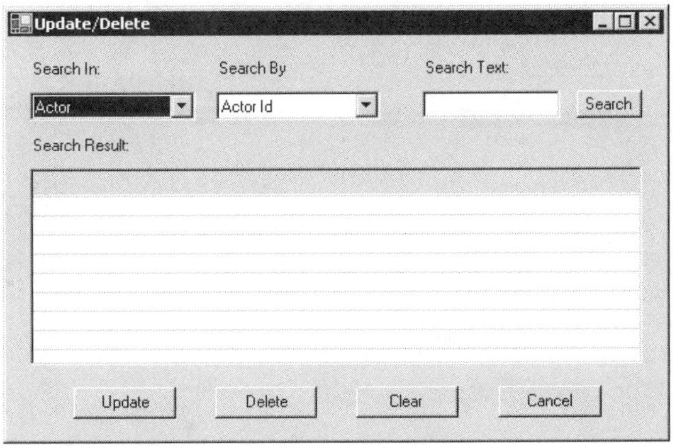

FIGURE 17-13 *The Update/Delete form*

Before adding controls to the Update/Delete form, you need to specify properties for the form. The properties you need to assign to the Update/Delete form are as follows:

Property	Value
Name	FrmUpdateDelete
Text	Update/Delete
Size	488, 320
WindowState	Normal

As shown in Figure 17-13, the Update/Delete form contains four labels. Table 17-22 lists the properties you need to assign to these labels.

Table 17-22 Properties Assigned to Labels

Control	Property	Value
Label 1	Name	LblSearchIn
Label 1	Text	Search In:
Label 1	Visible	True
Label 2	Name	LblSearchBy
Label 2	Text	Search By:
Label 2	Visible	True
Label 3	Name	LblSearchText
Label 3	Text	Search Text:
Label 3	Visible	True
Label 4	Name	LblSearchResult
Label 4	Text	Search Result:
Label 4	Visible	True

The Update/Delete form contains a text box and two combo boxes. Table 17-23 lists the properties you need to assign to the text box and combo boxes.

Table 17-23 Properties Assigned to the Text Box and Combo Boxes

Control	Property	Value
Text box 1	Name	TxtSearchText
Text box 1	Visible	True
Combo box 1	Name	CmbSearchIn
Combo box 1	Visible	True
Combo box 1	DropDownStyle	DropDownList
Combo box 2	Name	CmbSearchBy
Combo box 2	Visible	True
Combo box 2	DropDownStyle	DropDownList

In addition to the properties mentioned in the preceding table, you also need to specify the Columns property for the CmbSearchIn combo box. You need to use the Columns property of a combo box to add items to the combo box. To add items to the CmbSearchIn combo box, click on the ellipsis button next to the (Collection) value in the Properties window. When you click on the ellipsis button, the String Collection Editor dialog box displays. In the String Collection Editor dialog box, add the items for the CmbSearchIn combo box. Figure 17-14 shows the String Collection Editor dialog box with the items of the CmbSearchIn combo box.

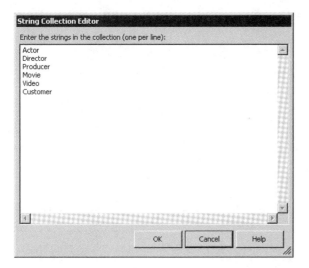

FIGURE 17-14 *The String Collection Editor dialog box*

You do not need to specify the `Columns` property for the `CmbSearchBy` combo box. This is because the items that need to be displayed in the `CmbSearchBy` combo box depend on the value selected by the user in the `CmbSearchIn` combo box. For example, if a user selects the Actor option in the `CmbSearchIn` combo box, the names of fields from the Actor table should be displayed in the `CmbSearchBy` combo box. Therefore, instead of specifying the items for the `CmbSearchBy` combo box at design time, you must populate the `CmbSearchBy` combo box at runtime. This can be done programmatically. You will learn how to specify the items for the `CmbSearchBy` combo box programmatically later in this book.

In addition to the combo boxes, the Update/Delete form contains a list view control. The properties you need to assign to the list view control are as follows:

Property	Value
Name	LvwSearchResult
View	Details
FullRowSelect	True
GridLines	True

In the list view control, you do not need to specify the `Columns` property. This is because the column headers that should display in the list view control depend on the value selected in the `CmbSearchIn` combo box. For example, if a user selects the Actor option from the `CmbSearchIn` combo box, column headers from that table should be displayed in the `LvwSearchResult` control. Therefore, as in the case of the `CmbSearchBy` combo box, you must specify the column headers of the `LvwSearchResult` control programmatically. You will learn about adding column headers to a list view control programmatically in subsequent chapters.

The Update/Delete form also contains five buttons. Table 17-24 lists the properties you need to assign to these buttons.

Table 17-24 Properties Assigned to Buttons

Control	Property	Value
Button 1	Name	CmdSearch
Button 1	Text	Search

Control	Property	Value
Button 1	Visible	True
Button 2	Name	CmdUpdate
Button 2	Text	Update
Button 2	Visible	True
Button 3	Name	CmdDelete
Button 3	Text	Delete
Button 3	Visible	True
Button 4	Name	CmdClear
Button 4	Text	Clear
Button 4	Visible	True
Button 5	Name	CmdCancel
Button 5	Text	Cancel
Button 5	Visible	True

As the name suggests, the Search button enables the administrator to search the database based on the criteria specified in the Update/Delete form. The search results are displayed in the list view control.

The Update button enables the administrator to edit records. To edit a record, the administrator can select the record in the list view control and click on the Update button. When the administrator clicks on the Update button, the selected record is displayed in a form. The form in which the record is displayed, however, depends on the type of record the administrator selects. For example, if the administrator selects a record from the Actor table and clicks on the Update button, the Update Actor form displays. Similarly, if the administrator selects a record from the Movie table and clicks on the Update button, the Update Movie form displays. You will learn more about the Update Actor and Update Movie forms in subsequent chapters. After the administrator makes the required modifications to the selected record, he or she can click on the Submit button in the form.

Alternatively, the administrator can click on the Delete button to delete the selected record from the database. To delete a record, the administrator can select the record from the list view control and click on the Delete button. When the administrator click on the Delete button, a message box confirming the deletion of the record displays.

The administrator can click on the Clear button to clear all the items from the list view control. In addition, the Cancel button enables the administrator to close the Update/Delete form.

The next section describes the Reports form.

The Reports Form

As the name suggests, the Reports form displays the various reports. There are three variations of the Reports form—Daily Sales, Movies in Demand, and Customer Details. The Reports form displays when the administrator selects any command from the Generate Reports menu of the Main form. When the administrator does this, the corresponding Reports form displays. For example, if the administrator selects the Daily Sales command from the Generate Reports menu, the Daily Sales Report form displays.

Figure 17-15 shows the Daily Sales Report form.

The properties you need to assign to the Reports form are as follows:

Property	Value
Name	FrmReport
Text	Reports
Size	472, 430
WindowState	Normal

As shown in Figure 17-15, the Reports form contains a menu control. To add a menu control to the Reports form, drag the MainMenu control from the Windows Form tab of the Toolbox to the form. After you add the MainMenu control to the Main form, you need to add the Exit menu to it. The properties you need to specify for the Exit menu are as follows:

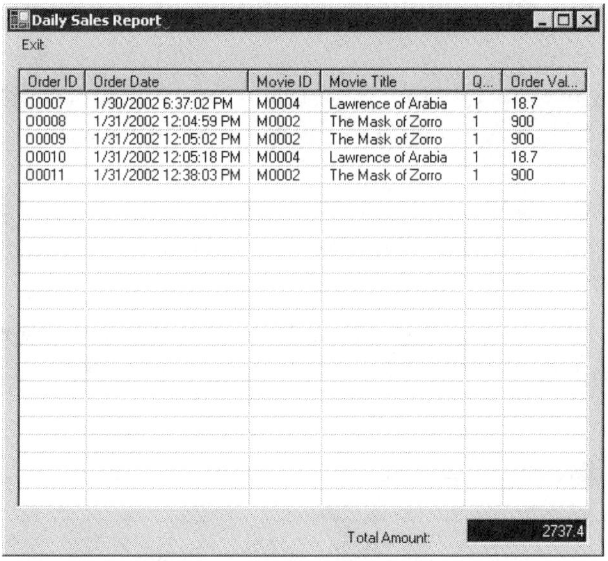

FIGURE 17-15 *The Daily Sales Report form*

Property	Value
Name	MmnuExit
Text	Exit

The Reports form also contains a list view control. The properties you need to assign to the list view control are as follows:

Property	Value
Name	LvwReport
View	Details
FullRowSelect	True
GridLines	True

In the Reports form, you do not need to specify the Columns property for the LvwReport control at the time of designing the form. Instead, you need to specify the column headers for the list view control programmatically. This is because the column headers that should display in the list view control in the Reports form depend on the command selected by the administrator in the Main form. For example, if the administrator selects the Daily Sales command from the Generate Reports menu, the list view control in the form should display columns that correspond to the Daily Sales report. Similarly, if the administrator selects the Customer Details command from the Generate Reports menu, the list view control in the form should display columns that correspond to Customer Details report. You will learn about programmatically adding column headers to a list view control in subsequent chapters.

In addition to the menu and the list view control, the Reports form contains a label and text box. The properties you need to assign to the label control are as follows:

Property	Value
Name	LblTotalAmountSale
Text	Total Sale:
Visible	True

The properties you need to assign to the text box are as follows:

Property	Value
Name	TxtTotalAmountSale
Visible	False

Summary

In this chapter, you learned to create the forms for the Administration module of the video kiosk application. You learned to create the Main, Insert Actor, Insert Director, Insert Producer, Insert Video, Insert Movie, and Insert Customer forms. You also learned to create the Update/Delete and Reports forms. This chapter also described the properties you need to assign to the various controls on the forms.

Chapter 18

Adding Functionality to the Main Form

In the preceding chapter, you learned to create the user interface for the Administration module of the video kiosk application. In this chapter and the next three, you will add functionality to forms in the Administration module.

As previously discussed, the Administration module consists of the following forms:

- ◆ The Main form
- ◆ The Insert Actor form
- ◆ The Insert Director form
- ◆ The Insert Producer form
- ◆ The Insert Video form
- ◆ The Insert Movie form
- ◆ The Insert Customer form
- ◆ The Update/Delete form
- ◆ The Reports form

In this chapter, you will learn to write code to add functionality to the Main form of the Administration module. To start with, let's review what the Main form looks like. See Figure 18-1.

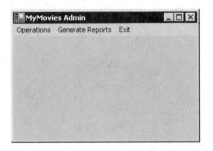

FIGURE 18-1 *The interface of the Main form*

As shown in Figure 18-1, the Main form contains a menu bar that displays the Operations, Generate Reports, and Exit menus. In addition, the administrator can use the menus in the Main form to access the other forms in the Administration module.

Before you look at the events you need to trap to add functionality to the Main form, take a look at the menu items in each menu. The Operations menu contains the Insert and Update/Delete commands. When the administrator clicks on the Insert command, a submenu displays. The Insert submenu displays the following commands:

- ◆ Actor
- ◆ Director
- ◆ Producer
- ◆ Video
- ◆ Movie
- ◆ Customer

As discussed in the preceding chapter, the administrator can click on any option in the Insert submenu to open the associated form. To do this, you need to trap the event generated when the command is selected. In other words, you need to trap the `Click` event for each command in the Insert submenu. Similarly, you need to trap the `Click` events for the commands in the other menus in the Main form.

Before you create functions, you need to declare the following variables in the Main form:

```
Public Shared ObjActor As FrmInsertActor
Public Shared ObjDirector As FrmInsertDirector
Public Shared ObjProducer As FrmInsertProducer
Public Shared ObjMovie As FrmInsertMovie
Public Shared ObjVideo As FrmInsertVideo
Public Shared ObjCustomer As FrmInsertCustomer
Public Shared ObjUpdateDelete As FrmUpdateDelete
Public Shared ObjReport As FrmReports
'Declares objects used to open other forms
```

The Main form consists of the following functions:

- ◆ `MitmActor_Click`
- ◆ `MitmDirector_Click`
- ◆ `MitmProducer_Click`

- ◆ MitmVideo_Click

- ◆ MitmMovie_Click

- ◆ MitmCustomer_Click

- ◆ MitmUpdateDelete_Click

- ◆ MitmDailySales_Click

- ◆ MitmMoviesInDemand_Click

- ◆ MitmCustDetails_Click

- ◆ MmnuExit_Click

The following sections describe the code for these functions.

The MitmActor_Click Function

The MitmActor_Click function executes when the administrator selects the Actor command from the Insert submenu.

The code for the MitmActor_Click function is as follows:

```
Private Sub MitmActor_Click(ByVal sender As System.Object, ByVal e As
System.EventArgs) Handles MitmActor.Click
        ObjActor = New FrmInsertActor()
'Declares ObjActor as an object of the FrmInsertActor class
        ObjActor.Show()
'Displays the Insert Actor form
End Sub
```

When the administrator selects the Actor command, the MitmActor_Click function opens the Insert Actor form. The administrator can use the Insert Actor form to add records to the Actor table in the Movies database.

The MitmDirector_Click Function

The MitmDirector_Click function executes when the administrator selects the Director command from the Insert submenu.

The code for the MitmDirector_Click function is as follows:

```
Private Sub MitmDirector_Click(ByVal sender As System.Object, ByVal e As
System.EventArgs) Handles MitmDirector.Click
        ObjDirector = New FrmInsertDirector()
'Declares ObjDirector as an object of the FrmInsertDirector class
        ObjDirector.Show()
'Displays the Insert Director form
End Sub
```

The MitmDirector_Click function opens the Insert Director form, which enables the administrator to add records to the Director table.

The MitmProducer_Click *Function*

As the name suggests, the MitmProducer_Click function executes when the administrator selects the Producer command from the Insert submenu.

The code for the MitmProducer_Click function is as follows:

```
Private Sub MitmProducer_Click(ByVal sender As System.Object, ByVal e As
System.EventArgs) Handles MitmProducer.Click
        ObjProducer = New FrmInsertProducer()
'Declares ObjProducer as an object of the FrmInsertProducer class
        ObjProducer.Show()
'Displays the Insert Producer form
End Sub
```

After the MitmProducer_Click function executes, the Insert Producer form displays. The Insert Producer form enables the administrator to add records to the Producer table.

The MitmVideo_Click *Function*

The MitmVideo_Click function executes when the administrator selects the Video option from the Insert submenu.

The code for the MitmVideo_Click function is as follows:

```
Private Sub MitmVideo_Click(ByVal sender As System.Object, ByVal e As
System.EventArgs) Handles MitmVideo.Click
```

```
        ObjVideo = New FrmInsertVideo()
'Declares ObjVideo as an object of the FrmInsertVideo class
        ObjVideo.Show()
'Displays the Insert Video form
End Sub
```

The `MitmDirector_Click` function displays the Insert Video form, which enables the administrator to add records to the Video table.

The MitmMovie_Click Function

The `MitmMovie_Click` function executes when the administrator selects the Movie command from the Insert menu. The code for the `MitmMovie_Click` function is as follows:

```
Private Sub MitmMovie_Click(ByVal sender As System.Object, ByVal e As
System.EventArgs) Handles MitmMovie.Click
        ObjMovie = New FrmInsertMovie()
'Declares ObjMovie as an object of the FrmInsertMovie class
        ObjMovie.Show()
'Opens the Insert Movie form
End Sub
```

The `MitmMovie_Click` function displays the Insert Movie form, which enables the administrator to insert records on the Movie table.

The MitmCustomer_Click Function

The `MitmCustomer_Click` function executes when the administrator selects the Customer command from the Insert submenu. The code for the `MitmCustomer-_Click` function is as follows:

```
Private Sub MitmCustomer_Click(ByVal sender As System.Object, ByVal e As
System.EventArgs) Handles MitmCustomer.Click
        ObjCustomer = New FrmInsertCustomer()
'Declares ObjCustomer as an object of the FrmInsertCustomer class
        ObjCustomer.Show()
'Displays the Insert Customer form
End Sub
```

When the `MitmCustomer_Click` function executes, the Insert Customer form opens. The Insert Customer form enables the administrator to add records to the Customer table.

The MitmUpdateDelete_Click *Function*

The `MitmUpdateDelete_Click` function executes when the administrator selects the Update/Delete command from the Operations menu. The code for the `MitmUpdateDelete_Click` function is as follows:

```
Private Sub MitmUpdateDelete_Click(ByVal sender As System.Object, ByVal e As
System.EventArgs) Handles MitmUpdateDelete.Click
        ObjUpdateDelete = New FrmUpdateDelete()
'Declares ObjUpdateDelete as an object of the FrmUpdateDelete class
        ObjUpdateDelete.Show()
'Opens the Update/Delete form
End Sub
```

The `MitmUpdateDelete_Click` function displays the Update/Delete form, which enables the administrator to modify and delete the records in the various tables in the database.

The MitmDailySales_Click *Function*

The `MitmDailySales_Click` function executes when the administrator selects the Daily Sales command from the Generate Reports menu. The code for this function is as follows:

```
Private Sub MitmDailySales_Click(ByVal sender As System.Object, ByVal e As
System.EventArgs) Handles MitmDailySales.Click
        ObjReport = New FrmReports()
'Declares ObjReport as an object of the FrmReports class
        ObjReport.IntReportType = 0
'Assigns a value of 0 to the IntReportType variable
        ObjReport.Show()
'Opens the Daily Sales report
End Sub
```

The `MitmDailySales_Click` function opens the Daily Sales report.

The **MitmMoviesInDemand_Click** *Function*

The `MitmMoviesInDemand_Click` function executes when the administrator selects the Movies in Demand command from the Generate Reports menu. The code for the `MitmMoviesInDemand_Click` function is as follows:

```
Private Sub MitmMoviesInDemand_Click(ByVal sender As System.Object, ByVal e As
System.EventArgs) Handles MitmMoviesInDemand.Click
        ObjReport = New FrmReports()
'Declares ObjReport as an object of the FrmReports class
        ObjReport.IntReportType = 1
'Assigns a value of 1 to the IntReportType variable
        ObjReport.Show()
'Opens the Movies In Demand report
End Sub
```

The `MitmMoviesInDemand_Click` function displays the Movies In Demand report.

The **MitmCustDetails_Click** *Function*

The `MitmCustDetails_Click` function executes when the administrator selects the Customer Details command from the Generate Reports menu. The code for the `MitmCustDetails_Click` function is as follows:

```
Private Sub MitmCustDetails_Click(ByVal sender As System.Object, ByVal e As
System.EventArgs) Handles MitmCustDetails.Click
        ObjReport = New FrmReports()
'Declares ObjReport as an object of the FrmReports class
        ObjReport.IntReportType = 2
'Assigns a value of 2 to the IntReportType variable
        ObjReport.Show()
'Displays the Customer Details report
End Sub
```

The `MitmCustDetails_Click` function displays the Customer Details report.

The MmnuExit_Click *Function*

The MmnuExit_Click function executes when the administrator selects the Exit menu command from the Main form.

```
Private Sub MmnuExit_Click(ByVal sender As System.Object, ByVal e As
System.EventArgs) Handles MmnuExit.Click
        Close()
'Closes the Main form
End Sub
```

The MmnuExit_Click function closes the Main form.

The Complete Code for the Main Form

In the preceding sections, you looked at the code associated with the events and functions in the Main form. Listing 18-1 provides the complete code for the Main form.

Listing 18-1 The Code for the Main Form

```
Public Class FrmMainAdmin
        Inherits System.Windows.Forms.Form

        Public Shared ObjActor As FrmInsertActor
        Public Shared ObjDirector As FrmInsertDirector
        Public Shared ObjProducer As FrmInsertProducer
        Public Shared ObjMovie As FrmInsertMovie
        Public Shared ObjVideo As FrmInsertVideo
        Public Shared ObjCustomer As FrmInsertCustomer
        Public Shared ObjUpdateDelete As FrmUpdateDelete
        Public Shared ObjReport As FrmReports

Windows Form Designer generated code
'Contains the code that specifies the size, location, and other properties, such as
font and name, for the controls on the form.
        Private Sub MitmActor_Click(ByVal sender As System.Object, ByVal e As
System.EventArgs) Handles MitmActor.Click
```

```
                 ObjActor = New FrmInsertActor()
                 ObjActor.Show()
End Sub


        Private Sub MitmDirector_Click(ByVal sender As System.Object, ByVal e As
System.EventArgs) Handles MitmDirector.Click
                    ObjDirector = New FrmInsertDirector()
                    ObjDirector.Show()
            End Sub


        Private Sub MitmProducer_Click(ByVal sender As System.Object, ByVal e As
System.EventArgs) Handles MitmProducer.Click
                    ObjProducer = New FrmInsertProducer()
                    ObjProducer.Show()
            End Sub


        Private Sub MitmVideo_Click(ByVal sender As System.Object, ByVal e As
System.EventArgs) Handles MitmVideo.Click
                    ObjVideo = New FrmInsertVideo()
                    ObjVideo.Show()
            End Sub


        Private Sub MitmMovie_Click(ByVal sender As System.Object, ByVal e As
System.EventArgs) Handles MitmMovie.Click
                    ObjMovie = New FrmInsertMovie()
                    ObjMovie.Show()
            End Sub


        Private Sub MitmCustomer_Click(ByVal sender As System.Object, ByVal e As
System.EventArgs) Handles MitmCustomer.Click
                    ObjCustomer = New FrmInsertCustomer()
                    ObjCustomer.Show()
                End Sub


        Private Sub MitmUpdateDelete_Click(ByVal sender As System.Object, ByVal e
As System.EventArgs) Handles MitmUpdateDelete.Click
                    ObjUpdateDelete = New FrmUpdateDelete()
                    ObjUpdateDelete.Show()
```

```
        End Sub


        Private Sub MitmDailySales_Click(ByVal sender As System.Object, ByVal e
As System.EventArgs) Handles MitmDailySales.Click
                ObjReport = New FrmReports()
                ObjReport.IntReportType = 0
                ObjReport.Show()
        End Sub


        Private Sub MitmMoviesInDemand_Click(ByVal sender As System.Object, ByVal e
As System.EventArgs) Handles MitmMoviesInDemand.Click
                ObjReport = New FrmReports()
                ObjReport.IntReportType = 1
                ObjReport.Show()
        End Sub


        Private Sub MitmCustDetails_Click(ByVal sender As System.Object, ByVal e
As System.EventArgs) Handles MitmCustDetails.Click
                ObjReport = New FrmReports()
                ObjReport.IntReportType = 2
                ObjReport.Show()
        End Sub


        Private Sub MmnuExit_Click(ByVal sender As System.Object, ByVal e As
System.EventArgs) Handles MmnuExit.Click
                Close()
        End Sub
End Class
```

Summary

In this chapter, you learned to add functionality to the Main form. This chapter also described the functions that you need to create to add functionality to the Main form. You also looked at the complete code for the Main form.

Chapter 19

In the preceding chapter, you learned to add functionality to the Main form. In this chapter, you will learn to add functionality to the Update/Delete form of the Administration module.

To start with, let's review the Update/Delete form as shown in Figure 19-1.

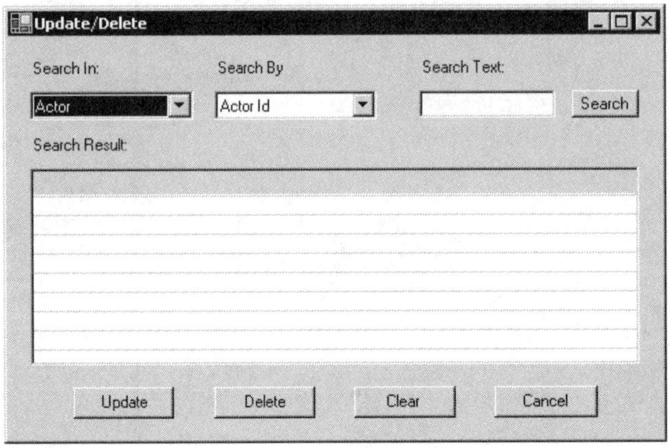

FIGURE 19-1 *The interface of the Update/Delete form*

The Update/Delete form enables the administrator to edit and delete records from the tables in the Movies database. To connect to the database from the Update/Delete form, you need to import the classes stored in the System.Data.SqlClient namespace. You can import the System.Data.SqlClient namespace by including the following statement in the Update/Delete form:

```
Imports System.Data.SqlClient
'Includes classes used by the SQL Server .NET data provider
```

In addition to the preceding statement, you need to include the following statements in the Update/Delete form:

```
Imports System.Data
'Includes the classes that make up the ADO.NET architecture
Imports System.String
'Includes the classes that enable you to work with strings
```

```
Imports System.Data.OleDb
'Includes classes used by the OLE DB .NET Data Provider
Imports System.Collections
'Includes the collection classes
Imports System.Data.SqlTypes
'Includes the classes for native data types within SQL Server
```

You also need to declare the following variables in the Update/Delete form:

```
Dim SqlConnection1 As New SqlConnection(StrConnectionString)
Dim SqlDataAdapter1 As New SqlDataAdapter()
Dim Result As Integer
```

Before you write code, take a look at the flow of the functions in the Update/Delete form. Figure 19-2 depicts this flow.

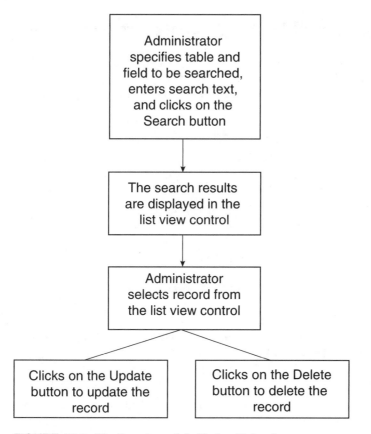

FIGURE 19-2 *The flow chart of the Update/Delete form*

The Update/Delete form consists of the following functions:

- ◆ `FrmUpdateDelete_Load`
- ◆ `CmbSearchIn_SelectedIndexChanged`
- ◆ `HandleComboIndexes()`
- ◆ `CmdSearch_Click`
- ◆ `CmdUpdate_Click`
- ◆ `CmdDelete_Click`
- ◆ `CmdClear_Click`
- ◆ `CmdCancel_Click`

The following sections describe the code for these functions.

The FrmUpdateDelete_Load Function

The `FrmUpdateDelete_Load` function executes when the Update/Delete form loads, and the Update/Delete form loads when the administrator selects the Update/Delete command from the Operations menu in the Main form.

The code for the `FrmUpdateDelete_Load` function is as follows:

```
Private Sub FrmUpdateDelete_Load(ByVal sender As System.Object, ByVal e As
System.EventArgs) Handles MyBase.Load
        CmbSearchIn.SelectedIndex = 0
'Specifies the Actor option as the selected option in the Search In combo box
        HandleComboIndexes()
'Calls the HandleComboIndexes function
End Sub
```

In the Update/Delete form, the `FrmUpdateDelete_Load` function performs the following tasks:

- ◆ It specifies that the Actor option is displayed in the Search In combo box when the Update/Delete form loads.
- ◆ It invokes the `HandleComboIndexes` function.

You will learn about the `HandleComboIndexes` function later in this chapter.

The CmbSearchIn_Selected IndexChanged *Function*

The CmbSearchIn_SelectedIndexChanged function executes when the administrator selects an option from the Search In combo box. This function also executes when the administrator changes the selected index in the Search In combo box.

The code for the CmbSearchIn_SelectedIndexChanged function is as follows:

```
Private Sub CmbSearchIn_SelectedIndexChanged(ByVal sender As System.Object, ByVal e
As System.EventArgs) Handles CmbSearchIn.SelectedIndexChanged
        HandleComboIndexes()
'Calls the HandleComboIndexes function
End Sub
```

When the administrator selects or changes the selection in the Search In combo box, the CmbSearchIn_SelectedIndexChanged function calls the HandleComboIndexes function.

The HandleComboIndexes() *Function*

As previously discussed, the items that need to be displayed in the Search By combo box depend on the value selected by the administrator in the Search In combo box. The HandleComboIndexes function populates the Search By combo box based on the option selected by the administrator in the Search In combo box. For example, if the administrator selects the Actor option in the Search In combo box, the HandleComboIndexes function populates the Search By combo box with the names of fields from the Actor table.

The code for the HandleComboIndexes function is as follows:

```
Private Sub HandleComboIndexes()
        Dim StrSearchIn As String
        Dim StrSearchBy As String
        Dim StrQuery As String
'Declares variables
        'Select the first item by default in "Search in" combo
        CmbSearchBy.Items.Clear()
'Removes all items from the Search By combo box
```

```
            StrSearchIn = CmbSearchIn.Text
    'Stores the option selected by the administrator in the Search In combo box in the
    StrSearchIn variable
            If (Compare(StrSearchIn, "Movie", True) = 0) Then
    'Checks if the administrator has selected the Movie option
                    CmbSearchBy.Items.Add("Movie Id")
                    CmbSearchBy.Items.Add("Movie Title")
                    CmbSearchBy.Items.Add("Release Year")
                    CmbSearchBy.Items.Add("Category")
    'Populates the Search By combo box with the names of the fields of the Movie table
            ElseIf (Compare(StrSearchIn, "Actor", True) = 0) Then
    'Checks if the administrator has selected the Actor option
                    CmbSearchBy.Items.Add("Actor Id")
                    CmbSearchBy.Items.Add("First Name")
                    CmbSearchBy.Items.Add("Last Name")
    'Populates the Search By combo box with the names of the fields of the Actor table
            ElseIf (Compare(StrSearchIn, "Director", True) = 0) Then
    'Checks if the administrator has selected the Director option
                    CmbSearchBy.Items.Add("Director Id")
                    CmbSearchBy.Items.Add("First Name")
                    CmbSearchBy.Items.Add("Last Name")
    'Populates the Search By combo box with the names of the fields of the Director
    table
            ElseIf (Compare(StrSearchIn, "Producer", True) = 0) Then
    'Checks if the administrator has selected the Producer option
                    CmbSearchBy.Items.Add("Producer Id")
                    CmbSearchBy.Items.Add("Name")
    'Populates the Search By combo box with the names of the fields of the Producer
    table
            ElseIf (Compare(StrSearchIn, "Video", True) = 0) Then
    'Checks if the administrator has selected the Video option
                    CmbSearchBy.Items.Add("Video Id")
                    CmbSearchBy.Items.Add("Format")
    'Populates the Search By combo box with the names of the fields of the Video table
            ElseIf (Compare(StrSearchIn, "Customer", True) = 0) Then
    'Checks if the administrator has selected the Customer option
                    CmbSearchBy.Items.Add("Customer Id")
                    CmbSearchBy.Items.Add("First Name")
```

```
                    CmbSearchBy.Items.Add("Last Name")
                    CmbSearchBy.Items.Add("State")
'Populates the Search By combo box with the names of the fields of the Customer
table
          Else
                    StrQuery = ""
          End If
          CmbSearchBy.SelectedIndex = 0
'Sets the first item in the Search By combo box as the selected option
End Sub
```

The CmdSearch_Click *Function*

The CmdSearch_Click function executes when the administrator clicks on the
Search button in the Update/Delete form. The CmdSearch_Click function populates the list view control based on the options selected by the administrator in the
Update/Delete form. The CmdSearch_Click function is populated based on the
option selected by the administrator in the Search In and Search By combo boxes
and the text entered in the Search Text text box.

The code for the CmdSearch_Click function is as follows:

```
Private Sub CmdSearch_Click(ByVal sender As System.Object, ByVal e As
System.EventArgs) Handles CmdSearch.Click
          Dim DsDataSet As DataSet
          Dim DrRowPicker As DataRow
          Dim StrSearchIn As String
          Dim StrSearchBy As String
          Dim StrQuery As String
          Dim BSearchStrEmpty As Boolean
'Declares variables
          BSearchStrEmpty = False
'Assigns a value of False to the BSearchStrEmpty variable

          If TxtSearchText.Text.Trim = "" Then
'Checks if the administrator has not entered any text in the Search Text text box
                    MessageBox.Show("Please enter some text to search.")
```

```
'Displays a message asking the administrator to enter text in the Search Text text
box
                BSearchStrEmpty = True
'Assigns a value of True to the BSearchStrEmpty variable
        End If


        StrSearchIn = CmbSearchIn.Text
'Stores the option selected by the administrator in the Search In combo box in the
StrSearchIn variable
        StrSearchBy = CmbSearchBy.Text
'Stores the option selected by the administrator in the Search By combo box in the
StrSearchBy variable


        If (Compare(StrSearchIn, "Movie", True) = 0) Then
'Checks if the administrator has selected the Movie option in the Search In combo
box
            Result = 0
'Assigns a value of 0 to the Result variable
            StrQuery = "SELECT DISTINCT MovID, MovTitle, DirID, ProdID, Duration,
Description, Category, ReleaseYear FROM Movie "
            If (Not BSearchStrEmpty) Then
                If (Compare(StrSearchBy, "Movie Id", True) = 0) Then
                    StrQuery += "WHERE MovID = '"
                    StrQuery += TxtSearchText.Text & "'"
                ElseIf (Compare(StrSearchBy, "Movie Title", True) = 0) Then
                    StrQuery += "WHERE MovTitle LIKE '"
                    StrQuery += TxtSearchText.Text & "%'"
                ElseIf (Compare(StrSearchBy, "Release Year", True) = 0) Then
                    StrQuery += "WHERE ReleaseYear = '"
                    StrQuery += TxtSearchText.Text & "'"
                ElseIf (Compare(StrSearchBy, "Category", True) = 0) Then
                    StrQuery += "WHERE Category = '"
                    StrQuery += TxtSearchText.Text & "'"
                End If
'Specifies the query to retrieve records from the Movie table based on the option
selected in the Search By combo box and the text entered in the Search Text text
box
            End If
```

```
        ElseIf (Compare(StrSearchIn, "Actor", True) = 0) Then
'Checks if the administrator has selected the Actor option in the Search In combo
box
            Result = 1
'Assigns a value of 1 to the Result variable
            StrQuery = "SELECT DISTINCT ActorID, FirstName, LastName FROM Actor "
            If (Not BSearchStrEmpty) Then
                If (Compare(StrSearchBy, "Actor Id", True) = 0) Then
                    StrQuery += "WHERE ActorID = '"
                    StrQuery += TxtSearchText.Text & "'"
                ElseIf (Compare(StrSearchBy, "First Name", True) = 0) Then
                    StrQuery += "WHERE FirstName LIKE '"
                    StrQuery += TxtSearchText.Text & "%'"
                ElseIf (Compare(StrSearchBy, "Last Name", True) = 0) Then
                    StrQuery += "WHERE LastName LIKE '"
                    StrQuery += TxtSearchText.Text & "%'"
                End If
'Specifies the query to retrieve records from the Actor table based on the option
selected in the Search By combo box and the text entered in the Search Text text
box
            End If
        ElseIf (Compare(StrSearchIn, "Director", True) = 0) Then
'Checks if the administrator has selected the Director option in the Search In
combo box
            Result = 2
'Assigns a value of 2 to the Result variable
            StrQuery = "SELECT DISTINCT DirID, FirstName, LastName FROM Director "
            If (Not BSearchStrEmpty) Then
                If (Compare(StrSearchBy, "Director Id", True) = 0) Then
                    StrQuery += "WHERE DirID = '"
                    StrQuery += TxtSearchText.Text & "'"
                ElseIf (Compare(StrSearchBy, "First Name", True) = 0) Then
                    StrQuery += "WHERE FirstName LIKE '"
                    StrQuery += TxtSearchText.Text & "%'"
                ElseIf (Compare(StrSearchBy, "Last Name", True) = 0) Then
                    StrQuery += "WHERE LastName LIKE '"
                    StrQuery += TxtSearchText.Text & "%'"
                End If
```

```
'Specifies the query to retrieve records from the Director table based on the
option selected in the Search By combo box and the text entered in the Search Text
text box
                End If
        ElseIf (Compare(StrSearchIn, "Producer", True) = 0) Then
'Checks if the administrator has selected the Producer option in the Search In
combo box
                Result = 3
'Assigns a value of 3 to the Result variable
                StrQuery = "SELECT DISTINCT ProdID, Name FROM Producer "
                If (Not BSearchStrEmpty) Then
                    If (Compare(StrSearchBy, "Producer ID", True) = 0) Then
                        StrQuery += "WHERE ProdID = '"
                        StrQuery += TxtSearchText.Text & "'"
                    ElseIf (Compare(StrSearchBy, "Name", True) = 0) Then
                        StrQuery += "WHERE Name LIKE '"
                        StrQuery += TxtSearchText.Text & "%'"
                    End If
'Specifies the query to retrieve records from the Producer table based on the
option selected in the Search By combo box and the text entered in the Search Text
text box
                End If
        ElseIf (Compare(StrSearchIn, "Video", True) = 0) Then
'Checks if the administrator has selected the Video option in the Search In combo
box
                Result = 4
'Assigns a value of 4 to the Result variable
                StrQuery = "SELECT DISTINCT VideoID, MovID, Format, Price FROM Video "
                If (Not BSearchStrEmpty) Then
                    If (Compare(StrSearchBy, "Video ID", True) = 0) Then
                        StrQuery += "WHERE VideoID = '"
                    ElseIf (Compare(StrSearchBy, "Format", True) = 0) Then
                        StrQuery += "WHERE Format = '"
                    End If
                    StrQuery += TxtSearchText.Text & "'"
                End If
'Specifies the query to retrieve records from the Video table based on the option
selected in the Search By combo box and the text entered in the Search Text text
box
```

```
            ElseIf (Compare(StrSearchIn, "Customer", True) = 0) Then
'Checks if the administrator has selected the Customer option in the Search In
combo box
                Result = 5
'Assigns a value of 5 to the Result variable
                StrQuery = "SELECT DISTINCT CustID, FirstName, LastName, Address,
City, State, Zip, Phone, Email FROM Customer "
                If (Not BSearchStrEmpty) Then
                    If (Compare(StrSearchBy, "Customer Id", True) = 0) Then
                        StrQuery += "WHERE CustID = '"
                        StrQuery += TxtSearchText.Text & "'"
                    ElseIf (Compare(StrSearchBy, "First Name", True) = 0) Then
                        StrQuery += "WHERE FirstName LIKE '"
                        StrQuery += TxtSearchText.Text & "%'"
                    ElseIf (Compare(StrSearchBy, "Last Name", True) = 0) Then
                        StrQuery += "WHERE LastName LIKE '"
                        StrQuery += TxtSearchText.Text & "%'"
                    ElseIf (Compare(StrSearchBy, "State", True) = 0) Then
                        StrQuery += "WHERE State = '"
                        StrQuery += TxtSearchText.Text & "'"
                    End If
'Specifies the query to retrieve records from the Customer table based on the
option selected in the Search By combo box and the text entered in the Search Text
text box
                End If
            Else
                Result = -1
'Assigns a value of -1 to the Result variable
                StrQuery = ""
'Assigns space to the StrQuery variable
            End If


            Dim SelectCmd1 As New SqlCommand(StrQuery, SqlConnection1)
'Declares SelectCmd1 as an object of the SqlCommand class and associates the object
with the SqlConnection1 object


            DsDataSet = New DataSet()
'Declares the dataset
```

```
        SqlDataAdapter1.SelectCommand = SelectCmd1
        SqlDataAdapter1.SelectCommand.CommandText = StrQuery
        SqlConnection1.Open()
'Establishes a connection with the database
        SqlDataAdapter1.Fill(DsDataSet, "SearchResultAdmin")
'Populates the SearchResultAdmin table in the DsDataSet dataset with the query
results

        LvwSearchResult.Items.Clear()
        LvwSearchResult.Columns.Clear()
'Clears the list view control

        Dim IntRowCount As Integer
        IntRowCount = 0
'Initializes the IntRowCount variable

        Dim IntKind As Integer
        IntKind = CInt(Result)
'Assigns the value of the Result variable to the IntKind variable

        Dim ColumnHeader1 As New ColumnHeader()
        Dim ColumnHeader2 As New ColumnHeader()
        Dim ColumnHeader3 As New ColumnHeader()
        Dim ColumnHeader4 As New ColumnHeader()
        Dim ColumnHeader5 As New ColumnHeader()
        Dim ColumnHeader6 As New ColumnHeader()
        Dim ColumnHeader7 As New ColumnHeader()
        Dim ColumnHeader8 As New ColumnHeader()
        Dim ColumnHeader9 As New ColumnHeader()
'Declares column header objects
        Dim StrMessage As String

        If (IntKind = 0) Then
'Checks if the query was executed on the Movie table
            StrMessage = "Couldn't find this movie."
'Assigns a value to the StrMessage variable based on the selection in the form
            LvwSearchResult.Columns.AddRange(New
```

```
System.Windows.Forms.ColumnHeader() {ColumnHeader1, ColumnHeader2, ColumnHeader3,
ColumnHeader4, ColumnHeader5, ColumnHeader6, ColumnHeader7, ColumnHeader8})
'Adds column headers to the list view control
            ColumnHeader1.Text = "Movie ID"
            ColumnHeader2.Text = "Movie Title"
            ColumnHeader3.Text = "Director ID"
            ColumnHeader4.Text = "Producer ID"
            ColumnHeader5.Text = "Duration"
            ColumnHeader6.Text = "Description"
            ColumnHeader7.Text = "Category"
            ColumnHeader8.Text = "Release Year"
'Sets the field names of the Movie table as the Text property for the column head-
ers
            ElseIf (IntKind = 1) Then
'Checks if the query was executed on the Actor table
            StrMessage = "Couldn't find this actor."
'Assigns a value to the StrMessage variable based on the selection in the form
            LvwSearchResult.Columns.AddRange(New
System.Windows.Forms.ColumnHeader() {ColumnHeader1, ColumnHeader2, ColumnHeader3})
'Adds column headers to the list view control
            ColumnHeader1.Text = "Actor ID"
            ColumnHeader2.Text = "First Name"
            ColumnHeader3.Text = "Last Name"
'Sets the field names of the Actor table as the Text property for the column
headers
            ElseIf (IntKind = 2) Then
'Checks if the query was executed on the Director table
            StrMessage = "Couldn't find this director."
'Assigns a value to the StrMessage variable based on the selection in the form
            LvwSearchResult.Columns.AddRange(New
System.Windows.Forms.ColumnHeader() {ColumnHeader1, ColumnHeader2, ColumnHeader3})
'Adds column headers to the list view control
            ColumnHeader1.Text = "Director ID"
            ColumnHeader2.Text = "First Name"
            ColumnHeader3.Text = "Last Name"
'Sets the field names of the Director table as the Text property for the column
headers
            ElseIf (IntKind = 3) Then
```

```
'Checks if the query was executed on the Procedure table
          StrMessage = "Couldn't find this producer."
'Assigns a value to the StrMessage variable based on the selection in the form
          LvwSearchResult.Columns.AddRange(New
System.Windows.Forms.ColumnHeader() {ColumnHeader1, ColumnHeader2})
'Adds column headers to the list view control
          ColumnHeader1.Text = "Producer ID"
          ColumnHeader2.Text = "Name"
'Sets the field names of the Procedure table as the Text property for the column
headers
       ElseIf (IntKind = 4) Then
'Checks if the query was executed on the Video table
          StrMessage = "Couldn't find this video."
'Assigns a value to the StrMessage variable based on the selection in the form
          LvwSearchResult.Columns.AddRange(New
System.Windows.Forms.ColumnHeader() {ColumnHeader1, ColumnHeader2, ColumnHeader3,
ColumnHeader4})
'Adds column headers to the list view control
          ColumnHeader1.Text = "Video ID"
          ColumnHeader2.Text = "Movie ID"
          ColumnHeader3.Text = "Format"
          ColumnHeader4.Text = "Price"
'Sets the field names of the Video table as the Text property for the column head-
ers
       ElseIf (IntKind = 5) Then
'Checks if the query was executed on the Customer table
          StrMessage = "Couldn't find this customer."
          LvwSearchResult.Columns.AddRange(New
System.Windows.Forms.ColumnHeader() {ColumnHeader1, ColumnHeader2, ColumnHeader3,
ColumnHeader4, ColumnHeader5, ColumnHeader6, ColumnHeader7, ColumnHeader8,
ColumnHeader9})
'Adds column headers to the list view control
          ColumnHeader1.Text = "Customer ID"
          ColumnHeader2.Text = "First Name"
          ColumnHeader3.Text = "Last Name"
          ColumnHeader4.Text = "Address"
          ColumnHeader5.Text = "City"
          ColumnHeader6.Text = "State"
```

```
                    ColumnHeader7.Text = "Zip"
                    ColumnHeader8.Text = "Phone"
                    ColumnHeader9.Text = "Email"
'Sets the field names of the Customer table as the Text property for the column
headers
            End If


            Dim StrValue0, StrValue1, StrValue2, StrValue3, StrValue4, StrValue5,
StrValue6, StrValue7, StrValue8 As String
            Dim IntCounter As Integer
'Declares variables


            'Display the records from the dataset
            For Each DrRowPicker In DsDataSet.Tables("SearchResultAdmin").Rows
                If (IntKind = 0) Then
'Checks if the query was executed on the Movie table
                    For IntCounter = 0 To 7
                        If (DrRowPicker.IsNull(IntCounter)) Then
'Checks if the dataset contains no records
                            If IntCounter = 0 Then
                                StrValue0 = ""
                            ElseIf IntCounter = 1 Then
                                StrValue1 = ""
                            ElseIf IntCounter = 2 Then
                                StrValue2 = ""
                            ElseIf IntCounter = 3 Then
                                StrValue3 = ""
                            ElseIf IntCounter = 4 Then
                                StrValue4 = ""
                            ElseIf IntCounter = 5 Then
                                StrValue5 = ""
                            ElseIf IntCounter = 6 Then
                                StrValue6 = ""
                            ElseIf IntCounter = 7 Then
                                StrValue7 = ""
                            End If
'Assigns a space to the string variables where the column has null value
                        Else
```

```
'Executes if the dataset contains records
                If IntCounter = 0 Then
                    StrValue0 = DrRowPicker(0)
                ElseIf IntCounter = 1 Then
                    StrValue1 = DrRowPicker(1)
                ElseIf IntCounter = 2 Then
                    StrValue2 = DrRowPicker(2)
                ElseIf IntCounter = 3 Then
                    StrValue3 = DrRowPicker(3)
                ElseIf IntCounter = 4 Then
                    StrValue4 = DrRowPicker(4)
                ElseIf IntCounter = 5 Then
                    StrValue5 = DrRowPicker(5)
                ElseIf IntCounter = 6 Then
                    StrValue6 = DrRowPicker(6)
                ElseIf IntCounter = 7 Then
                    StrValue7 = DrRowPicker(7)
                End If
'Picks up the values from the dataset and stores the values in string variables
                End If
            Next

                Dim StrSearchRow As String() = {StrValue0, StrValue1, StrValue2,
StrValue3, StrValue4, StrValue5, StrValue6, StrValue7}
'Picks up the values from the string variables and stores the values in a single
string variable
                LvwSearchResult.Items.Add(New ListViewItem(StrSearchRow))
'Displays the row in the list view control
            ElseIf (IntKind = 1) Then
'Checks if the query was executed on the Actor table
                For IntCounter = 0 To 2
                    If (DrRowPicker.IsNull(IntCounter)) Then
'Checks if the dataset contains no records
                        If IntCounter = 0 Then
                            StrValue0 = ""
                        ElseIf IntCounter = 1 Then
                            StrValue1 = ""
                        ElseIf IntCounter = 2 Then
```

```
                                StrValue2 = ""
                    End If
'Assigns a space to the string variables where the column has null value
                        Else
'Executes if the dataset contains records
                            If IntCounter = 0 Then
                                StrValue0 = DrRowPicker(IntCounter)
                            ElseIf IntCounter = 1 Then
                                StrValue1 = DrRowPicker(IntCounter)
                            ElseIf IntCounter = 2 Then
                                StrValue2 = DrRowPicker(IntCounter)
                            End If
'Picks up the values from the dataset and stores the values in string variables
                        End If
                Next

                    Dim StrSearchRow As String() = {StrValue0, StrValue1, StrValue2}
'Picks up the values from the string variables and stores the values in a single
string variable
                    LvwSearchResult.Items.Add(New ListViewItem(StrSearchRow))
'Displays the row in the list view control

                ElseIf (IntKind = 2) Then
'Checks if the query was executed on the Director table
                    For IntCounter = 0 To 2
                        If (DrRowPicker.IsNull(IntCounter)) Then
'Checks if the dataset contains no records
                            If IntCounter = 0 Then
                                StrValue0 = ""
                            ElseIf IntCounter = 1 Then
                                StrValue1 = ""
                            ElseIf IntCounter = 2 Then
                                StrValue2 = ""
                            End If
'Assigns a space to the string variables where the column has null value
                        Else
'Executes if the dataset contains records
                            If IntCounter = 0 Then
```

```
                                StrValue0 = DrRowPicker(0)
                    ElseIf IntCounter = 1 Then
                            StrValue1 = DrRowPicker(1)
                    ElseIf IntCounter = 2 Then
                            StrValue2 = DrRowPicker(2)
                    End If
'Picks up the values from the dataset and stores the values in string variables
                    End If
            Next


            Dim StrSearchRow As String() = {StrValue0, StrValue1, StrValue2}
'Picks up the values from the string variables and stores the values in a single
string variable
            LvwSearchResult.Items.Add(New ListViewItem(StrSearchRow))
'Displays the row in the list view control


        ElseIf (IntKind = 3) Then
'Checks if the query was executed on the Producer table
            For IntCounter = 0 To 1
                If (DrRowPicker.IsNull(IntCounter)) Then
'Checks if the dataset contains no records
                    If IntCounter = 0 Then
                        StrValue0 = ""
                    ElseIf IntCounter = 1 Then
                        StrValue1 = ""
                    End If
'Assigns a space to the string variables where the column has null value
                Else
'Executes if the dataset contains records
                    If IntCounter = 0 Then
                        StrValue0 = DrRowPicker(0)
                    ElseIf IntCounter = 1 Then
                        StrValue1 = DrRowPicker(1)
                    End If
'Picks up the values from the dataset and stores the values in string variables
                    End If
                Next
                Dim StrSearchRow As String() = {StrValue0, StrValue1}
```

```
'Picks up the values from the string variables and stores the values in a single
string variable
                    LvwSearchResult.Items.Add(New ListViewItem(StrSearchRow))
'Displays the row in the list view control


                ElseIf (IntKind = 4) Then
'Checks if the query was executed on the Video table
                    For IntCounter = 0 To 3
                        If (DrRowPicker.IsNull(IntCounter)) Then
'Checks if the dataset contains no records
                            If IntCounter = 0 Then
                                StrValue0 = ""
                            ElseIf IntCounter = 1 Then
                                StrValue1 = ""
                            ElseIf IntCounter = 2 Then
                                StrValue2 = ""
                            ElseIf IntCounter = 3 Then
                                StrValue3 = ""
                            End If
'Assigns a space to the string variables where the column has null value
                        Else
'Executes if the dataset contains records
                            If IntCounter = 0 Then
                                StrValue0 = DrRowPicker(0)
                            ElseIf IntCounter = 1 Then
                                StrValue1 = DrRowPicker(1)
                            ElseIf IntCounter = 2 Then
                                StrValue2 = DrRowPicker(2)
                            ElseIf IntCounter = 3 Then
                                StrValue3 = DrRowPicker(3)
                            End If
'Picks up the values from the dataset and stores the values in string variables
                        End If
                    Next


                Dim StrSearchRow As String() = {StrValue0, StrValue1, StrValue2,
StrValue3}
```

```
'Picks up the values from the string variables and stores the values in a single
string variable
                    LvwSearchResult.Items.Add(New ListViewItem(StrSearchRow))
'Displays the row in the list view control


            ElseIf (IntKind = 5) Then
'Checks if the query was executed on the Customer table
            For IntCounter = 0 To 8
                If (DrRowPicker.IsNull(IntCounter)) Then
'Checks if the dataset contains no records
                    If IntCounter = 0 Then
                        StrValue0 = ""
                    ElseIf IntCounter = 1 Then
                        StrValue1 = ""
                    ElseIf IntCounter = 2 Then
                        StrValue2 = ""
                    ElseIf IntCounter = 3 Then
                        StrValue3 = ""
                    ElseIf IntCounter = 4 Then
                        StrValue4 = ""
                    ElseIf IntCounter = 5 Then
                        StrValue5 = ""
                    ElseIf IntCounter = 6 Then
                        StrValue6 = ""
                    ElseIf IntCounter = 7 Then
                        StrValue7 = ""
                    ElseIf IntCounter = 8 Then
                        StrValue8 = ""
                    End If
'Assigns a space to the string variables where the column has null value
                Else
'Executes if the dataset contains records
                    If IntCounter = 0 Then
                        StrValue0 = DrRowPicker(0)
                    ElseIf IntCounter = 1 Then
                        StrValue1 = DrRowPicker(1)
                    ElseIf IntCounter = 2 Then
                        StrValue2 = DrRowPicker(2)
                    ElseIf IntCounter = 3 Then
```

```
                              StrValue3 = DrRowPicker(3)
                      ElseIf IntCounter = 4 Then
                              StrValue4 = DrRowPicker(4)
                      ElseIf IntCounter = 5 Then
                              StrValue5 = DrRowPicker(5)
                      ElseIf IntCounter = 6 Then
                              StrValue6 = DrRowPicker(6)
                      ElseIf IntCounter = 7 Then
                              StrValue7 = DrRowPicker(7)
                      ElseIf IntCounter = 8 Then
                              StrValue8 = DrRowPicker(8)
                      End If
'Picks up the values from the dataset and stores the values in string variables
                  End If
              Next


              Dim StrSearchRow As String() = {StrValue0, StrValue1, StrValue2,
StrValue3, StrValue4, StrValue5, StrValue6, StrValue7, StrValue8}
'Picks up the values from the string variables and stores the values in a single
string variable
              LvwSearchResult.Items.Add(New ListViewItem(StrSearchRow))
'Displays the row in the list view control
          End If


          IntRowCount += 1
'Increments the IntRowCount variable by 1
      Next


      If IntRowCount = 0 Then
          MessageBox.Show(StrMessage)
'Displays a message if no rows were found in the dataset
      End If


      SqlConnection1.Close()
'Closes the SqlConnection1 object
      SqlDataAdapter1.Dispose()
'Closes the SqlDataAdapter1 object
End Sub
```

The CmdUpdate_Click *Function*

As previously discussed, the administrator can click on the Update button in the Update/Delete form to update a record. In addition, when the administrator clicks on the Update button, the CmdUpdate_Click function executes. The CmdUpdate_Click function opens the record selected by the administrator in a form. The administrator can then edit the record. However, the form that displays when the administrator clicks on the Update button depends on the type of record selected by the administrator. For example, if the record selected by the administrator is contained in the Actor table, the Update Actor form displays when the administrator clicks on the Update button. Similarly, if the record selected by the administrator is contained in the Movie table, the Update Movie form displays. The Update Actor and Update Movie forms are identical to the Insert Actor and Insert Movie forms, respectively.

The code for the CmdUpdate_Click function is as follows:

```
Private Sub CmdUpdate_Click(ByVal sender As System.Object, ByVal e As
System.EventArgs) Handles CmdUpdate.Click
        Dim LstViewCollection As ListView.SelectedListViewItemCollection
'Declares LstViewCollection as an object of the SelectedListViewItemCollection
class
        LstViewCollection = New
ListView.SelectedListViewItemCollection(LvwSearchResult)
'Stores the item selected by the administrator in the LstViewCollection object

        Dim IntTotalSelectedCount As Integer
        IntTotalSelectedCount = LstViewCollection.Count()
'Stores the number of items selected by the administrator in the
IntTotalSelectedCount variable
        If (IntTotalSelectedCount < 1) Then
'Checks if the administrator has not selected any items in the list view control
            MessageBox.Show("You have not selected any records.")
'Displays a message asking the administrator to select a record
            Return
        ElseIf IntTotalSelectedCount > 1 Then
'Checks if the administrator has not selected multiple items from the list view
control
            Return
```

```
        End If

        Dim StrQuery, StrTemp, StrIDToUpdate As String
        Dim IntKind As Integer
        IntKind = CInt(Result)
'Stores the value of the Result variable in the IntKind variable

        Dim ObjActor As FrmInsertActor
        Dim ObjDirector As FrmInsertDirector
        Dim ObjProducer As FrmInsertProducer
        Dim ObjMovie As FrmInsertMovie
        Dim ObjVideo As FrmInsertVideo
        Dim ObjCustomer As FrmInsertCustomer
'Declares objects

        Dim StrUpdateID As String = LstViewCollection.Item(0).Text()
'Stores the text of the item selected by the administrator in the StrUpdateID
variable
        If (IntKind = 0) Then
'Checks if the query was executed on the Movie table
            ObjMovie = New FrmInsertMovie()
'Declares ObjMovie as an object of the FrmInsertMovie class
            ObjMovie.SetUpdateID(StrUpdateID)
'Calls the SetUpdateID function and passes the text of the selected item to the
function
            ObjMovie.Show()
'Displays the Insert Movie form
        ElseIf (IntKind = 1) Then
'Checks if the query was executed on the Actor table
            ObjActor = New FrmInsertActor()
'Declares ObjActor as an object of the FrmInsertActor class
            ObjActor.SetUpdateID(StrUpdateID)
'Calls the SetUpdateID function and passes the text of the selected item to the
function
            ObjActor.Show()
'Opens the Insert Actor form
        ElseIf (IntKind = 2) Then
'Checks if the query was executed on the Director table
```

```
                ObjDirector = New FrmInsertDirector()
'Declares ObjDirector as an object of the FrmInsertDirector class
                ObjDirector.SetUpdateID(StrUpdateID)
'Calls the SetUpdateID function and passes the text of the selected item to the
function
                ObjDirector.Show()
'Displays the Insert Director form
        ElseIf (IntKind = 3) Then
'Checks if the query was executed on the Producer table
                ObjProducer = New FrmInsertProducer()
'Declares ObjProducer as an object of the FrmInsertProducer class
                ObjProducer.SetUpdateID(StrUpdateID)
'Calls the SetUpdateID function and passes the text of the selected item to the
function
                ObjProducer.Show()
'Displays the Insert Producer form
        ElseIf (IntKind = 4) Then
'Checks if the query was executed on the Video table
                ObjVideo = New FrmInsertVideo()
'Declares ObjVideo as an object of the FrmInsertVideo class
                ObjVideo.SetUpdateID(StrUpdateID)
'Calls the SetUpdateID function and passes the text of the selected item to the
function
                ObjVideo.Show()
'Displays the Insert Video form
        ElseIf (IntKind = 5) Then
'Checks if the query was executed on the Customer table
                ObjCustomer = New FrmInsertCustomer()
'Declares ObjCustomer as an object of the FrmInsertCustomer class
                ObjCustomer.SetUpdateID(StrUpdateID)
'Calls the SetUpdateID function and passes the text of the selected item to the
function
                ObjCustomer.Show()
'Displays the Insert Customer form
        End If
End Sub
```

The CmdDelete_Click *Function*

The administrator also can delete records by using the Update/Delete form. To delete a record, the administrator needs to click on the Delete button in the Update/Delete form. When the administrator clicks on the Delete button, the CmdDelete_Click function executes.

The CmdDelete_Click function prompts the administrator to confirm the deletion of the selected record. If the administrator clicks on the Yes button in the message box, the selected record is deleted from the database.

The code of the CmdDelete_Click function is as follows:

```
Private Sub CmdDelete_Click(ByVal sender As System.Object, ByVal e As
System.EventArgs) Handles CmdDelete.Click
        Dim LstViewCollection As ListView.SelectedListViewItemCollection
'Declares LstViewCollection as an object of the SelectedListViewItemCollection
class
        LstViewCollection = New
ListView.SelectedListViewItemCollection(LvwSearchResult)
'Stores the item selected by the administrator in the LstViewCollection object

        Dim IntTotalSelectedCount As Integer
        IntTotalSelectedCount = LstViewCollection.Count()
'Stores the number of items selected by the administrator in the
IntTotalSelectedCount variable

        If (IntTotalSelectedCount < 1) Then
'Checks if the administrator has not selected any items in the list view control
            MessageBox.Show("You have not selected any records.")
'Displays a message asking the administrator to select a record
            Return
        End If

Dim IntRes As DialogResult
        IntRes = MessageBox.Show("Are you sure you want to delete this record?",
"", MessageBoxButtons.YesNo)
'Displays a message confirming the deletion of the selected record
        If (IntRes = DialogResult.No) Then
```

```
            Return
        End If


        Dim IntCounter As Integer
        Dim StrIDToDelete As String
        For IntCounter = 0 To IntTotalSelectedCount - 1
            StrIDToDelete += "'"
'Adds a single quotation mark
            StrIDToDelete += LstViewCollection.Item(0).Text
'Adds the ID of the record to be deleted to the StrIDToDelete variable
            StrIDToDelete += "'"
'Adds another quotation mark
            If (IntCounter < IntTotalSelectedCount - 1) Then
                StrIDToDelete += ","
'Adds a comma
            End If
            LstViewCollection.Item(0).Remove()
'Removes the item from the list view control
        Next


        Dim StrQuery, StrTemp As String
        Dim IntKind As Integer
        IntKind = CInt(Result)
'Stores the value of the Result variable in the IntKind variable


        If (IntKind = 0) Then
'Checks if the selected record is contained in the Movie table
            StrQuery = "DELETE FROM movie WHERE MovID IN ("
            StrQuery += StrIDToDelete & ")"
'Specifies the query to delete records from the Movie table where the IDs of the
selected records match those in the table
        ElseIf (IntKind = 1) Then
'Checks if the selected record is contained in the Actor table
            StrQuery = "DELETE FROM actor WHERE ActorID IN ("
            StrQuery += StrIDToDelete & ")"
'Specifies the query to delete records from the Actor table where the IDs of the
selected records match those in the table
        ElseIf (IntKind = 2) Then
```

```
'Checks if the selected record is contained in the Director table
        StrQuery = "DELETE FROM director WHERE DirID IN ("
        StrQuery += StrIDToDelete & ")"
'Specifies the query to delete records from the Director table where the IDs of the
selected records match those in the table
        ElseIf (IntKind = 3) Then
'Checks if the selected record is contained in the Producer table
        StrQuery = "DELETE FROM producer WHERE ProdID IN ("
        StrQuery += StrIDToDelete & ")"
'Specifies the query to delete records from the Producer table where the IDs of the
selected records match those in the table
        ElseIf (IntKind = 4) Then
'Checks if the selected record is contained in the Video table
        StrQuery = "DELETE FROM video WHERE VideoID IN ("
        StrQuery += StrIDToDelete & ")"
'Specifies the query to delete records from the Video table where the IDs of the
selected records match those in the table
        ElseIf (IntKind = 5) Then
'Checks if the selected record is contained in the Customer table
        StrQuery = "DELETE FROM customer WHERE CustID IN ("
        StrQuery += StrIDToDelete & ")"
'Specifies the query to delete records from the Customer table where the IDs of the
selected records match those in the table
        End If


        Dim DeleteCmd1 As New SqlCommand(StrQuery, SqlConnection1)
'Declares DeleteCmd1 as an object of the SqlCommand class and associates the object
with the SqlConnection1 object


        SqlDataAdapter1.DeleteCommand = DeleteCmd1
        Try
            SqlConnection1.Open()
'Establishes a connection with the database
            SqlDataAdapter1.DeleteCommand.ExecuteNonQuery()
'Executes the query
        Catch MyException As SqlException
            MessageBox.Show(("Source: " & MyException.Source & ControlChars.Cr & _
```

```
                  "Number: " & MyException.Number.ToString() & ControlChars.Cr &

       _

                  "State: " & MyException.State.ToString() & ControlChars.Cr &

       _

                  "Class: " & MyException.Class.ToString() & ControlChars.Cr &

       _

                  "Server: " & MyException.Server & ControlChars.Cr & _
                  "Message: " & MyException.Message & ControlChars.Cr & _
                  "Procedure: " & MyException.Procedure & ControlChars.Cr & _
                  "Line: " & MyException.LineNumber.ToString()))


             SqlConnection1.Close()
'Closes the SqlConnection1 object
             SqlDataAdapter1.Dispose()
'Closes the SqlDataAdapter1 object
             Return
         End Try
End Sub
```

The CmdClear_Click *Function*

The CmdClear_Click function executes when the administrator clicks on the Clear button in the Update/Delete form.

The code for the CmdClear_Click function is as follows:

```
Private Sub CmdClear_Click(ByVal sender As System.Object, ByVal e As
System.EventArgs) Handles CmdClear.Click
          LvwSearchResult.Items.Clear()
End Sub
```

The CmdClear_Click function clears the list view control.

The CmdCancel_Click *Function*

The CmdCancel_Click function executes when the administrator clicks on the Cancel button in the Update/Delete form.

The code for the `CmdCancel_Click` function is as follows:

```
Private Sub CmdCancel_Click(ByVal sender As System.Object, ByVal e As
System.EventArgs) Handles CmdCancel.Click
        Me.Close()
End Sub
```

The `CmdCancel_Click` function closes the Update/Delete form.

Complete Code for the Update/Delete Form

In the preceding sections, you looked at the code associated with the events and functions in the Update/Delete form. Listing 19-1 provides the complete code for the Update/Delete form.

Listing 19-1 The Code for the Update/Delete Form

```
Imports System.Data
Imports System.String
Imports System.Data.OleDb
Imports System.Collections
Imports System.Data.SqlClient
Imports System.Data.SqlTypes


Public Class FrmUpdateDelete
        Inherits System.Windows.Forms.Form
        Dim SqlConnection1 As New SqlConnection(StrConnectionString)
        Dim SqlDataAdapter1 As New SqlDataAdapter()
        Dim Result As Integer

Windows Form Designer generated code
'Contains the code that specifies the size, location, and other properties, such as
font and name, for the controls on the form.
        Private Sub FrmUpdateDelete_Load(ByVal sender As System.Object, ByVal e
As System.EventArgs) Handles MyBase.Load
                CmbSearchIn.SelectedIndex = 0
```

```
            HandleComboIndexes()
    End Sub


    Private Sub CmbSearchIn_SelectedIndexChanged(ByVal sender As
System.Object, ByVal e As System.EventArgs) Handles CmbSearchIn.SelectedIndexChanged
            HandleComboIndexes()
    End Sub


    Private Sub HandleComboIndexes()
            Dim StrSearchIn As String
            Dim StrSearchBy As String
            Dim StrQuery As String

            CmbSearchBy.Items.Clear()

            StrSearchIn = CmbSearchIn.Text
            If (Compare(StrSearchIn, "Movie", True) = 0) Then
                    CmbSearchBy.Items.Add("Movie Id")
                    CmbSearchBy.Items.Add("Movie Title")
                    CmbSearchBy.Items.Add("Release Year")
                    CmbSearchBy.Items.Add("Category")
            ElseIf (Compare(StrSearchIn, "Actor", True) = 0) Then
                    CmbSearchBy.Items.Add("Actor Id")
                    CmbSearchBy.Items.Add("First Name")
                    CmbSearchBy.Items.Add("Last Name")
            ElseIf (Compare(StrSearchIn, "Director", True) = 0) Then
                    CmbSearchBy.Items.Add("Director Id")
                    CmbSearchBy.Items.Add("First Name")
                    CmbSearchBy.Items.Add("Last Name")
            ElseIf (Compare(StrSearchIn, "Producer", True) = 0) Then
                    CmbSearchBy.Items.Add("Producer Id")
                    CmbSearchBy.Items.Add("Name")
            ElseIf (Compare(StrSearchIn, "Video", True) = 0) Then
                    CmbSearchBy.Items.Add("Video Id")
                    CmbSearchBy.Items.Add("Format")
            ElseIf (Compare(StrSearchIn, "Customer", True) = 0) Then
                    CmbSearchBy.Items.Add("Customer Id")
                    CmbSearchBy.Items.Add("First Name")
```

```vbnet
                            CmbSearchBy.Items.Add("Last Name")
                            CmbSearchBy.Items.Add("State")
            Else
                            StrQuery = ""
            End If


                CmbSearchBy.SelectedIndex = 0
        End Sub


        Private Sub CmdSearch_Click(ByVal sender As System.Object, ByVal e As
System.EventArgs) Handles CmdSearch.Click
                Dim DsDataSet As DataSet
                Dim DrRowPicker As DataRow
                Dim StrSearchIn As String
                Dim StrSearchBy As String
                Dim StrQuery As String
                Dim BSearchStrEmpty As Boolean
                BSearchStrEmpty = False

                If TxtSearchText.Text.Trim = "" Then
                        MessageBox.Show("Please enter some text to search.")
                        BSearchStrEmpty = True
                End If

                StrSearchIn = CmbSearchIn.Text
                StrSearchBy = CmbSearchBy.Text


                If (Compare(StrSearchIn, "Movie", True) = 0) Then
                            Result = 0
                            StrQuery = "SELECT DISTINCT MovID, MovTitle, DirID,
ProdID, Duration, Description, Category, ReleaseYear FROM Movie "
                            If (Not BSearchStrEmpty) Then
                                    If (Compare(StrSearchBy, "Movie Id",
True) = 0) Then

                                            StrQuery += "WHERE MovID = '"
                                            StrQuery +=
TxtSearchText.Text & "'"
```

```
                                ElseIf (Compare(StrSearchBy, "Movie Title",
True) = 0) Then

                                    StrQuery += "WHERE MovTitle LIKE
' "

                                    StrQuery += TxtSearchText.Text
& "%'"
                                ElseIf (Compare(StrSearchBy, "Release Year",
True) = 0) Then

                                    StrQuery += "WHERE ReleaseYear
= ' "

                                    StrQuery += TxtSearchText.Text
& "'"
                                ElseIf (Compare(StrSearchBy, "Category", True)
= 0) Then

                                    StrQuery += "WHERE Category =
' "

                                    StrQuery +=
TxtSearchText.Text & "'"
                                End If
                        End If
                ElseIf (Compare(StrSearchIn, "Actor", True) = 0) Then
                        Result = 1
                        StrQuery = "SELECT DISTINCT ActorID, FirstName,
LastName FROM Actor "
                        If (Not BSearchStrEmpty) Then
                                If (Compare(StrSearchBy, "Actor Id", True) =
0) Then

                                    StrQuery += "WHERE ActorID = '"
                                    StrQuery += TxtSearchText.Text
& "'"
                                ElseIf (Compare(StrSearchBy, "First Name",
True) = 0) Then

                                    StrQuery += "WHERE FirstName LIKE
' "

                                    StrQuery += TxtSearchText.Text
& "%'"
```

```
                                        ElseIf (Compare(StrSearchBy, "Last Name",
True) = 0) Then

                                            StrQuery += "WHERE LastName
LIKE '"

                                            StrQuery += TxtSearchText.Text
& "%'"
                                    End If
                            End If
                ElseIf (Compare(StrSearchIn, "Director", True) = 0) Then
                        Result = 2
                        StrQuery = "SELECT DISTINCT DirID, FirstName,
LastName FROM Director "
                        If (Not BSearchStrEmpty) Then
                                If (Compare(StrSearchBy, "Director Id",
True) = 0) Then

                                        StrQuery += "WHERE DirID = '"
                                        StrQuery += TxtSearchText.Text
& "'"
                                    ElseIf (Compare(StrSearchBy, "First
Name", True) = 0) Then

                                        StrQuery += "WHERE FirstName
LIKE '"

                                        StrQuery += TxtSearchText.Text
& "%'"
                                    ElseIf (Compare(StrSearchBy, "Last
Name", True) = 0) Then

                                        StrQuery += "WHERE LastName
LIKE '"

                                        StrQuery +=
TxtSearchText.Text & "%'"
                                    End If
                            End If
                    ElseIf (Compare(StrSearchIn, "Producer", True) = 0) Then
                        Result = 3
                        StrQuery = "SELECT DISTINCT ProdID, Name FROM
Producer "
                        If (Not BSearchStrEmpty) Then
```

```
                                                        If (Compare(StrSearchBy, "Producer ID",
True) = 0) Then
                                                                StrQuery += "WHERE ProdID = '"
                                                                StrQuery += TxtSearchText.Text
& "'"
                                                        ElseIf (Compare(StrSearchBy, "Name",
True) = 0) Then
                                                                StrQuery += "WHERE Name LIKE '"
                                                                StrQuery += TxtSearchText.Text
& "%'"
                                                End If
                                        End If
                        ElseIf (Compare(StrSearchIn, "Video", True) = 0) Then
                                Result = 4
                                StrQuery = "SELECT DISTINCT VideoID, MovID, Format,
Price FROM Video "
                                If (Not BSearchStrEmpty) Then
                                                If (Compare(StrSearchBy, "Video ID",
True) = 0) Then
                                                                StrQuery += "WHERE VideoID = '"
                                                ElseIf (Compare(StrSearchBy, "Format",
True) = 0) Then
                                                                StrQuery += "WHERE Format = '"
                                                End If
                                                StrQuery += TxtSearchText.Text
& "'"
                                End If
                        ElseIf (Compare(StrSearchIn, "Customer", True) = 0) Then
                                Result = 5
                                StrQuery = "SELECT DISTINCT CustID, FirstName,
LastName, Address, City, State, Zip, Phone, Email FROM Customer "
                                If (Not BSearchStrEmpty) Then
                                                If (Compare(StrSearchBy, "Customer Id", True)
= 0) Then
                                                                StrQuery += "WHERE CustID = '"
                                                                StrQuery += TxtSearchText.Text
& "'"
```

```
                                        ElseIf (Compare(StrSearchBy, "First Name",
True) = 0) Then

                                                StrQuery += "WHERE FirstName
LIKE '"

                                                StrQuery += TxtSearchText.Text
& "%'"

                                        ElseIf (Compare(StrSearchBy, "Last Name",
True) = 0) Then

                                                StrQuery += "WHERE LastName
LIKE '"

                                                StrQuery += TxtSearchText.Text
& "%'"

                                        ElseIf (Compare(StrSearchBy, "State",
True) = 0) Then

                                                StrQuery += "WHERE State = '"
                                                StrQuery += TxtSearchText.Text
& "'"

                                End If
                        End If
                Else
                        Result = -1
                        StrQuery = ""
                End If

                Dim SelectCmd1 As New SqlCommand(StrQuery, SqlConnection1)
                DsDataSet = New DataSet()

                SqlDataAdapter1.SelectCommand = SelectCmd1
                SqlDataAdapter1.SelectCommand.CommandText = StrQuery
                SqlConnection1.Open()
                SqlDataAdapter1.Fill(DsDataSet, "SearchResultAdmin")

                LvwSearchResult.Items.Clear()
                LvwSearchResult.Columns.Clear()

                Dim IntRowCount As Integer
                IntRowCount = 0
```

```
Dim IntKind As Integer
IntKind = CInt(Result)

Dim ColumnHeader1 As New ColumnHeader()
Dim ColumnHeader2 As New ColumnHeader()
Dim ColumnHeader3 As New ColumnHeader()
Dim ColumnHeader4 As New ColumnHeader()
Dim ColumnHeader5 As New ColumnHeader()
Dim ColumnHeader6 As New ColumnHeader()
Dim ColumnHeader7 As New ColumnHeader()
Dim ColumnHeader8 As New ColumnHeader()
Dim ColumnHeader9 As New ColumnHeader()
Dim StrMessage As String

If (IntKind = 0) Then
            StrMessage = "Couldn't find this movie."
            LvwSearchResult.Columns.AddRange(New
System.Windows.Forms.ColumnHeader() {ColumnHeader1, ColumnHeader2, ColumnHeader3,
ColumnHeader4, ColumnHeader5, ColumnHeader6, ColumnHeader7, ColumnHeader8})
            ColumnHeader1.Text = "Movie ID"
            ColumnHeader2.Text = "Movie Title"
            ColumnHeader3.Text = "Director ID"
            ColumnHeader4.Text = "Producer ID"
            ColumnHeader5.Text = "Duration"
            ColumnHeader6.Text = "Description"
            ColumnHeader7.Text = "Category"
            ColumnHeader8.Text = "Release Year"
    ElseIf (IntKind = 1) Then
            StrMessage = "Couldn't find this actor."
            LvwSearchResult.Columns.AddRange(New
System.Windows.Forms.ColumnHeader() {ColumnHeader1, ColumnHeader2, ColumnHeader3})
            ColumnHeader1.Text = "Actor ID"
            ColumnHeader2.Text = "First Name"
            ColumnHeader3.Text = "Last Name"
    ElseIf (IntKind = 2) Then
            StrMessage = "Couldn't find this director."
            LvwSearchResult.Columns.AddRange(New
```

```
System.Windows.Forms.ColumnHeader() {ColumnHeader1, ColumnHeader2, ColumnHeader3})
                        ColumnHeader1.Text = "Director ID"
                        ColumnHeader2.Text = "First Name"
                        ColumnHeader3.Text = "Last Name"
            ElseIf (IntKind = 3) Then
                        StrMessage = "Couldn't find this producer."
                        LvwSearchResult.Columns.AddRange(New
System.Windows.Forms.ColumnHeader() {ColumnHeader1, ColumnHeader2})
                        ColumnHeader1.Text = "Producer ID"
                        ColumnHeader2.Text = "Name"
            ElseIf (IntKind = 4) Then
                        StrMessage = "Couldn't find this video."
                        LvwSearchResult.Columns.AddRange(New
System.Windows.Forms.ColumnHeader() {ColumnHeader1, ColumnHeader2, ColumnHeader3,
ColumnHeader4})
                        ColumnHeader1.Text = "Video ID"
                        ColumnHeader2.Text = "Movie ID"
                        ColumnHeader3.Text = "Format"
                        ColumnHeader4.Text = "Price"
            ElseIf (IntKind = 5) Then
                        StrMessage = "Couldn't find this customer."
                        LvwSearchResult.Columns.AddRange(New
System.Windows.Forms.ColumnHeader() {ColumnHeader1, ColumnHeader2, ColumnHeader3,
ColumnHeader4, ColumnHeader5, ColumnHeader6, ColumnHeader7, ColumnHeader8,
ColumnHeader9})
                        ColumnHeader1.Text = "Customer ID"
                        ColumnHeader2.Text = "First Name"
                        ColumnHeader3.Text = "Last Name"
                        ColumnHeader4.Text = "Address"
                        ColumnHeader5.Text = "City"
                        ColumnHeader6.Text = "State"
                        ColumnHeader7.Text = "Zip"
                        ColumnHeader8.Text = "Phone"
                        ColumnHeader9.Text = "Email"
            End If
```

```
Dim StrValue0, StrValue1, StrValue2, StrValue3, StrValue4,
StrValue5, StrValue6, StrValue7, StrValue8 As String
                Dim IntCounter As Integer

                For Each DrRowPicker In
DsDataSet.Tables("SearchResultAdmin").Rows
                    If (IntKind = 0) Then
                            For IntCounter = 0 To 7
                                If
(DrRowPicker.IsNull(IntCounter)) Then
                                    If IntCounter = 0
Then
                                            StrValue0
= ""
                                    ElseIf IntCounter
= 1 Then
                                            StrValue1
= ""
                                    ElseIf IntCounter
= 2 Then
                                            StrValue2
= ""
                                    ElseIf IntCounter
= 3 Then
                                            StrValue3
= ""
                                    ElseIf IntCounter
= 4 Then
                                            StrValue4
= ""
                                    ElseIf IntCounter
= 5 Then
                                            StrValue5
= ""
                                    ElseIf IntCounter
= 6 Then
                                            StrValue6
= ""
```

```
            ElseIf IntCounter = 7 Then
                StrValue7 = ""
            End If
        Else
            If IntCounter = 0 Then
                StrValue0 = DrRowPicker(0)
            ElseIf IntCounter = 1 Then
                StrValue1 = DrRowPicker(1)
            ElseIf IntCounter = 2 Then
                StrValue2 = DrRowPicker(2)
            ElseIf IntCounter = 3 Then
                StrValue3 = DrRowPicker(3)
            ElseIf IntCounter = 4 Then
                StrValue4 = DrRowPicker(4)
            ElseIf IntCounter = 5 Then
                StrValue5 = DrRowPicker(5)
            ElseIf IntCounter = 6 Then
                StrValue6 = DrRowPicker(6)
            ElseIf IntCounter = 7 Then
                StrValue7 = DrRowPicker(7)
```

```
                                                      End If
                                     End If
                        Next

                                     Dim StrSearchRow As String() =
{StrValue0, StrValue1, StrValue2, StrValue3, StrValue4, StrValue5, StrValue6,
StrValue7}
                                         LvwSearchResult.Items.Add(New
ListViewItem(StrSearchRow))
                        ElseIf (IntKind = 1) Then
                              For IntCounter = 0 To 2
                                    If
(DrRowPicker.IsNull(IntCounter)) Then
                                                If IntCounter = 0
Then
                                                      StrValue0
= ""
                                                ElseIf IntCounter
= 1 Then
                                                      StrValue1
= ""
                                                ElseIf IntCounter
= 2 Then
                                                      StrValue2
= ""
                                                End If
                                    Else
                                                If IntCounter = 0
Then
                                                      StrValue0
= DrRowPicker(IntCounter)
                                                ElseIf IntCounter
= 1 Then
                                                      StrValue1
= DrRowPicker(IntCounter)
                                                ElseIf IntCounter
= 2 Then
```

```
                                                                    StrValue2
= DrRowPicker(IntCounter)
                                                            End If
                                                    End If
                                        Next

                                        Dim StrSearchRow As String() =
{StrValue0, StrValue1, StrValue2}
                                        LvwSearchResult.Items.Add(New
ListViewItem(StrSearchRow))
                                ElseIf (IntKind = 2) Then
                                        For IntCounter = 0 To 2
                                                If
(DrRowPicker.IsNull(IntCounter)) Then
                                                        If IntCounter = 0
Then
                                                                StrValue0
= ""
                                                        ElseIf IntCounter
= 1 Then
                                                                StrValue1
= ""
                                                        ElseIf IntCounter
= 2 Then
                                                                StrValue2
= ""
                                                        End If
                                                Else
                                                        If IntCounter = 0
Then
                                                                StrValue0
= DrRowPicker(0)
                                                        ElseIf IntCounter
= 1 Then
                                                                StrValue1
= DrRowPicker(1)
                                                        ElseIf IntCounter
= 2 Then
```

```vb
                                                    StrValue2 = DrRowPicker(2)
                                                End If
                                            End If
                                Next

                                Dim StrSearchRow As String() = {StrValue0, StrValue1, StrValue2}
                                LvwSearchResult.Items.Add(New ListViewItem(StrSearchRow))
                        ElseIf (IntKind = 3) Then
                            For IntCounter = 0 To 1
                                If (DrRowPicker.IsNull(IntCounter)) Then
                                    If IntCounter = 0 Then
                                        StrValue0 = ""
                                    ElseIf IntCounter = 1 Then
                                        StrValue1 = ""
                                    End If
                                Else
                                    If IntCounter = 0 Then
                                        StrValue0 = DrRowPicker(0)
                                    ElseIf IntCounter = 1 Then
                                        StrValue1 = DrRowPicker(1)
                                    End If
                                End If
                            Next
                            Dim StrSearchRow As String() = {StrValue0, StrValue1}
                            LvwSearchResult.Items.Add(New
```

```
ListViewItem(StrSearchRow))
                              ElseIf (IntKind = 4) Then
                                   For IntCounter = 0 To 3
                                        If
(DrRowPicker.IsNull(IntCounter)) Then
                                             If IntCounter = 0
Then
                                                  StrValue0
= ""
                                             ElseIf IntCounter
= 1 Then
                                                  StrValue1
= ""
                                             ElseIf IntCounter
= 2 Then
                                                  StrValue2
= ""
                                             ElseIf IntCounter
= 3 Then
                                                  StrValue3
= ""
                                             End If
                                        Else
                                             If IntCounter = 0
Then
                                                  StrValue0
= DrRowPicker(0)
                                             ElseIf IntCounter
= 1 Then
                                                  StrValue1
= DrRowPicker(1)
                                             ElseIf IntCounter
= 2 Then
                                                  StrValue2
= DrRowPicker(2)
                                             ElseIf IntCounter
= 3 Then
```

```
                                                       StrValue3
= DrRowPicker(3)
                                                   End If
                                          End If
                              Next

                              Dim StrSearchRow As String() =
{StrValue0, StrValue1, StrValue2, StrValue3}
                              LvwSearchResult.Items.Add(New
ListViewItem(StrSearchRow))
                    ElseIf (IntKind = 5) Then
                         For IntCounter = 0 To 8
                              If
(DrRowPicker.IsNull(IntCounter)) Then
                                   If IntCounter = 0
Then
                                        StrValue0
= ""
                                   ElseIf IntCounter
= 1 Then
                                        StrValue1
= ""
                                   ElseIf IntCounter
= 2 Then
                                        StrValue2
= ""
                                   ElseIf IntCounter
= 3 Then
                                        StrValue3
= ""
                                   ElseIf IntCounter
= 4 Then
                                        StrValue4
= ""
                                   ElseIf IntCounter
= 5 Then
                                        StrValue5
= ""
```

```
                                            ElseIf IntCounter
= 6 Then
                                                StrValue6
= ""
                                            ElseIf IntCounter
= 7 Then
                                                StrValue7
= ""
                                            ElseIf IntCounter
= 8 Then
                                                StrValue8
= ""
                                            End If
                            Else
                            If IntCounter = 0
Then
                                                StrValue0
= DrRowPicker(0)
                                            ElseIf IntCounter
= 1 Then
                                                StrValue1
= DrRowPicker(1)
                                            ElseIf IntCounter
= 2 Then
                                                StrValue2
= DrRowPicker(2)
                                            ElseIf IntCounter
= 3 Then
                                                StrValue3
= DrRowPicker(3)
                                            ElseIf IntCounter
= 4 Then
                                                StrValue4
= DrRowPicker(4)
                                            ElseIf IntCounter
= 5 Then
                                                StrValue5
= DrRowPicker(5)
```

```
                                                    ElseIf IntCounter
= 6 Then
                                                        StrValue6
= DrRowPicker(6)
                                                    ElseIf IntCounter
= 7 Then
                                                        StrValue7
= DrRowPicker(7)
                                                    ElseIf IntCounter
= 8 Then
                                                        StrValue8
= DrRowPicker(8)
                                                End If
                            End If
                Next


                        Dim StrSearchRow As String() =
{StrValue0, StrValue1, StrValue2, StrValue3, StrValue4, StrValue5, StrValue6,
StrValue7, StrValue8}
                        LvwSearchResult.Items.Add(New
ListViewItem(StrSearchRow))
                    End If

                IntRowCount += 1
            Next

            If IntRowCount = 0 Then
                    MessageBox.Show(StrMessage)
            End If

            SqlConnection1.Close()
            SqlDataAdapter1.Dispose()
        End Sub


        Private Sub CmdUpdate_Click(ByVal sender As System.Object, ByVal e As
System.EventArgs) Handles CmdUpdate.Click
                Dim LstViewCollection As ListView.SelectedListViewItemCollection
```

```
LstViewCollection = New
ListView.SelectedListViewItemCollection(LvwSearchResult)

    Dim IntTotalSelectedCount As Integer
    IntTotalSelectedCount = LstViewCollection.Count()
    If (IntTotalSelectedCount < 1) Then
            MessageBox.Show("You have not selected any records.")
            Return
    ElseIf IntTotalSelectedCount > 1 Then
            Return
    End If

    Dim StrQuery, StrTemp, StrIDToUpdate As String
    Dim IntKind As Integer
    IntKind = CInt(Result)

    Dim ObjActor As FrmInsertActor
    Dim ObjDirector As FrmInsertDirector
    Dim ObjProducer As FrmInsertProducer
    Dim ObjMovie As FrmInsertMovie
    Dim ObjVideo As FrmInsertVideo
    Dim ObjCustomer As FrmInsertCustomer

    Dim StrUpdateID As String = LstViewCollection.Item(0).Text()
    If (IntKind = 0) Then
            ObjMovie = New FrmInsertMovie()
            ObjMovie.SetUpdateID(StrUpdateID)
            ObjMovie.Show()
    ElseIf (IntKind = 1) Then
            ObjActor = New FrmInsertActor()
            ObjActor.SetUpdateID(StrUpdateID)
            ObjActor.Show()
    ElseIf (IntKind = 2) Then
            ObjDirector = New FrmInsertDirector()
            ObjDirector.SetUpdateID(StrUpdateID)
            ObjDirector.Show()
    ElseIf (IntKind = 3) Then
```

```
                    ObjProducer = New FrmInsertProducer()
                    ObjProducer.SetUpdateID(StrUpdateID)
                    ObjProducer.Show()
        ElseIf (IntKind = 4) Then
                        ObjVideo = New FrmInsertVideo()
                        ObjVideo.SetUpdateID(StrUpdateID)
                        ObjVideo.Show()
        ElseIf (IntKind = 5) Then
                        ObjCustomer = New FrmInsertCustomer()
                        ObjCustomer.SetUpdateID(StrUpdateID)
                        ObjCustomer.Show()
            End If
    End Sub


        Private Sub CmdDelete_Click(ByVal sender As System.Object, ByVal e As
System.EventArgs) Handles CmdDelete.Click
                    Dim LstViewCollection As
ListView.SelectedListViewItemCollection
                    LstViewCollection = New
ListView.SelectedListViewItemCollection(LvwSearchResult)


                Dim IntTotalSelectedCount As Integer
                IntTotalSelectedCount = LstViewCollection.Count()
                If (IntTotalSelectedCount < 1) Then
                        MessageBox.Show("You have not selected any records.")
                    Return
                End If


                Dim IntRes As DialogResult
                IntRes = MessageBox.Show("Are you sure you want to delete
this record?", "", MessageBoxButtons.YesNo)
                If (IntRes = DialogResult.No) Then
                        Return
                End If


                Dim IntCounter As Integer
                Dim StrIDToDelete As String
```

```
For IntCounter = 0 To IntTotalSelectedCount - 1
        StrIDToDelete += "'"
        StrIDToDelete += LstViewCollection.Item(0).Text
        StrIDToDelete += "'"
        If (IntCounter < IntTotalSelectedCount - 1) Then
                StrIDToDelete += ","
        End If
        LstViewCollection.Item(0).Remove()
Next

Dim StrQuery, StrTemp As String
Dim IntKind As Integer
IntKind = CInt(Result)

If (IntKind = 0) Then
        StrQuery = "DELETE FROM movie WHERE MovID IN ("
        StrQuery += StrIDToDelete & ")"
ElseIf (IntKind = 1) Then
        StrQuery = "DELETE FROM actor WHERE ActorID IN ("
        StrQuery += StrIDToDelete & ")"
ElseIf (IntKind = 2) Then
        StrQuery = "DELETE FROM director WHERE DirID IN ("
        StrQuery += StrIDToDelete & ")"
ElseIf (IntKind = 3) Then
        StrQuery = "DELETE FROM producer WHERE ProdID IN ("
        StrQuery += StrIDToDelete & ")"
ElseIf (IntKind = 4) Then
        StrQuery = "DELETE FROM video WHERE VideoID IN ("
        StrQuery += StrIDToDelete & ")"
ElseIf (IntKind = 5) Then
        StrQuery = "DELETE FROM customer WHERE CustID IN ("
        StrQuery += StrIDToDelete & ")"
End If

Dim DeleteCmd1 As New SqlCommand(StrQuery, SqlConnection1)
SqlDataAdapter1.DeleteCommand = DeleteCmd1
```

```vbnet
            Try
                        SqlConnection1.Open()
                        SqlDataAdapter1.DeleteCommand.ExecuteNonQuery()
                        Catch MyException As SqlException
                        MessageBox.Show(("Source: " & MyException.Source &
ControlChars.Cr & _
                                        "Number: " &
MyException.Number.ToString() & ControlChars.Cr & _
                                        "State: " & MyException.State.ToString()
& ControlChars.Cr & _
                                        "Class: " & MyException.Class.ToString()
& ControlChars.Cr & _
                                        "Server: " & MyException.Server &
ControlChars.Cr & _
                                        "Message: " & MyException.Message &
ControlChars.Cr & _
                                        "Procedure: " & MyException.Procedure &
ControlChars.Cr & _
                                        "Line: " &
MyException.LineNumber.ToString()))

                        SqlConnection1.Close()
                        SqlDataAdapter1.Dispose()
                        Return
                End Try
        End Sub


        Private Sub CmdClear_Click(ByVal sender As System.Object, ByVal e As
System.EventArgs) Handles CmdClear.Click
                    LvwSearchResult.Items.Clear()
        End Sub


        Private Sub CmdCancel_Click(ByVal sender As System.Object, ByVal e As
System.EventArgs) Handles CmdCancel.Click
                    Me.Close()
        End Sub
End Class
```

Summary

In this chapter, you learned to add functionality to the Update/Delete form. This chapter also described the functions you need to create to add functionality to the Update/Delete form. You also looked at the complete code for the Update/Delete form.

Chapter 20

*Adding
Functionality to
the Insert Forms*

In the preceding chapter, you learned to add functionality to the Update/Delete form. In this chapter, you will learn to add functionality to the Insert forms. The Insert forms enable you to add records to the various tables in the Movies database.

This chapter describes how to add functionality to the following forms:

- ◆ The Insert Actor form
- ◆ The Insert Director form
- ◆ The Insert Producer form
- ◆ The Insert Video form
- ◆ The Insert Movie form
- ◆ The Insert Customer form

The following sections discuss each of these forms.

The Insert Actor Form

As the name suggests, the Insert Actor form enables the administrator to add records to the Actor table. Let's review the form shown in Figure 20-1.

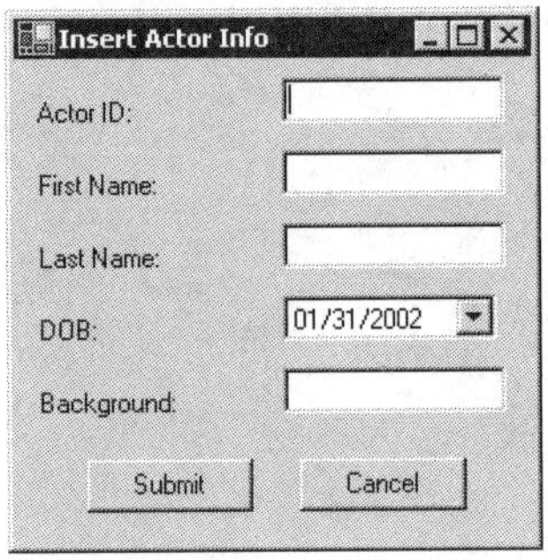

FIGURE 20-1 *The interface of the Insert Actor form*

As with the other forms, you need to include the following statements in the Insert Actor form:

```
Imports System.Data
Imports System.Data.SqlClient
Imports System.Data.SqlTypes
```

The variables you need to declare in the Insert Actor form are as follows:

```
Dim SqlDataAdapter1 As New SqlDataAdapter()
Dim SqlConnection1 As New SqlConnection(StrConnectionString)
Private StrIDToUpdate As String
'Used to check if the form is opened from the Update/Delete form
```

You need to create the following functions in the Insert Actor form:

- ◆ SetUpdateID
- ◆ FrmInsertActor_Load
- ◆ CmdSubmit_Click
- ◆ CmdCancel_Click

The preceding functions are discussed in the following sections.

The *SetUpdateID* Function

As mentioned in the preceding chapter, the SetUpdateID function is called when the administrator selects a record in the Update/Delete form and clicks on the Update button. The Update/Delete form passes the text of the item selected by the administrator to the SetUpdateID function.

The SetUpdateID function of the Insert Actor form executes if the administrator selects a record contained in the Actor table and clicks on the Update button. Next, the SetUpdateID function executes and stores the item selected by the administrator in the StrIDToUpdate variable.

```
Public Sub SetUpdateID(ByVal StrUpID As String)
        StrIDToUpdate = StrUpID
'Stores the item selected by the administrator in the StrIDToUpdate variable
End Sub
```

The *FrmInsertActor_Load* Function

The FrmInsertActor_Load function executes when the Insert Actor form is loaded. This function checks to see if the Insert Actor form is opened from the

Update/Delete form. If the Insert Actor form is invoked from the Update/Delete form, the `FrmInsertActor_Load` function retrieves the details for the record selected by the administrator and displys the details in the form. In addition to displaying the records, the `FrmInsertActor_Load` function also changes the caption of the form to Update Actor Info and disables the Actor ID text box.

The code for this function is as follows:

```
Private Sub FrmInsertActor_Load(ByVal sender As System.Object, ByVal e As
System.EventArgs) Handles MyBase.Load
        DtpDOB.Format = DateTimePickerFormat.Custom
'Specifies that the DtpDOB date time picker control displays the date-time value in
a customized format
        DtpDOB.CustomFormat = "MM/dd/yyyy"
'Sets the format for the DtpDOB date time picker control to MM/dd/yyyy

        If StrIDToUpdate <> "" Then
'Checks if the form was opened from the Update/Delete form
            Me.Text = "Update Actor Info"
'Changes the Text property of the form
            TxtActorID.Enabled = False
'Disables the Actor ID text box

        Dim SelectString As String
        SelectString = "SELECT ActorID, FirstName, LastName, DOB, Background
FROM Actor WHERE ActorID = '" & StrIDToUpdate & "'"
'Specifies the query to retrieve the record from the Actor table

        Dim SelectCmd1 As New SqlCommand(SelectString, SqlConnection1)
'Creates an instance of the SqlCommand class

        Dim DsDataSet As DataSet
        DsDataSet = New DataSet()
'Creates the dataset
        SqlDataAdapter1.SelectCommand = SelectCmd1
        SqlDataAdapter1.SelectCommand.CommandText = SelectString
        Try

            SqlConnection1.Open()
```

```
'Establishes the connection
                SqlDataAdapter1.Fill(DsDataSet, "Result")
'Populates the Result table in the DsDataSet dataset with the query results
            Catch MyException As SqlException
                MessageBox.Show(("Source: " & MyException.Source & ControlChars.Cr & _
                        "Number: " & MyException.Number.ToString() &
ControlChars.Cr & _
                        "State: " & MyException.State.ToString() &
ControlChars.Cr & _
                        "Class: " & MyException.Class.ToString() &
ControlChars.Cr & _
                        "Server: " & MyException.Server & ControlChars.Cr & _
                        "Message: " & MyException.Message & ControlChars.Cr & _
                        "Procedure: " & MyException.Procedure & ControlChars.Cr & _
                        "Line: " & MyException.LineNumber.ToString()))


                SqlConnection1.Close()
'Closes the SqlConnection1 object
                SqlDataAdapter1.Dispose()
'Releases the resources used by the SqlDataAdapter1 object
                Return
            End Try


            TxtActorID.DataBindings.Add(New Binding("Text", DsDataSet,
"Result.ActorID"))
            TxtFName.DataBindings.Add(New Binding("Text", DsDataSet,
"Result.FirstName"))
            TxtLName.DataBindings.Add(New Binding("Text", DsDataSet,
"Result.LastName"))
            DtpDOB.DataBindings.Add(New Binding("Text", DsDataSet, "Result.DOB"))
            TxtBackground.DataBindings.Add(New Binding("Text", DsDataSet,
"Result.Background"))
'Binds the controls in the form with the fields in the dataset


            SqlConnection1.Close()
'Closes the SqlConnection1 object
```

```
                SqlDataAdapter1.Dispose()
'Releases the resources used by the SqlDataAdapter1 object
            End If
    End Sub
```

The *CmdSubmit_Click* Function

The CmdSubmit_Click function executes when the administrator clicks on the Submit button in the Insert Actor form.

The code for the CmdSubmit_Click function is as follows:

```
Private Sub CmdSubmit_Click(ByVal sender As System.Object, ByVal e As
System.EventArgs) Handles CmdSubmit.Click
        If TxtActorID.Text.Trim = "" Then
'Checks if the administrator has not entered any text in the Actor ID text box
            MessageBox.Show("Please enter the actor ID.")
'Displays a message asking the administrator to enter text in the Actor ID text box
            TxtActorID.Focus()
'Sets the focus on the Actor ID text box
            Return
        End If


        If TxtFName.Text.Trim = "" Then
'Checks if the administrator has not entered any text in the First Name text box
            MessageBox.Show("Please enter the first name.")
'Displays a message asking the administrator to enter text in the First Name text
box
            TxtFName.Focus()
'Sets the focus on the First Name text box
            Return
        End If


        If TxtLName.Text.Trim = "" Then
'Checks if the administrator has not entered any text in the Last Name text box
            MessageBox.Show("Please enter the last name.")
'Displays a message asking the administrator to enter text in the Last Name text
box
            TxtLName.Focus()
```

```
'Sets the focus on the Last Name text box
            Return
        End If


        If StrIDToUpdate <> "" Then
'If the record needs to be updated
            Dim UpdString As String
            UpdString = "UPDATE Actor SET ActorID = @ActorID, FirstName =
@FirstName, LastName = @LastName, DOB = @" & _
            "DOB, Background = @Background WHERE ActorID = '" & StrIDToUpdate & "'"
'Specifies the query to update the record with the specified Actor ID
            Dim UpdateCmd1 As New SqlCommand(UpdString, SqlConnection1)
'Creates an instance of the SqlCommand class


            SqlDataAdapter1.UpdateCommand = UpdateCmd1
            SqlDataAdapter1.UpdateCommand.Parameters.Add(New
System.Data.SqlClient.SqlParameter("@ActorID", System.Data.SqlDbType.Char, 5,
"ActorID"))
            SqlDataAdapter1.UpdateCommand.Parameters(0).Value = TxtActorID.Text
            SqlDataAdapter1.UpdateCommand.Parameters.Add(New
System.Data.SqlClient.SqlParameter("@FirstName", System.Data.SqlDbType.VarChar, 50,
"FirstName"))
            SqlDataAdapter1.UpdateCommand.Parameters(1).Value = TxtFName.Text
            SqlDataAdapter1.UpdateCommand.Parameters.Add(New
System.Data.SqlClient.SqlParameter("@LastName", System.Data.SqlDbType.VarChar, 50,
"LastName"))
            SqlDataAdapter1.UpdateCommand.Parameters(2).Value = TxtLName.Text
            SqlDataAdapter1.UpdateCommand.Parameters.Add(New
System.Data.SqlClient.SqlParameter("@DOB", System.Data.SqlDbType.DateTime, 8, "DOB"))
            SqlDataAdapter1.UpdateCommand.Parameters(3).Value = DtpDOB.Text
            SqlDataAdapter1.UpdateCommand.Parameters.Add(New
System.Data.SqlClient.SqlParameter("@Background", System.Data.SqlDbType.VarChar,
255, "Background"))
            SqlDataAdapter1.UpdateCommand.Parameters(4).Value = TxtBackground.Text
'Associates the named parameter variables with the fields in the table
```

```
'Assigns the values specified by the administrator in the controls to the named
parameter variables

            Try
                    SqlConnection1.Open()
'Establishes a connection
                    SqlDataAdapter1.UpdateCommand.ExecuteNonQuery()
'Executes the query

            Catch MyException As SqlException
                MessageBox.Show(("Source: " & MyException.Source & ControlChars.Cr & _
                        "Number: " & MyException.Number.ToString() &
ControlChars.Cr & _
                        "State: " & MyException.State.ToString() &
ControlChars.Cr & _
                        "Class: " & MyException.Class.ToString() &
ControlChars.Cr & _
                        "Server: " & MyException.Server & ControlChars.Cr & _
                        "Message: " & MyException.Message & ControlChars.Cr & _
                        "Procedure: " & MyException.Procedure & ControlChars.Cr & _
                        "Line: " & MyException.LineNumber.ToString()))

                    SqlConnection1.Close()
'Closes the SqlConnection1 object
                    SqlDataAdapter1.Dispose()
'Releases the resources used by the SqlDataAdapter1object
                    Return
            End Try
            MessageBox.Show("The record has been updated.")
        Else
'Executes if the record needs to be added
            Dim InsString As String
            InsString = "INSERT INTO Actor(ActorID, FirstName, LastName, DOB,
Background) VALUES (@ActorID" & _
                ", @FirstName, @LastName, @DOB, @Background); SELECT ActorID,
FirstName, LastName" & _
```

```
                ", DOB, Background FROM Actor WHERE (ActorID = @ActorID)"
'Specifies the query to add a record to the Actor table
                Dim InsertCmd1 As New SqlCommand(InsString, SqlConnection1)
'Creates an instance of the SqlCommand class


                SqlDataAdapter1.InsertCommand = InsertCmd1
'Specifies the query stored in the InsertCmd1 variable as the query to be executed


                SqlDataAdapter1.InsertCommand.Connection = SqlConnection1
                SqlDataAdapter1.InsertCommand.Parameters.Add(New
SqlParameter("@ActorID", System.Data.SqlDbType.VarChar, 5, "ActorID"))
                SqlDataAdapter1.InsertCommand.Parameters(0).Value = TxtActorID.Text
                SqlDataAdapter1.InsertCommand.Parameters.Add(New
SqlParameter("@FirstName", System.Data.SqlDbType.VarChar, 50, "FirstName"))
                SqlDataAdapter1.InsertCommand.Parameters(1).Value = TxtFName.Text
                SqlDataAdapter1.InsertCommand.Parameters.Add(New
SqlParameter("@LastName", System.Data.SqlDbType.VarChar, 50, "LastName"))
                SqlDataAdapter1.InsertCommand.Parameters(2).Value = TxtLName.Text
                SqlDataAdapter1.InsertCommand.Parameters.Add(New SqlParameter("@DOB",
System.Data.SqlDbType.DateTime, 8, "DOB"))
                SqlDataAdapter1.InsertCommand.Parameters(3).Value = DtpDOB.Text
                SqlDataAdapter1.InsertCommand.Parameters.Add(New
SqlParameter("@Background", System.Data.SqlDbType.VarChar, 255, "Background"))
                SqlDataAdapter1.InsertCommand.Parameters(4).Value = TxtBackground.Text
'Associates the named parameter variables with the fields in the table
'Assigns the values specified by the administrator in the controls to the named
parameter variables


                Try
                    SqlConnection1.Open()
'Establishes the connection with the database
                    SqlDataAdapter1.InsertCommand.ExecuteNonQuery()
'Executes the query
                Catch MyException As SqlException
                    MessageBox.Show(("Source: " & MyException.Source & ControlChars.Cr & _
                            "Number: " & MyException.Number.ToString() & ControlChars.Cr
& _
```

```
                              "State: " & MyException.State.ToString() & ControlChars.Cr
          & _
                              "Class: " & MyException.Class.ToString() & ControlChars.Cr
          & _
                               "Server: " & MyException.Server & ControlChars.Cr & _
                               "Message: " & MyException.Message & ControlChars.Cr & _
                               "Procedure: " & MyException.Procedure & ControlChars.Cr & _
                               "Line: " & MyException.LineNumber.ToString()))

                    SqlConnection1.Close()
          'Closes the SqlConnection1 object
                        SqlDataAdapter1.Dispose()
          'Releases the resources used by the SqlDataAdapter1 object
                        Return
                   End Try

                   MessageBox.Show("The record has been added.", "Record added",
          MessageBoxButtons.OK, MessageBoxIcon.Information)
          'Displays a message informing the administrator that the record was added to the
          Actor table
                End If

                    SqlConnection1.Close()
          'Closes the SqlConnection1 object
                        SqlDataAdapter1.Dispose()
          'Releases the resources used by the SqlDataAdapter1 object
                   Me.Close()
          End Sub
```

The *CmdCancel_Click* Function

The CmdCancel_Click function executes when the administrator clicks on the Cancel button in the Insert Actor form.

The code for the CmdCancel_Click function is as follows:

```
Private Sub CmdCancel_Click(ByVal sender As System.Object, ByVal e As
System.EventArgs) Handles CmdCancel.Click
```

```
        Me.Close()
'Closes the form
End Sub
```

When the `CmdCancel_Click` function executes, the Insert Actor form closes.

The Complete Code for the Insert Actor Form

In the preceding sections, you looked at the code associated with the events and functions in the Insert Actor form. Listing 20-1 provides the complete code for the Insert Actor form.

Listing 20-1 The Code for the Insert Actor Form

```
Imports System.Data
Imports System.Data.SqlClient
Imports System.Data.SqlTypes


Public Class FrmInsertActor
    Inherits System.Windows.Forms.Form
    Dim SqlDataAdapter1 As New SqlDataAdapter()
    Dim SqlConnection1 As New SqlConnection(StrConnectionString)
    Private StrIDToUpdate As String


Windows Form Designer generated code

    Public Sub SetUpdateID(ByVal StrUpID As String)
        StrIDToUpdate = StrUpID
    End Sub


    Private Sub FrmInsertActor_Load(ByVal sender As System.Object, ByVal e As
System.EventArgs) Handles MyBase.Load
        DtpDOB.Format = DateTimePickerFormat.Custom
        DtpDOB.CustomFormat = "MM/dd/yyyy"
        If StrIDToUpdate <> "" Then
            Me.Text = "Update Actor Info"
            TxtActorID.Enabled = False
            Dim SelectString As String
```

```vb
        SelectString = "SELECT ActorID, FirstName, LastName, DOB, Background FROM
Actor WHERE ActorID = '" & StrIDToUpdate & "'"

        Dim SelectCmd1 As New SqlCommand(SelectString, SqlConnection1)

        Dim DsDataSet As DataSet
        DsDataSet = New DataSet()
        SqlDataAdapter1.SelectCommand = SelectCmd1
        SqlDataAdapter1.SelectCommand.CommandText = SelectString
        Try

            SqlConnection1.Open()
            SqlDataAdapter1.Fill(DsDataSet, "Result")
        Catch MyException As SqlException
            MessageBox.Show(("Source: " & MyException.Source & ControlChars.Cr & _
                "Number: " & MyException.Number.ToString() & ControlChars.Cr & _
                "State: " & MyException.State.ToString() & ControlChars.Cr & _
                "Class: " & MyException.Class.ToString() & ControlChars.Cr & _
                "Server: " & MyException.Server & ControlChars.Cr & _
                "Message: " & MyException.Message & ControlChars.Cr & _
                "Procedure: " & MyException.Procedure & ControlChars.Cr & _
                "Line: " & MyException.LineNumber.ToString()))

            SqlConnection1.Close()
            SqlDataAdapter1.Dispose()
            Return
        End Try


        TxtActorID.DataBindings.Add(New Binding("Text", DsDataSet,
    "Result.ActorID"))
        TxtFName.DataBindings.Add(New Binding("Text", DsDataSet,
    "Result.FirstName"))
        TxtLName.DataBindings.Add(New Binding("Text", DsDataSet,
    "Result.LastName"))
        DtpDOB.DataBindings.Add(New Binding("Text", DsDataSet, "Result.DOB"))
        TxtBackground.DataBindings.Add(New Binding("Text", DsDataSet,
    "Result.Background"))
```

```
        SqlConnection1.Close()
        SqlDataAdapter1.Dispose()
    End If
End Sub


Private Sub CmdSubmit_Click(ByVal sender As System.Object, ByVal e As
System.EventArgs) Handles CmdSubmit.Click
    If TxtActorID.Text.Trim = "" Then
        MessageBox.Show("Please enter the actor ID.")
        TxtActorID.Focus()
        Return
    End If
    If TxtFName.Text.Trim = "" Then
        MessageBox.Show("Please enter the first name.")
        TxtFName.Focus()
        Return
    End If
    If TxtLName.Text.Trim = "" Then
        MessageBox.Show("Please enter the last name.")
        TxtLName.Focus()
        Return
    End If
    If StrIDToUpdate <> "" Then
        Dim UpdString As String
        UpdString = "UPDATE Actor SET ActorID = @ActorID, FirstName = @FirstName,
LastName = @LastName, DOB = @DOB, Background = @Background WHERE ActorID = '" &
StrIDToUpdate & "'"

        Dim UpdateCmd1 As New SqlCommand(UpdString, SqlConnection1)

        SqlDataAdapter1.UpdateCommand = UpdateCmd1
        SqlDataAdapter1.UpdateCommand.Parameters.Add(New
System.Data.SqlClient.SqlParameter("@ActorID", System.Data.SqlDbType.Char, 5,
"ActorID"))
        SqlDataAdapter1.UpdateCommand.Parameters(0).Value = TxtActorID.Text
        SqlDataAdapter1.UpdateCommand.Parameters.Add(New
System.Data.SqlClient.SqlParameter("@FirstName", System.Data.SqlDbType.VarChar, 50,
"FirstName"))
```

```vb
        SqlDataAdapter1.UpdateCommand.Parameters(1).Value = TxtFName.Text
        SqlDataAdapter1.UpdateCommand.Parameters.Add(New
System.Data.SqlClient.SqlParameter("@LastName", System.Data.SqlDbType.VarChar, 50,
"LastName"))
        SqlDataAdapter1.UpdateCommand.Parameters(2).Value = TxtLName.Text
        SqlDataAdapter1.UpdateCommand.Parameters.Add(New
System.Data.SqlClient.SqlParameter("@DOB", System.Data.SqlDbType.DateTime, 8, "DOB"))
        SqlDataAdapter1.UpdateCommand.Parameters(3).Value = DtpDOB.Text
        SqlDataAdapter1.UpdateCommand.Parameters.Add(New
System.Data.SqlClient.SqlParameter("@Background", System.Data.SqlDbType.VarChar,
255, "Background"))
        SqlDataAdapter1.UpdateCommand.Parameters(4).Value = TxtBackground.Text

    Try
        SqlConnection1.Open()
        SqlDataAdapter1.UpdateCommand.ExecuteNonQuery()
    Catch MyException As SqlException
        MessageBox.Show((("Source: " & MyException.Source & ControlChars.Cr & _
        "Number: " & MyException.Number.ToString() & ControlChars.Cr & _
        "State: " & MyException.State.ToString() & ControlChars.Cr & _
        "Class: " & MyException.Class.ToString() & ControlChars.Cr & _
        "Server: " & MyException.Server & ControlChars.Cr & _
        "Message: " & MyException.Message & ControlChars.Cr & _
        "Procedure: " & MyException.Procedure & ControlChars.Cr & _
        "Line: " & MyException.LineNumber.ToString())))

        SqlConnection1.Close()
        SqlDataAdapter1.Dispose()
        Return
    End Try
    MessageBox.Show("The record has been updated.")
Else
    Dim InsString As String
    InsString = "INSERT INTO Actor(ActorID, FirstName, LastName, DOB,
Background) VALUES (@ActorID, @FirstName, @LastName, @DOB, @Background); SELECT
ActorID, FirstName, LastName, DOB, Background FROM Actor WHERE (ActorID =
@ActorID)"
```

```
Dim InsertCmd1 As New SqlCommand(InsString, SqlConnection1)

SqlDataAdapter1.InsertCommand = InsertCmd1

SqlDataAdapter1.InsertCommand.Connection = SqlConnection1
SqlDataAdapter1.InsertCommand.Parameters.Add(New SqlParameter("@ActorID",
System.Data.SqlDbType.VarChar, 5, "ActorID"))
SqlDataAdapter1.InsertCommand.Parameters(0).Value = TxtActorID.Text
SqlDataAdapter1.InsertCommand.Parameters.Add(New
SqlParameter("@FirstName", System.Data.SqlDbType.VarChar, 50, "FirstName"))
SqlDataAdapter1.InsertCommand.Parameters(1).Value = TxtFName.Text
SqlDataAdapter1.InsertCommand.Parameters.Add(New SqlParameter("@LastName",
System.Data.SqlDbType.VarChar, 50, "LastName"))
SqlDataAdapter1.InsertCommand.Parameters(2).Value = TxtLName.Text
SqlDataAdapter1.InsertCommand.Parameters.Add(New SqlParameter("@DOB",
System.Data.SqlDbType.DateTime, 8, "DOB"))
SqlDataAdapter1.InsertCommand.Parameters(3).Value = DtpDOB.Text
SqlDataAdapter1.InsertCommand.Parameters.Add(New
SqlParameter("@Background", System.Data.SqlDbType.VarChar, 255, "Background"))
SqlDataAdapter1.InsertCommand.Parameters(4).Value = TxtBackground.Text

Try
    SqlConnection1.Open()
    SqlDataAdapter1.InsertCommand.ExecuteNonQuery()
Catch MyException As SqlException
    MessageBox.Show(("Source: " & MyException.Source & ControlChars.Cr & _
        "Number: " & MyException.Number.ToString() & ControlChars.Cr & _
        "State: " & MyException.State.ToString() & ControlChars.Cr & _
        "Class: " & MyException.Class.ToString() & ControlChars.Cr & _
        "Server: " & MyException.Server & ControlChars.Cr & _
        "Message: " & MyException.Message & ControlChars.Cr & _
        "Procedure: " & MyException.Procedure & ControlChars.Cr & _
        "Line: " & MyException.LineNumber.ToString()))

    SqlConnection1.Close()
    SqlDataAdapter1.Dispose()
    Return
End Try
```

```
        MessageBox.Show("The record has been added.", "Record added",
MessageBoxButtons.OK, MessageBoxIcon.Information)
        End If

        SqlConnection1.Close()
        SqlDataAdapter1.Dispose()
        Me.Close()
    End Sub

    Private Sub CmdCancel_Click(ByVal sender As System.Object, ByVal e As
System.EventArgs) Handles CmdCancel.Click
        Me.Close()
    End Sub
End Class
```

The Insert Director Form

The Insert Director form enables the administrator to add records to the Director table. Let's review the interface of the Insert Director form shown below.

FIGURE 20-2 *The interface of the Insert Director form*

As with the Insert Actor form, you need to include the following statements in the Insert Director form:

```
Imports System.Data
Imports System.Data.SqlClient
Imports System.Data.SqlTypes
```

In addition to importing namespaces, you need to declare the following variables in the Insert Director form:

```
Dim SqlDataAdapter1 As New SqlDataAdapter()
Dim SqlConnection1 As New SqlConnection(StrConnectionString)
Private StrIDToUpdate As String
'Used to check if the form is opened from the Update/Delete form
```

You need to create the following functions in the Insert Actor form:

- ◆ SetUpdateID
- ◆ FrmInsertDirector_Load
- ◆ CmdSubmit_Click
- ◆ CmdCancel_Click

Note that the functions you need to create to add functionality to the Insert Director form are similar to the ones you need to create for the Insert Actor form. In addition, the functions in the Insert Director form perform the same tasks as the Insert Actor form's functions, which have already been explained in detail in this chapter. Listing 20-2 provides the complete code for the Insert Director form.

Listing 20-2 The Code for the Insert Director Form

```
Imports System.Data
Imports System.Data.SqlClient
Imports System.Data.SqlTypes


Public Class FrmInsertDirector
    Inherits System.Windows.Forms.Form
    Private StrIDToUpdate As String
    Dim SqlConnection1 As New SqlConnection(StrConnectionString)
    Dim SqlDataAdapter1 As New SqlDataAdapter()

Windows Form Designer generated code

    Public Sub SetUpdateID(ByVal StrUpID As String)
        StrIDToUpdate = StrUpID
    End Sub
```

```
Private Sub CmdSubmit_Click(ByVal sender As System.Object, ByVal e As
System.EventArgs) Handles CmdSubmit.Click
    If TxtDirectorID.Text.Trim = "" Then
        MessageBox.Show("Please enter director ID.")
        TxtDirectorID.Focus()
        Return
    End If
    If TxtFName.Text.Trim = "" Then
        MessageBox.Show("Please enter first name.")
        TxtFName.Focus()
        Return
    End If
    If TxtLName.Text.Trim = "" Then
        MessageBox.Show("Please enter last name.")
        TxtLName.Focus()
        Return
    End If
    If StrIDToUpdate <> "" Then
        Dim UpdString As String
        UpdString = "UPDATE Director SET DirID = @DirID, FirstName = @FirstName,
LastName = @LastName, DOB = @DOB, Background = @Background WHERE DirID = '" &
StrIDToUpdate & "'"

        Dim UpdateCmd1 As New SqlCommand(UpdString, SqlConnection1)

        SqlDataAdapter1.UpdateCommand = UpdateCmd1
        SqlDataAdapter1.UpdateCommand.Parameters.Add(New
System.Data.SqlClient.SqlParameter("@DirID", System.Data.SqlDbType.Char, 5,
"DirID"))
        SqlDataAdapter1.UpdateCommand.Parameters(0).Value = TxtDirectorID.Text
        SqlDataAdapter1.UpdateCommand.Parameters.Add(New
System.Data.SqlClient.SqlParameter("@FirstName", System.Data.SqlDbType.VarChar, 50,
"FirstName"))
        SqlDataAdapter1.UpdateCommand.Parameters(1).Value = TxtFName.Text
        SqlDataAdapter1.UpdateCommand.Parameters.Add(New
System.Data.SqlClient.SqlParameter("@LastName", System.Data.SqlDbType.VarChar, 50,
"LastName"))
        SqlDataAdapter1.UpdateCommand.Parameters(2).Value = TxtLName.Text
```

```
        SqlDataAdapter1.UpdateCommand.Parameters.Add(New
System.Data.SqlClient.SqlParameter("@DOB", System.Data.SqlDbType.DateTime, 8, "DOB"))
        SqlDataAdapter1.UpdateCommand.Parameters(3).Value = DtpDOB.Text
        SqlDataAdapter1.UpdateCommand.Parameters.Add(New
System.Data.SqlClient.SqlParameter("@Background", System.Data.SqlDbType.VarChar,
255, "Background"))
        SqlDataAdapter1.UpdateCommand.Parameters(4).Value = TxtBackground.Text

    Try
        SqlConnection1.Open()
        SqlDataAdapter1.UpdateCommand.ExecuteNonQuery()
    Catch MyException As SqlException
        MessageBox.Show(("Source: " & MyException.Source & ControlChars.Cr & _
        "Number: " & MyException.Number.ToString() & ControlChars.Cr & _
        "State: " & MyException.State.ToString() & ControlChars.Cr & _
        "Class: " & MyException.Class.ToString() & ControlChars.Cr & _
        "Server: " & MyException.Server & ControlChars.Cr & _
        "Message: " & MyException.Message & ControlChars.Cr & _
        "Procedure: " & MyException.Procedure & ControlChars.Cr & _
        "Line: " & MyException.LineNumber.ToString()))

        SqlConnection1.Close()
        SqlDataAdapter1.Dispose()
        Return
    End Try
    MessageBox.Show("The record has been Updated")
Else
    Dim InsString As String
    InsString = "INSERT INTO Director(DirID, FirstName, LastName, DOB,
Background) VALUES (@DirID, @FirstName, @LastName, @DOB, @Background); SELECT
DirID, FirstName, LastName, DOB, Background FROM Director WHERE (DirID = @DirID)"

    Dim InsertCmd1 As New SqlCommand(InsString, SqlConnection1)

    SqlDataAdapter1.InsertCommand = InsertCmd1
    SqlDataAdapter1.InsertCommand.Connection = SqlConnection1
```

```vb
            SqlDataAdapter1.InsertCommand.Parameters.Add(New SqlParameter("@DirID",
    System.Data.SqlDbType.VarChar, 5, "DirID"))
            SqlDataAdapter1.InsertCommand.Parameters(0).Value = TxtDirectorID.Text
            SqlDataAdapter1.InsertCommand.Parameters.Add(New
    SqlParameter("@FirstName", System.Data.SqlDbType.VarChar, 50, "FirstName"))
            SqlDataAdapter1.InsertCommand.Parameters(1).Value = TxtFName.Text
            SqlDataAdapter1.InsertCommand.Parameters.Add(New SqlParameter("@LastName",
    System.Data.SqlDbType.VarChar, 50, "LastName"))
            SqlDataAdapter1.InsertCommand.Parameters(2).Value = TxtLName.Text
            SqlDataAdapter1.InsertCommand.Parameters.Add(New SqlParameter("@DOB",
    System.Data.SqlDbType.DateTime, 8, "DOB"))
            SqlDataAdapter1.InsertCommand.Parameters(3).Value = DtpDOB.Text
            SqlDataAdapter1.InsertCommand.Parameters.Add(New
    SqlParameter("@Background", System.Data.SqlDbType.VarChar, 255, "Background"))
            SqlDataAdapter1.InsertCommand.Parameters(4).Value = TxtBackground.Text

        Try
            SqlConnection1.Open()
            SqlDataAdapter1.InsertCommand.ExecuteNonQuery()
        Catch MyException As SqlException
            MessageBox.Show(("Source: " & MyException.Source & ControlChars.Cr & _
            "Number: " & MyException.Number.ToString() & ControlChars.Cr & _
            "State: " & MyException.State.ToString() & ControlChars.Cr & _
            "Class: " & MyException.Class.ToString() & ControlChars.Cr & _
            "Server: " & MyException.Server & ControlChars.Cr & _
            "Message: " & MyException.Message & ControlChars.Cr & _
            "Procedure: " & MyException.Procedure & ControlChars.Cr & _
            "Line: " & MyException.LineNumber.ToString()))

            SqlConnection1.Close()
            SqlDataAdapter1.Dispose()
            Return
        End Try
        MessageBox.Show("The record has been added.", "Record added",
    MessageBoxButtons.OK, MessageBoxIcon.Information)
        End If
        SqlConnection1.Close()
        SqlDataAdapter1.Dispose()
```

```
        Me.Close()
    End Sub


    Private Sub CmdCancel_Click(ByVal sender As System.Object, ByVal e As
System.EventArgs) Handles CmdCancel.Click
        Me.Close()
    End Sub


    Private Sub FrmInsertDirector_Load(ByVal sender As System.Object, ByVal e As
System.EventArgs) Handles MyBase.Load
        DtpDOB.Format = DateTimePickerFormat.Custom
        DtpDOB.CustomFormat = "MM/dd/yyyy"
        If StrIDToUpdate <> "" Then
            Me.Text = "Update Director Info"
            TxtDirectorID.Enabled = False

        Dim SelectString As String
        SelectString = "SELECT DirID, FirstName, LastName, DOB, Background FROM
Director WHERE DirID = '" & StrIDToUpdate & "'"

        Dim SelectCmd1 As New SqlCommand(SelectString, SqlConnection1)

        Dim DsDataSet As DataSet
        DsDataSet = New DataSet()
        SqlDataAdapter1.SelectCommand = SelectCmd1
        SqlDataAdapter1.SelectCommand.CommandText = SelectString
        Try

            SqlConnection1.Open()
            SqlDataAdapter1.Fill(DsDataSet, "Result")
        Catch MyException As SqlException
            MessageBox.Show(("Source: " & MyException.Source & ControlChars.Cr & _
                "Number: " & MyException.Number.ToString() & ControlChars.Cr & _
                "State: " & MyException.State.ToString() & ControlChars.Cr & _
                "Class: " & MyException.Class.ToString() & ControlChars.Cr & _
                "Server: " & MyException.Server & ControlChars.Cr & _
                "Message: " & MyException.Message & ControlChars.Cr & _
                "Procedure: " & MyException.Procedure & ControlChars.Cr & _
```

```
                    "Line: " & MyException.LineNumber.ToString()))


                SqlConnection1.Close()
                SqlDataAdapter1.Dispose()
                Return
            End Try


            TxtDirectorID.DataBindings.Add(New Binding("Text", DsDataSet,
"Result.DirID"))
            TxtFName.DataBindings.Add(New Binding("Text", DsDataSet,
"Result.FirstName"))
            TxtLName.DataBindings.Add(New Binding("Text", DsDataSet,
"Result.LastName"))
            DtpDOB.DataBindings.Add(New Binding("Text", DsDataSet, "Result.DOB"))
            TxtBackground.DataBindings.Add(New Binding("Text", DsDataSet,
"Result.Background"))


            SqlConnection1.Close()
            SqlDataAdapter1.Dispose()
        End If
    End Sub
End Class
```

The Insert Producer Form

The Insert Producer form enables the administrator to add records to the Producer table. Figure 20-3 shows the interface of the Insert Producer form.

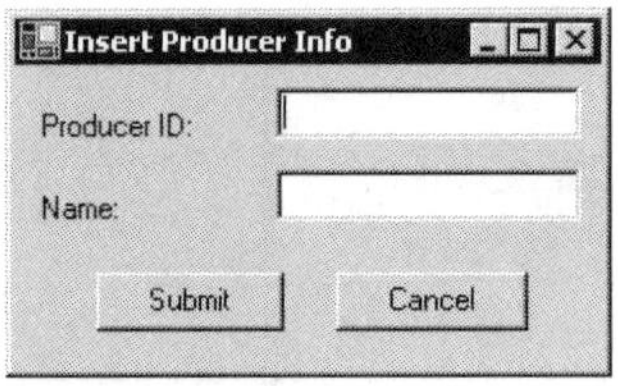

FIGURE 20-3 *The interface of the Insert Producer form*

As with the forms already discussed in this chapter, you need to include the following statements in the Insert Producer form:

```
Imports System.Data
Imports System.Data.SqlClient
Imports System.Data.SqlTypes
```

In addition to importing namespaces, you need to declare the following variables in the Insert Producer form:

```
Dim SqlDataAdapter1 As New SqlDataAdapter()
Dim SqlConnection1 As New SqlConnection(StrConnectionString)
Private StrIDToUpdate As String
'Used to check if the form is opened from the Update/Delete form
```

You need to create the following functions in the Insert Producer form:

- ◆ SetUpdateID
- ◆ FrmInsertProducer_Load
- ◆ CmdSubmit_Click
- ◆ CmdCancel_Click

The functions you need to create to add functionality to the Insert Producer form are similar to the ones you need to create for the other forms. Listing 20-3 provides the complete code for the Insert Producer form.

Listing 20-3 The Code for the Insert Producer Form

```
Imports System.Data
Imports System.Data.SqlClient
Imports System.Data.SqlTypes


Public Class FrmInsertProducer
    Inherits System.Windows.Forms.Form
    Dim SqlConnection1 As New SqlConnection(StrConnectionString)
    Dim SqlDataAdapter1 As New SqlDataAdapter()
    Private StrIDToUpdate As String


Windows Form Designer generated code
```

```vb
Public Sub SetUpdateID(ByVal StrUpID As String)
    StrIDToUpdate = StrUpID
End Sub


Private Sub CmdSubmit_Click(ByVal sender As System.Object, ByVal e As
System.EventArgs) Handles CmdSubmit.Click
    If TxtProducerID.Text.Trim = "" Then
        MessageBox.Show("Please enter Producer ID")
        TxtProducerID.Focus()
        Return
    End If


    If TxtName.Text.Trim = "" Then
        MessageBox.Show("Please enter the producer name.")
        TxtName.Focus()
        Return
    End If


    If StrIDToUpdate <> "" Then
        Dim UpdString As String
        UpdString = "UPDATE Producer SET ProdID = @ProdID, Name = @Name WHERE
ProdID = '" & StrIDToUpdate & "'"


        Dim UpdateCmd1 As New SqlCommand(UpdString, SqlConnection1)


        SqlDataAdapter1.UpdateCommand = UpdateCmd1
        SqlDataAdapter1.UpdateCommand.Parameters.Add(New
System.Data.SqlClient.SqlParameter("@ProdID", System.Data.SqlDbType.VarChar, 5,
"ProdID"))
        SqlDataAdapter1.UpdateCommand.Parameters(0).Value = TxtProducerID.Text
        SqlDataAdapter1.UpdateCommand.Parameters.Add(New
System.Data.SqlClient.SqlParameter("@Name", System.Data.SqlDbType.VarChar, 25,
"Name"))
        SqlDataAdapter1.UpdateCommand.Parameters(1).Value = TxtName.Text
        Try
            SqlConnection1.Open()
            SqlDataAdapter1.UpdateCommand.ExecuteNonQuery()
        Catch MyException As SqlException
```

```
        MessageBox.Show(("Source: " & MyException.Source & ControlChars.Cr & _
            "Number: " & MyException.Number.ToString() & ControlChars.Cr & _
            "State: " & MyException.State.ToString() & ControlChars.Cr & _
            "Class: " & MyException.Class.ToString() & ControlChars.Cr & _
            "Server: " & MyException.Server & ControlChars.Cr & _
            "Message: " & MyException.Message & ControlChars.Cr & _
            "Procedure: " & MyException.Procedure & ControlChars.Cr & _
            "Line: " & MyException.LineNumber.ToString()))


        SqlConnection1.Close()
        SqlDataAdapter1.Dispose()
        Return
    End Try
    MessageBox.Show("The record has been Updated")
Else
    Dim InsString As String
    InsString = "INSERT INTO Producer(ProdID, Name) VALUES (@ProdID, @Name);
SELECT ProdID, Name FROM Producer WHERE (ProdID = @ProdID)"


    Dim InsertCmd1 As New SqlCommand(InsString, SqlConnection1)


    SqlDataAdapter1.InsertCommand = InsertCmd1


    SqlDataAdapter1.InsertCommand.Connection = SqlConnection1
    SqlDataAdapter1.InsertCommand.Parameters.Add(New SqlParameter("@ProdID",
System.Data.SqlDbType.VarChar, 5, "ProdID"))
    SqlDataAdapter1.InsertCommand.Parameters(0).Value = TxtProducerID.Text
    SqlDataAdapter1.InsertCommand.Parameters.Add(New SqlParameter("@Name",
System.Data.SqlDbType.VarChar, 25, "Name"))
    SqlDataAdapter1.InsertCommand.Parameters(1).Value = TxtName.Text


    Try
        SqlConnection1.Open()
        SqlDataAdapter1.InsertCommand.ExecuteNonQuery()
    Catch MyException As SqlException
        MessageBox.Show(("Source: " & MyException.Source & ControlChars.Cr & _
            "Number: " & MyException.Number.ToString() & ControlChars.Cr & _
            "State: " & MyException.State.ToString() & ControlChars.Cr & _
```

```vb
            "Class: " & MyException.Class.ToString() & ControlChars.Cr & _
            "Server: " & MyException.Server & ControlChars.Cr & _
            "Message: " & MyException.Message & ControlChars.Cr & _
            "Procedure: " & MyException.Procedure & ControlChars.Cr & _
            "Line: " & MyException.LineNumber.ToString()))

            SqlConnection1.Close()
            SqlDataAdapter1.Dispose()
            Return
        End Try
        MessageBox.Show("The record has been added.", "Record added",
MessageBoxButtons.OK, MessageBoxIcon.Information)
        End If

            SqlConnection1.Close()
            SqlDataAdapter1.Dispose()
            Me.Close()
    End Sub


    Private Sub CmdCancel_Click(ByVal sender As System.Object, ByVal e As
System.EventArgs) Handles CmdCancel.Click
        Me.Close()
    End Sub


    Private Sub FrmInsertProducer_Load(ByVal sender As System.Object, ByVal e As
System.EventArgs) Handles MyBase.Load
        If StrIDToUpdate <> "" Then
            Me.Text = "Update Producer Info"
            TxtProducerID.Enabled = False
            Dim SelectString As String
            SelectString = "SELECT ProdID, Name FROM Producer WHERE ProdID = '" &
StrIDToUpdate & "'"
            Dim SelectCmd1 As New SqlCommand(SelectString, SqlConnection1)
            Dim DsDataSet As DataSet
            DsDataSet = New DataSet()
            SqlDataAdapter1.SelectCommand = SelectCmd1
            SqlDataAdapter1.SelectCommand.CommandText = SelectString
            Try
```

```
        SqlConnection1.Open()
        SqlDataAdapter1.Fill(DsDataSet, "Result")
    Catch MyException As SqlException
        MessageBox.Show(("Source: " & MyException.Source & ControlChars.Cr & _
        "Number: " & MyException.Number.ToString() & ControlChars.Cr & _
        "State: " & MyException.State.ToString() & ControlChars.Cr & _
        "Class: " & MyException.Class.ToString() & ControlChars.Cr & _
        "Server: " & MyException.Server & ControlChars.Cr & _
        "Message: " & MyException.Message & ControlChars.Cr & _
        "Procedure: " & MyException.Procedure & ControlChars.Cr & _
        "Line: " & MyException.LineNumber.ToString()))

        SqlConnection1.Close()
        SqlDataAdapter1.Dispose()
        Return
    End Try

    TxtProducerID.DataBindings.Add(New Binding("Text", DsDataSet,
"Result.ProdID"))
    TxtName.DataBindings.Add(New Binding("Text", DsDataSet, "Result.Name"))

    SqlConnection1.Close()
    SqlDataAdapter1.Dispose()
  End If
End Sub
End Class
```

The Insert Video Form

The administrator can use the Insert Video form to add records to the Video table. Figure 20-4 shows the Insert Video form.

In the Insert Video form, you need to import the same namespaces as in the forms discussed earlier. In addition, you need to declare the same variables as were declared in the earlier forms.

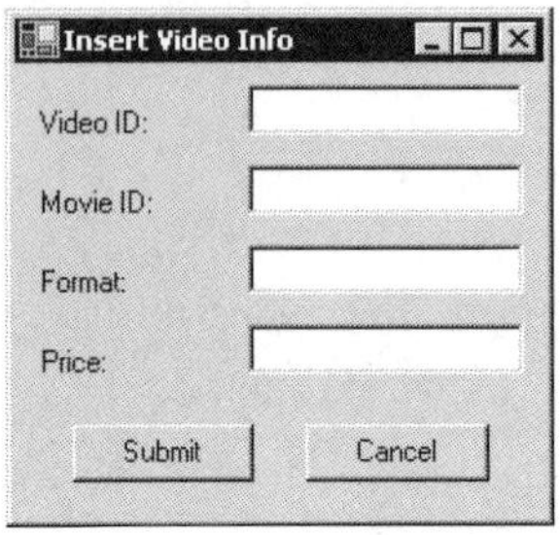

FIGURE 20-4 *The interface of the Insert Video form*

Similar to the forms already discussed, the Insert Video form also contains the following functions:

- ◆ SetUpdateID
- ◆ FrmInsertVideo_Load
- ◆ CmdSubmit_Click
- ◆ CmdCancel_Click

The complete code for the Insert Video form is provided in Listing 20-4.

Listing 20-4 The Code for the Insert Video Form

```
Imports System.Data
Imports System.Data.SqlClient
Imports System.Data.SqlTypes

Public Class FrmInsertVideo
    Inherits System.Windows.Forms.Form
    Private StrIDToUpdate As String
    Dim SqlConnection1 As New SqlConnection(StrConnectionString)
    Dim SqlDataAdapter1 As New SqlDataAdapter()

Windows Form Designer generated code

    Public Sub SetUpdateID(ByVal StrUpID As String)
        StrIDToUpdate = StrUpID
    End Sub
```

```vb
Private Sub CmdSubmit_Click(ByVal sender As System.Object, ByVal e As
System.EventArgs) Handles CmdSubmit.Click
    If TxtVideoID.Text.Trim = "" Then
        MessageBox.Show("Please enter video ID.")
        TxtVideoID.Focus()
        Return
    End If
    If TxtMovieID.Text.Trim = "" Then
        MessageBox.Show("Please enter the movie ID.")
        TxtMovieID.Focus()
        Return
    End If
    If TxtPrice.Text.Trim = "" Then
        MessageBox.Show("Please enter price for the video.")
        TxtPrice.Focus()
        Return
    End If


    If StrIDToUpdate <> "" Then
        Dim UpdString As String
        UpdString = "UPDATE Video SET MovID = @MovID, Format = @Format, Price =
@Price WHERE VideoID = '" & StrIDToUpdate & "'"

        Dim UpdateCmd1 As New SqlCommand(UpdString, SqlConnection1)

        SqlDataAdapter1.UpdateCommand = UpdateCmd1
        SqlDataAdapter1.UpdateCommand.Parameters.Add(New
System.Data.SqlClient.SqlParameter("@MovID", System.Data.SqlDbType.VarChar, 5, "MovID"))
        SqlDataAdapter1.UpdateCommand.Parameters(0).Value = TxtMovieID.Text
        SqlDataAdapter1.UpdateCommand.Parameters.Add(New
System.Data.SqlClient.SqlParameter("@Format", System.Data.SqlDbType.VarChar, 4,
"Format"))
        SqlDataAdapter1.UpdateCommand.Parameters(1).Value = TxtFormat.Text
        SqlDataAdapter1.UpdateCommand.Parameters.Add(New
System.Data.SqlClient.SqlParameter("@Price", System.Data.SqlDbType.Money, 8, "Price"))
        SqlDataAdapter1.UpdateCommand.Parameters(2).Value = TxtPrice.Text
```

```
    Try
        SqlConnection1.Open()
        SqlDataAdapter1.UpdateCommand.ExecuteNonQuery()
    Catch MyException As SqlException
        MessageBox.Show(("Source: " & MyException.Source & ControlChars.Cr & _
            "Number: " & MyException.Number.ToString() & ControlChars.Cr & _
            "State: " & MyException.State.ToString() & ControlChars.Cr & _
            "Class: " & MyException.Class.ToString() & ControlChars.Cr & _
            "Server: " & MyException.Server & ControlChars.Cr & _
            "Message: " & MyException.Message & ControlChars.Cr & _
            "Procedure: " & MyException.Procedure & ControlChars.Cr & _
            "Line: " & MyException.LineNumber.ToString()))

        SqlConnection1.Close()
        SqlDataAdapter1.Dispose()
        Return
    End Try
    MessageBox.Show("The record has been Updated")
Else
    Dim InsString As String
    InsString = "INSERT INTO Video(VideoID, MovID, Format, Price) VALUES
(@VideoID, @MovID, @Format, @Price); SELECT VideoID, MovID, Format, Price FROM
Video WHERE (VideoID = @VideoID)"

    Dim InsertCmd1 As New SqlCommand(InsString, SqlConnection1)

    SqlDataAdapter1.InsertCommand = InsertCmd1
    SqlDataAdapter1.InsertCommand.Connection = SqlConnection1
    SqlDataAdapter1.InsertCommand.Parameters.Add(New SqlParameter("@VideoID",
System.Data.SqlDbType.VarChar, 5, "VideoID"))
    SqlDataAdapter1.InsertCommand.Parameters(0).Value = TxtVideoID.Text
    SqlDataAdapter1.InsertCommand.Parameters.Add(New SqlParameter("@MovID",
System.Data.SqlDbType.VarChar, 5, "MovID"))
    SqlDataAdapter1.InsertCommand.Parameters(1).Value = TxtMovieID.Text
    SqlDataAdapter1.InsertCommand.Parameters.Add(New SqlParameter("@Format",
System.Data.SqlDbType.VarChar, 4, "Format"))
    SqlDataAdapter1.InsertCommand.Parameters(2).Value = TxtFormat.Text
```

```vbnet
        SqlDataAdapter1.InsertCommand.Parameters.Add(New SqlParameter("@Price",
System.Data.SqlDbType.Money, 8, "Price"))
        SqlDataAdapter1.InsertCommand.Parameters(3).Value = TxtPrice.Text

        Try

            SqlConnection1.Open()
            SqlDataAdapter1.InsertCommand.ExecuteNonQuery()
        Catch MyException As SqlException
            MessageBox.Show(("Source: " & MyException.Source & ControlChars.Cr & _
                "Number: " & MyException.Number.ToString() & ControlChars.Cr & _
                "State: " & MyException.State.ToString() & ControlChars.Cr & _
                "Class: " & MyException.Class.ToString() & ControlChars.Cr & _
                "Server: " & MyException.Server & ControlChars.Cr & _
                "Message: " & MyException.Message & ControlChars.Cr & _
                "Procedure: " & MyException.Procedure & ControlChars.Cr & _
                "Line: " & MyException.LineNumber.ToString()))

            SqlConnection1.Close()
            SqlDataAdapter1.Dispose()
            Return
        End Try
        MessageBox.Show("The record has been added", "Record added",
MessageBoxButtons.OK, MessageBoxIcon.Information)
    End If

    SqlConnection1.Close()
    SqlDataAdapter1.Dispose()
    Me.Close()
End Sub


Private Sub CmdCancel_Click(ByVal sender As System.Object, ByVal e As
System.EventArgs) Handles CmdCancel.Click
    Me.Close()
End Sub
```

```vbnet
    Private Sub FrmInsertVideo_Load(ByVal sender As System.Object, ByVal e As
System.EventArgs) Handles MyBase.Load
        If StrIDToUpdate <> "" Then
            Me.Text = "Update Video Info"
            TxtVideoID.Enabled = False

            Dim SelectString As String
            SelectString = "SELECT VideoID, MovID, Format, Price FROM Video WHERE
VideoID = '" & StrIDToUpdate & "'"

            Dim SelectCmd1 As New SqlCommand(SelectString, SqlConnection1)

            Dim DsDataSet As DataSet
            DsDataSet = New DataSet()
            SqlDataAdapter1.SelectCommand = SelectCmd1
            SqlDataAdapter1.SelectCommand.CommandText = SelectString
            Try
                SqlConnection1.Open()
                SqlDataAdapter1.Fill(DsDataSet, "Result")
            Catch MyException As SqlException
                MessageBox.Show(("Source: " & MyException.Source & ControlChars.Cr & _
                "Number: " & MyException.Number.ToString() & ControlChars.Cr & _
                "State: " & MyException.State.ToString() & ControlChars.Cr & _
                "Class: " & MyException.Class.ToString() & ControlChars.Cr & _
                "Server: " & MyException.Server & ControlChars.Cr & _
                "Message: " & MyException.Message & ControlChars.Cr & _
                "Procedure: " & MyException.Procedure & ControlChars.Cr & _
                "Line: " & MyException.LineNumber.ToString()))

                SqlConnection1.Close()
                SqlDataAdapter1.Dispose()
                Return
            End Try

            TxtVideoID.DataBindings.Add(New Binding("Text", DsDataSet,
    "Result.VideoID"))
            TxtMovieID.DataBindings.Add(New Binding("Text", DsDataSet,
    "Result.MovID"))
```

```
        TxtFormat.DataBindings.Add(New Binding("Text", DsDataSet,
"Result.Format"))
        TxtPrice.DataBindings.Add(New Binding("Text", DsDataSet, "Result.Price"))

        SqlConnection1.Close()
        SqlDataAdapter1.Dispose()
    End If
End Sub


End Class
```

The Insert Movie Form

The Insert Video form enables the administrator to add records to the Movie table. Figure 20-5 displays the Insert Movie form.

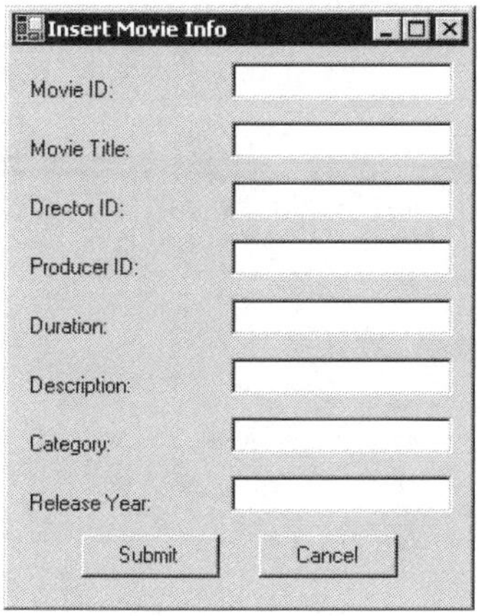

FIGURE 20-5 *The interface of the Insert Movie form*

Just as you imported namespaces and declared variables in the preceding forms, you need to do so in the Insert Movie form. In the Insert Movie form, you need to import the same namespaces and declare the same variables as you declared in the earlier forms.

The Insert Movie form also contains the following functions:

◆ SetUpdateID

◆ FrmInsertVideo_Load

◆ CmdSubmit_Click

◆ CmdCancel_Click

Listing 20-5 provides the complete code for the Insert Movie form.

Listing 20-5 The Code for the Insert Movie Form

```
Imports System.Data
Imports System.Data.SqlClient
Imports System.Data.SqlTypes


Public Class FrmInsertMovie
    Inherits System.Windows.Forms.Form
    Private StrIDToUpdate As String
    Dim SqlConnection1 As New SqlConnection(StrConnectionString)
    Dim SqlDataAdapter1 As New SqlDataAdapter()


Windows Form Designer generated code

    Public Sub SetUpdateID(ByVal StrUpID As String)
        StrIDToUpdate = StrUpID
        End Sub


    Private Sub CmdSubmit_Click(ByVal sender As System.Object, ByVal e As
System.EventArgs) Handles CmdSubmit.Click
        If TxtMovieID.Text.Trim = "" Then
            MessageBox.Show("Please enter the movie ID.")
            TxtMovieID.Focus()
            Return
        End If
        If TxtMovieTitle.Text.Trim = "" Then
            MessageBox.Show("Please enter the movie title.")
            TxtMovieTitle.Focus()
            Return
        End If
```

```vbnet
        If TxtDirectorID.Text.Trim = "" Then
            MessageBox.Show("Please enter the director ID.")
            TxtDirectorID.Focus()
            Return
        End If
        If TxtProducerID.Text.Trim = "" Then
            MessageBox.Show("Please enter the producer ID.")
            TxtProducerID.Focus()
            Return
        End If


        If TxtDuration.Text.Trim = "" Then
            MessageBox.Show("Please enter the duration of movie.")
            TxtDuration.Focus()
            Return
        End If


        If TxtRelYear.Text.Trim = "" Then
            MessageBox.Show("Please enter year of release of the movie.")
            TxtRelYear.Focus()
            Return
        End If


        If StrIDToUpdate <> "" Then
            Dim UpdString As String
            UpdString = "UPDATE Movie SET MovID = @MovID, MovTitle = @MovTitle, DirID
= @DirID, ProdID = @ProdID, Duration = @Duration, Description = @Description,
Category = @Category, ReleaseYear = @ReleaseYear WHERE MovID = '" & StrIDToUpdate & "'"


            Dim UpdateCmd1 As New SqlCommand(UpdString, SqlConnection1)


            SqlDataAdapter1.UpdateCommand = UpdateCmd1
            SqlDataAdapter1.UpdateCommand.Parameters.Add(New
System.Data.SqlClient.SqlParameter("@MovID", System.Data.SqlDbType.VarChar, 5, "MovID"))
            SqlDataAdapter1.UpdateCommand.Parameters(0).Value = TxtMovieID.Text
            SqlDataAdapter1.UpdateCommand.Parameters.Add(New
```

```
System.Data.SqlClient.SqlParameter("@MovTitle", System.Data.SqlDbType.VarChar, 40,
"MovTitle"))
        SqlDataAdapter1.UpdateCommand.Parameters(1).Value = TxtMovieTitle.Text
        SqlDataAdapter1.UpdateCommand.Parameters.Add(New
System.Data.SqlClient.SqlParameter("@DirID", System.Data.SqlDbType.VarChar, 5,
"DirID"))
        SqlDataAdapter1.UpdateCommand.Parameters(2).Value = TxtDirectorID.Text
        SqlDataAdapter1.UpdateCommand.Parameters.Add(New
System.Data.SqlClient.SqlParameter("@ProdID", System.Data.SqlDbType.VarChar, 5,
"ProdID"))
        SqlDataAdapter1.UpdateCommand.Parameters(3).Value = TxtProducerID.Text
        SqlDataAdapter1.UpdateCommand.Parameters.Add(New
System.Data.SqlClient.SqlParameter("@Duration", System.Data.SqlDbType.Int,
"Duration"))
        SqlDataAdapter1.UpdateCommand.Parameters(4).Value = TxtDuration.Text
        SqlDataAdapter1.UpdateCommand.Parameters.Add(New
System.Data.SqlClient.SqlParameter("@Description", System.Data.SqlDbType.VarChar,
255, "Description"))
        SqlDataAdapter1.UpdateCommand.Parameters(5).Value = TxtDescription.Text
        SqlDataAdapter1.UpdateCommand.Parameters.Add(New
System.Data.SqlClient.SqlParameter("@Category", System.Data.SqlDbType.VarChar, 20,
"Category"))
        SqlDataAdapter1.UpdateCommand.Parameters(6).Value = TxtCategory.Text
        SqlDataAdapter1.UpdateCommand.Parameters.Add(New
System.Data.SqlClient.SqlParameter("@ReleaseYear", System.Data.SqlDbType.Int,
"ReleaseYear"))
        SqlDataAdapter1.UpdateCommand.Parameters(7).Value = TxtRelYear.Text

    Try
        SqlConnection1.Open()
        SqlDataAdapter1.UpdateCommand.ExecuteNonQuery()
    Catch MyException As SqlException
        MessageBox.Show(("Source: " & MyException.Source & ControlChars.Cr & _
        "Number: " & MyException.Number.ToString() & ControlChars.Cr & _
        "State: " & MyException.State.ToString() & ControlChars.Cr & _
        "Class: " & MyException.Class.ToString() & ControlChars.Cr & _
        "Server: " & MyException.Server & ControlChars.Cr & _
        "Message: " & MyException.Message & ControlChars.Cr & _
```

```
            "Procedure: " & MyException.Procedure & ControlChars.Cr & _
            "Line: " & MyException.LineNumber.ToString()))

            SqlConnection1.Close()
            SqlDataAdapter1.Dispose()
            Return
        End Try
        MessageBox.Show("The record has been Updated")
    Else
        Dim InsString As String
        InsString = "INSERT INTO Movie(MovID, MovTitle, DirID, ProdID, Duration,
Description, Category, ReleaseYear) VALUES (@MovID, @MovTitle, @DirID, @ProdID,
@Duration, @Description, @Category, @ReleaseYear); SELECT MovID, MovTitle, DirID,
ProdID, Duration, Description, Category, ReleaseYear FROM Movie WHERE (MovID =
@MovID)"

        Dim InsertCmd1 As New SqlCommand(InsString, SqlConnection1)

        SqlDataAdapter1.InsertCommand = InsertCmd1
        SqlDataAdapter1.InsertCommand.Parameters.Add(New
System.Data.SqlClient.SqlParameter("@MovID", System.Data.SqlDbType.VarChar, 5,
"MovID"))
        SqlDataAdapter1.InsertCommand.Parameters(0).Value = TxtMovieID.Text
        SqlDataAdapter1.InsertCommand.Parameters.Add(New
System.Data.SqlClient.SqlParameter("@MovTitle", System.Data.SqlDbType.VarChar, 40,
"MovTitle"))
        SqlDataAdapter1.InsertCommand.Parameters(1).Value = TxtMovieTitle.Text
        SqlDataAdapter1.InsertCommand.Parameters.Add(New
System.Data.SqlClient.SqlParameter("@DirID", System.Data.SqlDbType.VarChar, 5,
"DirID"))
        SqlDataAdapter1.InsertCommand.Parameters(2).Value = TxtDirectorID.Text
        SqlDataAdapter1.InsertCommand.Parameters.Add(New
System.Data.SqlClient.SqlParameter("@ProdID", System.Data.SqlDbType.VarChar, 5,
"ProdID"))
        SqlDataAdapter1.InsertCommand.Parameters(3).Value = TxtProducerID.Text
        SqlDataAdapter1.InsertCommand.Parameters.Add(New
System.Data.SqlClient.SqlParameter("@Duration", System.Data.SqlDbType.Int, 4,
"Duration"))
```

```
        SqlDataAdapter1.InsertCommand.Parameters(4).Value = TxtDuration.Text
        SqlDataAdapter1.InsertCommand.Parameters.Add(New
System.Data.SqlClient.SqlParameter("@Description", System.Data.SqlDbType.VarChar,
255, "Description"))
        SqlDataAdapter1.InsertCommand.Parameters(5).Value = TxtDescription.Text
        SqlDataAdapter1.InsertCommand.Parameters.Add(New
System.Data.SqlClient.SqlParameter("@Category", System.Data.SqlDbType.VarChar, 20,
"Category"))
        SqlDataAdapter1.InsertCommand.Parameters(6).Value = TxtCategory.Text
        If TxtRelYear.Text = "" Then
            TxtRelYear.Text = "Null"
        End If
        SqlDataAdapter1.InsertCommand.Parameters.Add(New
System.Data.SqlClient.SqlParameter("@ReleaseYear", System.Data.SqlDbType.Int, 4,
"ReleaseYear"))
        SqlDataAdapter1.InsertCommand.Parameters(7).Value = TxtRelYear.Text

        Try

            SqlConnection1.Open()
            SqlDataAdapter1.InsertCommand.ExecuteNonQuery()
        Catch MyException As SqlException
            MessageBox.Show(("Source: " & MyException.Source & ControlChars.Cr & _
            "Number: " & MyException.Number.ToString() & ControlChars.Cr & _
            "State: " & MyException.State.ToString() & ControlChars.Cr & _
            "Class: " & MyException.Class.ToString() & ControlChars.Cr & _
            "Server: " & MyException.Server & ControlChars.Cr & _
            "Message: " & MyException.Message & ControlChars.Cr & _
            "Procedure: " & MyException.Procedure & ControlChars.Cr & _
            "Line: " & MyException.LineNumber.ToString()))
        Catch MyException As Exception
            MessageBox.Show(MyException.Message)
            SqlConnection1.Close()
            SqlDataAdapter1.Dispose()
            Return
        End Try
        MessageBox.Show("The record has been added.", "Record added",
MessageBoxButtons.OK, MessageBoxIcon.Information)
```

```
    End If

    SqlConnection1.Close()
    SqlDataAdapter1.Dispose()

    Me.Close()
End Sub

Private Sub CmdCancel_Click(ByVal sender As System.Object, ByVal e As
System.EventArgs) Handles CmdCancel.Click
    Me.Close()
End Sub

Private Sub FrmInsertMovie_Load(ByVal sender As System.Object, ByVal e As
System.EventArgs) Handles MyBase.Load
    If StrIDToUpdate <> "" Then
        Me.Text = "Update Movie Info"
        TxtMovieID.Enabled = False

        Dim SelectString As String
        SelectString = "SELECT MovID, MovTitle, DirID, ProdID, Duration,
Description, Category, ReleaseYear FROM Movie WHERE MovID = '" & StrIDToUpdate & "'"

        Dim SelectCmd1 As New SqlCommand(SelectString, SqlConnection1)

        Dim DsDataSet As DataSet
        DsDataSet = New DataSet()
        SqlDataAdapter1.SelectCommand = SelectCmd1
        SqlDataAdapter1.SelectCommand.CommandText = SelectString
        Try
            SqlConnection1.Open()
            SqlDataAdapter1.Fill(DsDataSet, "Result")
        Catch MyException As SqlException
            MessageBox.Show(("Source: " & MyException.Source & ControlChars.Cr & _
            "Number: " & MyException.Number.ToString() & ControlChars.Cr & _
            "State: " & MyException.State.ToString() & ControlChars.Cr & _
            "Class: " & MyException.Class.ToString() & ControlChars.Cr & _
```

```
                    "Server: " & MyException.Server & ControlChars.Cr & _
                    "Message: " & MyException.Message & ControlChars.Cr & _
                    "Procedure: " & MyException.Procedure & ControlChars.Cr & _
                    "Line: " & MyException.LineNumber.ToString()))

                SqlConnection1.Close()
                SqlDataAdapter1.Dispose()
                Return
            End Try


            TxtMovieID.DataBindings.Add(New Binding("Text", DsDataSet,
        "Result.MovID"))
            TxtMovieTitle.DataBindings.Add(New Binding("Text", DsDataSet,
        "Result.MovTitle"))
            TxtDirectorID.DataBindings.Add(New Binding("Text", DsDataSet,
        "Result.DirID"))
            TxtProducerID.DataBindings.Add(New Binding("Text", DsDataSet,
        "Result.ProdID"))
            TxtDuration.DataBindings.Add(New Binding("Text", DsDataSet,
        "Result.Duration"))
            TxtDescription.DataBindings.Add(New Binding("Text", DsDataSet,
        "Result.Description"))
            TxtCategory.DataBindings.Add(New Binding("Text", DsDataSet,
        "Result.Category"))
            TxtRelYear.DataBindings.Add(New Binding("Text", DsDataSet,
        "Result.ReleaseYear"))

            SqlConnection1.Close()
            SqlDataAdapter1.Dispose()
        End If
    End Sub
End Class
```

The Insert Customer Form

The administrator can use the Insert Customer form to add records to the Customer table. Figure 20-6 shows the Insert Customer form.

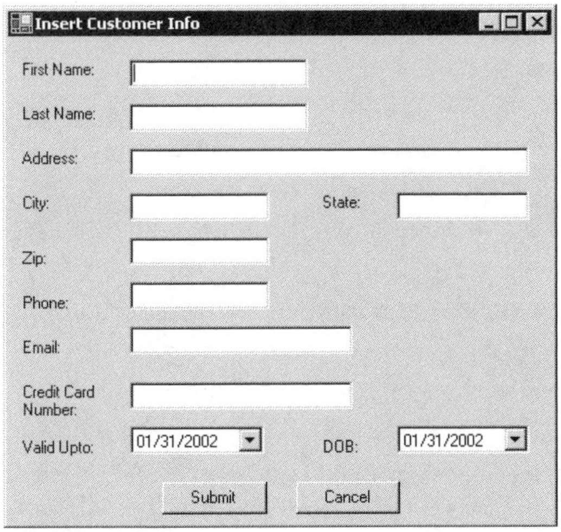

FIGURE 20-6 *The interface of the Insert Customer form*

Before you write the code for the Insert Customer form, you need to import namespaces and declare the variables in the form.

Similar to the forms already discussed, the Insert Customer form contains the following functions:

- ◆ SetUpdateID
- ◆ FrmInsertVideo_Load
- ◆ CmdSubmit_Click
- ◆ CmdCancel_Click

The complete code for the Insert Customer form is provided in Listing 20-6.

Listing 20-6 The Code for the Insert Customer Form

```
Imports System.Data
Imports System.Data.SqlClient
Imports System.Data.SqlTypes
```

```vb
Public Class FrmInsertCustomer
    Inherits System.Windows.Forms.Form
    Private StrIDToUpdate As String
    Dim SqlConnection1 As New SqlConnection(StrConnectionString)
    Dim SqlDataAdapter1 As New SqlDataAdapter()


Windows Form Designer generated code

    Public Sub SetUpdateID(ByVal StrUpID As String)
        StrIDToUpdate = StrUpID
    End Sub


    Private Sub CmdSubmitReg_Click(ByVal sender As System.Object, ByVal e As
System.EventArgs) Handles CmdSubmitReg.Click
        If TxtFName.Text.Trim = "" Then
            MessageBox.Show("Please enter the first name.")
            TxtFName.Focus()
            Return
        End If
        If TxtLName.Text.Trim = "" Then
            MessageBox.Show("Please enter the last name.")
            TxtLName.Focus()
            Return
        End If
        If TxtAddress.Text.Trim = "" Then
            MessageBox.Show("Please enter the address.")
            TxtAddress.Focus()
            Return
        End If
        If (TxtCCNumber.Text.Trim = "") Then
            MessageBox.Show("Please enter the credit card number.", "Message Box",
MessageBoxButtons.OK)
            TxtCCNumber.Focus()
            Return
        ElseIf (TxtCCNumber.Text.Trim.Length <> 16) Then
            MessageBox.Show("Invalid credit card number. Please re-enter the credit
card number.", "Message Box", MessageBoxButtons.OK)
            TxtCCNumber.Focus()
```

```
        Return
    End If
    If (CDate(DtpCCValidUpto.Text) < Now()) Then
        MessageBox.Show("Invalid date")
        DtpCCValidUpto.Focus()
        Return
    End If



    If StrIDToUpdate <> "" Then
        Dim UpdString As String
        UpdString = "UPDATE Customer SET FirstName = @FirstName, LastName =
@LastName, Address = @Address, City = @City, State = @State, Zip = @Zip, Phone =
@Phone, EMail = @EMail, DOB = @DOB, CreditCardNum = @CreditCardNum,
CreditCardValidUpto = @CreditCardValidUpto WHERE CustID = " & StrIDToUpdate


        Dim UpdateCmd1 As New SqlCommand(UpdString, SqlConnection1)


        SqlDataAdapter1.UpdateCommand = UpdateCmd1
        SqlDataAdapter1.UpdateCommand.Parameters.Add(New
System.Data.SqlClient.SqlParameter("@FirstName", System.Data.SqlDbType.VarChar, 50,
"FirstName"))
        SqlDataAdapter1.UpdateCommand.Parameters(0).Value = TxtFName.Text
        SqlDataAdapter1.UpdateCommand.Parameters.Add(New
System.Data.SqlClient.SqlParameter("@LastName", System.Data.SqlDbType.VarChar, 50,
"LastName"))
        SqlDataAdapter1.UpdateCommand.Parameters(1).Value = TxtLName.Text
        SqlDataAdapter1.UpdateCommand.Parameters.Add(New
System.Data.SqlClient.SqlParameter("@Address", System.Data.SqlDbType.VarChar, 25,
"Address"))
        SqlDataAdapter1.UpdateCommand.Parameters(2).Value = TxtAddress.Text
        SqlDataAdapter1.UpdateCommand.Parameters.Add(New
System.Data.SqlClient.SqlParameter("@City", System.Data.SqlDbType.VarChar, 25,
"City"))
        SqlDataAdapter1.UpdateCommand.Parameters(3).Value = TxtCity.Text
        SqlDataAdapter1.UpdateCommand.Parameters.Add(New
System.Data.SqlClient.SqlParameter("@State", System.Data.SqlDbType.VarChar, 15,
"State"))
```

```
        SqlDataAdapter1.UpdateCommand.Parameters(4).Value = TxtState.Text
        SqlDataAdapter1.UpdateCommand.Parameters.Add(New
System.Data.SqlClient.SqlParameter("@Zip", System.Data.SqlDbType.VarChar, 7, "Zip"))
        SqlDataAdapter1.UpdateCommand.Parameters(5).Value = TxtZip.Text
        SqlDataAdapter1.UpdateCommand.Parameters.Add(New
System.Data.SqlClient.SqlParameter("@Phone", System.Data.SqlDbType.VarChar, 10,
"Phone"))
        SqlDataAdapter1.UpdateCommand.Parameters(6).Value = TxtPhone.Text
        SqlDataAdapter1.UpdateCommand.Parameters.Add(New
System.Data.SqlClient.SqlParameter("@EMail", System.Data.SqlDbType.VarChar, 50,
"EMail"))
        SqlDataAdapter1.UpdateCommand.Parameters(7).Value = TxtEmail.Text
        SqlDataAdapter1.UpdateCommand.Parameters.Add(New
System.Data.SqlClient.SqlParameter("@DOB", System.Data.SqlDbType.DateTime, 8, "DOB"))
        SqlDataAdapter1.UpdateCommand.Parameters(8).Value = DtpDOB.Text
        SqlDataAdapter1.UpdateCommand.Parameters.Add(New
System.Data.SqlClient.SqlParameter("@CreditCardNum", System.Data.SqlDbType.VarChar,
16, "CreditCardNum"))
        SqlDataAdapter1.UpdateCommand.Parameters(9).Value = TxtCCNumber.Text
        SqlDataAdapter1.UpdateCommand.Parameters.Add(New
System.Data.SqlClient.SqlParameter("@CreditCardValidUpto",
System.Data.SqlDbType.DateTime, 8, "CreditCardValidUpto"))
          SqlDataAdapter1.UpdateCommand.Parameters(10).Value =
DtpCCValidUpto.Text

    Try
        SqlConnection1.Open()
        SqlDataAdapter1.UpdateCommand.ExecuteNonQuery()
    Catch MyException As SqlException
        MessageBox.Show(("Source: " & MyException.Source & ControlChars.Cr & _
        "Number: " & MyException.Number.ToString() & ControlChars.Cr & _
        "State: " & MyException.State.ToString() & ControlChars.Cr & _
        "Class: " & MyException.Class.ToString() & ControlChars.Cr & _
        "Server: " & MyException.Server & ControlChars.Cr & _
        "Message: " & MyException.Message & ControlChars.Cr & _
        "Procedure: " & MyException.Procedure & ControlChars.Cr & _
        "Line: " & MyException.LineNumber.ToString()))
```

```
            SqlConnection1.Close()
            SqlDataAdapter1.Dispose()
            Return
        End Try
        MessageBox.Show("The record has been Updated")
    Else
        Dim InsString As String
        InsString = "INSERT INTO Customer(FirstName, LastName, Address, City,
State, Zip, Phone, EMail, DOB, CreditCardNum, CreditCardValidUpto) VALUES
(@FirstName, @LastName, @Address, @City, @State, @Zip, @Phone, @EMail, @DOB,
@CreditCardNum, @CreditCardValidUpto)"
        Dim InsertCmd1 As New SqlCommand(InsString, SqlConnection1)

        SqlDataAdapter1.InsertCommand = InsertCmd1
        SqlDataAdapter1.InsertCommand.Parameters.Add(New
System.Data.SqlClient.SqlParameter("@FirstName", System.Data.SqlDbType.VarChar, 50,
"FirstName"))
        SqlDataAdapter1.InsertCommand.Parameters(0).Value = TxtFName.Text
        SqlDataAdapter1.InsertCommand.Parameters.Add(New
System.Data.SqlClient.SqlParameter("@LastName", System.Data.SqlDbType.VarChar, 50,
"LastName"))
        SqlDataAdapter1.InsertCommand.Parameters(1).Value = TxtLName.Text
        SqlDataAdapter1.InsertCommand.Parameters.Add(New
System.Data.SqlClient.SqlParameter("@Address", System.Data.SqlDbType.VarChar, 25,
"Address"))
        SqlDataAdapter1.InsertCommand.Parameters(2).Value = TxtAddress.Text
        SqlDataAdapter1.InsertCommand.Parameters.Add(New
System.Data.SqlClient.SqlParameter("@City", System.Data.SqlDbType.VarChar, 25,
"City"))
        SqlDataAdapter1.InsertCommand.Parameters(3).Value = TxtCity.Text
        SqlDataAdapter1.InsertCommand.Parameters.Add(New
System.Data.SqlClient.SqlParameter("@State", System.Data.SqlDbType.VarChar, 15,
"State"))
        SqlDataAdapter1.InsertCommand.Parameters(4).Value = TxtState.Text
        SqlDataAdapter1.InsertCommand.Parameters.Add(New
System.Data.SqlClient.SqlParameter("@Zip", System.Data.SqlDbType.VarChar, 7, "Zip"))
        SqlDataAdapter1.InsertCommand.Parameters(5).Value = TxtZip.Text
```

```
            SqlDataAdapter1.InsertCommand.Parameters.Add(New
System.Data.SqlClient.SqlParameter("@Phone", System.Data.SqlDbType.VarChar, 10,
"Phone"))
            SqlDataAdapter1.InsertCommand.Parameters(6).Value = TxtPhone.Text
            SqlDataAdapter1.InsertCommand.Parameters.Add(New
System.Data.SqlClient.SqlParameter("@EMail", System.Data.SqlDbType.VarChar, 50,
"EMail"))
            SqlDataAdapter1.InsertCommand.Parameters(7).Value = TxtEmail.Text
            SqlDataAdapter1.InsertCommand.Parameters.Add(New
System.Data.SqlClient.SqlParameter("@DOB", System.Data.SqlDbType.DateTime, 8,
"DOB"))
            SqlDataAdapter1.InsertCommand.Parameters(8).Value = DtpDOB.Text
            SqlDataAdapter1.InsertCommand.Parameters.Add(New
System.Data.SqlClient.SqlParameter("@CreditCardNum", System.Data.SqlDbType.VarChar,
16, "CreditCardNum"))
            SqlDataAdapter1.InsertCommand.Parameters(9).Value = TxtCCNumber.Text
            SqlDataAdapter1.InsertCommand.Parameters.Add(New
System.Data.SqlClient.SqlParameter("@CreditCardValidUpto",
System.Data.SqlDbType.DateTime, 8, "CreditCardValidUpto"))
            SqlDataAdapter1.InsertCommand.Parameters(10).Value = DtpCCValidUpto.Text

        Try
            SqlConnection1.Open()
            SqlDataAdapter1.InsertCommand.ExecuteNonQuery()
        Catch MyException As SqlException
            MessageBox.Show(("Source: " & MyException.Source & ControlChars.Cr & _
            "Number: " & MyException.Number.ToString() & ControlChars.Cr & _
            "State: " & MyException.State.ToString() & ControlChars.Cr & _
            "Class: " & MyException.Class.ToString() & ControlChars.Cr & _
            "Server: " & MyException.Server & ControlChars.Cr & _
            "Message: " & MyException.Message & ControlChars.Cr & _
            "Procedure: " & MyException.Procedure & ControlChars.Cr & _
            "Line: " & MyException.LineNumber.ToString()))

            SqlConnection1.Close()
            SqlDataAdapter1.Dispose()
            Return
        End Try
```

```
        MessageBox.Show("The record has been added", "Record added",
MessageBoxButtons.OK, MessageBoxIcon.Information)
    End If

    SqlConnection1.Close()
    SqlDataAdapter1.Dispose()
    Me.Close()
End Sub


Private Sub CmdCancel_Click(ByVal sender As System.Object, ByVal e As
System.EventArgs) Handles CmdCancel.Click
    Me.Close()
End Sub


Private Sub FrmInsertCustomer_Load(ByVal sender As System.Object, ByVal e As
System.EventArgs) Handles MyBase.Load

    DtpDOB.Format = DateTimePickerFormat.Custom
    DtpDOB.CustomFormat = "MM/dd/yyyy"
    DtpCCValidUpto.Format = DateTimePickerFormat.Custom
    DtpCCValidUpto.CustomFormat = "MM/dd/yyyy"

    If StrIDToUpdate <> "" Then
        Me.Text = "Update Customer Info"

        Dim SelectString As String
        SelectString = "SELECT FirstName, LastName, Address, City, State, Zip,
Phone, EMail, DOB, CreditCardNum, CreditCardValidUpto FROM Customer WHERE CustID =
'" & StrIDToUpdate & "'"

        Dim SelectCmd1 As New SqlCommand(SelectString, SqlConnection1)

        Dim DsDataSet As DataSet
        DsDataSet = New DataSet()

        SqlDataAdapter1.SelectCommand = SelectCmd1
        SqlDataAdapter1.SelectCommand.CommandText = SelectString
        Try
```

```
    SqlConnection1.Open()
    SqlDataAdapter1.Fill(DsDataSet, "Result")
Catch MyException As SqlException
    MessageBox.Show(("Source: " & MyException.Source & ControlChars.Cr & _
    "Number: " & MyException.Number.ToString() & ControlChars.Cr & _
    "State: " & MyException.State.ToString() & ControlChars.Cr & _
    "Class: " & MyException.Class.ToString() & ControlChars.Cr & _
    "Server: " & MyException.Server & ControlChars.Cr & _
    "Message: " & MyException.Message & ControlChars.Cr & _
    "Procedure: " & MyException.Procedure & ControlChars.Cr & _
    "Line: " & MyException.LineNumber.ToString()))

    SqlConnection1.Close()
    SqlDataAdapter1.Dispose()
    Return
End Try


    TxtFName.DataBindings.Add(New Binding("Text", DsDataSet,
"Result.FirstName"))
    TxtLName.DataBindings.Add(New Binding("Text", DsDataSet,
"Result.LastName"))
    TxtAddress.DataBindings.Add(New Binding("Text", DsDataSet,
"Result.Address"))
    TxtCity.DataBindings.Add(New Binding("Text", DsDataSet, "Result.City"))
    TxtState.DataBindings.Add(New Binding("Text", DsDataSet, "Result.State"))
    TxtZip.DataBindings.Add(New Binding("Text", DsDataSet, "Result.Zip"))
    TxtPhone.DataBindings.Add(New Binding("Text", DsDataSet, "Result.Phone"))
    TxtEmail.DataBindings.Add(New Binding("Text", DsDataSet, "Result.Email"))
    DtpDOB.DataBindings.Add(New Binding("Text", DsDataSet, "Result.DOB"))
    TxtCCNumber.DataBindings.Add(New Binding("Text", DsDataSet,
"Result.CreditCardNum"))
    DtpCCValidUpto.DataBindings.Add(New Binding("Text", DsDataSet,
"Result.CreditCardValidUpto"))

    SqlConnection1.Close()
    SqlDataAdapter1.Dispose()
End If
```

```
    End Sub
End Class
```

Summary

In this chapter, you learned to add functionality to the Insert forms. This chapter also described the functions you need to create to add functionality to the each Insert form. This chapter also provided the complete code for each Insert form.

Chapter 21

**Adding
Functionality to
the Reports Form**

In the preceding chapter, you learned to add functionality to the Insert forms. In this chapter, you will learn to add functionality to the Reports form of the Administration module.

The Reports form displays reports related to daily sales, movies in demand, and customer details. However, these reports are not displayed simultaneously in the Reports form. In other words, there are three variations of the Reports form—Daily Sales, Movies in Demand, and Customer Details.

Figure 21-1 shows the Daily Sales Report form.

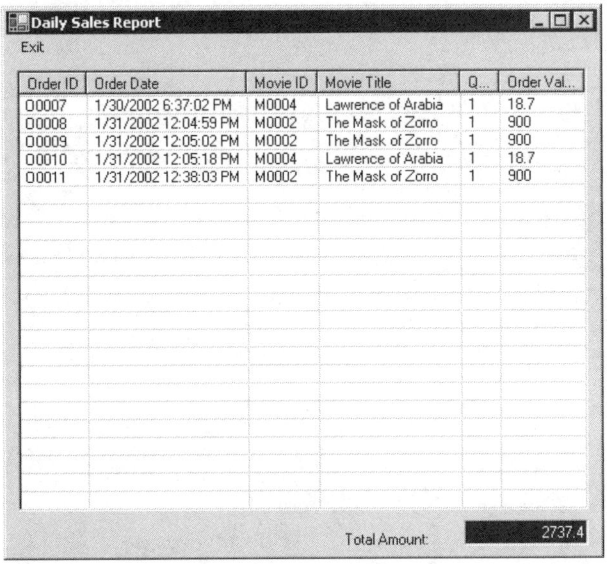

FIGURE 21-1 *The interface of the Daily Sales Report form*

Figure 21-2 shows the Movies In Demand Report form.

Figure 21-3 shows the Customer Details Report form.

The Reports form displays when the administrator selects any command from the Generate Reports menu of the Main form. The Reports form that displays depends on the option selected by the administrator.

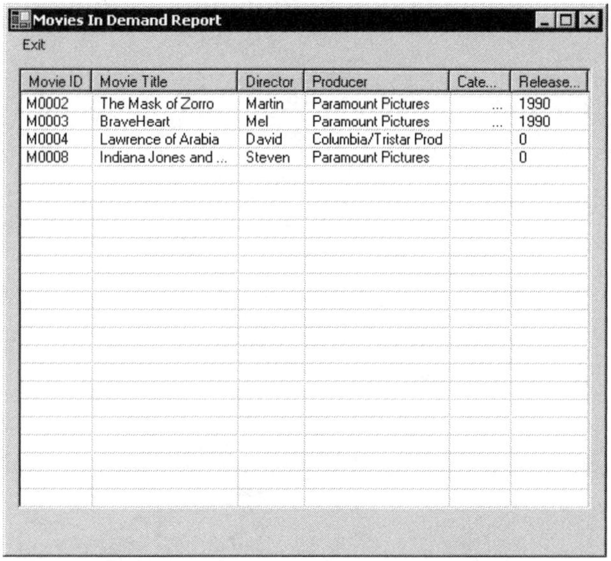

FIGURE 21-2 *The interface of the Movies In Demand Report form*

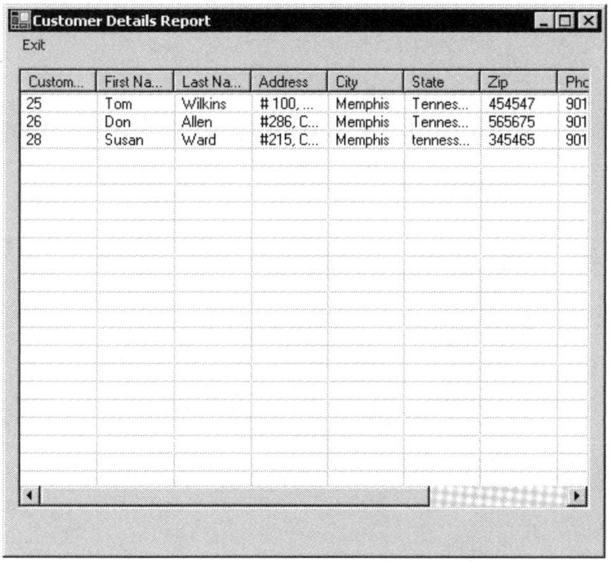

FIGURE 21-3 *The interface of the Customer Details Report form*

To display records from the database, you need to use the SQL Server .NET data provider in the Reports form. To use the SQL Server .NET data provider, you need to import the classes stored in the `System.Data.SqlClient` namespace. You can import the System.Data.SqlClient namespace by including the following statement in the Reports form:

```
Imports System.Data.SqlClient
'Includes classes used by the SQL Server .NET data provider
```

In addition to the preceding statement, you need to include the following statements in the Reports form:

```
Imports System.Data
'Includes the classes that make up the ADO.NET architecture
Imports System.Data.SqlTypes
'Includes the classes for native data types within SQL Server
```

In addition, to connect to the Movies database from the Reports form, you need to use an object of the SqlConnection class. To transfer data from the Main form to a dataset and vice versa, you need to use an object of the SqlDataAdapter class.

You need to declare the following variables in the Reports form:

```
Dim SqlConnection1 As New SqlConnection(StrConnectionString)
'Declares the connection object
Dim SqlDataAdapter1 As New SqlDataAdapter()
'Declares the data adapter
Dim DsDataSet As DataSet
'Declares the dataset
Public Shared IntReportType As Integer
'Declares a variable that is accessible across instances
```

The Reports form consists of the following functions:

- ◆ FrmReport_Load
- ◆ MmnuExit_Click

The following sections describe the code for these functions.

The FrmReport_Load Function

The FrmReport_Load function executes when the Reports form loads. The Reports form loads when the administrator selects any command from the Generate Reports menu in the Main form.

As previously mentioned, there are three variations of the Reports form. The Reports form that displays when the administrator selects an option from the Generate Reports menu depends on the command selected by the administrator. For example, if the administrator selects the Daily Sales command, the Daily Sales report displays. If the administrator selects the Movies In Demand command, the Movies In Demand report displays. In addition, if the administrator selects the Customer Details command, the Customer Details report displays.

This implies that you need to populate the Reports form programmatically. To do this, when the administrator selects a command from the Generate Reports menu, the `IntReportType` variable is assigned a value. For example, if the administrator selects the Daily Sales command, the `IntReportType` variable is assigned a value of 0. Similarly, if the administrator selects the Movies In Demand command, the `IntReportType` variable is assigned a value of 1. If the administrator selects the Customer Details command, the `IntReportType` variable is assigned a value of 2.

The `FrmReport_Load` function checks the value of the `IntReportType` variable and populates the Reports form. The code for the `FrmReport_Load` function is as follows:

```
Private Sub FrmReport_Load(ByVal sender As System.Object, ByVal e As
System.EventArgs) Handles MyBase.Load
        Dim DblSum As Double
        Dim RowPicker1 As DataRow
        Dim RowPicker2 As DataRow
        Dim StrQuery As String
'Declares variables
        LvwReport.Items.Clear()
'Clears the list view control

        DsDataSet = New DataSet()
'Creating the dataset

    Try
        Dim ColumnHeader1 As New ColumnHeader()
        Dim ColumnHeader2 As New ColumnHeader()
        Dim ColumnHeader3 As New ColumnHeader()
        Dim ColumnHeader4 As New ColumnHeader()
```

```
            Dim ColumnHeader5 As New ColumnHeader()
            Dim ColumnHeader6 As New ColumnHeader()
            Dim ColumnHeader7 As New ColumnHeader()
            Dim ColumnHeader8 As New ColumnHeader()
            Dim ColumnHeader9 As New ColumnHeader()
            Dim ColumnHeader10 As New ColumnHeader()
'Declares column headers

            If (IntReportType = 2) Then
'Checks if the administrator selected the Customer Details command
            Text = "Customer Details Report"
'Specifies the Text property of the Reports form
            TxtTotalAmountSale.Enabled = False
'Disables the Total Amount text box
            LblTotalAmountSale.Visible = False
'Hides the Total Amount label
            LvwReport.Columns.AddRange(New System.Windows.Forms.ColumnHeader()
{ColumnHeader1, ColumnHeader2, ColumnHeader3, ColumnHeader4, ColumnHeader5,
ColumnHeader6, ColumnHeader7, ColumnHeader8, ColumnHeader9, ColumnHeader10})
'Adds column headers to the list view control
            ColumnHeader1.Text = "Customer ID"
            ColumnHeader2.Text = "First Name"
            ColumnHeader3.Text = "Last Name"
            ColumnHeader4.Text = "Address"
            ColumnHeader5.Text = "City"
            ColumnHeader6.Text = "State"
            ColumnHeader7.Text = "Zip"
            ColumnHeader8.Text = "Phone"
            ColumnHeader9.Text = "Email"
            ColumnHeader10.Text = "Date of Birth"
'Specifies the column headers for the list view control

            StrQuery = "SELECT CustID, FirstName, LastName, Address, City,
State, Zip, Phone, Email, DOB FROM Customer a WHERE ( (SELECT COUNT(*) FROM Orders
WHERE a.CustID = Orders.CustID) >= 5)"
'Specifies the query to retrieve the details of customers who have placed more than
5 orders
```

```
                Dim SelectCmd0 As New SqlCommand(StrQuery, SqlConnection1)
'Declares SelectCmd0 as an object of the SqlCommand class and associates it with
the SqlConnection1 object
                DsDataSet = New DataSet()
'Creates the dataset


                SqlDataAdapter1.SelectCommand = SelectCmd0
                SqlDataAdapter1.SelectCommand.CommandText = StrQuery


                SqlConnection1.Open()
'Establishes a connection with the database
                SqlDataAdapter1.Fill(DsDataSet, "CustomerReport")
'Populates the CustomerReport table in the DsDataSet dataset with the query results


                For Each RowPicker1 In DsDataSet.Tables("CustomerReport").Rows
                    Dim StrCustomerDetails As String() = {RowPicker1("CustID"),
RowPicker1("FirstName"), RowPicker1("LastName"), RowPicker1("Address"),
RowPicker1("City"), RowPicker1("State"), RowPicker1("Zip"), RowPicker1("Phone"),
RowPicker1("Email"), RowPicker1("DOB")}
'Retrieves the records from the dataset
                        LvwReport.Items.Add(New ListViewItem(StrCustomerDetails))
'Displays the records in the list view control
                    Next
                ElseIf (IntReportType = 1) Then
'Checks if the administrator selected the Movies In Demand command
                    Text = "Movies In Demand Report"
'Specifies the Text property of the Reports form
                    TxtTotalAmountSale.Enabled = False
'Disables the Total Amount text box
                    LblTotalAmountSale.Visible = False
'Shows the Total Amount label
                    LvwReport.Columns.AddRange(New System.Windows.Forms.ColumnHeader()
{ColumnHeader1, ColumnHeader2, ColumnHeader3, ColumnHeader4, ColumnHeader5,
ColumnHeader6})
'Adds column headers to the list view control
                        ColumnHeader1.Text = "Movie ID"
                        ColumnHeader2.Text = "Movie Title"
                        ColumnHeader3.Text = "Director"
```

```
                ColumnHeader4.Text = "Producer"
                ColumnHeader5.Text = "Category"
                ColumnHeader6.Text = "Release Year"
'Specifies the column headers for the list view control
                    'Make Query string
                StrQuery = "SELECT a.MovID, a.MovTitle, b.FirstName, c. Name,
a.Category, a.ReleaseYear FROM Movie a, Director b, Producer c WHERE MovID IN
(SELECT movid FROM Video WHERE videoid IN (SELECT b.VideoID FROM Orders a,
OrderDetail b WHERE a.OrderID=b.OrderID AND a.OrderDate > DateADD(day, -7,
GetDate()) GROUP BY b.VideoID )) AND a.DirID = b.DirID AND a.ProdID = c.ProdID"
'Specifies the query to retrieve the details of movies


                Dim SelectCmd1 As New SqlCommand(StrQuery, SqlConnection1)
'Declares SelectCmd1 as an object of the SqlCommand class and associates it with
the SqlConnection1 object


                SqlDataAdapter1.SelectCommand = SelectCmd1
                SqlDataAdapter1.SelectCommand.CommandText = StrQuery


                SqlConnection1.Open()
'Establishes a connection with the database
                SqlDataAdapter1.Fill(DsDataSet, "MoviesInDemandReport")
'Populates the MoviesInDemandReport table in the DsDataSet dataset with the query
results


                For Each RowPicker1 In
DsDataSet.Tables("MoviesInDemandReport").Rows
                    Dim StrCategory As String
                    If RowPicker1.IsNull(4) Then
'Checks of the Category field is null
                        StrCategory = ""
                    Else
                        StrCategory = RowPicker1(4)
'Stores the value in the Category field in the StrCategory variable
                    End If


                    Dim IntRelYear As Integer
                    If RowPicker1.IsNull(5) Then
```

```
'Checks of the Release Year field is null
                        IntRelYear = 0
'Assigns a value of 0 to the IntRelYear variable
                    Else
                        IntRelYear = RowPicker1(5)
'Stores the value in the Release Year field in the IntRelYear variable
                    End If


                    Dim StrSalesDetails As String() = {RowPicker1(0), RowPicker1(1),
RowPicker1(2), RowPicker1(3), StrCategory, IntRelYear}
'Retrieves the records from the dataset
                    LvwReport.Items.Add(New ListViewItem(StrSalesDetails))
'Displays the records in the list view control
                Next
            Else
'Executes if the administrator selects the Daily Sales command
                Text = "Daily Sales Report"
'Specifies the Text property of the Reports form
                TxtTotalAmountSale.Visible = True
'Enables the Total Amount text box
                LblTotalAmountSale.Visible = True
'Shows the Total Amount label
                LvwReport.Columns.AddRange(New System.Windows.Forms.ColumnHeader()
{ColumnHeader1, ColumnHeader2, ColumnHeader3, ColumnHeader4, ColumnHeader5,
ColumnHeader6})
'Adds column headers to the list view control
                ColumnHeader1.Text = "Order ID"
                ColumnHeader2.Text = "Order Date"
                ColumnHeader3.Text = "Movie ID"
                ColumnHeader4.Text = "Movie Title"
                ColumnHeader5.Text = "Quantity Ordered"
                ColumnHeader6.Text = "Order Value"
'Specifies the column headers for the list view control

                StrQuery = "SELECT DISTINCT a.OrderID, a.OrderDate, d.MovID,
d.MovTitle, a.TotalQtyOrdered, a.OrderValue FROM Orders a, OrderDetail b, Video c,
Movie d WHERE a.OrderID = b.OrderID AND b.VideoID = c.VideoID AND c.MovID = d.MovID
AND a.OrderDate > DateADD(day, -1, GetDate()) ORDER BY a.OrderID"
```

```
'Specifies the query to retrieve the details of the sales on a particular date

                Dim SelectCmd3 As New SqlCommand(StrQuery, SqlConnection1)
'Declares SelectCmd3 as an object of the SqlCommand class and associates it with
the SqlConnection1 object

                SqlDataAdapter1.SelectCommand = SelectCmd3
                SqlDataAdapter1.SelectCommand.CommandText = StrQuery
                SqlDataAdapter1.Fill(DsDataSet, "SalesReport")
'Populates the SalesReport table in the DsDataSet dataset with the query results

                For Each RowPicker1 In DsDataSet.Tables("SalesReport").Rows
                    Dim StrSalesDetails As String() = {RowPicker1(0),
RowPicker1(1), RowPicker1(2), RowPicker1(3), RowPicker1(4), RowPicker1(5)}
'Retrieves the records from the dataset
                    LvwReport.Items.Add(New ListViewItem(StrSalesDetails))
'Displays the records in the list view control
                    DblSum = DblSum + RowPicker1(5)
'Calculates the total sale value
                Next

                TxtTotalAmountSale.Text = DblSum
'Displays the total sale value in the Total Amount text box

            End If
        Catch MyException As Exception
            MsgBox("Error Occurred:" & vbLf & MyException.ToString)
        End Try

        'Closing the connection
        SqlConnection1.Close()
'Closes the SqlConnection1 object
        SqlDataAdapter1.Dispose()
'Releases the resources used by the SqlDataAdapter1 object
    End Sub
```

The MmnuExit_Click *Function*

The MmnuExit_Click function executes when the administrator selects the Exit menu from the Reports form. As the name suggests, the MmnuExit_Click function closes the Reports form.

The code for the MmnuExit_Click function is as follows:

```
Private Sub MmnuExit_Click(ByVal sender As System.Object, ByVal e As
System.EventArgs) Handles MmnuExit.Click
        Me.Close()
'Closes the form
End Sub
```

The Complete Code for the Reports Form

In the previous sections, you looked at the code associated with the events and functions in the Reports form. Listing 21-1 lists the complete code for the Reports form.

Listing 21-1 The Code for the Reports Form

```
Imports System.Data
Imports System.Data.SqlClient
Imports System.Data.SqlTypes

Public Class FrmReports
        Inherits System.Windows.Forms.Form
        Dim SqlConnection1 As New SqlConnection(StrConnectionString)
        Dim SqlDataAdapter1 As New SqlDataAdapter()
        Dim DsDataSet As DataSet
        Public Shared IntReportType As Integer
Windows Form Designer generated code
'Contains the code that specifies the size, location, and other properties, such as
font and name, for the controls on the form.
```

```vb
        Private Sub FrmReport_Load(ByVal sender As System.Object, ByVal e As
System.EventArgs) Handles MyBase.Load
                Dim DblSum As Double
                Dim RowPicker1 As DataRow
                Dim RowPicker2 As DataRow
                Dim StrQuery As String

                LvwReport.Items.Clear()

                DsDataSet = New DataSet()

                Try
                        Dim ColumnHeader1 As New ColumnHeader()
                        Dim ColumnHeader2 As New ColumnHeader()
                        Dim ColumnHeader3 As New ColumnHeader()
                        Dim ColumnHeader4 As New ColumnHeader()
                        Dim ColumnHeader5 As New ColumnHeader()
                        Dim ColumnHeader6 As New ColumnHeader()
                        Dim ColumnHeader7 As New ColumnHeader()
                        Dim ColumnHeader8 As New ColumnHeader()
                        Dim ColumnHeader9 As New ColumnHeader()
                        Dim ColumnHeader10 As New ColumnHeader()

                        If (IntReportType = 2) Then
                                Text = "Customer Details Report"
                                TxtTotalAmountSale.Enabled = False
                                LblTotalAmountSale.Visible = False
                                LvwReport.Columns.AddRange(New
System.Windows.Forms.ColumnHeader() {ColumnHeader1, ColumnHeader2, ColumnHeader3,
ColumnHeader4, ColumnHeader5, ColumnHeader6, ColumnHeader7, ColumnHeader8,
ColumnHeader9, ColumnHeader10})
                                ColumnHeader1.Text = "Customer ID"
                                ColumnHeader2.Text = "First Name"
                                ColumnHeader3.Text = "Last Name"
                                ColumnHeader4.Text = "Address"
                                ColumnHeader5.Text = "City"
                                ColumnHeader6.Text = "State"
                                ColumnHeader7.Text = "Zip"
```

```
                                      ColumnHeader8.Text = "Phone"
                                      ColumnHeader9.Text = "Email"
                                      ColumnHeader10.Text = "Date of Birth"

                                      StrQuery = "SELECT CustID, FirstName,
LastName, Address, City, State, Zip, Phone, Email, DOB FROM Customer a WHERE (
(SELECT COUNT(*) FROM Orders WHERE a.CustID = Orders.CustID) >= 5)"

                                      Dim SelectCmd0 As New
SqlCommand(StrQuery, SqlConnection1)
                                      DsDataSet = New DataSet()

                                      SqlDataAdapter1.SelectCommand = SelectCmd0

SqlDataAdapter1.SelectCommand.CommandText = StrQuery

                                      SqlConnection1.Open()
                                      SqlDataAdapter1.Fill(DsDataSet,
"CustomerReport")

                                      For Each RowPicker1 In
DsDataSet.Tables("CustomerReport").Rows
                                          Dim StrCustomerDetails As
String() = {RowPicker1("CustID"), RowPicker1("FirstName"), RowPicker1("LastName"),
RowPicker1("Address"), RowPicker1("City"), RowPicker1("State"), RowPicker1("Zip"),
RowPicker1("Phone"), RowPicker1("Email"), RowPicker1("DOB")}
                                              LvwReport.Items.Add(New
ListViewItem(StrCustomerDetails))
                                  Next
                          ElseIf (IntReportType = 1) Then
                                      Text = "Movies In Demand Report"
                                      TxtTotalAmountSale.Enabled = False
                                      LblTotalAmountSale.Visible = False
                                      LvwReport.Columns.AddRange(New
System.Windows.Forms.ColumnHeader() {ColumnHeader1, ColumnHeader2, ColumnHeader3,
ColumnHeader4, ColumnHeader5, ColumnHeader6})
                                      ColumnHeader1.Text = "Movie ID"
```

```
ColumnHeader2.Text = "Movie Title"
ColumnHeader3.Text = "Director"
ColumnHeader4.Text = "Producer"
ColumnHeader5.Text = "Category"
ColumnHeader6.Text = "Release Year"

StrQuery = "SELECT a.MovID, a.MovTitle,
b.FirstName, c. Name, a.Category, a.ReleaseYear FROM Movie a, Director b, Producer
c WHERE MovID IN (SELECT movid FROM Video WHERE videoid IN (SELECT b.VideoID FROM
Orders a, OrderDetail b WHERE a.OrderID=b.OrderID AND a.OrderDate > DateADD(day, -
7, GetDate()) GROUP BY b.VideoID )) AND a.DirID = b.DirID AND a.ProdID = c.ProdID"
Dim SelectCmd1 As New
SqlCommand(StrQuery, SqlConnection1)
SqlDataAdapter1.SelectCommand = SelectCmd1

SqlDataAdapter1.SelectCommand.CommandText = StrQuery

SqlConnection1.Open()
SqlDataAdapter1.Fill(DsDataSet,
"MoviesInDemandReport")

For Each RowPicker1 In
DsDataSet.Tables("MoviesInDemandReport").Rows
Dim StrCategory As String
If RowPicker1.IsNull(4) Then
StrCategory = ""
Else
StrCategory =
RowPicker1(4)

End If

Dim IntRelYear As Integer
If RowPicker1.IsNull(5) Then
IntRelYear = 0
Else
IntRelYear =
RowPicker1(5)
```

```
                                            End If

                                            Dim StrSalesDetails As
String() = {RowPicker1(0), RowPicker1(1), RowPicker1(2), RowPicker1(3), StrCategory,
IntRelYear}
                                                    LvwReport.Items.Add(New
ListViewItem(StrSalesDetails))
                                    Next
                    Else
                                    Text = "Daily Sales Report"
                                    TxtTotalAmountSale.Visible = True
                                    LblTotalAmountSale.Visible = True
                                    LvwReport.Columns.AddRange(New
System.Windows.Forms.ColumnHeader() {ColumnHeader1, ColumnHeader2, ColumnHeader3,
ColumnHeader4, ColumnHeader5, ColumnHeader6})
                                            ColumnHeader1.Text = "Order ID"
                                            ColumnHeader2.Text = "Order Date"
                                            ColumnHeader3.Text = "Movie ID"
                                            ColumnHeader4.Text = "Movie Title"
                                            ColumnHeader5.Text = "Quantity Ordered"
                                            ColumnHeader6.Text = "Order Value"

                                            StrQuery = "SELECT DISTINCT a.OrderID,
a.OrderDate, d.MovID, d.MovTitle, a.TotalQtyOrdered, a.OrderValue FROM Orders a,
OrderDetail b, Video c, Movie d WHERE a.OrderID = b.OrderID AND b.VideoID =
c.VideoID AND c.MovID = d.MovID  AND a.OrderDate > DateADD(day, -1, GetDate())
ORDER BY a.OrderID"
                                    Dim SelectCmd3 As New
SqlCommand(StrQuery, SqlConnection1)

                                    SqlDataAdapter1.SelectCommand =
SelectCmd3

SqlDataAdapter1.SelectCommand.CommandText = StrQuery
                                    SqlDataAdapter1.Fill(DsDataSet,
"SalesReport")
```

```
                                        For Each RowPicker1 In
DsDataSet.Tables("SalesReport").Rows
                                                    Dim StrSalesDetails As
String() = {RowPicker1(0), RowPicker1(1), RowPicker1(2), RowPicker1(3),
RowPicker1(4), RowPicker1(5)}

                                                    LvwReport.Items.Add(New
ListViewItem(StrSalesDetails))

                                                    DblSum = DblSum +
RowPicker1(5) 'Calculating the total Sale Value
                                        Next

                                        TxtTotalAmountSale.Text = DblSum


                            End If
                    Catch MyException As Exception
                                MsgBox("Error Occurred:" & vbLf &
MyException.ToString)
                    End Try

                    SqlConnection1.Close()
                    SqlDataAdapter1.Dispose()
            End Sub


            Private Sub MmnuExit_Click(ByVal sender As System.Object, ByVal e As
System.EventArgs) Handles MmnuExit.Click
                        Me.Close()
            End Sub
End Class
```

Summary

In this chapter, you learned to add functionality to the Reports form. This chapter also described the function you need to create to add functionality to the Reports form. This chapter also provided the complete code for the Reports form.

PART IV

Professional Project 3

Project 3

**Creating Web
Applications**

Project 3 Overview

In Part III of this book, you learned to create a Windows application for a video company. Now the same company requires a Web application that can be accessed by the customers. In other words, the company requires a Web site named MyMovies.com that can be accessed by any customer and at any time. In this project, you will create the MyMovies Web application that provides the same functionality as the MyMovies Windows application created in Part III.

Similar to the MyMovies Windows application, the MyMovies Web application is designed for the customers and administrators of the video stores. In addition, this application provides the same features as the Windows application, such as allowing customers to search for movies and purchase them. Customers can also search the database for movies based on various criteria. The administrator can use the MyMovies Web application to maintain and update the various tables in the database and to generate reports.

The MyMovies Web application is an application developed by using Visual Basic.NET and ASP.NET. Similar to the Windows application, this application also stores all the client- and movie-specific details in a Microsoft SQL 2000 database. The key concepts used to create the MyMovies Web application are as follows:

◆ Visual Basic.NET

◆ Web services

◆ Working with Web forms

◆ Creating Web applications using ASP.NET

In the project, you will learn the basic concepts of ASP.NET and create the MyMovies Web application.

Chapter 22

Project Case Study—Creating a Web Application for the MyMovies Video Kiosk

In Part III of the book, you learned how to create a VB.NET Windows application for the MyMovies company. Starting with this chapter, you will learn to create Web applications in Visual Basic.NET. Before actually creating a project, however, you first need to look at the existing Windows application that MyMovies has started using at its stores. This chapter describes the MyMovies video kiosk Windows application and discusses why there is a need to switch to a Web application.

MyMovies Video Kiosk:
Windows Application

As discussed in Chapter 9, "Project Case Study—Creating a Video Kiosk," MyMovies is a video company based in New Jersey. The company sells movie videos and also provides information about movies. The company owns a chain of stores in various cities across the United States.

The company changed its old system of paper catalogs and installed a Windows application for customers at its stores. This application is a big hit with all the customers visiting the video stores. The company conducted a customer survey and found that the customers want a system they can use to browse through catalogs and place orders sitting in their homes. This means that there is a demand for a Web application that can be accessed from anywhere and at any time.

MyMovies Web Application:
The Solution

As mentioned in the preceding section, the solution is to create a Web application that can provide the same functionality as the Windows application. In other words, customers should be able to use an application that will be running on a Web server. In addition, this application should provide the same features as the Windows application, such as enabling customers to log on and search for a movie of their choice and buy it as well. Customers should also be able to view details about a specific movie, actor, or director. This information can be stored in a Microsoft SQL 2000 database. Therefore, what is required is a Web application that can provide a simple and interactive interface.

Because you are already familiar with a typical project cycle for developing an application (as discussed in Chapter 9), this chapter will just discuss the functionality required for this application.

Requirements Analysis

The company formed a team to study various video Web applications and named the team "VideoWeb." The VideoWeb team analyzed the various existing video Web applications and came up with the following recommendations for the MyMovies video Web application.

The Web application should:

◆ Be easy to use in terms of navigation and provide enough tips

◆ Be simple, fast, and interactive

◆ Enable a customer to log in before placing an order for a video

◆ Enable a customer to view his or her order details

◆ Provide a feature to search for a particular movie based on a criteria, such as a movie, director, or actor's name

◆ Provide enough information about a movie to attract a customer to buy it

◆ Enable an administrator to maintain the various tables in the database and also generate reports

After analyzing these requirements, the VideoWeb team decided to make the following two Web-page interfaces for the video kiosk application:

◆ A customer interface

◆ An admin interface

Customers will use the customer interface to browse the movie database for the required information. They also will be able to search for specific information using the various criteria and will be able to purchase videos. The system administrators of MyMovies will use the admin interface to maintain the database and keep it updated.

The customer interface Web page will address the following requirements:

◆ It will provide an easy method for browsing the movie information.

◆ It will offer an option to search based on various criteria.

◆ It will provide a registration form that accepts information about a customer, such as his or her name, address, and e-mail address.

◆ It will enable a customer to view his or her order details.

The admin interface Web page will address the following requirements:

◆ It will provide a simple and easy method for maintaining and updating the various tables in the movie database.

◆ It will generate reports showing collated data such as daily sales, movies in demand, and details of regular customers.

In short, what is required is a Web site with the name "MyMovies.com" that can be accessed by any customer and at any time. Access to the admin interface, however, should be restricted to the administrators at MyMovies.

High-Level Design

As discussed in Chapter 9, in the high-level design phase, the team decides on the functionality of the system. In addition, the various data input and output formats are finalized, and the operating requirements are identified.

Figure 22-1 displays the Web page for the customer interface. Because this is the first Web page of the Web application, it will be referred to as the home page. This page provides options for registered customers as well as new customers.

A registered customer needs to enter his or her customer ID in the Login box on the left side of the Web page and then click on the Login button. This will display a welcome message to the registered customers, as shown in Figure 22-2.

When a customer clicks the Search hyperlink on the left side of the Web page, a new Web page appears, as shown in Figure 22-3. This page enables customers to search for movies of their choice and then select movies they want to buy.

Note that this screen provides a Search Text text box in which customers can enter the text for which they want to search, and they also can select a category from the Browse By drop-down list. Clicking the Search button displays the results in the middle of the Web page, as shown in Figure 22-4. This Web page

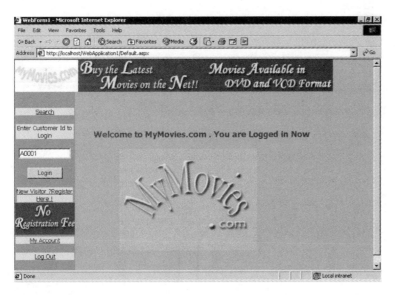

FIGURE 22-1 *The home page for the customer interface*

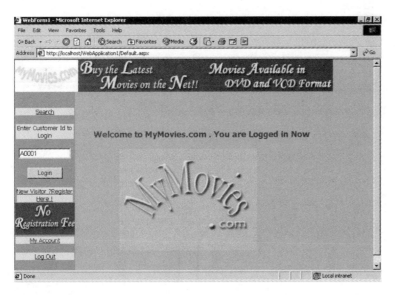

FIGURE 22-2 *A welcome message for registered customers*

also provides a Show All Records button that displays all the movies available in the store. Also note the credit card details that appear in the Web page for a registered customer.

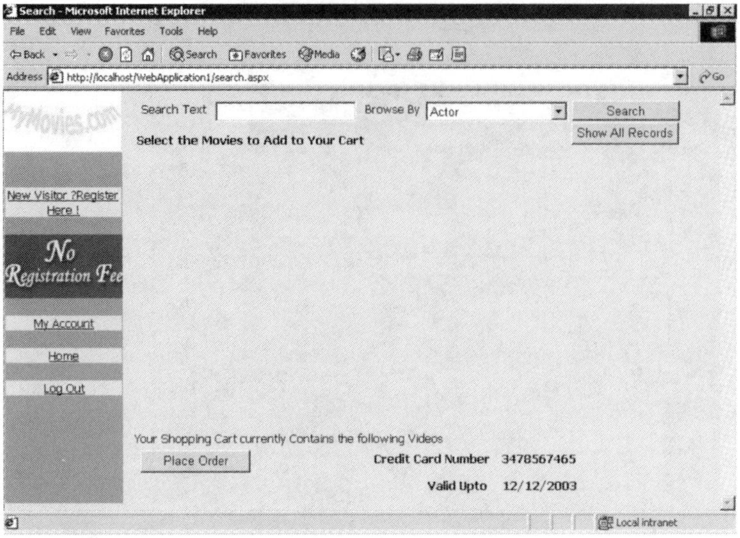

FIGURE 22-3 *The search Web page*

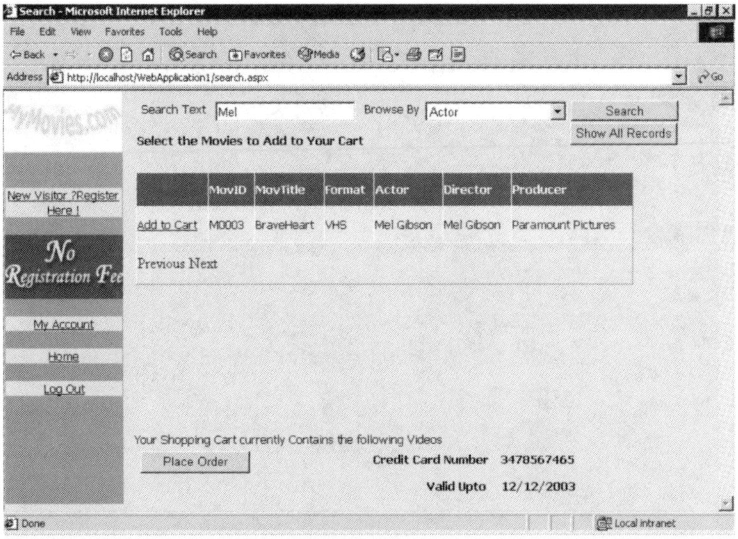

FIGURE 22-4 *The search results in the Web page*

Clicking on the Add to Cart link next to each movie record adds the video to the shopping cart, as shown in Figure 22-5.

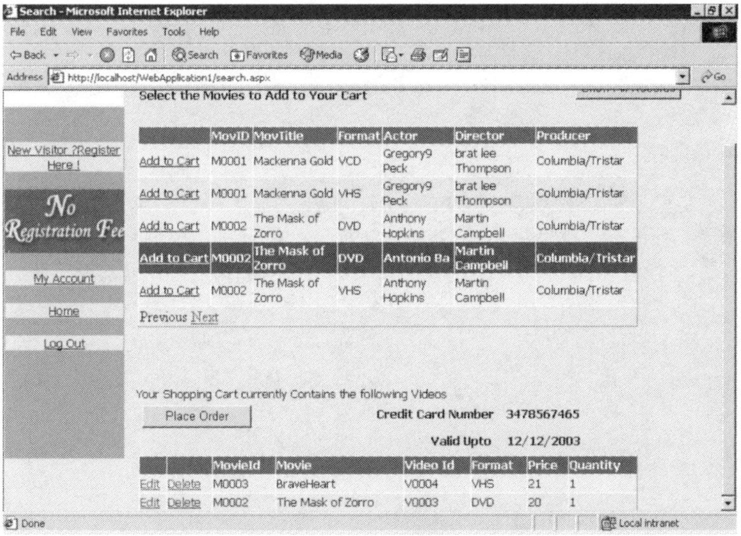

FIGURE 22-5 *The shopping cart displaying the selected videos*

Customers can click on the Place Order button to place the order, and the data gets updated in the database.

Let's now understand how a customer who has not registered will use this application. Let's go back to the home page of the customer interface (refer back to Figure 22-1). An unregistered customer can view the various videos available in the store but will not be able to place an order. To view videos, customers need to click on the Search hyperlink on the left side of the Web page. This displays the same Web page that a registered customer will see, and it enables an unregistered customer to search for a video (refer back to Figure 22-3). The only difference is the message an unregistered customer will get after clicking on the Add to Cart link. This message is shown in Figure 22-6.

The home page of the customer interface enables a new customer to log in. For this, there is a New Visitor? Register Here! link in the left panel of the home page. Clicking this link displays the Customer Registration page, as shown in Figure 22-7.

The Customer Registration page also appears if the customer clicks the Register button shown in the home page of the customer interface (refer back to Figure 22-1).

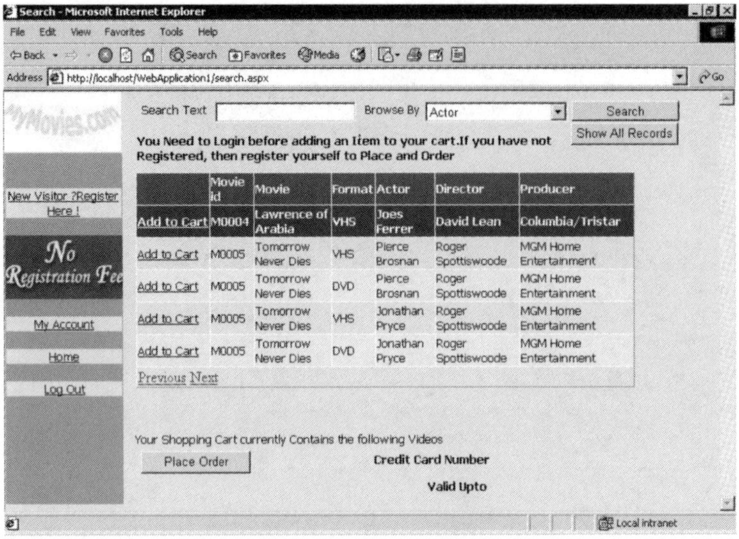

FIGURE 22-6 *The message that an unregistered customer gets after clicking the* Add to Cart *link*

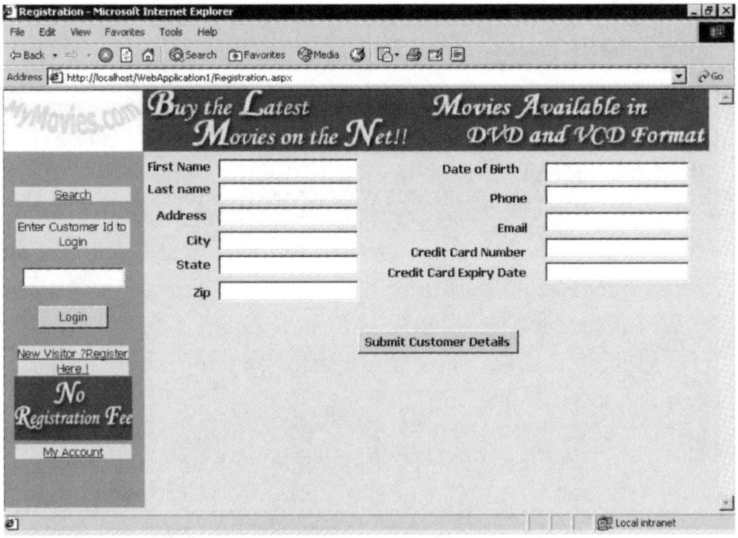

FIGURE 22-7 *The Customer Registration page*

In addition to the aforementioned pages, there is another Web page that displays the account details for a registered customer using the Web service. Figure 22-8 displays this page.

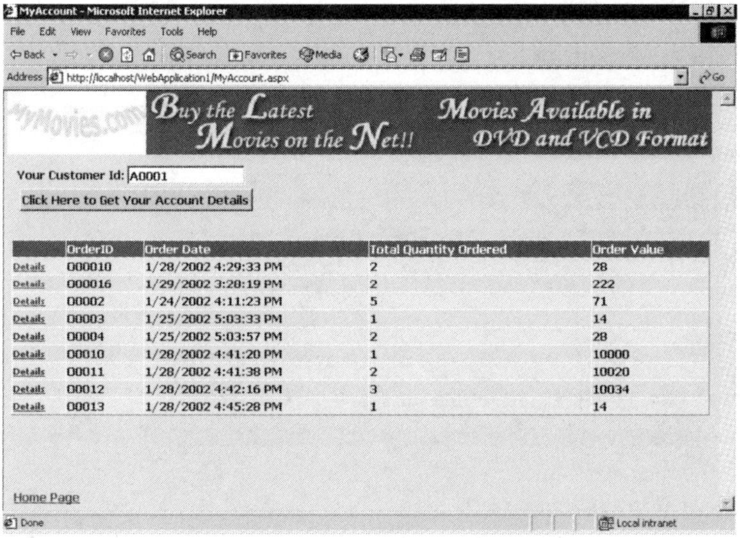

FIGURE 22-8 *A registered customer's account details page*

For the admin interface, there will be a home page like the one shown in Figure 22-9.

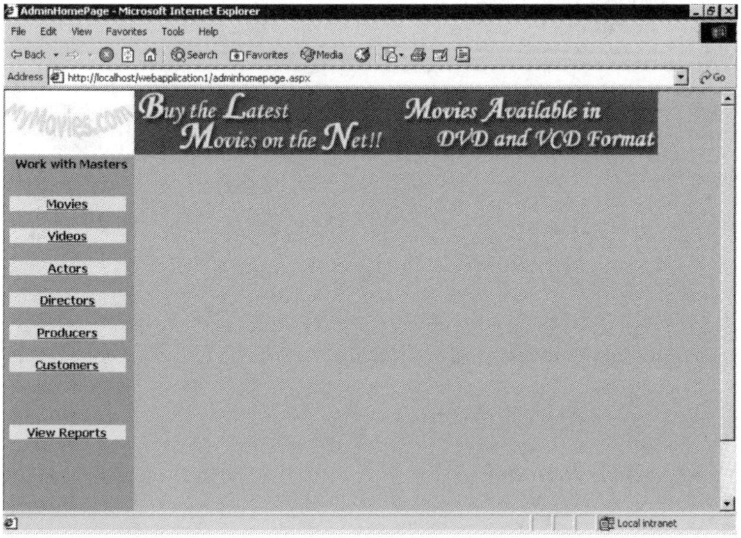

FIGURE 22-9 *The admin interface home page*

This page provides various links in the left panel that can be used by the administrator to maintain various tables and to view reports. Figure 22-10 displays the page that appears when the `Videos` link is clicked.

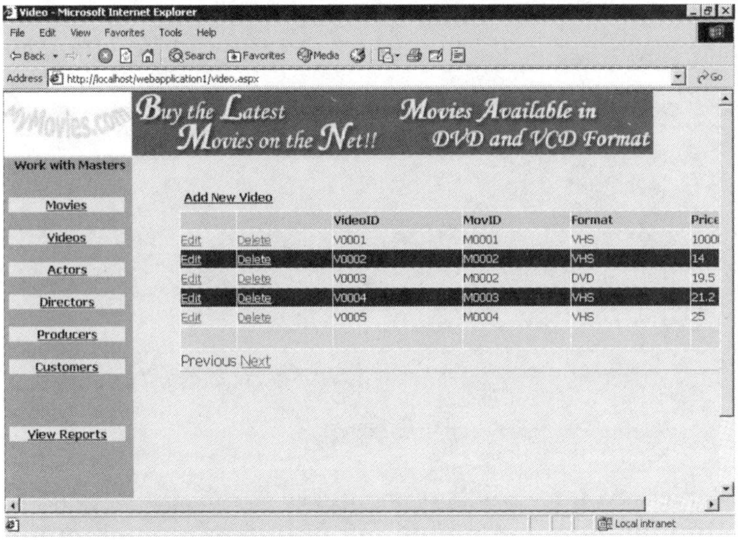

FIGURE 22-10 *The Videos page*

Note the `Add New Video` link on the page and the links to update and delete records. Figure 22-11, on page 537, displays the Web page that appears when the `View Reports` link is clicked.

This page provides three buttons to view different reports. Figure 22-12, on page 537, displays the Movies in Demand report.

The database schema for this application is the same as the one discussed in Chapter 9. For more information, refer to Chapter 9.

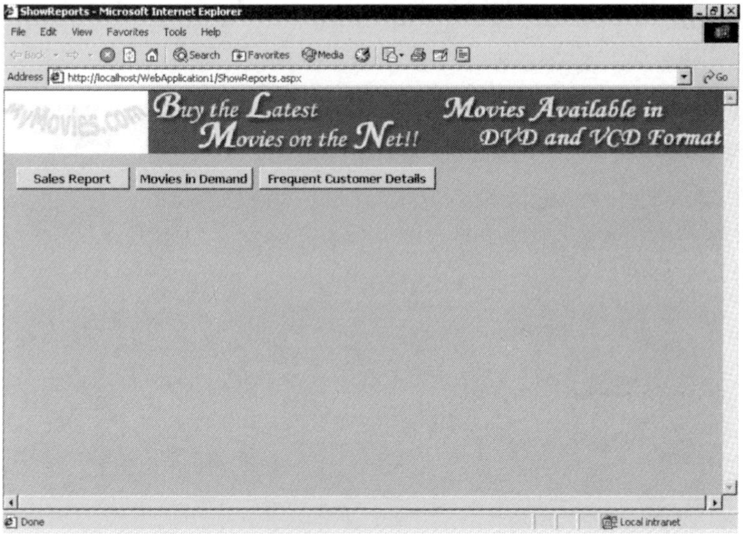

FIGURE 22-11 *The View Report page*

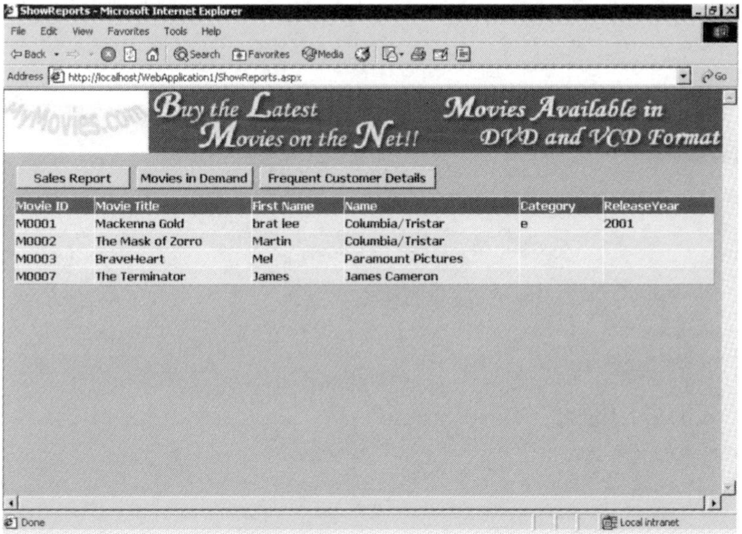

FIGURE 22-12 *The Movies In Demand report page*

Summary

In this chapter, you learned that the MyMovies video company requires a Web application that can be accessed from anywhere and at any time. Then you looked at the various requirements for this solution and were introduced to the various screens required for the application.

In the next chapter, you will learn basic concepts of ASP.NET, which is used to create Web applications. In subsequent chapters, you will learn how to develop this Web application.

Chapter 23

Before you actually go about creating the MyMovies video kiosk Web application, let's first understand the basics of ASP.NET. This will help you understand the creation of Web applications in a better way.

The .NET framework includes tools that ease the creation of Web services. ASP.NET is the latest offering from Microsoft toward the creation of a new paradigm for server-side scripting. This chapter will cover the basics of ASP.NET, which provides a complete framework for the development of Web applications.

This chapter introduces you to ASP.NET, the platform requirements for ASP.NET applications, and the ASP.NET architecture. In addition, the chapter introduces Web forms of ASP.NET applications, a new addition to ASP.NET.

Introducing ASP.NET

ASP.NET differs in some ways from earlier versions of ASP. ASP.NET has new features such as better language support, a new set of controls, XML-based components, and more secure user authentication. ASP.NET also provides increased performance by executing ASP code.

Usually a software product undergoes many evolutionary phases. In each release version of the software product, the software vendor fixes the bugs from previous versions and adds new features. ASP 1.0 was released in 1996. Since then, two more versions of ASP (2.0 and 3.0) have been released. In various versions of ASP, new features have been added. However, the basic methodology used for creating applications has not changed.

ASP.NET provides a unique approach toward Web application development, so one might say that ASP.NET has started a new revolution in the world of Web application development. ASP.NET is based on the Microsoft .NET framework. The .NET framework is based on the common language runtime (CLR). Therefore, it imparts all of the CLR benefits to ASP.NET applications. These CLR benefits include automatic memory management, support for multiple languages, secure user authentication, ease in configuration, and ease in deployment.

ASP.NET provides these benefits:

◆ *Support for various programming languages.* ASP.NET provides better programming-language support than ASP. It uses the new ADO.NET. Earlier versions of ASP support only scripting languages such as VBScript and JScript. Using these scripting languages, you can write applications used to perform server-side processing, but this has two major drawbacks. First, scripting languages are interpreted and not compiled. Therefore, the errors can only be checked at runtime. This affects the performance of Web applications. Second, scripting languages are not strongly typed. The scripting languages do not have a built-in set of predefined data types. This requires developers to cast the existing objects of the language to their expected data type. Thus, these objects can be validated only at runtime. This validation leads to a low performance of Web applications. ASP.NET continues to support scripting languages, but it supports complete Visual Basic for server-side programming. ASP.NET also provides support for C# (pronounced *C sharp*) and C++. This benefit helps you select a language according to your level of expertise and ease.

◆ *Cross-language development.* ASP.NET provides flexibility to extend objects created in one language to another language. For example, if you have created an object in C++, ASP.NET enables you to extend this object in Visual Basic.NET.

◆ *Content and application logic separation.* The earlier versions of ASP have the content to be presented to users (for example, HTML code) and programming logic (for example, ASP scripts) integrated. This creates several restrictions. The problem increases many folds if these Web pages are to be frequently updated. In addition, due to the integration of the code and the UI, the use of different design tools is restricted.

ASP.NET, however, relieves you from all your worries regarding integration of content with application logic. ASP.NET helps you separate the content from the application logic. Therefore, the designer can design the UI while the programmer builds the programming logic for the UI for the same Web page. The required updates to the Web page can be done without any confusion. In addition, the designer can use standard design tools to create the UI. This is because the content is separated from the application logic used at the backend.

◆ *Secure user authentication.* ASP.NET provides form-based user authentication. It also supports cookie management and automatic redirecting of unauthorized users to your login page. It provides user accounts and roles to each user, and the roles enable you to access different codes and executables stored on a Web server.

◆ *New server processing architecture.* Earlier versions of ASP render the content of a Web page in the order in which it is written. Therefore, the programmer has to keep the position of the code rendering on the Web page in mind. In ASP, you need to write code for all actions occur on your Web page. In fact, you even need to write code for displaying HTML output.

ASP.NET has introduced new server-based controls. These controls are declared and programmed on the server side and are event driven by the client. This frees the programmers from considering the rendering position while designing programming logic, thereby enabling programmers to concentrate on programming logic only. ASP.NET control objects can be controlled by using scripting languages. ASP.NET provides a set of object-oriented controls (such as list boxes, validation controls, data grid controls, and data) and everything you expect from a dataset control. In addition, all ASP.NET objects can expose events that can easily be processed by ASP.NET code. Therefore, this makes the coding easy and well organized.

◆ *Improved debugging and tracing.* The key elements of an application development cycle are debugging and tracing. ASP.NET uses the .NET framework, which contains Visual Studio. Therefore, you can use the built-in Visual Studio.NET debugging tools for tracing your Web pages. ASP did not provide debugging support.

◆ *More control over application configuration.* You don't have to touch the registry to modify configuration settings. Plain text files are used for the configuration of ASP.NET. You can also upload or change the configuration files while the application is running. Therefore, you need not restart the server. Also, this does not modify the registry.

◆ *Easier application deployment.* ASP.NET provides ease in deployment by ensuring that you need not restart the server to deploy or replace compiled code. ASP.NET simply redirects all new requests to the new code. You just need to copy the directory to Internet Information Server (IIS) to deploy an ASP.NET application.

◆ *Improved caching features.* ASP.NET includes improved caching features than those present in earlier versions of ASP. ASP.NET provides following caches:

  ◆ *Page-level caching.* This enables you to cache a complete page.

  ◆ *Fragment caching.* This enables you to cache portions of a page.

  ◆ *The Cache API.* This exposes the cache engine to programmers to cache their own objects.

  The use of these caching features in ASP.NET results in increased speed and performance of your Web pages.

Most of the codes written in earlier versions of ASP will not run under ASP.NET. To overcome this problem, ASP.NET uses the new file extension .ASPX. Applications with this extension will run side by side with standard ASP applications on the same server.

ASP.NET Programming Models

The .NET framework software development kit (SDK) is used to develop Web applications, which run on the .NET framework SDK on a platform with IIS. To correlate the different subsystems involved in creating, building, testing, and deploying ASP.NET applications, you need to understand the ASP.NET architecture, which is shown in Figure 23-1.

ASP.NET consists of two programming models that you can use to create your Web applications:

◆ *Web forms.* This programming model enables you to create form-based Web pages. This is a powerful feature provided by ASP.NET that enables you to create dynamic Web pages for Web applications. To create Web forms, you can use server controls to create UI components. Then you can program them at the server side.

◆ *Web services.* This programming model enables you to remotely perform some functionality at the server side. In ASP.NET, Web services play an important role in integrating applications across different platforms. This is because Web services are not bound to a specific technology. In addition, Web services help in the exchange of data in a client-server or a server-server architecture. Web services use standards such as HTTP and XML messaging to enable data exchange.

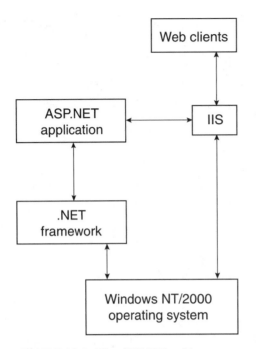

FIGURE 23-1 *The ASP.NET architecture*

To create your Web applications, you can use either of these programming models or a combination of the two. Both of these models use the CLR benefits of the .NET framework. Therefore, these models enable you to develop secure, scalable, and high-performance applications.

ASP.NET Platform Requirements

ASP.NET is a part of the .NET framework SDK, which can be downloaded from **http://msdn.Microsoft.com/downloads**. Files required for creating, building, and testing .NET applications are included in the .NET framework SDK. You need to install Internet Explorer 5.5 or later on your computer to use the .NET framework SDK. The following Windows platforms support the .NET framework SDK:

◆ Windows XP Professional

◆ Windows 2000

◆ Windows NT 4.0 with Service Pack 6a

◆ Windows 98

> ### TIP
>
> ASP.NET applications can be created on Windows 98 and Windows Me platforms, but you must have a Web server installed on your computer to run them. You need to install IIS for platforms such as Windows 98, Windows Me, and Windows XP Professional. IIS is installed automatically when Windows 2000 Server or Windows NT 4.0 (with Service Pack 6a) is installed.

The .NET framework SDK provides you with tools to develop and test your ASP.NET applications. However, while using the .NET framework SDK, you can develop ASP.NET applications by using text editors and command-line compilers only. Moreover, you need to manually copy your files to IIS for deploying your applications.

You can install Visual Studio.NET to enable you to develop applications faster, easier, and more conveniently. Visual Studio.NET provides many handy tools that make application development an enchanting experience. The following are some of the tools that Visual Studio.NET provides:

◆ Smart code editors that have features such as statement completion and syntax checking.

◆ Visual designers that save your time and effort by enabling you to drag and drop controls while writing code for controls. Therefore, you need not type code to add each control to your page.

◆ Built-in compilers and debuggers that do not require compilation of applications to be done using the command prompt.

Creating Web Forms

ASP.NET includes a technology called Web forms that enables you to create dynamic Web pages faster. Using Web forms, you can create form-based Web pages. Web pages created using Web forms are called *Web forms pages* and look like the Web pages created in earlier versions of ASP. However, the overall experience of users with Web forms pages is much different and better as a result of the use of the CLR and other .NET features to create these Web forms. You need to be familiar with the features of Web forms before you actually go and create them in ASP.NET. The following lists introduce you to the features of Web forms.

Web forms:

♦ Use the .NET framework that runs on a Web server to create dynamic Web forms pages.

♦ Use the features of the CLR such as type safety and inheritance.

♦ Enable you to use a rich set of controls to design a user interface. In addition, you can extend the Web forms.

Web forms pages are:

♦ Designed and programmed by using the Rapid Application Development (RAD) tools that Visual Studio.NET includes. The RAD tools help in developing rich user interfaces quickly.

♦ Not dependent on the client in which they're displayed.

♦ Compatible with any Web browser or mobile device.

Web Forms Components

The most important feature of ASP.NET is that it separates the content from the application logic. You can implement this feature by using Web forms. In Web forms, there are two components:

♦ *User interface.* This component presents content to the users. It consists of a file that contains static HTML code or XML code and server controls. This file is stored with the .ASPX extension and is called the *page* file.

♦ *Programming logic.* This component is used to take care of user interactions with Web forms pages. Any of the .NET programming languages, such as Visual Basic .NET or C#, can be used to write the logic for Web forms page.

You can write the programming logic for the Web page in the .ASPX file. This logic does not mix with the HTML code as it used to in earlier versions of ASP. This model of writing programming logic is called the *code-inline model*.

Another model of writing programming logic for a Web page is the *code-behind model*. For this model, you write the page logic in a file called the *code-behind file*.

The choice between the two models depends on the programmer's preference. Programmers who use the usual methodology of application development with ASP prefer the code-inline method. However, once these programmers start using the code-behind method, they'll find the method more convenient.

▲ TIP

A Web forms page is a combination of a page file and a code-behind file.

Designing Web Forms

In this section, you will design a simple ASP.NET Web forms application to understand how an application is created in ASP.NET. You need to perform the following steps:

1. Start Visual Studio.NET and choose File, New, Project to open the New Project dialog box.

2. Next you need to select the project type. To do so, select a project type in the Project Types pane. The choices are Visual Basic Projects, Visual C# Projects, or Visual C++ Projects. For this example, select Visual Basic Projects.

3. You are creating an ASP.NET Web application. Therefore, select ASP.NET Web Application in the Templates pane.

4. Next you need to specify a name for your project and the name of the computer on which IIS is installed. To specify these, type the name of the computer in the Location box followed by the name of your project. The name of the project should be descriptive. For this example, enter the following in the Location box:

   http://*<name of the computer >*/MyFirstApplication

5. Click on OK to complete the procedure of creating the application.

Figure 23-2 displays how the Visual Studio.NET window will look after you have performed the preceding steps.

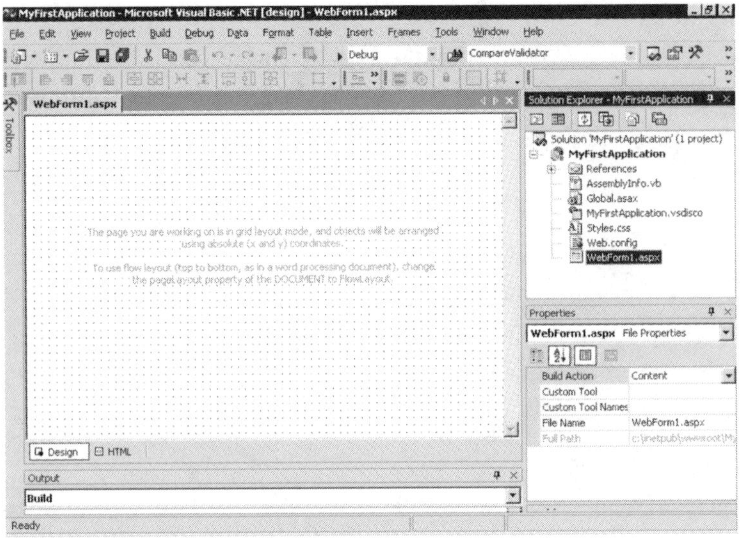

FIGURE 23-2 *The Visual Studio.NET window*

Note that Figure 23-2 displays a default Web form called *WebForm1*. Next you need to add controls and buttons to the Web form you have created. You can rename a Web form. To do so, right-click on the Web form in the Solution Explorer and choose Rename from the context menu.

The ASP.NET Web application template also generates different files in addition to a Web form. Table 23-1 lists the name of the files generated and the content in these files.

Table 23-1 Files and Their Content

File Name	Contains
Web.config	Application configuration information
Global.asax	Application-level event handlers
Licenses.lics	License information
MyFirstApplication.vsdisco	Informational links to ASP.NET Web services to be used in your application
AsemblyInfo.vb	Information, such as versioning and dependencies, for your assembly
Styles.css	Default HTML style settings

In addition to the files listed in Table 23-1, the ASP.NET Web application template adds the references to namespaces, which are contained in the References folder. A folder called bin is also created. This folder contains the .DLL files used in an application. The bin folder is not visible in the Solution Explorer. To view the bin folder, you need to click the Show All Files icon in the Solution Explorer window.

The page file, named as WebForm1.aspx, of the Web form you created is displayed in the Solution Explorer window (refer back to Figure 23-2) in the Design view. Therefore, you can place controls directly on the form by dragging and dropping controls from the Toolbox. By default, the page file is displayed in the grid layout. This makes it easy for you to accurately position the controls on the page. You can also use the flow layout for designing your page. This layout enables you to directly add text to your page. You can change the layout in which your page is displayed by selecting the page in the Design view and pressing the F4 key. This activates the Properties window for the page. In this window, you can select FlowLayout in the pageLayout property.

While you design the form in the Design view, the HTML code for the page is automatically generated. To view the HTML code, you have to use the HTML view. Programmers who find it convenient to work with HTML can edit the HTML code in the HTML view. In fact, you can write the programming logic for the page in the HTML view. To change the view from Design to HTML or vice versa, click the Design or HTML tab at the bottom of the page file.

A code-behind file also exists, in addition to the page file, for your Web form application. This file is not currently displayed in the Solutions Explorer window. You can view this file by clicking the Show All File icon in the Solution Explorer window. In addition, you can also view the code-behind file by pressing the F7 key when the page file is open.

Now that you have designed the look of your Web forms page, you need to add the functionality to it. You can do so by using the HTML view of the page file or the code-behind file. First, however, you need to understand the automatically generated code in these files before you can modify these files.

If you use the HTML view for the page, it displays the following code:

```
<%@ Page Language="vb" AutoEventWireup="false" codebehind="WebForm1.aspx.vb"
Inherits="MyFirstApplication.WebForm1"%>
```

In the preceding code, the @ Page directive specifies the page attributes and how they will affect the creation of your page. The Language attribute specifies the supported .NET language for your page. The AutoEventWireup attribute specifies whether the page events are automatically wired. If you assign a false value, it indicates that a developer should enable the page events. Next the codebehind attribute is used. This attribute specifies the name of the code-behind file for your page. The preceding code also contains the Inherits attribute. This attribute is used to specify the name of the code-behind class that a page inherits.

In the <Head> element of the HTML code, you can write the programming logic for your page. You have to use the <Script> tag to add the programming logic. Consider the following code:

```
<Script runat="server" language="vb">
          'Code statements
</Script>
```

This code uses the <Script> tag to add the programming logic. The code statement runat="server" is used to specify that the code will run at the server side. The next statement in the code, language="vb", specifies that Visual Basic.NET is used for adding the programming logic. The language specified in this attribute should be supported by the .NET framework.

Next, the controls or text are added to the <Body> element. These are added in the <% %> block. The code is also generated for the code-behind file. The code snippet generated in the WebForm1.aspx.vb file is displayed:

```
Public Class WebForm1
    Inherits System.Web.UI.Page
```

The first line of the code specifies that class named WebForm1 is inherited from the Page class. The Page class is a part of the System.Web.UI namespace.

This code also contains two methods, InitializeComponent and Page_Init.

◆ InitializeComponent contains the code to initialize the page components such as controls.

◆ Page_Init is the event handler for the Init event of the page. This method calls the InitializeComponent method.

Next, the Page_Load method is used to handle the Load event of your page. You can also add event handlers for the controls you have used on your page.

Now you will create a simple application that displays a welcome message. To begin the procedure for the creation of the application, open the Properties window for the WebForm1 page. To set the background color, set the bgColor property to #ffcccc. Next open the code-behind file for your application. In this example, open the WebForm1.aspx.vb file. This file will be used to modify the existing code. You need to write the following code in the Page_Load method:

```
Private Sub Page_Load(ByVal sender As System.Object, ByVal e As System.EventArgs)
Handles
MyBase.Load
    Dim UserName As String
    UserName = Request.QueryString("Name")
        Response.Write("<Center>" + "<B>Welcome</B>" + "<B> " + UserName + "</B>" +
"</Center>")
        Response.Write("<Center>" + "<B>This is your first Web application!!!</B>"
+ "</Center>")
End Sub
```

To run the application, press Ctrl+F5. The preceding code displays a message to the user when the user supplies his or her name. Figure 23-3 displays the output that appears when a user has entered the following URL:

**http://*<name of the computer>*/MyFirstApplication/WebForm1.aspx?
Name=Robert**

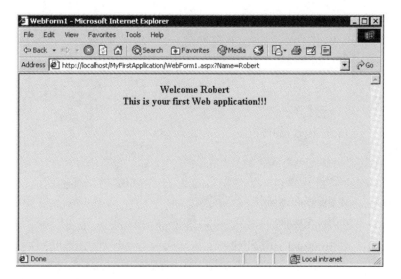

FIGURE 23-3 *The output in Internet Explorer*

Many times, an application contains many different Web forms. When you develop an application, it will be very tedious to develop the entire application to check the functionality of a specific page. In this situation, you can browse the specific page without developing the entire application. To browse a specific page, right-click the .ASPX file and select View in Browser.

IIS Application Root Directory

In Visual Studio.NET, when you are creating an ASP.NET application, you need to specify the name of the project and the location. You can specify the location as **http://_localhost_** or **http://**<*name of the computer*>.

The location contains the name of the computer and no reference to the directory path. This makes it difficult to locate the application at a later stage. You need not worry, however, when you are developing an ASP.NET application project because an application root directory with the project name is created in the default Web site of the IIS server. This application directory is called the IIS application root. This directory maps to the physical location of the directory on the server, which is available at the path <*drive name*>**:\inetpub\wwwroot**<*name of the project*>. All the files generated and developed in the .NET framework are included in the IIS application root directory.

If you want to trace an application named `MyFirstApplication` that you created using ASP.NET, you can trace the IIS application root directory for it. You can trace the IIS application root directory by opening the IIS Microsoft Management Console (MMC) by choosing Start, Programs, Administrative Tools, Internet Services Manager. Figure 23-4 shows the `MyFirstApplication` directory selected in the IIS MMC.

As you can see in Figure 23-4, three types of folders exist in the Default Web Site directory:

◆ *Explorer-style folders.* These folders exist as physical directories in IIS. Examples include `vti_pvt` and `vti_txt`.

◆ *Explorer-style folders with HTML circles.* These folders represent virtual directories. An example is `vti_bin`.

◆ *Web application folders.* These folders appear as package icons. If you create a virtual directory, the directory is automatically treated as a Web application folder. For example, if you create an ASP.NET application

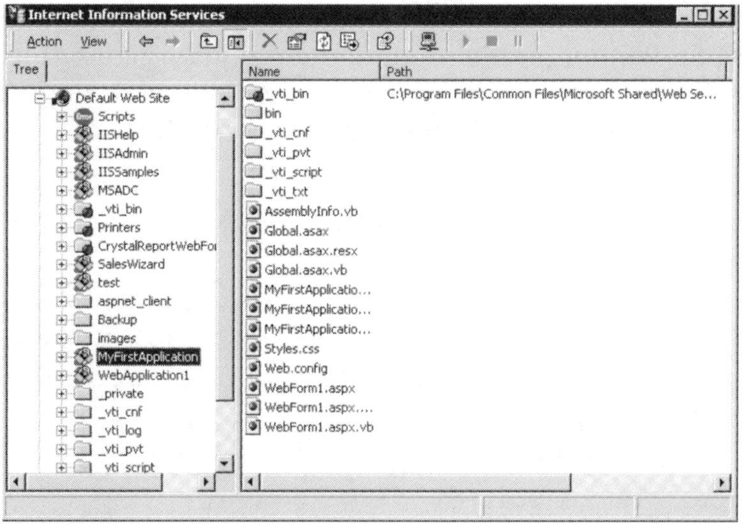

FIGURE 23-4 *The IIS MMC displaying an application root directory*

named `MyApplication`, a Web application folder named `MyApplication`
is automatically created in IIS.

If you are creating your ASP.NET application in Visual Studio.NET, the application root directory is created automatically for you. If you are creating your ASP.NET application using a text editor such as TextPad, however, you have to create the application root directory. You can do this in one of the following ways:

◆ Create a virtual directory

◆ Mark a folder as an application

The next two sections will show you how to create the application root directory using these ways.

Creating a Virtual Directory

Let's say you've created a Web forms page named MyPage.aspx in C:/MyWeb. You need to publish this page to deploy it on a Web site. This can be done by creating a *Web virtual directory*. These virtual directories are not located at the physical structure of the root directory of the Web server. In fact, the actual directory can be created at a completely different physical location, or it could be on a remote computer. Therefore, different virtual directories can point to the same set of files. If you create your ASP.NET applications in directories different from the root directory of the Web server, the virtual directories are a handy feature. If you create a virtual directory and point it to your application stored in a directory other than the root directory of the Web server, the virtual directory becomes your application root directory. To create virtual directories in the IIS MMC, you need to follow these steps:

1. Open the IIS MMC from the Internet Service Manager and right-click on Default Web Site.

2. Choose New, Virtual Directory from the context menu. This will initiate the Virtual Directory Creation Wizard. You need to follow the onscreen prompts to finish creating the virtual directory. (These are described in steps 3 through 7.)

3. Click Next on the Welcome screen to view the next screen. You're prompted to enter an alias for the virtual directory.

4. Type a name for your virtual directory; let's say you enter MyWeb. The name that you enter for your virtual directory appears in the IIS MMC. Click Next.

5. The next screen asks you to enter the name of the content directory you want to publish on the Web site. In the Directory box, type the name of the directory that contains your ASP.NET Web forms page and other related files. Click Next.

6. The next screen asks you to set the access permissions for the virtual directory. Select the access permissions. You can only assign permissions such as Read and Run scripts (such as ASP). Click Next and the final screen appears.

7. Click Finish to complete the process.

Figure 23-5 displays the MyWeb application root.

Marking a Folder as an Application

The next method used to creating an application root is to mark a folder containing your ASP.NET application files as an application. To do this, you need to create a folder that you want to mark as an application in c:\inetpub\wwwroot. You create the folder and name MyFolder. If you launch the IIS MMC, you'll see MyFolder displayed under the Default Web Site.

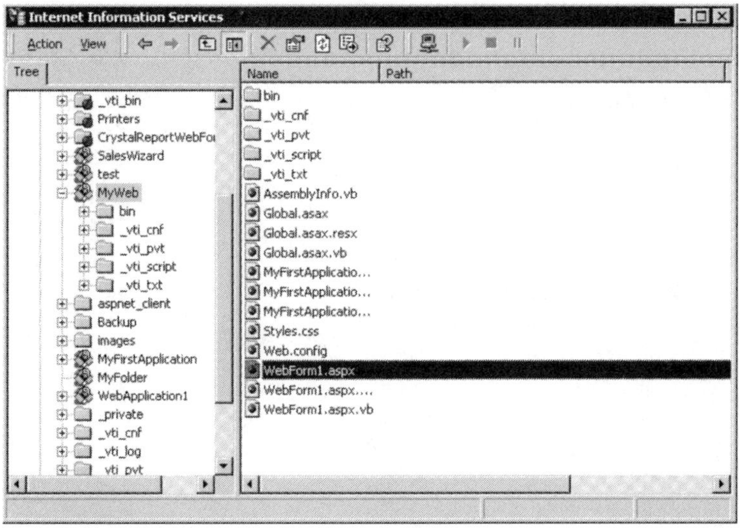

FIGURE 23-5 *The* MyWeb *application root displays the WebForm1.aspx file*

> ### TIP
>
> If the IIS MMC is already launched, select the Default Web Site and click the Refresh button on the Toolbar.

You have created a folder. To mark this folder as an application, you need to convert it to an application. To do so, right-click MyFolder and choose Properties from the context menu. The Properties dialog box will appear, as shown in Figure 23-6.

The Properties dialog box displays the local path and permissions for the selected folder. To convert this folder to an application, click the Create button under Application Settings. This makes available the boxes that were unavailable before the Create button was clicked. Next click on OK to complete the process. You'll see that the folder icon for MyFolder has changed to a package icon, indicating that it is now converted to an application.

The next section discusses the various controls you can use to design your ASP.NET Web applications.

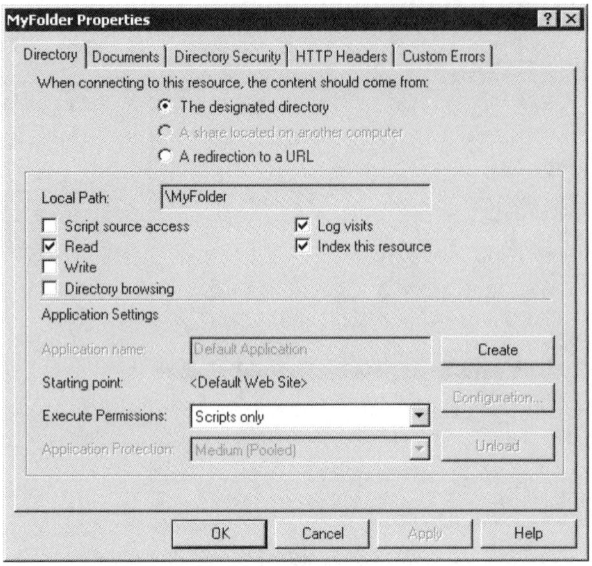

FIGURE 23-6 *The Properties dialog box for* MyFolder

ASP.NET Server Controls

You can design well-structured user interfaces for your Web forms pages by using ASP.NET. This technology provides you with a rich set of server controls for creating interactive and dynamic Web forms pages. These controls adopt a server-side programming model in which users at the client side interact with server controls to generate several events, which are handled at the server side. An example is the events that occur when a client browser requests a page. This page is compiled into an object called Page. The Page object has server controls compiled as objects within the Page object. Whenever the page is requested, the server controls are compiled and executed on the server that hosts the page. This method in ASP.NET is more dynamic than the normal HTML controls. This is because the HTML controls do not have any interaction with the server after they are rendered on the page, whereas server controls allow access to the properties, methods, and events at the server side.

Types of Server Controls

The .NET framework supports HTML server controls and Web server controls. The following list defines these controls:

◆ *HTML server controls.* The HTML server controls are the HTML elements you can use in a server-side code. These server controls are part of the `System.Web.UI.HtmlControls` namespace and are derived from the `HtmlControl` base class.

◆ *Web server controls.* The ASP.NET Web forms server controls are part of the `System.Web.UI.WebControls` namespace. These controls are also called Web controls. They are derived from the `WebControl` base class. In addition to the basic controls that the ASP.NET Web forms server controls include, the following Web controls are also included:

◆ *List controls.* These controls are used to create lists. You can bind these lists to a data source. For example, these controls can be used to create ListBox and DropDownList controls.

◆ *Validation controls.* These controls are used to check and validate the values entered in other controls used on a page. For example, Required-FieldValidator and CustomValidator are validation controls.

◆ *Rich controls.* These are special controls used to create task-specific output. For example, these controls can be used to create Calendar and AdRotator controls.

◆ *User controls.* You can create controls as Web forms pages and also embed these controls in other Web forms pages.

Table 23-2 lists the various HTML server controls and their corresponding tags.

Table 23-2 HTML Server Controls and Their Corresponding HTML Tags

HTML Server Control	HTML Tag
HtmlForm	`<form>`
HtmlInputText	`<input type = "text">` and `<input type = "password">`
HtmlInputButton	`<input type = "button">`
HtmlInputCheckBox	`<input type = "check">`
HtmlInputRadioButton	`<input type = "radio">`
HtmlInputImage	`<input type = "image">`
HtmlAnchor	`<a>`

continues

Table 23-2 *(continued)*

HTML Server Control	HTML Tag
HtmlButton	`<button>`
HtmlTable	`<table>`
HtmlTableRow	`<tr>`
HtmlTableCell	`<td>`

Differences Between HTML Server Controls and Web Controls

When creating Web applications, you need to choose between HTML server controls and Web controls. The choice depends on your requirements and the functionality required in each server control. This decision can be made if you understand the functionality of both types of server controls. The following list compares the two controls on certain factors:

◆ *Mapping to HTML tags.* HTML server controls map directly to HTML tags. The HTML tags are converted to server controls by using the `runat="server"` attribute. This makes it easier to migrate from ASP to ASP.NET. Web controls do not map directly to HTML tags. Therefore, you need to include controls from a third party.

◆ *Object model.* For HTML server controls, an HTML-centric object model is used in which a control has a set of attributes. These attributes use string name/value pairs that are not strongly typed. For Web controls, a Visual Basic–like programming model is used in which each Web control has a set of standard properties.

◆ *Target browser.* For HTML server controls, the generated HTML is not changed depending on the target browser. Therefore, you need to ensure that the controls are rendered in both up-level and down-level browsers. For Web controls, the rendered output adjusts automatically depending on the target browser. This ensures that the controls are rendered in both up-level and down-level browsers.

Adding Web Controls to Forms

When creating Web forms, you can add server controls either at design time or at runtime. To add server controls at design time, you can use either Toolbox or the HTML view of the .ASPX file. The server controls can also be added programmatically at runtime. This can be done using the `<Script>` tag in the .ASPX file or in the code-behind file. The following sections describe the ways in which you can add server controls to your Web forms.

Using the Toolbox

The Toolbox includes a wide set of controls that are grouped under different categories for convenient access. You can access the Toolbox from the extreme left of the Visual Studio.NET window. If it is not available there, you need to launch it by selecting View, Toolbox. The following are the different categories in the Toolbox:

- *Web Forms.* This category contains all Web controls, including validation controls and rich Web controls. This category is very frequently used when designing Web forms pages.
- *HTML.* This category consists of all the HTML server controls.
- *Data.* This category contains data objects, which are used to implement data access and manipulation functionality.
- *Component.* This category contains a set of components that can be used to add time-based functionality to your forms. This Toolbox category has standard available components, and you can add other components.
- *Clipboard Ring.* This category stores text items. Any text that you cut or copy becomes a part of this category. You can use this category to more multiple code snippets from one part of the Code Editor to another.
- *General.* This category initially displays only a Pointer tool. You can add controls to this category such as button and custom controls.

You can create Web forms server controls by either dragging or drawing controls from the Toolbox to the Web form. This adds the control with its default size. Different controls have different default sizes. To add a control to your form, you can even double-click the control and specify the location coordinates in the form. Adding controls to the form by using the Toolbox generates an ASP.NET code for the controls in the HTML view of the .ASPX file.

Using the HTML View of the .ASPX File

You can also add server controls by specifying the ASP.NET code for the controls directly in the HTML view of the .ASPX file of your Web form. For example, you can add a text box by using the following ASP.NET code:

```
<asp:TextBox id = "MyTextBox" runat = "server" Text = "Greetings"></asp:TextBox>
```

You can view the control's rendered output in the Design view.

Using the Code-Behind File

ASP.NET enables you to add server controls even at runtime. You can do so by creating an instance of the Control class that inherits the WebControl base class. Suppose you want to create a text box at runtime. You can use the following Visual Basic code:

```
Dim Text_Box As New TextBox()
Controls.Add(Text_Box)
```

In the preceding code, the control is added to the form by using the Add method of the Controls class.

Setting Properties of Web Controls

Server controls have common properties called *base properties* that are inherited from the WebControl base class. Apart from the base properties, each control has its own set of properties. You can set a control's properties at design time or runtime. To set the properties at design time, you can use the Properties window or the ASP.NET code to set a control's properties. To view the Properties window, right-click on the control for which you want to set the properties and, from the context menu, select Properties. In addition, you can display the Properties window of the control by selecting Properties Window from the View menu or by pressing the F4 key. Figure 23-7 displays the Properties window for a text box.

ASP.NET enables you to set the properties of Web controls by directly editing the ASP.NET code in the HTML view. Suppose you want to set the Enabled property of a text box in the .ASPX file. For that, you would use the following code:

```
<asp:TextBox Id = "Text_Box" runat = "server" Enabled = False></asp:TextBox>
```

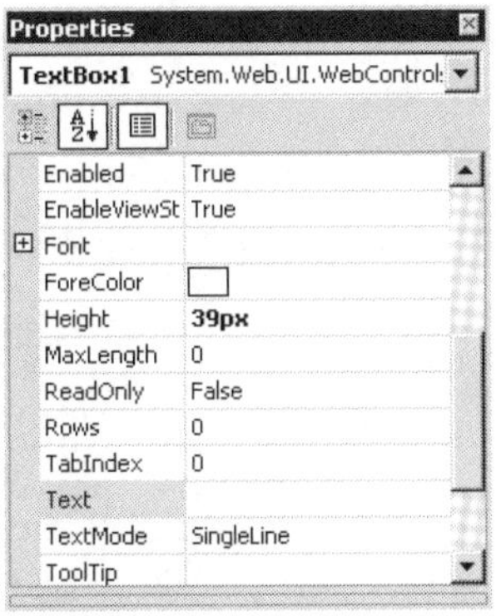

FIGURE 23-7 *The Properties window for a text box*

Sometimes you might need to set properties of controls at runtime. The following syntax is used to set a control's property programmatically:

```
ControlID.PropertyName = Value
```

Let's say you want to display a control only when a certain condition is met. You would need to set the Visible property of the control to True programmatically. The following code illustrates this example:

```
Text_Box.Enabled = True
```

In this code snippet, the Enabled property is the property of the control. The ControlID is represented by Text_Box. This code snippet is used to set the value of the Enabled property to True for the control with the ID Text_Box.

Handling Events of Web Controls

In ASP.NET, the controls inherit a set of events from the WebControl class. Each control also has its own set of events that you can handle by using either the code-behind file or the .ASPX file. Let's look at this with more detail. A button has its own click event. You can handle this event in either the code-behind file or the .ASPX file. To open the code-behind file, you can either use the Solution Explorer window or press F7. Now you need to write the handler for a control's event. To do so, select the name of the control from the Class Name list. Next select the event from the Method Name list.

Consider this example: The ID of the button is AcceptButton, select AcceptButton from the Class Name list and Click from the Method Name list. This automatically generates the following code:

```
Private Sub AcceptButton_Click(ByVal sender As Object, ByVal e As System.EventArgs)
Handles AcceptButton.Click
            'Code statements
End Sub
```

In this code, the procedure AcceptButton_Click is the event handler for the Click event of the button with the ID AcceptButton. This procedure accepts two arguments. The first argument contains an object called an event sender. The second argument contains the data for the event. The Handles keyword is used to associate the Click event with the event handler (that is, AcceptButton_Click). Next you can modify the code in the event handler to add the desired tasks. You test the code by accessing the form from a Web browser.

You can also create event handlers for server controls by using the .ASPX file. Consider the preceding example of a button with the ID AcceptButton. The creation and association of the event handler with the Click event is done in two steps:

1. Edit the code for the control in the .ASPX file. This is used to specify the event handler for the Click event.

   ```
   <asp:Button Id = "AcceptButton" runat = "server" OnClick =
   "AcceptButton_Click"></asp:Button>
   ```

   In this code snippet, OnCick = "AcceptButton_Click" is the event that should be called when the Click event of the button is generated.

2. Next you need to write the AcceptButton_Click event handler in the .ASPX file.

Some Commonly Used Web Controls

All Web controls inherit from the WebControl class. Therefore, all controls have a set of common properties, methods, and events. In addition, all controls have their own specific properties, methods, and events. Table 23-3 looks at the commonly used properties, methods, and events for some Web controls.

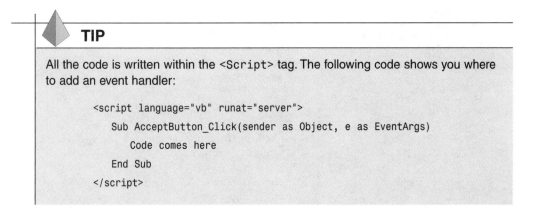

> ## ▲ TIP
>
> All the code is written within the `<Script>` tag. The following code shows you where to add an event handler:
>
> ```vb
> <script language="vb" runat="server">
>     Sub AcceptButton_Click(sender as Object, e as EventArgs)
>         Code comes here
>     End Sub
> </script>
> ```

Table 23-3 Properties, Methods, and Events of the *WebControl* Class

Property/Method/Event	Description
`AccessKey` property	This is used to get or set the keyboard shortcut to access the control.
`BackColor` property	This is used to get or set the background color of the control.
`BorderColor` property	This is used to get or set the border color of the control.
`BorderStyle` property	This is used to set the border style of the control as double, solid, or dotted.
`Controls` property	This is used to return an object of the `ControlCollection` class.
`DataBind` method	This is used to bind data from a data source to a server control and all its child controls.
`DataBinding` event	This is generated when the control is being bound to a data source.
`Enabled` property	This accepts a `Boolean` value indicating whether the control is enabled.
`EnableViewState` property	This accepts a `Boolean` value indicating whether the control maintains its view state.
`Font` property	This is used to get or set the font information, such as font name and size, of the control.
`ForeColor` property	This is used to get or set the foreground color of the control.

continues

Table 23-3 *(continued)*

Property/Method/Event	Description
`Height` property	This is used to get or set the height of the control.
`ID` property	This is used to get or set the identifier of the control.
`TabIndex` property	This is used to get or set the tab index of the control.
`ToolTip` property	This is used to get or set the pop-up text displayed upon moving the mouse pointer over the control.
`Visible` property	This accepts a `Boolean` value. A `True` value indicates that the control is rendered as UI on the page; a `False` value indicates that the control isn't rendered on the page.
`Width` property	This is used to get or set the width of the control.

Validation Controls

Many Web pages require user input to be validated before this input is fed into a database. In ASP.NET, this validation is done using validation controls, which are one of the new features that have been introduced in ASP.NET. They are very useful because you don't have to write validation code. Suppose you want to validate the user input in a text box. You can add a validation control to your page and associate it with the control you want to validate. This section covers more details about validation and how it is used in Web forms.

What Are Validation Controls?

ASP.NET provides six validation controls. All validation controls are inherited from the `BaseValidator` class. You can use this class to implement the other validation controls because this is an abstract class that forms the core of validation. The following are the types of ASP.NET validation controls:

◆ `RequiredFieldValidator` is used to validate a control to check whether it is empty or not.

◆ `CompareValidator` is used to compare values in different controls to check whether the two values match.

◆ RangeValidator is used to check whether the value in a control is in the specified text or numeric range.

◆ RegularExpressionValidator is used to check whether the value in a control matches a specified regular expression.

◆ CustomValidator is used to perform validation on a control by using user-defined functions.

◆ ValidationSummary is used to display all the validation error messages grouped together.

Let's now discuss how validation works. It is actually a four-step process, as follows:

1. You add a validation control. Next you need to associate it with another control that requires validation. Specifying the ControlToValidate property of the validation control does this.

2. A page with different controls and validations attached to the controls is displayed to a user. Now the user enters values in different controls and submits the completed form. Values entered by the user are passed to the appropriate validation controls. This means that the validation control attached to the respective control validates the value entered for this control.

3. Validation controls validate the values passed to the controls.

4. After the validation is done, the value for the IsValid property of each validation control attached to the control is set to either True or False. If the value is True, it indicates that the validation succeeded. A False value indicates that the validation failed. After all the validations have succeeded, the page data is processed at the server.

Using Validation Controls

To use validation controls, you need to create an ASP.NET Web form project. Lets create a project named SampleValidation. You also need to design a basic form that contains several controls to accept user input. Let's design a form named CheckForm. This form accepts the necessary information from a customer who wants to buy a CD from a video portal. You can specify IDs for different controls on the form. You can use Table 23-4 as a reference.

> ### TIP
>
> A failure of a single validation makes the value of the IsValid property False. If this occurs, the page data is not processed at the server, and the page is sent back to the client browser with the validation errors.
>
> This indicates that the validation controls perform validation checks at the server side. You can also use validation controls to perform validation checks using client scripts. These are called *client-side validations*. This type of validation is possible only if the client browser supports Dynamic Hypertext Markup Language (DHTML).
>
> In client-side validation, the form is not processed at the server side. The error messages are displayed to a user as soon as the user moves out of the control that contains the error. Client-side validation reduces cycle time and improves performance.

Table 23-4 Sample Form Control IDs

Control	Text	ID
Button	Accept	AcceptButton
Label	Message	MessageLabel
Text box	Confirm password	ConfirmBox
Text box	Customer ID	CustIDBox
Text box	Number of CDs	NumberOfCDsBox
Text box	Password	PasswordBox
Text box	Telephone number	TelephoneNumberBox
Text box	Username	UserNameBox

Let's now look at how to use various controls.

RequiredFieldValidator

This control is used to check that the control being validated contains a value. You use this control to validate whether a user has entered the required information in a text box. You can add the RequiredFieldValidator control from the Web forms tab of the Toolbox. Table 23-5 displays the values set for properties of this validation control.

Table 23-5 Setting Properties for the RequiredFieldValidator Control

Property	Value
ID	UserNameRequiredFieldValidator
ControlToValidate	UserNameBox
ErrorMessage	Enter your user name.
Display	Dynamic

You can add the RequiredFieldValidator control and set its properties. The corresponding ASP.NET code for the control is automatically generated. You can see this code in the HTML view of the .ASPX file. After setting the properties of the RequiredFieldValidator control, you need to write the following code for the `Click` event of the Accept button:

```
Private Sub AcceptButton_Click(ByVal sender As System.Object, ByVal e As
System.EventArgs) Handles
AcceptButton.Click
      If Page.IsValid = True Then
          'Specify a message to be displayed on the label
          MessageLabel.Text = "Welcome " + UserNameBox.Text
          'Make the label visible
          MessageLabel.Visible = True
      End If
End Sub
```

You have done the coding for the RequiredFieldValidator control. When you execute the application, you'll see that the control isn't rendered on the page. However, if you click the Accept button without entering any details in the `UserNameBox` text box, an error message displays.

CompareValidator

Let's see how the CompareValidator control is used. This control compares the value entered in a control with the value in another control or a specific value. You can compare these values by using any operator available with the control, such as `Equal`, `NotEqual`, `GreaterThan`, and `LessThan`. ASP.NET enables you to compare values of different types such as `String`, `Integer`, `Double`, `Date`, and `Currency`.

Table 23-6 displays some of the common properties of the CompareValidator control.

Table 23-6 Some Properties of the CompareValidator Control

Property	Description
ControlToValidate	This is used to get or set the ID of the control with the value you want to validate.
ControlToCompare	This is used to get or set the ID of the control with the value you want to compare.
Display	This is used to get or set one of the values. You can set `Static`, `Dynamic`, or `None`. The default value is `Static`.
ErrorMessage	This is used to set the text for the error message.
Operator	This is used for comparisons. The value for this property can be `Equal`, `NotEqual`, `LessThan`, or `GreaterThan`. The default value is `Equal`.
Type	This specifies the data type of the value you want to compare. This property can have the value `String`, `Integer`, `Currency`, `Date`, or `Double`. The default value is `String`.
ValueToCompare	This is used to get or set a specific value that you want to compare.

Let's implement the CompareValidator control in the `CheckForm` form. In this form, you need to compare the value entered in the `Password` text box and the `ConfirmBox` text box. To do so, you need to add the CompareValidator control to the form.

You can even write an equivalent ASP.NET code to add the control. The following is the equivalent code to add the control:

```
<asp:CompareValidator
id = "PasswordValidator" runat = "server"
ControlToCompare = "Password_Box"
ControlToValidate = "Confirm_Box"
ErrorMessage = "Please retype the password."
```

```
Display = "Dynamic">
</asp:CompareValidator>
You also need to edit the code for the Click event of the Accept button.
Private Sub AcceptButton_Click(ByVal sender As System.Object, ByVal e As
System.EventArgs) Handles AcceptButton.Click
        If Page.IsValid = True Then
            'Specify a message to be displayed on the label
            MessageLabel.Text = "Welcome " + UserNameBox.Text + ", You are
    authorized to use the services provided by the video kiosk."
            'Make the label visible
            MessageLabel.Visible = True
        End If
End Sub
```

When you enter different passwords in the `Password` and `ConfirmBox` text boxes and click the Accept button, an error message displays.

RangeValidator

You can implement the RangeValidator control to check whether a value falls within a specified range of values. You can specify the range by setting maximum and minimum values. These can be constant values from other controls. The RangeValidator control has multiple properties including `ControlToValidate`, `ErrorMessage`, and `Display`. Let's look at some of the other properties:

- The `MaximumValue` property is used to set the upper limit value of the validation range.

- The `MinimumValue` property is used to set the lower limit value of the validation range.

- `Type` is used to set the data type for the values that are compared. You can set one of the following data types: `String`, `Integer`, `Double`, `Date`, or `Currency`.

In the `CheckForm` form, you can use the RangeValidator control to validate the `NumberOfCDsBox` text box that accepts the value for the number of CDs to be bought. The kiosk doesn't issue more than four CDs to a user. You have to specify the range between 1 and 4.

You can add the RangeValidator control by using the Toolbox. Table 23-7 displays the values for the different properties of the control.

Table 23-7 Properties Set for the RangeValidator Control

Property	Value
ID	BooksRangeValidator
ControlToValidate	NumberOfCDsBox
MaximumValue	4
MinimumValue	1
Type	Integer
ErrorMessage	The number of CDs must be between 1 and 4.
Display	Dynamic

When you execute the application, enter the number of CDs outside the range of 1 and 4. Now click the Accept button. This displays an error message.

RegularExpressionValidator

You can use the RegularExpressionValidator control to validate a value entered in a control against some specific expression. This specific expression validation is used to validate certain data such as telephone numbers, ZIP codes, social security numbers, and e-mail addresses.

The RegularExpressionValidator control uses the `ControlToValidate`, `ErrorMessage`, and `Display` properties. It also uses a property called `ValidationExpression`. This property is used to validate user input data against some pattern of a specific expression.

Let's use this validation in the `CheckForm` form. You can implement this validation for the `TelephoneNumber` text box. You need to validate this number against a fixed pattern of U.S. telephone numbers. In addition, the different parts of the telephone number must be separated by hyphens.

You can add the RegularExpressionValidator control by using the Toolbox. The properties set for the control are displayed in Table 23-8.

Table 23-8 Properties Set for the RegularExpressionValidator Control

Property	Value
ID	TelephoneRegularExpressionValidator
ControlToValidate	TelephoneNumberBox
ValidationExpression	[0-9]{3}-[0-9]{3}\s[0-9]{4}
ErrorMessage	Please retype the telephone number.
Display	Dynamic

You need to understand the value [0-9]{3}-[0-9]{3}\s[0-9]{4} for the ValidationExpression property. The first part [0-9] represents any digit between 0 and 9. {3} indicates that three digits are required for the first part. Next, a hyphen is placed. This indicates that a hyphen is required. In the middle part, \s indicates that a space is required. This means that the next three digits are followed by a space. The final part [0-9]{4} indicates a four-digit number in which each number is in the range of 0 to 9.

Now you execute the application. Enter a telephone number that does not match the specified pattern and click the Accept button. This displays an error message.

CustomValidator

This control enables you to validate a value entered in a control by using a user-defined function. Consider this example: You validate a control to ensure that the control accepts only odd numbers. This is only possible by writing a code for detecting an odd number. Therefore, you have to use the CustomValidator control. This control enables you to use validation functions at the client side as well as the server side. The CustomValidator control has a property called ClientValidationFunction. This property is used to get or set the client script function that is called automatically to validate the control. To write the validation code, you can use any scripting language such as JavaScript or VBScript.

For server-side validation, the CustomValidator control raises the ServerValidate event. You must write code in the event handler for this control. You can do this by using either the code-behind file or the HTML view of the .ASPX file.

Let's implement the CustomValidator control in the CheckForm form. You can use this validation control to validate the Member Number text box. You can add the

CustomValidator control to the CheckForm form. Table 23-9 displays the values set for the properties used in the CustomValidator control.

Table 23-9 Properties Set for the CustomValidator Control

Property	Value
ID	NumberCustomValidator
ControlToValidate	CustIDBox
ClientValidationFunction	CustIsValidFun
ErrorMessage	This is an invalid customer ID, please retype.
Display	Dynamic

The value for the ClientValidationFunction property is set to CustIsValidFun. This is the name of the client script function. This function is invoked when the control with ID CustIDBox is validated. You can write this function using VBScript. Let's add the following validation code in the .ASPX file of the CheckForm form:

```
<script language="vbscript">
   Sub CustIsValidFun (source,arguments)
     if(arguments.Value)="KBL77777" Then
       arguments.IsValid=true
     Else
       arguments.IsValid=false
     End If
   End Sub
</script>
```

The CustIsValidFun function accepts two parameters, source and argument. The source parameter gets the control ID from the ControlToValidate property of the CustomValidator control. The arguments parameter contains the actual information about the value being entered in the control. Therefore, in the following function, the value entered in the control with the ID CustIDBox is matched against a value. If the two values match, the IsValid property is set to True. If the value of the function is returned as True, the validation succeeds.

When you execute the application, the page is displayed in the browser. If you enter an incorrect value in the CustIDBox text box, an error message displays.

ValidationSummary

You can use the ValidationSummary control to display all the validation errors in the page. This control enables you to display the summary of errors in a list, a bulleted list, or paragraph format. In addition, it provides you with an option to display the summary of errors inline or as a pop-up message box.

Table 23-10 lists some of the common properties of the ValidationSummary control.

Table 23-10 Properties of the ValidationSummary Control

Property	Description
DisplayMode	This is used to get or set the display mode of the validation summary. This property accepts one of three values: List, BulletList, or SingleParagraph.
HeaderText	This is used to get or set the text to be displayed at the top of the validation summary.
ShowSummary	This is used to get or set a Boolean value that indicates whether the validation summary is displayed inline. The default value is True.
ShowSummaryBox	This is used to get or set a Boolean value that indicates whether the validation summary is displayed as a pop-up message box. The default value is False.

You can add the ValidationSummary control to the CheckForm form by using the Toolbox. The ASP.NET code for the ValidationSummary control is as follows:

```
<asp:ValidationSummary
id="ValidationSummary1" runat="server"
HeaderText="The following errors were encountered">
</asp:ValidationSummary>
```

You can display the validation summary as a pop-up message box by setting the value of the ShowSummaryBox property to True.

When you execute the application, the form displays. If you enter invalid data in any of the controls of the form and click the Accept button, the page displays an inline validation summary.

Using Multiple Validation Controls

You know how to use different validation controls in isolation. In some applications, however, you need a control for multiple conditions. Consider this example: You want the value of a control to be within a specific range. In addition, you also require that the value of the control pass a custom validation test. To test multiple conditions for a control's value, you need to associate multiple validation controls to a single control.

In most cases, you use the RequiredFieldValidator control in combination with other validation controls. Let's go back to the CheckForm form example. If a user does not enter any value in the two password boxes and clicks on the Accept button, the comparison validation test does not fail. This is because there is no value in the two password boxes. You have to add a validation control to avoid such a situation. Therefore, you need to use the RequiredFieldValidator control in conjunction with the CompareValidator control.

It is quite easy to use multiple validation controls for the same control. You simply have to add all the validation controls you require for a control to the form. Next you have to set the ControlToValidate property of all the validation controls as the ID of the control you want to be validated.

Table 23-11 displays the values you need to associate for the CheckForm form. These values are used to add multiple validations to the form.

Table 23-11 Properties Set for the Second RequireFieldValidator Control

Property	Value
ID	PasswordRequiredFieldValidator
ControlToValidate	ConfirmBox
ErrorMessage	Enter your password
Display	Dynamic

If you don't enter the value for the two password fields and submit the form, a message `Enter your password` will display.

Summary

This chapter covered the basics of ASP.NET and the platform requirements for ASP.NET applications. It also covered the details about the ASP.NET architecture and introduced you to Web forms ASP.NET applications. This chapter also covered the different types of server controls and validation controls that you can use in your page. ASP.NET provides structured framework for the complete development of Web applications.

Chapter 24

In the preceding chapter, you were introduced to ASP.NET. You learned how to develop a Web application using the various server controls. In this chapter, you will learn to configure and secure ASP.NET applications.

You define the configuration for an application to define its behavior. With the explosive growth of the Internet and its far-reaching access, you need to improve the performance of your Web application. You can improve application performance by using caching, which will be covered in this chapter. In addition to being fast, a Web site needs to be secure. This is because a nonsecure site will not hold any value to a user. Therefore, you need to give a lot of consideration to the security aspects of your Web application. In this chapter, you will also learn about the various security mechanisms available with ASP.NET.

Configuring ASP.NET Applications

The various details you provide when you create an application are called its configuration information. Consider this example: When a new application such as Microsoft Outlook is installed, you provide information about the user and the mail server to be used. Similarly, the configuration information of a Web application includes details such as session timeout, security options, and error handling. In this section, you will learn about the basics of configuring ASP.NET applications.

The properties and behavior of ASP.NET applications are determined by the settings defined inside the configuration files. These files are XML based. Therefore, you can access and set the configuration settings without writing any scripts. There are two types of configuration files:

- *machine.config.* This is the machine configuration file that gets installed on the server when Visual Studio.NET is installed. The machine.config file contains the default configuration for all Web applications hosted on the server. There can be only one machine.config file on the server. This file is located in the %runtime install path%/config directory.

◆ *Web.config*. Some files are automatically created when you create an ASP.NET application project. One of these files is the Web.config file, which is created in the root directory of the application. This file contains settings specific to an individual application. You can override the default settings by changing the settings in the Web.config file. You can have multiple Web.config files, one for each application on the server.

Let's now take a look at some of the advantages of configuring applications in ASP.NET. First, the files configured in ASP.NET are XML based, thus making them easy to read and write. In addition, the changes made to the configuration files take effect immediately. Second, the configuration settings are applied in a hierarchical manner. Therefore, you can have different settings for different applications and different settings for different parts of the same application. Finally, the ASP.NET configuration system is extensible. This implies that you can create custom configuration handlers.

Let's ask a simple question. Would you like to visit a site that contains excellent information and provides effective services but is extremely slow? The answer is a simple "No." The solution to this problem is a mechanism called *caching*. In the following section, you will learn about caching in ASP.NET.

Caching in ASP.NET

A Web application that is slow can result in users' dissatisfaction and can prove to be a complete failure. An effective solution is caching. Caching improves performance by storing frequently accessed data in memory. Therefore, frequently accessed pages are retrieved from the cache directly instead of reloading the page from the Web server. Data, especially static data, can quickly be displayed using caching. Caching is also beneficial with nonstatic data. You can specify the validity period of data in the expiration policy of the requested page. The client request is serviced using the cache for the specified duration in the expiration policy. After the expiration date, the request from the client is redirected to the Internet.

ASP.NET caches frequently accessed pages in memory or on local hard disks. As a result, a request from an application on the Web server is processed only once and is cached for future use. Once the request is cached, any further requests for the same page are processed from the cache instead of from the Web server. This saves time and improves performance.

The Web application can cache frequently accessed data at the client side or at the server side. The cached information can be stored in any of the following locations:

◆ *Client.* You can have your application cache the frequently accessed data in temporary files on the client computer or on the hard disk. The subsequent request for the cached data is serviced directly from the memory or from the hard disk of the client. Most Web browsers perform client-side caching. However, the drawback of storing cached data on the client is that it cannot be shared among multiple users.

◆ *Dedicated server.* A proxy server, such as Microsoft Proxy Server, can be used for caching. Although most Web browsers take care of client-side caching, you need to specify a dedicated server to share the cached information among multiple users. A proxy server can act as an intermediary between the Internet and a user workstation. When there is a request from the client, the proxy server checks the cache for the requested page. If the page is available within the cache, it is sent to the client. If not, the proxy server redirects the request to the Internet.

◆ *Reverse proxy.* The proxy server solves the problem of sharing data among many users. However, having a single proxy server to handle client requests increases the load on it. To prevent this from happening, you need to balance the load on one proxy server. Consider this example: A proxy server named PS1 handles requests for a Web application. You can reduce the load on PS1 by placing another proxy server named PS2 ahead of PS1. All client requests for PS1 are routed through PS2. This is called reverse proxy.

ASP.NET provides three types of caching that can be used by Web applications:

◆ *Output caching.* This is used to cache a dynamic response to a client request. Output caching is enabled by default. For the response to be cached, however, it must have a valid expiration policy. For example, a Web page that is accessed from a database has to be re-created for each request. This increases the load on the network traffic and on the server. With output caching enabled, however, the page needs to be retrieved only after its expiration date. You can set the expiration policy by using the directives at the page level. The directives use certain attributes to determine the behavior of the output cache. These directives include `duration`, `location`, and `VaryByParam`. Consider the following example:

```
<%@ OutputCache duration="60" VaryByParam="Name" %>
```

The `duration` attribute specifies the expiration time for a Web page. In the preceding code, the value of the `duration` attribute is specified as `60`, so the cached information is retained for 60 seconds. After the specified time, the cache expires, and any subsequent request is directed to the Web server.

The `location` attribute specifies the location of the cached information. This attribute can take the values `client`, `downstream`, `server`, `any`, and `none`. The value `client` indicates that the output cache is located on the client. The value `downstream` indicates that the output cache is located on the server (other than the origin server) where the request is processed. Specifying the value as `server` means that output cache is located on the Web server. The value `any` specifies that output cache could be located on either the client or the Web server. You can use the value `none` to indicate that output caching has not been enabled for the page.

The `VaryByParam` attribute specifies a list of strings separated by semicolons. These strings are used to vary the output cache. The strings represent the query strings sent with the client request. For example, in the preceding code, the data is cached based on the name of the user that's passed as a query string variable to the page URL.

◆ *Fragment caching.* There are times when you want to cache the entire page but only part of the page needs to be placed in memory. In such situations, you can use fragment caching. Fragment caching helps you cache specific portions of the page but not the entire page. For this purpose, you can identify data that is important and needs to be cached, or you can cache different regions of a page.

◆ *Data caching.* ASP.NET provides the cache mechanism to store frequently accessed data in memory. This is done using memory variables on the server side. ASP.NET provides a cache engine that can be used by the pages to store and retrieve data across the client requests. This cache is specific to a page, and the life of the cache is equivalent to the life of the page. This means that once the page is restarted, the cache is re-created. Programmers can easily use the cache to store and retrieve the stored data.

Visual Studio.NET provides the `Cache` class to implement the cache for a Web application. This class is included in the `System.Web.Caching` namespace. This class stores all the cached items and also provides properties, such as `Count` and `Item`, that you can use to access the cached items. This class also provides methods to add and remove items from the cache.

You can also use ASP.NET cache to maintain a page's data based on the changes made to the page during its lifetime. For this purpose, ASP.NET supports three types of dependencies that enable you to validate specific data within the cache depending on the changes made to the page. You can also use these dependencies to invalidate specific data.

The three types of dependencies are as follows:

◆ File-based dependency
◆ Key-based dependency
◆ Time-based dependency

File-based dependency is used to invalidate a specific item in the cache based on the changes made to a file on the disk. In *key-based dependency*, the cache item is invalidated based on another cache item. This dependency is useful in situations in which one set of data depends on another. For example, the commission of a salesperson depends on the sales made. *Time-based dependency* terminates the cache data at a specific time. There are two options on which you can base a time-based dependency. The first option is called *absolute expiration*. This option represents the time when the cache item is removed. The second option is called *sliding*. Using this option, you can reset the cache expiration time with each request.

In the preceding section, you were introduced to the concept of caching. Caching is important to improve the performance of your Web pages. In the following section, you will be introduced to another important concept—application security. The security of data on the Internet is the most important concern of both Web developers and users. Adequate authentication is an essential ingredient for the success of a Web application.

ASP.NET Application Security Mechanisms

Applications on the Internet need to be secure for users to access and use the information on them. The security aspect of Web development requires maximum attention from a Web developer. The security of an application ensures not only that it is protected from hackers but also that the information accessible to users is restricted.

As you are aware, an ASP.NET application is deployed on the Internet Information Server (IIS). Therefore, the security mechanisms available on the IIS are also applicable to the ASP.NET Web application. In addition, ASP.NET provides its own security mechanism that helps you further secure your Web application.

Let's take a look at the security mechanisms available with IIS. The IIS Server 5.0 provides four built-in types of security mechanisms, as follows:

◆ *Anonymous authentication.* This is the default authentication mechanism used by IIS. In this authentication, the user does not provide a username or a password. In fact, the user is authenticated using a default logon name and password.

◆ *Basic authentication.* In this authentication mechanism, a user is required to specify a logon name and password. This mechanism is not very safe, however, because the user's details are sent over the Internet in an unencrypted form.

◆ *Digest authentication.* Digest authentication is similar to basic authentication. The only difference is that digest authentication sends the user's details over the Internet in an encrypted form. Therefore, it is more secure than basic authentication.

◆ *Integrated Windows authentication.* This authentication requires the user to have a valid account with the Windows 2000 domain. The integrated Windows authentication mechanism is useful when the number of users accessing the application is relatively low.

In addition to the security measures provided by IIS, three other security mechanisms are provided by ASP.NET: Forms authentication, passport authentication, and Windows authentication. Your choice of the ASP.NET authentication depends on the IIS authentication used. If you have chosen to use any other IIS authentication mechanism other than anonymous, you will most likely use the

Windows authentication provided by ASP.NET. Otherwise, you can use either forms or passport authentication.

Here is some more information about ASP.NET authentication mechanisms:

◆ *Forms authentication.* In this scheme of authentication, a simple HTML form on the client side is used to collect user credentials. The HTML form submits the user credentials to the application for authentication. If the user is authenticated, the application issues a cookie to the user. Forms authentication is also called *cookie-based authentication*. If the requested resource does not contain the cookie, the application redirects the user to the logon page. The user credentials are stored by the application in many ways, such as in a SQL database. The advantage of this authentication mechanism is that it can be used for both authentication and personalization. In addition, forms authentication does not require the corresponding Windows account. However, it is possible to replay the request during the lifetime of the cookie unless authentication such as Secure Socket Layer is used.

To implement the forms authentication, you need to create your own logon page and redirect URL for users who are not authorized. In addition, you must create your own scheme for account authentication.

◆ *Passport authentication.* This is a centralized authentication service provided by Microsoft. Passport authentication offers a single logon and profile services for member sites. You can subscribe to this site by signing a contract with Microsoft through its Web site **www.microsoft.com/myservices**. When you use passport authentication, you spend less on hardware infrastructure and require fewer people to run your Web application. In addition, you can cater to a larger audience using passport authentication. The steps that take place in passport authentication are as follows:

1. A user requests a protected resource. The request does not contain the passport ticket, so the server returns the user to the Passport Logon Service along with the encrypted parameters about the request.

2. The user then issues the request to the logon server with the supplied query string.

3. The Passport logon server then presents the user with the logon form. The user completes the form and sends it back to the server.

4. The server then redirects the user to the required request, along with the authentication ticket encrypted within the request.

The main advantage of passport authentication is that it requires single sign-in across multiple domains. In addition, it is compatible with all browsers. However, passport authentication depends on external sources for the authentication process.

To use passport authentication, you must download the Passport development kit (SDK) and use the documentation provided to implement passport authentication.

♦ *Windows authentication.* Windows authentication depends on the IIS to provide authenticated users. After a user is authenticated by the IIS using any of its authentication mechanisms, it passes a security token to ASP.NET. This token is used by ASP.NET to authenticate the user. One advantage of Windows authentication is that you need not write any custom authentication code. However, this means that you need to manage individual Windows user accounts. To implement Windows authentication, you must change the Web application's configuration file.

Summary

In this chapter, you learned about different concepts of ASP.NET and about configuring ASP.NET applications. By configuring applications, you can define the behavior of the application. You learned about improving the performance of your Web application. You learned that by caching recently requested information, you can improve the response time of the application for users. At the end of the chapter, you learned about different security mechanisms that can be applied to ASP.NET applications. The security mechanisms include anonymous, basic, digest, and integrated Windows authentication. You also learned about ASP.NET security mechanisms such as forms authentication, passport authentication, and Windows authentication.

Chapter 25

The Internet (or the Web, as it is commonly called) has evolved tremendously and has revolutionized the way business happens these days. Almost everyone has used the Internet at least once in one way or another. In other words, the Internet has become an integral part of our lives, and it is commonly used in both households and business offices. The ever-changing business scenario has become more and more dependent on the Web for any data transactions or for communication between applications. As a result, the focus of software development is shifting from desktop applications to applications that can access data through the Internet. These applications are mainly *distributed applications*—scalable applications in which data is shared across applications.

Take the case of a distributed application, which consists of a client application that interacts with a middleware application that contains the business logic for the entire business solution that you've created. This intermediate application in turn interacts with the underlying databases that store the data for the application. Therefore, as you can see, a business solution on the whole comprises a number of applications and databases. These applications and databases may be present on a single computer, but in large-scale business operations, they generally are distributed across different computers connected over a network. In such cases, these applications may be created by using different programming languages and, in the worst scenario, on different platforms. However, to build a complete business solution, it is essential that you integrate these applications. This integration is made simpler with the use of Web services.

In this chapter, you first will be introduced to the basics of Web services. Then you'll learn about the architecture and working of a Web service. This chapter also introduces the technologies used in a Web service, such as eXtensible Markup Language (XML), Simple Object Access Protocol (SOAP), Web Services Description Language (WSDL), and Universal Description Discovery and Integration (UDDI). Finally, you will learn to create a simple Web service in Visual Studio.NET.

Introduction to Web Services

As previously discussed, a Web service is used to integrate different applications that access data through the Internet. To do this, methods in a Web service are called over the Internet, and can then be accessed by applications developed on different platforms. In other words, a Web service is a reusable component (such as a method) that can be used by any Web application running on the Internet. In addition, a Web service can be used by a Windows application. These applications are called *Web service client applications.*

Before .NET came into the picture for developing Web services, DLL files or components were used to create distributed applications. To communicate with a client application, however, these components use protocols such as the Remote Procedure Call (RPC), Distributed Component Object Model (DCOM), Remote Method Invocation (RMI), or Internet Inter-ORB Protocol (IIOP). Therefore, communication between a client application and a component depends on various factors such as hardware platform, programming languages, vendor implementations, and data-encryption schemes. This means that transferring data between two applications requires a similar infrastructure at the two application sites. However, this scenario cannot be obtained while working with Internet applications. An Internet application can be accessed by various client applications. Therefore, it is essential to build components that can be used to create distributed applications that can be accessed from various platforms. To do this, you can use Web services. Web services enable you to create platform-independent distributed applications. The capability is mainly due to the support of a Web service for Internet standards such as HTTP and XML. (For more information on XML, see Chapter 30, "Getting Started with XML.")

In addition to integrating applications built on different platforms, a Web service enables you to integrate business solutions for one or more organizations. This means you can create a Web service specific to your organization, or you can customize a Web service created by another organization to your specific requirements. You can also create a Web service that can be used by a single application or that can be called on the Internet to be used by multiple applications. To call a Web service from the Internet, the Web service client needs to know the location of the Web service as well as the input and output information required for accessing the Web service.

A Web service that you create can be a simple one-method service. For example, consider a situation in which you want to know the current time in a particular state. You can create a method in a Web service that returns the current time in the state you choose. You can pass the state for which you want to know the current time as a parameter to the method. A method created in a Web service is called a *Web method*. You will learn about Web methods in detail later in this chapter.

In addition to performing simple tasks by using a Web service method, you can create Web methods that perform complex tasks. In such cases, a Web service may consist of several Web methods performing complex tasks. For example, consider a situation in which you need to validate the username and password entered by a user to log on to a site. This is a very common scenario because almost all Web sites require a method to validate the username and password. Therefore, in such a case, you can create a Web service that performs data validations. In addition, the Web service you create can be used to validate data for various Web sites. You can then customize the Web service according the requirements based on your database schema. In this case, the Web site that uses the Web service to perform data validations is called a Web service client application, and the application that hosts the Web service is called a *Web service provider application*.

The data validation scenario discussed involves various applications and an underlying database. For example, the Web site that needs to perform data validation is a Web application that interacts with a database. The database can be created using SQL, Access, Oracle, or any other relational database management system (RDBMS). In addition, for the Web application to perform validations based on the data in the database, the Web application uses another application. In this case, the other application required to perform validations is a Web service. Therefore, as you can see, multiple applications are involved in a complete business solution. To integrate these applications, a Web service can be used. Let's now see how a Web service can provide integration of multiple applications.

A Web service uses XML and any other Internet standard (such as HTTP) to create an infrastructure that helps you integrate applications built on multiple platforms. Due to the support of Web services for XML, these Web services are often referred to as *XML Web services*.

An XML Web service uses Simple Object Access Protocol (SOAP) messaging to communicate and transfer data across applications. SOAP messaging allows a great deal of abstraction between a Web service client and a Web service provider.

This means that using the XML messaging technique enables you to create a client and a service provider independent of each other.

By now, you must have an idea of the need for a Web service. Let's now discuss the architecture of a Web service.

Web Services Architecture

As previously mentioned, a Web service can be an intermediate application that allows a Web service client application to access data from an underlying database. To do this, the Web service architecture internally consists of four layers, as follows:

◆ *The data layer.* The data layer is the first layer in the Web service architecture. This layer contains the data that the Web client application needs to access.

◆ *The data access layer.* The layer above the data layer is the data access layer. This layer contains the business logic or code that allows the Web client application to access the data in the data layer. In addition to storing data, the data access layer is used to secure the data present in the data layer.

◆ *The business layer.* The third layer in the Web service architecture is the business layer. This layer contains the code required for implementing the Web service. The business layer, in turn, is divided into the business logic and business façade layers. The business logic layer contains all the services provided in a Web service, but the business façade layer acts as an interface of the Web service.

◆ *The listener layer.* As the name suggests, the listener layer receives the requests sent by users for a Web service. In addition to receiving the message, the listener layer also parses the received messages and dispatches the request to the appropriate method in the business facade layer.

The Web service architecture is explained in Figure 25-1.

The next section looks at how the Web service works based on the Web service architecture.

The Web Service Architecture

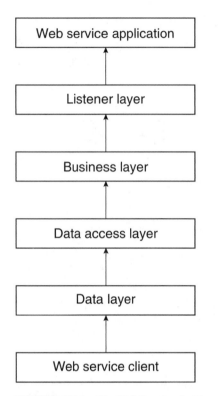

FIGURE 25-1 *The Web Service Architecture*

How Web Services Work

Let's understand how a Web service works. First, the client application sends a request for a service. The request is made to the Web service in the form of an XML message using a transfer protocol such as HTTP. This scenario is somewhat similar to a method call statement that you use to call a particular method. The request for the service is passed to the listener layer, which forwards the request to the Web service provider application. The request is then processed by the Web service provider application. Processing the request includes the data access layer retrieving the data requested by the client application. This data is then passed to the listener layer, which forwards it to the client application. Figure 25-2 shows the working of a Web service.

Take a look at the working of a Web service in detail. When a client application sends a request for a service, you may need to pass arguments. To pass arguments

The Working of a Web Service

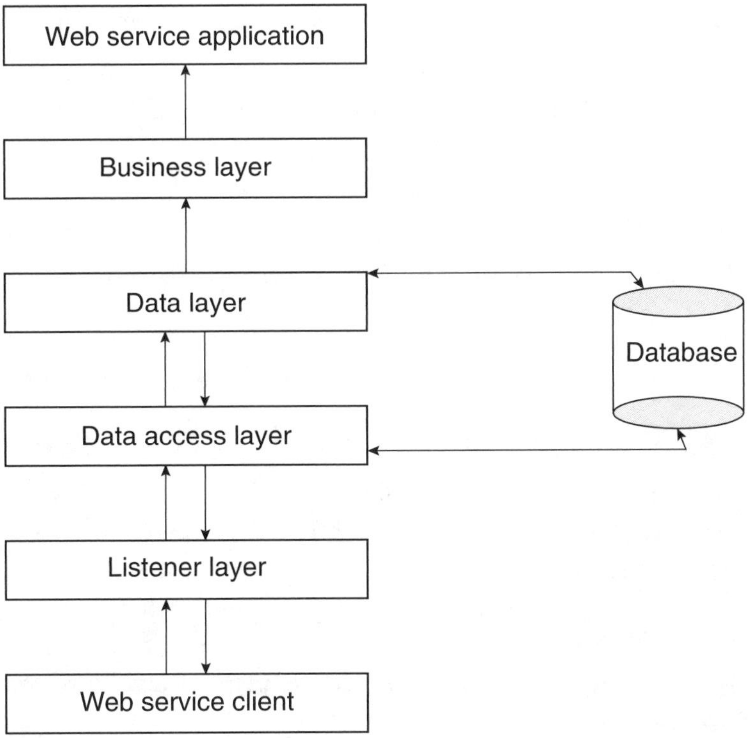

FIGURE 25-2 *The working of a Web service*

over the network, the arguments are packaged as a SOAP message and are passed to the Web method by using a network protocol. You will learn about SOAP in detail later in this chapter.

Then the Web service decodes the SOAP message to retrieve the arguments passed to the Web method. Once the arguments are passed to the Web method, the method is executed, and the return value is passed to the Web client application.

The following steps explain how a request for a Web service from a user is received and processed:

1. The client application sends a request for a Web service.

2. The listener layer receives the request.

3. The listener layer, after receiving the message, calls for the business facade layer.

4. The business facade layer sends the request to the data access layer.

5. The data access layer applies the business logic.

6. After applying the business logic, the data access layer sends the message back to the business facade layer.

7. The business facade layer sends the message to the listener layer.

8. The listener layer sends the data to the Web services client. Having learned about the working of a Web service, let's now look at the technologies used by a Web service.

Technologies Used in Web Services

You can create Web services using any language provided by the .NET framework, such as Visual C#.NET, Visual Basic.NET, and Visual C++.NET. For an application to be able to access a Web service, however, the client application needs to meet certain requirements. These requirements include a standard format for describing Web services, a standard format for representing data transfer, and a standard for sending methods (and the results returned by the methods) across the network. In addition, to be able to access a Web service, the Web client application needs to identify a method for locating the Web service and passing inputs to the Web methods.

As a solution to these requirements, technologies such as XML, WSDL, and SOAP have been developed. These technologies are discussed in the following sections.

XML in a Web Service

XML is a markup language used to describe data in a particular format. This data can be accessed by any application built on any platform. XML enables you to transfer data in a format that is independent of the platform. Therefore, XML is a widely-used technology that transfers data across Internet applications. XML documents store data in the form of text. This makes the XML document easily understood by applications built on different platforms. Moreover, content stored in an XML document is easily transferred over the network.

Now that you've had an overview of XML in general, let's see how a Web service uses XML. When a Web service client application calls a Web service, the client application passes arguments to the Web method. The Web service processes the Web methods and returns a result to the client application. Since the client application can be built using any platform, the data returned by the Web service is in the form of XML.

WSDL in a Web Service

The Web Services Description Language (WSDL) is a markup language that defines a Web service. WSDL is an XML file that contains information about a Web service. This information includes the Web services called by a Web site, the methods included in each of the Web services, and the parameters you need to pass to the Web methods. In addition, WSDL includes information about the results returned when a request is processed by a Web service. For example, WSDL defines the type of values returned by a Web method. Therefore, WSDL is a vocabulary defined for the creation of a Web service that the developer may need to use when creating a Web service.

In addition to storing information about the Web methods, WSDL stores information about the format used by a user to access a Web service and specifies the location at which the Web service is available. Therefore, WSDL describes the entire mechanism involved in the transfer of data from a Web service client to the Web service and vice versa.

For example, a Web service client application needs to call a Web method that validates the username and password entered by the user. The Web method is created in a Web service. To call this Web method, the Web service client sends a request to the Web service. The request sent to the Web method is specified by WSDL. The request sent to the Web service is in the form of XML messages. In this case, WSDL stores the format in which the request is sent.

In addition, when a Web method is called, you need to pass the username and password as parameters. The information about the type and format of the parameters is stored in a WSDL file. When the request is processed and the result is returned, WSDL stores the format and other information about the results returned.

SOAP in a Web Service

To transfer data from a Web service client to a Web service and vice versa, the SOAP transfer protocol is used. SOAP is a protocol based on XML that is used by a client application to access a Web service. In addition to XML, SOAP uses HTTP for the transfer of data. When a client sends a request, the request is in the form of a SOAP message. The SOAP message also includes the parameters and the method call statement. Based on the information in the SOAP message, the appropriate Web method is called.

As previously discussed, SOAP is a standard protocol used for communication between a Web service client and a Web service. However, SOAP does not define syntax to be followed when transferring data. Instead, SOAP provides a mechanism for packaging data to be transferred across a network. In addition, SOAP is a transfer protocol based on simple Internet standards. The transfer of data using SOAP takes place in the form of a SOAP package. A SOAP package includes an envelope that encapsulates the data to be exchanged.

In addition to these technologies, Web services use Universal Description Discovery and Integration (UDDI) to identify the Web services provided by various Web service providers. The following section discusses UDDI in detail.

UDDI in a Web Service

When you develop a Web service, you need to register the Web service in a UDDI directory. This implies that UDDI provides a mechanism for Web service providers to register their Web services. When a Web service is registered with a UDDI directory, an entry for the Web service is created. A UDDI directory maintains an XML file for each Web service registered with the UDDI directory. This XML file contains a pointer to the Web service registered in the directory. In addition, the UDDI directory also contains pointers to the WSDL document for a Web service. To do this, the Web service provider first needs to describe the Web service in a WSDL document. After a WSDL document is created, the Web service can be registered with the UDDI directory. This makes the Web service easily accessible to the Web service clients because the client applications can discover and identify a Web service from a UDDI directory.

Consider the earlier example of the Web service used to perform user validation. Once you have created the Web service and described it in a WSDL document, you can register the Web service with the UDDI directory. Then any user that wants to use the Web method can search on the UDDI directory for the required method. The UDDI directory returns the list of Web services registered with the UDDI directory. The user can then select the required Web method from the list of available Web services.

A UDDI directory contains white pages, yellow pages, and green pages. The white pages contain information about the organization that provides the Web service. This information includes the name, address, and other contact numbers of the Web service provider company. The yellow pages in a UDDI directory contain information about the companies based on geographical taxonomies. The green pages provide the service interface for the client applications that access the Web service.

The following section discusses how Web services fit into the .NET framework.

Web Services in the .NET Framework

The .NET framework provides a complete framework for developing Web services. This means that in the .NET framework, you can not only create Web services but also deploy, use, and maintain them. The .NET framework provides tools and technologies you can use to develop a Web service. The next section discuses how to create a Web service in Visual Studio.NET.

Similar to creating a Windows application and a Web application, Visual Studio.NET provides you with a template to create a Web service. The template for creating a Web service is provided in the New Project dialog box. To access the Web service template, perform the following steps:

1. Create a new project using the File, New option. In the displayed list, select the Project option. The New Project dialog box displays.
2. In the right pane of the New Project dialog box, select the ASP.NET Web Service project template option. In the Location text box, type the address of the Web server on which you will develop the Web service.

In this case, the development server is the local computer. You can also specify the name of the Web service, SampleWebService, in the Location text box.

> **TIP**
>
> The Web server you specify as the development server must have the .NET frame-work and IIS 5.0 or later installed on it. If you have IIS 5.0 installed on your local com-puter, you can specify the path in the Location text box of the local computer.

A Web service with the name MyWebService is created. MyWebService contains the files and references required for the Web service. A description of these files is given in Table 25-1.

Table 25-1 Files in a Web Service

File	Description
AssemblyInfo.cs	Contains the metadata of the assembly for the project.
Service1.asmx.cs	Contains the code for the class declared in the Web service.
Service1.asmx	Is the entry point of the Web service and contains information about the processing directive of the Web service. The processing directive identifies the class in which the code for the Web service is implemented.
Global.asax.cs	Contains the code for handling the events generated in the application.
Global.asax	Contains information about handling the events generated in the application.
Web.config	Contains information about the configuration settings of ASP.NET resources.
SampleWebService.csproj.webinfo	Contains information about the location of the project on the development server.
SampleWebService.vsdisco	Contains the description of the Web service that is required by the client application to access the Web service. The file contains descriptions of the methods and interfaces used in the Web service to enable program-mers to communicate with these resources.

File	Description
SampleWebService.sln	Contains the metadata of the solution. If your local server is your development server, the MyWebService.sln file exists on the local server.
SampleWebService.csproj	Contains information about the list of files related to a project.

When you create a Web service, the Component Designer view for Service1.asmx is displayed. The Service1.asmx.cs file contains the code for the Web service. You will learn about the default code generated by Visual Studio.NET later in this chapter.

In the .NET framework, you can create complex Web services that an application can use to access data over the Internet. You will learn about creating complex Web services later in this project. In this chapter, however, let's create a simple Web service that will help you have a better understanding of how to create a Web service.

Creating a Simple Web Service in the .NET Framework

This section will show you how to create a simple Web service in the .NET framework. This Web service will contain a default HelloWorld Web method.

The following tasks will be involved when creating the Web service:

- ◆ Create a blank Web service project.
- ◆ Create the appropriate Web methods in the Web service.
- ◆ Compile and test the Web service.

Let's name this Web service as MyFirstWebService. You can create a Web service by using the ASP.NET Web Service template in the New Project dialog box. In the Location text box of the New Project dialog box, specify the name of the Web service as MyFirstWebService.

When you click on the OK button in the New Project dialog box, Visual Studio.NET creates a virtual directory with the name of your Web service. If a Web service with the specified name already exists, Visual Studio.NET prompts you to specify another name for your Web service. Figure 25-3 shows the screen that appears when you create a Web service.

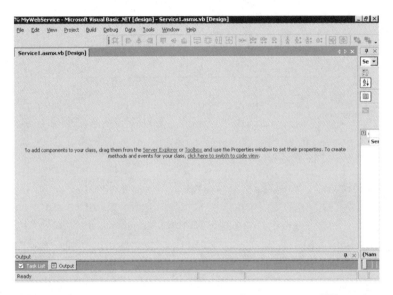

FIGURE 25-3 *The first screen that appears when you create a Web service*

Note that the Web service does not have any user interface or a form. The default file displayed when Visual Studio.NET creates a Web service is Service1.asmx. Table 25-1 already explained the default files generated by Visual Studio.NET.

After creating the Web service, you need to add the Web methods to the Web service. The code behind the Web service is written in the Service1.asmx.vb file. To access the Service1.asmx.vb file, press the F7 key or double-click the Service1.asmx file.

As you can see in the Service1.asmx.vb file, Visual Studio.NET generates a default code for your Web service. Figure 25-4 displays the screen you will see upon clicking the link for the Code view in the Design view of the Service1.asmx.vb file.

Note that you get a default Web method named HelloWorld that you can use. Make the following changes to the code:

```
<WebService(Namespace:="http://localhost/MyFirstService")> _
Public Class Service1
```

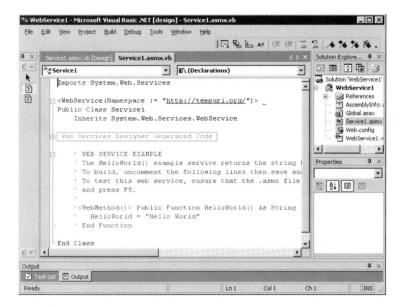

FIGURE 25-4 *The default code for a Web service*

```
    Inherits System.Web.Services.WebService
<WebMethod(Description:="Wow... This is my first Web service...")> Public Function
HelloWorld() As String
        HelloWorld = "Hello World"
End Function
```

> **NOTE**
>
> The Service1.asmx file uses two files named Service1.asmx.vb and
> Service1.asmx.resx. The Service1.asmx.vb file contains the Visual Basic.NET code,
> and the Service1.asmx.resx file contains resources related to the Web service. These
> files are not visible by default. To view these files, click the Show All Files button in
> the Solution Explorer. Now click the plus symbol next to the Service1.asmx file. The
> Service1.asmx.vb file appears as a child node. To view the Service1.asmx.res file,
> click the plus symbol next to the Service1.asmx.vb file.

Now that your Web service is ready, let's test it to make sure it is running fine.

To test a Web service application, you do not need to explicitly create a client that uses the Web service. You can test the Web service and its methods by executing the Web service from Visual Studio.NET. Figure 25-5 depicts the Web page displayed when Web service is executed for testing.

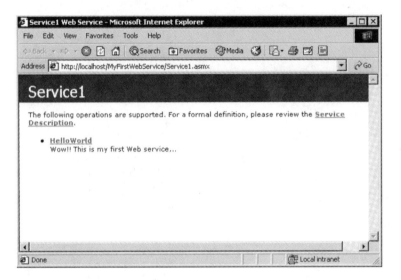

FIGURE 25-5 *The Web service interface in the browser*

This Web page lists all the methods provided by the Web service along with their descriptions. The Address bar in Internet Explorer shows the address of the location where your Web service has been deployed. To test the HelloWorld method, click HelloWorld. This form also displays the description of the HelloWorld method that you specified in the WebMethod attribute of the HelloWorld method. This Web page also displays the SOAP request and response snippets for the Web method.

Figure 25-6 depicts the Web page displayed when you click the HelloWorld Web method link.

This completes the process of creating a simple Web service.

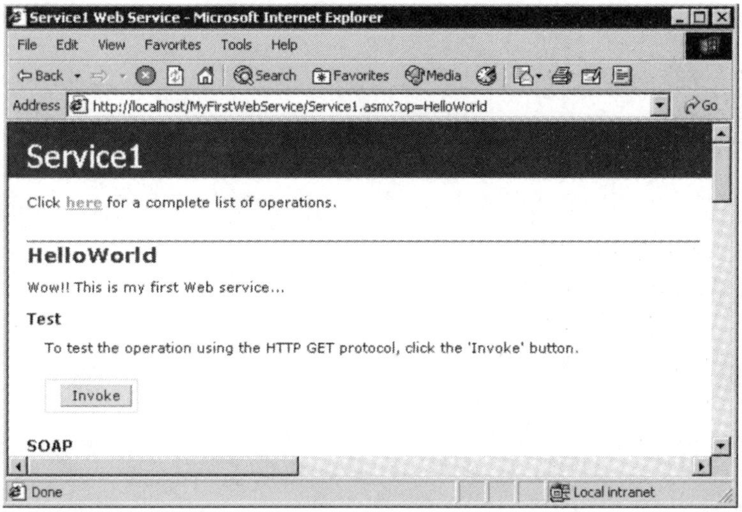

FIGURE 25-6 *The form displayed when you click the* HelloWorld *Web method link*

Summary

In this chapter, you learned about distributed applications, and the concept of Web services was introduced. Next you learned about the architecture of a Web service. Based on this architecture, you learned about the working of a Web service. You also learned about the role of XML, WSDL, SOAP, and UDDI in a Web service. Based on this knowledge, you learned to create a simple Web service using Visual Studio.NET.

Chapter 26

**Designing the
Customer
Interface**

In Chapter 22, "Project Case Study—Creating a Web Application for the MyMovies Video Kiosk," you learned about the video kiosk Web application. For the rest of this project, you will learn to create the video kiosk Web application. As discussed in Chapter 22, the video kiosk Web application is divided into two interfaces: the customer interface and the admin interface.

In this chapter, you will learn to design the customer interface of the video kiosk Web application. You will learn about the Web forms you need for this interface. In addition, you will learn about the controls for each form of the application and the properties you need to set.

Typically, an ASP.NET application contains one or more Web forms. A Web form is used to create programmable Web pages. Web forms enable you to create form-based Web pages.

As discussed in the Chapter 22, the customer interface of the video kiosk Web application consists of the following Web pages:

◆ The home page
◆ The Search page
◆ The Account Details page
◆ The Customer Registration page

The following sections describe each of these pages in detail. To start with, take a look at how to design the home page of the customer interface.

The Home Page

As the name suggests, the home page is the first Web page a customer will see. The home page is the central location from which customers can browse for movies, place orders for movies, and register themselves. Figure 26-1 shows the home page.

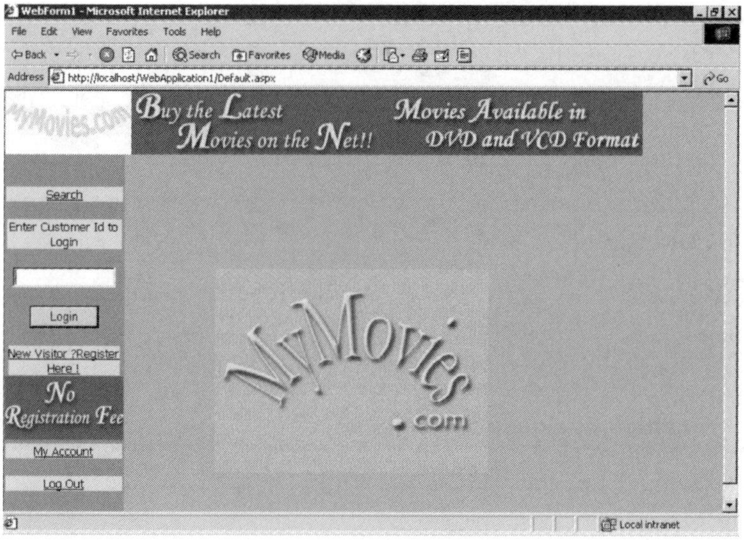

FIGURE 26-1 *The interface of the home page*

To create the home page, you need to add controls to the Web form. Before adding controls, you need to specify some properties for the Web form. The properties you need to assign to the home Web form are listed in Table 26-1.

Table 26-1 Properties of the Home Web Form

Form	Property	Value
Home form	pageLayout	GridLayout
Home form	bgColor	#dda0dd

As shown in Figure 26-1, the home Web form contains different Web controls for registered customers and new customers. If customers are registered users, they can log in using their assigned customer ID, view the details of their accounts, search the site, and ultimately log out. Only a registered customer is allowed to place orders. Customers can enter their customer identification numbers in the Cus-tomer ID text box and can click on the Login button to log in. After a registered customer has logged in, he or she can click on the Search hyperlink to display the Search page. The Search page enables a customer to search for movies. If a cus-tomer is not a registered user, the customer can click on either the New Visitor? Register Here! hyperlink or the Search hyperlink. If the customer clicks on the

New Visitor? Register Here! hyperlink, the Customer Registration page displays. A customer can use this page to register and obtain a customer identification number. Alternatively, a customer can click on the Search hyperlink to search for movies without registering. Therefore, the customer interface allows a customer to browse for movies regardless of whether the customer is a registered user or not. You will learn more about the Customer Registration and search Web forms later in this chapter.

Most of the Web controls on this page are contained in a panel to align them. Table 26-2 lists the properties of the panel.

Table 26-2 Properties Assigned to the Panel

Control	Property	Value
Panel 1	ID	Panel1
Panel 1	Height	385px
Panel 1	HorizontalAlign	Center
Panel 1	Width	132px
Panel 1	BackColor	MediumOrchid

The home Web form contains two labels. The first label displays the caption for the text box that takes the customer ID to log in, and the second label display a Welcome message when the customer has successfully logged in. Table 26-3 lists the properties of these labels.

Table 26-3 Properties Assigned to the Labels

Control	Property	Value
Label 1	ID	Label1
Label 1	Text	Enter Customer Id to Login
Label 1	BackColor	#FFCOFF
Label 1	Font	Tahoma, Smaller
Label 1	Width	126px
Label 2	ID	Label2

Control	Property	Value
Label 2	Text	Welcome to MyMovies.com . You are Logged in Now
Label 2	Font	Tahoma, Larger
Label 2	ForeColor	DarkViolet
Label 2	Visible	False

In addition to the labels, the Panel1 panel contains a text box and a button. The ID property of the text box is set to TxtCustomerID, and the Width property is set to 113px. The Text property of the button is set to Login, the ID property is set to CmdLogin, and the Width property is set to 76px.

The home Web form also displays four hyperlinks. The NavigateUrl property of each Hyperlink control contains the name of the page that should open when the hyperlink is clicked. Table 26-4 describes the properties for the hyperlinks on the home Web form.

Table 26-4 Properties Assigned to the Hyperlinks

Control	Property	Value
Hyperlink 1	ID	HyperLink1
Hyperlink 1	Text	Search
Hyperlink 1	BackColor	#FFC0FF
Hyperlink 1	Font	Tahoma, Smaller
Hyperlink 1	ForeColor	Black
Hyperlink 1	Width	128px
Hyperlink 1	NavigateUrl	search.aspx
Hyperlink 2	ID	HyperLink2
Hyperlink 2	Text	New Visitor ?Register Here !
Hyperlink 2	BackColor	#FFC0FF

continues

Table 26-4 *(continued)*

Control	Property	Value
Hyperlink 2	Font	Tahoma, Smaller
Hyperlink 2	ForeColor	Black
Hyperlink 2	Width	122px
Hyperlink 2	NavigateUrl	Registration.aspx
Hyperlink 3	ID	HyperLink3
Hyperlink 3	Text	MyAccount
Hyperlink 3	BackColor	#FFC0FF
Hyperlink 3	Font	Tahoma, Smaller
Hyperlink 3	ForeColor	Black
Hyperlink 3	Width	128px
Hyperlink 3	NavigateUrl	MyAccount.aspx
Hyperlink 4	ID	HyperLink4
Hyperlink 4	Text	Log Out
Hyperlink 4	BackColor	#FFC0FF
Hyperlink 4	Font	Tahoma, Smaller
Hyperlink 4	ForeColor	Black
Hyperlink 4	Width	128px
Hyperlink 4	NavigateUrl	#

The home Web form also contains three Image controls. The first Image control displays the caption for the home page, the second displays the banner, and the third displays another caption in the panel. Table 26-5 lists the properties of the Image controls.

Table 26-5 Properties Assigned to the Image Controls

Control	Property	Value
Image 1	ID	Image1
Image 1	ImageUrl	Center1.jpg

Control	Property	Value
Image 1	Height	221px
Image 1	Width	298px
Image 2	ID	Image2
Image 2	ImageUrl	Fee.jpg
Image 3	ID	Image3
Image 3	ImageUrl	Bar.jpg
Image 3	Height	69px
Image 3	Width	690px

Finally, the home page also contains two Validation controls. The first Validation control checks for a blank customer ID, and the second checks for an incorrect value for the customer ID. Table 26-6 lists the properties of Validation controls.

Table 26-6 Properties Assigned to the Validation Controls

Control	Property	Value
RequiredFieldValidator 1	ID	RequiredField Validator1
RequiredFieldValidator 1	Error message	Customer Id Cannot be blank
RequiredFieldValidator 1	Font	Tahoma,Larger
RequiredFieldValidator 1	ForeColor	DarkViolet
RequiredFieldValidator 1	ControlToValidate	TxtCustomerID
RequiredFieldValidator 1	Width	290px
CustomValidator 1	ID	CustomValidator1
CustomValidator 1	Error message	Customer Id Entered is Incorrect
CustomValidator 1	Font	Tahoma,Larger
CustomValidator 1	ForeColor	DarkViolet

continues

Table 26-6 (continued)

Control	Property	Value
CustomValidator 1	ControlToValidate	TxtCustomerID
CustomValidator 1	Width	323px

As the name suggests, customers can use the Log Out hyperlink to log out. When a customer enters a valid customer identification number in the Customer ID text box and clicks on the Login button, a welcome message displays. When a customer clicks on the Search hyperlink, the Search page displays. The Search page also displays when a new customer clicks on the Search hyperlink. The next section describes the Search page.

The Search Page

As the name suggests, the Search page of the customer interface enables customers to search for movies. Figure 26-2 shows the Search page.

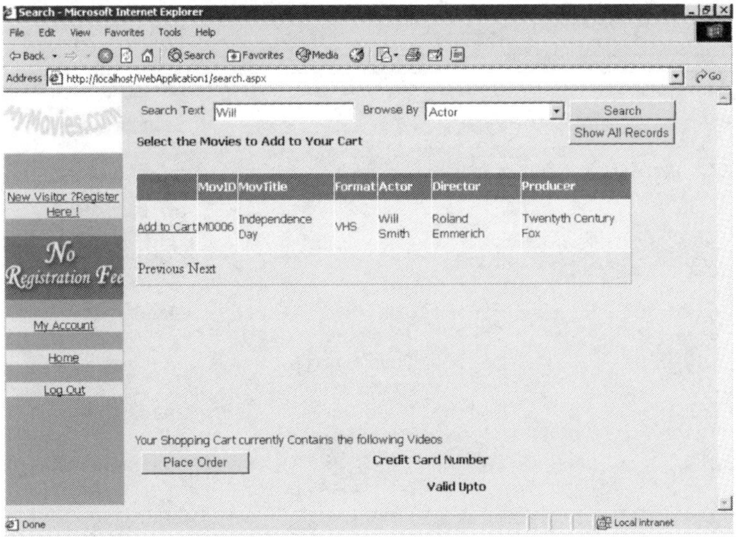

FIGURE 26-2 *The Search page*

To start with, take a look at the properties of the Search Web form. The page-Layout property of the Search Web form has been changed to GridLayout, and the bgColor property has been changed to #ffc0ff.

The Search page also consists of the panel created for the home page. The difference is that the `LblCustomerID` label and the `TxtCustomerID` are removed. Also, a few properties of the image in the banner have been changed, and a hyperlink that links to the home page has been added to the panel. Table 26-7 lists the properties of the image in the banner.

Table 26-7 Properties Assigned to the Image

Control	Property	Value
Image 1	ID	Image1
Image 1	ImageUrl	myMovie_Logo copy.jpg
Image 1	BackColor	DarkViolet
Image 1	Height	65px
Image 1	Width	130px

As shown in Figure 26-2, the Search Web form contains nine labels. Table 26-8 lists the properties of the labels.

Table 26-8 Properties Assigned to the Labels

Control	Property	Value
Label 1	ID	LblSearchText
Label 1	Text	Search Text:
Label 1	Font	Tahoma,Smaller
Label 2	ID	LblBrowseBy
Label 2	Text	Browse By:
Label 2	Font	Tahoma,Smaller
Label 3	ID	LblSelectMovies
Label 3	Text	Select the Movies to Add to Your Cart
Label 3	BackColor	#FFCOFF

continues

Table 26-8 *(continued)*

Control	Property	Value
Label 3	Font	Tahoma,Smaller
Label 3	Height	38px
Label 3	Width	461px
Label 4	ID	LblMsg
Label 4	Text	Your Shopping Cart currently Contains the following Videos
Label 4	BackColor	#FFCOFF
Label 4	Font	Tahoma,Smaller
Label 4	Width	340px
Label 5	ID	LblCCNum
Label 5	Text	Credit Card Number
Label 5	Font	Tahoma,Smaller
Label 5	Width	136px
Label 6	ID	LblCCNo
Label 6	Font	Tahoma,Smaller
Label 6	Width	124px
Label 7	ID	Label1
Label 7	Text	Valid Upto
Label 7	Font	Tahoma,Smaller
Label 7	Width	124px
Label 8	ID	LblValidUpto
Label 8	Font	Tahoma,Smaller
Label 8	Width	122px
Label 9	ID	Label2
Label 9	Font	Tahoma,Smaller

Control	Property	Value
Label 9	ForeColor	Red
Label 9	Visible	False
Label 9	Width	284px

The Search Web form also contains a text box and a combo box. Table 26-9 lists the properties of the text box and combo box.

Table 26-9 Properties Assigned to the Text Box and the Combo Box

Control	Property	Value
Text box	Name	txtSearch
Combo box	Name	lstSearch
Combo box	Width	155px

In addition to these properties, you need to specify the Items property for the combo box. When you select the Items property, an ellipsis button appears next to the (Collection) value, as shown in Figure 26-3. You need to click on the ellipsis button to add items to the Browse By combo box.

FIGURE 26-3 *The* Items *property of the combo box*

When you click on the ellipsis button, the ListItem Collection Editor dialog box displays (see Figure 26-4). You can add items to the combo box by using this dialog box.

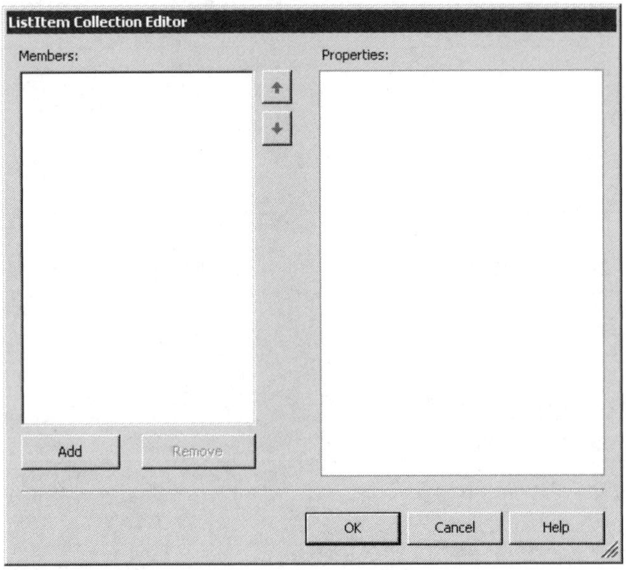

FIGURE 26-4 *The ListItem Collection Editor dialog box*

Using the ListItem Collection Editor dialog box, you can specify the items for the combo box. To add an item to the combo box, click on the Add button in the List-Item Collection Editor dialog box. When you click on the Add button, a ListItem object is added to the Members pane, as shown in Figure 26-5.

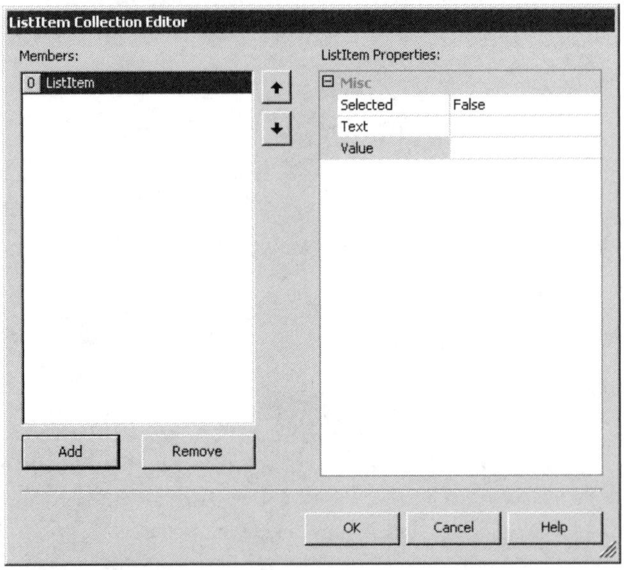

FIGURE 26-5 *A column added to the list view control*

Note that the properties for the selected item appear in the right pane in the List-Item Collection Editor dialog box. To edit the item name, you need to modify the Text property of the column header, as shown in Figure 26-6.

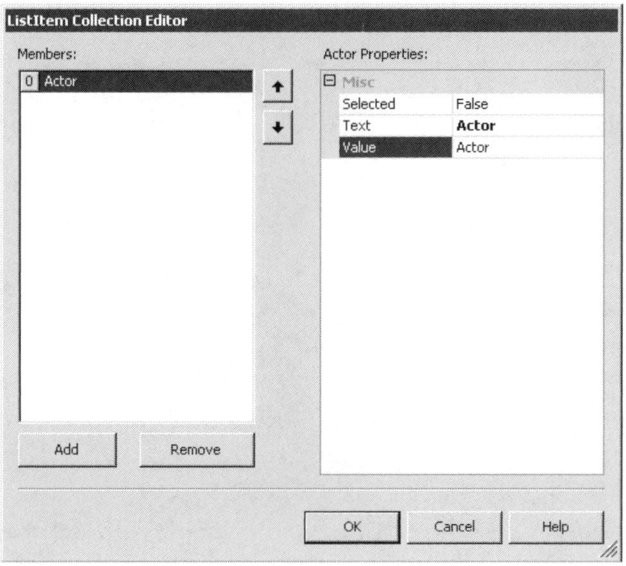

FIGURE 26-6 *Modify the* Text *property for the ListItem*

Now add the required number of columns and modify the Text property for each column. The properties you need to specify for the column headers are:

ListItem	Value of Text Property
ListItem 1	Actor
ListItem 2	Director
ListItem 3	Movie
ListItem 4	Producer

Figure 26-7 shows the ListItem Collection Editor dialog box with all the columns.

After you add the items to the combo box, you need to click on the OK button in the ListItem Collection Editor dialog box.

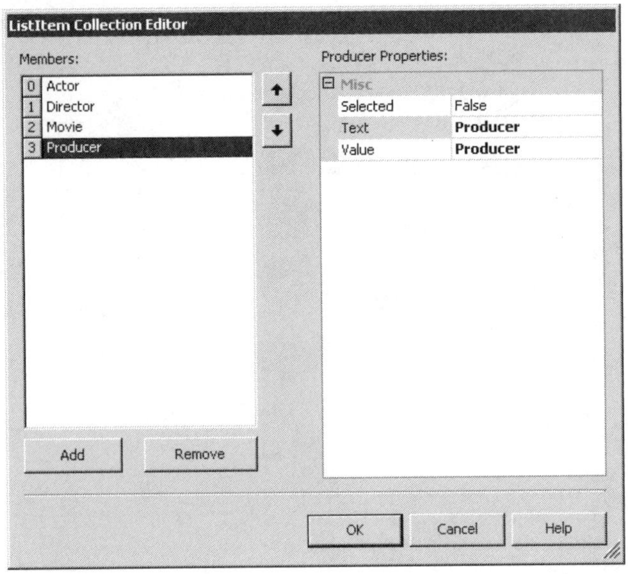

FIGURE 26-7 *The ListItem Collection Editor dialog box with all the items*

In addition to the combo box and the text box, the Search Web form also contains two DataGrid controls. Table 26-10 lists the properties assigned to the DataGrid controls on the Search Web form.

Table 26-10 Properties Assigned to the DataGrid Controls

Control	Property	Value
DataGrid 1	ID	DataGrid1
DataGrid 1	Height	122px
DataGrid 1	Width	542px
DataGrid 1	Height	122px
DataGrid 1	AllowPaging	True
DataGrid 1	BackColor	#FFCCFF (Under AlternatingItemStyle)
DataGrid 1	Wrap	False (Under AlternatingItemStyle)
DataGrid 1	Wrap	False (Under EditItemStyle)

Control	Property	Value
DataGrid 1	Wrap	False (Under `EditItemStyle`)
DataGrid 1	BackColor	Lavender (Under `ItemStyle`)
DataGrid 1	Font	Tahoma,Smaller (Under `ItemStyle`)
DataGrid 1	ForeColor	Black (Under `ItemStyle`)
DataGrid 1	HorizontalAlign	Left (Under `ItemStyle`)
DataGrid 1	Wrap	False (Under `ItemStyle`)
DataGrid 1	NextPageText	Next (Under `PagerStyle`)
DataGrid 1	PrevPageText	Previous (Under `PagerStyle`)
DataGrid 1	BackColor	#990033 (Under `SelectedItemStyle`)
DataGrid 1	ForeColor	White (Under `SelectedItemStyle`)
DataGrid 1	Wrap	False (Under `SelectedItemStyle`)
DataGrid 2	ID	DataGrid3
DataGrid 2	AutoGenerateColumns	False
DataGrid 2	Width	541px
DataGrid 2	Height	61px
DataGrid 2	PageSize	5
DataGrid 2	Font	Tahoma,Smaller (Under `AlternatingItemStyle`)

continues

Table 26-10 *(continued)*

Control	Property	Value
DataGrid 2	Wrap	False (Under AlternatingItemStyle)
DataGrid 2	BackColor	DarkViolet (Under HeaderStyle)
DataGrid 2	Font	Tahoma, Smaller (Under HeaderStyle)
DataGrid 2	ForeColor	White (Under HeaderStyle)
DataGrid 2	BackColor	Lavender (Under ItemStyle)
DataGrid 2	Font	Tahoma, Smaller (Under ItemStyle)
DataGrid 2	HorizontalAlign	Left (Under ItemStyle)
DataGrid 2	Wrap	False (Under ItemStyle)
DataGrid 2	NextPageText	Next (Under PagerStyle)
DataGrid 2	PrevPageText	Previous (Under PagerStyle)
DataGrid 2	BackColor	#990033 (Under SelectedItemStyle)

In addition to the properties in Table 26-10, you also need to specify the Columns property of the DataGrid control that shows the search results. When you select the Columns property, an ellipsis button appears next to the (Collection) value, as shown in Figure 26-8. You need to click on the ellipsis button to add column headers to DataGrid1.

When you click on the ellipsis button, the DataGrid Properties dialog box displays (see Figure 26-9). You can add columns to the DataGrid control by using this dialog box.

FIGURE 26-8 *The* Columns *property of the DataGrid control*

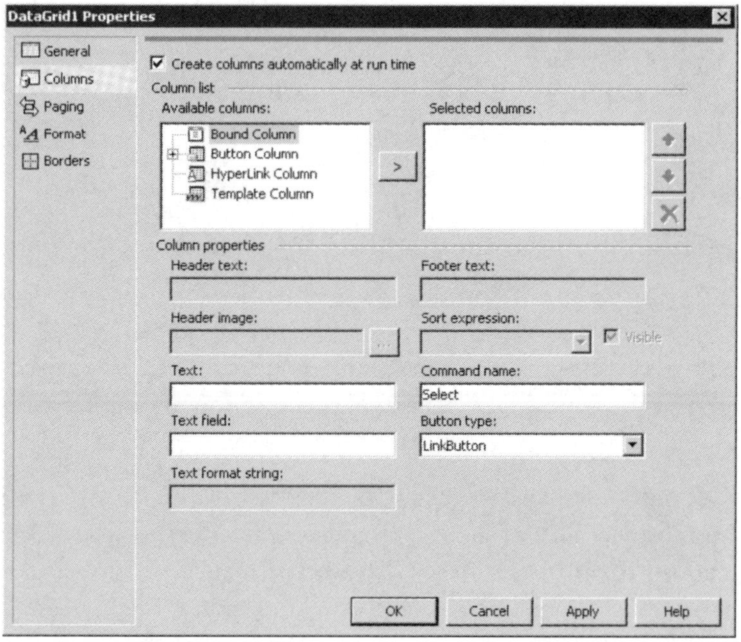

FIGURE 26-9 *The DataGrid Properties dialog box*

Using the DataGrid Properties dialog box, you can specify the items for the combo box. To add a column to the DataGrid control, click on the Add button in the DataGrid Properties dialog box. To add a column that contains a hyperlink, select Hyperlink Column in the Available columns pane and click on the Add button. A Hyperlink Column entry is added to the Selected columns pane, as shown in Figure 26-10.

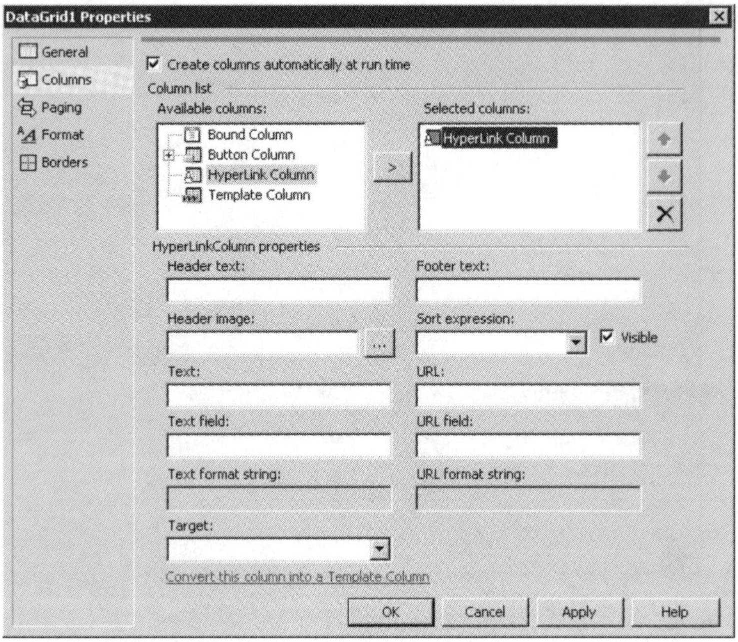

FIGURE 26-10 *A column added to the DataGrid control*

Note that the properties for the selected column appear in the DataGrid Properties dialog box. To edit the column name, you need to modify the `Text` property of the column header, as shown in Figure 26-11.

Click on the OK button to close the dialog box. Similarly, you need to specify the column text and headers for `DataGrid3`, which contains the details of the shopping cart. To do so, select `DataGrid3` and open the DataGrid Properties dialog box. The first two columns you add should contain the `Edit` and `Delete` hyperlinks. Such a column can be added by using the Button Column node. To add a column that contains the `Edit` hyperlink, select Edit, Update, Cancel from the Button Column node in the Available columns pane and click on the Add button. A Button Column is added to the Selected columns pane, as shown in Figure 26-12.

Note that the properties for the selected column appear in the DataGrid Properties dialog box. Similarly, you need to add a Delete column to the Selected columns pane. After this you need to add a bound column to the grid. A bound column is used to add data columns from a data source. To add a bound column, select Bound Column from the Available columns pane and click on the Add but-

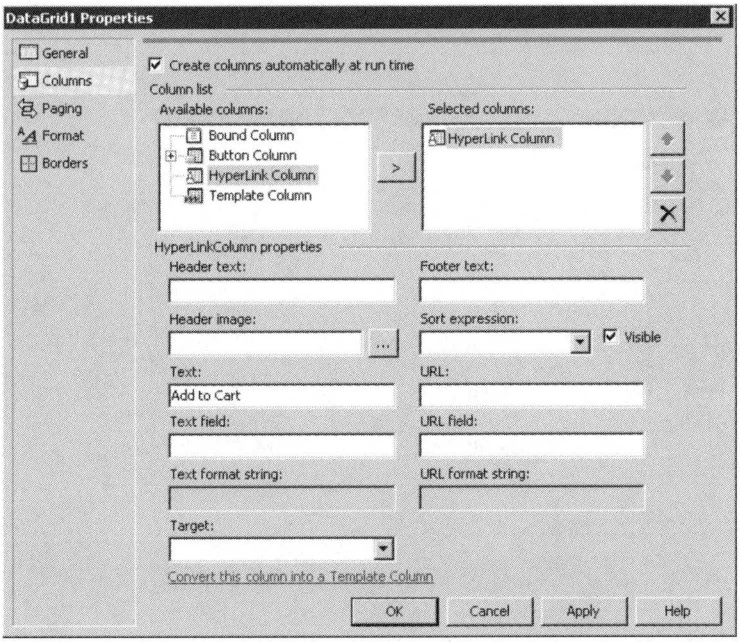

FIGURE 26-11 *Modifying the* Text *property for the Hyperlink Column*

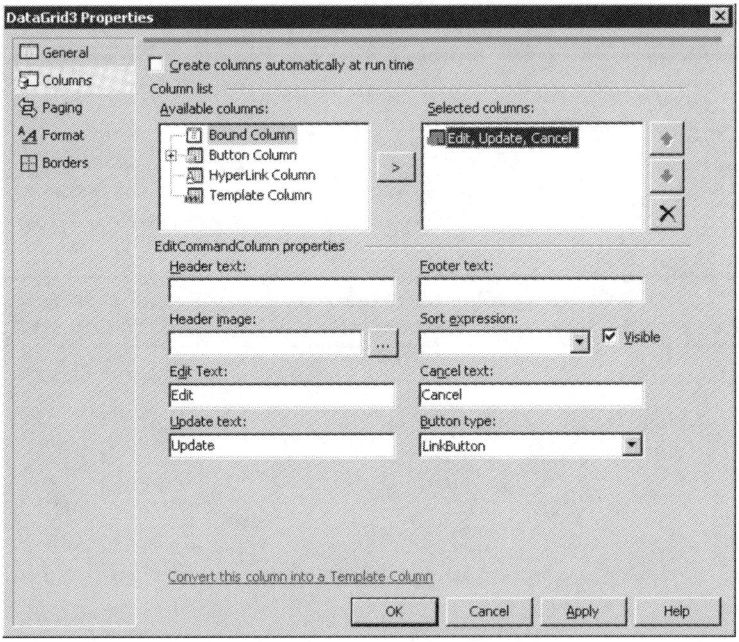

FIGURE 26-12 *Adding a column to the DataGrid control*

ton. To edit the column name, you need to modify the Header text and Data Field properties of the column, as shown in Figure 26-13.

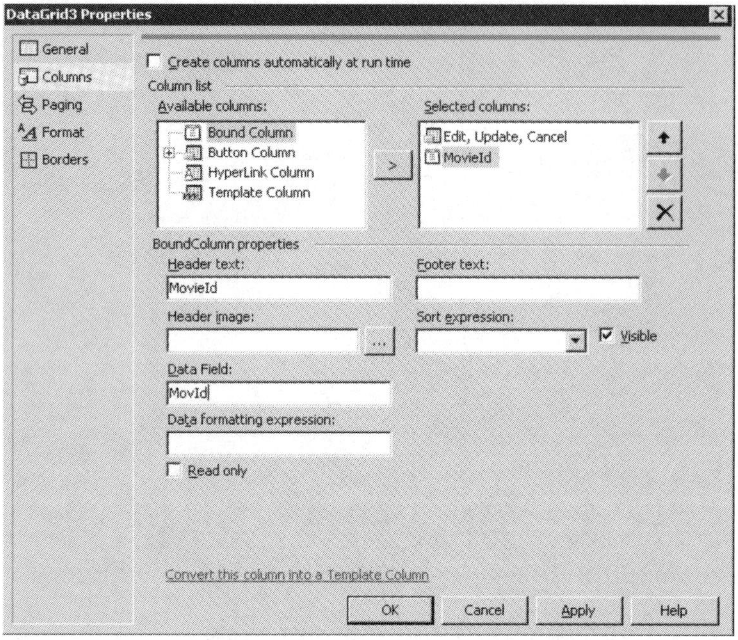

FIGURE 26-13 *Modifying the* Header text *and* Data Field *properties of the Bound Column*

Now add the required number of columns and modify the Header text and Data Field properties for each column. The following are the properties you need to specify for the columns:

Bound Column	Value of Header text Property	Value of Data Field Property
Bound Column 1	MovieId	MovId
Bound Column 2	Movie	Movie
Bound Column 3	VideoId	VideoId
Bound Column 4	Format	Format
Bound Column 5	Price	Price
Bound Column 6	Quantity	Quantity

Figure 26-14 shows the DataGrid Properties dialog box with all the columns.

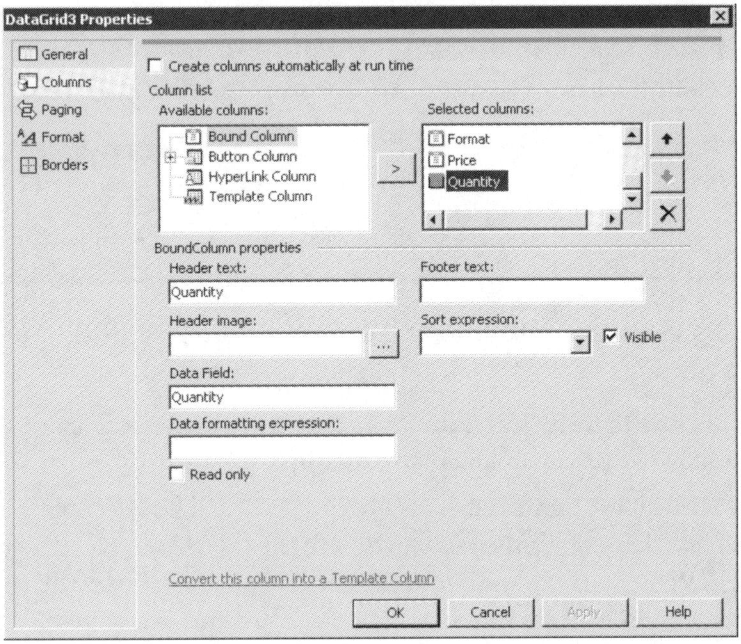

FIGURE 26-14 *The DataGrid Properties dialog box for* DataGrid3

After you add the items to the grid, you need to click on the OK button in the DataGrid Properties dialog box.

The Search Web form also contains three buttons. Table 26-11 lists the properties assigned to the buttons on the Search Web form.

Table 26-11 Properties Assigned to the Buttons

Control	Property	Value
Button 1	ID	CmdSearch
Button 1	Text	Search
Button 1	Height	22px
Button 1	Width	115px
Button 2	ID	CmdShowAllRecords

continues

Table 26-11 (continued)

Control	Property	Value
Button 2	Text	Show All Records
Button 2	Width	115px
Button 3	ID	CmdPlaceOrder
Button 3	Text	Place Order
Button 3	Width	119px

Customers can use the Search button to browse the movies database. To search for a movie, a customer needs to perform the following steps:

1. Type the text to be searched in the Search Text text box. This text could be the name of an actor, director, producer, or movie.

2. Select a category from the Browse By combo box. The selection in this combo box determines the table to be searched. For example, if a customer selects the Actor option in the Browse By combo box, the text that the customer types in the Search Text text box is searched in the Actor table in the database.

3. Click on the Search button.

When a customer clicks on the Search button, the results are displayed in the list view control. These results are based on the selection and the text entered in the text box. For example, if a customer enters Harrison in the text box, selects Actor from the Browse By combo box, and clicks on the Search button, the Search page appears as shown in Figure 26-15.

Alternatively, a customer can also display all movie records by clicking on the Show All Records button.

Only five records are displayed at a time as the search results. To view the next five records, a customer can click on the Next hyperlink. After the DataGrid control displays the search results, a customer can click on the Add to Cart hyperlink to add a video to his or her shopping cart. To search for a movie, a customer needs to perform the following steps:

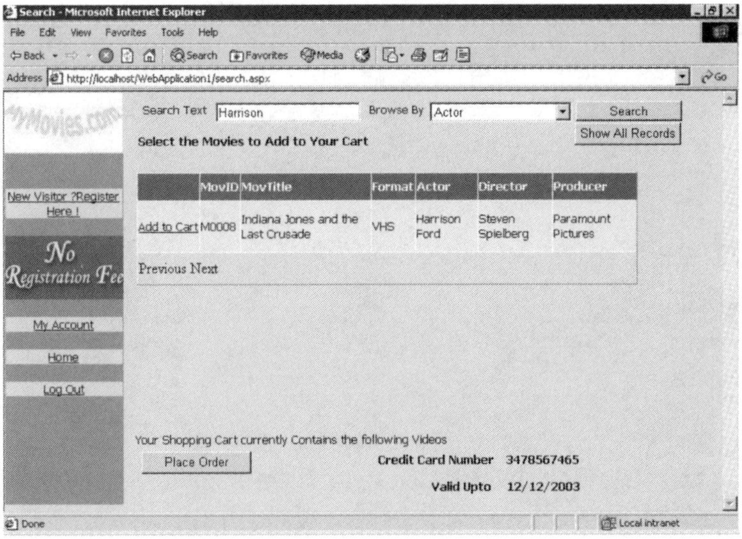

FIGURE 26-15 *The Search page with results*

1. Click on the Add to Cart hyperlink next to the desired video. The videos in the shopping cart are displayed in DataGrid2.

2. To change the quantity of a particular video, click on Edit next to the desired video in DataGrid3 and change the quantity.

3. Click on the Update hyperlink.

After adding one or more videos to the cart, a customer can click on the Place Order button to purchase a movie.

The Account Details Page

The Account Details page enables customers to view the placed orders for movies. Figure 26-16 shows the Account Details page.

The Account Details Web form contains a label and a text box. Table 26-12 lists the properties of the label and the text box.

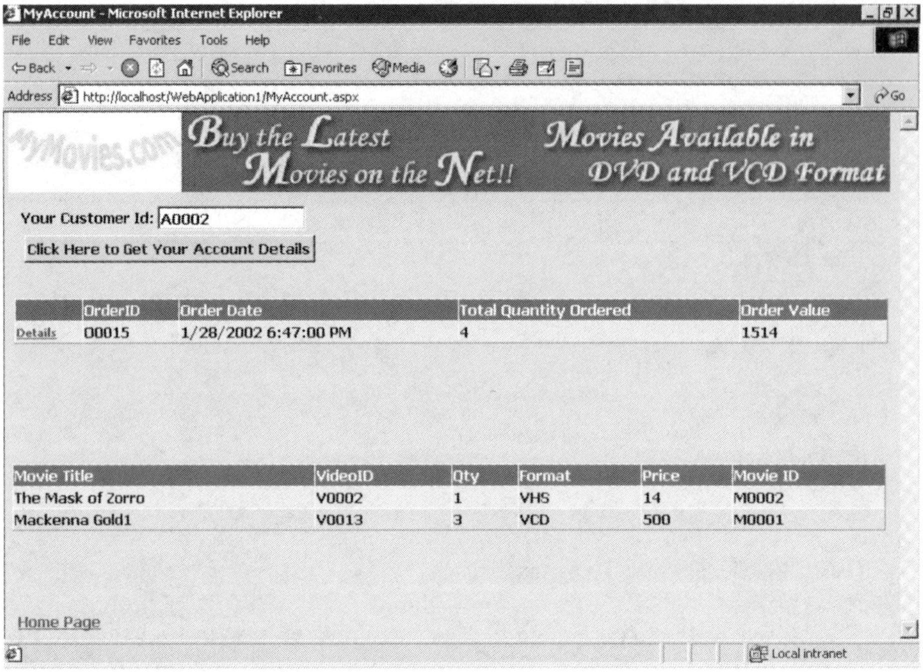

FIGURE 26-16 *The Account Details page*

Table 26-12 Properties Assigned to the Label and the Text Box

Control	Property	Value
Label 1	ID	Label1
Label 1	Text	Your Customer Id:
Label 1	Font	Tahoma,Smaller
Label 1	Height	1px
Label 1	Width	126px
Text box 1	ID	txtCustID
Text box 1	Font	Tahoma, Smaller
Text box 1	Height	21px
Text box 1	Width	129px

The Account Details Web form also contains a RequiredValidator control and a CustomValidator control. Table 26-13 lists the properties of the Validation controls.

Table 26-13 Properties Assigned to the Validation Controls

Control	Property	Value
RequiredFieldValidator 1	ID	RequiredFieldValidator1
RequiredFieldValidator 1	Error message	Customer Id Cannot be blank
RequiredFieldValidator 1	Font	Tahoma,Larger
RequiredFieldValidator 1	ForeColor	DarkViolet
RequiredFieldValidator 1	ControlToValidate	txtCustID
RequiredFieldValidator 1	Width	290px
CustomValidator 1	ID	CustomValidator1
CustomValidator 1	Error message	Customer Id Entered is Incorrect
CustomValidator 1	Font	Tahoma,Larger
CustomValidator 1	ForeColor	DarkViolet
CustomValidator 1	ControlToValidate	txtCustID
CustomValidator 1	Width	323px

In addition to these controls, the Account Details Web form also contains two DataGrid controls. Table 26-14 lists the properties assigned to the DataGrid controls on the Account Details Web form.

Table 26-14 Properties Assigned to the DataGrid Controls

Control	Property	Value
DataGrid 1	ID	dgAccountDetails
DataGrid 1	Height	13px
DataGrid 1	Width	760px

continues

Table 26-14 *(continued)*

Control	Property	Value
DataGrid 1	Height	122px
DataGrid 1	DataKeyField	OrderID
DataGrid 1	BackColor	#FFCCFF (Under AlternatingItemStyle)
DataGrid 1	Font	Tahoma, Smaller (Under AlternatingItemStyle)
DataGrid 1	Wrap	False (Under AlternatingItemStyle)
DataGrid 1	BackColor	DarkViolet (Under HeaderStyle)
DataGrid 1	Font	Tahoma, Smaller (Under HeaderStyle)
DataGrid 1	ForeColor	White (Under HeaderStyle)
DataGrid 1	BackColor	Lavender (Under ItemStyle)
DataGrid 1	Font	Tahoma, Smaller (Under ItemStyle)
DataGrid 1	ForeColor	Black (Under ItemStyle)
DataGrid 1	HorizontalAlign	Left (Under ItemStyle)
DataGrid 1	Wrap	False (Under ItemStyle)
DataGrid 1	NextPageText	Next (Under PagerStyle)
DataGrid 1	PrevPageText	Previous (Under PagerStyle)
DataGrid 1	BackColor	#990033 (Under SelectedItemStyle)

Control	Property	Value
DataGrid 1	ForeColor	White (Under SelectedItemStyle)
DataGrid 1	Wrap	False (Under SelectedItemStyle)
DataGrid 2	ID	DataGrid2
DataGrid 2	AutoGenerateColumns	False
DataGrid 2	Width	541px
DataGrid 2	Height	61px
DataGrid 2	PageSize	5
DataGrid 2	Font	Tahoma,Smaller (Under AlternatingItemStyle)
DataGrid 2	Wrap	False (Under AlternatingItemStyle)
DataGrid 2	BackColor	DarkViolet (Under HeaderStyle)
DataGrid 2	Font	Tahoma,Smaller (Under HeaderStyle)
DataGrid 2	ForeColor	White (Under HeaderStyle)
DataGrid 2	BackColor	Lavender (Under ItemStyle)
DataGrid 2	Font	Tahoma,Smaller (Under ItemStyle)
DataGrid 2	HorizontalAlign	Left (Under ItemStyle)
DataGrid 2	Wrap	False (Under ItemStyle)
DataGrid 2	NextPageText	Next (Under PagerStyle)

continues

Table 26-14 *(continued)*

Control	Property	Value
DataGrid 2	PrevPageText	Previous (Under PagerStyle)
DataGrid 2	BackColor	#990033 (Under SelectedItemStyle)

The first column of the dgAccountDetails grid is a button column. You can use the DataGrid Properties dialog box to add the Select button column and to set its Text property to Details. A customer can go back to the home page by clicking on the Home Page hyperlink. Table 26-15 describes the properties for the hyperlinks on the Account Details Web form.

Table 26-15 Properties Assigned to the Hyperlink

Control	Property	Value
Hyperlink 1	ID	HyperLink1
Hyperlink 1	Text	Home Page
Hyperlink 1	Font	Tahoma, X-Smaller
Hyperlink 1	Height	15px
Hyperlink 1	Width	170px
Hyperlink 1	NavigateUrl	Default.aspx

The next section describes the Customer Registration page.

The Customer Registration Page

As the name suggests, the Customer Registration Web form enables a customer to register. Figure 26-17 shows the Customer Registration Web form.

The Customer Registration page displays when a customer clicks on the New Visitor? Register Here! hyperlink on the home page or the Search page. To start with, take a look at the properties of the Customer Registration Web form. The pageLayout property of the form has been set to GridLayout, and the

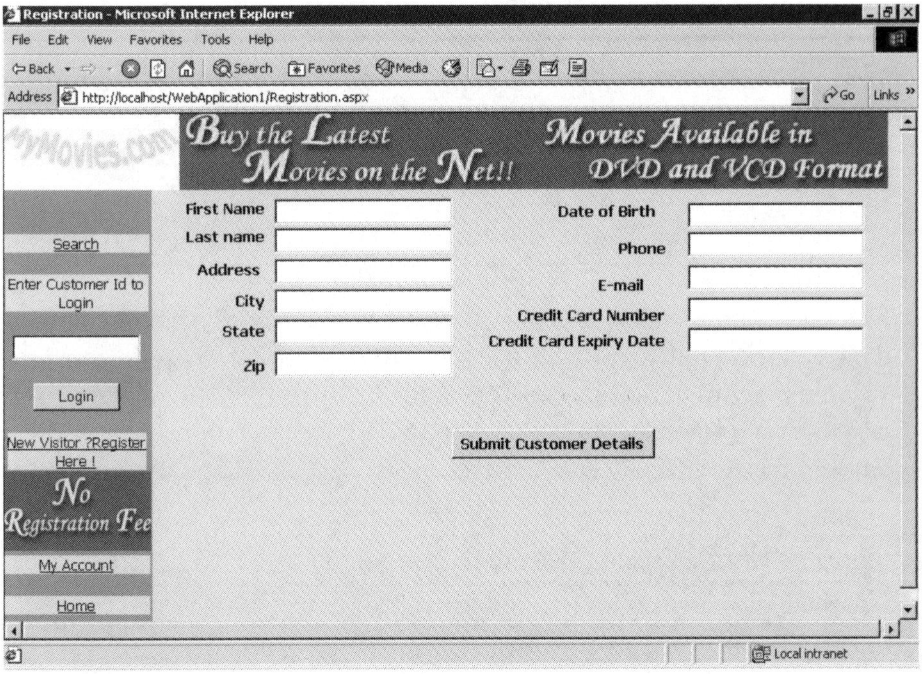

FIGURE 26-17 *The Customer Registration Web form*

bgColor property has been changed to #ffcoff. As shown in Figure 26-17, the Customer Registration Web form contains multiple text boxes and labels. Table 26-16 lists the properties assigned to the labels.

Table 26-16 Properties Assigned to the Labels

Control	Property	Value
Label 1	ID	LblFName
Label 1	Text	First Name
Label 1	Font	Tahoma, Smaller
Label 2	ID	LblLName
Label 2	Text	Last Name
Label 2	Font	Tahoma, Smaller
Label 3	ID	LblAddress

continues

Table 26-16 *(continued)*

Control	Property	Value
Label 3	Text	Address
Label 3	Font	Tahoma, Smaller
Label 4	ID	LblCity
Label 4	Text	City
Label 4	Font	Tahoma, Smaller
Label 5	ID	LblState
Label 5	Text	State
Label 5	Font	Tahoma, Smaller
Label 6	ID	LblZip
Label 6	Text	Zip:
Label 6	Font	Tahoma, Smaller
Label 7	ID	LblPhone
Label 7	Text	Phone:
Label 7	Font	Tahoma, Smaller
Label 8	ID	LblEmail
Label 8	Text	Email
Label 8	Font	Tahoma, Smaller
Label 9	ID	LblCCNum
Label 9	Text	Credit Card Number
Label 9	Font	Tahoma, Smaller
Label 10	ID	LblCCExp
Label 10	Text	Valid Upto:
Label 10	Font	Tahoma, Smaller
Label 11	ID	LblDOB
Label 11	Text	DOB:
Label 11	Font	Tahoma, Smaller

Control	Property	Value
Label 12	ID	lblError
Label 12	Text	Errors Occurred
Label 12	Font	Tahoma, Smaller
Label 12	Visible	False
Label 12	Width	361px

Table 26-17 lists the properties assigned to the text boxes in the Customer Registration Web form.

Table 26-17 Properties Assigned to the Text Boxes

Control	Property	Value
Text box 1	ID	txtFname
Text box 1	TabIndex	1
Text box 2	ID	txtLname
Text box 2	TabIndex	2
Text box 3	Name	txtAdd
Text box 3	TabIndex	3
Text box 4	Name	txtCity
Text box 4	TabIndex	4
Text box 5	Name	txtState
Text box 5	TabIndex	5
Text box 6	Name	txtZip
Text box 6	TabIndex	6
Text box 7	Name	txtDOB
Text box 7	TabIndex	7
Text box 8	Name	txtPhone
Text box 8	TabIndex	8

continues

Table 26-17 _(continued)_

Control	Property	Value
Text box 9	Name	txtEmail
Text box 9	TabIndex	9
Text box 10	Name	txtCCNo
Text box 10	TabIndex	10
Text box 11	Name	txtExpDate
Text box 11	TabIndex	11

The Customer Registration Web form also contains the Submit Customer Details button to submit the details entered by the customer. Table 26-18 lists the properties of the buttons on the Customer Registration Web form.

Table 26-18 Properties Assigned to Buttons

Control	Property	Value
Button 1	ID	CmdCustDetails
Button 1	Text	Submit Customer Details
Button 1	Height	25px
Button 1	Width	175px
Button 1	Font	Tahoma, Smaller

Customers can use the Submit Customer Details button to update the database with the information entered in the Customer Registration Web form. If the values entered in the text boxes are not valid or if the required fields are left blank, a message box appears showing the summary of all the errors that occurred. This is accomplished by using a ValidationSummary control. The properties for the ValidationSummary control are listed in Table 26-19.

Table 26-19 Properties Assigned to the ValidationSummary Control

Control	Property	Value
ValidationSummary 1	ID	ValidationSummary1
ValidationSummary 1	ForeColor	Red
ValidationSummary 1	ShowMessageBox	True
ValidationSummary 1	ShowSummary	False
ValidationSummary 1	Width	188px

Summary

In this chapter, you learned to create the Web forms for the customer interface of the video kiosk Web application. You learned to create the home, Search, Customer Registration, and Account Details Web forms. This chapter also described the properties you need to assign to the various controls on the Web forms. The next chapter will discuss the functionality you need to add to the customer interface.

Chapter 27

*Adding
Functionality to
the Customer
Interface*

In the preceding chapter, you learned how to design the customer interface of the MyMovies video kiosk Web application. In this chapter, you will learn about the functionality involved in the customer interface. To start with, let's look at the customer interface, as shown in Figure 27-1.

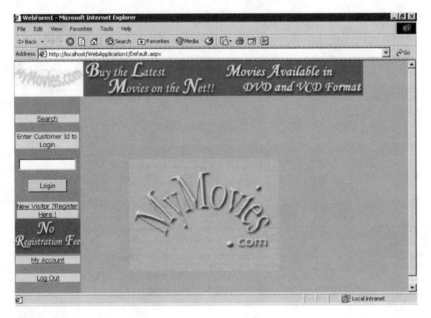

FIGURE 27-1 *The customer interface*

There are two ways to approach this interface: one for a registered customer and another for an unregistered customer. Let's begin exploring the functionality of the interface for an unregistered user.

Coding for the Customer Registration Page

If you are an unregistered user, you need to click on the New Visitor? Register Here! link in the left panel of the Web application. When you click on this link, you are directed to the Customer Registration page, which is shown in Figure 27-2.

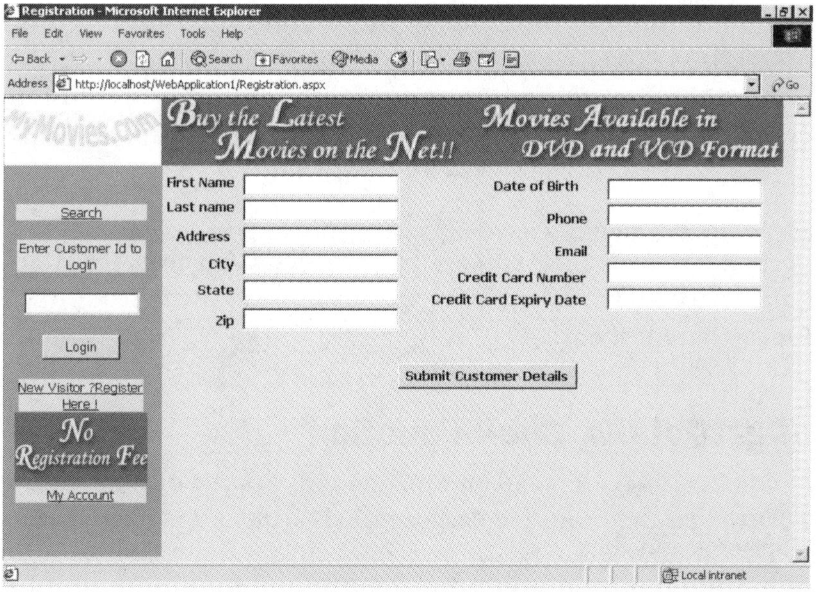

FIGURE 27-2 *The Customer Registration page*

An unregistered user has to fill in his or her personal details as specified in the form. When entering information, invalid information in any specified control is marked with a red asterisk. This red asterisk denotes the presence of the RequiredFieldValidator, RegularExpressionValidator, or CompareValidator class, which in turn validates the input to the specified control to which it is linked. If the user has not entered valid data in all of the controls, he or she is not allowed to enter his or her details in the underlying data source. After the user has entered the details in the form, the ValidationSummary class marks the summary of invalid information. Therefore, users are not allowed to enter invalid details in the underlying database.

There are two functions you need to code to add functionality to the Customer Registration page, Page_Load and CmdCustDetails_Click. The following sections explain these two functions in detail.

The *Page_Load* Function

The Page_Load function executes when the registration form loads. The code for this function is as follows:

```
Private Sub Page_Load(ByVal sender As System.Object, ByVal e As
System.EventArgs) Handles MyBase.Load
        'Put user code to initialize the page here
        CompareValidator2.ValueToCompare = Today
End Sub
```

This function sets the ValueToCompare property of the CompareValidator control to the current date. This date is compared with the date entered in the Credit Card Expiry Date text box.

The *CmdCustDetails_Click* Function

When a user has entered all valid information and clicks on the Submit Customer Details button on the form, the CmdCustDetails_Click function is called. The code for this function is as follows:

```
Private Sub CmdCustDetails_Click(ByVal sender As System.Object, ByVal e
As System.EventArgs) Handles CmdCustDetails.Click
        Dim strConnectionString As String = Application("strConnect")
        Dim sqlString As String
        Dim MyConnection As New SqlConnection(strConnectionString)
        Dim CustID As String
        Try
            lblError.Visible = False
            MyConnection.Open()
            Dim cmdCust As SqlCommand
            cmdCust = New SqlCommand("Select
            IsNull(Max(convert(int,substring(CustID,2,4))),0)+1 as CustID
            from Customer", MyConnection)
            Dim myReader As SqlDataReader =
            cmdCust.ExecuteReader(CommandBehavior.SingleRow)
            While myReader.Read()
                CustID = myReader.GetInt32(0).ToString
            End While
            CustID = "A000" + CStr(CustID)
```

```
MyConnection.Close()
Dim myCommand As SqlCommand
Dim insertCmd As String
' Check that four of the input values are not empty. If any of them
' is empty, show a message to the user and rebind the DataGrid.
insertCmd = "insert into Customer values (@CustID,
@LastName,@FirstName,@Address,@City,@State,@Zip,@Phone,@Email,@DOB,"
 & "@CreditCardNum,@CreditCardValidUpto);"
' Initialize the SqlCommand with the new SQL string.
MyConnection.Open()
myCommand = New SqlCommand(insertCmd, MyConnection)
myCommand.Parameters.Add(New SqlParameter("@CustID",
SqlDbType.VarChar, 11))
myCommand.Parameters.Add(New SqlParameter("@LastName",
SqlDbType.VarChar, 50))
myCommand.Parameters.Add(New SqlParameter("@FirstName",
SqlDbType.VarChar, 50))
myCommand.Parameters.Add(New SqlParameter("@Address",
SqlDbType.VarChar, 25))
myCommand.Parameters.Add(New SqlParameter("@City",
SqlDbType.VarChar, 25))
myCommand.Parameters.Add(New SqlParameter("@State",
SqlDbType.VarChar, 15))
myCommand.Parameters.Add(New SqlParameter("@Zip", SqlDbType.VarChar,
7))
myCommand.Parameters.Add(New SqlParameter("@Phone",
SqlDbType.VarChar, 10))
myCommand.Parameters.Add(New SqlParameter("@Email",
SqlDbType.VarChar, 50))
myCommand.Parameters.Add(New SqlParameter("@DOB",
SqlDbType.DateTime, 8))
myCommand.Parameters.Add(New SqlParameter("@CreditCardNum",
SqlDbType.VarChar, 16))
myCommand.Parameters.Add(New SqlParameter("@CreditCardValidUpto",
SqlDbType.DateTime, 8))

myCommand.Parameters("@CustID").Value = CustID
myCommand.Parameters("@FirstName").Value = txtFname.Text
```

```
    myCommand.Parameters("@LastName").Value = txtLName.Text
    myCommand.Parameters("@Address").Value = txtAdd.Text
    myCommand.Parameters("@City").Value = txtCity.Text
    myCommand.Parameters("@State").Value = txtState.Text
    myCommand.Parameters("@Zip").Value = txtZip.Text
    myCommand.Parameters("@Phone").Value = txtPhone.Text
    myCommand.Parameters("@Email").Value = txtEMail.Text
    myCommand.Parameters("@CreditCardNum").Value = txtCCNo.Text
    myCommand.Parameters("@DOB").Value = txtDOB.Text
    myCommand.Parameters("@CreditCardValidUpto").Value = txtExpDate.Text

    myCommand.ExecuteNonQuery()
    MyConnection.Close()
    lblError.Visible = True
    lblError.Text = "Customer Created Successfully. Customer Id is " +
    CustID
Catch
    lblError.Visible = True
    Exit Sub
End Try
End Sub
```

This function performs the following tasks:

◆ The `Visible` property of the `lblError` label is set to `False`. The function establishes a new SQL connection with the underlying database. This is done through the following statements:

```
Dim strConnectionString As String = Application("strConnect")
Dim MyConnection As New SqlConnection(strConnectionString)
MyConnection.Open()
```

The preceding statements define a connection string and establish a new SQL connection using the connection string. The connection is opened by the `Open` method of the `SqlConnection` class.

◆ The function also extracts the maximum value of the `CustID` field from the `Customer` table and increments it by 1. This is done because a new customer is being added to the `Customer` table.

```
cmdCust = New SqlCommand("Select IsNull(Max(convert(int,substring
(CustID,2,4))),0)+1 as CustID from Customer", MyConnection)
```

◆ The following code snippet creates a new value for the `CustID` field:

```
Dim myReader As SqlDataReader =
cmdCust.ExecuteReader(CommandBehavior.SingleRow)
While myReader.Read()
CustID = myReader.GetInt32(0).ToString
End While
CustID = "A000" + CStr(CustID)
```

◆ Next, a `SqlCommand` object is used to insert the new record in the `Customer` table. It takes the values for the various fields through the controls specified in the registration form, except for the `CustID` value, which is calculated in the preceding code. The code snippet for this purpose is as follows:

```
Dim myCommand As SqlCommand
Dim insertCmd As String
' Check that four of the input values are not empty. If any of
them
' is empty, show a message to the user and rebind the
DataGrid.
insertCmd = "insert into Customer values (@CustID,
@LastName,@FirstName,@Address,@City,@State,@Zip,@Phone,@Email,@DOB,"
    & "@CreditCardNum,@CreditCardValidUpto);"
' Initialize the SqlCommand with the new SQL string.
MyConnection.Open()
myCommand = New SqlCommand(insertCmd, MyConnection)
myCommand.Parameters.Add(New SqlParameter("@CustID",
SqlDbType.VarChar, 11))
myCommand.Parameters.Add(New SqlParameter("@LastName",
SqlDbType.VarChar, 50))
myCommand.Parameters.Add(New SqlParameter("@FirstName",
SqlDbType.VarChar, 50))
myCommand.Parameters.Add(New SqlParameter("@Address",
SqlDbType.VarChar, 25))
myCommand.Parameters.Add(New SqlParameter("@City",
SqlDbType.VarChar, 25))
myCommand.Parameters.Add(New SqlParameter("@State",
SqlDbType.VarChar, 15))
```

```
                    myCommand.Parameters.Add(New SqlParameter("@Zip",
SqlDbType.VarChar, 7))
                    myCommand.Parameters.Add(New SqlParameter("@Phone",
                    SqlDbType.VarChar, 10))
                    myCommand.Parameters.Add(New SqlParameter("@Email",
                    SqlDbType.VarChar, 50))
                    myCommand.Parameters.Add(New SqlParameter("@DOB",
                    SqlDbType.DateTime, 8))
                    myCommand.Parameters.Add(New SqlParameter("@CreditCardNum",
                    SqlDbType.VarChar, 16))
                    myCommand.Parameters.Add(New
SqlParameter("@CreditCardValidUpto",
                    SqlDbType.DateTime, 8))

                    myCommand.Parameters("@CustID").Value = CustID
                    myCommand.Parameters("@FirstName").Value = txtFname.Text
                    myCommand.Parameters("@LastName").Value = txtLName.Text
                    myCommand.Parameters("@Address").Value = txtAdd.Text
                    myCommand.Parameters("@City").Value = txtCity.Text
                    myCommand.Parameters("@State").Value = txtState.Text
                    myCommand.Parameters("@Zip").Value = txtZip.Text
                    myCommand.Parameters("@Phone").Value = txtPhone.Text
                    myCommand.Parameters("@Email").Value = txtEMail.Text
                    myCommand.Parameters("@CreditCardNum").Value = txtCCNo.Text
                    myCommand.Parameters("@DOB").Value = txtDOB.Text
                    myCommand.Parameters("@CreditCardValidUpto").Value =
txtExpDate.Text
                    myCommand.ExecuteNonQuery()
                    MyConnection.Close()
```

◆ Finally, the customer ID for the user is displayed on the screen. The customer uses this ID to log in to the site for further operations.

This section covered an unregistered user registering and obtaining a customer ID, which he or she can use to log in to the site. The next section discusses how a customer logs in and shops for movies of his or her choice.

Coding for the Customer Login Interface

For registered customers, there is a text box in the left panel of the customer interface where they can enter their login ID. (The login ID is the same as the customer ID.) The customer login interface is shown in Figure 27-3.

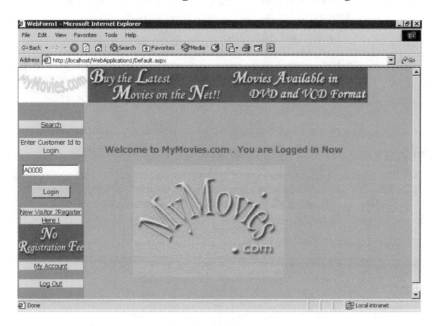

FIGURE 27-3 *The customer login interface*

In previous chapters, you have already seen the design of the customer login interface for the MyMovies video kiosk Web application. The interface has a text box and the Login button. In addition, there are the following controls:

◆ The RequiredFieldValidator control associated with the text box ensures that the customer does not leave the text box blank. It displays the message `Customer ID Cannot Be Blank` if left blank.

◆ The CustomValidator control checks whether the customer ID entered is valid. If the customer ID does not match, the message `Customer ID Entered Is Incorrect` is displayed.

◆ If the customer ID is valid, this interface displays the message: `Welcome to MyMovies.com. You are Logged in Now.`

The CustomValidator controls provide you with customized validation logic. They perform validation on the server and provide client-side validation. At this point, however, only server-side validation will be discussed. For creating a server-side validation function, you need a handler for the `ServerValidate` event. The string value that needs to be validated is accessed by the `ServerValidateEvent-Args` object's `Value` property. It is passed to the event handler as a parameter. The validation result is stored in the `ServerValidateEventArgs` object's `IsValid` property. The CustomValidator controls check the `IsValid` property. If it is false, it displays the text set in its `Text` property.

The next section will discuss the functionality of the third case, in which the customer ID entered is valid. The `CustomValidator1_ServerValidate` function of the `Index` class validates the specified customer ID against the `Customer` table.

The *CustomValidator1_ServerValidate* Function

The code for the `CustomValidator1_ServerValidate` function is as follows:

```
Private Sub CustomValidator1_ServerValidate(ByVal source As System.Object, ByVal
args As System.Web.UI.WebControls.ServerValidateEventArgs) Handles
CustomValidator1.ServerValidate
        Dim sConnectionString As String
        Dim sqlString As String

        Dim MyConnection As SqlConnection
        Dim MyDataAdapter As SqlDataAdapter
        Dim DS As New DataSet()

        sConnectionString = Application("strConnect")
        sqlString = "Select * from Customer where CustID='" + args.Value + "'"
        'Open the connection

        MyConnection = New SqlConnection(sConnectionString)
        MyDataAdapter = New SqlDataAdapter(sqlString, MyConnection)

        MyDataAdapter.Fill(DS, "Customer")
        If DS.Tables("Customer").DefaultView.Count = 0 Then
            args.IsValid = False
            Session("UserLoggedIn") = "No"
```

```
        Else
            args.IsValid = True

            Label2.Visible = True
            Session("UserLoggedIn") = "Yes"
            Session("CustID") = args.Value
            sqlString = "Select * from Customer where CustID='" +
            args.Value + "'"
            Dim myCommand As New SqlCommand(sqlString, MyConnection)
            MyConnection.Open()
            Dim myReader As SqlDataReader
            myReader = myCommand.ExecuteReader()
            ' Always call Read before accessing data.
            While myReader.Read()
                Session("CCNum") = myReader.GetString(10).Trim
                Session("ValidUpTo") = myReader.GetDateTime(11)
            End While
        End If
End Sub
```

Before explaining the preceding code, it is necessary for you to understand the difference between `Application` and `Session` objects. The `Application` object stores data that can be accessed from anywhere in the Web application. The `Session` object stores data that is accessible by the user session that creates the specified object. For example, in the preceding code, there will be a separate `Session` object for every user. See the following code statements:

```
sConnectionString = Application("strConnect")
Session("UserLoggedIn") = "Yes"
Session("CustID") = args.Value
Session("CCNum") = myReader.GetString(10).Trim
Session("ValidUpTo") = myReader.GetDateTime(11)
```

From these statements, you can interpret that the `Application` object is being used to establish a connection with the underlying database that can be used by any module of the Web application. On the other hand, there are separate `Session` objects that store data, such as `CustID` (customer ID), `CCNum` (credit card number), and `ValidUpTo` (expiry date for credit card) fields that have specific values for every user that logs in to the Web application. `Session` objects are destroyed when the customer logs out from the application. Therefore, Session objects are customer specific.

The preceding ServerValidate function code performs the following tasks in the given application:

◆ A connection is established with the underlying database.

◆ An object of data adapter is instantiated.

```
MyDataAdapter = New SqlDataAdapter(sqlString, MyConnection)
```

◆ The data adapter fetches records in the dataset by executing the sqlString. The SQL command in the sqlString is as follows:

```
sqlString = "Select * from Customer where CustID='" + args.Value + "'"
```

◆ The data adapter's Fill method is used to populate dataset object (DS).

```
MyDataAdapter.Fill(DS, "Customer")
```

◆ The number of records present in the Customer table of the dataset is checked. If no records are present with the particular CustID entered by the user, the value for the UserLoggedIn Session variable is set to No. The IsValid property of the ServerValidateEventArgs object is set to False.

```
If DS.Tables("Customer").DefaultView.Count = 0 Then
    args.IsValid = False
    Session("UserLoggedIn") = "No"
```

◆ If the records are greater than 0, the value of the UserLoggedIn Session variable is set to Yes. The IsValid property of the ServerValidate-EventArgs object is set to True. Then, in accordance with the customer ID, the relevant credit card number and its corresponding validity date are fetched from the database and stored in the respective session variables.

```
    Else
        args.IsValid = True
            Label2.Visible = True
        Session("UserLoggedIn") = "Yes"
        Session("CustID") = args.Value
        sqlString = "Select * from Customer where CustID='" + args.Value + "'"
        Dim myCommand As New SqlCommand(sqlString, MyConnection)
```

```
            MyConnection.Open()
            Dim myReader As SqlDataReader
            myReader = myCommand.ExecuteReader()
            ' Always call Read before accessing data.
            While myReader.Read()
                Session("CCNum") = myReader.GetString(10).Trim
                Session("ValidUpTo") = myReader.GetDateTime(11)
            End While
    End If
```

After the customer has logged in to the Web application, he or she can search for movies of his or her choice and place orders accordingly. When the customer clicks on the Search hyperlink in the left pane, he or she is directed to the Search.aspx page. The functionality of the Search page is discussed in the next section.

Coding for the Search Page

Figure 27-4 displays the Search page.

The Search page contains the following functions:

- ◆ Page_Load
- ◆ DataGrid1_PageIndexChanged
- ◆ CmdShowAllRecords_Click
- ◆ CmdSearch_Click
- ◆ DataGrid1_ItemCommand
- ◆ DataGrid3_CancelCommand
- ◆ DataGrid3_EditCommand
- ◆ DataGrid3_UpdateCommand
- ◆ DataGrid3_DeleteCommand
- ◆ CmdPlaceOrder_Click

The following sections cover each of these functions in detail.

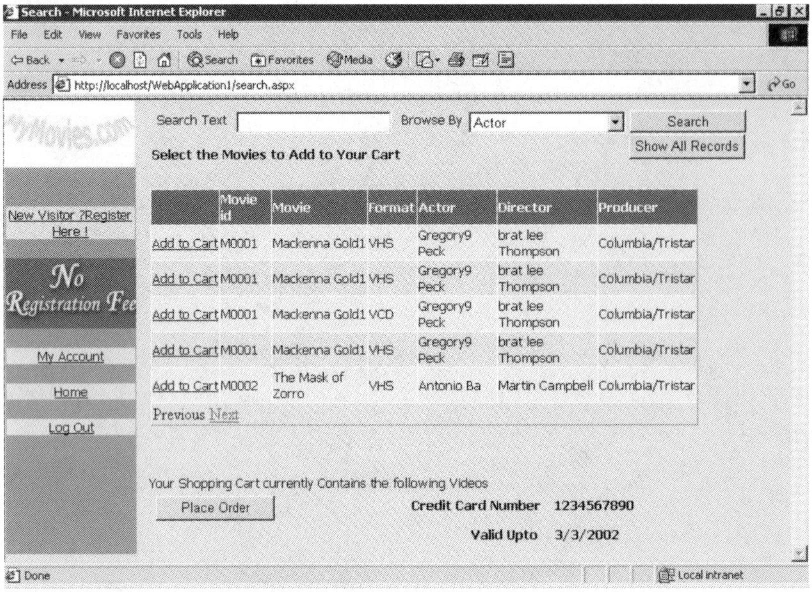

FIGURE 27-4 *The Search page*

The *Page_Load* Function

Both customers and unregistered users can access the Search page. The difference is that customers can place orders, whereas the unregistered users can only view the movies available. To shop for movies, you need to log in to the Web application or register yourself as a customer with the application. The functionality for this logic is placed in the Page_Load function.

When the Search page loads in the browser, the Page_Load function is called by default. The code for the function is as follows:

```
Private Sub Page_Load(ByVal sender As System.Object, ByVal e As
System.EventArgs) Handles MyBase.Load
        If Session("UserLoggedIn") <> "Yes" Then
            'Do not allow the user to place an order.
            lblCCNo.Text = ""
            lblValidUpTo.Text = ""
        Else
            lblCCNo.Text = Session("CCNum")
            lblValidUpTo.Text = Session("ValidUpTo")
```

```
            End If
            If Session("LoadPage") = "Yes" Then
                Call LoadGrid()
            End If
    End Sub
    'Code for the LoadGrid function
    Private Function LoadGrid()
            Dim strConnectionString = Application("strConnect")


            Dim MyConnection As New SqlConnection(strConnectionString)
            Dim strCmdText As String
            Dim MyDataAdapter As SqlDataAdapter
            Dim MyDataSet As New DataSet()
            Try
                strCmdText = "SELECT Movie.MovID as [Movie id], Movie.MovTitle as
    [Movie],Video.Format, Actor.FirstName +' '+Actor.LastName AS Actor, Di" & _
                        "rector.FirstName +' '+ Director.LastName AS Director,
    Producer.Name AS Producer " & _
                        "FROM Actor INNER JOIN ActorMovie ON Actor.ActorID =
    ActorMovie.Acto" & _
                        "rID INNER JOIN Movie ON ActorMovie.MovID = Movie.MovID
    INNER JOIN Director ON Mo" & _
                        "vie.DirID = Director.DirID INNER JOIN Producer ON
    Movie.ProdID = Producer.ProdID INNER JOIN Video ON Movie.MovID = Video.MovID"


                MyDataAdapter = New SqlDataAdapter(strCmdText, MyConnection)
                MyDataAdapter.Fill(MyDataSet)
                DataGrid1.DataSource = MyDataSet
                DataGrid1.DataBind()
                Session("LoadPage") = "No"
            Catch
                LblSelectMovies.Text = "Errors Occured."
                Exit Function
            End Try
    End Function
```

The preceding code performs the following tasks:

◆ If the value contained in the session variable `UserLoggedIn` is not `Yes`, it indicates that the user is not logged in. In this case, the labels for credit card number and validity date are set to blank. This functionality is explained by the following code:

```
If Session("UserLoggedIn") <> "Yes" Then
        lblCCNo.Text = ""
        lblValidUpTo.Text = ""
```

◆ If the customer logs in, the labels for credit card number and validity date take their values from the respective `Session` objects that were created in the `CustomValidator1_ServerValidate` function. The code snippet for this is as follows:

```
        lblCCNo.Text = Session("CCNum")
        lblValidUpTo.Text = Session("ValidUpTo")
```

◆ If the value of the session variable `LoadPage` is `Yes`, the function named `LoadGrid()` is called. This function fetches all the available records depending on the filter specified, such as Actor, Movie, Producer, or Director. All the fetched records are populated in a dataset. This dataset is then bound to `DataGrid1`.

```
If Session("LoadPage") = "Yes" Then
    Call LoadGrid()
End If
```

The *DataGrid1_PageIndexChanged* Function

The code for the `DataGrid1_PageIndexChanged` function is as follows:

```
Private Sub DataGrid1_PageIndexChanged(ByVal source As Object, ByVal e As
System.Web.UI.WebControls.DataGridPageChangedEventArgs) Handles
DataGrid1.PageIndexChanged

        DataGrid1.CurrentPageIndex = e.NewPageIndex
        DataGrid1.DataBind()
        Call CmdShowAllRecords_Click(source, e)
End Sub
```

Whenever a user clicks the `Next` or `Previous` hyperlinks, the `PageIndexChanged` event is triggered. As a result, the `CurrentPageIndex` property of `DataGrid1` is set.

The *CmdShowAllRecords _Click* Function

This function is called when the customer clicks the Show All Records button. In this case, no filter is set while retrieving records; all the records in the underlying database are displayed. The session variable `PageLoad` is set to `Yes`. The `Page_Load` function that displays all the records is called. Finally, the `txtSearch.Text` property is set to blank because the customer needs no filter in his or her search.

```
Private Sub CmdShowAllRecords _Click(ByVal sender As System.Object, ByVal e As
System.EventArgs) Handles Button1.Click
        Session("LoadPage") = "Yes"
        Call Page_Load(sender, e)
        txtSearch.Text = ""
End Sub
```

The *CmdSearch_Click* Function

When the customer selects the search criteria from the drop-down list box and clicks the Search button, this function is called. The customer has the option of viewing records based on any actor, video, movie, or director choice. When the customer clicks the Search button, the records are displayed in the data grid below. The code for the `CmdSearch_Click` function is as follows:

```
Private Sub CmdSearch_Click(ByVal sender As System.Object, ByVal e As
System.EventArgs) Handles CmdSearch.Click
        Dim strConnectionString = Application("strConnect")
        Dim MyConnection As New SqlConnection(strConnectionString)
        Dim strCmdText As String
        Dim MyDataAdapter As SqlDataAdapter
        Dim MyDataSet As New DataSet()
        Dim strCriteria As String
        Dim strType As String
        strType = lstSearch.SelectedItem.Text

        Select Case strType
            Case "Actor"
                strCriteria = " Where Actor.FirstName+Actor.LastName Like'%" +
                txtSearch.Text + "%'"
            Case "Director"
```

```
                              strCriteria = " Where Director.FirstName+Director.LastName
                              Like'%" + txtSearch.Text + "%'"
                    Case "Producer"
                              strCriteria = " Where Producer.Name Like'%" + txtSearch.Text +
                              "%'"
                    Case "Movie"
                              strCriteria = " Where Movie.MovTitle Like'%" + txtSearch.Text +
                              "%'"
          End Select

          strCmdText = "SELECT Distinct Movie.MovID, Movie.MovTitle,Video.Format,
          Actor.FirstName +' '+Actor.LastName AS Actor, Di" & _
                    "rector.FirstName +' '+ Director.LastName AS Director,
Producer.Name AS Producer" & _
                    " FROM Actor INNER JOIN ActorMovie ON Actor.ActorID =

ActorMovie.Acto" & _
                    "rID INNER JOIN Movie ON ActorMovie.MovID = Movie.MovID INNER JOIN
Director ON Mo" & _
                    "vie.DirID = Director.DirID INNER JOIN Producer ON Movie.ProdID
= Producer.ProdID INNER JOIN Video ON Movie.MovID = Video.MovID" & _
                    "" + strCriteria

          MyDataAdapter = New SqlDataAdapter(strCmdText, MyConnection)
          MyDataAdapter.Fill(MyDataSet)
          DataGrid1.DataSource = MyDataSet
          DataGrid1.DataBind()
End Sub
```

The preceding function performs the following tasks:

◆ The text of the selected item in the lstSearch list box is captured in a string variable called strType. Depending on the value in strType, the where clause of the Select statement is decided and stored in the str-Criteria variable. The value that the customer enters in the txtSearch text box is appended to the where clause in the strCriteria variable.

◆ The strCmdText variable contains the Select statement and the JOIN queries that retrieve records from the related tables in the database. A

DataAdapter object is created and uses the query in the strCmdText variable to populate the dataset.

◆ The dataset that is formed contains the filtered records from the tables in the database acts as a data source for the data grid. The records are displayed in the DataGrid1 object.

The *DataGrid1_ItemCommand* Function

The DataGrid1 object's ItemCommand event is raised when the Add To Cart hyperlink is clicked in the DataGrid1 control. The code for the same is as follows:

```
Private Sub DataGrid1_ItemCommand(ByVal source As Object, ByVal e As
System.Web.UI.WebControls.DataGridCommandEventArgs) Handles
DataGrid1.ItemCommand
        Dim strCmd As String
        If Session("UserLoggedIn") <> "Yes" Then
            'Do Not Allow the User to Place an Order.
            'DataGrid1.Columns(0).Visible = False
            strCmd = e.CommandName.ToString
            If strCmd = "Page" Then
                Exit Sub
            Else
                Dim strLabelText As String
                strLabelText = LblSelectMovies.Text()
                LblSelectMovies.Text = "You Need to Login before adding an Item to
your
cart. If you have not Registered, then register yourself to Place and Order"
            End If
        Else

            strCmd = e.CommandName.ToString
            If strCmd = "Page" Then
                Exit Sub
            End If
            'Dim key As String = DataGrid1.DataKeys(e.Item.ItemIndex).ToString
            Dim key As String = e.Item.Cells(1).Text()
            Dim movie As String
            Dim videoId As String
```

```
Dim format As String = e.Item.Cells(3).Text()
Dim Price As Integer
Dim strConnectionString = Application("strConnect")

Dim mySelectQuery As String = "SELECT Movie.MovID, Movie.MovTitle,
Video.VideoID,Video.Format, Video.Price FROM Movie INNER JOIN Video ON
Movie.MovID = dbo.Video.MovID where Movie.MovID='" & key & "' and
Video.Format='" + format + "'"
Dim myConnection As New SqlConnection(strConnectionString)
Dim myCommand As New SqlCommand(mySelectQuery, myConnection)
myConnection.Open()
Dim myReader As SqlDataReader
myReader = myCommand.ExecuteReader()
' Always call Read before accessing data.
While myReader.Read()
    'Console.WriteLine((myReader.GetInt32(0) & ", " &
myReader.GetString(1)))
        movie = myReader.GetString(1)
        videoId = myReader.GetString(2)
        format = myReader.GetString(3)
        Price = myReader.GetDecimal(4)
End While
' Always call Close when done reading.
myReader.Close()
' Close the connection when done with it.
myConnection.Close()
Dim dr As DataRow
If Session("ShoppingCart") Is Nothing Then
    'Cart.Columns.Add(New DataColumn("Quantity", GetType(String)))
    Cart.Columns.Add(New DataColumn("MovID", GetType(String)))
    Cart.Columns.Add(New DataColumn("Movie", GetType(String)))
    Cart.Columns.Add(New DataColumn("VideoID",
    GetType(String)))
    Cart.Columns.Add(New DataColumn("Format", GetType(String)))
    Cart.Columns.Add(New DataColumn("Price", GetType(String)))
    Cart.Columns.Add(New DataColumn("Quantity", GetType(String)))
    Session("ShoppingCart") = Cart
Else
```

```
            Cart = CType(Session("ShoppingCart"), DataTable)
        End If
        Dim i As Integer
        'For i = 1 To 9
        dr = Cart.NewRow()
        dr(0) = key
        dr(1) = movie
        dr(2) = videoId
        dr(3) = format
        dr(4) = Price
        dr(5) = 1
        Cart.Rows.Add(dr)
        CartView = New DataView(Cart)
        CartView.Sort = "MovID"
        Session("ShoppingCart") = Cart
        Cart = CType(Session("ShoppingCart"), DataTable)
        CartView = New DataView(Cart)
        BindGrid()
    End If
End Sub
Sub BindGrid()
    DataGrid3.DataSource = CartView
    DataGrid3.DataBind()
End Sub
```

In the preceding code, if the value of the UserLoggedIn session variable is not Yes, it indicates that the customer has not logged in and is just browsing the movie records in the application. In this case, when the customer clicks on the Add To Cart hyperlink in the DataGrid1 control, this message displays: You Need to Login before adding an Item to your cart. If you have not Registered, then register yourself to Place an Order. This is the text contained in LblSelectMovies.Text property of the Search page.

If the customer has logged in and clicks on the Add to Cart hyperlink, the particular record for which the button was clicked is retrieved. The columns MovieId, Movie, VideoID, Format, Price, and Quantity are picked up from the underlying tables of the database through a SQL query and are displayed in the DataGrid3 control.

The `BindGrid` method binds the controls of the `DataGrid3` object to the data source specified by the `DataSource` property. `CartView` is a data view created on the `Cart` table. The data source for the `DataGrid3` controls is the `CartView`, which is sorted on the `MovID` field.

The `DataSet(Cart)` used to populate `DataGrid3` is also stored in the session variable `ShoppingCart`. This implies that it can be further used in that session.

The customer can edit or delete the item present in the `DataGrid3` control. The functions called when this is done are explained in the following sections.

The *DataGrid3_CancelCommand* Function

This function is called when the Cancel button is clicked in the `DataGrid3` control.

```
Private Sub DataGrid3_CancelCommand(ByVal source As Object, ByVal e As
System.Web.UI.WebControls.DataGridCommandEventArgs) Handles
DataGrid3.CancelCommand
        Label6.Text = ""
        Label6.Visible = False
        DataGrid3.EditItemIndex = -1
        BindGrid()
End Sub
```

When the customer clicks on the Edit button in the `DataGrid3` control, it is replaced by the Update and Cancel buttons. When the customer clicks on the Cancel button, the preceding function is called. The text in the `Label6` control is not visible, and the `EditItemIndex` property of `DataGrid3` is set to -1.

To edit the DataGrid control, you can use the `DataGrid.EditItemIndex` property. This property is used to get or set the index of an item located in the DataGrid control. This property is used when `EditCommandColumnObject` is a part of DataGrid control.

After you set this property, the DataGrid control will allow you to edit the corresponding item. For example, if you set the property as 2, the item that possesses the index number 2 will be available for editing. However, this will not be the case if the value of the property is set to −1. In such a situation, none of the items located in the DataGrid control will be available for editing. Moreover, if the value of this property is set as any number less than −1, you might encounter an exception.

The *DataGrid3_EditCommand* Function

The `DataGrid3_EditCommand` function is called when the `DataGrid3.EditCommand` event occurs. This event occurs when the Edit button is clicked for an item in the `DataGrid3` control. The code for the function is as follows:

```
Private Sub DataGrid3_EditCommand(ByVal source As Object, ByVal e As
System.Web.UI.WebControls.DataGridCommandEventArgs) Handles
DataGrid3.EditCommand
        DataGrid3.EditItemIndex = e.Item.ItemIndex
        BindGrid()
End Sub
```

The parameter passed to the function is an object of the `DataGridCommandEvent-Args` type. This parameter contains all information for the event. The index of the item that calls this function is stored in the `EditItemIndex` property of the `Data-Grid3` control. Finally, the `BindGrid` function is called.

The *DataGrid3_UpdateCommand* Function

The `DataGrid3_UpdateCommand` function is called when the `UpdateCommand` event occurs. This event occurs when the Update button is clicked for an item in the `DataGrid3` control. The code for the function is as follows:

```
Private Sub DataGrid3_UpdateCommand(ByVal source As Object, ByVal e As
System.Web.UI.WebControls.DataGridCommandEventArgs) Handles
DataGrid3.UpdateCommand
        ' For bound columns, the edited value is stored in a TextBox.
        ' The TextBox is the 0th element in the column's cell.

        Dim MovID As String = e.Item.Cells(2).Text
        Dim movie As String = e.Item.Cells(3).Text
        Dim videoId As String = e.Item.Cells(4).Text
        Dim Format As String = e.Item.Cells(5).Text
        'Dim txtPrice As TextBox = CType(e.Item.Cells(6).Controls(0), TextBox)
        Dim txtQty As TextBox = CType(e.Item.Cells(7).Controls(0), TextBox)
```

```
Dim Price As String = e.Item.Cells(6).Text
Dim Qty As String = txtQty.Text
'Dim Qty As String = e.Item.Cells(7).Text
'Qty = e.Item.Cells(7).Text
Dim myvar As Boolean
myvar = IsNumeric(txtQty.Text)
If myvar = False Then
    Label6.Visible = True
    Label6.Text = "Quantity should be a positive Numeric value"
    Exit Sub
ElseIf Qty <= 0 Then
    Label6.Visible = True
    Label6.Text = "Quantity should be a positive Numeric value"
    Exit Sub
Else
    Label6.Visible = False
End If
Dim dr As DataRow


' With a database, use an update command to update the data. Because
' the data source in this example is an in-memory DataTable, delete the
' old row and replace it with a new one.
Dim item1 As String = e.Item.Cells(2).Text
Cart = Session("ShoppingCart")
CartView = New DataView(Cart)
CartView.RowFilter = "MovID='" & item1 & "'"
If CartView.Count > 0 Then
    CartView.Delete(0)
End If
CartView.RowFilter = ""
' Add new entry.
dr = Cart.NewRow()
dr("MovID") = MovID
dr("Movie") = movie
dr("VideoID") = videoID
dr("Format") = Format
```

```
        dr("Price") = Price
        dr("Quantity") = Qty
        Cart.Rows.Add(dr)

        DataGrid3.EditItemIndex = -1
        BindGrid()

End Sub
```

In the preceding code, the values in the cells of the selected record are stored into respective string variables. The customer can update the quantity of a specified record. The updated quantity is validated. The dataset from the session variable ShoppingCart is fetched into another dataset, Cart. The updated row in this dataset is detected using Movie ID and is removed from the dataset.

Next, the updated row that contains the updated quantity is added to the dataset. This dataset is put back into the session variable.

The *DataGrid3_DeleteCommand* Function

The DataGrid3_DeleteCommand function is called when the DataGrid3.- DeleteCommand event occurs. This event occurs when the Delete button is clicked for an item in the DataGrid3 control. The code for the function is as follows:

```
Private Sub DataGrid3_DeleteCommand(ByVal source As Object, ByVal e As
System.Web.UI.WebControls.DataGridCommandEventArgs) Handles
DataGrid3.DeleteCommand
        Dim dr As DataRow

        Dim item1 As String = e.Item.Cells(2).Text
        Cart = Session("ShoppingCart")
        CartView = New DataView(Cart)
        CartView.RowFilter = "MovID='" & item1 & "'"
        If CartView.Count > 0 Then
            CartView.Delete(0)
        End If
        CartView.RowFilter = ""
        BindGrid()
    End Sub
```

The *CmdPlaceOrder_Click* Function

The CmdPlaceOrder_Click function is called when the customer has placed all the desired items in the cart and then clicks on the Place Order button. The code for the function is as follows:

```
Private Sub CmdPlaceOrder _Click(ByVal sender As Object, ByVal e As
System.EventArgs)
Handles CmdPlaceOrder.Click
        Dim intCount As Integer
        Dim intTotalQty As Integer
        Dim OrderValue As Integer
        intCount = CartView.Count
        If intCount = 0 Then
            Label2.Visible = True
            Label2.Text = "Select some Videos before placing an Order"
            Exit Sub
        Else
            Label6.Visible = False
            Dim intQty As Integer

            OrderValue = 0
            Dim intPrice As Integer
            intTotalQty = 0
            Dim j As Integer
            For j = 0 To intCount - 1
                intPrice = CartView.Table.Rows(j)(4)
                intQty = CartView.Table.Rows(j)(5)
                intTotalQty = intTotalQty + CartView.Table.Rows(j)(5)
                OrderValue = OrderValue + (intQty * intPrice)
            Next j

        End If
        Dim strConnectionString = Application("strConnect")
        Dim MyConnection As New SqlConnection(strConnectionString)
        MyConnection.Open()

        Dim mySelectQuery As String = "Select
IsNull(Max(convert(int,substring(OrderID,2,4))),0)+1 as orderId from Orders"
```

```
        Dim myCommand As New SqlCommand(mySelectQuery, MyConnection)

        Dim myReader As SqlDataReader
        Dim OrderID As String
        myReader = myCommand.ExecuteReader()
        ' Always call Read before accessing data.

        While myReader.Read()
            OrderID = "O000" + CStr(myReader.GetInt32(0))
        End While
        ' always call Close when done reading.
        myReader.Close()
        ' Close the connection when done with it.
        MyConnection.Close()

        Dim cmdInsert As SqlCommand
        Dim strCustID As String
        strCustID = Session("CustID")
        Dim strInsert As String
        MyConnection.Open()

        strInsert = "Insert Into Orders Values('" + OrderID + "','" + Now +
"','" + strCustID + "'," + CStr(intTotalQty) + "," + CStr(OrderValue) + ")"
        cmdInsert = New SqlCommand(strInsert, MyConnection)
        cmdInsert.ExecuteNonQuery()

        cmdInsert = Nothing
        MyConnection.Close()

        Dim strVideoID As String
        Dim strQuantity As String
        MyConnection.Open()
        Dim i As Integer
        For i = 0 To intCount - 1
            strVideoID = CartView.Table.Rows(i)(2)
            strQuantity = CartView.Table.Rows(i)(5)
            strInsert = "Insert Into
OrderDetails(OrderID,VideoID,Qty) Values('" + OrderID + "','" +
```

```
strVideoID + "','" + strQuantity + "')"
        cmdInsert = New SqlCommand(strInsert, MyConnection)
        cmdInsert.ExecuteNonQuery()
        cmdInsert = Nothing


    Next i
    MyConnection.Close()
End Sub
```

The preceding code performs the following tasks:

- If the customer has not added any items to the cart, it can be checked by the Count property of the CartView object. If it is 0, the Label2.Text property is set to Select some Videos before placing an Order.

- The price and quantity of all the items ordered is retrieved from the CartView object and placed into two integer variables. The total quantity and order value are calculated and captured into numeric variables.

- A connection with the underlying database is maintained. The maximum value of OrderID is retrieved from the Orders table and is incremented by 1 to form the new order ID for the order placed. This order ID is captured in a string variable.

- Next, a new record with the order ID, total quantity, and order value is inserted in the Orders table by using the SqlCommand object.

- The value in the VideoID and Quantity fields is retrieved from the Card-View object and is stored into string variables. Finally, a new record is inserted in the OrderDetails table with the new OrderID, VideoID, and Quantity. The record is inserted by using the SqlCommand object. This is true for all orders placed.

After the customer has performed search operations and placed orders to the application, he or she can check his or her respective account. When the customer clicks on the My Account hyperlink in the left panel, he or she is directed to the MyAccount.aspx page. The functionality of the Account Details page is discussed in the next section.

Coding for the Account Details Page

The Account Details page looks like Figure 27-5.

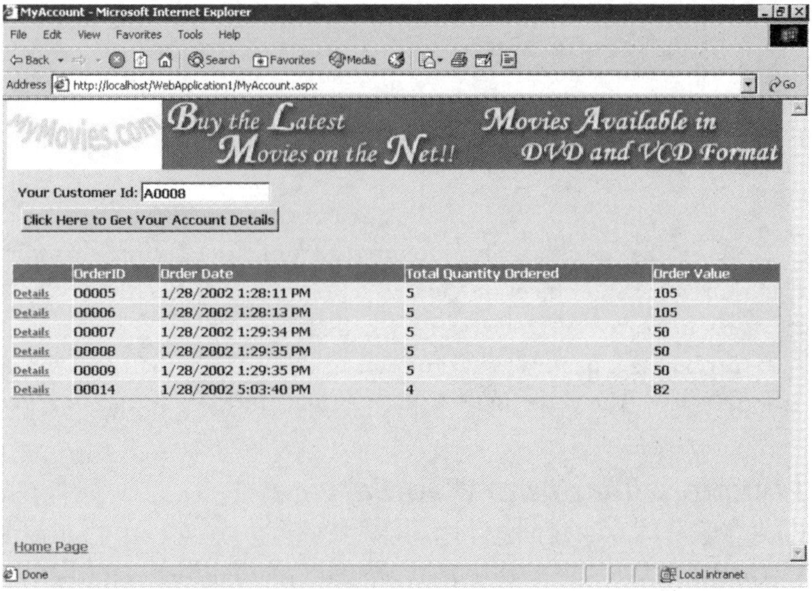

FIGURE 27-5 *The Account Details page*

The customer has to enter his or her customer ID and then click on the Click Here to Get Your Account Details button. The account details are displayed in the grid. The Account Details page contains the following functions.

◆ btnGetData_Click

◆ dgAccountDetails_ItemCommand

◆ CustomValidator1_ServerValidate

Each of these functions is explained in the following sections.

The *btnGetData_Click* Function

The btnGetData_Click function is called when the Click Here to Get Your Account Details button is clicked. The code for the function is as follows:

```
Private Sub btnGetData_Click(ByVal sender As System.Object, ByVal e As
System.EventArgs) Handles btnGetData.Click
        Dim MyDataSet As DataSet
        Dim accountWeb As New localhost.MyMoviesAccDet()
        Try
            MyDataSet = accountWeb.GetMyAccount(txtCustID.Text)
```

```
            dgAccountDetails.DataSource = MyDataSet
            dgAccountDetails.DataBind()
        Catch
            Exit Sub
        End Try
    End Sub
```

This function uses a Web service for fetching customer details into this form. The accountWeb variable is an object of the MyMoviesAccDet Web service. The GetMy-Account method of the Web service is called by passing the text from the txtCustID text box as a parameter. To understand the functionality of the preceding function, let's see the code and functionality of the Web service involved.

The Functionality of the Web Service

As discussed in Chapter 25, "Web Services," Visual Studio.NET provides you with an ASP.NET Web service project template that enables you to create Web services in Visual Basic or C#. When you use this built-in template, your final application consists of a set of predefined files that you can use to code the Web service, depending on your requirements. To create a Web service by using an ASP.NET Web service template, you need to perform the following steps:

1. Click File, New, Project. The New Project dialog box appears on the screen.

2. Select either the Visual Basic Projects or Visual C# Projects folder from the dialog box. The available templates appear in the box.

3. Click on the ASP.NET Web Service icon. A Web service with the default name of WebService1 is created for you. Visual Studio creates the files needed to support a Web service. These files are visible in the Solution Explorer.

After the Web project has been created, you need to code the Web service methods. For clients to access these methods, you can use the WebMethod attribute that is placed before the declaration of the method. The code for the MyMovies-AccDet.asmx file is as follows:

```
Public Class MyMoviesAccDet Inherits System.Web.Services.WebService
<WebMethod()> Public Function GetMyAccount(ByVal CustomerID As String) As DataSet
        Dim MyConnStr As String
        Dim MySql As String
```

```
        Dim MyConn As SqlConnection
        Dim MyDataAdapter As SqlDataAdapter
        Dim MyDataSet As New DataSet()
        'set the connection string
        MyConnStr = Application("strConnect")
        'set the select statement
        MySql = "SELECT Orders.OrderID, Orders.OrderDate AS [Order Date],
Orders.TotalQtyOrdered as [Total Quantity Ordered], Orders.OrderValue as [Order
Value] FROM Orders WHERE orders.CustID = '" + CustomerID + "'"
        'open the connection
        MyConn = New SqlConnection(MyConnStr)
        MyDataAdapter = New SqlDataAdapter(MySql, MyConn)
        MyDataAdapter.Fill(MyDataSet)
        Return MyDataSet

    End Function
    <WebMethod()> Public Function GetMyAccountDetails(ByVal OrderID As String) As
DataSet
        Dim MyConnStr As String
        Dim MySql As String
        Dim MyConn As SqlConnection
        Dim MyDataAdapter As SqlDataAdapter
        Dim MyDataSet As New DataSet()
        'set the connection string
        MyConnStr = Application("strConnect")
        'set the select statement
        MySql = "SELECT Movie.MovTitle as [Movie Title], OrderDetails.VideoID,
OrderDetails.Qty, Video.Format, Video.Price, Movie.MovID AS [Movie ID] FROM
OrderDetails INNER JOIN Video ON OrderDetails.VideoID = Video.VideoID INNER JOIN
Movie ON Video.MovID = Movie.MovID WHERE OrderDetails.OrderID = '" + OrderID +
"'"
        'open the connection
        MyConn = New SqlConnection(MyConnStr)
        MyDataAdapter = New SqlDataAdapter(MySql, MyConn)
        MyDataAdapter.Fill(MyDataSet)
        Return MyDataSet
    End Function
End Class
```

The Web service contains two Web methods: GetMyAccount and GetMyAccount-Details. Let's discuss the functionality of these methods in detail.

The GetMyAccount method is called when the btnGetData_Click function is executed. It takes the customer ID as a parameter, which is captured through the Text property of the txtCustID text box. A connection with the underlying database is started. A SQL Select query fetches the OrderID, OrderDate, TotalQty-Ordered, and OrderValue fields from the Orders table where the CustID field matches with the CustomerID parameter passed to the function. The DataAdapter object uses its Fill method to populate the dataset, which is then returned back to the calling method (btnGetData_Click).

The GetMyAccountDetails method takes as a parameter the OrderID passed to it by the calling method. A connection with the underlying database is started. A SQL Select and JOIN query fetches the respective fields from the OrderDetails, Video, and Movie tables where the OrderID field matches with the OrderID parameter passed to the function. The DataAdapter object uses its Fill method to populate the dataset, which is then returned back to the calling method.

The *dgAccountDetails_ItemCommand* Function

This function is called when the customer clicks the Details button of the dgAccountDetails grid. This function handles the ItemCommand event raised by the DataGrid object. The function receives a parameter of type DataGridCommand-EventArgs containing data related to this event. The code for the function is as follows:

```
Private Sub dgAccountDetails_ItemCommand(ByVal source As Object, ByVal e As
System.Web.UI.WebControls.DataGridCommandEventArgs) Handles
dgAccountDetails.ItemCommand
        Dim key As String = dgAccountDetails.DataKeys(e.Item.ItemIndex).ToString
        Dim MyDataSet As DataSet
        Dim accountDetWeb As New localhost.MyMoviesAccDet()

        MyDataSet = accountDetWeb.GetMyAccountDetails(key)
        DataGrid1.DataSource = MyDataSet
        DataGrid1.DataBind()
    End Sub
```

The preceding code captures the index of the item that acts as the command source in the DataGrid control. The `DataKeys` method of the DataGrid control captures the key field in the data source specified by the `DataSource` property. Therefore, the `OrderID` is captured in the string variable defined by the name `key`. This `OrderID` is passed to the Web service method, `GetMyAccountDetails`. The method returns a dataset that acts as the data source for the controls in the `Data Grid` object. Therefore, the records in the dataset, returned by the Web service method, are displayed in the grid.

The *CustomValidator1_ServerValidate* Function

The `CustomValidator1_ServerValidate` function validates the customer ID. The code for the function is as follows:

```
Private Sub CustomValidator1_ServerValidate(ByVal source As System.Object,
ByVal args As System.Web.UI.WebControls.ServerValidateEventArgs) Handles
CustomValidator1.ServerValidate
        Dim sConnectionString As String
        Dim sqlString As String

        Dim MyConnection As SqlConnection
        Dim MyDataAdapter As SqlDataAdapter
        Dim DS As New DataSet()

        sConnectionString = Application("strConnect")
        sqlString = "Select * from Customer where CustID='" + args.Value + "'"
        'Opening the connection

        MyConnection = New SqlConnection(sConnectionString)
        MyDataAdapter = New SqlDataAdapter(sqlString, MyConnection)

        MyDataAdapter.Fill(DS, "Customer")
        If DS.Tables("Customer").DefaultView.Count = 0 Then
            CustomValidator1.ErrorMessage = "This Customer Id Does not Exist"
            args.IsValid = False

        Else
            args.IsValid = True
```

```
    End If

End Sub
```

The customer ID entered by the user is validated using a CustomValidator control. A connection with the underlying database is established. The `DataAdapter` object, defined in the preceding code, populates the dataset with records from the `Customer` table that have the same `CustID` as the one stored in the `args.Value` property. If the `Customer` table in the dataset contains 0 records, the `CustomValidator1` control displays the message `This Customer Id Does not Exist`. Therefore, this function validates the application for a correct Customer ID entered.

After the customer has completed his or her operations in the Web application, he or she can log out by clicking the `Log out` hyperlink in the left panel of the Web application. The welcome message disappears from the home page, and the `Session` objects created for the particular customer are destroyed.

Summary

In this chapter, you learned about the functionality of the customer interface of the MyMovies video kiosk Web application. You learned about the various functions, both user defined and built-in, that impart functionality to the application.

Chapter 28

**Designing the
Admin Interface**

In Chapter 26, "Designing the Customer Interface," you learned how to create the customer interface of the video kiosk Web application. In this chapter, you will learn to create the admin interface, including the pages associated with it and the properties and controls associated with each page.

The admin interface of the video kiosk application consists of the following pages:

- The AdminHomePage page
- The Movies page
- The Video page
- The Actors page
- The Director page
- The Producer page
- The Customer page
- The ShowReports page

The following sections discuss each of these pages in detail.

The AdminHomePage Page

The AdminHomePage page is the first page of the admin interface. This page is the central location from which an administrator can modify the tables at the backend. In addition, the page also enables the administrator to view reports. Figure 28-1 shows the user interface of the home page.

Figure 28-2 shows AdminHomePage in the Design view.

The properties of the AdminHomePage Web form are listed in Table 28-1.

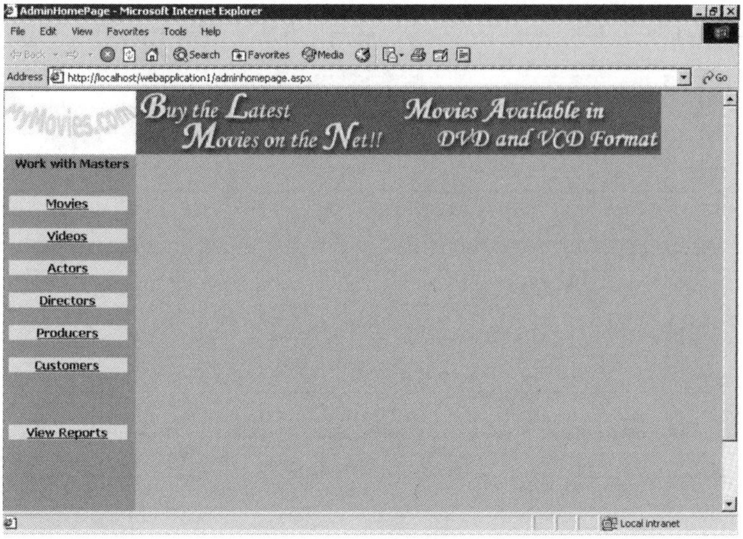

FIGURE 28-1 *The interface of the AdminHomePage page*

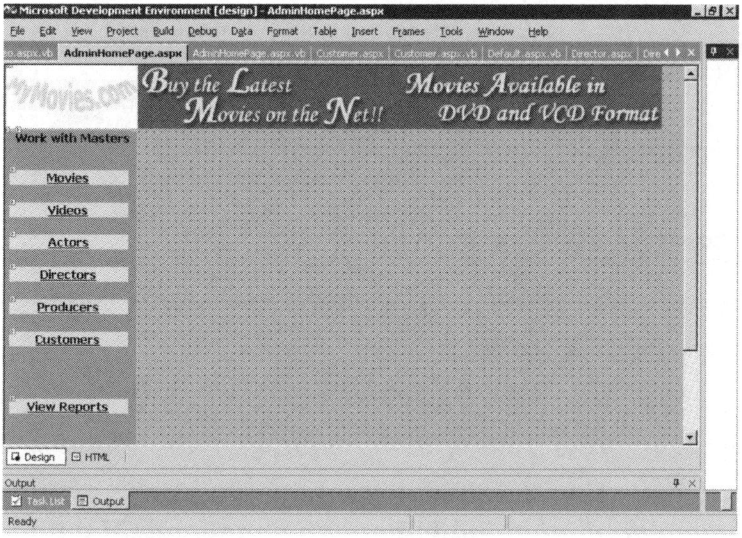

FIGURE 28-2 *The Design view of the AdminHomePage Web form*

Table 28-1 Properties Assigned to the AdminHomePage Web Form

Web Form	Property	Value
AdminHomePage	bgColor	#dda0dd
AdminHomePage	pageLayout	GridLayout

The AdminHomePage Web form contains an Image control. This Image control displays the banner on the page. Table 28-2 lists the properties of the Image control.

Table 28-2 Properties Assigned to the Image Control

Control	Property	Value
Image 1	ID	Image3
Image 1	ImageUrl	Bar.jpg
Image 1	Height	69px
Image 1	Width	710px

As shown in Figure 28-2, the AdminHomePage Web form contains hyperlinks that an administrator can use to move to the Movies, Actor, Director, Producer, Customer, Video, and ShowReports pages. These hyperlinks are placed on a panel. The properties of the panel are listed in Table 28-3.

Table 28-3 Properties Assigned to the Panel

Control	Property	Value
Panel 1	ID	Panel1
Panel 1	Height	410px
Panel 1	HorizontalAlign	Center
Panel 1	Width	145px
Panel 1	BackColor	MediumOrchid

The panel contains a label with the text Work with Masters. Table 28-4 lists the properties of this label.

Table 28-4 Properties Assigned to the Label

Control	Property	Value
Label 1	ID	lblMasters
Label 1	Font	Tahoma, Smaller
Label 1	Text	Work with Masters
Label 1	Height	23px
Label 1	Width	125px

It is under this label that all hyperlinks are placed. The NavigateUrl property of each Hyperlink control contains the name of the page that should open when the hyperlink is clicked. Table 28-5 lists the properties of these hyperlinks.

Table 28-5 Properties Assigned to the Hyperlinks

Control	Property	Value
Hyperlink 1	ID	HyperLink1
Hyperlink 1	BackColor	#FFC0FF
Hyperlink 1	Font	Tahoma, Smaller
Hyperlink 1	ForeColor	Black
Hyperlink 1	NavigateUrl	Movies.aspx
Hyperlink 1	Text	Movies
Hyperlink 1	Height	8px
Hyperlink 1	Width	128px
Hyperlink 2	ID	HyperLink2
Hyperlink 2	BackColor	#FFC0FF
Hyperlink 2	Font	Tahoma, Smaller
Hyperlink 2	ForeColor	Black
Hyperlink 2	Text	Actors
Hyperlink 2	NavigateUrl	actors.aspx
Hyperlink 3	ID	HyperLink3

continues

Table 28-5 *(continued)*

Control	Property	Value
Hyperlink 3	BackColor	#FFC0FF
Hyperlink 3	Font	Tahoma, Smaller
Hyperlink 3	ForeColor	Black
Hyperlink 3	Text	Producers
Hyperlink 3	NavigateUrl	Producer.aspx
Hyperlink 4	ID	HyperLink4
Hyperlink 4	BackColor	#FFC0FF
Hyperlink 4	Font	Tahoma, Smaller
Hyperlink 4	ForeColor	Black
Hyperlink 4	Height	3px
Hyperlink 4	Text	Videos
Hyperlink 4	NavigateUrl	video.aspx
Hyperlink 5	ID	HyperLink5
Hyperlink 5	BackColor	#FFC0FF
Hyperlink 5	Font	Tahoma, Smaller
Hyperlink 5	ForeColor	Black
Hyperlink 5	Text	Directors
Hyperlink 5	NavigateUrl	Director.aspx
Hyperlink 7	ID	HyperLink7
Hyperlink 7	BackColor	#FFC0FF
Hyperlink 7	Font	Tahoma, Smaller
Hyperlink 7	ForeColor	Black
Hyperlink 7	Text	Customers
Hyperlink 7	NavigateUrl	customer.aspx
Hyperlink 8	ID	HyperLink8
Hyperlink 8	BackColor	#FFC0FF

Control	Property	Value
Hyperlink 8	Font	Tahoma, Smaller
Hyperlink 8	ForeColor	Black
Hyperlink 8	Text	View Reports
Hyperlink 8	NavigateUrl	ShowReports.aspx

When an administrator clicks on a hyperlink, the page associated with the hyperlink opens.

The Movies Page

When an administrator clicks on the Movies hyperlink, the Movies page opens. Figure 28-3 displays the Design view of the Movies Web form.

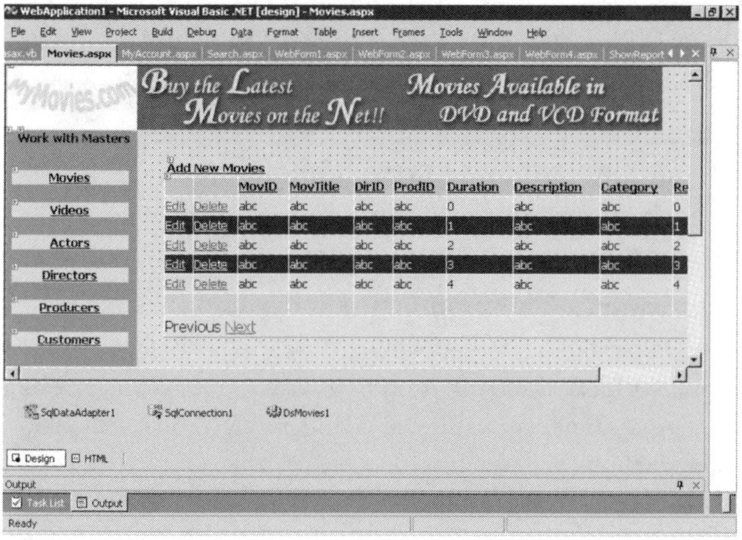

FIGURE 28-3   *The Design view of the Movies Web form*

As you can see, the Web form contains a SqlDataAdapter, a SqlConnection, and a DataSet object. You create a SqlAdapter object by performing the following steps:

1. Select and drag the `SqlDataAdapter` control from the Data tab of the Toolbox to the Web form. When you do so, an instance of the `Sql-DataAdapter` class is added to the Web form, and the first screen of the Data Adapter Configuration Wizard appears (see Figure 28-4).

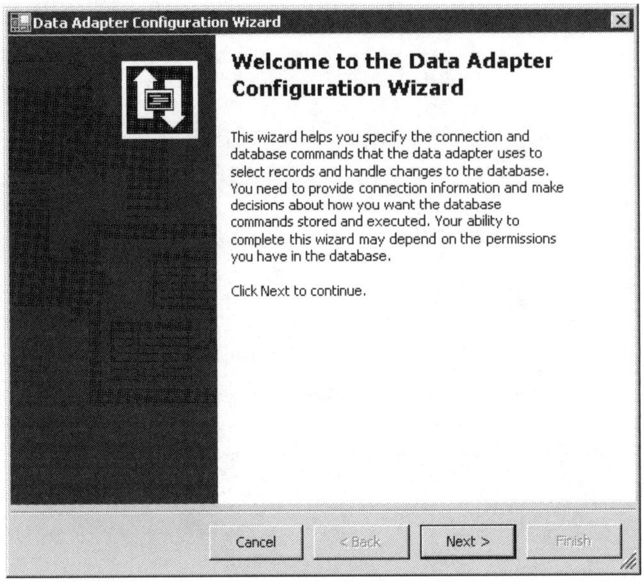

FIGURE 28-4 *The first screen of the Data Adapter Configuration Wizard*

2. Click on the Next button and then click on the Next button again.

3. Select the Use SQL statements option in the third screen of the Data Adapter Configuration Wizard and then click on the Next button.

4. Click on the Query Builder button to use the Query Builder. The Add Table dialog box appears, as shown in Figure 28-5. Select the Movie table and click on the Add button to display the columns of the selected table. Click on the Close button to close the Add Table dialog box.

5. In the Query Builder, check all the columns of the Movie table. Click on the OK button to close the Query Builder and return to the wizard. The query you designed appears on the screen.

6. Click on the Next button to open the last screen of the wizard, which provides a list of the tasks that the wizard has performed.

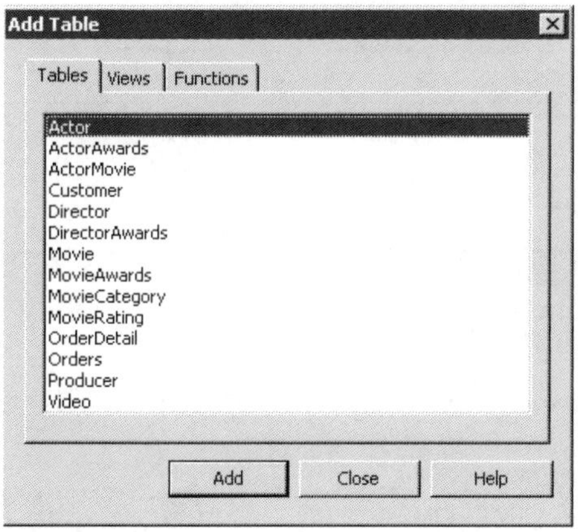

FIGURE 28-5 *The Add Table dialog box*

7. Click on the Finish button in the last screen to complete the process of configuring the data adapter. When you click on the Finish button, the selected settings are applied to the data adapter, and an instance of the connection object and the data adapter object appear on the Web form.

The Generate DataSet hyperlink in the properties window of the `DataAdapter` object has been used to generate the dataset.

The page contains a DataGrid control. This DataGrid control displays the details of five movies at a time. You use the `Next` and `Previous` links in the DataGrid control to view the next or previous set of records. The control also enables you to edit and delete the movie records. Table 28-6 lists the properties of the DataGrid control.

Table 28-6 Properties Assigned to the DataGrid Control

Control	Property	Value
DataGrid 1	ID	DataGrid1
DataGrid 1	AllowPaging	True
DataGrid 1	AllowSorting	True
DataGrid 1	DataKeyField	MovID
DataGrid 1	DataMember	Movie
DataGrid 1	DataSource	DsMovies1

continues

Table 28-6 (continued)

Control	Property	Value
DataGrid 1	Font	Tahoma, Small
DataGrid 1	Height	174px
DataGrid 1	PageSize	5
DataGrid 1	ShowFooter	True
DataGrid 1	Width	658px

As you can see, on the left side of the page, there is a panel that contains hyperlinks to various pages. The Movies page has a hyperlink, Add New Movies. The properties of this hyperlink are listed in Table 28-7.

Table 28-7 Properties Assigned to the Hyperlink

Control	Property	Value
Hyperlink 9	ID	HyperLink9
Hyperlink 9	BackColor	#FFC0FF
Hyperlink 9	Font	Tahoma, Smaller
Hyperlink 9	ForeColor	Black
Hyperlink 9	NavigateUrl	AddNewMovies.aspx
Hyperlink 9	Text	Add New Movies
Hyperlink 9	Height	8px
Hyperlink 9	Width	128px

When you click on the Add New Movies hyperlink, the AddNewMovies page opens. Figure 28-6 displays the user interface of the AddNewMovies page.

The AddNewMovies page is used to accept details of a new movie from the administrator and add the record to the database when the Add New Record button is clicked. As you can see in Figure 28-6, the Web form contains a Sql-DataAdapter object, a SqlConnection object, two datasets, and various labels, text boxes, and combo boxes. Table 28-8 lists the properties of the labels in the AddNewMovies Web form.

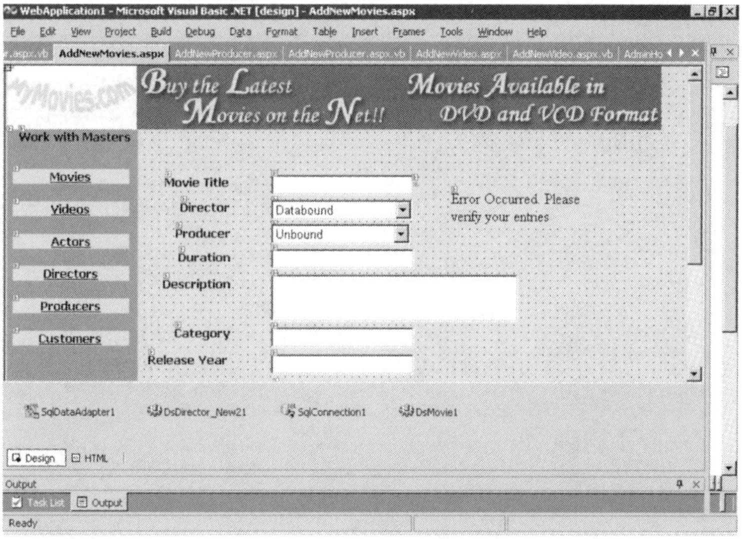

FIGURE 28-6 *The Design view of the AddNewMovies Web form*

Table 28-8 Properties Assigned to Labels

Control	Property	Value
Label 1	ID	Label1
Label 1	BackColor	#FFC0FF
Label 1	Font	Tahoma, Smaller
Label 1	ForeColor	Black
Label 1	Text	Description
Label 2	ID	Label2
Label 2	BackColor	#FFC0FF
Label 2	Font	Tahoma, Smaller
Label 2	ForeColor	Black
Label 2	Text	Movie Title
Label 2	Width	71px
Label 3	ID	Label3
Label 3	BackColor	#FFC0FF

continues

Table 28-8 *(continued)*

Control	Property	Value
Label 3	Font	Tahoma, Smaller
Label 3	ForeColor	Black
Label 3	Text	Director
Label 3	Width	54px
Label 4	ID	Label4
Label 4	BackColor	#FFC0FF
Label 4	Font	Tahoma, Smaller
Label 4	ForeColor	Black
Label 4	Text	Producer
Label 4	Width	59px
Label 5	ID	Label5
Label 5	BackColor	#FFC0FF
Label 5	Font	Tahoma, Smaller
Label 5	ForeColor	Black
Label 5	Text	Duration
Label 6	ID	Label6
Label 6	BackColor	#FFC0FF
Label 6	Font	Tahoma, Smaller
Label 6	ForeColor	Black
Label 6	Text	Category
Label 7	ID	Label7
Label 7	BackColor	#FFC0FF
Label 7	Font	Tahoma, Smaller
Label 7	ForeColor	Black
Label 7	Text	Realese Year
Label 7	Width	90px

Control	Property	Value
Label 8	ID	Label8
Label 8	Height	37px
Label 8	Font	Tahoma, Smaller
Label 8	ForeColor	Black
Label 8	Text	Error Occurred. Please verify your entries.
Label 8	Width	90px

The page contains text boxes and combo boxes to accept the new movie details from the administrator. The properties of the text boxes in the Web form are listed in Table 28-9.

Table 28-9 Properties Assigned to Text Boxes

Control	Property	Value
Text box 1	ID	txtMovie
Text box 2	ID	txtDuration
Text box 3	ID	txtDesc
Text box 3	Height	51px
Text box 3	Rows	4
Text box 3	Width	268px
Text box 4	ID	txtCat
Text box 5	ID	txtRelYear

To ensure that the txtMovie box is not left blank, a RequiredFieldValidator control is used. The properties of the RequiredFieldValidator control are listed in Table 28-10.

Table 28-10 Properties Assigned to RequiredFieldValidator Control

Control	Property	Value
RequiredFieldValidator1	ID	RequiredField Validator1
RequiredFieldValidator1	ControlToValidate	txtMovie
RequiredFieldValidator1	ErrorMessage	Movie Title Cannot be Blank
RequiredFieldValidator1	ForeColor	Red
RequiredFieldValidator1	Text	*

The AddNewMovies Web form has two combo boxes. The properties of these combo boxes are listed in Table 28-11.

Table 28-11 Properties Assigned to Combo Boxes

Control	Property	Value
cmbDirector	ID	cmbDirector
cmbDirector	DataMember	Director
cmbDirector	DataSource	DsDirector_New21
cmbDirector	DataValueField	DirID
cmbDirector	Width	153px
cmbProducer	ID	cmbProducer
cmbProducer	Width	151px

The AddNewMovie Web form has a ValidationSummary control that is used to display the errors on the page in a message box. The properties of the Validation-Summary control are listed in Table 28-12.

Table 28-12 Properties Assigned to the ValidationSummary Control

Control	Property	Value
ValidationSummary 1	ID	ValidationSummary1
ValidationSummary 1	ShowMessageBox	True

Control	Property	Value
ValidationSummary 1	ShowSummary	False
ValidationSummary 1	Width	81px

After the administrator enters the details of a movie and clicks on the Add New Record button, the movie is added to the database if the details specified by the administrator are valid. Table 28-13 lists the properties of the button.

Table 28-13 Properties Assigned to the Button

Control	Property	Value
Button 1	ID	Button1
Button 1	Text	Add New Record

The Video Page

When an administrator clicks on the Videos hyperlink in the AdminHomePage page, the Video page opens. The Design view of this page is shown in Figure 28-7, shown on page 688.

The Video page, in addition to containing the hyperlinks to the master tables, contains a DataGrid control that displays the video records five at a time. The DataGrid control enables you to edit and delete the records. In addition, you can also view the previous or next set of video records. Table 28-14 lists the properties of the DataGrid control.

Table 28-14 Properties Assigned to the DataGrid Control

Control	Property	Value
DataGrid 1	ID	DataGrid1
DataGrid 1	AllowPaging	True
DataGrid 1	AllowSorting	True
DataGrid 1	AutoGenerateColumns	False

continues

Table 28-14 *(continued)*

Control	Property	Value
DataGrid 1	DataKeyField	VideoID
DataGrid 1	DataMember	Video
DataGrid 1	DataSource	DsVideo2
DataGrid 1	Font	Tahoma, Small
DataGrid 1	Height	174px
DataGrid 1	PageSize	5
DataGrid 1	ShowFooter	True
DataGrid 1	Width	658px

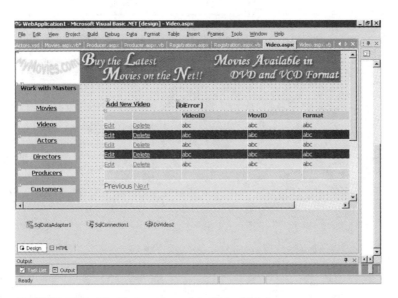

FIGURE 28-7 *The Design view of the Video Web form*

The Video Web form contains a `SqlDataAdapter` object, a `SqlConnection` object, and a `DataSet` object. When creating the `SqlDataAdapter` object, the Video table has to be specified in the DataAdapter Configuration Wizard.

The Web form contains two labels, `lblMasters` and `lblError`. The `lblMasters` label displays the `Work with Masters` text and is placed above the hyperlinks, as shown in Figure 28-7. The `lblError` label is used to display an error message if an error occurs. The properties of the labels are listed in Table 28-15.

Table 28-15 Properties Assigned to Labels

Control	Property	Value
Label 1	ID	lblMasters
Label 1	Font	Tahoma, Smaller
Label 1	Height	23px
Label 1	Text	Work with Masters
Label 1	Width	125px
Label 2	ID	lblError
Label 2	BackColor	#FFC0FF
Label 2	Font	Tahoma, Smaller
Label 2	ForeColor	Black
Label 2	Width	244px

The Video page has a hyperlink, `Add New Video`. The properties of this hyperlink are listed in Table 28-16.

Table 28-16 Properties Assigned to the Hyperlink

Control	Property	Value
Hyperlink 9	ID	HyperLink9
Hyperlink 9	BackColor	#FFC0FF
Hyperlink 9	Font	Tahoma, Smaller
Hyperlink 9	ForeColor	Black
Hyperlink 9	NavigateUrl	AddNewVideo.aspx
Hyperlink 9	Text	Add New Video
Hyperlink 9	Height	8px
Hyperlink 9	Width	128px

When you click on the Add New Video hyperlink, the AddNewVideo page opens. Figure 28-8 displays the Design view of the AddNewVideo Web form.

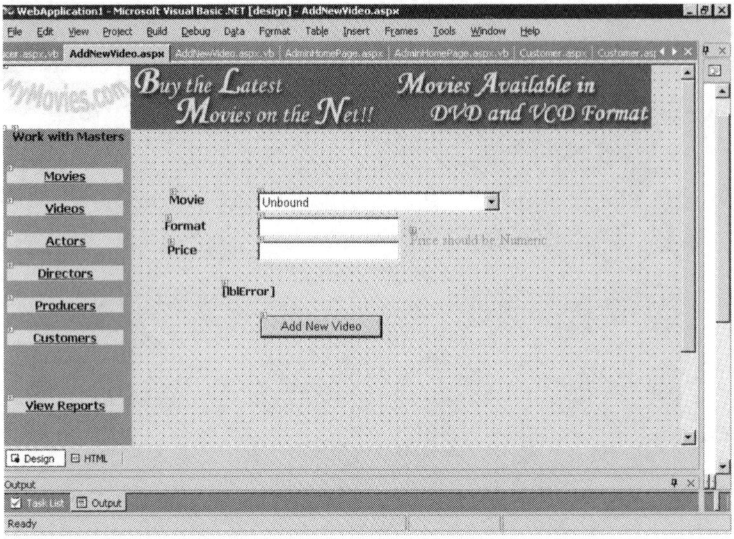

FIGURE 28-8 *The Design view of the AddNewVideo Web form*

The Web form is used to accept details from the administrator and to add the record to the database when the Add New Video button is clicked. As shown in Figure 28-8, the page contains labels, text boxes, and a combo box. Table 28-17 lists the properties of the labels in the AddNewVideo Web form.

Table 28-17 Properties Assigned to Labels

Control	Property	Value
Label 1	ID	lblMasters
Label 1	Font	Tahoma, Smaller
Label 1	Height	23px
Label 1	Text	Work with Masters
Label 1	Width	125px
Label 2	ID	lblError
Label 2	BackColor	#FFC0FF
Label 2	Font	Tahoma, Smaller

Control	Property	Value
Label 2	ForeColor	Black
Label 2	Width	244px
Label 3	ID	Label3
Label 3	BackColor	#FFC0FF
Label 3	Font	Tahoma, Smaller
Label 3	ForeColor	Black
Label 3	Text	Movie
Label 3	Width	54px
Label 4	ID	Label4
Label 4	BackColor	#FFC0FF
Label 4	Font	Tahoma, Smaller
Label 4	ForeColor	Black
Label 4	Text	Format
Label 4	Width	59px
Label 5	ID	Label5
Label 5	BackColor	#FFC0FF
Label 5	Font	Tahoma, Smaller
Label 5	ForeColor	Black
Label 5	Text	Price

The Web form also contains a combo box that contains a list of movies. The properties of the combo box are listed in Table 28-18.

Table 28-18 Properties Assigned to the Combo Box

Control	Property	Value
Combo box 1	ID	cmbMovie
Combo box 1	DataValueField	DirID
Combo box 1	Width	264px

There also are two text boxes on the Web form. These text boxes accept the format and price of the video. The properties of these text boxes are listed in Table 28-19.

Table 28-19 Properties Assigned to Text Boxes

Control	Property	Value
Text box 1	ID	txtFormat
Text box 2	ID	txtPrice

To ensure that the value entered in the txtPrice box is numeric, a CompareValidator control has been used. The properties of the CompareValidator control are listed in Table 28-20.

Table 28-20 Properties Assigned to the CompareValidator Control

Control	Property	Value
CompareValidator 1	ID	CompareValidator1
CompareValidator 1	ControlToValidate	txtPrice
CompareValidator 1	ErrorMessage	Price should be Numeric
CompareValidator 1	Operator	DataTypeCheck
CompareValidator 1	Type	Currency
CompareValidator 1	ValueToCompare	1
CompareValidator 1	Width	158px

After the administrator enters the details of a video and clicks on the Add New Video button, the video is added to the database if the details specified by the administrator are valid. Table 28-21 lists the properties of the button.

Table 28-21 Properties Assigned to the Button

Control	Property	Value
Button 1	ID	Button1
Button 1	Text	Add New Video

The Actors Page

When an administrator clicks on the Actors hyperlink in the AdminHomePage page, the Actors page opens. The Design view of the Actors Web form is shown in Figure 28-9.

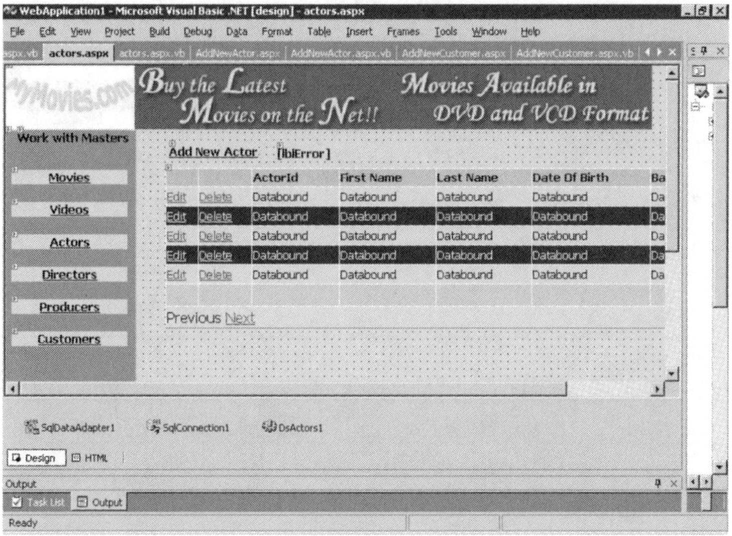

FIGURE 28-9   *The Design view of the Actors Web form*

The Actors Web form contains a SqlDataAdapter object, a SqlConnection object, and a dataset. When creating the SqlDataAdapter object, the Actor table has to be specified in the DataAdapter Configuration Wizard.

The Actors page, in addition to containing the hyperlinks to the master tables, contains a DataGrid control that displays the actor records five at a time. The DataGrid control enables you to edit and delete the records. In addition, you can also view the previous or next set of actor records. Table 28-22 lists the properties of the DataGrid control.

Table 28-22 Properties Assigned to the DataGrid Control

Control	Property	Value
DataGrid 1	ID	DataGrid1
DataGrid 1	AllowPaging	True
DataGrid 1	AllowSorting	True
DataGrid 1	AutoGenerateColumns	False
DataGrid 1	Font	Tahoma, Small
DataGrid 1	Height	174px
DataGrid 1	PageSize	5
DataGrid 1	ShowFooter	True
DataGrid 1	Width	658px

The Web form contains two labels, lblMasters and lblError. The lblMasters label displays the Work with Masters text and is placed above the hyperlink (refer back to Figure 28-6). The lblError label is used to display an error message if an error occurs. The properties of the labels are listed in Table 28-23.

Table 28-23 Properties Assigned to the Labels

Control	Property	Value
Label 1	ID	lblMasters
Label 1	Font	Tahoma, Smaller
Label 1	Height	23px
Label 1	Text	Work with Masters
Label 1	Width	125px
Label 2	ID	lblError
Label 2	BackColor	#FFC0FF
Label 2	Font	Tahoma, Smaller
Label 2	ForeColor	Black
Label 2	Width	244px

The Actors page has a hyperlink, Add New Actor. The properties of this hyperlink are listed in Table 28-24.

Table 28-24 Properties Assigned to the Hyperlink

Control	Property	Value
Hyperlink	ID	HyperLink9
Hyperlink	BackColor	#FFC0FF
Hyperlink	Font	Tahoma, Smaller
Hyperlink	ForeColor	Black
Hyperlink	NavigateUrl	AddNewActor.aspx
Hyperlink	Text	Add New Actor
Hyperlink	Height	8px
Hyperlink	Width	128px

When you click on the Add New Actor hyperlink, the AddNewActor page opens. Figure 28-10 displays the Design view of the AddNewActor Web form.

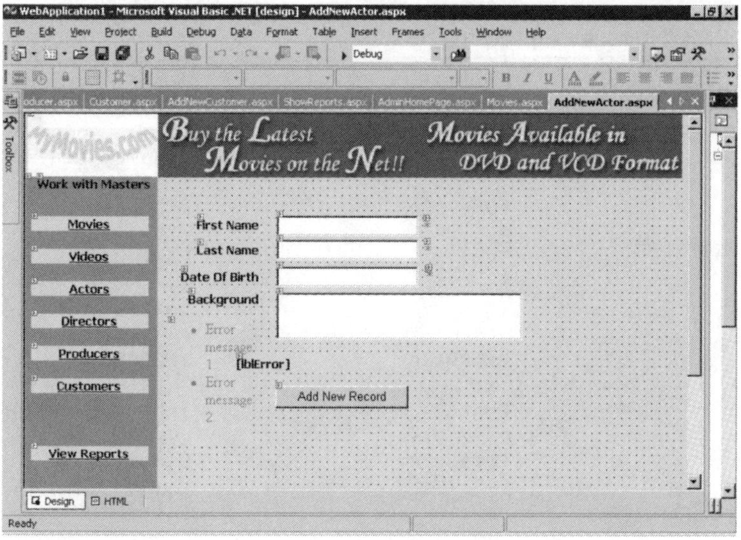

FIGURE 28-10 *The Design view of the AddNewActor Web form*

The Web form is used to accept details from the administrator and to add the record to the database when the Add New Actor button is clicked. As you can see, the page contains labels and text boxes. Table 28-25 lists the properties of the labels in the AddNewActor Web form.

Table 28-25 Properties Assigned to the Labels

Control	Property	Value
Label 1	ID	lblError
Label 1	BackColor	#FFC0FF
Label 1	Font	Tahoma, Smaller
Label 1	ForeColor	Black
Label 1	Width	244px
Label 2	ID	LblFName
Label 2	BackColor	#FFC0FF
Label 2	Font	Tahoma, Smaller
Label 2	ForeColor	Black
Label 2	Text	First Name
Label 3	ID	LblLName
Label 3	BackColor	#FFC0FF
Label 3	Font	Tahoma, Smaller
Label 3	ForeColor	Black
Label 3	Text	Last Name
Label 4	ID	LblDOB
Label 4	BackColor	#FFC0FF
Label 4	Font	Tahoma, Smaller
Label 4	ForeColor	Black
Label 4	Text	Date Of Birth
Label 5	ID	LblBackGround
Label 5	BackColor	#FFC0FF

Control	Property	Value
Label 5	Font	Tahoma, Smaller
Label 5	ForeColor	Black
Label 5	Text	Background

There also are four text boxes on the Web form. These text boxes accept the details of an actor. The properties of these text boxes are listed in Table 28-26.

Table 28-26 Properties Assigned to Text Boxes

Control	Property	Value
Text box 1	ID	txtFname
Text box 1	TabIndex	1
Text box 2	ID	txtLname
Text box 2	TabIndex	2
Text box 3	ID	txtDOB
Text box 3	TabIndex	3
Text box 4	ID	txtBGround
Text box 4	Height	51px
Text box 4	Rows	4
Text box 4	TabIndex	4
Text box 4	Width	268px

To ensure that the First Name, Last Name, and Date of Birth fields are not left blank, the RequiredFieldValidator controls are used. The properties of the RequiredFieldValidator controls are listed in Table 28-27.

Table 28-27 Properties Assigned to the RequiredFieldValidator Controls

Control	Property	Value
RequiredFieldValidator 1	ID	RequiredField Validator1
RequiredFieldValidator 1	ControlToValidate	txtFname
RequiredFieldValidator 1	ErrorMessage	First Name Cannot be Blank
RequiredFieldValidator 1	ForeColor	Red
RequiredFieldValidator 1	Text	*
RequiredFieldValidator 2	ID	RequiredField Validator2
RequiredFieldValidator 2	ControlToValidate	txtDOB
RequiredFieldValidator 2	ErrorMessage	Date of Birth cannot be Blank
RequiredFieldValidator 2	ForeColor	Red
RequiredFieldValidator 2	Text	*
RequiredFieldValidator 3	ID	RequiredField Validator3
RequiredFieldValidator 3	ControlToValidate	txtLname
RequiredFieldValidator 3	ErrorMessage	Last Name Cannot be Blank
RequiredFieldValidator 3	ForeColor	Red
RequiredFieldValidator 3	Text	*

The AddNewActor Web form has a ValidationSummary control that is used to display the errors on the page in a message box. The properties of the Validation-Summary control are listed in Table 28-28.

Table 28-28 Properties Assigned to the ValidationSummary Control

Control	Property	Value
ValidationSummary 1	ID	ValidationSummary1
ValidationSummary 1	ShowMessageBox	True

Control	Property	Value
ValidationSummary 1	ShowSummary	False
ValidationSummary 1	Width	81px

After the administrator enters the details of an actor and clicks on the Add New Record button, the record is added to the database if the details specified by the administrator are valid. Table 28-29 lists the properties of the button.

Table 28-29 Properties Assigned to the Button

Control	Property	Value
Button 1	ID	CmdAddNewRecord
Button 1	Text	Add New Record

The Director Page

The Director page opens when a user clicks on the Directors hyperlink. The Design view of the Director Web form is shown in Figure 28-11.

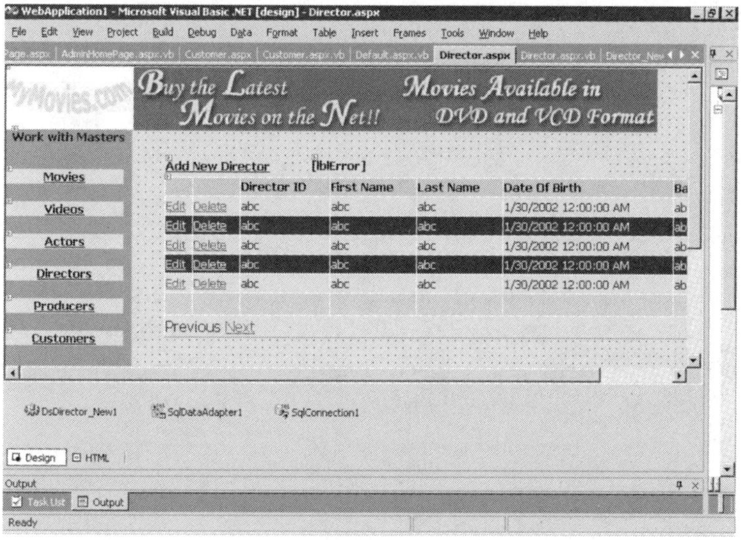

FIGURE 28-11 *The Design view of the Director Web form*

The Director Web form contains a `SqlDataAdapter` object, a `SqlConnection` object, and a dataset. When creating the `SqlDataAdapter` object, the Director table has to be specified in the DataAdapter Configuration Wizard.

The Director page, in addition to containing the hyperlinks to the master tables, contains a DataGrid control that displays the director records five at a time. The DataGrid control enables you to edit and delete the records. In addition, you can also view the previous or next set of records. Table 28-30 lists the properties of the DataGrid control.

Table 28-30 Properties Assigned to the DataGrid Control

Control	Property	Value
DataGrid 1	ID	DataGrid1
DataGrid 1	AllowPaging	True
DataGrid 1	AllowSorting	True
DataGrid 1	AutoGenerateColumns	False
DataGrid 1	DataKeyField	DirID
DataGrid 1	DataMember	Director
DataGrid 1	DataSource	DsDirector_New1
DataGrid 1	Font	Tahoma, Small
DataGrid 1	Height	174px
DataGrid 1	PageSize	5
DataGrid 1	ShowFooter	True
DataGrid 1	Width	658px

The Web form contains two labels, `lblMasters` and `lblError`. The `lblMasters` label displays the `Work with Masters` text and is placed above the hyperlinks (refer back to Figure 28-7). The `lblError` label is used to display an error message if an error occurs. The properties of the labels are listed in Table 28-31.

Table 28-31 Properties Assigned to the Labels

Control	Property	Value
Label 1	ID	lblMasters
Label 1	Font	Tahoma, Smaller
Label 1	Height	23px
Label 1	Text	Work with Masters
Label 1	Width	125px
Label 2	ID	lblError
Label 2	BackColor	#FFC0FF
Label 2	Font	Tahoma, Smaller
Label 2	ForeColor	Black
Label 2	Width	316px

The Director page has a hyperlink, Add New Director. The properties of this hyperlink are listed in Table 28-32.

Table 28-32 Properties Assigned to the Hyperlink

Control	Property	Value
Hyperlink	ID	HyperLink9
Hyperlink	BackColor	#FFC0FF
Hyperlink	Font	Tahoma, Smaller
Hyperlink	ForeColor	Black
Hyperlink	NavigateUrl	AddNewDirector.aspx
Hyperlink	Text	Add New Director
Hyperlink	Height	8px
Hyperlink	Width	128px

When you click on the Add New Director hyperlink, the AddNewDirector page opens. Figure 28-12 displays the Design view of the AddNewDirector page.

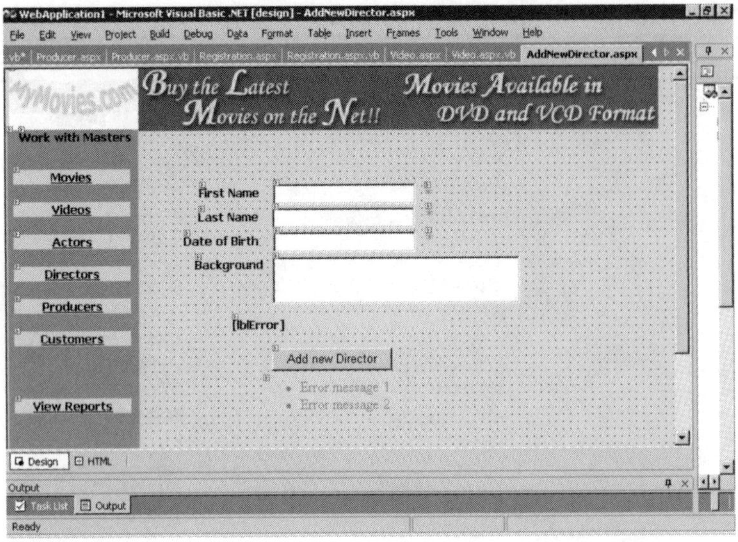

FIGURE 28-12 *The Design view of the AddNewDirector Web form*

The Web form is used to accept details from the administrator and to add the record to the database when the Add New Director button is clicked. As you can see, the page contains labels and text boxes. Table 28-33 lists the properties of the labels in the AddNewDirector page.

Table 28-33 Properties Assigned to the Labels

Control	Property	Value
Label 1	ID	LblBackGround
Label 1	BackColor	#FFC0FF
Label 1	Font	Tahoma, Smaller
Label 1	ForeColor	Black
Label 1	Text	Background
Label 2	ID	LblFName
Label 2	BackColor	#FFC0FF
Label 2	Font	Tahoma, Smaller
Label 2	ForeColor	Black
Label 2	Text	First Name

Control	Property	Value
Label 2	Width	71px
Label 3	ID	LblLName
Label 3	BackColor	#FFC0FF
Label 3	Font	Tahoma, Smaller
Label 3	ForeColor	Black
Label 3	Text	Last Name
Label 3	Width	77px
Label 4	ID	LblDOB
Label 4	BackColor	#FFC0FF
Label 4	Font	Tahoma, Smaller
Label 4	ForeColor	Black
Label 4	Text	Date Of Birth
Label 5	ID	lblError
Label 5	BackColor	#FFC0FF
Label 5	Font	Tahoma, Smaller
Label 5	ForeColor	Black
Label 5	Visible	False
Label 5	Width	237px

There are also four text boxes on the Web form that accept the details of a director. The properties of these text boxes are listed in Table 28-34.

Table 28-34 Properties Assigned to the Text Boxes

Control	Property	Value
Text box 1	ID	txtFName
Text box 2	ID	txtLname
Text box 3	ID	txtDOB

continues

Table 28-34 (continued)

Control	Property	Value
Text box 4	ID	txtBGround
Text box 4	Height	51px
Text box 4	Rows	4
Text box 4	Width	268px

To ensure that the First Name, Last Name, and Date of Birth fields are not left blank, RequiredFieldValidator controls are used. The properties of the Required-FieldValidator controls are listed in Table 28-35.

Table 28-35 Properties Assigned to the RequiredFieldValidator Controls

Control	Property	Value
RequiredFieldValidator 1	ID	RequiredField Validator1
RequiredFieldValidator 1	ControlToValidate	txtFName
RequiredFieldValidator 1	ErrorMessage	First Name cannot be Blank
RequiredFieldValidator 1	ForeColor	Red
RequiredFieldValidator 1	Text	*
RequiredFieldValidator 2	ID	RequiredFieldV alidator2
RequiredFieldValidator 2	ControlToValidate	txtLName
RequiredFieldValidator 2	ErrorMessage	Last name Cannot be Blank
RequiredFieldValidator 2	ForeColor	Red
RequiredFieldValidator 2	Text	*
RequiredFieldValidator 3	ID	RequiredField Validator3
RequiredFieldValidator 3	ControlToValidate	txtDOB

Control	Property	Value
RequiredFieldValidator 3	ErrorMessage	Date of Birth Cannot be Blank
RequiredFieldValidator 3	ForeColor	Red
RequiredFieldValidator 3	Text	*

The AddNewDirector Web form has a ValidationSummary control that is used to display the errors on the page in a message box. The properties of the ValidationSummary control are listed in Table 28-36.

Table 28-36 Properties Assigned to the ValidationSummary Control

Control	Property	Value
ValidationSummary 1	ID	ValidationSummary1
ValidationSummary 1	ShowMessageBox	True
ValidationSummary 1	ShowSummary	False

After the administrator enters the details of a director and clicks on the Add New Director button, the record is added to the database if the details specified by the administrator are valid. Table 28-37 lists the properties of the button.

Table 28-37 Properties Assigned to the Button

Control	Property	Value
Button 1	ID	CmdAddNewDir
Button 1	Text	Add New Director
Button 1	Width	131px

The Producer Page

The Producer page opens when a user clicks on the Producers hyperlink. The Design view of the Producer Web form is shown in Figure 28-13.

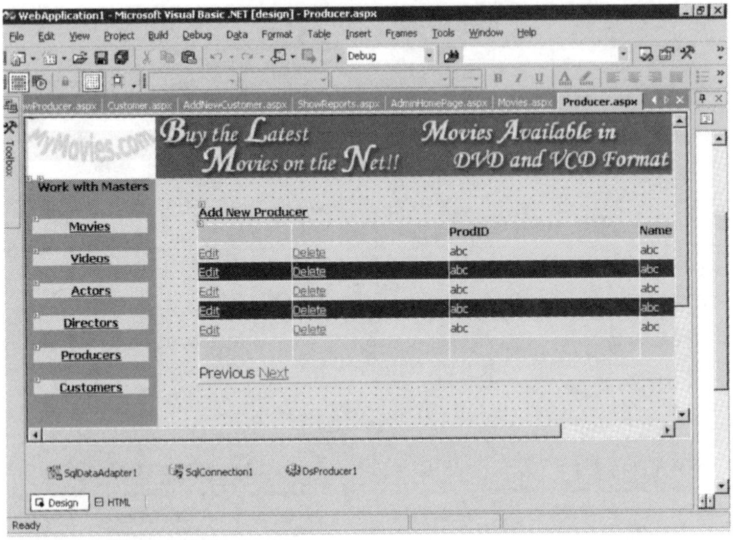

FIGURE 28-13 *The Design view of the Producer Web form*

The Producer Web form contains a `SqlDataAdapter` object, a `SqlConnection` object, and a dataset. When creating the `SqlDataAdapter` object, the `Producer` table has to be specified in the DataAdapter Configuration Wizard.

The Producer page, in addition to containing the hyperlinks to the master tables, contains a DataGrid control that displays the producer records five at a time. The DataGrid control enables you to edit and delete the records. In addition, you can also view the previous or next set of records. Table 28-38 lists the properties of the DataGrid control.

Table 28-38 Properties Assigned to the DataGrid Control

Control	Property	Value
DataGrid 1	ID	DataGrid1
DataGrid 1	AllowPaging	True
DataGrid 1	AllowSorting	True
DataGrid 1	AutoGenerateColumns	False
DataGrid 1	DataKeyField	ProdID
DataGrid 1	DataMember	Producer

Control	Property	Value
DataGrid 1	DataSource	DsProducer1
DataGrid 1	Font	Tahoma, Small
DataGrid 1	Height	174px
DataGrid 1	PageSize	5
DataGrid 1	ShowFooter	True
DataGrid 1	Width	658px

The Web form contains a label, lblMasters. The lblMasters label displays the Work with Masters text and is placed above the hyperlinks (refer to Figure 28-9).

The Producer page has a hyperlink, Add New Producer. The properties of this hyperlink are listed in Table 28-39.

Table 28-39 Properties Assigned to the Hyperlink

Control	Property	Value
Hyperlink	ID	HyperLink9
Hyperlink	BackColor	#FFC0FF
Hyperlink	Font	Tahoma, Smaller
Hyperlink	ForeColor	Black
Hyperlink	NavigateUrl	AddNewProducer.aspx
Hyperlink	Text	Add New Producer
Hyperlink	Height	8px
Hyperlink	Width	128px

When you click on the Add New Producer hyperlink, the AddNewProducer page opens. Figure 28-14 displays the Design view of the AddNewProducer page.

The Web form is used to accept details from the administrator and to add the record to the database when the Add New Producer button is clicked. Figure 28-13 shows the AddNewProducer page in the Design view. As you can see, the page

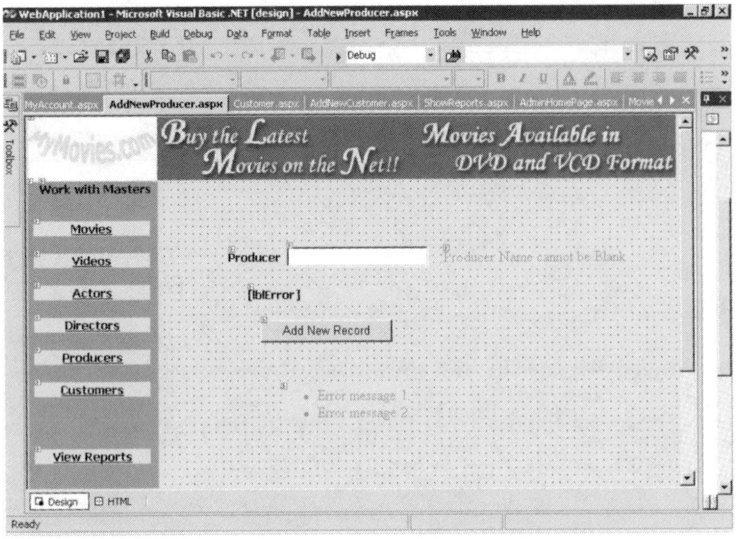

FIGURE 28-14 *The Design view of the AddNewProducer Web form*

contains labels and text boxes. Table 28-40 lists the properties of the labels in the AddNewProducer page.

Table 28-40 Properties Assigned to the Labels

Control	Property	Value
Label 1	ID	Label1
Label 1	Font	Tahoma, Smaller
Label 1	Text	Producer
Label 1	Width	63px
Label 2	ID	lblError
Label 2	Font	Tahoma, Smaller
Label 2	Width	171px

There is a text box on the Web form that accepts the name of the producer. The ID property of this text box is txtName. To ensure that the Producer field is not left blank, the RequiredFieldValidator control is used. The properties of the RequiredFieldValidator control are listed in Table 28-41.

Table 28-41 Properties Assigned to the RequiredFieldValidator Control

Control	Property	Value
RequiredFieldValidator 1	ID	RequiredField Validator1
RequiredFieldValidator 1	ControlToValidate	txtName
RequiredFieldValidator 1	ErrorMessage	Producer Name cannot be Blank

The AddNewProducer Web form has a ValidationSummary control that is used to display the errors on the page in a message box. The properties of the ValidationSummary control are listed in Table 28-42.

Table 28-42 Properties Assigned to the ValidationSummary Control

Control	Property	Value
ValidationSummary 1	ID	ValidationSummary1
ValidationSummary 1	ShowMessageBox	True
ValidationSummary 1	ShowSummary	False

After the administrator enters the details of a producer and clicks on the Add New Record button, the record is added to the database if the details specified by the administrator are valid. Table 28-43 lists the properties of the button.

Table 28-43 Properties Assigned to the Button

Control	Property	Value
Button 1	ID	CmdAddNewProducer
Button 1	Text	Add New Record

The Customer Page

The Customer page opens when a user clicks on the Customers hyperlink. The Design view of the Customer Web form is shown in Figure 28-15.

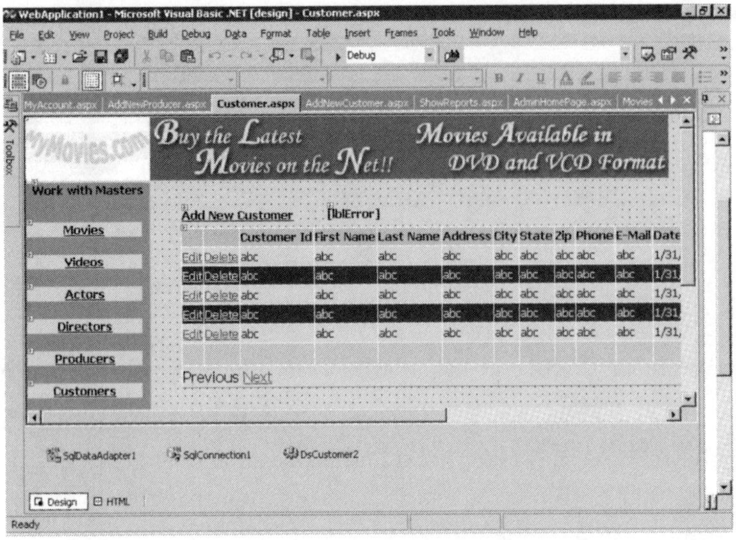

FIGURE 28-15 *The Design view of the Customer Web form*

The Customer Web form contains a SqlDataAdapter object, a SqlConnection object, and a dataset. When creating the SqlDataAdapter object, the Customer table has to be specified in the DataAdapter Configuration Wizard.

The Customer page, in addition to containing the hyperlinks to the master tables, contains a DataGrid control that displays the customer records five at a time. The DataGrid control enables you to edit and delete the records. In addition, you can also view the previous or next set of records. Table 28-44 lists the properties of the DataGrid control.

Table 28-44 Properties Assigned to the DataGrid Control

Control	Property	Value
DataGrid 1	ID	DataGrid1
DataGrid 1	AllowPaging	True
DataGrid 1	AllowSorting	True
DataGrid 1	AutoGenerateColumns	False
DataGrid 1	DataKeyField	CustID
DataGrid 1	DataMember	Customer

Control	Property	Value
DataGrid 1	DataSource	DsCustomer2
DataGrid 1	Font	Tahoma, Small
DataGrid 1	Height	174px
DataGrid 1	PageSize	5
DataGrid 1	ShowFooter	True
DataGrid 1	Width	658px

The Web form contains two labels, lblMasters and lblError. The lblMasters label displays the Work with Masters text and is placed above the hyperlinks. The lblError label is used to display an error message if an error occurs. The properties of the labels are listed in Table 28-45.

Table 28-45 Properties Assigned to the Labels

Control	Property	Value
Label 1	ID	lblMasters
Label 1	Font	Tahoma, Smaller
Label 1	Height	23px
Label 1	Text	Work with Masters
Label 1	Width	125px
Label 2	ID	lblError
Label 2	BackColor	#FFC0FF
Label 2	Font	Tahoma, Smaller
Label 2	ForeColor	Black
Label 2	Width	316px

The Customer page has a hyperlink, Add New Customer. The properties of this hyperlink are listed in Table 28-46.

Table 28-46 Properties Assigned to the Hyperlink

Control	Property	Value
Hyperlink 9	ID	HyperLink9
Hyperlink 9	BackColor	#FFC0FF
Hyperlink 9	Font	Tahoma, Smaller
Hyperlink 9	ForeColor	Black
Hyperlink 9	NavigateUrl	AddNew Customer.aspx
Hyperlink 9	Text	Add New Customer
Hyperlink 9	Height	8px
Hyperlink 9	Width	128px

When you click on the Add New Customer hyperlink, the AddNewCustomer page opens. Figure 28-16 displays the Design view of the AddNewCustomer Web form.

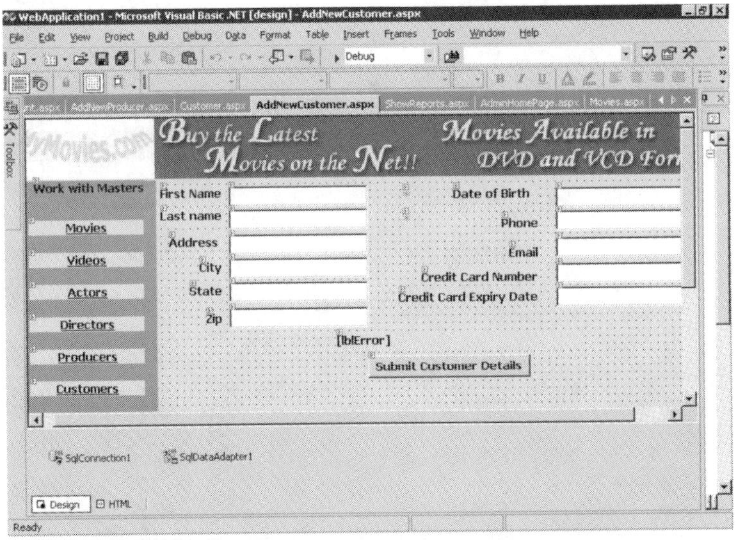

FIGURE 28-16 *The Design view of the AddNewCustomer page*

The Web form is used to accept details from the administrator and to add the record to the database when the Submit Customer Details button is clicked. The details of this Web form were discussed in Chapter 26.

The ShowReports Page

The ShowReports page opens when a user clicks on the View Reports hyperlink. The user interface of the ShowReports page is shown in Figure 28-17.

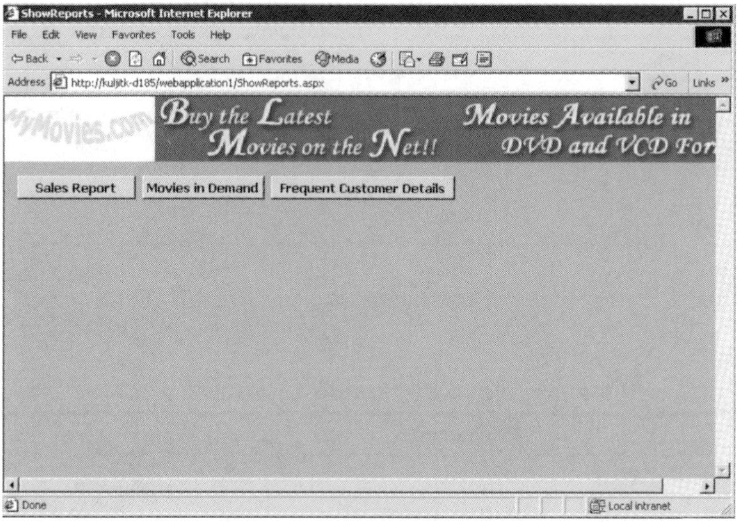

FIGURE 28-17 *The user interface of the ShowReports page*

The Design view of the page is shown in Figure 28-18.

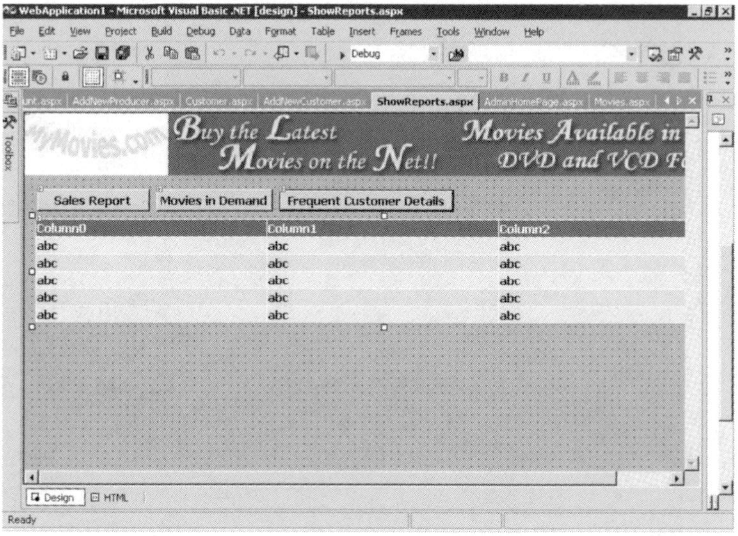

FIGURE 28-18 *The Design view of the ShowReports page*

As you can see, the page contains three buttons and a DataGrid control. When you click on a button, the relevant details appear in the DataGrid. The properties of the DataGrid are listed in Table 28-47.

Table 28-47 Properties Assigned to the DataGrid Control

Control	Property	Value
DataGrid 1	ID	dgAccountDetails
DataGrid 1	Height	13px
DataGrid 1	Width	760px

Table 28-48 lists the properties of the buttons in the ShowReports page.

Table 28-48 Properties Assigned to the Button

Control	Property	Value
Button 1	ID	CmdSalesReport
Button 1	Font	Tahoma, Smaller
Button 1	Height	24px
Button 1	Text	Sales Report
Button 1	Width	122px
Button 2	ID	CmdMoviesInDemand
Button 2	Font	Tahoma, Smaller
Button 2	Height	24px
Button 2	Text	Movies in Demand
Button 2	Width	127px
Button 3	ID	CmdFrequent CustDetails
Button 3	Font	Tahoma, Smaller
Button 3	Height	24px

Control	Property	Value
Button 3	Text	Frequent Customer Details
Button 3	Width	192px

Summary

In this chapter, you learned about the Web pages that make up the admin interface. You also learned about the properties that are required to be set for the controls on each Web page.

Chapter 29

Adding Functionality to the Admin Interface

The preceding chapter introduced you to the design of the admin interface of the MyMovies video kiosk Web application. As discussed in that chapter, the Web application consists of several Web pages. In this chapter, you will write the code to add functionality to these pages.

As discussed in the preceding chapter, the AdminHomePage page consists of the hyperlinks Movies, Videos, Actors, Directors, Producers, Customers, and View Reports (as shown in Figure 29-1.)

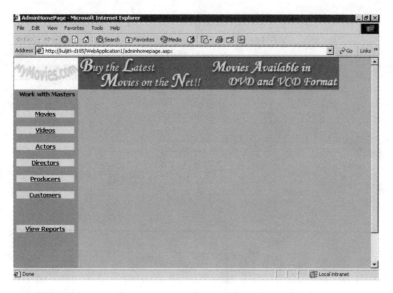

FIGURE 29-1 *The interface of the AdminHomePage page*

When the user clicks any of the hyperlinks, the application loads the corresponding page. When you create hyperlinks on the AdminHomePage, Visual Basic.NET adds the following code for the form by default:

```
Public Class AdminHomePage
    Inherits System.Web.UI.Page
    Protected WithEvents HyperLink1 As System.Web.UI.WebControls.HyperLink
    Protected WithEvents Panel3 As System.Web.UI.WebControls.Panel
    Protected WithEvents HyperLink4 As System.Web.UI.WebControls.HyperLink
```

```
Protected WithEvents HyperLink2 As System.Web.UI.WebControls.HyperLink
Protected WithEvents HyperLink5 As System.Web.UI.WebControls.HyperLink
Protected WithEvents HyperLink3 As System.Web.UI.WebControls.HyperLink
Protected WithEvents HyperLink7 As System.Web.UI.WebControls.HyperLink
Protected WithEvents HyperLink8 As System.Web.UI.WebControls.HyperLink
Protected WithEvents lblMasters As System.Web.UI.WebControls.Label
Protected WithEvents Image3 As System.Web.UI.WebControls.Image
End Class
```

The preceding code indicates that the mentioned controls exist on the form. Because you already know how to create the hyperlinks for the various pages, let's now write the code for the pages. Let's begin by writing the code for the page associated with the Movies hyperlink.

The Code for the *Movies Hyperlink*

In the preceding chapter, you created the SqlConnection string object and configured the SqlDataAdapter and the dataset. Now you need to write the code to populate the DataGrid object when the page is loaded. In addition, you need to bind the dataset with the DataGrid control. Write the following code for the tasks that need to be performed when the Movies page is loaded in the browser:

```
Private Sub Page_Load(ByVal sender As System.Object, ByVal e As
System.EventArgs)
    Handles MyBase.Load
        'Put user code to initialize the page here
        SqlDataAdapter1.Fill(DsMovies1)
        If Not IsPostBack Then
            DataGrid1.DataBind()
        End If
End Sub
```

The preceding code uses the SqlDataAdapter1.Fill method to fill the dataset DsMovies1. Then the IsPost property is used to check whether the page is being loaded for the first time or was loaded after a client request (such as to move to the next or previous pages). If the page was not loaded earlier, the application will bind the DataGrid control to the data source you specified while configuring the data connection.

After you have populated the dataset, you need to write the code to insert, modify, or delete records stored in the data table. In addition, you need to write the code for when the user cancels the update of a particular record. You also will write the code to move to the next or previous pages. You'll write the code to insert a new record a little later in this chapter. The next section discusses the code for modifying a record.

The Code for the *Edit* Hyperlink

When modifying a record, you can choose to either update the change or cancel it. When the form loads in the browser, the form will contain an option to edit the record. Recall that, when designing the form, you set the DataGrid's property to first display the Edit hyperlink. Then, when the Edit hyperlink is clicked, the links for Update and Cancel display. Hence, let's first write the code for the Edit hyperlink.

When a user clicks on the Edit hyperlink, the data grid automatically displays the Update and Cancel hyperlinks for the record. However, before that happens, the code needs to trap the index value of the record that the user wants to edit. To accomplish this, you need to write the following code.

```
Private Sub DataGrid1_EditCommand(ByVal source As Object, ByVal e As
System.Web.UI.WebControls.DataGridCommandEventArgs) Handles
DataGrid1.EditCommand
        DataGrid1.EditItemIndex = e.Item.ItemIndex
        DataGrid1.DataBind()
End Sub
```

The preceding code uses the e.Item.ItemIndex property to get the index value of the record that the user wants to edit. As previously mentioned, when the user clicks the Edit hyperlink, the links for Update and Cancel become visible. You'll now write the code for updating a record.

The Code for the *Update* Hyperlink

The function to update the DataGrid control accepts two parameters—the source and the event that the application raises when the Update hyperlink is clicked. To update a record, you need to write the following code:

```
Private Sub DataGrid1_UpdateCommand(ByVal source As Object, ByVal e As
System.Web.UI.WebControls.DataGridCommandEventArgs) Handles DataGrid1.UpdateCommand
        Dim key As String = DataGrid1.DataKeys(e.Item.ItemIndex).ToString
        Dim tb As TextBox
        Dim strMovTitle, strDirId, strProdId, strDuration, strDesc, strCat,
        strRelYear As String
        'Gets the value from the text box control in the third column
        tb = CType(e.Item.Cells(3).Controls(0), TextBox)
        strMovTitle = tb.Text
        'Gets the value from the text box control in the fourth column
        tb = CType(e.Item.Cells(4).Controls(0), TextBox)
        strDirId = tb.Text

        ' Gets the value from the text box control in the fifth column
        tb = CType(e.Item.Cells(5).Controls(0), TextBox)
        strProdId = tb.Text

        ' Gets the value from the text box control in the sixth column
        tb = CType(e.Item.Cells(6).Controls(0), TextBox)
        strDuration = tb.Text

        ' Gets the value from the text box control in the seventh column
        tb = CType(e.Item.Cells(7).Controls(0), TextBox)
        strDesc = tb.Text

        'Gets the value from the text box control in the eighth column
        tb = CType(e.Item.Cells(8).Controls(0), TextBox)
        strCat = tb.Text

        ' Gets the value from the text box in the ninth column
        tb = CType(e.Item.Cells(9).Controls(0), TextBox)
        strRelYear = tb.Text

        Dim r As dsMovies.MovieRow
        r = DsMovies1.Movie.FindByMovID(key)

        r.MovTitle = strMovTitle
        r.DirID = strDirId
```

```
        r.ProdID = strProdId
        r.Duration = strDuration
        r.Description = strDesc
        r.Category = strCat
        r.ReleaseYear = strRelYear

        SqlDataAdapter1.Update(DsMovies1)
        DataGrid1.EditItemIndex = -1

        ' Refresh the grid
        DataGrid1.DataBind()
    End Sub
```

The preceding code defines two variables key and tb of type String and TextBox, respectively. The variable key will store the index value of the record you are updating. The code also defines the variables strMovTitle, strDirId, strProdId, strDuration, strDesc, strCat, and strRelYear of the String data type. Next, the CType function converts the data stored in the cells of the data grid to TextBox type. Next, the values of the strMovTitle, strDirId, strProdId, strDuration, strDesc, strCat, and strRelYear variable are assigned to the different fields of the datarow. After storing the values that you want to update in the strMovTitle, strDirId, strProdId, strDuration, strDesc, strCat, and strRelYear variables, you need to search the record in the dataset and then update the table with the same. To do so, a variable r has been defined of the type datarow (MovieRow of the dataset dsMovies). After defining the variable, the code has been specified to find the MovieID stored in the variable key using the FindByMovID method. Next, it has been specified to store the values in the strMovTitle, strDirId, strProdId, str-Duration, strDesc, strCat, and strRelYear variables in the MovTitle, DirID, ProdID, Duration, Description, Category, and ReleaseYear fields of the data table. Finally, the method SqlDataAdapter1.Update(DsMovies1) updates the values in the dataset.

After you have saved the new values in the data table, you need to refresh the data grid and set the EditItemIndex property to -1. The EditItemIndex property stores the index value of the record being edited. Therefore, after you have edited and updated the changes, you need to set the EditItemIndex to its default value -1. Finally, the code to refresh the data grid has been added by binding it to the dataset.

In addition to updating a record, the user can also choose to cancel editing the record. In the following section, you will write the code for the Cancel hyperlink.

The Code for the *Cancel* Hyperlink

To cancel editing the record, you need to write the following code:

```
Private Sub DataGrid1_CancelCommand(ByVal source As Object, ByVal e As
System.Web.UI.WebControls.DataGridCommandEventArgs) Handles
DataGrid1.CancelCommand
        DataGrid1.EditItemIndex = -1
        DataGrid1.DataBind()
End Sub
```

The preceding code simply resets the EditItemIndex property of the DataGrid1 to -1 and refreshes the data grid. Recall that, at design time, you specified that if the user clicks the Cancel hyperlink, the page will close the window that shows the Update and Cancel options and will display only the link for editing the record.

The Code for Deleting a Record

In the previous section, you wrote the code to modify a record. You will first store the index value for the record that needs to be deleted in a variable and then search for the record with the same index value in the data table. You will then delete the record by using the Delete method of the datarow (here it is MovieRow). Then you'll update the dataset by using SqlDataAdapter1.Update(DsMovies1, "Movie"). Finally, you'll refresh the data grid. Let's now write the code to delete a record.

```
Private Sub DataGrid1_DeleteCommand(ByVal source As Object, ByVal e As
System.Web.UI.WebControls.DataGridCommandEventArgs) Handles
DataGrid1.DeleteCommand
        Dim key As String = DataGrid1.DataKeys(e.Item.ItemIndex).ToString
        Dim r As dsMovies.MovieRow
        r = DsMovies1.Movie.FindByMovID(key)
        r.Delete()
        SqlDataAdapter1.Update(DsMovies1, "Movie")
        DataGrid1.DataBind()
End Sub
```

Next you need to specify the code for navigating the pages in a data grid.

Navigating the Pages of a Data Grid

Recall that, at design time, you specified that the data grid should display five records on a page. In addition, you attached the Previous and Next hyperlinks to the dataset. Now you need to specify that, when the user clicks the Next or Previous hyperlinks, the data grid will display the next or previous page. To specify this functionality, you need to trap the PageIndexChanged event for the DataGrid control. This event is raised when one of selections for navigating a page is clicked. Let's now write the code for navigating the pages of a data grid.

```
Private Sub DataGrid1_PageIndexChanged(ByVal source As Object, ByVal e As
System.Web.UI.WebControls.DataGridPageChangedEventArgs) Handles
DataGrid1.PageIndexChanged
        DataGrid1.CurrentPageIndex = e.NewPageIndex
        DataGrid1.DataBind()
End Sub
```

The preceding code traps the index value of the page to which the user wants to navigate and displays the page with the same index value.

The Code for Inserting a Record

When the user clicks the Add New Movies hyperlink, the application loads the AddNewMovies page (see Figure 29-2.)

When the page is loaded in the browser, you need to ensure that the combo lists for the Director and Producer fields are already populated. To populate the combo lists, you need to write the code in the Page_Load event for the form. Because you need to populate two combo boxes, you need to use two different datasets. This is an opportunity for you to learn how to create a typed dataset and a programmatically created dataset. Recall that you created a typed dataset while designing the form. To programmatically create the other dataset, write the following code:

```
Private Sub Page_Load(ByVal sender As System.Object, ByVal e As
System.EventArgs)Handles MyBase.Load
        'Put user code to initialize the page here
        Dim strConnectionString = Application("strConnect")
```

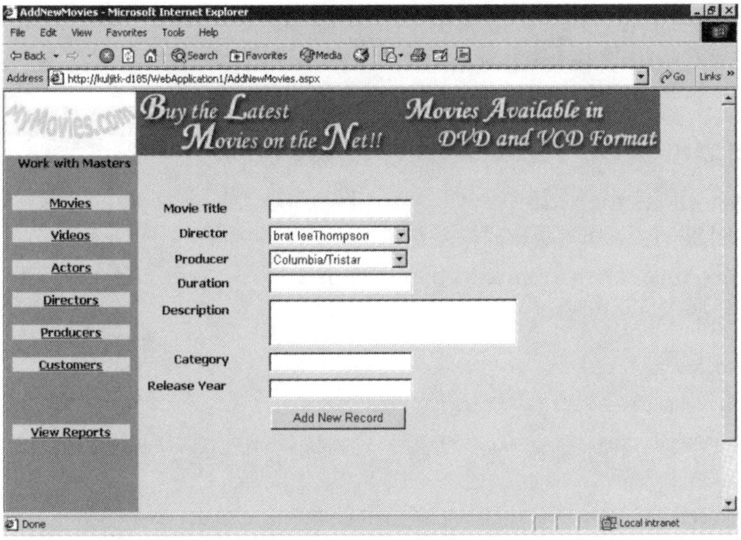

FIGURE 29-2 *The interface of the AddNewMovies page*

```
        Dim MyConnection As New SqlConnection(strConnectionString)
        Dim strCmdText As String
        Dim MyDataAdapter As SqlDataAdapter
MyDataAdapter = New SqlDataAdapter("Select ProdId,Name from Producer",
MyConnection)
        Dim MyDataSet As New DataSet()
        MyDataAdapter.Fill(MyDataSet)
        cmbProducer.DataSource = MyDataSet
        cmbProducer.DataMember = MyDataSet.Tables(0).ToString
        cmbProducer.DataTextField = "Name"
        cmbProducer.DataValueField = "ProdId"
        cmbProducer.DataBind()
        SqlDataAdapter1.Fill(DsDirector_New21)
        cmbDirector.DataBind()
End Sub
```

The preceding code creates a connection object called `MyConnection` and a `Sql-DataAdapter` object called MyDataAdapter. Then, using the `SqlDataAdapter`, the code retrieves the `ProdId` and `Name` fields from the `Producer` table. Then the `Sql-DataAdapter` has been used to fill the dataset MyDataSet. After the dataset has been populated, it has been used to fill the combo box `cmbDirector`. The method `cmbProducer.DataBind()` is used to bind the dataset with the combo box control.

Now that you have populated the combo boxes, you'll learn how to write the code to add the new record when the Add New Record button is clicked.

The Code for the Add New Record Button

When the user clicks the Add New Record button, you need to ensure that the record is added to the data table. Note that the Movie ID needs to be in a predefined format. To meet the aforementioned requirements, write the following code for the Add New Record button.

```
Private Sub Button1_Click(ByVal sender As System.Object, ByVal e As
System.EventArgs) Handles Button1.Click
        Dim strConnectionString As String = Application("strConnect")
        Dim sqlString As String
        Dim MyConnection As New SqlConnection(strConnectionString)
        Dim MovieId As String


        Try
            Label8.Visible = False
            MyConnection.Open()
            Dim cmdMovie As SqlCommand
            cmdMovie = New SqlCommand("Select
            IsNull(Max(convert(int,substring(MovID,2,4))),0)+1 as MovieId from
Movie", MyConnection)
            Dim myReader As SqlDataReader =
            cmdMovie.ExecuteReader(CommandBehavior.SingleRow)
            While myReader.Read()
                MovieId = myReader.GetInt32(0).ToString
            End While
            MovieId = "M00" + CStr(MovieId)
            MyConnection.Close()
            Dim myCommand As SqlCommand
            Dim insertCmd As String
            insertCmd = "insert into Movie values (@MovieId, @MovTitle,
            @DirId,@ProdId," _
                & "@Duration,@Description,@Category,@ReleaseYear);"
            ' Initialize the SqlCommand with the new SQL string.
            MyConnection.Open()
```

```
            myCommand = New SqlCommand(insertCmd, MyConnection)
            ' Create new parameters for the SqlCommand object and
            ' initialize them to the input-form field values.
            myCommand.Parameters.Add(New SqlParameter("@MovieId", _
            SqlDbType.VarChar, 11))
            myCommand.Parameters("@MovieId").Value = MovieId
            myCommand.Parameters.Add(New SqlParameter("@MovTitle", _
            SqlDbType.VarChar, 40))
            myCommand.Parameters("@MovTitle").Value = txtMovie.Text
            myCommand.Parameters.Add(New SqlParameter("@DirId", _
            SqlDbType.VarChar, 20))
            myCommand.Parameters("@DirId").Value =
            cmbDirector.SelectedItem.Value
            myCommand.Parameters.Add(New SqlParameter("@ProdId", _
            SqlDbType.VarChar, 20))
            myCommand.Parameters("@ProdId").Value =
            cmbProducer.SelectedItem.Value
            myCommand.Parameters.Add(New SqlParameter("@Duration", _
            SqlDbType.Int, 4))
            myCommand.Parameters("@Duration").Value = txtDuration.Text
            myCommand.Parameters.Add(New SqlParameter("@Description", _
            SqlDbType.VarChar, 40))
            myCommand.Parameters("@Description").Value = txtDesc.Text
            myCommand.Parameters.Add(New SqlParameter("@Category", _
            SqlDbType.VarChar, 40))
            myCommand.Parameters("@Category").Value = txtCat.Text
            myCommand.Parameters.Add(New SqlParameter("@ReleaseYear", _
            SqlDbType.Int, 4))
            myCommand.Parameters("@ReleaseYear").Value = txtRelYear.Text
            'Test whether the new row can be added and display the appropriate
            ' message 'box to the user.
            myCommand.ExecuteNonQuery()
            myCommand.Connection.Close()
        Catch eException As System.Exception
            ' Error occured
            Label8.Visible = True
            Label8.Text = eException.Source.ToString
            Exit Sub
```

```
            End Try
        End Sub
End Class
```

The preceding code first creates a connection object. Then, using a SQL query, the code retrieves the maximum MovieID value. Then the code has been specified for autogeneration of the movie ID. Using the SQL query, the maximum movie_id is picked from the Movie table in the database, and the value is incremented by 1. Then the movie ID is stored in the required format in the string variable MovieID. Next, a command object and the parameters for the fields are created. Then the values that you need to enter for the parameters are specified. The parameters in the method myCommand.Parameters.Add associate the named paramter variables with the fields in the data table. Finally, the code is specified to execute the query and, on successful execution of the query, close the connection. If the query is not executed, the application will raise an exception.

You have now completed creating the forms for the first hyperlink. The programming logic for the other forms is the same.

The Code for the Videos Hyperlink

As previously mentioned, the logic for the Videos hyperlink is almost the same as the Movies hyperlink. When the user clicks the Videos hyperlink, the application loads the Video.aspx page (see Figure 29-3.)

When the Video.aspx page is loaded in the browser, the code needs to populate the dataset. The code also needs to check whether the page is being loaded for the first time or is being loaded after a client request. If the page is loaded for the first time, the application needs to bind the DataGrid control to the data source. Let's now write the code for the Page_Load event of the form:

```
Private Sub Page_Load(ByVal sender As System.Object, ByVal e As
System.EventArgs) Handles MyBase.Load
        SqlDataAdapter1.Fill(DsVideo2)
        If Not IsPostBack Then
            DataGrid1.DataBind()
        End If
End Sub
```

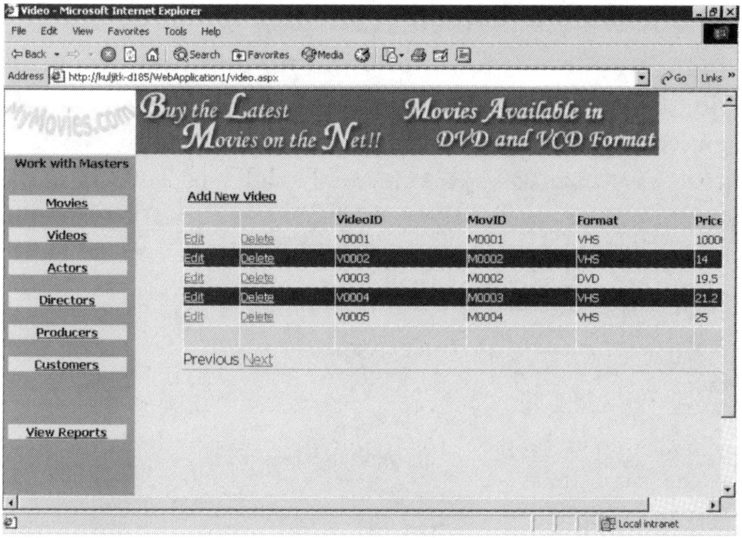

FIGURE 29-3 *The interface of the Video page*

Next you will take a look at the code for the hyperlink for editing records.

The Code for Editing a Video Record

As in the case of the Movies page, the code for the Edit hyperlink needs to store the index value for the record that the user wants to edit. To do so, write the following code:

```
Private Sub DataGrid1_EditCommand(ByVal source As Object, ByVal e As
System.Web.UI.WebControls.DataGridCommandEventArgs) Handles
DataGrid1.EditCommand
        DataGrid1.EditItemIndex = e.Item.ItemIndex
        DataGrid1.DataBind()
End Sub
```

Now that you have written the code for the Edit hyperlink, you need to specify the actions that need to take place when the user modifies the values in the cells and clicks on the Update hyperlink.

The Code for Updating a Video Record

The code for the Update hyperlink needs to store the values changed by the user in the data table. To update the data table, the code first needs to point to the record that the user has chosen to edit. The code then needs to assign the values stored in strMovID, strFormat, and strPrice in the different fields of the datarow. After this is done, the code needs to refresh the data grid and set the EditItem-Index property to -1. To perform this functionality, the code is as follows:

```
Private Sub DataGrid1_UpdateCommand(ByVal source As Object, ByVal e As
System.Web.UI.WebControls.DataGridCommandEventArgs) Handles
DataGrid1.UpdateCommand
        Try
                Dim key As String = DataGrid1.DataKeys(e.Item.ItemIndex).ToString
                Dim tb As TextBox

                Dim strMovId, strFormat, strPrice As String
                ' Gets the value from the text box control in the third column
                tb = CType(e.Item.Cells(3).Controls(0), TextBox)
                strMovId = tb.Text

                ' Gets the value from the text box control in the fourth column
                tb = CType(e.Item.Cells(4).Controls(0), TextBox)
                strFormat = tb.Text

                ' Gets the value from the text box control in the fifth column
                tb = CType(e.Item.Cells(5).Controls(0), TextBox)
                strPrice = tb.Text

                Dim r As dsVideo.VideoRow
                r = DsVideo2.Video.FindByVideoID(key)
                r.MovID = strMovId
                r.Format = strFormat
                r.Price = strPrice

                SqlDataAdapter1.Update(DsVideo2)
                DataGrid1.EditItemIndex = -1
```

```
                    ' Refresh the grid
            DataGrid1.DataBind()
            Catch eException As System.Exception
                'Error occured
                lblError.Visible = True
                lblError.Text = eException.Source.ToString
                Exit Sub
            End Try
    End Sub
```

Next you will take a look at the code you need to specify for the Cancel hyperlink.

The Code for the *Cancel* Hyperlink

Users can choose not to save the changes they have made in the form. To do so, the user can click the Cancel hyperlink. Upon clicking Cancel, any changes that the user has made to the form page are not saved in the data table. The following code performs this functionality:

```
Private Sub DataGrid1_CancelCommand(ByVal source As Object, ByVal e As
    System.Web.UI.WebControls.DataGridCommandEventArgs) Handles
    DataGrid1.CancelCommand
        DataGrid1.EditItemIndex = -1
        DataGrid1.DataBind()
End Sub
```

To complete this form page, you need to specify the functionality for moving to the next or previous page set of records.

The Code to Navigate the Pages

To navigate the pages of a data grid, you need to update the value of the CurrentPageIndex property of the data grid. The following code traps the PageIndexChanged event and navigates to the required page:

```
Private Sub DataGrid1_PageIndexChanged(ByVal source As Object, ByVal e As
System.Web.UI.WebControls.DataGridPageChangedEventArgs) Handles
DataGrid1.PageIndexChanged
        DataGrid1.CurrentPageIndex = e.NewPageIndex
        DataGrid1.DataBind()
    End Sub
```

To complete the functionality for this form, you need to write the code for the Add New Video button.

The Code for the Add New Video Button

When the user clicks on the Add New Video button, the AddNewVideo.aspx page will be displayed in the browser window, as shown in Figure 29-4.

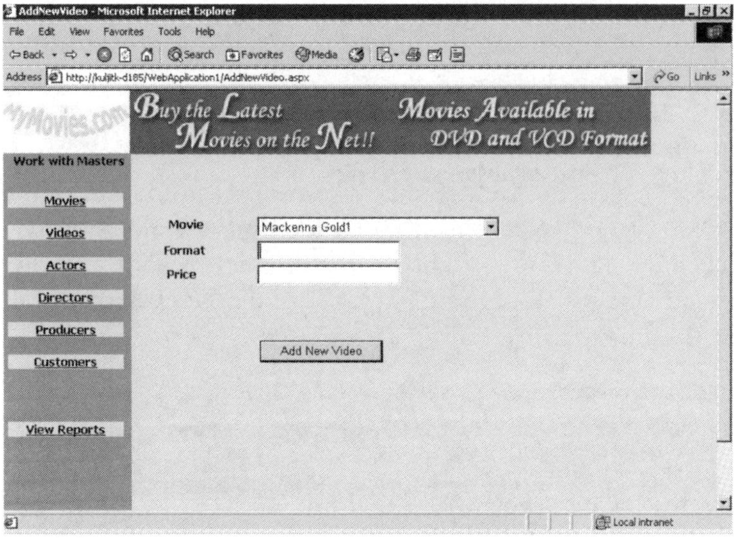

FIGURE 29-4 *The interface of the AddNewVideo page*

As in the case of the Add New Movie button, when the user clicks on the Add New Video button, the new values need to be stored in the data table at the backend. Write the following code in the Page_Load event of the AddNewVideo page:

```
Private Sub Page_Load(ByVal sender As System.Object, ByVal e As
System.EventArgs) Handles MyBase.Load
        'Put user code to initialize the page here
        Dim strConnectionString = Application("strConnect")

        Dim MyConnection As New SqlConnection(strConnectionString)
        Dim strCmdText As String
        Dim MyDataAdapter As SqlDataAdapter
```

```
MyDataAdapter = New SqlDataAdapter("Select MovId,MovTitle from Movie",
MyConnection)

Dim MyDataSet As New DataSet()
MyDataAdapter.Fill(MyDataSet)
cmbMovie.DataSource = MyDataSet
cmbMovie.DataMember = MyDataSet.Tables(0).ToString
cmbMovie.DataTextField = "MovTitle"
cmbMovie.DataValueField = "MovId"
cmbMovie.DataBind()


End Sub
```

The preceding code contains the statements to connect to the database using a connection string in the Page_Load event. In addition, it contains the code for populating the combo box cmbMovie.

The following is the code you need to specify in the Click event of the Add New Video button:

```
Private Sub Button1_Click(ByVal sender As System.Object, ByVal e As
System.EventArgs) Handles Button1.Click
        Dim strConnectionString As String = Application("strConnect")
        Dim sqlString As String
        Dim MyConnection As New SqlConnection(strConnectionString)
        Dim VideoId As String

        Try
            lblError.Visible = False
            MyConnection.Open()
            Dim cmdVideo As SqlCommand
            cmdVideo = New SqlCommand("Select
            IsNull(Max(convert(int,substring(VideoID,2,4))),0)+1 as VideoId from
            Video", MyConnection)
            Dim myReader As SqlDataReader =
            cmdVideo.ExecuteReader(CommandBehavior.SingleRow)
            While myReader.Read()
                VideoId = myReader.GetInt32(0).ToString
            End While
```

```
        VideoId = "V00" + CStr(VideoId)
        MyConnection.Close()
        Dim myCommand As SqlCommand
        Dim insertCmd As String
        ' Check that four of the input values are not empty. If any of them
        '  is empty, show a message to the user and rebind the DataGrid.
        insertCmd = "insert into Video values (@VideoId,
        @MovId,@Format,@Price);"
        ' Initialize the SqlCommand with the new SQL string.
        MyConnection.Open()
        myCommand = New SqlCommand(insertCmd, MyConnection)
        ' Create new parameters for the SqlCommand object and
        ' initialize them to the input-form field values.
        myCommand.Parameters.Add(New SqlParameter("@VideoId", _
        SqlDbType.VarChar, 11))
        myCommand.Parameters("@VideoId").Value = VideoId
        myCommand.Parameters.Add(New SqlParameter("@MovId", _
        SqlDbType.VarChar, 40))
        myCommand.Parameters("@MovId").Value = cmbMovie.SelectedItem.Value
        myCommand.Parameters.Add(New SqlParameter("@Format", _
        SqlDbType.VarChar, 40))
        myCommand.Parameters("@Format").Value = txtFormat.Text
        myCommand.Parameters.Add(New SqlParameter("@Price", _
        SqlDbType.Money, 8))
        myCommand.Parameters("@Price").Value = txtPrice.Text
        ' Test whether the new row can be added and  display the
        ' appropriate message box to the user.
        'myCommand.Connection.Open()
        myCommand.ExecuteNonQuery()
        myCommand.Connection.Close()
        lblError.Visible = True
        lblError.Text = "Video Added Successfully"
    Catch eException As System.Exception
        'Error occured
        lblError.Visible = True
        lblError.Text = eException.Source.ToString
        Exit Sub
```

```
        End Try
End Sub
```

The preceding code uses a SQL query to retrieve the maximum VideoID value. The maximum video ID is picked from the Video table in the database, and the value is incremented by 1. Then the video ID is stored in the required format in the string variable VideoID. Next, a command object and the parameters for the fields are created. Then the values for the parameters are specified. The parameters in the method myCommand.Parameters.Add associate the named parameter variables with the fields in the data table. Finally, the code is specified to execute the query and, on successful execution of the query, close the connection. If the query is not executed, the application will raise an exception.

The Video page is now ready. The code for the other pages, with the exception of the code for the Show Reports page, is similar to the two pages you have created. Because the functionality is the same, the code will not be explained in detail.

Let's now write the code for the page associated with the Actors hyperlink.

The Code for the Actors Hyperlink

As in the preceding two cases, when the user clicks the Actors hyperlink, the corresponding page is loaded in the browser. On the page, the use can opt to insert, modify, or delete a record. The user can also navigate the pages. When the user clicks on the Edit hyperlink, the hyperlinks for Update and Cancel become available. The page that loads when the user clicks the Actors hyperlink is shown in Figure 29-5.

The code for the Actors page is as follows:

```
Private Sub Page_Load(ByVal sender As System.Object, ByVal e As
System.EventArgs) Handles MyBase.Load
        Me.SqlConnection1.ConnectionString = Application("strConnect")
        SqlDataAdapter1.Fill(DsActors1)
        DataGrid1.DataSource = DsActors1
        If Not IsPostBack Then
            DataGrid1.DataBind()
        End If

End Sub
```

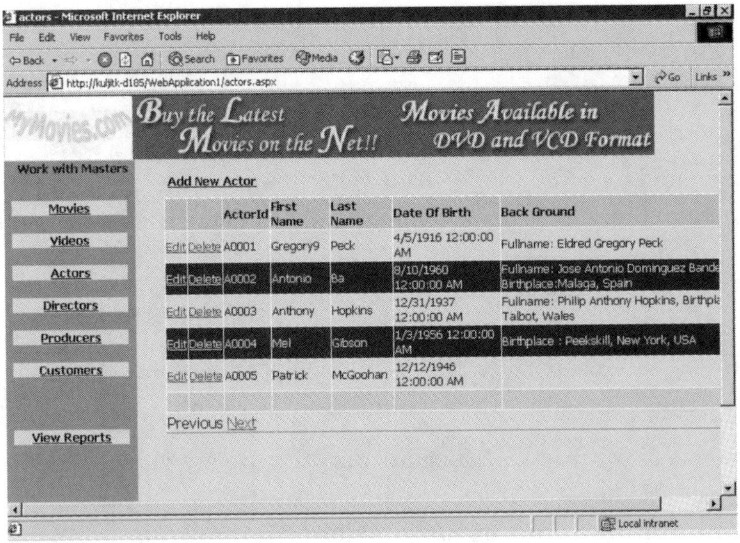

FIGURE 29-5 *The interface of the Actors page*

```
Private Sub DataGrid1_EditCommand(ByVal source As Object, ByVal e As
  System.Web.UI.WebControls.DataGridCommandEventArgs) Handles
  DataGrid1.EditCommand
        DataGrid1.EditItemIndex = e.Item.ItemIndex
        DataGrid1.DataBind()
End Sub


Private Sub DataGrid1_CancelCommand(ByVal source As Object, ByVal e As
System.Web.UI.WebControls.DataGridCommandEventArgs) Handles
DataGrid1.CancelCommand
        DataGrid1.EditItemIndex = -1
        DataGrid1.DataBind()
End Sub

    Private Sub DataGrid1_UpdateCommand(ByVal source As Object, ByVal e As
    System.Web.UI.WebControls.DataGridCommandEventArgs) Handles
    DataGrid1.UpdateCommand
        Try
            Dim key As String = e.Item.Cells(2).Text
            Dim tb As TextBox
            Dim strFirstName, strLastName, dtmDOB, strBackGround As String
```

```vbnet
            ' Gets the value from the text box control in the third column
            tb = CType(e.Item.Cells(3).Controls(0), TextBox)
            strFirstName = tb.Text


            ' Gets the value from the text box control in the fourth column
            tb = CType(e.Item.Cells(4).Controls(0), TextBox)
            strLastName = tb.Text


            ' Gets the value from the text box control in the fifth column
            tb = CType(e.Item.Cells(5).Controls(0), TextBox)
            'dtmDOB = IIf(tb.Text = "", System.DBNull.Value.Value, tb.Text)
            dtmDOB = tb.Text


            ' Gets the value from the text box control in the sixth column
            tb = CType(e.Item.Cells(6).Controls(0), TextBox)
            strBackGround = tb.Text


            Dim r As dsActors.ActorRow
            r = DsActors1.Actor.FindByActorID(key)


            r.FirstName = strFirstName
            r.LastName = strLastName
            r.DOB = dtmDOB
            r.Background = strBackGround


            SqlDataAdapter1.Update(DsActors1)
            DataGrid1.EditItemIndex = -1


            ' Refresh the grid
            DataGrid1.DataBind()
        Catch eException As System.Exception
            'Error occured
            lblError.Visible = True
            lblError.Text = eException.Source.ToString
            Exit Sub
        End Try
    End Sub
```

```
Private Sub DataGrid1_DeleteCommand(ByVal source As Object, ByVal e As
System.Web.UI.WebControls.DataGridCommandEventArgs) Handles
    DataGrid1.DeleteCommand
        Try
            Dim key As String = e.Item.Cells(2).Text
            Dim r As dsActors.ActorRow
            r = DsActors1.Actor.FindByActorID(key)
            r.Delete()
            SqlDataAdapter1.Update(DsActors1, "Actor")
            DataGrid1.DataBind()
        Catch eException As System.Exception
            'Error occured
            lblError.Visible = True
            lblError.Text = eException.Source.ToString
            Exit Sub
        End Try
    End Sub


    Private Sub DataGrid1_PageIndexChanged(ByVal source As Object, ByVal e As
    System.Web.UI.WebControls.DataGridPageChangedEventArgs) Handles
    DataGrid1.PageIndexChanged
        DataGrid1.CurrentPageIndex = e.NewPageIndex
        DataGrid1.DataBind()
    End Sub


    Private Sub Button2_Click(ByVal sender As System.Object, ByVal e As
System.EventArgs)
        SqlDataAdapter1.Update(DsActors1, "Actor")
        DataGrid1.DataBind()
    End Sub
End Class
```

The preceding code defines the functionality to modify, edit, cancel, delete, and navigate records. However, you still need to add the code for inserting a record. When inserting a new record, the code needs to update the record in the data table. Before the record is updated, however, don't forget to add the validation to check that all mandatory fields are filled. The user interface for the form to add a new actor is shown in Figure 29-6.

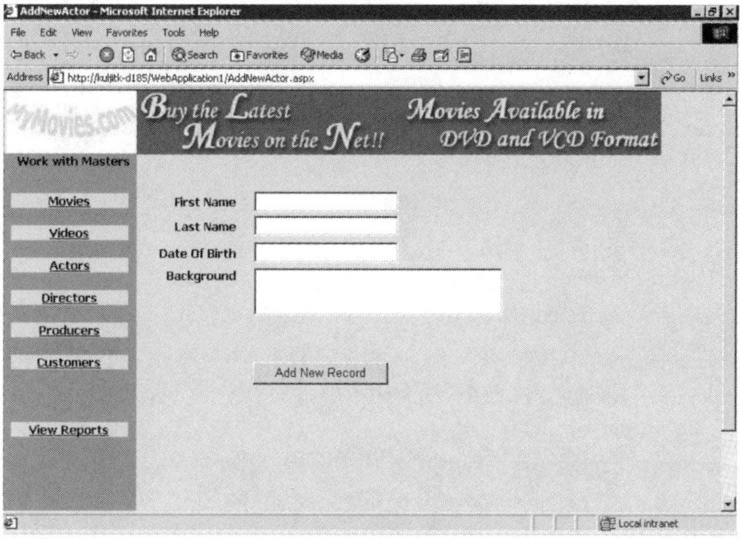

FIGURE 29-6 *The interface of the AddNewActor page*

The code for adding a new record for an actor is as follows:

```
Private Sub CmdAddNewRecord_Click(ByVal sender As System.Object, ByVal e As
System.EventArgs) Handles CmdAddNewRecord.Click
        Try
            Dim strConnectionString As String = Application("strConnect")
            Dim sqlString As String
            Dim MyConnection As New SqlConnection(strConnectionString)
            Dim ActorId As String
            MyConnection.Open()
            Dim cmdActor As SqlCommand
            cmdActor = New SqlCommand("Select
             IsNull(Max(convert(int,substring(ActorID,2,4))),0)+1 as ActorId
             from Actor", MyConnection)
            Dim myReader As SqlDataReader =
             cmdActor.ExecuteReader(CommandBehavior.SingleRow)
            While myReader.Read()
                ActorId = myReader.GetInt32(0).ToString
            End While
            ActorId = "A00" + CStr(ActorId)
            MyConnection.Close()
            Dim myCommand As SqlCommand
```

```
        Dim insertCmd As String
        ' Check that four of the input values are not empty. If any of them
        '  is empty, show a message to the user and rebind the DataGrid.
        insertCmd = "insert into Actor values (@ActorId, @FName, @LName," _
            & "@DOB, @Background);"
        ' Initialize the SqlCommand with the new SQL string.
        MyConnection.Open()
        myCommand = New SqlCommand(insertCmd, MyConnection)
        ' Create new parameters for the SqlCommand object and
        ' initialize them to the input-form field values.
        myCommand.Parameters.Add(New SqlParameter("@ActorId", _
            SqlDbType.VarChar, 11))
        myCommand.Parameters("@ActorId").Value = ActorId
        myCommand.Parameters.Add(New SqlParameter("@FName", _
            SqlDbType.VarChar, 40))
        myCommand.Parameters("@FName").Value = txtFname.Text
        myCommand.Parameters.Add(New SqlParameter("@LName", _
            SqlDbType.VarChar, 20))
        myCommand.Parameters("@LName").Value = txtLname.Text
        myCommand.Parameters.Add(New SqlParameter("@DOB", _
            SqlDbType.DateTime, 12))
        myCommand.Parameters("@DOB").Value = txtDOB.Text
        myCommand.Parameters.Add(New SqlParameter("@BackGround", _
            SqlDbType.VarChar, 40))
        myCommand.Parameters("@BackGround").Value = txtBGround.Text
        ' Test whether the new row can be added and  display the
        ' appropriate message box to the user.
        myCommand.ExecuteNonQuery()
        myCommand.Connection.Close()
        lblError.Visible = True
        lblError.Text = "Actor added Successfully"
    Catch eException As System.Exception
        'Error occured
        lblError.Visible = True
        lblError.Text = eException.Source.ToString
        Exit Sub
    End Try
End Sub
```

The Code for the Directors Hyperlink

When the user clicks the Directors hyperlink, the Director.aspx page is loaded in the browser, as shown in Figure 29-7.

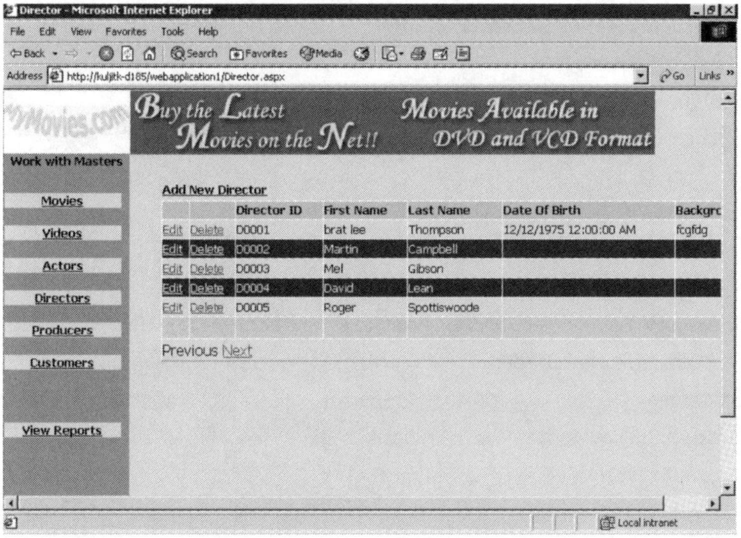

FIGURE 29-7 *The interface of the Director page*

The following is the code for editing, updating, canceling, deleting, and navigating records:

```
Private Sub Page_Load(ByVal sender As System.Object, ByVal e As
System.EventArgs) Handles MyBase.Load
        'Put user code to initialize the page here
        SqlDataAdapter1.Fill(DsDirector_New1)
        If Not IsPostBack Then
            DataGrid1.DataBind()
        End If
End Sub
Private Sub DataGrid1_DeleteCommand(ByVal source As Object, ByVal e As
System.Web.UI.WebControls.DataGridCommandEventArgs) Handles
DataGrid1.DeleteCommand
        Try
            Dim key As String = DataGrid1.DataKeys(e.Item.ItemIndex).ToString
```

```vb
            Dim r As dsDirector_New.DirectorRow
            r = DsDirector_New1.Director.FindByDirID(key)
            r.Delete()
            SqlDataAdapter1.Update(DsDirector_New1, "Director")
            DataGrid1.DataBind()
        Catch eException As System.Exception
            ' Error occured
            lblError.Visible = True
            lblError.Text = eException.Source.ToString
            Exit Sub
    End Try


    End Sub
    Private Sub DataGrid1_EditCommand(ByVal source As Object, ByVal e As
    Sstem.Web.UI.WebControls.DataGridCommandEventArgs) Handles
    DataGrid1.EditCommand
        DataGrid1.EditItemIndex = e.Item.ItemIndex
        DataGrid1.DataBind()
    End Sub
    Private Sub DataGrid1_CancelCommand(ByVal source As Object, ByVal e As
    System.Web.UI.WebControls.DataGridCommandEventArgs) Handles
        DataGrid1.CancelCommand


        DataGrid1.EditItemIndex = -1
        DataGrid1.DataBind()
        'Call cmdLoad_Click(source, e)
    End Sub
    Private Sub DataGrid1_PageIndexChanged(ByVal source As Object, ByVal e As
    System.Web.UI.WebControls.DataGridPageChangedEventArgs) Handles
    DataGrid1.PageIndexChanged
        DataGrid1.CurrentPageIndex = e.NewPageIndex
        DataGrid1.DataBind()
    End Sub
    Private Sub DataGrid1_UpdateCommand(ByVal source As Object, ByVal e As
    System.Web.UI.WebControls.DataGridCommandEventArgs) Handles
    DataGrid1.UpdateCommand
        Dim key As String = DataGrid1.DataKeys(e.Item.ItemIndex).ToString
        Dim tb As TextBox
```

```
'Update for Actors
'_ _ _ _ _ _ _ _ _ _ _ _ _ _ _ _ _ _ _ _ _ _ _ _ _ _ _ _ _ _ _ _ _
Dim strDirId, strFname, strLname, strDOB, strBGround As String

' Gets the value from the text box control in the third column

tb = CType(e.Item.Cells(3).Controls(0), TextBox)
strFname = tb.Text

' Gets the value from the text box control in the fourth column
tb = CType(e.Item.Cells(4).Controls(0), TextBox)
strLname = tb.Text

' Gets the value from the text box control in the fifth column
tb = CType(e.Item.Cells(5).Controls(0), TextBox)
strDOB = IIf(tb.Text = "", System.DBNull.Value, tb.Text)

' Gets the value from the text box control in the sixth column
tb = CType(e.Item.Cells(6).Controls(0), TextBox)
strBGround = tb.Text


Dim r As dsDirector_New.DirectorRow
r = DsDirector_New1.Director.FindByDirID(key)
r.FirstName = strFname
r.LastName = strLname
r.DOB = strDOB
r.Background = strBGround

SqlDataAdapter1.Update(DsDirector_New1)
DataGrid1.EditItemIndex = -1

' Refresh the grid
DataGrid1.DataBind()
End Sub
```

When the user clicks on the Add New Director button, the page shown in Figure 29-8 is loaded in the browser.

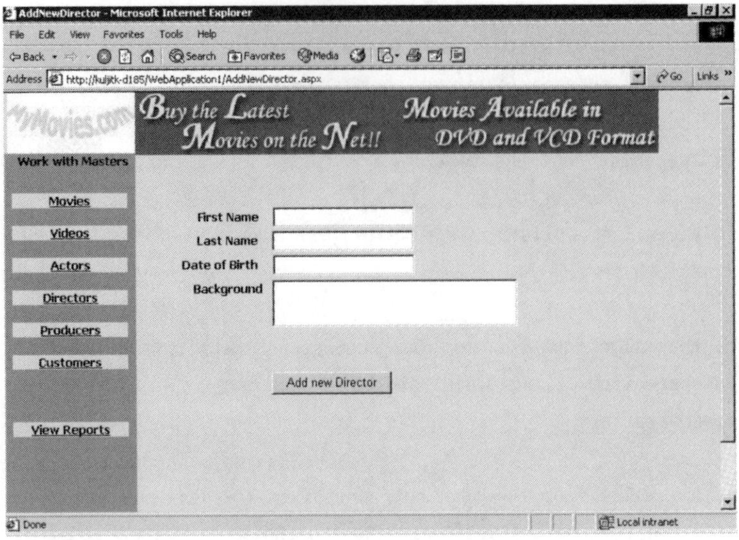

FIGURE 29-8 *The interface of the AddNewDirector page*

The code for the adding a new record for a director is as follows:

```
Private Sub CmdAddNewDir_Click(ByVal sender As System.Object, ByVal e As
System.EventArgs) Handles CmdAddNewDir.Click
        Dim strConnectionString As String = Application("strConnect")
        Dim sqlString As String
        Dim MyConnection As New SqlConnection(strConnectionString)
        Dim DirId As String

        Try
            lblError.Visible = False
            MyConnection.Open()
            Dim cmdDirector As SqlCommand
            cmdDirector = New SqlCommand("Select
            IsNull(Max(convert(int,substring(DirID,2,4))),0)+1 as DirId from
Director",
            MyConnection)
            Dim myReader As SqlDataReader =
            cmdDirector.ExecuteReader(CommandBehavior.SingleRow)
            While myReader.Read()
                DirId = myReader.GetInt32(0).ToString
```

```
          End While
          DirId = "D00" + CStr(DirId)
          MyConnection.Close()
          Dim myCommand As SqlCommand
          Dim insertCmd As String
          ' Check that four of the input values are not empty. If any of them
          '  is empty, show a message to the user and rebind the DataGrid.
          insertCmd = "insert into Director values (@DirId,
          @FirstName,@LastName,@DOB,@BackGround);"
          ' Initialize the SqlCommand with the new SQL string.
          MyConnection.Open()
          myCommand = New SqlCommand(insertCmd, MyConnection)
          ' Create new parameters for the SqlCommand object and
          ' initialize them to the input-form field values.
          myCommand.Parameters.Add(New SqlParameter("@DirId", _
              SqlDbType.VarChar, 11))
          myCommand.Parameters("@DirId").Value = DirId
          myCommand.Parameters.Add(New SqlParameter("@FirstName", _
              SqlDbType.VarChar, 40))
          myCommand.Parameters("@FirstName").Value = txtFName.Text
          myCommand.Parameters.Add(New SqlParameter("@LastName", _
              SqlDbType.VarChar, 40))
          myCommand.Parameters("@LastName").Value = txtLName.Text
          myCommand.Parameters.Add(New SqlParameter("@DOB", _
              SqlDbType.DateTime, 8))
          myCommand.Parameters("@DOB").Value = txtDOB.Text
          myCommand.Parameters.Add(New SqlParameter("@BackGround", _
              SqlDbType.VarChar, 255))
          myCommand.Parameters("@BackGround").Value = txtBGround.Text


          ' Test whether the new row can be added and  display the
          ' appropriate message box to the user.
          myCommand.ExecuteNonQuery()
          myCommand.Connection.Close()
          lblError.Visible = True
          lblError.Text = "Director Added Successfully"
      Catch eException As System.Exception
          ' Error occured
```

```
            lblError.Visible = True
            lblError.Text = eException.Source.ToString
            Exit Sub
        End Try
    End Sub
```

The Code for the Producers Hyperlink

When the user clicks the Producers hyperlink, the Producer.aspx page (shown in Figure 29-9) is loaded in the browser.

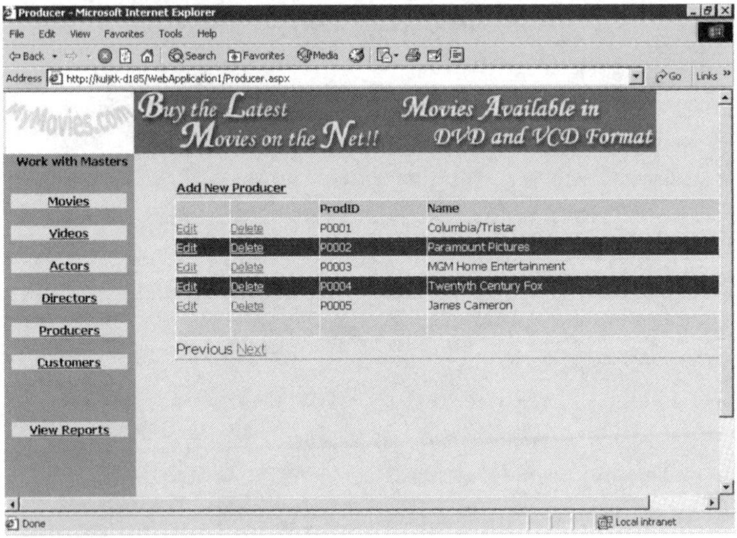

FIGURE 29-9 *The interface of the Producer page*

The code for the page is as follows:

```
Private Sub Page_Load(ByVal sender As System.Object, ByVal e As
System.EventArgs) Handles MyBase.Load
        'Put user code to initialize the page here
        SqlDataAdapter1.Fill(DsProducer1)
        If Not IsPostBack Then
            DataGrid1.DataBind()
        End If
```

```
End Sub
Private Sub DataGrid1_PageIndexChanged(ByVal source As Object, ByVal e As
System.Web.UI.WebControls.DataGridPageChangedEventArgs) Handles
DataGrid1.PageIndexChanged
        DataGrid1.CurrentPageIndex = e.NewPageIndex
        DataGrid1.DataBind()
End Sub
Private Sub DataGrid1_DeleteCommand(ByVal source As Object, ByVal e As
System.Web.UI.WebControls.DataGridCommandEventArgs) Handles
DataGrid1.DeleteCommand
        Dim key As String = DataGrid1.DataKeys(e.Item.ItemIndex).ToString
        Dim r As dsProducer.ProducerRow
        r = DsProducer1.Producer.FindByProdID(key)
        r.Delete()
        SqlDataAdapter1.Update(DsProducer1, "Producer")
        DataGrid1.DataBind()
End Sub
Private Sub DataGrid1_EditCommand(ByVal source As Object, ByVal e As
System.Web.UI.WebControls.DataGridCommandEventArgs) Handles
DataGrid1.EditCommand
        DataGrid1.EditItemIndex = e.Item.ItemIndex
        DataGrid1.DataBind()
End Sub
Private Sub DataGrid1_CancelCommand(ByVal source As Object, ByVal e As
System.Web.UI.WebControls.DataGridCommandEventArgs) Handles
DataGrid1.CancelCommand
        DataGrid1.EditItemIndex = -1
        DataGrid1.DataBind()
        'Call cmdLoad_Click(source, e)
End Sub

Private Sub DataGrid1_UpdateCommand(ByVal source As Object, ByVal e As
System.Web.UI.WebControls.DataGridCommandEventArgs) Handles
DataGrid1.UpdateCommand
        Dim key As String = DataGrid1.DataKeys(e.Item.ItemIndex).ToString
        Dim tb As TextBox
        'Update for Actors
        Dim strName As String
```

```
' Gets the value from the text box control in the third column
tb = CType(e.Item.Cells(3).Controls(0), TextBox)
strName = tb.Text

Dim r As dsProducer.ProducerRow
r = DsProducer1.Producer.FindByProdID(key)
r.ProdID = key
r.Name = strName

SqlDataAdapter1.Update(DsProducer1)
DataGrid1.EditItemIndex = -1
' Refresh the grid
DataGrid1.DataBind()
```
End Sub

When the user clicks on the Add New Producer hyperlink, the AddNewProducer.aspx page is loaded in the browser, as shown in Figure 29-10.

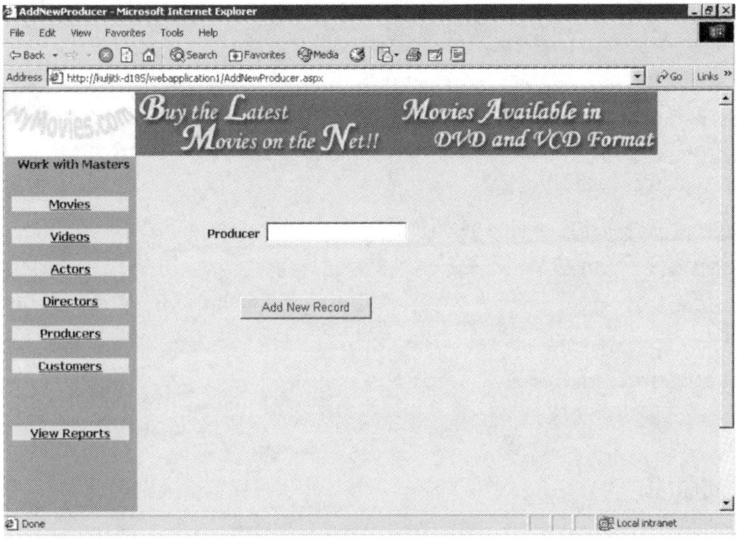

FIGURE 29-10 _The interface of the AddNewProducer page_

The following code adds the record for a new producer:

```
Private Sub Page_Load(ByVal sender As System.Object, ByVal e As
System.EventArgs) Handles MyBase.Load
```

```
        'Put user code to initialize the page here
End Sub


Private Sub CmdAddNewProducer_Click(ByVal sender As System.Object, ByVal e As
System.EventArgs) Handles CmdAddNewProducer.Click
        Dim strConnectionString As String = Application("strConnect")
        Dim sqlString As String
        Dim MyConnection As New SqlConnection(strConnectionString)
        Dim ProdId As String

        Try
            lblError.Visible = False
            MyConnection.Open()
            Dim cmdProducer As SqlCommand
            cmdProducer = New SqlCommand("Select
            IsNull(Max(convert(int,substring(ProdID,2,4))),0)+1 as ProducerId
            from Producer", MyConnection)
            Dim myReader As SqlDataReader =
            cmdProducer.ExecuteReader(CommandBehavior.SingleRow)
            While myReader.Read()
                ProdId = myReader.GetInt32(0).ToString
            End While
            ProdId = "P00" + CStr(ProdId)
            MyConnection.Close()
            Dim myCommand As SqlCommand
            Dim insertCmd As String
            ' Check that four of the input values are not empty. If any of them
            'is empty, show a message to the user and rebind the DataGrid.
            insertCmd = "insert into Producer values (@ProdId, @Name);"
            'Initialize the SqlCommand with the new SQL string.
            MyConnection.Open()
            myCommand = New SqlCommand(insertCmd, MyConnection)
            ' Create new parameters for the SqlCommand object and
            ' initialize them to the input-form field values.
            myCommand.Parameters.Add(New SqlParameter("@ProdId", _
                SqlDbType.VarChar, 11))
            myCommand.Parameters("@ProdId").Value = ProdId
            myCommand.Parameters.Add(New SqlParameter("@Name", _
```

```
            SqlDbType.VarChar, 40))
        myCommand.Parameters("@Name").Value = txtName.Text
        ' Test whether the new row can be added and  display the
        ' appropriate message box to the user.
        myCommand.ExecuteNonQuery()
        myCommand.Connection.Close()
        lblError.Visible = True
        lblError.Text = "Producer Added Successfully"
    Catch eException As System.Exception
        ' Error occured
        lblError.Visible = True
        lblError.Text = eException.Source.ToString
        Exit Sub
    End Try
End Sub
```

Next you will take a look at how to write the code for the Customers hyperlink.

The Code for the Customers Hyperlink

When the user clicks on the Customers hyperlink, the Customer.aspx page is loaded in the browser, as shown in Figure 29-11.

The code for adding the functionality for the page is as follows:

```
Private Sub Page_Load(ByVal sender As System.Object, ByVal e As
System.EventArgs) Handles MyBase.Load
        'Put user code to initialize the page here
        SqlDataAdapter1.Fill(DsCustomer2)
        If Not IsPostBack Then
            DataGrid1.DataBind()
        End If
End Sub
Private Sub DataGrid1_DeleteCommand(ByVal source As Object, ByVal e As
System.Web.UI.WebControls.DataGridCommandEventArgs) Handles
DataGrid1.DeleteCommand
        Dim key As String = DataGrid1.DataKeys(e.Item.ItemIndex).ToString
        Dim r As dsCustomer.CustomerRow
        r = DsCustomer2.Customer.FindByCustID(key)
```

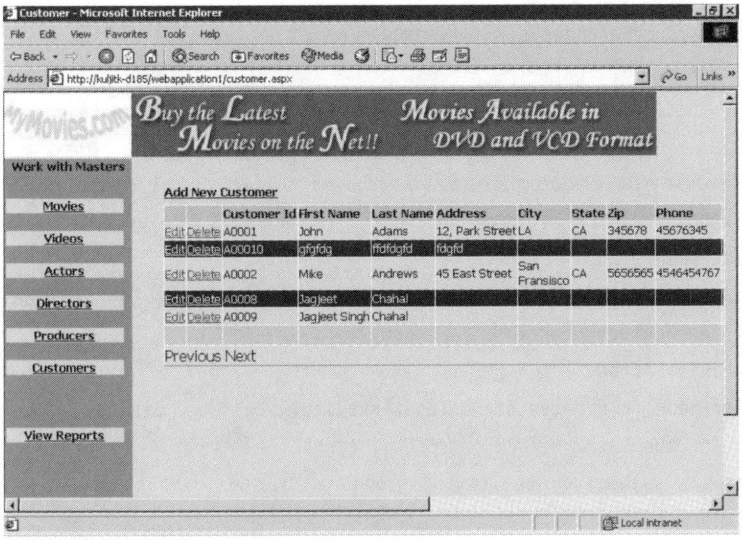

FIGURE 29-11 *The interface of the Customer page*

```
        r.Delete()
        SqlDataAdapter1.Update(DsCustomer2, "Customer")
        DataGrid1.DataBind()
End Sub


Private Sub DataGrid1_CancelCommand(ByVal source As Object, ByVal e As
System.Web.UI.WebControls.DataGridCommandEventArgs) Handles
DataGrid1.CancelCommand
        DataGrid1.EditItemIndex = -1
        DataGrid1.DataBind()
    End Sub


Private Sub DataGrid1_EditCommand(ByVal source As Object, ByVal e As
System.Web.UI.WebControls.DataGridCommandEventArgs) Handles
DataGrid1.EditCommand
        DataGrid1.EditItemIndex = e.Item.ItemIndex
        DataGrid1.DataBind()
End Sub


Private Sub DataGrid1_PageIndexChanged(ByVal source As Object, ByVal e As
System.Web.UI.WebControls.DataGridPageChangedEventArgs) Handles
```

```
DataGrid1.PageIndexChanged
        DataGrid1.CurrentPageIndex = e.NewPageIndex
        DataGrid1.DataBind()
End Sub


Private Sub DataGrid1_UpdateCommand(ByVal source As Object, ByVal e As
System.Web.UI.WebControls.DataGridCommandEventArgs) Handles
DataGrid1.UpdateCommand
        Dim key As String = DataGrid1.DataKeys(e.Item.ItemIndex).ToString
        Dim tb As TextBox
        'Update for Actors
        Dim strFname, strLName, strAddress, strCity, strState, StrZip,
strPhone,         strEmail, strDOB, strCCNum, strVal As String
        ' Gets the value from the text box control in the third column
        tb = CType(e.Item.Cells(3).Controls(0), TextBox)
        strFname = tb.Text


        ' Gets the value from the text box control in the fourth column
        tb = CType(e.Item.Cells(4).Controls(0), TextBox)
        strLName = tb.Text


        ' Gets the value from the text box control in the fifth column
        tb = CType(e.Item.Cells(5).Controls(0), TextBox)
        strAddress = tb.Text


        tb = CType(e.Item.Cells(6).Controls(0), TextBox)
        strCity = tb.Text


        tb = CType(e.Item.Cells(7).Controls(0), TextBox)
        strState = tb.Text


        tb = CType(e.Item.Cells(8).Controls(0), TextBox)
        StrZip = tb.Text


        tb = CType(e.Item.Cells(9).Controls(0), TextBox)
        strPhone = tb.Text


        tb = CType(e.Item.Cells(10).Controls(0), TextBox)
```

```
        strEmail = tb.Text

        tb = CType(e.Item.Cells(11).Controls(0), TextBox)
        strDOB = tb.Text

        tb = CType(e.Item.Cells(12).Controls(0), TextBox)
        strCCNum = tb.Text

        tb = CType(e.Item.Cells(13).Controls(0), TextBox)
        strVal = tb.Text

        Dim r As dsCustomer.CustomerRow
        r = DsCustomer2.Customer.FindByCustID(key)
        r.CustID = key
        r.FirstName = strFname
        r.LastName = strLName
        r.Address = strAddress
        r.City = strCity
        r.State = strState
        r.Zip = strZIP
        r.Phone = strPhone
        r.EMail = strEmail
        r.DOB = strDOB
        r.CreditCardNum = strCCNum
        r.CreditCardValidUpto = strVal
        SqlDataAdapter1.Update(DsCustomer2)
        DataGrid1.EditItemIndex = -1
        ' Refresh the grid
        DataGrid1.DataBind()
End Sub
```

When the user clicks on the Add New Customer button, the page AddNewCustomer.aspx is loaded in the browser, as shown in Figure 29-12 on page 754.

The code for adding the functionality for the AddNewCustomer page is as follows:

```
Private Sub Page_Load(ByVal sender As System.Object, ByVal e As
System.EventArgs) Handles MyBase.Load
```

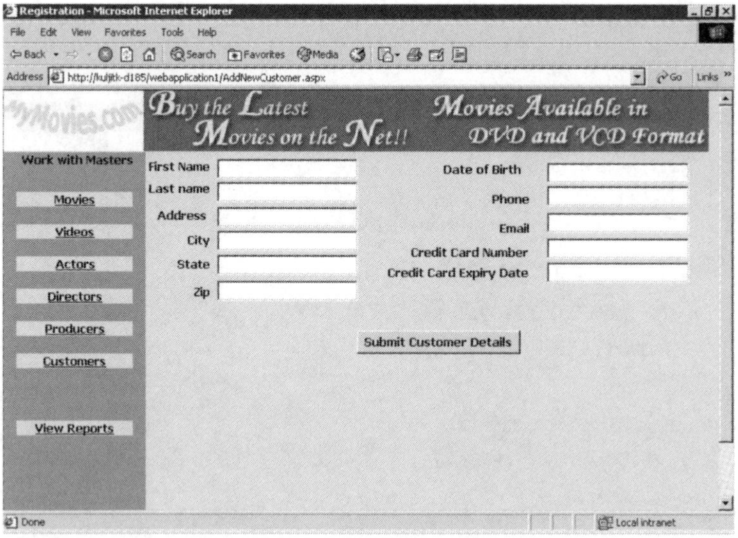

FIGURE 29-12 *The interface of the AddNewCustomer page*

```
        'Put user code to initialize the page here
        CompareValidator2.ValueToCompare = Today
End Sub


Private Sub Button2_Click(ByVal sender As System.Object, ByVal e As
System.EventArgs) Handles Button2.Click
        Dim strConnectionString As String = Application("strConnect")
        Dim sqlString As String
        Dim MyConnection As New SqlConnection(strConnectionString)
        Dim CustId As String
        Try
            lblError.Visible = False
            MyConnection.Open()
            Dim cmdCust As SqlCommand
            cmdCust = New SqlCommand("Select
            IsNull(Max(convert(int,substring(CustID,2,4))),0)+1 as CustId from
            Customer", MyConnection)
            Dim myReader As SqlDataReader =
            cmdCust.ExecuteReader(CommandBehavior.SingleRow)
            While myReader.Read()
                CustId = myReader.GetInt32(0).ToString
```

```
End While
CustId = "A000" + CStr(CustId)

MyConnection.Close()

Dim myCommand As SqlCommand
Dim insertCmd As String
' Check that four of the input values are not empty. If any of them
'  is empty, show a message to the user and rebind the DataGrid.
insertCmd = "insert into Customer values (@CustId,

@LastName,@FirstName,@Address,@City,@State,@Zip,@Phone,
@Email,@DOB," _
 & "@CreditCardNum,@CreditCardValidUpto);"
' Initialize the SqlCommand with the new SQL string.
MyConnection.Open()
myCommand = New SqlCommand(insertCmd, MyConnection)
myCommand.Parameters.Add(New SqlParameter("@CustId",
SqlDbType.VarChar,
11))
myCommand.Parameters.Add(New SqlParameter("@LastName",
SqlDbType.VarChar, 50))
myCommand.Parameters.Add(New SqlParameter("@FirstName",
 SqlDbType.VarChar, 50))
myCommand.Parameters.Add(New SqlParameter("@Address",
SqlDbType.VarChar,
25))
myCommand.Parameters.Add(New SqlParameter("@City",
SqlDbType.VarChar, 25))
myCommand.Parameters.Add(New SqlParameter("@State",
SqlDbType.VarChar, 15))
myCommand.Parameters.Add(New SqlParameter("@Zip", SqlDbType.VarChar,
7))
myCommand.Parameters.Add(New SqlParameter("@Phone",
SqlDbType.VarChar, 10))
myCommand.Parameters.Add(New SqlParameter("@Email",
SqlDbType.VarChar, 50))
myCommand.Parameters.Add(New SqlParameter("@DOB",
```

```
            SqlDbType.DateTime,  8))
            myCommand.Parameters.Add(New SqlParameter("@CreditCardNum",
            SqlDbType.VarChar, 16))
            myCommand.Parameters.Add(New SqlParameter("@CreditCardValidUpto",
             SqlDbType.DateTime, 8))


            myCommand.Parameters("@CustId").Value = CustId
            myCommand.Parameters("@FirstName").Value = txtFname.Text
            myCommand.Parameters("@LastName").Value = txtLName.Text
            myCommand.Parameters("@Address").Value = txtAdd.Text
            myCommand.Parameters("@City").Value = txtCity.Text
            myCommand.Parameters("@State").Value = txtState.Text
            myCommand.Parameters("@Zip").Value = txtZip.Text
            myCommand.Parameters("@Phone").Value = txtPhone.Text
            myCommand.Parameters("@Email").Value = txtEMail.Text
            myCommand.Parameters("@CreditCardNum").Value = txtCCNo.Text
            myCommand.Parameters("@DOB").Value = txtDOB.Text
            myCommand.Parameters("@CreditCardValidUpto").Value = txtExpDate.Text


            myCommand.ExecuteNonQuery()
            MyConnection.Close()
            lblError.Visible = True
            lblError.Text = "Customer Created Successfully. Customer Id is " +
            CustId
        Catch
            lblError.Visible = True
            lblError.Text = "Error Occurred"
            Exit Sub
        End Try
    End Sub
```

In the preceding sections, you wrote the code for the form pages associated with the Movies, Customers, Videos, Directors, and Producers hyperlinks. To complete the functionality for the admin interface, you now need to write the code for the page associated with the View Reports hyperlink.

The Code for the
View Reports *Hyperlink*

When the user clicks on the View Reports hyperlink, the page ShowReports.aspx is loaded in the browser, as shown in Figure 29-13.

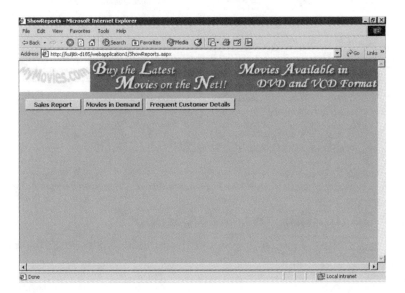

FIGURE 29-13 *The interface of the ShowReports page*

Note that page contains three buttons: Sales Report, Movies in Demand, and Frequent Customer Details. When the user clicks on the buttons, the data for the report associated with the button is displayed in the data grid. For example, when the user clicks on the Movies in Demand button, the corresponding report (shown in Figure 29-14) will be displayed in the data grid.

Let's write the code to display the report associated with the Sales Report button. When the user clicks on the button, the code needs to perform the same check for all the rows in the data table. As you know, to perform repetitive tasks such as performing the same check for all the rows in the data table, you need to create a function and then call that function. Hence, before writing the code for the Sales Report button, you need to define a function.

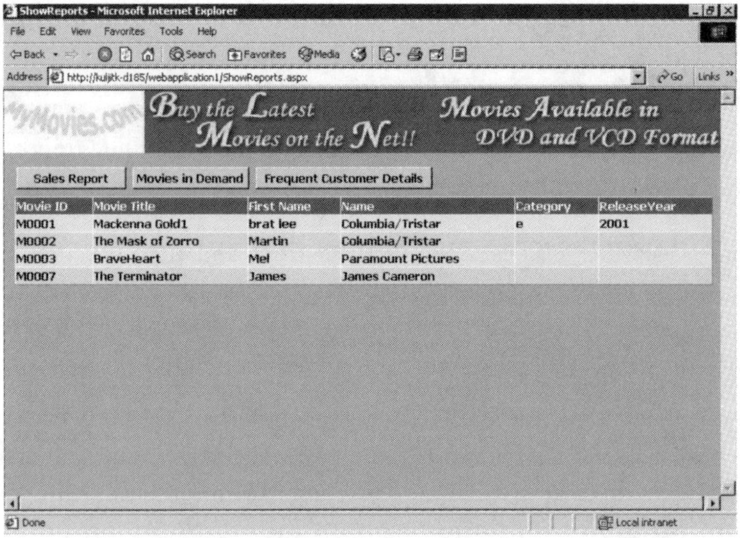

FIGURE 29-14 *The interface of the ShowReports page showing the Movies in Demand report*

The Code for Generating the Sales Report

As previously mentioned, you first need to write the code for the `GetSalesReport` function. The same code follows:

```
Public Function GetSalesReport() As DataSet
        Dim MyConnStr As String
        Dim MySql As String
        Dim MyConn As SqlConnection
        Dim MyDataAdapter As SqlDataAdapter
        Dim MyDataSet As New DataSet()
        'Set the connection string
        MyConnStr = "data source=localhost;initial
        catalog=Movies;persist security info=False;user id=sa;packet size=4096"
        'Set the select statement
        MySql = "SELECT Orders.OrderID, Orders.OrderDate, Movie.MovID,
        Movie.MovTitle,
        OrderDetails.Qty, (OrderDetails.Qty * Video.Price) as OrderValue"
        MySql = MySql + " FROM Orders INNER JOIN OrderDetails ON Orders.OrderID =
        OrderDetails.OrderID INNER JOIN Video ON OrderDetails.VideoID =
Video.VideoID
        INNER JOIN Movie ON Video.MovID = Movie.MovID"
```

```
      'open the connection
      MyConn = New SqlConnection(MyConnStr)
      MyDataAdapter = New SqlDataAdapter(MySql, MyConn)
      MyDataAdapter.Fill(MyDataSet)
      Return MyDataSet
  End Function
```

The preceding code first defines a connection string and then specifies a SQL query to retrieve the values for OrderID, OrderDate, MovieID, MovTitle, Qty, and OrderValue from three tables: Orders, OrderDetails, and Movie. After retrieving the values, the connection is opened and the dataset populated.

Now let's write the code for the Sales Report button. When the user clicks on the Sales Report button, the code should call the GetSalesReport function and then bind the DataGrid control to the dataset MyDataSet. Write the following code in the Click event of the CmdSalesReport function:

```
Private Sub CmdSalesReport_Click(ByVal sender As System.Object, ByVal e As
System.EventArgs) Handles CmdSalesReport.Click
      Dim MyDataSet As DataSet
      MyDataSet = GetSalesReport()
      dgAccountDetails.DataSource = MyDataSet
      dgAccountDetails.DataBind()
End Sub
```

The preceding code calls the GetSalesReport function and sets the data source of the DataGrid control to the dataset returned by this function.

Next you need to write the code for generating the Movies in Demand report.

The Code for Generating the Movies in Demand Report

When the user clicks on the Movies in Demand button, the code needs to retrieve the records for movies that were ordered in the past seven days. As you did previously, you will first write a function that checks the data table for movies that were ordered in the past seven days. The following is the code for the GetMoviesInDemand function:

```
Public Function GetMoviesInDemand() As DataSet
      Dim MyConnStr As String
      Dim MySql As String
```

```
        Dim MyConn As SqlConnection
        Dim MyDataAdapter As SqlDataAdapter
        Dim MyDataSet As New DataSet()
        'Set the connection string
        MyConnStr = "data source=localhost;initial catalog=Movies;persist security
          info=False;user id=sa;packet size=4096"
        'Set the select statement
        MySql = "SELECT a.MovID as [Movie ID], a.MovTitle as [Movie Title],
b.FirstName as [First
        Name], c. Name, a.Category, a.ReleaseYear FROM Movie a, Director b,
Producer c
        WHERE MovID IN (select movid from Video where videoid in (select
        OrderDetails.VideoID from Orders, OrderDetails WHERE OrderDate >
DateADD(day, -7,
         GetDate()) AND Orders.OrderID = OrderDetails.OrderID GROUP BY VideoID )) AND
         a.DirID = b.DirID AND a.ProdID = c.ProdID"
        'Open the connection
        MyConn = New SqlConnection(MyConnStr)
        MyDataAdapter = New SqlDataAdapter(MySql, MyConn)
        MyDataAdapter.Fill(MyDataSet)
        Return MyDataSet
End Function
```

Now you need to write the code to call the function and populate the dataset when the user clicks on the Movies in Demand button. To specify this functionality, write the following code in the Click event of the CmdMoviesInDemand function:

```
Private Sub CmdMoviesInDemand_Click(ByVal sender As System.Object, ByVal e As
System.EventArgs)Handles CmdMoviesInDemand.Click
        Dim MyDataSet As DataSet
        MyDataSet = GetMoviesInDemand()
        dgAccountDetails.DataSource = MyDataSet
        dgAccountDetails.DataBind()
End Sub
```

The preceding code is similar to the code you wrote for the Sales Report button. It uses `MyDataSet` to store the result returned by the `GetMoviesInDemand` function. Then it specifies the data source of the DataGrid control as the dataset returned by the function.

Next you will take a look at how to write the code for the Frequent Customer Details button.

The Code for Generating the Frequent Customer Details Report

The code for generating this report is similar to the code you wrote in the preceding two sections. Hence, it will not be explained here. The code for the `Get-CustomerDetails` function and the `Click` event of the `CmdFrequentCustDetails` function is as follows:

```
Public Function GetCustomerDetails() As DataSet
        Dim MyConnStr As String
        Dim MySql As String
        Dim MyConn As SqlConnection
        Dim MyDataAdapter As SqlDataAdapter
        Dim MyDataSet As New DataSet()
        'Set the connection string
        MyConnStr = "data source=localhost;initial catalog=Movies;persist security
        info=False;user id=sa;packet size=4096"
        'Set the select statement
        MySql = "SELECT CustID as [Customer ID], FirstName as [First Name],
LastName as [Last
        Name], Address, City, State, Zip, Phone, Email, DOB FROM Customer a WHERE (
        (SELECT COUNT(*) FROM Orders WHERE a.CustID = Orders.CustID) > 5)"
        'Open the connection
        MyConn = New SqlConnection(MyConnStr)
        MyDataAdapter = New SqlDataAdapter(MySql, MyConn)
        MyDataAdapter.Fill(MyDataSet)
        Return MyDataSet

    End Function
```

```
Private Sub CmdFrequentCustDetails _Click(ByVal sender As System.Object, ByVal e As
System.EventArgs) Handles CmdFrequentCustDetails.Click
        Dim MyDataSet As DataSet
        MyDataSet = GetCustomerDetails()
        dgAccountDetails.DataSource = MyDataSet
        dgAccountDetails.DataBind()
End Sub
```

To complete this form, you just need to write the code to navigate the pages of the DataGrid control.

Navigating the Pages of the DataGrid Control

Recall that, while designing the form, you specified that five records should be displayed on a page. To navigate the different pages of the grid, write the following code in the PageIndexChanged event for the DataGrid control:

```
Private Sub dgAccountDetails_PageIndexChanged(ByVal source As Object, ByVal e As
System.Web.UI.WebControls.DataGridPageChangedEventArgs) Handles
dgAccountDetails.PageIndexChanged
        dgAccountDetails.CurrentPageIndex = e.NewPageIndex
        dgAccountDetails.DataBind()
End Sub
```

The form attached to the View Reports link is now complete. The entire code for the form is provided here for your reference:

```
Private Sub Page_Load(ByVal sender As System.Object, ByVal e As
System.EventArgs) Handles MyBase.Load
        'Put user code to initialize the page here

End Sub
Public Function GetSalesReport() As DataSet
        Dim MyConnStr As String
        Dim MySql As String
        Dim MyConn As SqlConnection
        Dim MyDataAdapter As SqlDataAdapter
        Dim MyDataSet As New DataSet()
        'Set the connection string
```

```
        MyConnStr = "data source=localhost;initial catalog=Movies;persist security
        info=False;user id=sa;packet size=4096"
        'Set the select statement
        MySql = "SELECT Orders.OrderID, Orders.OrderDate, Movie.MovID, Movie.MovTitle,
        OrderDetails.Qty, (OrderDetails.Qty * Video.Price) as OrderValue"
        MySql = MySql + " FROM Orders INNER JOIN OrderDetails ON Orders.OrderID =
        OrderDetails.OrderID INNER JOIN Video ON OrderDetails.VideoID = Video.VideoID
        INNER JOIN Movie ON Video.MovID = Movie.MovID"
        'open the connection
        MyConn = New SqlConnection(MyConnStr)
        MyDataAdapter = New SqlDataAdapter(MySql, MyConn)
        MyDataAdapter.Fill(MyDataSet)
        Return MyDataSet


    End Function


    Private Sub CmdSalesReport _Click(ByVal sender As System.Object, ByVal e As
System.EventArgs)
        Handles CmdSalesReport.Click
        Dim MyDataSet As DataSet
        MyDataSet = GetSalesReport()
        dgAccountDetails.DataSource = MyDataSet
        dgAccountDetails.DataBind()
    End Sub


    Private Sub CmdMoviesInDemand_Click(ByVal sender As System.Object, ByVal e As
System.EventArgs)
        Handles CmdMoviesInDemand.Click
        Dim MyDataSet As DataSet
        MyDataSet = GetMoviesInDemand()
        dgAccountDetails.DataSource = MyDataSet
        dgAccountDetails.DataBind()
    End Sub
    Public Function GetMoviesInDemand() As DataSet
        Dim MyConnStr As String
        Dim MySql As String
        Dim MyConn As SqlConnection
```

```
        Dim MyDataAdapter As SqlDataAdapter
        Dim MyDataSet As New DataSet()
        'set the connection string
        MyConnStr = "data source=localhost;initial catalog=Movies;persist security
        info=False;user id=sa;packet size=4096"
        'set the select statement
        MySql = "SELECT a.MovID as [Movie ID], a.MovTitle as [Movie Title],
b.FirstName as [First
        Name], c. Name, a.Category, a.ReleaseYear FROM Movie a, Director b, Producer
c
        WHERE MovID IN (select movid from Video where videoid in (select
        OrderDetails.VideoID from Orders, OrderDetails WHERE OrderDate > DateADD(day,
-7,
        GetDate()) AND Orders.OrderID = OrderDetails.OrderID GROUP BY VideoID )) AND
        a.DirID = b.DirID AND a.ProdID = c.ProdID"
        'open the connection
        MyConn = New SqlConnection(MyConnStr)
        MyDataAdapter = New SqlDataAdapter(MySql, MyConn)
        MyDataAdapter.Fill(MyDataSet)
        Return MyDataSet

    End Function
    Public Function GetCustomerDetails() As DataSet
        Dim MyConnStr As String
        Dim MySql As String
        Dim MyConn As SqlConnection
        Dim MyDataAdapter As SqlDataAdapter
        Dim MyDataSet As New DataSet()
        'set the connection string
        MyConnStr = "data source=localhost;initial catalog=Movies;persist security
        info=False;user id=sa;packet size=4096"
        'set the select statement
        MySql = "SELECT CustID as [Customer ID], FirstName as [First Name], LastName
as [Last
            Name], Address, City, State, Zip, Phone, Email, DOB FROM Customer a WHERE (
            (SELECT COUNT(*) FROM Orders WHERE a.CustID = Orders.CustID) > 5)"
```

```
            'open the connection
            MyConn = New SqlConnection(MyConnStr)
            MyDataAdapter = New SqlDataAdapter(MySql, MyConn)
            MyDataAdapter.Fill(MyDataSet)
            Return MyDataSet

    End Function


        Private Sub CmdFrequentCustDetails _Click(ByVal sender As System.Object,
ByVal e As System.EventArgs)
            Handles CmdFrequentCustDetails.Click
            Dim MyDataSet As DataSet
            MyDataSet = GetCustomerDetails()
            dgAccountDetails.DataSource = MyDataSet
            dgAccountDetails.DataBind()
        End Sub


    Private Sub dgAccountDetails_PageIndexChanged(ByVal source As Object, ByVal e As
    System.Web.UI.WebControls.DataGridPageChangedEventArgs) Handles
    dgAccountDetails.PageIndexChanged
        dgAccountDetails.CurrentPageIndex = e.NewPageIndex
        dgAccountDetails.DataBind()
    End Sub
End Class
```

With this code, you have completed the functionality for the admin interface.

Summary

In this chapter, you learned how to add functionality to the admin interface. You looked at the code for the various hyperlinks on the AdminHomePage. You also learned about the code to insert, modify, and delete records from the various tables in the database at the backend.

PART V

Professional Project 4

Project 4

Creating a Word-to-XML Converter Application

Project 4 Overview

The My Movies project is used to considerably reduce the processing time for a sales order. The application converts a Word file to XML format, which can be accessed by users from anywhere and on any platform. The application uses several built-in functions to read and convert XML text. The application first prompts the user for the directory where the file will be placed. After the user has specified the directory, the application validates whether the path is valid. If the directory structure is valid, the application enables the FileSystem Watcher; otherwise, it raises an error message. If the directory is valid, the application hides the form and displays the notification icon on the status bar. It then checks whether the user has added the file to the source directory. The application then checks the format of the file and converts it into an XML file. In addition, it moves and saves the XML file in the processed directory.

To add the preceding functionality, you'll use several controls. These controls are as follows:

◆ The TabControl

◆ The ImageList control

◆ The ErrorProvider control

◆ The FileSystem Watcher control

◆ The NotifyIcon control

When creating the application, you'll use the following concepts:

◆ The .NET framework

◆ Visual Basic.NET

◆ XML basics

◆ Converting Word data to the XML format

Chapter 30

Getting Started with XML

Earlier in the book, you learned how to create the MyMovies Web application required by the MyMovies company. The company now requires an application to convert a Word memo file into an XML document. Before you start creating the application, however, you need to understand what exactly XML is.

In this chapter, you will learn about XML, which stands for eXtensible Markup Language. It is defined and standardized by the World Wide Web Consortium (W3C). In this chapter, you will learn the differences between XML and HTML. You will also learn about XML-related specifications, including Document Type Definitions (DTDs), namespaces, Designer, the document object model (DOM), Reader, Writer, schemas, and eXtensible Stylesheet Language Transformations (XSLT). In addition, you will learn about the basic rules for a well-formed XML document. XML documents must meet all syntactical requirements specified by W3C. Therefore, you will also learn to perform XML data validation using DTD, XML-Data Reduced (XDR), and XML Schema Definition (XSD) validation services. In addition, you will learn to convert relational data to the XML format to help Web applications share data with other similar applications. You can also use XML to display dynamic data. This can be done using data binding, which will also be explained in this chapter.

In the .NET framework, XML provides a comprehensive and integrated set of classes and APIs that help you work with XML data and documents. Some of the XML class groups discussed in this chapter include:

◆ Writing XML

◆ Validating XML

◆ `XmlReader`, `XmlWriter`

◆ `XpathNavigator`

◆ `XslTransform` and XSL Transformations (XSLT)

◆ `XslSchema` and the XML Schema Definition language (XSD)

What is XML?

As everyone knows, HTML is a very popular markup language. There are millions or more Web pages based on HTML. In addition, HTML enjoys a wide range of support, including browsers, editors, e-mail software, databases, and more. To meet the demanding needs of the Web, HTML has been extended over the years. In fact, HTML has grown into a complex language with the inclusion of many new tags.

This alone, however, did not offer appropriate solutions to the growing needs of modern-day Web applications. For example, electronic-commerce applications required tags for product references, prices, addresses, and others. This implied that more new tags needed to be created, which would not do any good to the already-burdened HTML language. Therefore, XML was introduced to address the shortcomings of HTML.

XML provides a set of rules to present structured data. Examples of structured data include spreadsheets, financial transactions, and technical drawings. Similar to HTML, XML also makes use of tags and attributes. In HTML, tags are used to control the display and appearance of data. In XML, however, tags are used to define the structure of data. XML is simple, platform-independent, and widely used. In XML, tags are used to delineate elements of data. The interpretation of data is not done by XML but by the application itself. For example, the <p> tag in XML need not indicate a paragraph. Depending on the content, it could mean a price, parameter, or person. You can define an unlimited number of tags in XML. Unlike in HTML, the rules for defining and using tags are more stringent in XML. One important point to remember is that XML was not introduced to replace HTML but to complement it.

First let's compare and contrast XML with HTML. You also need to know how to write an XML code and view its output.

XML vs. HTML

XML became a popular markup language because HTML was successful. However, there are some differences between the two, as follows:

◆ HTML is designed to display data. XML is designed to describe and focus on data.

- In HTML, you can only use predefined tags, which are limited in number. In XML, the author of the document can define an unlimited number of tags.

- In XML, all tags must have a closing tag. In addition, all attributes in XML need to be enclosed within either single or double quotes. Requirements such as these are not essential in HTML. For example, the following statement in XML is acceptable:

```
<IMG source="logo.gif"> </IMG>
```

The following statement, however, is only acceptable in HTML:

```
<IMG source="logo.gif">
```

- The tag names in XML are case sensitive, whereas in HTML they are not. For example, in XML, the <p> tag and the <P> tag are two different tags.

- In XML, nested tags whose closing tags overlap are not allowed. However, nested tags are common in HTML. For example, code such as the following cannot be used in XML:

```
<IMG source="logo.gif"> <SPAN>The logo. </IMG></SPAN>
```

To make the difference between HTML and XML clear, look at the output of two sample codes. First, the following HTML document named Employees.html is created in Notepad to display employee details in a numbered list:

```
<HTML>
<HEAD> <TITLE> Employee Details </TITLE> </HEAD>
<BODY>
<OL>
    <LI> <B> Employee ID: </B> EMP1  <B> Employee Name : </B> Mark Greg </LI>
    <LI> <B> Employee ID: </B> EMP2  <B> Employee Name : </B> Mary Robert </LI>
</OL>
</BODY>
</HTML>
```

When you open this HTML document in a Web browser, you see the output shown in Figure 30-1.

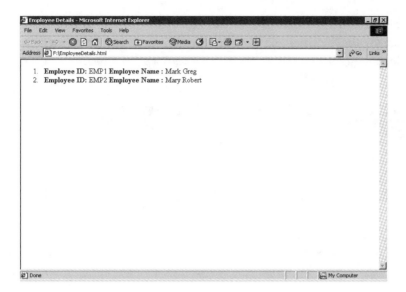

FIGURE 30-1 *Output of the HTML code*

Next create an XML document named Employees.xml in Notepad to describe the data in a structured manner as displayed in the preceding HTML document:

```
<?xml version="1.0"?>
<Employees>
    <Employee>
        <Id> EMP1 </Id>
        <LastName> Mark </LastName>
        <FirstName> Greg   </FirstName>
    </Employee>
    <Employee>
        <Id> EMP2 </Id>
        <LastName> Susan</LastName>
        <FirstName> Ward</FirstName>
    </Employee>
</Employees>
```

NOTE

Remember that XML is case sensitive. Therefore, the <Employee> tag is not the same as the <employee> tag. Be careful when you code in XML.

In the preceding code, the first line `<?xml version= "1.0"?>` is an XML declaration statement that notifies the browser that the document being processed is an XML document. When you open this XML document in Internet Explorer, the document appears as shown in Figure 30-2.

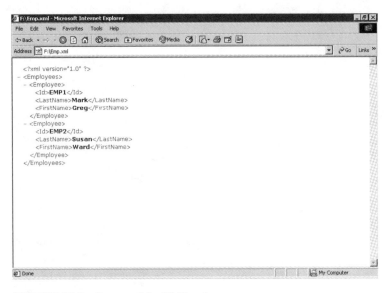

FIGURE 30-2 *Output of the XML code*

Notice that the document in Figure 30-2 is displayed in a structured manner in the form of a tree. Each tag that contains subtags can be expanded or collapsed. All XML documents are displayed in a similar manner.

By now, the basic functionality of XML and its differences with HTML should be clear. Because XML is integrated in .NET, later in this chapter you'll learn how to create an XML document in the .NET framework using the XML Designer.

In the next section, you will learn about some of the benefits of XML.

Benefits of XML

XML offers many advantages to programmers, including the following:

◆ *Simplicity.* Information stored in an XML document is easy to understand. In addition, computers can easily process the information.

- *Extensibility.* In XML, there is no restriction on the number of tags to be used. Therefore, new tags can be created according to specific requirements.

- *Self-explanatory.* Information in an XML document is self-descriptive. This is because the XML document contains metadata in the form of tags and attributes. For example, <product> is a tag in XML and clearly describes what it contains.

- *Machine-readable content.* The tags and attributes in an XML document provide context information about the document. This can lead to the use of highly efficient search engines.

- *Segregate content from presentation.* In XML, the focus is more on the information itself rather than its presentation. The presentation of an XML document is decided by using external style sheets. Style sheets contain styling instructions that help you view the document and apply appropriate style to it.

- *Openness.* XML is a W3C standard. Therefore, it finds universal acceptance within the software industry.

The next section provides an overview of a simple XML document.

Overview of an XML Document

An XML document primarily consists of the following:

- Tags
- Text
- Attributes

Tags define the data elements, and text defines the actual content of the XML document. The structure of an XML document contains a start tag that defines the name of the data element, the text to be contained in the data element, and the end tag.

For example:

```
<Employee> Susan Ward </Employee>
```

In this example, the tag <Employee> is the start tag or the data element. The name Susan Ward is the text contained in the element. </Employee> defines the end tag.

You can also use nested tags in XML. Consider an example in which an organization needs to store details about employees in each of its departments separately. The XML for this requirement can be written as follows:

```
<Department>
  <Finance>
    <Employee>
      <Empname> Susan Ward </Empname>
      <Dateofjoining> 03/20/01</Dateofjoining>
      </Employee>

    ...

  </Finance>
  <HumanResource>
    <Employee>
      <Empname> Ron Floyd </Empname>
      <Dateofjoining> 03/12/01 </Dateofjoining>
    </Employee>

    ...

    </HumanResource>
  </Department>
```

Attributes of an XML document provide more information about the element and are used inside the start tag. All values of the attributes must be enclosed within quotes.

An attribute in an XML document can be written as in the following example:

```
<div class="preface">
```

In this example, `class` is the attribute of the `div` element. The value of the `class` attribute is `preface`.

Basic Rules for a Well-Formed XML Document

In the preceding section, you learned about the constituents of an XML document. In this section, you will learn about well-formed XML documents. XML documents are well formed if they follow certain rules. Well-formed XML documents are defined by their use, not by any specific standards. The rules for a well-formed XML document are as follows:

◆ Every XML document must have a root element that contains all the other elements in the document.

◆ All tags opened in XML must also be closed. Tags must be explicitly specified because they are not inferred in XML. Consider this example:

```
<L1> the items purchased
<L2> the first item
```

This is acceptable in HTML. In XML, however, this is an ambiguous reference because the `<L1>` tag is not closed. In XML, you can infer the second tag to be the continuation of the first or a new tag altogether. Therefore, you need to explicitly close all open tags. The preceding example can be rewritten in XML as follows:

```
<L1> the items purchased </L1>
<L2> the first item </L2>
```

◆ In XML, empty tags must be closed using a forward slash (/). Empty tags are those that do not contain any value but might contain attributes. The values of attributes are specified within the opening and closing angular brackets of the empty tag. The forward slash must be placed before the closing angular bracket. For example:

```
<graphic name="logo.gif"/>
```

In this example, `<graphic>` is the empty tag that contains the attribute name. The value of the attribute is specified as a GIF image.

◆ In XML, the value of an element's attribute must be enclosed within double quotation marks. XML does not allow any value of an attribute to be specified outside the double quotation marks. Consider the example `<Employee name="susan"/>`. In this example, susan is the value for the attribute name of the `<Employee>` tag.

◆ The tags in XML must be nested correctly. This means that all opening tags must be closed in the reverse order in which they were opened. Consider an example:

```
<Employee> Susan <Role>Systems Analyst </Employee></Role>.
```

In this example, the order of the tags' closing is not valid because the `<Employee>` tag is closed before the `<Role>` tag. The following is the correct sequence:

```
<Employee> Susan <Role>Systems Analyst </Role></Employee>.
```

♦ The tags in XML must match each other. This implies that both the opening and closing tags must correspond in every aspect. This is because XML tags are case sensitive. Any difference between the tags results in an error. Consider an example:

```
<L1> the items purchased </l1>
```

This example would produce an error because the tags are not similar.

Now that you know how to create a well-formed XML document, you will move on to XML specifications. XML specifications offer more than just a well-formed document. The following section discusses some of these specifications.

XML Specifications

You are now familiar with the concept of a well-formed XML document, but you also need to provide the document with a meaningful structure. Similarly, you also need to maintain some form of consistency with respect to elements in an XML document. These and many other requirements can be met using certain specifications related to XML. These specifications include the following:

♦ *Document Type Definitions (DTDs)* specify the rules for XML documents. They make it easier for everyone to understand the structure and logic of your XML documents.

♦ *XML namespaces* are used to avoid conflicting names and to assign a unique name to each element when you define multiple elements in an XML document.

♦ The *document object model (DOM)* enables navigation and modification in an XML document, including adding, updating, or deleting the content of elements. In addition, this also enables you to access XML data programmatically.

♦ *eXtensible Stylesheet Language Transformations (XSLT)* are the style sheets provided by the W3C to format XML documents.

♦ *XML schemas* can be considered a superset of DTDs and are also used to define the structure of XML documents.

These specifications are discussed in greater detail in the following sections.

Document Type Definitions (DTDs)

A DTD represents a set of rules that defines the structure and logic of XML documents. The documents that store these rules are called DTD documents and have the extension DTD.

To better understand the concept of DTD documents, compare them to the creation of tables in a database. When you create a table in a database system, you specify the columns, the data types for different columns, the validation rules for data within columns, and so on. Similarly, you can specify rules that can be used in XML documents—such as tags and attributes—by using a DTD document. DTD documents can be considered to be rulebooks for XML documents.

> ### TIP
>
> It's not essential for you to create a DTD document for your XML documents. However, a DTD document can be important to users who need to understand the structure of your XML documents or who need to create an XML document similar to the one you've already created. These users can refer to your DTD document to understand the structure and logic of your XML documents.

When you create a DTD document for an XML document, the XML document is checked against the rules specified in the DTD document. If the XML document adheres to all the DTD rules, the document is considered valid. Otherwise, the XML document fails to generate the desired output.

To explain how to create a DTD, let's continue with the same Employee example discussed previously. Type the following code in Notepad and save the file as Employees.dtd to create a DTD document that you will use later in this chapter.

```
<!ELEMENT Employees (Employee)+>
<!ELEMENT Employee (Id, LastName, FirstName)>
<!ELEMENT Id (#PCDATA)>
<!ELEMENT LastName (#PCDATA)>
<!ELEMENT FirstName (#PCDATA)>
```

The DTD document declares five elements: Employees, Employee, Id, LastName, and FirstName. Each element declaration statement has three parameters: the keyword ELEMENT, the name of the element, and the content type of the element.

Therefore, when you consider the preceding code, the first declaration creates an element called `Employees` and defines the content type as `(Employee)+`.

NOTE

The + symbol indicates that the `Employees` element can contain multiple `Employee` elements.

Similarly, the content type for the `Employee` element is declared in such a way that it must contain three elements: `Id`, `LastName`, and `FirstName`. The `Id`, `LastName`, and `FirstName` elements can each contain character data. Character data is represented by the keyword (`#PCDATA`).

If you want to use the rules declared in a DTD document, you must include it with the XML document you create. To include the DTD document in an XML document, use the following statement:

```
<!DOCTYPE Employees SYSTEM "Employees.DTD">
```

Now you will learn how you can include a DTD document in an XML code and also the effect the DTD has on the XML document. Create an XML document in Notepad named EmployeeDTD.xml and type the following code:

```
<?xml version="1.0"?>
<!DOCTYPE Employees SYSTEM "Employees.DTD">
<Employees>
    <Employee>
        <Id> E001 </Id>
        <Name> Susan Ward </Name>
    </Employee>
</Employees>
```

When you view this XML document in a browser, the browser reports an error because the XML document isn't valid. According to the DTD document, the `<Employee>` element contains three elements: `<Id>`, `<LastName>`, and `<FirstName>`. However, the XML document you created doesn't conform to this rule and therefore doesn't pass the validation test.

> **NOTE**
>
> When you view the file in a browser, you might actually see an XML-based tree struc-
> ture. This is because MSXML is a DOM-enabled parser. The error will occur if you
> use XML DOM objects and set the `validateOnParse` flag to `true` in a script. There-
> fore, to access an XML document and to validate it, you need to use the DOM
> objects provided by MSXML. The following is a sample script you can run; enter the
> name of the XML file you want to validate.

```
<html>
<head>
<script>
function validate()
{
var xmldoc = new ActiveXObject("Microsoft.XMLDOM");
xmldoc.async = false;
xmldoc.validateOnParse=true;
xmldoc.load(TxtXMLFileName.value);
var error=xmldoc.parseError;
transformedwindow=window.open('Transformed.htm','_new','location=0,status=1,
toolbar=0,menuBar=0,
scrollBars=0,directories=0,resizable=0,width=600,height=600');
    if(error!="")
    {
    transformedwindow.document.write('<HTML><TITLE>DTD
Validator</Title><BODY><P><b>Error
    Validating the document</b></p><br>');
    transformedwindow.document.write('<b>Error URL: </b><br>' + error.url +
'<br>');
    transformedwindow.document.write('<b>Error Line: </b><br>' + error.line +
'<br>');
    transformedwindow.document.write('<b>Error Position: </b><br>' +
error.linepos + '<br>');
    transformedwindow.document.write('<b>Error Reason: </b><br>' + error.reason
+ '<br>');
    transformedwindow.document.write('</BODY></HTML>');
    }
```

continues

NOTE *(continued)*

```
    else
    {
    transformedwindow.document.write('<HTML><TITLE>DTD
Validator</Title><BODY><b>No Error
    </b><br>');
        transformedwindow.document.write('</BODY></HTML>');
        }
    }
    </script>
    <body>
    Enter XML Document Name: <input type="text" name="TxtXMLFileName">
    <input type="button" onclick="javascript:validate()" value="Load">
    </body>
    </html>
```

You'll learn about XML DOM later in this chapter.

XML Namespaces

As previously mentioned, you can define your own elements to describe the data while creating XML documents. You can also use elements that you define outside your XML document, such as in a DTD document. However, defining multiple elements might create a problem: You might end up defining the same element twice. For example, when defining the data structure to present employee details, you might define the <Name> element twice: once to qualify the employee name and a second time to qualify the department name. This situation is not unlikely when you have a large number of elements to define. It leads to name collisions, and your XML document cannot be processed for correct output. To avoid such situations, W3C recommends the use of XML namespaces. XML namespaces are a collection of unique elements identified by *uniform resource identifiers (URI)*, and they are declared by using the keyword xmlns.

To continue with the same example, you can use the following statement to declare an XML namespace for the <Name> element that defines the department name:

```
xmlns:DepartmentName="http://www.dn.com/dn"
```

In this statement, `DepartmentName` is an alias for the `<Name>` element, and `http://www.dn.com/dn` is the URI. Later, when you want to use the `<Name>` element to qualify a department name, you must prefix it with the alias `Department-Name`, as in the following statement:

```
<DepartmentName: Name>
```

> ### NOTE
>
> When you specify a namespace URI, the browser does not search the URI or the documents at the specified URL. In fact, the URI just serves as a unique identifier.

The XML Document Object Model (DOM)

To access and display XML data in your Web applications, you need to use the XML Web server control and set its specific properties at the design time. There might be situations when you want to display the XML data based on some conditions. In such cases, you'll have to access the XML data programmatically. To do that, you must employ the XML DOM. The DOM is an in-memory, cached tree representation of an XML document that enables the navigation and modification of a document including adding, updating, or deleting content of elements. The DOM represents data as a hierarchy of object nodes.

> ### TIP
>
> The Microsoft .NET framework SDK implements the W3C DOM (Core) Level 1 (information available at **www.w3.org/TR/REC-DOM-Level-1/level-one-core.html**) and the DOM Core (information available at **www.w3.org/TR/DOM-Level-2-Core/core.html**).

At the top of the hierarchy lies the XML document. To implement XML DOM, the .NET framework provides a set of classes that enable you to access the XML data programmatically included in the `System.Xml` namespace. Some of the classes in the `System.Xml` namespace are as follows:

◆ `XmlDocument` represents a complete XML document and provides a means to view and manipulate the nodes of the entire XML document. The `Xml-Document` class is contained in the `System.Xml.XmlDocument` namespace.

◆ XmlDataDocument enables you to store and manipulate XML and relational data into a data set. This class is derived from the XmlDocument class.

◆ XmlDocumentType represents the DTD used by an XML document.

◆ XmlNode supports methods for performing operations on the document as a whole, such as loading or saving an XML file.

◆ XmlTextReader represents a reader that performs a fast, noncached, forward-only read operation on an XML document.

◆ XmlTextWriter represents a writer that performs a fast, noncached, forward-only generation of streams and files that contain XML data.

◆ XmlElement represents a single element from an XML document.

◆ XmlAttribute represents a single attribute of an element.

XmlNode and XmlDocument have methods and properties to do the following:

◆ Access and modify nodes specific to a DOM, such as attribute nodes, element nodes, entity reference nodes, and so on

◆ Retrieve entire nodes as well as the information the node contains, such as the text in an element node

Two other classes are widely used with XML implementations. These are the XmlReader class and the XmlWriter class.

The XmlReader *Class*

XmlReader is an abstract base class that provides noncached, forward-only, read-only access to XML data. The XmlReader reads a stream or an XML document to check whether the document is well made and generates XmlExceptions if an error is encountered. The XmlReader implements namespace requirements documented as recommendations by the W3C.

Because the XmlReader class is an abstract base class, it enables you to customize your own type of reader or extend the functionality of current implementations of other derived classes such as XmlTextReader, XmlValidatingReader, and XmlNodeReader.

The XmlReader has various properties and methods associated with it. It has methods to do the following:

◆ Read XML content and extract data from complete XML documents such as XML text files

◆ Skip over elements and their content, such as unwanted records
◆ Determine whether an element has content or is empty
◆ Determine the depth of the XML element stack
◆ Read attributes of elements

The XmlReader has properties that return information, such as:

◆ The name of the current node
◆ The content of the current node

Implementations of XmlReader enhance the base class functionality to extend support to various situational requirements. The common implementations of Xml-Reader can offer fast access to data without validation or complete data validation. The following list describes some implementations of XmlReader:

◆ *The* XmlTextReader *class.* Reads data extremely fast. It is a forward-only reader with methods that return data on content and node types. Has no DTD or schema support.

◆ *The* XmlNodeReader *class.* Provides a parser over an XML DOM API, like the XmlNode tree. Takes in an XmlNode as a parameter and returns all nodes that it finds in the DOM tree. Has no DTD or schema validation support but can resolve entities defined in a DTD.

◆ *The* XmlValidatingReader *class.* Provides a fully compliant validating or nonvalidating XML parser with DTD, XSD schema, or XDR schema support.

◆ *Custom XML readers.* Allows developer-defined derivations of the XmlReader.

The XmlWriter *Class*

XmlWriter also is an abstract base class, and it defines an interface for creating XML documents. The XmlWriter provides a forward-only, read-only, noncached way of generating XML streams, which help you build XML documents that conform to the W3C and namespace recommendations.

The XmlWriter has methods and properties that enable you to do the following:

◆ Create well-made XML documents
◆ Specify whether the XML document should support namespaces
◆ Write multiple documents to one output stream
◆ Manage the output, determine the progress of the output, and close the output

◆ Report the current namespace prefix

◆ Write valid and qualified names

However, the `XmlWriter` does not check for the following:

◆ Invalid element and attribute names

◆ Unicode characters that do not match the encoding

◆ Duplicate attributes

The `XmlWriter` has one implementation, the `XmlTextWriter`.

Simple API for XML

One of the main advantages of the DOM is that it is a hierarchical representation of XML object nodes and enables modification of each node. At times, however, this could act to your disadvantage, especially if your document is large.

When you use the DOM to manipulate an XML file, the DOM reads the file, breaks it up into individual objects (such as elements, attributes, and comments), and then creates a tree structure of the document in memory. The benefit to using the DOM is that you can reference and manipulate each object, called a *node*, individually. However, creating a tree structure for a document, especially a large document, requires significant amounts of memory.

The Simple API for XML (SAX) is an interface that enables you to write applications to read data in an XML document. SAX2, the latest version of SAX, provides a simple, fast, low-overhead alternative to processing through the DOM.

Unlike the DOM, SAX2 is events based. This means that SAX2 generates events as it finds specific symbols in an XML document. One major advantage of SAX2 is that it reads a section of an XML document, generates an event, and then moves on to the next section. This kind of serial processing of documents enables SAX2 to use less memory than the DOM and therefore is better for processing large documents. SAX2 can create applications that abort processing when a particular piece of information is found.

You can choose SAX over DOM in the following situations:

◆ When your documents are extremely large

◆ When you want to abort processing a document when a specific piece of information is found

- When you want to retrieve specific bits of information

- When you want to create a document structure with only high-level objects and not with low-level elements, attributes, and instructions (as in the DOM)

- When you cannot afford the DOM due to high memory requirements against low availability

eXtensible Style Sheet Language Transformations

As previously discussed, the basic aim of XML is to describe structured data rather than focus on the presentation of data. XML documents do not contain any tags that define the format of the data to be displayed. This fact has its unique advantages and helps XML documents remain platform independent. However, you can apply any format to the data and display the same data in multiple formats by using special style sheets.

W3C has specified a style sheet called *eXtensible Stylesheet Language Transformations (XSLT)* that is specifically designed for XML documents. The goal of XSLT is to transform the content of a source XML document into another document that is different in format or structure, such as transforming an XML document into HTML for displaying it in Web applications. In the .NET framework, the XslTransform class, found in the System.Xml.Xsl namespace, is an XSLT processor that implements the functionality of this specification. To create an XSL style sheet in the .NET framework, use the XSL or XSLT file in the Add New Item dialog box. For example, the following code defines a style sheet named Employees.xslt for the Employees.xml document:

```
<xsl:stylesheet version="1.0" xmlns:xsl="http://www.w3.org/1999/XSL/Transform"
xmlns="http://www.w3.org/TR/xhtml1/strict">
<xsl:output method="xml" encoding="iso-8859-1" />
<xsl:template match="/">
    <OL>
        <xsl:for-each select='Employees/Employee'>
            <LI>
                <b>
                    Employee Id :
                    <xsl:value-of select='Id' /> <br />
                </b>
```

```
                    Last Name :
                    <xsl:value-of select='LastName' /> <br />
                    First Name :
                    <xsl:value-of select='FirstName' /> <br />
              <hr />
          </LI>
      </xsl:for-each>
  </OL>
</xsl:template>
</xsl:stylesheet>
```

In the preceding code:

◆ The `<xsl:template>` element enables you to create a template to display the data in the required format.

◆ The `<xsl:for-each>` element is used to perform a task repeatedly.

◆ The `<xsl:value-of>` element is used to retrieve the data from individual elements.

After you create the XSLT file, include this file with your XML file to apply the format. To do this step, open the Employees.xml file in the XML view and, after the first line, add the following line:

```
<?xml-stylesheet type="text/xsl" href="Employees.xslt"?>
```

When you browse the Employees.xml file in a browser, the output looks formatted and appears as shown in Figure 30-3.

XSLT uses XPath to select parts of an XML document that are to be formatted. XPath is a query language used to navigate nodes of a XML document tree.

The following is a list of classes commonly used when working with XSLT and XPath:

◆ `XPathNavigator` is an API that provides a cursor-style model for navigating over a data store. For editing the store, you need to use the `Xml-Document` class.

◆ `IXPathNavigable` is an interface that provides a `CreateNavigator` method to an `XPathNavigator` for the data store.

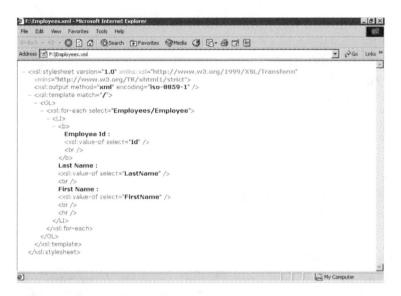

FIGURE 30-3 *The Employees.xml file as displayed in the browser after including an XSLT style sheet*

- ◆ XmlDocument enables editing of a document. It implements IXPathNavigable to enable editing of document scenarios where XSLT is subsequently required.

- ◆ XmlDataDocument is a subclass of the XmlDocument class. It bridges the relational database and XML worlds by using a DataSet to optimize storage of structured data within the XML document according to specified mappings on the DataSet. It implements the IXPathNavigable class to allow document scenarios where XSLT can be performed over relational data retrieved from a database.

- ◆ XPathDocument provides a performance cache to optimize XslTransform processing and XPath queries. It implements IXPathNavigable.

- ◆ XPathNodeIterator provides navigation over an XPath nodeset. All XPath selection methods on the XPathNavigator return an XPathNodeIterator. Multiple XPathNodeIterators can be created over the same store, each representing a selected set of nodes.

XML Schemas

The XSD language enables you to define the structure and data types for XML documents. To understand the concept of schemas, let's again draw a comparison to a database system. You might know about database schemas that define and validate the tables, columns, and data types that make up the database. Like database schemas, XML schemas also define and validate the content and structure of XML documents and can be used to maintain consistency among various XML documents. XML schema files have the XSD extension.

NOTE

The schema element definition in an XML document must include the namespace **http://www.w3.org/2001/XMLSchema**.

DTDs are also used to define the structure of XML documents. The question that arises here is this: How are XML schemas different from DTDs? XML schemas are not really different from DTDs, they just offer greater functionality. XML schemas can be considered to be supersets of DTDs. XML schemas offer the following advantages over DTDs:

◆ DTDs help you specify whether an element can be empty or can contain character data or other elements. In contrast, XML schemas enable you to specify whether an element can contain an integer, float, or string value.

◆ Unlike DTDs, which have their own syntax, XML schemas use the XML syntax, so you don't have to learn a new syntax to create XML schemas.

XML schemas contain attribute and element declarations and type definitions for elements. Two basic types of elements can be declared: `simpleType` elements and `complexType` elements. These element types can be used to define custom data types in addition to the built-in data types provided by XSD, such as `integer` and `string`. These two data types can be defined as follows:

◆ `simpleType`. A type definition for a value that can be used as the content (`textOnly`) of an element or attribute. This data type cannot contain other elements or attributes.

◆ `complexType`. A type definition for elements that contain elements and attributes. This data type can contain elements and attributes.

The element declarations in a schema define the elements, their contents, and attributes that can be used, as well as the rules for their appearance in an XML document that uses the defined schema. An element declaration can contain either a `simpleType` or `complexType` element.

If elements and attributes are defined within the `complexType` element, the number of elements can be controlled. You can use the `minOccurs` and `maxOccurs` attributes to define the number of occurrences of an element in an XML document based on the schema.

The following list describes the elements with XSD:

- `all` allows the elements in the group to appear (or not appear) in any order in the containing element.
- `any` enables any element from the specified namespace(s) to appear in the containing `complexType`, `sequence`, `all`, or `choice` element.
- `anyAttribute` enables any attribute from the specified namespace(s) to appear in the containing `complexType` element.
- `annotation` defines an annotation.
- `appinfo` specifies information to be used by applications within an annotation element.
- `attribute` declares an attribute.
- `attributeGroup` groups a set of attribute declarations so that they can be incorporated as a group into complex type definitions.
- `choice` allows one and only one of the elements contained in the group to be present within the containing element.
- `complexContent` contains extensions or restrictions on a complex type that contains mixed content or elements only.
- `complexType` defines a complex type, which determines the set of attributes and the content of an element.
- `documentation` specifies information to be read or used by users within the annotation element.
- `element` declares an element.
- `extension` contains extensions on `complexContent` or `simpleContent`, which can also extend a complex type.

◆ `field` specifies an XML Path Language (XPath) expression that specifies the value (or one of the values) used to define an identity constraint (`unique`, `key`, and `keyref` elements).

◆ `group` groups a set of element declarations so that they can be incorporated as a group into complex type definitions.

◆ `import` identifies a namespace whose schema components are referenced by the containing schema.

◆ `include` includes the specified schema document in the target namespace of the containing schema.

◆ `key` specifies that an attribute or element value (or set of values) must be a key within the specified scope.

◆ `keyref` specifies that an attribute or element value (or set of values) corresponds with those of the specified key or unique element.

◆ `list` defines a `simpleType` element as a list of values of a specified data type.

◆ `notation` contains the definition of a notation.

◆ `redefine` allows simple and complex types, groups, and attribute groups that are obtained from external schema files to be redefined in the current schema.

◆ `restriction` (XSD) defines constraints on a `simpleType`, `simpleContent`, or `complexContent` definition.

◆ `schema` contains the definition of a schema.

◆ `selector` specifies an `XPath` expression that selects a set of elements for an identity constraint (`unique`, `key`, and `keyref` elements).

◆ `sequence` requires the elements in the group to appear in the specified sequence within the containing element.

◆ `simpleContent` either contains the extensions or restrictions on a `complexType` element with character data or contains a `simpleType` element as content and contains no elements.

◆ `simpleType` defines a simple type, which determines the constraints on and information about the values of attributes or elements with text-only content.

◆ `union` defines a `simpleType` element as a collection of values from specified simple data types.

◆ `unique` specifies that an attribute or element value (or a combination of attribute or element values) must be unique within the specified scope.

The Schema Object Model (SOM)

The schema object model (SOM) provides a set of classes in the `System.Xml.Schema` namespace that is fully compliant with the W3C XML schema recommendation specifications. These classes enable you to programmatically create a schema in memory that you can compile and validate.

The SOM provides the following features:

◆ It loads and saves valid XSD schemas to and from files.

◆ It provides an easy way to create memory resident schemas using strongly typed classes.

◆ It interacts with the `XmlSchemaCollection` class to cache and retrieve schemas.

◆ It interacts with the `XmlValidatingReader` class (through the `XmlSchemaCollection` class) to validate schemas against XML documents.

◆ It enables developers to build editors for creating and maintaining schemas.

The Schema Designer

To understand the concept of XML schemas in the .NET framework, let's use the XML Designer to create an XML schema for the Employees.xml document. You'll work on the same document you created earlier in this chapter.

The XML Schema Designer provides a set of visual tools for working with XML schemas and documents. The XML Designer supports the XSD language as defined by the WC3. It does not support DTDs or other XML schema languages such as XDR.

The XML Schema Designer provides three views you can work with:

◆ *Schema view.* Provides a visual representation of the elements, attributes, and types for creating and modifying XML schemas. In this view, you can construct schemas and datasets by dropping elements on the design surface from either the XML Schema tab of the Toolbox or from Server Explorer.

◆ *Data view.* Provides a data grid that can be used to modify XML documents. In this view, you can modify the actual content of an XML file as opposed to tags and structures.

◆ *XML view.* Provides an editor for editing XML source code and provides IntelliSense and color coding, including complete Word and List members.

To create a schema using the XML Schema Designer, open the project and follow these steps:

1. Open the Add New Item dialog box by choosing Project and then Add New Item.

2. Select XML Schema in the Templates pane, enter the name of the file (Employees.xsd), and click on Open.

   The Designer opens in the Schema view. In this view, you can design the schema visually by using the Toolbox. The Designer also provides the XML view that you can use to write the XML code to create the XML schema.

3. Switch to the XML view and write the following code to define the structure of the XML data represented in the Employees.xml document:

```
<?xml version="1.0" encoding="utf-8" ?>
<xsd:schema xmlns:xsd="http://www.w3.org/2001/XMLSchema">
    <xsd:element name="Employees" type="EmployeeInfo" />
        <xsd:complexType name="EmployeeInfo">
            <xsd:sequence>
                <xsd:element name="Employee" type="Details" minOccurs="0"
maxOccurs="unbounded" />
            </xsd:sequence>
        </xsd:complexType>
        <xsd:complexType name="Details">
            <xsd:sequence>
                <xsd:element name="Id" type="xsd:string" />
                <xsd:element name="LastName" type="xsd:string" />
                <xsd:element name="FirstName" type="xsd:string" />
            </xsd:sequence>
        </xsd:complexType>
    </xsd:schema>
```

In the preceding code:

◆ The XML schema elements are defined in the XML schema name-space.

◆ The `<xsd:element>` element describes the data it contains.

◆ The `<xsd:complexType>` element can contain additional elements and attributes.

4. Switch to the Schema view. You see the schema, as shown in Figure 30-4.

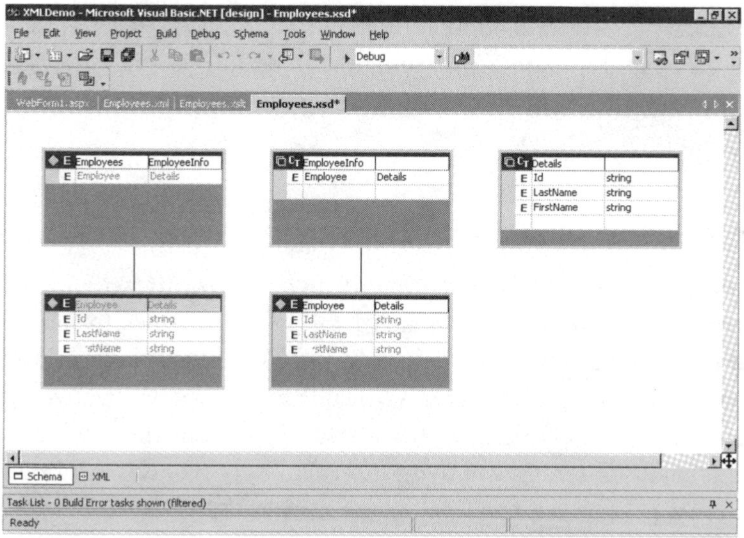

FIGURE 30-4 *The Schema view of the Employees.xsd file*

Validating XML Data

A well-formed XML document must meet all the syntactical requirements specified by the W3C. It also must conform to constraints defined by its DTD or schema that are used to define document structure, element relationships, data types, and content constraints. Therefore, you need to validate the XML document to ensure that it is well formed, has a DTD or schema attached, and follows the rules specified in them.

Validation of XML documents ensures that elements and attributes are used correctly. It also ensures that the relationship between them is correct. By validating XML data, you can ensure that the data types specified in the document are correct.

XML data can be validated using either a DTD or a schema. A DTD, which was introduced in W3C XML 1.0., defines the validation rules for an XML document. An XML processor uses the DTD at runtime to validate the XML document.

Schemas are an alternative to DTDs because they solve the limitations presented by DTDs. For more information on schemas, refer to the "XML Related Specifications" section earlier in this chapter.

Validation of XML documents is enforced by the `XmlValidatingReader` class. This class provides DTD, XDR, and XSD schema validation services implementing the validity constraints defined by the W3C. The `XmlValidatingReader` class also enforces XML validation. Validation is performed in a forward-only manner over a stream of XML. The `XmlValidatingReader` also supports the ability to parse XML fragments with `XmlParserContext` class.

DTD Validation

DTD validation is implemented using the validity constraints defined in the W3C. As previously discussed, DTDs use a formal set of rules to describe the structure and syntax of compliant XML documents. DTDs specify content and values allowed for the XML document. XML documents are associated with and validated against the DTD defined in the `<!DOCTYPE>` declaration, which can be either an inline DTD or a reference to an external DTD file. For information on inline and external DTDs, you can refer to the section "XML Specifications" earlier in this chapter.

XDR Validation

XML-Data Reduced (XDR) schema validation is implemented using the validity constraints defined in the Microsoft XML parser (MSXML) schema specification. XDR schemas are recognized by the use of the `MSXML x-schema:namespace` prefix. To implement the XDR validation, you need to create a file with the XDR extension. This file should contain the validation rules, which you can use to validate your XML document.

XSD Validation

The XML Schema Definition language (XSD) helps you define the structure and data types for XML documents. An XML schema defines the elements, attributes, and data types used in a document, as per the W3C recommendations. An XML schema consists of a top-level schema element that contains the type definitions and element and attribute declarations.

The XSD validation is implemented using the validity constraints specified by the W3C. All XSD schemas must include the namespace: **http://w3c.ord/2001/ XMLSchema**.

In this section, you have learned about XML data validation. Validation is important in XML because of its flexible syntax for describing the content of a document. Therefore, it is important to verify that a document adheres to the format you require.

Consider this situation: If your Web application accesses data from a database system (such as Oracle) and also needs to share data with other applications, you would want to convert relational data into XML format. By doing this, you can share data across varied platforms. In the following section, you will learn about integrating XML with relational data.

XML Integration with Relational Data

Traditionally, relational databases have been used for storing data. However, they have some limitations. For example, the cost of deploying and maintaining a database is high. Another limitation is the complexity of deploying applications pertaining to various operating systems and databases.

You can use XML to solve the problems faced by relational databases because it provides cost-effective data-storage solutions. Data stored in XML documents can be used across different platforms. In addition, it can be used with XSLT to transform and render data to various devices such as browsers and mobile devices.

XML provides two approaches for presenting relational data. The first approach is one-to-many relationships, which is represented by using separate tables of rows that are related by common columns. The second approach is nested relationships. This is represented hierarchically by parent elements that contain nested child elements.

To convert relational data into XML format, you need to follow these steps:

1. Establish a connection with a database server.
2. Retrieve data from the table.
3. Convert relational data into XML format.

In this section, you learned to convert relation data into XML format. However, with the growing use of XML in Web applications, programmers need to access and manipulate the content of XML documents. There are certain standard ways to access this content, such as the W3C DOM API. However, APIs such as these are used for lower-level XML manipulation. Programmers can develop custom APIs to access the data, but this is a cumbersome task. One effective solution for this problem is data binding. In the following section, you will learn about the concept of data binding in XML.

Data Binding with an XML Document

Data binding is the process of mapping the components of a given data format into a specific representation for a given programming language. This representation depicts the intended meaning of the data format. Data binding enables programmers to work in the native code of the language and preserves the meaning of the original data.

An XML document represents a number of different data types such as `strings` and `integers`. These data types are grouped together in a logical hierarchy that represents some meaning to the domain for which the XML data is intended. In an ideal situation, interaction with the XML content should be as objects and data structures native to the programming language used. In addition, the interaction should be in a manner that closely reflects the meaning of the data. This would make programming with XML more natural and less tedious and would improve code readability and maintainability. This is possible through data binding.

Data binding enables you to represent data and structure in the natural format of the programming language of your choice. It also represents data in a manner that depicts the intended meaning.

The XML-based applications that are written today do some form of data binding. For example, when you convert the value of an attribute to an integer or create an object to represent an element structure, you are performing data binding.

Summary

In this chapter, you learned about XML. You started with the basics and then moved on to some advanced concepts. You learned about the origin of XML, the difference between XML and HTML, and the benefits of XML. Then you learned to create an XML document and were introduced to the rules for creating a well-formed XML document. This chapter also discussed XML specifications and their integration with .NET. The various specifications covered included DTDs, DOM, namespaces, XSLT, and schemas. How to validate XML document was the next topic. At the end of the chapter, you learned how to convert relational data into XML format and about data binding with an XML document.

Chapter 31

Project Case Study—Word-to-XML Converter Application

In previous chapters, you learned how to create a Windows application and also a Web application. In this lesson, you'll create another Windows application that will convert a Word document into XML format and then save it as an XML file. In addition, you'll use controls such as TabControl and ImageList in your application.

Project Case Study

MyMovies is a video company based in New York. The company sells DVDs, CDs, and LCDs of movies. MyMovies is a popular chain that has multiple stores throughout the United States. In recent months, however, sales at MyMovies have shown a slight drop. The management at MyMovies is vigilant and has commissioned a faultfinding team to identify the reasons for the drop in sales.

The faultfinding team first studies the project life cycle at MyMovies. The project life cycle is as follows:

- When a customer requests a video, the retail outlets issue a memo in a Word document.

- The retail outlets also send a memo to the sales department at the head office.

- At the sales department, an operator makes an entry of the record in a database.

- The sales department then sends a memo to the inventory department to check the status of the product.

- After checking the status, the inventory department sends a memo back to the sales department.

- Based on the availability of the product, the sales department dispatches the product.

Because the entire process is manual, it takes almost three weeks. Due to this long cycle time, the faultfinding team finds that MyMovies customers are now turning to a new company that dispatches the movies within a week. The faultfinding team has recommended that management work on reducing the cycle time for dispatch of documents.

Based on the faultfinding team's recommendations, management has decided to automate the sales process. This task is assigned to a development team consisting of three members. Michael Fisher is the project manager of the team, while Mary Jones and Tim Smith are the two application developers.

The development team has decided on the following strategy to automate the sales process:

- When a customer issues an order, the retail outlets will send a memo to the sales department at the head office over the intranet.
- The memo will be stored in a specified directory on the main server.
- The format of the memo will then be validated.
- After the format is validated, the entry of the document will be made in an XML document.

The preceding process is an automated process that reduces the cycle time to a week. The development team decides to use XML as the format for transferring and storing data because XML files are platform independent and light in weight.

To carry out the entire process, the development team plans to create a Windows application and name it as the MyMovies project. The following section discusses the stages in the life cycle of the MyMovies project.

Project Life Cycle

In previous chapters, you looked at the phases of a development life cycle (DLC). Therefore, this chapter will not cover the DLC again. Instead, it will discuss the requirements analysis done by the development team and the design of the application that was approved by the project manager.

Requirements Analysis

Requirements analysis is one of the most important phases of the development life cycle. The first step in any DLC is to analyze the customer's requirements. Then, based on a clear understanding of the requirements, you need to define the design and functionality of the DLC. The requirements analysis for the problem faced by MyMovies is based on the following problem statement, as stated by the management at MyMovies:

> *"We need to reduce our cycle time by one-third to get a competitive edge. It is therefore essential that we devise a simple, automated process that reduces our effort as well as out cycle time."*

Upon analyzing the problem statement, the development team has defined the following list of tasks that the application needs to perform:

◆ The organization needs to ensure that the sales data is entered in a pre-defined format.

◆ The data needs to be stored in a specified directory.

◆ The application needs to automate the process of generating the XML file so that it can be easily accessed and processed by the other divisions.

Solution to the Problem

After analyzing the requirements, the development team has decided to create a Windows application that performs the following functions:

◆ The cash memo will be stored in a specified directory on the main server.

◆ The application will then validate the format of the cash memo.

◆ If the validation of the cash memo returns false, the application will generate an error and create an event log.

◆ If the validation of the cash memo returns true, indicating that the cash memo is in the correct format, an entry of the cash memo will be added to an XML document.

High-Level Design

In this phase, the development team creates the design of the Windows application. The MyMovies form consists of a Windows form. The layout for the form is shown in Figure 31-1.

To create the layout of the MyMovies application (as shown in Figure 31-1), you need to insert a TabControl, two labels, two text boxes, and a check box. For the other tabbed pages in the application, you need to insert four labels, a text box, a list box, and four buttons. In previous lessons, you learned how to insert text box,

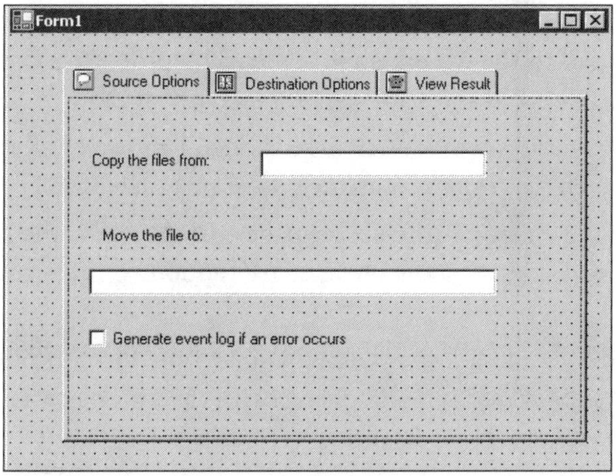

FIGURE 31-1 *The layout of the MyMovies form*

label, and check box controls. Now you will learn to insert a TabControl and define its properties.

A TabControl

A TabControl is a Windows forms control that you can use to create multiple tabs. You can add pictures and other controls to the tabs, and you can use the TabControl to create dialog boxes or forms that contain several options that can be grouped in different pages. For example, you can use a TabControl to create a dialog box in which the font options are listed on one control and the page-layout options are listed on the other.

The most important property of a TabControl is `TabPages`. The tab pages contain individual tabs, and each tab is a `TabPage` object. When the tab is clicked, the `Click` event for that `TabPage` object is raised.

To create a TabControl in Visual Studio.NET, drag the control from the Windows Forms toolbox to the form. Let's now create a TabControl for the application:

1. Drag a TabControl from the Windows Forms toolbox to the Windows form.
2. You now need to add pages to the TabControl. Let's now add tab pages.
3. In the Properties window, click on the ellipsis button of the `TabPages` property.

4. To add a page to the control, click the Add button. A tabbed page with an index of 0 is added to the Members text box. The properties of the tabbed page are displayed in the TabPage1 Properties window.

5. In the TabPage1 Properties window, change the `Text` property of the tabbed page to `Source Options` and change `Name` to `TabSource`.

6. When you change the name of the tabbed page to `TabSource`, the name of the TabPage1 Properties window changes to TabSource Properties window.

7. Repeat steps 4 and 5 to add another tabbed page to the form. Name the new tabbed page `TabDestination` and change the `Text` property to `Destination Options`.

8. Repeat steps 4 and 5 to add another tabbed page to the form. Name the new tabbed page `TabViewResult` and change the `Text` property to `View Result`. You can change the order in which the tabbed pages display by clicking on either the up- or down-arrow button.

9. Click on the OK button to close the TabPage Collection Editor dialog box.

Figure 31-2 shows the TabPage Collection Editor dialog box.

To make your tab pages more interesting and easily identifiable, you can add images to them. To do this, you need to change the `ImageIndex` property in the TabPage Collection Editor. Before you do that, however, you need to add an ImageList to the form. The next section looks at adding ImageList to the form.

The ImageList Control

The ImageList control stores images that can be used in other controls. Using an ImageList enables you to write the code for a single catalog of images that you can use in several controls. For example, you can use an ImageList to add the same icon images to both a label and Toolbar control.

You can use the ImageList control to add images to several controls. These controls include the ListView, TreeView, Toolbar, TabControl, button, check box, radio button, and label controls.

The key property of the ImageList is `Images`, which is used to associate pictures to the ImageList control. Two other properties, `ColorDepth` and `ImageSize`, also

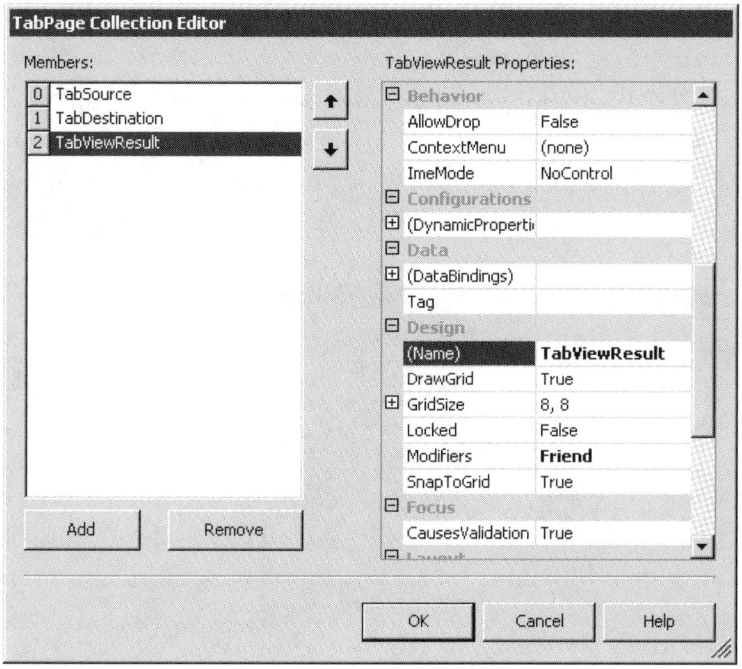

FIGURE 31-2 *The TabPage Collection Editor dialog box*

are frequently used. The `ColorDepth` property determines the colors that render the image, and the `ImageSize` property determines the size of the image.

To add an ImageList to the form, drag an ImageList from the Windows Forms toolbox to the form. The ImageList is added to the component tray of the form. To this point, the ImageList does not contain any images. To add images, you need to change the `Images` property of the ImageList. When you add images to the ImageList, they are added to a collection object of the control.

To add images to an ImageList in Visual Studio.NET, perform the following steps:

1. Click on the ellipsis button of the `Images` property. The Image Collection Editor dialog box opens.

2. Click on the Add button to add an image to the Members text box. You can browse for the image to add it to the ImageList. The image you add is included in the `System.Drawing` namespace. The index value of the first image added is 0. As you add more images to the ImageList , the

index value increases. For this form, you need to add two more images later.

3. Click on the OK button to close the Image Collection Editor dialog box.

Figure 31-3 shows the Bitmap image added to the Image Collection Editor dialog box.

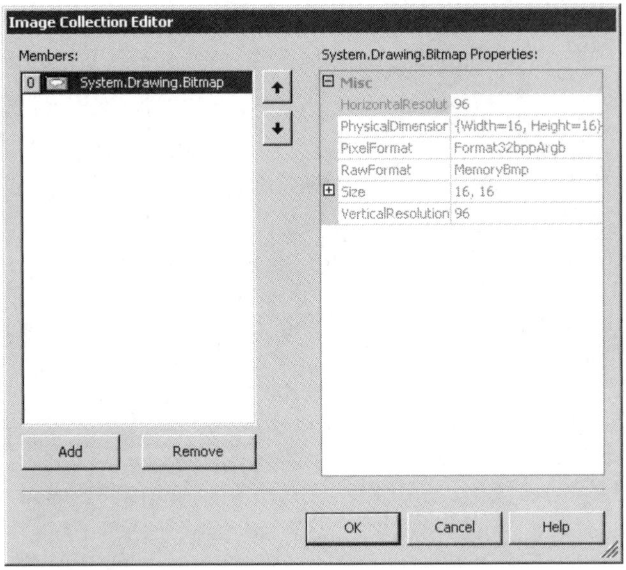

FIGURE 31-3 *The Image Collection Editor dialog box*

To add the image in the `ImageList` property of the TabControl, perform the following steps:

1. Click on the drop-down arrow button of the `ImageList` property of the TabControl.

2. From the drop-down list, select the ImageList1 option. The Bitmap image is not currently visible on the tabbed pages. To display the image on the tabbed pages, you need to modify the properties of the tabbed pages in the TabPage Collection Editor page.

3. Click on the ellipsis button of the `TabPages` property of the TabControl to display the properties of the tabbed pages. The `TabSource` tabbed page is selected by default.

4. Click on the drop-down button of the ImageIndex property.

5. From the drop-down list, select 0.

6. Repeat steps 3 and 4 to add images to the TabDestination and Tab-ViewResult tabbed pages. The images get added to the tabbed pages.

The next section shows you how to add labels and text boxes to the tabbed pages.

Adding Controls to Tabbed Pages

The TabControl you created contains three tabbed pages: Source Options, Destination Options, and View Result. Let's first add controls to the Source Options page.

The Source Options page consists of a check box, two labels, and two textboxes. You can add these controls to the TabSource tabbed page by dragging the controls from the Windows Forms toolbox. The properties you need to set for the controls are provided in Table 31-1.

Table 31-1 Properties Assigned to the Controls on the *TabSource* Tabbed Page

Control	Property	Value
Label 1	ID	Label1
Label 1	Text	Copy the files from:
Label 2	ID	Label2
Label 2	Text	Move the file to:
Text box 1	Text	TxtSource
Text box 2	Text	TxtProcessedFile
Check box	ID	OptGenerateLog
Check box	Text	Generate event log if an error occurs

Now compare your form with Figure 31-4.

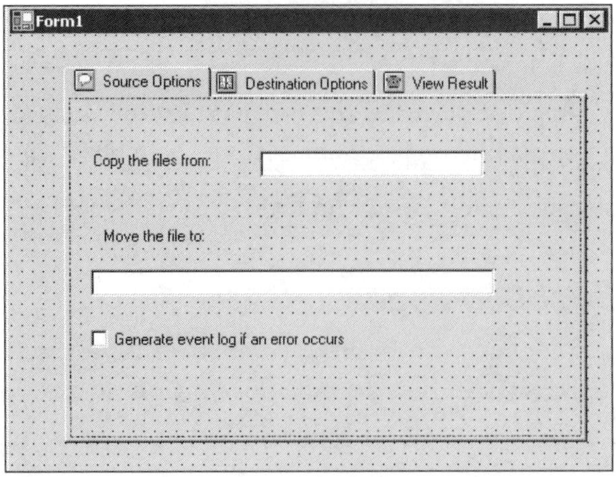

FIGURE 31-4 *The* TabSource *page with the controls*

Similarly, you can add controls to the TabDestination page. The TabDestination page contains a label, a text box, a list box, a group box, and two buttons. The properties you need to set for the controls on the TabDestination page are provided in Table 31-2.

Table 31-2 Properties Assigned to the Controls on the *TabDestination* Tabbed Page

Control	Property	Value
Label 1	Name	Label2
Label 1	Text	Destination Directory
Text box	Text	TxtDestination
List box	Name	LstEvents
Group box	Name	GroupEventLog
Group box	Text	Event Log
Button 1	Name	BtnRefresh
Button 1	Text	Refresh Log
Button 2	Name	BtnOK
Button 2	Text	OK

Control	Property	Value
Button 3	Name	BtnExit
Button 3	Text	Exit

Figure 31-5 shows the controls added to the TabDestination page.

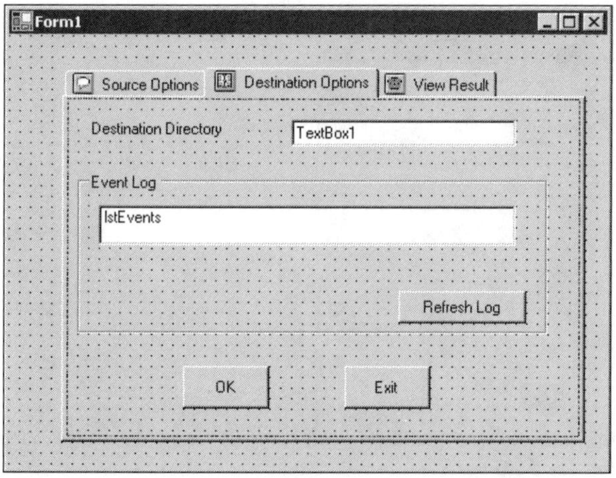

FIGURE 31-5 *The* TabDestination *page with the controls*

Let's now add controls to the last tabbed page—the View Result tabbed page. The View Result tabbed page consists of a label and a button. Table 31-3 shows the properties of the controls you need.

Table 31-3 Properties Assigned to the Controls on the *TabViewResult* Tabbed Page

Control	Property	Value
Label 1	Name	LblSummary
Label 2	Name	LinkLabel1
Label 2	Text	View in Internet Explorer
Label 2	ActiveLinkColor	Red
Label 2	LinkColor	0, 0, 255

continues

Table 31-3 (continued)

Control	Property	Value
Button	Name	BtnSummary
Button	Text	View Summary

Figure 31-6 shows the controls added to the `TabViewResult` page.

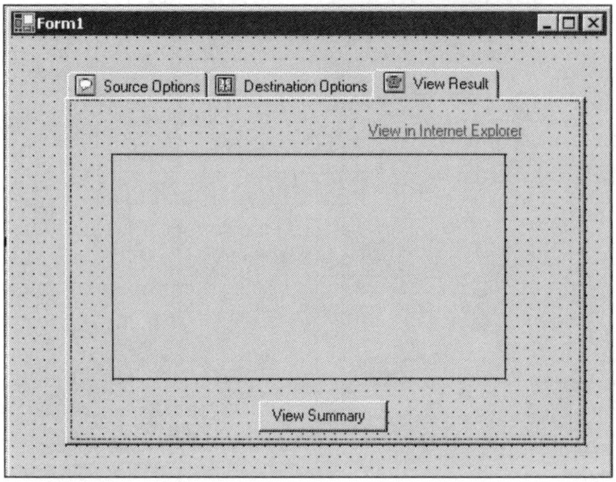

FIGURE 31-6 *The* TabViewResult *page with the controls*

Low-Level Design

After creating the design of a form in the high-level design phase, the development team next creates a detailed design of software modules. These software modules are then used to create a detailed structure of the application. In addition to creating software modules, the team decides the flow and interaction of each module. This includes creating flowcharts for each module.

Based on the high-level design of the MyMovies form, the development team creates the flowchart for the form, as shown in Figure 31-7.

Having decided on the interface and the software module, the development team proceeds with construction and testing of the Windows application. After the application is tested and the errors in the application are detected and removed, the application is deployed at the client site. The next chapter will cover how to write the code and deploy the MyMovies application.

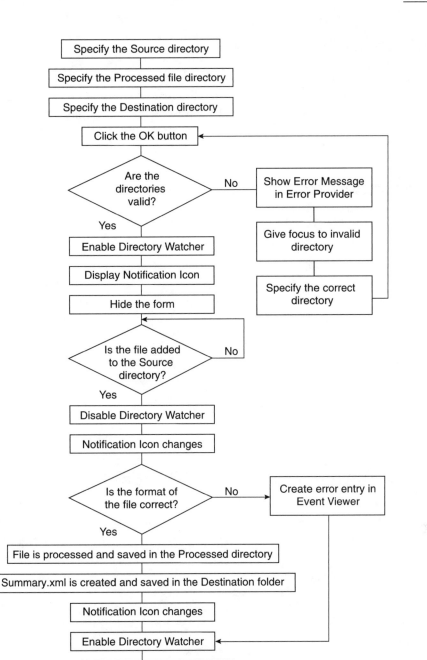

FIGURE 31-7 *Flowchart of the MyMovies application*

Summary

In this chapter, you were introduced to the project case study. You analyzed the requirements of MyMovies and learned to create detailed high-level and low-level designs for the application. You will learn to create and deploy the application in the next chapter.

Chapter 32

Coding the Converter Application

The preceding chapter introduced you to the design of the MyMovies project. You also saw the flowchart that showed you the sequence of events. This chapter deals with writing the programming logic for the MyMovies project.

Writing the Programming Logic for the Application

Before you write the programming logic for the MyMovies project, let's see how the application will work:

1. The first step when the user runs the application is to specify the path of the Source, Processed, and Destination directories. By default, the application will show the path as D:\My Movies\Source, D:\My Movies\Processed, and D:\My Movies\Destination, respectively. The user can opt to either use the default directory or change the directory.

2. After the user has specified the directories and clicks the OK button, the application checks to see if the directory structure is valid.

3. If the directory structure is not valid, the application raises an error message. The application also gives focus to the invalid directory. If the directory structure is valid, the application enables the FileSystem Watcher.

4. The application then hides the form and displays a notification icon on the status bar.

5. The application then checks whether the user has added the file to the Source directory.

6. When the user copies the memo file to the Source directory, the application disables the FileSystem Watcher until processing is on. In addition, the notification icon changes to a processing icon.

7. The application then checks the format of the memo file, and if the format is correct, the application processes the memo file. The file extracts data from the memo file and then saves the information in an XML

document called Summary.xml. The Summary.xml file is stored in the destination directory specified by the user.

8. Alternatively, if the format is incorrect or if the path specified for the source, destination, or processed files is incorrect, the application generates an error in the Event Viewer.

9. After creating the Summary.xml document, the application changes the notification icon again and enables the FileSystem Watcher so that it can check the directory for any new file.

10. Finally, the application displays the result on the ViewResult tab. The user can also choose to view the application in Internet Explorer by clicking the View in Internet Explorer hyperlink.

Now that you are familiar with how the application works, let's begin coding the application.

Coding the Application

The first step is to write the code for the task that will be performed when the user runs the application. This task is written in the form's Load event. Let's do this now.

Coding the Form's *Load* Event

When the user runs the application, you need to ensure that the default path for the source, destination, and processed directories is displayed in the TxtSource, TxtDestination, and TxtProcessedFile text boxes, respectively. Recall that in the preceding lesson, you added the mentioned text box to the form. In addition, you need to ensure that the OptGenerateLog check box is selected by default. To add the default values for the application, you need to write the following code:

```
Private Sub Form1_Load(ByVal sender As System.Object, ByVal e As System.EventArgs)
Handles MyBase.Load
        TxtSource.Text = "D:\My Movies\Source\"
        TxtProcessedFile.Text = " D:\My Movies\Processed\"
        TxtDestination.Text = " D:\My Movies\Destination\"
        OptGenerateLog.Checked = True
End Sub
```

When the application is run, the default values are added to the MyMovies form. Figures 32-1 and 32-2 show the default values for the Source, Destination, and Processed directories.

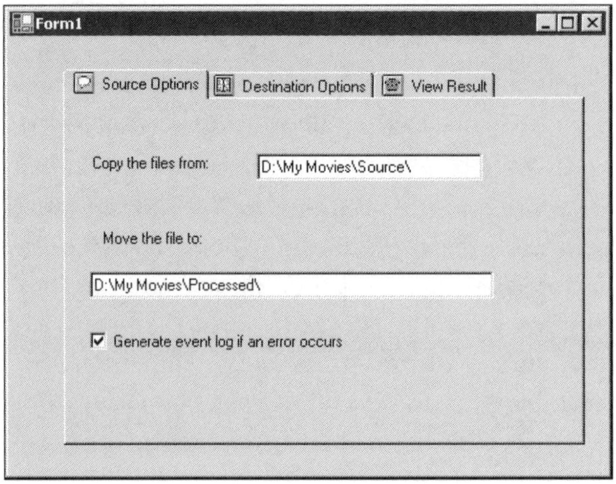

FIGURE 32-1 *The* TabSource *page at runtime*

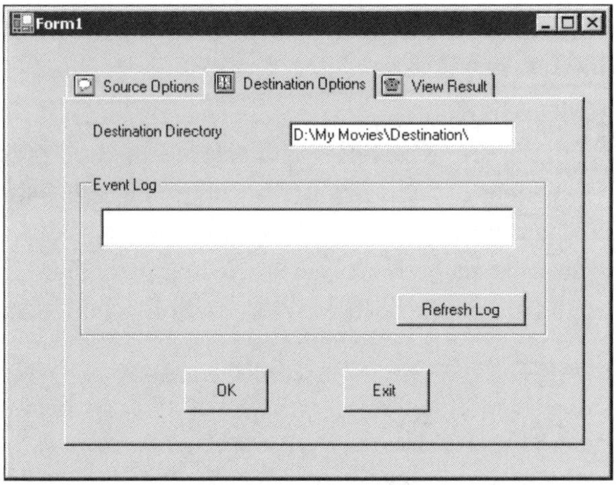

FIGURE 32-2 *The* TabDestination *page at runtime*

The user can either choose the default path or specify a new path. After specifying the path for the source, destination, and processed directories, the user needs to click the OK button. The application will then validate the path of the directories. Now let's write the code for the OK button.

Coding the OK Button

When a user clicks on the OK button, the application validates the path of the source, destination, and processed directories. If the directory paths are incorrect, the application generates an error message. You can display the error message in a message box or by using the ErrorProvider control. The advantage of using the ErrorProvider control over displaying the error message in a message box is that in a message box, once the message is dismissed, the error message is no longer available. Alternatively, the ErrorProvider control displays the error icon next to the control in which the error occurs. In addition, when the user positions the mouse pointer over the error icon, a ToolTip showing the error string appears.

To use the ErrorProvider control, however, you need to add the control to the form. Let's do this now.

The ErrorProvider Control

The ErrorProvider control is used to validate the data entered by a user. The ErrorProvider displays an error message in a nonobstructive way if the data entered by the user is not in the specified format.

To insert an ErrorProvider control into the form, drag the ErrorProvider control to the Windows form. Next you need to specify the icon that will be displayed when an error occurs. By default, Visual Studio.NET displays the icon shown in Figure 32-3.

You can change the icon, however, by changing the Icon property of the Error-Provider control. In addition to displaying the icon, the ErrorProvider control also displays an error message when the user points toward the error message icon. To display the error message, you use the SetError method. The SetError method accepts two parameters: the name of the control with which the error message is attached and the string that will be displayed when the user points the mouse toward the error message icon. Let's now add an ErrorProvider control to the form.

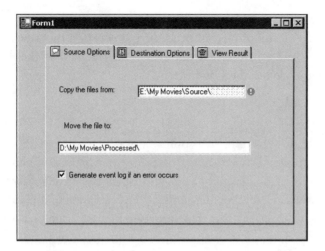

FIGURE 32-3 *The Windows form showing the error message icon*

1. Drag the ErrorProvider control from the Windows Forms toolbox to the form.

2. Change the Name property of the ErrorProvider control to ErrMessage.

   You now need to specify an error message and associate it with the controls that need to be validated. You'll specify the error message and associate it with the TxtSource, TxtDestination, and TxtProcessedFile text boxes.

3. Now you need to add the following code to the Click event of the OK button to display the specified error message if the directory structure is not correct:

```
Private Sub BtnOK_Click(ByVal sender As System.Object, ByVal e As System.EventArgs)
Handles BtnOK.Click

        If (Directory.Exists(TxtSource.Text) = False) Then
            ErrMessage.SetError(TxtSource, "Invalid source directory")
            TxtSource.Focus()
            TabControl1.SelectedTab = TabSource
            Return
        Else
            ErrMessage.SetError(TxtSource, "")
        End If
```

```
        If (Directory.Exists(TxtDestination.Text) = False) Then
            ErrMessage.SetError(TxtDestination, "Invalid destination directory")
            TxtDestination.Focus()
            TabControl1.SelectedTab = TabDestination
            Return
        Else
            ErrMessage.SetError(TxtDestination, "")
        End If


        If (Directory.Exists(TxtProcessedFile.Text) = False) Then
            ErrMessage.SetError(TxtProcessedFile, "Invalid processed file directory")
            TxtProcessedFile.Focus()
            TabControl1.SelectedTab = TabSource
            Return
        Else
            ErrMessage.SetError(TxtProcessedFile, "")
        End If
End Sub
```

The preceding code checks to see if the specified directory exists. If the Directory.Exists command returns false, the code will generate an error message. The SetError method is used to attach the error message to a control. As previously mentioned, the SetError method accepts two parameters: the name of the control and the error string. In the preceding code, the SetError method is used to associate the text boxes with the error message. The Focus() method is used to set the focus on the specified control. The command sets the focus of the application on the TxtSource, TxtDestination, or TxtProcessed text boxes, depending on the text box whose path is not in the specified format. The command TabControl1.SelectedTab is used to set the focus of the control on the tab page on which the error occurs. For example, if the error occurs in the TxtSource control, the TabControl1.SelectedTab command is set to TabControl1.SelectedTab=TabSource. TabSource is the tab page on which the TxtSource control is present. The Else clause of the If construct specifies a null value for the message string. This implies that if the directory paths are correct, the message string will be empty, and no error message will display.

Enhancing the Form

Let's make the form a little more interesting. To do so, add the code to change the color of the text box if the directory path entered by the user is incorrect. To add this functionality, you need to add the following code in the `KeyUp` event of the text box in which you want to change the code. Let's now add the code for the `TxtSource` text box.

```
Private Sub TxtSource_KeyUp(ByVal sender As Object, ByVal e As
System.Windows.Forms.KeyEventArgs) Handles
TxtSource.KeyUp
        If (Directory.Exists(TxtSource.Text)) Then
            TxtSource.BackColor = Color.White
        Else
            TxtSource.BackColor = Color.BlanchedAlmond
        End If
End Sub
```

Now add the code to change the color of the `TxtDestination` and `TxtProcessed-File` text boxes. Don't forget to specify the name of the text box. Now that you have written the code for validating the directory path, you need to enable the FileSystem Watcher and display the notification icon in the status bar.

In addition, you will hide the form until the memo file is being processed. Let's now add a FileSystem Watcher component to the form. You use a FileSystem Watcher component to track any changes made to files or directories of a file system.

The FileSystem Watcher Control

The FileSystem Watcher control, as previously mentioned, is used to track changes made to a file system and then react to those changes. For example, if a number of users are working on a file, you can use the FileSystem Watcher to track changes made to the shared file. In this example, you will use the FileSystem Watcher to detect whether a file is added to the Source directory. Whenever the FileSystem Watcher detects that a file is added to the Source directory, it will initiate the processing for the file. Let's now add the FileSystem Watcher to the form. To add and configure the FileSystem Watcher, perform the following steps:

1. Drag a FileSystem Watcher component from the Components toolbox.

2. Change the `Name` property of the FileSystem Watcher to `FileWatcher` and the `Filter` property to `*.doc`.

   By setting the filter property to `*.doc`, you can limit the FileSystem Watcher to look for only Word documents. I have done this because, for this application, you know that the memo file will always be in Word format. Now you need to enable the FileSystem Watcher.

3. To enable the FileSystem Watcher component, add the following statement to the `Click` event of the OK button. Note that you need to add the code below the code `ErrMessage.SetError(TxtProcessedFile, "")` that you added in the previous section.

   ```
   FileWatcher .EnableRaisingEvents=True
   ```

   Now that you have enabled the FileSystem Watcher, you need to specify the component that the FileSystem Watcher needs to monitor.

4. To specify the path of the directory that the FileSystem Watcher needs to monitor, add the following statement to the `Click` event of the OK button.

   ```
   FileWatcher .Path=TxtSource.Text
   ```

   The preceding code associates the FileSystem Watcher to the TxtSource control. You will now add a NotifyIcon Control to the form.

The NotifyIcon Control

The NotifyIcon control is used to indicate that a process is running in the background. In this example, the NotifyIcon control is used to display a different icon, which shows that the application is processing the memo file. The icon will be displayed on the status bar.

Two key properties you need to set while using the NotifyIcon control are `Icons` and `Visible`. The `Icons` property specifies the icon that appears in the status bar. The `Visible` property determines whether the icon will be visible at a particular time or not.

In addition to these two properties, you need to add the icon files to the bin folder of your application. Let's now perform the steps to add the NotifyIcon control to your form:

1. Drag the NotifyIcon control from the Windows Forms toolbox to the form.

2. Change the Name property of the NotifyIcon control to `IconNotify`.

3. To create an instance of the icon file in the bin folder, add the following code in the Declaration section:

```
Private m_ready As New System.Drawing.Icon("Ready.ICO")
Private m_Error As New System.Drawing.Icon("Error.ICO")
Private m_Info As New System.Drawing.Icon("Info.ICO")
```

In the preceding code, `New System.Drawing.Icon` is the default name-space for the icon files.

4. To display the notification icon, add the following code to the `Click` event of the OK button. Add it below the code you added in the previous section.

```
IcoNotify.Icon=m_Ready
IcoNotify.Visible=True
```

Until the process is on, the user does not need to see the application. Therefore, you can hide the application from the Taskbar.

5. To hide the application, add the following code to the `Click` event of the OK button.

```
Me.ShowInTaskbar = False
Me.Hide()
```

The entire code for the OK button is as follows:

```
Private Sub BtnOK_Click(ByVal sender As System.Object, ByVal e As System.EventArgs)
Handles BtnOK.Click
        If (Directory.Exists(TxtSource.Text) = False) Then
            ErrMessage.SetError(TxtSource, "Invalid source directory")
            TxtSource.Focus()
            TabControl1.SelectedTab = TabSource
            Return
        Else
            ErrMessage.SetError(TxtSource, "")
        End If

        If (Directory.Exists(TxtDestination.Text) = False) Then
```

```
            ErrMessage.SetError(TxtDestination, "Invalid destination directory")
            TxtDestination.Focus()
            TabControl1.SelectedTab = TabDestination
            Return
        Else
            ErrMessage.SetError(TxtDestination, "")
        End If

        If (Directory.Exists(TxtProcessedFile.Text) = False) Then
            ErrMessage.SetError(TxtProcessedFile, "Invalid processed file directory")
            TxtProcessedFile.Focus()
            TabControl1.SelectedTab = TabSource
            Return
        Else
            ErrMessage.SetError(TxtProcessedFile, "")
            FileWatcher .Path = TxtSource.Text
            FileWatcher .EnableRaisingEvents = True
            IcoNotify.Icon = m_ready
            IcoNotify.Visible = True
            Me.ShowInTaskbar = False
            Me.Hide()
        End If
    End Sub
```

After writing the code for validating the directory structure and displaying the notification icon, let's move a step further and write the code for converting the text stored in the Word document to an XML file. In addition, you'll trap any errors generated while processing the Word documents in the Windows Event Viewer.

To convert the text to XML, you need to check when a new file is copied to the Source folder and then start the processing. To see if a new file has been added to the Source directory, you need to write the code in the Created event of the FileSystem Watcher class.

The *Created* Event

As previously mentioned, the FileSystem Watcher is used to track the changes made in a directory or file. When a change takes place in the directory or file, the FileSystem Watcher generates various events such as `Created`, `Deleted`, or `Renamed`. For this application, the `Created` event is used. The `Created` event will track when a new file is added to a directory specified in the `FullPath` property of the event. The `FullPath` property stores the path of the file or directory in which the change takes place. In the `Created` event property, you will write the code to extract data from the Word document and then write the same data in an XML file. In addition, you need to write the code to disable the FileSystem Watcher when the file is being processed. To perform these tasks, write the following code in the `Created` event of the FileSystem Watcher:

```
Private Sub FileWatcher_Created(ByVal sender As Object, ByVal e As
System.IO.FileSystemEventArgs) Handles
FileWatcher .Created
FileWatcher .EnableRaisingEvents = False
        IconNotify.Icon = m_Info
        IconNotify.Text = "Processed: " + e.Name
            'e.Name contains the name of the affected file
End Sub
```

In the preceding code, the `FileWatcher.EnableRaisingEvents` property is set to `False`. This disables the FileSystem Watcher until it is explicitly enabled again. To enable the FileSystem Watcher, you need to set the `FileWatcher.EnableRaising-Events` property to `True`. The `Icon` property of the NotifyIcon control is set as `m_Info`. Recall that in the preceding section, you assigned the path of the Info image file to the variable `m_info`. The code `IconNotify.Text = "Processed: " + e.Name` will display the ToolTip as `Processed`, along with the name of the affected file after the file is processed.

Extracting Data from a Word Document

Your application is now ready for processing. To access the Word document stored in the Source directory, you need to create an instance of Microsoft Word by using the `Word.ApplicationClass` class. After you have created an instance of the Word application, you can create an instance of the document by using the `Word.Docu-mentClass` class. To create instances of the Word application as well as the Word document, write the following code in the `Created` event of the `FileSys-temWatcher` component:

```
Dim wdApp As New Word.ApplicationClass()
Dim wdDoc As New Word.DocumentClass()
```

After creating an instance of the Word document, you need to open the document file. To so this, use the `Open()` method of the `Document` class. The following code specifies the path of the document you need to open:

```
Dim FileName As Object = e.FullPath
```

The preceding code opens the Word document and stores its content in the instance of the `WordDocumentClass`. However, you do not require all of the information. For this example, you just need the quantity and memo number. Figure 32-4 shows the sample cash memo document you will use to convert to an XML document.

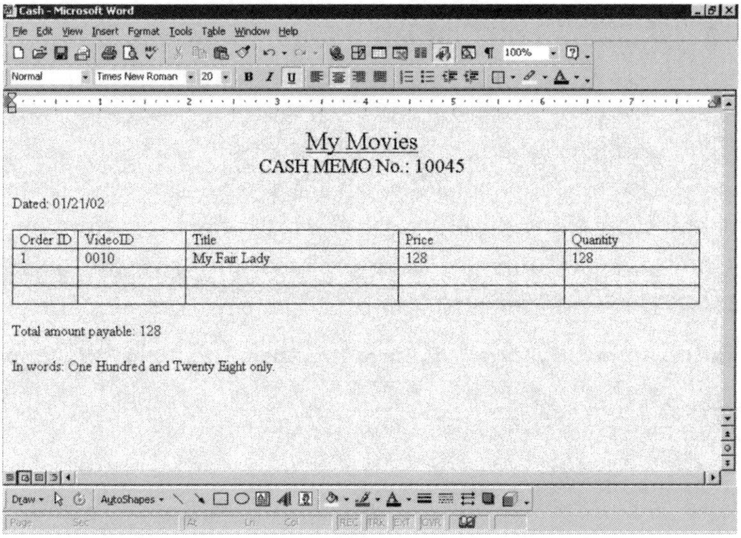

FIGURE 32-4 *A sample cash memo document*

Let's now write the code to retrieve the data stored in the cash memo document. As previously mentioned, you will retrieve specific data: The value for the memo number and the quantity fields. To retrieve the required information, add the following code to the `Created` event:

```
Try
            wdDoc = wdApp.Documents.Open(FileName)
            'creates an instance of the WordRange to store the content of the Word
docs
        Dim WdRange As Word.Range
            WdRange = wdDoc.Paragraphs.Item(2).Range

            Dim MemoNum, Quantity As String
            Dim ParaCount As String
            MemoNum = WdRange.Text
            MemoNum = MemoNum.Substring(15, 5)
            ParaCount = wdDoc.Paragraphs.Count
            ParaCount = ParaCount - 2
            WdRange = wdDoc.Paragraphs.Item(ParaCount).Range
            WdRange.MoveEnd("1", "-1")
            Quantity = WdRange.Text
            Quantity = Quantity.Substring(23)
```

The preceding code creates an object of the type `Word.Range`. The object `WdRange` stores the content of the Word document. Then the `Item` property of the `Paragraphs` collection is used to retrieve the data from a specified paragraph. As you can see in Figure 32-4, the `Cash Memo No.` is the second paragraph in the cash memo document. Therefore, you need to retrieve the content of the second paragraph of the cash memo document by using the `Range` property. The content that is retrieved is then stored in `WdRange`.

The `Text` property of the `WdRange` object stores the text of the paragraph in a `String`-type variable `strMemo`. Until now, the `strMemo` variable has stored the entire content of the second paragraph. However, to retrieve the value of the `Cash Memo No.` field, use the `Substring()` method. The `Substring()` method takes two parameters: the starting position from which the text is to be retrieved and the number of characters to be retrieved.

Similarly, you can store the text of the `Quantity` field in another `String`-type variable, `StrQuantity`. The `Quantity` field is the second-to-last paragraph in the cash memo document. Therefore, you need to declare an `Integer` variable, `IntParacount`, that stores the number of paragraphs in a document. Use the `Count` property of the `Paragraphs` collection to count the number of paragraphs in the document.

Converting Data to XML Format

You will now write the data stored in the Word document to XML format. The first step when writing data in XML format is to create an instance of the XML-TextWriter class. To create an instance of this class, you need to write the following code in the Created event of the WatchDir control:

```
Dim XmlWrite As XmlTextWriter
```

Now you can use XMLTextWriter to write data to the XML document. Before you do that, however, you need to specify the path where the XML file will be stored. To specify the destination of the XML file, you need to specify the following code:

```
XmlWrite = New XmlTextWriter(TxtDestination.Text + "Summary.xml", Nothing)
XmlWrite.Formatting = Formatting.Indented
```

The preceding code specifies the path of the XML file as the path stored in the TxtDestination text box. Summary.xml specifies the name of the XML file. The keyword Nothing specifies that the default encoding style is being used for the XML file. Formatting.Indented specifies the indentation setting for the elements in the XML file.

Next you need to write to the XML file. Let's now write the code to add data to the XML file.

```
XmlWrite.WriteComment("Summary of sales at My Movies")
          XmlWrite.WriteStartElement("Sales")
          XmlWrite.WriteStartElement("Date")
          XmlWrite.WriteAttributeString("Date", Convert.ToString(DateTime.Today))
          XmlWrite.WriteElementString("Memo", MemoNum)
          XmlWrite.WriteElementString("Quantity", Quantity)
          XmlWrite.WriteEndElement()
          XmlWrite.WriteEndElement()
```

In the preceding code, the WriteStartElement method is used to specify the start elements as Sales and Date. You will now write the code to handle any errors that might occur when running the application. The errors generated when running the application are tracked in the Event Log. Let's now look at handling exceptions using the Event Log.

Displaying the Error Message in the Event Log

You can track the performance of the software and hardware events running in the system by using the Event Viewer. The Event Viewer is a tool that helps administrators track errors in a system. You can access the Event Viewer by choosing Administrative Tools in the Control Panel. Then double-click the Event Viewer to open the Event Viewer window. The Event Viewer window lists all the tasks performed by different applications on your system. You can read or write to the Event Viewer by using the Event Log component. To include the EventLog component, drag it from the Components toolbox to the form. Change the Name property of the control to eventLog.

To add an error entry in the eventLog component, you need to catch any exception generated by the application. You write exceptions to the Event Viewer by using the WriteEntry() method. Before you do that, however, you need to create an instance of the event log.

Let's now write the code to write an error log to the Event Viewer. In addition, you will also specify the code to change the icon if an error occurs. Write the code in the Created event:

```
Dim evlog As New EventLog()
        evlog.Log = "Application"
        evlog.MachineName = "."


Catch Exc As Exception
            IcoNotify.Icon = m_Error
            IcoNotify.Text = "Error in " + e.Name

        If (OptGenerateLog.Checked = True) Then
            evlog.WriteEntry(e.Name + ": " + Exc.Message)
```

In the preceding code, the Error.ico notification icon is displayed, and a ToolTip displaying the error message is added to the notification icon. The code then checks to see whether the OptGenerateLog check box is selected. If the user selected the check box, the error entry is written to the Event Viewer. However, the user may choose to uncheck the check box. This would prevent the error entry from being written to the Event Viewer.

After writing the data to an XML document, you need to close the object of the XmlTextWriter class by using the Close() method. In addition, you need to exit the Microsoft Word application. You can do this by using the `Quit()` method. You also need to enable the FileSystem Watcher component to enable it to monitor the Source directory.

```
Finally
        wdApp.Quit()
        watchDir.EnableRaisingEvents = True
    End Try
```

After the file is processed, you can move the file that the directory specified in the `TxtProcessedFile` text box. To do this, add the following code to the `Created` event:

```
tryagain:
    Try
        File.Move(e.FullPath, TxtProcessedFile.Text + e.Name)
    Catch

        GoTo tryagain
    End Try
```

The `File.Move()` method call statement is enclosed in the `Try` block. This is because the application moves the processed file to the processed directory only after the file has been processed. The `Move()` method is used to move the processed file to the directory specified in the `TxtProcessedFile` text box. The path of the Source directory and Destination directory are passed as parameters to the `Move()` method.

The events generated are visible in the Microsoft Windows Event Viewer. However, you will now add the code for displaying the entries generated in the Event Viewer in a list box.

Displaying Event Entries in a List Box

In the preceding lesson, you created a list box to display the event entries from the Event Viewer. Let's now add code to the `Refresh Log` button. When a user clicks on the `Refresh Log` button, the event entries from the Event Viewer are picked and displayed in the `LstEvents` list box. To do so, add the following code to the `Click` event of the `Refresh Log` button.

```
Private Sub BtnRefresh_Click(ByVal sender As Object, ByVal e As System.EventArgs)
Handles BtnRefresh.Click
        LstEvents.Items.Clear()
        Dim evlog As New EventLog()
        evlog.Log = "Application"
        evlog.MachineName = "."
        evlog.Source = "MyApp"
        Dim LogEntry As EventLogEntry
        For Each LogEntry In evlog.Entries
            If (LogEntry.Source = "MyApp") Then
                LstEvents.Items.Add(LogEntry.Message)
            End If
        Next
End Sub
```

The preceding code uses the `Clear()` method to clear the content of the `LstEvents` list box. It then sets the `Log` property of the `EventLog` class to the `Application Log` node of the Event Viewer. Specifying the `MachineName` property of the `EventLog` class to dot (.) indicates that the event log is created in the Event Viewer of the user's machine.

Next, the `For…Each` loop is used to write all the event entries to the `LstEvents` list box. The `Add()` method of the `ListBox` class adds an entry as an item to the `LstEvents` list box.

In addition to creating a list box to view the event entries for the application, you can display the contents of the Summary.xml document in a label.

Displaying Data from the Summary.xml Document in a Label

To display the data from the Summary.xml document in a label, you need to read data from the XML document. To do this, create an instance of the `StreamReader` class, `StrRead`. The `StreamReader` class is a class in the `System.IO` namespace and implements the `System.IO.TextReader` class. The `TextReader` class represents a reader used to read the characters in a byte stream. To create an instance of the `StreamReader` class, use the following statement:

```
Dim StrRead As StreamReader
```

After creating the instance, you can use it to read the contents of the Summary.xml document in the directory specified in the TxtDestination text box. To read the data from the Summary.xml document, use the following statement:

```
StrRead = New StreamReader(TxtDestination.Text + "Summary.xml")
```

To read the data in the Summary.xml document, use the ReadToEnd() method of the StreamReader class. To display the text in the label , type the following statements in the Click event of the BtnSummary button.

```
Private Sub BtnSummary_Click(ByVal sender As System.Object, ByVal e As
System.EventArgs) Handles BtnSummary.Click
        Dim StrRead As StreamReader
        Try
            StrRead = New StreamReader(TxtDestination.Text + "Summary.xml")
            LblSummary.Text = StrRead.ReadToEnd
        StrRead.Close()
End Sub
```

After displaying the data in the label, you need to close the object of the Stream-Reader class. You can close the StrRead object by using the Close() method of the StreamReader class. The Close() method closes the object and releases any resources associated with the StrRead object.

Figure 32-5, on page 836, shows the label displaying the data from the Summary.xml document.

When reading data from an XML document, if the application generates an exception, you can display the exception in a message box, as shown in the following statement:

```
Catch Exc As Exception
            MessageBox.Show("An error was returned: " + Exc.Message + "Please
check the destination folder for
                        summary")
        End Try
```

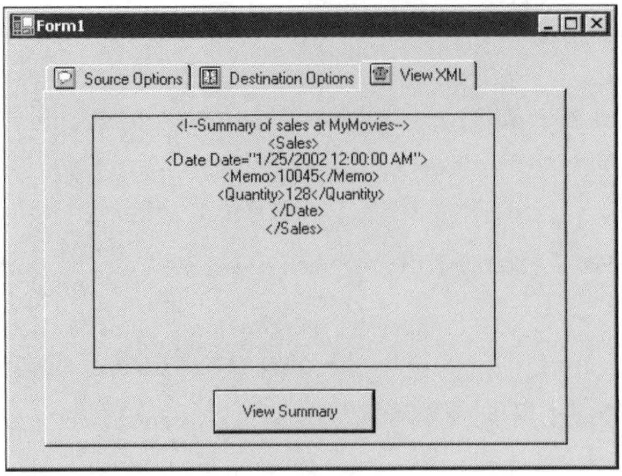

FIGURE 32-5 *The label displaying the data from the Summary.xml document*

Coding the Exit Button

Add the following code to the Click event of the Exit button. This code will enable the application to terminate when the user clicks on the Exit button.

```
Private Sub BtnExit_Click(ByVal sender As Object, ByVal e As System.EventArgs)
Handles BtnExit.Click
        Application.Exit()
End Sub
```

Listing 32-1 provides the complete code for the MyMovies.vb file.

Listing 32-1 MyMovies.vb

```
Imports System
Imports System.IO
Imports System.Collections
Imports System.Drawing
Imports System.ComponentModel
Imports System.Windows.Forms
Imports System.Data
Imports System.Diagnostics
Imports System.Xml


Public Class Form1
    Inherits System.Windows.Forms.Form
```

```
        Private m_ready As New System.Drawing.Icon("Ready.ICO")
        Private m_Error As New System.Drawing.Icon("Error.ICO")
        Friend WithEvents IcoNotify As System.Windows.Forms.NotifyIcon
        Friend WithEvents BtnOK As System.Windows.Forms.Button
        Friend WithEvents BtnSummary As System.Windows.Forms.Button
        Friend WithEvents LblSummary As System.Windows.Forms.Label
        Friend WithEvents LinkLabel1 As System.Windows.Forms.LinkLabel
        Friend WithEvents TabDestination As System.Windows.Forms.TabPage
        Friend WithEvents TabViewResult As System.Windows.Forms.TabPage
        Friend WithEvents Button1 As System.Windows.Forms.Button
        Friend WithEvents ErrorProvider1 As System.Windows.Forms.ErrorProvider
        Private m_Info As New System.Drawing.Icon("Info.ICO")


#Region " Windows Form Designer generated code "

        Public Sub New()
            MyBase.New()


            'This call is required by the Windows Form Designer.
            InitializeComponent()


            'Add any initialization after the InitializeComponent() call


        End Sub


        'Form overrides dispose to clean up the component list.
        Protected Overloads Overrides Sub Dispose(ByVal disposing As Boolean)
            If disposing Then
                If Not (components Is Nothing) Then
                    components.Dispose()
                End If
            End If
            MyBase.Dispose(disposing)
        End Sub
        Friend WithEvents TabControl1 As System.Windows.Forms.TabControl
        Friend WithEvents TabSource As System.Windows.Forms.TabPage
        Friend WithEvents ImageList1 As System.Windows.Forms.ImageList
        Friend WithEvents Label1 As System.Windows.Forms.Label
```

```vbnet
    Friend WithEvents Label3 As System.Windows.Forms.Label
    Friend WithEvents TxtSource As System.Windows.Forms.TextBox
    Friend WithEvents TxtProcessedFile As System.Windows.Forms.TextBox
    Friend WithEvents Label2 As System.Windows.Forms.Label
    Friend WithEvents TxtDestination As System.Windows.Forms.TextBox
    Friend WithEvents grpEventLog As System.Windows.Forms.GroupBox
    Friend WithEvents BtnRefresh As System.Windows.Forms.Button
    Friend WithEvents LstEvents As System.Windows.Forms.ListBox
    Friend WithEvents OptGenerateLog As System.Windows.Forms.CheckBox
    Friend WithEvents ErrMessage As System.Windows.Forms.ErrorProvider
    Friend WithEvents BtnExit As System.Windows.Forms.Button
    Friend WithEvents watchDir As System.IO.FileSystemWatcher


    'Required by the Windows Form Designer
    Private components As System.ComponentModel.IContainer


    'NOTE: The following procedure is required by the Windows Form Designer
    'It can be modified using the Windows Form Designer.
    'Do not modify it using the code editor.
    <System.Diagnostics.DebuggerStepThrough()> Private Sub InitializeComponent()
        Me.components = New System.ComponentModel.Container()
        Dim resources As System.Resources.ResourceManager = New
System.Resources.ResourceManager(GetType(Form1))
        Me.TabControl1 = New System.Windows.Forms.TabControl()
        Me.TabSource = New System.Windows.Forms.TabPage()
        Me.OptGenerateLog = New System.Windows.Forms.CheckBox()
        Me.TxtProcessedFile = New System.Windows.Forms.TextBox()
        Me.TxtSource = New System.Windows.Forms.TextBox()
        Me.Label3 = New System.Windows.Forms.Label()
        Me.Label1 = New System.Windows.Forms.Label()
        Me.TabDestination = New System.Windows.Forms.TabPage()
        Me.BtnExit = New System.Windows.Forms.Button()
        Me.BtnOK = New System.Windows.Forms.Button()
        Me.LstEvents = New System.Windows.Forms.ListBox()
        Me.grpEventLog = New System.Windows.Forms.GroupBox()
        Me.BtnRefresh = New System.Windows.Forms.Button()
        Me.TxtDestination = New System.Windows.Forms.TextBox()
        Me.Label2 = New System.Windows.Forms.Label()
```

```
        Me.TabViewResult = New System.Windows.Forms.TabPage()
        Me.LinkLabel1 = New System.Windows.Forms.LinkLabel()
        Me.LblSummary = New System.Windows.Forms.Label()
        Me.BtnSummary = New System.Windows.Forms.Button()
        Me.ImageList1 = New System.Windows.Forms.ImageList(Me.components)
        Me.ErrMessage = New System.Windows.Forms.ErrorProvider()
        Me.watchDir = New System.IO.FileSystemWatcher()
        Me.IcoNotify = New System.Windows.Forms.NotifyIcon(Me.components)
        Me.Button1 = New System.Windows.Forms.Button()
        Me.ErrorProvider1 = New System.Windows.Forms.ErrorProvider()
        Me.TabControl1.SuspendLayout()
        Me.TabSource.SuspendLayout()
        Me.TabDestination.SuspendLayout()
        Me.grpEventLog.SuspendLayout()
        Me.TabViewResult.SuspendLayout()
        CType(Me.watchDir, System.ComponentModel.ISupportInitialize).BeginInit()
        Me.SuspendLayout()
        '
        'TabControl1
        '
        Me.TabControl1.Controls.AddRange(New System.Windows.Forms.Control()
{Me.TabSource, Me.TabDestination, Me.TabViewResult})
        Me.TabControl1.ImageList = Me.ImageList1
        Me.TabControl1.Location = New System.Drawing.Point(40, 24)
        Me.TabControl1.Name = "TabControl1"
        Me.TabControl1.SelectedIndex = 0
        Me.TabControl1.Size = New System.Drawing.Size(392, 280)
        Me.TabControl1.TabIndex = 0
        '
        'TabSource
        '
        Me.TabSource.Controls.AddRange(New System.Windows.Forms.Control()
{Me.OptGenerateLog, Me.TxtProcessedFile, Me.TxtSource, Me.Label3, Me.Label1})
        Me.TabSource.ImageIndex = 0
        Me.TabSource.Location = New System.Drawing.Point(4, 23)
        Me.TabSource.Name = "TabSource"
        Me.TabSource.Size = New System.Drawing.Size(384, 253)
        Me.TabSource.TabIndex = 0
```

```
Me.TabSource.Text = "Source Options"
'
'OptGenerateLog
'
Me.OptGenerateLog.Location = New System.Drawing.Point(16, 168)
Me.OptGenerateLog.Name = "OptGenerateLog"
Me.OptGenerateLog.Size = New System.Drawing.Size(304, 24)
Me.OptGenerateLog.TabIndex = 4
Me.OptGenerateLog.Text = "Generate event log if an error occurs"
'
'TxtProcessedFile
'
Me.TxtProcessedFile.Location = New System.Drawing.Point(16, 128)
Me.TxtProcessedFile.Name = "TxtProcessedFile"
Me.TxtProcessedFile.Size = New System.Drawing.Size(304, 20)
Me.TxtProcessedFile.TabIndex = 3
Me.TxtProcessedFile.Text = ""
'
'TxtSource
'
Me.TxtSource.Location = New System.Drawing.Point(144, 40)
Me.TxtSource.Name = "TxtSource"
Me.TxtSource.Size = New System.Drawing.Size(168, 20)
Me.TxtSource.TabIndex = 2
Me.TxtSource.Text = ""
'
'Label3
'
Me.Label3.Location = New System.Drawing.Point(24, 96)
Me.Label3.Name = "Label3"
Me.Label3.Size = New System.Drawing.Size(184, 16)
Me.Label3.TabIndex = 1
Me.Label3.Text = "Move the processed source file to:"
'
'Label1
'
Me.Label1.Location = New System.Drawing.Point(16, 40)
Me.Label1.Name = "Label1"
```

```
        Me.Label1.Size = New System.Drawing.Size(104, 16)
        Me.Label1.TabIndex = 0
        Me.Label1.Text = "Copy the files from:"
        '
        'TabDestination
        '
        Me.TabDestination.Controls.AddRange(New System.Windows.Forms.Control()
{Me.BtnExit, Me.BtnOK, Me.LstEvents, Me.grpEventLog, Me.TxtDestination, Me.Label2})
        Me.TabDestination.ImageIndex = 1
        Me.TabDestination.Location = New System.Drawing.Point(4, 23)
        Me.TabDestination.Name = "TabDestination"
        Me.TabDestination.Size = New System.Drawing.Size(384, 253)
        Me.TabDestination.TabIndex = 1
        Me.TabDestination.Text = "Destination Options"
        '
        'BtnExit
        '
        Me.BtnExit.Location = New System.Drawing.Point(208, 200)
        Me.BtnExit.Name = "BtnExit"
        Me.BtnExit.Size = New System.Drawing.Size(64, 32)
        Me.BtnExit.TabIndex = 8
        Me.BtnExit.Text = "Exit"
        '
        'BtnOK
        '
        Me.BtnOK.Location = New System.Drawing.Point(88, 200)
        Me.BtnOK.Name = "BtnOK"
        Me.BtnOK.Size = New System.Drawing.Size(64, 32)
        Me.BtnOK.TabIndex = 7
        Me.BtnOK.Text = "OK"
        '
        'LstEvents
        '
        Me.LstEvents.Location = New System.Drawing.Point(24, 80)
        Me.LstEvents.Name = "LstEvents"
        Me.LstEvents.Size = New System.Drawing.Size(312, 30)
        Me.LstEvents.TabIndex = 6
        '
```

```vbnet
'grpEventLog
'
Me.grpEventLog.Controls.AddRange(New System.Windows.Forms.Control()
{Me.BtnRefresh})
Me.grpEventLog.Location = New System.Drawing.Point(8, 56)
Me.grpEventLog.Name = "grpEventLog"
Me.grpEventLog.Size = New System.Drawing.Size(352, 120)
Me.grpEventLog.TabIndex = 3
Me.grpEventLog.TabStop = False
Me.grpEventLog.Text = "Event Log"
'
'BtnRefresh
'
Me.BtnRefresh.Location = New System.Drawing.Point(240, 88)
Me.BtnRefresh.Name = "BtnRefresh"
Me.BtnRefresh.Size = New System.Drawing.Size(96, 24)
Me.BtnRefresh.TabIndex = 4
Me.BtnRefresh.Text = "Refresh Log"
'
'TxtDestination
'
Me.TxtDestination.Location = New System.Drawing.Point(168, 16)
Me.TxtDestination.Name = "TxtDestination"
Me.TxtDestination.Size = New System.Drawing.Size(168, 20)
Me.TxtDestination.TabIndex = 1
Me.TxtDestination.Text = "TextBox1"
'
'Label2
'
Me.Label2.Location = New System.Drawing.Point(16, 16)
Me.Label2.Name = "Label2"
Me.Label2.Size = New System.Drawing.Size(120, 16)
Me.Label2.TabIndex = 0
Me.Label2.Text = "Destination Directory"
'
'TabViewResult
'
Me.TabViewResult.Controls.AddRange(New System.Windows.Forms.Control()
```

```
{Me.Button1, Me.LinkLabel1, Me.LblSummary, Me.BtnSummary})
        Me.TabViewResult.ImageIndex = 2
        Me.TabViewResult.Location = New System.Drawing.Point(4, 23)
        Me.TabViewResult.Name = "TabViewResult"
        Me.TabViewResult.Size = New System.Drawing.Size(384, 253)
        Me.TabViewResult.TabIndex = 2
        Me.TabViewResult.Text = "View Result"
        '
        'LinkLabel1
        '
        Me.LinkLabel1.Location = New System.Drawing.Point(224, 16)
        Me.LinkLabel1.Name = "LinkLabel1"
        Me.LinkLabel1.Size = New System.Drawing.Size(136, 23)
        Me.LinkLabel1.TabIndex = 3
        Me.LinkLabel1.TabStop = True
        Me.LinkLabel1.Text = "View in Internet Explorer"
        '
        'LblSummary
        '
        Me.LblSummary.BorderStyle = System.Windows.Forms.BorderStyle.FixedSingle
        Me.LblSummary.Location = New System.Drawing.Point(32, 40)
        Me.LblSummary.Name = "LblSummary"
        Me.LblSummary.Size = New System.Drawing.Size(296, 184)
        Me.LblSummary.TabIndex = 2
        Me.LblSummary.TextAlign = System.Drawing.ContentAlignment.TopCenter
        '
        'BtnSummary
        '
        Me.BtnSummary.Location = New System.Drawing.Point(112, 280)
        Me.BtnSummary.Name = "BtnSummary"
        Me.BtnSummary.Size = New System.Drawing.Size(120, 32)
        Me.BtnSummary.TabIndex = 1
        Me.BtnSummary.Text = "View Summary"
        '
        'ImageList1
        '
        Me.ImageList1.ColorDepth = System.Windows.Forms.ColorDepth.Depth8Bit
        Me.ImageList1.ImageSize = New System.Drawing.Size(16, 16)
```

```
        Me.ImageList1.ImageStream =
CType(resources.GetObject("ImageList1.ImageStream"),
System.Windows.Forms.ImageListStreamer)
        Me.ImageList1.TransparentColor = System.Drawing.Color.Transparent
        '
        'watchDir
        '
        Me.watchDir.EnableRaisingEvents = True
        Me.watchDir.Filter = "*.doc"
        Me.watchDir.SynchronizingObject = Me
        '
        'IcoNotify
        '
        Me.IcoNotify.Text = "NotifyIcon1"
        Me.IcoNotify.Visible = True
        '
        'Button1
        '
        Me.Button1.Location = New System.Drawing.Point(144, 240)
        Me.Button1.Name = "Button1"
        Me.Button1.TabIndex = 4
        Me.Button1.Text = "BtnSummary"
        '
        'ErrorProvider1
        '
        Me.ErrorProvider1.DataMember = Nothing
        '
        'Form1
        '
        Me.AutoScaleBaseSize = New System.Drawing.Size(5, 13)
        Me.ClientSize = New System.Drawing.Size(448, 325)
        Me.Controls.AddRange(New System.Windows.Forms.Control() {Me.TabControl1})
        Me.Name = "Form1"
        Me.Text = "Form1"
        Me.TabControl1.ResumeLayout(False)
        Me.TabSource.ResumeLayout(False)
        Me.TabDestination.ResumeLayout(False)
        Me.grpEventLog.ResumeLayout(False)
```

```
        Me.TabViewResult.ResumeLayout(False)
        CType(Me.watchDir, System.ComponentModel.ISupportInitialize).EndInit()
        Me.ResumeLayout(False)

    End Sub

#End Region

    Private Sub TabControl1_SelectedIndexChanged(ByVal sender As System.Object,
ByVal e As System.EventArgs) Handles TabControl1.SelectedIndexChanged

    End Sub

    Private Sub Form1_Load(ByVal sender As System.Object, ByVal e As
System.EventArgs) Handles MyBase.Load
        TxtSource.Text = "D:\MarkUp Movies\Source\"
        TxtProcessedFile.Text = "D:\MarkUp Movies\Processed\"
        TxtDestination.Text = "D:\MarkUp Movies\Destination\"
        OptGenerateLog.Checked = True
    End Sub

    Private Sub BtnOK_Click(ByVal sender As System.Object, ByVal e As
System.EventArgs) Handles BtnOK.Click

        If (Directory.Exists(TxtSource.Text) = False) Then
            ErrMessage.SetError(TxtSource, "Invalid source directory")
            TxtSource.Focus()
            TabControl1.SelectedTab = TabSource
            Return
        Else
            ErrMessage.SetError(TxtSource, "")
        End If

        If (Directory.Exists(TxtDestination.Text) = False) Then
            ErrMessage.SetError(TxtDestination, "Invalid destination directory")
            TxtDestination.Focus()
            TabControl1.SelectedTab = TabDestination
```

```
            Return
        Else
            ErrMessage.SetError(TxtDestination, "")
        End If


        If (Directory.Exists(TxtProcessedFile.Text) = False) Then
            ErrMessage.SetError(TxtProcessedFile, "Invalid processed file directory")
            TxtProcessedFile.Focus()
            TabControl1.SelectedTab = TabSource
            Return
        Else
            ErrMessage.SetError(TxtProcessedFile, "")
            watchDir.Path = TxtSource.Text
            watchDir.EnableRaisingEvents = True
            IcoNotify.Icon = m_ready
            IcoNotify.Visible = True
            Me.ShowInTaskbar = False
            Me.Hide()
        End If


    End Sub


    Private Sub TxtSource_KeyUp(ByVal sender As Object, ByVal e As
System.Windows.Forms.KeyEventArgs)
    Handles TxtSource.KeyUp
        If (Directory.Exists(TxtSource.Text)) Then
            TxtSource.BackColor = Color.White
        Else
            TxtSource.BackColor = Color.BlanchedAlmond


        End If
    End Sub


    Private Sub TxtDestination_KeyUp(ByVal sender As Object, ByVal e As
System.Windows.Forms.KeyEventArgs)
    Handles TxtDestination.KeyUp
        If (Directory.Exists(TxtSource.Text)) Then
```

```
            TxtDestination.BackColor = Color.White
        Else
            TxtDestination.BackColor = Color.BlanchedAlmond
        End If
    End Sub


    Private Sub TxtProcessedFile_KeyUp(ByVal sender As Object, ByVal e As
System.Windows.Forms.KeyEventArgs) Handles TxtProcessedFile.KeyUp
        If (Directory.Exists(TxtSource.Text)) Then
            TxtProcessedFile.BackColor = Color.White
        Else
            TxtProcessedFile.BackColor = Color.BlanchedAlmond

        End If
    End Sub


    Private Sub IcoNotify_DoubleClick(ByVal sender As Object, ByVal e As
System.EventArgs) Handles IcoNotify.DoubleClick
        IcoNotify.Visible = False
        Me.ShowInTaskbar = True
        Me.Show()
    End Sub


    Private Sub BtnExit_Click(ByVal sender As Object, ByVal e As System.EventArgs)
Handles BtnExit.Click
        Application.Exit()
    End Sub


    Private Sub watchDir_Created(ByVal sender As Object, ByVal e As
System.IO.FileSystemEventArgs) Handles watchDir.Created

        Dim evlog As New EventLog()
        evlog.Log = "Application"
        evlog.MachineName = "."
        evlog.Source = "MyApp"
        watchDir.EnableRaisingEvents = False
        IcoNotify.Icon = m_Info
        IcoNotify.Text = "Processed: " + e.Name
```

```
Dim wdApp As New Word.ApplicationClass()
Dim wdDoc As New Word.DocumentClass()
Dim FileName As Object = e.FullPath
Dim XmlWrite As XmlTextWriter


Try
     wdDoc = wdApp.Documents.Open(FileName)
'creates an instance of the WordRange to store the content of the Word docs
     Dim WdRange As Word.Range
     WdRange = wdDoc.Paragraphs.Item(2).Range

     Dim MemoNum, Quantity As String
     Dim ParaCount As String
     MemoNum = WdRange.Text
     MemoNum = MemoNum.Substring(15, 5)
     ParaCount = wdDoc.Paragraphs.Count
     ParaCount = ParaCount - 2
     WdRange = wdDoc.Paragraphs.Item(ParaCount).Range
     WdRange.MoveEnd("1", "-1")
     Quantity = WdRange.Text
     Quantity = Quantity.Substring(23)

     XmlWrite = New XmlTextWriter(TxtDestination.Text + "Summary.xml", Nothing)

     XmlWrite.Formatting = Formatting.Indented

     XmlWrite.WriteComment("Summary of sales at My Movies")
     XmlWrite.WriteStartElement("Sales")
     XmlWrite.WriteStartElement("Date")
     XmlWrite.WriteAttributeString("Date", Convert.ToString(DateTime.Today))

     XmlWrite.WriteElementString("Memo", MemoNum)
     XmlWrite.WriteElementString("Quantity", Quantity)

     XmlWrite.WriteEndElement()
     XmlWrite.WriteEndElement()
     XmlWrite.Flush()
```

```
            XmlWrite.Close()
            IcoNotify.Icon = m_ready
            LinkLabel1.Tag = TxtDestination.Text + "Summary.xml"

        Catch Exc As Exception
            IcoNotify.Icon = m_Error
            IcoNotify.Text = "Error in " + e.Name

            If (OptGenerateLog.Checked = True) Then
                evlog.WriteEntry(e.Name + ": " + Exc.Message)
            End If
        Finally

            wdApp.Quit()
            watchDir.EnableRaisingEvents = True

        End Try
tryagain:
        Try
            File.Move(e.FullPath, TxtProcessedFile.Text + e.Name)
        Catch

            GoTo tryagain
        End Try
    End Sub


    Private Sub BtnViewSummary_Click(ByVal sender As System.Object, ByVal e As
System.EventArgs)

    End Sub


    Private Sub BtnRefresh_Click(ByVal sender As Object, ByVal e As
System.EventArgs) Handles BtnRefresh.Click
        LstEvents.Items.Clear()
        Dim evlog As New EventLog()
        evlog.Log = "Application"
        evlog.MachineName = "."
```

```vbnet
            evlog.Source = "MyApp"
        Dim LogEntry As EventLogEntry
        For Each LogEntry In evlog.Entries
            If (LogEntry.Source = "MyApp") Then
                LstEvents.Items.Add(LogEntry.Message)
            End If
        Next
    End Sub


    Private Sub TabSource_Click(ByVal sender As System.Object, ByVal e As
System.EventArgs) Handles TabSource.Click

    End Sub


    Private Sub BtnSummary_Click(ByVal sender As System.Object, ByVal e As
System.EventArgs) Handles BtnSummary.Click
        Dim StrRead As StreamReader
        Try
            StrRead = New StreamReader(TxtDestination.Text + "Summary.xml")

            LblSummary.Text = StrRead.ReadToEnd
            StrRead.Close()

        Catch Exc As Exception
            MessageBox.Show("An error was returned: " + Exc.Message + "Please
check the destination folder for summary")

        End Try
    End Sub


    Private Sub TxtProcessedFile_TextChanged(ByVal sender As System.Object, ByVal e
As System.EventArgs)
    Handles TxtProcessedFile.TextChanged

    End Sub
```

```vbnet
    Private Sub LblSummary_Click(ByVal sender As System.Object, ByVal e As
System.EventArgs) Handles
    LblSummary.Click

    End Sub


    Private Sub LinkLabel1_LinkClicked(ByVal sender As System.Object, ByVal e As
        System.Windows.Forms.LinkLabelLinkClickedEventArgs) Handles
LinkLabel1.LinkClicked
        If LinkLabel1.Tag = Nothing Then
            MessageBox.Show("              No File Found in Destination Directory
")
            Exit Sub
        End If

        Try
            System.Diagnostics.Process.Start(LinkLabel1.Tag)
        Catch exp As Exception
            MsgBox(exp.Message.ToString)
        End Try

    End Sub


    Private Sub watchDir_Changed(ByVal sender As System.Object, ByVal e As
System.IO.FileSystemEventArgs) Handles watchDir.Changed

    End Sub


    Private Sub IcoNotify_MouseDown(ByVal sender As System.Object, ByVal e As
System.Windows.Forms.MouseEventArgs) Handles IcoNotify.MouseDown

    End Sub
End Class
```

Summary

In this chapter, you learned to add the code for the Windows application. In addition, you learned to use controls such as ErrorProvider, FileSystemWatcher, and NotifyIcon. You also learned to convert data stored in a Word document to the XML format.

PART VI

Professional Project 5

Project 5

Project 5 Overview

Mobile Web applications enable users on the move to access data on their handheld devices. This project will introduce you to creating a mobile Web application. You'll create a quiz that the employees of Markup Toys, a fictitious company, can access from anywhere in the world. The company hopes that the application will provide an interesting recreation for employees away from home. The application will first accept the user's name and store the name in a session variable. Then the application will display a set of five questions that the users can attempt to answer. Finally, after the user has attempted the questions, the application will display the user's name and score. In addition, it will also display the name of the employee who has scored the highest score so far. To display the name of the user who has scored the highest score, the application will interact with a SQL 2000 database.

The key concepts you will use to create the application are as follows:

◆ The .NET framework

◆ Visual Basic.NET

◆ The Wireless Application Protocol

◆ Mobile Web forms

◆ Connecting to a database

This project will explain how to create a mobile Web application. You will begin by learning about the project case study, then about designing the forms, and then about adding the code for the application.

Chapter 33

**Project Case
Study—
MobileQuiz
Application**

This chapter takes up the example of a fictitious company by the name Markup Toys. Let's assume that Markup Toys is a leading toy manufacturing company in the United States. The company maintains high quality standards, and this has led to its rapid growth. The company at present has a team of 300 dedicated employees. The company head office is in New York, and its retail outlets are located across the United States.

The company has now decided to expand its operations to the Middle East and Southeast Asia. The expansion plans have led to frequent traveling by a number of company employees. Top management officials realize that the job is stressful. In its continuous endeavor to make the job less stressful for its employees, management has decided to create an application to provide a source of entertainment for employees. Because many of the company's employees are on the move, management wants the application to be accessible on a mobile phone. Management has approved a small quiz that poses a set of five interesting questions. Management wants the questions to cover varied topics. For this, the data for the application needs to be updated daily. Employees can access the quiz from anywhere in the world on their handheld devices. The application will pose five new questions to users every day. In addition, the application will also display the user's score, the highest score of the day, and the name of the person with the highest score. These pieces of information will be stored in and retrieved from a database.

After analyzing the various available technologies, management has decided to develop the application using Visual Basic.NET. This is because the .NET framework makes it easy to develop applications for the distributed Web environment, and it supports cross-platform execution. Moreover, the .NET framework makes data available anytime, anywhere, and on any device. In addition, because the data in the database needs to be updated daily, easy connectivity is needed between the backend and front end. Visual Basic.NET offers this easy connectivity.

For the development of this application, a three-member team has been formed. The team is called the MobileApplicationTeam and consists of the following members:

◆ Patie Jason, the project manager of the development team
◆ Helina Smithson

◆ Joel Hallary

◆ you

All the members of the MobileApplicationTeam are experienced programmers who have developed applications using Visual Basic.NET and Microsoft SQL 2000. You are a part of the development team and are responsible for developing the mobile Web application.

To start the development of the application, the members of the MobileApplicationTeam have determined the development life cycle of the mobile Web application project. This life cycle is discussed in the following section.

Project Life Cycle of Markup Toys

Every project has a development life cycle. In most cases, the life cycle of a project consists of three phases:

◆ Project initiation

◆ Project execution

◆ Project deployment

Since you are familiar with these phases (refer to Chapter 9, "Project Case Study—Creating a Video Kiosk"), this section will just discuss the various stages of the project execution phase and how they pertain to this chapter's sample company.

Requirements Analysis

In this stage of the example, the MobileApplicationTeam gathers information from management officials regarding the requirements for the mobile Web application. To do so, the team interviews these officials to understand their areas of interest and to chalk out the type of questions the officials would like to attempt. In addition, the MobileApplicationTeam looks into existing applications on the company Web site to ascertain what features these applications were not offering. Then the team analyzes its findings and arrives at a consensus regarding the requirements for the mobile Web application. As per the results of the requirements analysis stage, the mobile Web application should enable a user to do the following:

- ◆ Attempt the questions
- ◆ Display new questions every day
- ◆ Display the score of the user
- ◆ Display the highest score attained by the user in a quiz
- ◆ Display the name of the employee who has attained the highest score

High-Level Design

In this stage of the example, the MobileApplicationTeam designs an application that accepts the user's name and then asks the user to attempt the questions. After the user attempts all the questions and clicks the Submit button, the application displays the name and score of the user. In addition, the application also interacts with the backend and retrieves the highest score and the name of the employee who attained that score.

The design for the application consists of seven forms, starting with a Welcome form. The subsequent forms display the questions for the quiz. The final form displays the user's score and the highest score attained by any user. Figure 33-1 shows the Welcome screen for the application. Users will be prompted to enter their names. The name field is a mandatory field.

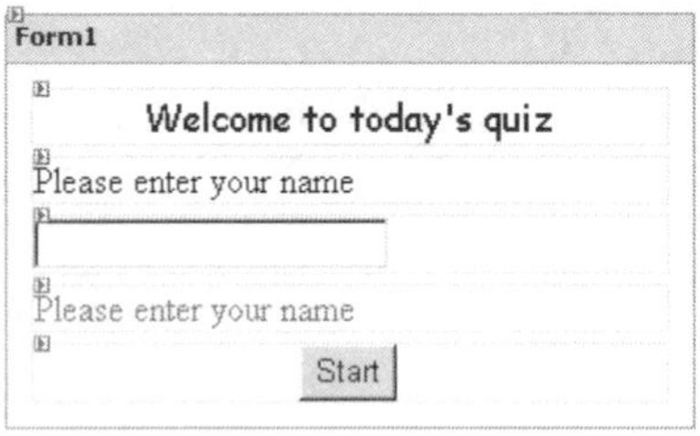

FIGURE 33-1 *The Welcome form*

The next form prompts users with the first question of the quiz. Each form holds a single question.

The forms for the subsequent questions are shown in the Figures 33-2–33-6.

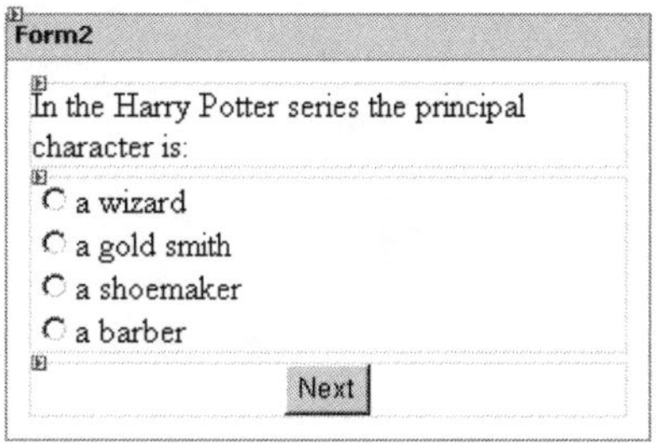

```
Form2

In the Harry Potter series the principal
character is:

  ○ a wizard
  ○ a gold smith
  ○ a shoemaker
  ○ a barber

              Next
```

FIGURE 33-2 *The second form*

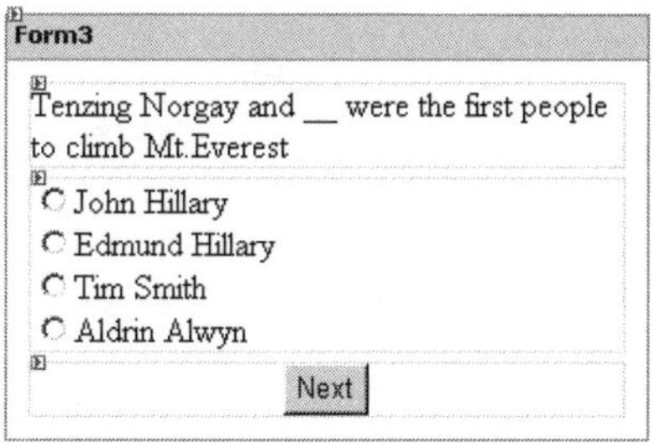

```
Form3

Tenzing Norgay and __ were the first people
to climb Mt.Everest

  ○ John Hillary
  ○ Edmund Hillary
  ○ Tim Smith
  ○ Aldrin Alwyn

              Next
```

FIGURE 33-3 *The third form*

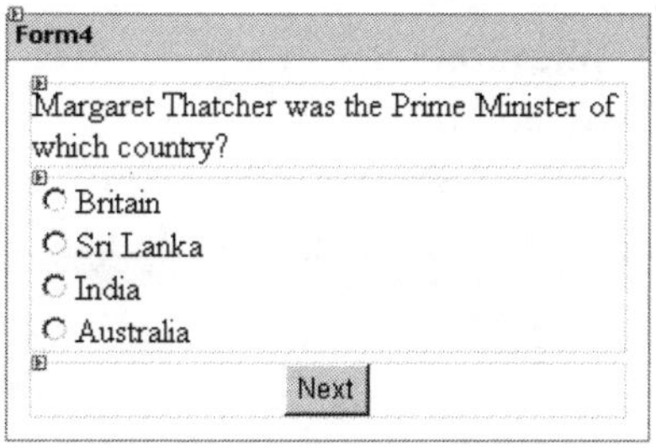

```
Form4

Margaret Thatcher was the Prime Minister of
which country?

  ○ Britain
  ○ Sri Lanka
  ○ India
  ○ Australia

              Next
```

FIGURE 33-4 *The fourth form*

```
Form5

Who created the cartoon character Goofy?

  ○ Walt Disney
  ○ Mickey Mouse
  ○ Tim Matthew

              Next
```

FIGURE 33-5 *The fifth form*

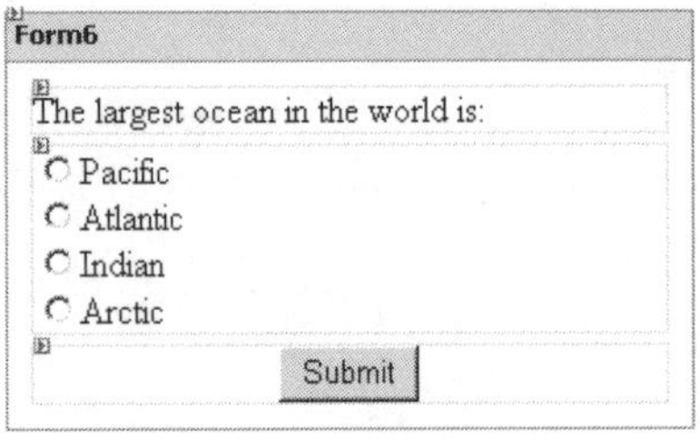

FIGURE 33-6 *The sixth form*

The last form will display the user's score. It will also display the name and score of the user with the highest score.

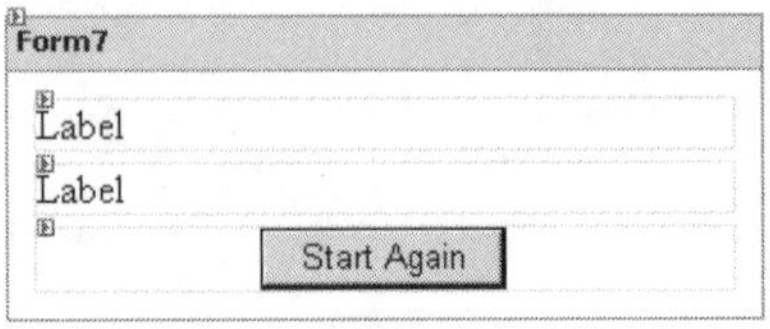

FIGURE 33-7 *The seventh form*

Low-Level Design

In this stage of our example, the MobileApplicationTeam made decisions about database connectivity and how to access the required information. The team also decided on the classes and methods to be used for developing the application. The data needed by the MobileApplicationTeam application is available in a single table database.

Testing

In this stage of the example, the quality assurance (QA) team of the company tested the functionality of the mobile Web application. The QA team tested the application in various scenarios such as different mobiles and handheld devices. The QA team listed all bugs in a report, which was given to the development team. The development team then fixed the bugs or provided valid reasons for not fixing a bug pointed out by the QA team.

Acceptance

In this stage, the company carries out testing of the project developed for the client. This testing is done according to the standards defined by the industry. Successful testing of the project in this stage signifies the final acceptance of the project before release to the client.

In the mobile Web application example, the QA team gave its final acceptance after being completely satisfied by the bug fixes incorporated by the development team. In addition, because the application was developed for the company's internal use, the QA team gave the final signoff.

In addition to deploying the application, the MobileApplicationTeam also provides any required after-deployment assistance to the users.

The Database Schema

As previously mentioned, the application interacts with a database to retrieve the name of the user and the highest score attained by the user. The database uses a table called UserRecord to store the data. The UserRecord table is stored in the master database, and the structure of this table is shown in Table 33-1.

Table 33-1 The *UserRecord* Table Structure

Column Name	Data Type
UserName	varchar(25)
MaxScore	int

Summary

In this chapter, you learned about the company Markup Toys. Then you learned about the company's need to create an application. The company named the application mobile Web and formed a three-member development team named MobileApplicationTeam. Next, you learned about the development life cycle of a project and how its phases pertained to the MobileApplicationTeam. In the next chapter, you will learn how to develop the mobile Web application.

Chapter 34

**Coding the
MobileQuiz
Application**

In Chapter 33, "Project Case Study—MobileQuiz Application," you learned about a mobile Web application. Now, in this chapter, you will learn how to create the application. First, however, I'll introduce you to the need for creating mobile Web applications. I'll also discuss the Wireless Application Protocol (WAP), the Mobile Internet Toolkit, and mobile Web forms.

Today's business world is very dynamic, and users need to access the Internet from anywhere and at any time. Mobile technology offers users around the world just that—the power to access the Internet from anywhere and at any time. However, most users are wary of accessing the Internet from their mobile phones. This is because:

◆ Mobile phones are limited by CPU, memory, or battery life.
◆ Mobile phones require higher bandwidths, which result in higher overhead costs.
◆ Web pages developed for the Internet don't fit the average mobile's screen.

It is because of these problems that mobile Web applications have not become very popular. The .NET technology, however, now gives you the power to change this. Using Visual Studio.NET, you can create mobile Web applications that can be easily accessed on any mobile phone. What's more, the information appears just as it appears in your browser window.

The following sections look at the two basic requirements for creating a mobile Web application—WAP and the Mobile Internet Toolkit.

An Introduction to WAP

The first requirement for mobile Web applications is a WAP-enabled mobile phone. WAP is a communication protocol that defines standards to connect wireless applications to the Internet. In addition to having a WAP-enabled mobile phone, the Web site you are accessing also should be WAP enabled.

A WAP-enabled device has microbrowser software that sends and receives requests for accessing a Web site. This section will now lead you a further into WAP and discuss how WAP-enabled Web sites communicate with the Internet.

To understand this concept, you first need to understand the WAP architecture. This architecture is similar to the Web architecture in that the client sends a request to the Web server and the Web server responds to the request of the client. Figure 34-1 illustrates the Web architecture, and Figure 34-2 illustrates the WAP architecture.

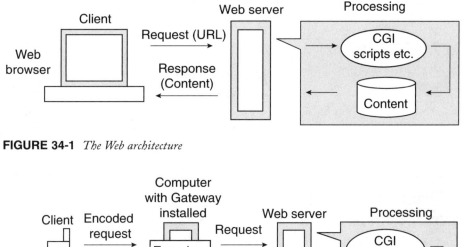

FIGURE 34-1 *The Web architecture*

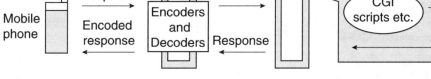

FIGURE 34-2 *The WAP architecture*

The only difference between the WAP architecture and the Web architecture is the presence of the WAP gateway. The WAP gateway is software that is placed between a network that supports WAP and the Internet. The following steps explain how a WAP-enabled device communicates with the Internet:

1. The client (mobile phone) sets up a connection with the WAP gateway and requests its content.

2. The WAP gateway converts the request into an Internet-understandable version. It then forwards the request to the Web server.

3. The Web server then sends the content to the gateway, which then converts it into WAP format, which is later sent to the mobile phone.

A WAP-enabled Web site is hosted to the client as a WML or WML Script file. WML scripting languages are used to write WAP content. These scripting languages are used to send and receive information on mobile phones. A WAP-enabled mobile phone has a microbrowser that is similar to other Web browsers and that displays the information a user receives.

The next section discusses the Mobile Internet Toolkit, which is the second requirement for creating a mobile Web application.

The Mobile Internet Toolkit

The other requirement is to install the Mobile Internet Toolkit on your computer. This is because, when you install Microsoft Visual Studio.NET, by default, you cannot create mobile Web applications. To be able to create mobile Web applications, you need to install the Mobile Internet Toolkit. This toolkit is available for free on the Microsoft Web site. You can download it from the following link:

http://msdn.microsoft.com/downloads/default.asp?url=/downloads/sample.asp?

The Mobile Internet Toolkit is based on the .NET framework and provides an easy-to-use visual interface for creating mobile Web applications. In addition, the Mobile Internet Toolkit enables you to create mobile Web applications that target a wide variety of mobile devices. This means you need to create just one mobile Web application for different wireless applications such as palm-held PCs and mobile phones.

The Mobile Internet Toolkit consists of server-side mobile Web Form controls and a Mobile Internet Designer that helps you create the user interface for your mobile Web application.

The following section explains mobile Web forms, the building blocks for a mobile Web application.

Mobile Web Forms

A mobile Web application consists of a mobile forms page that contains several mobile controls. A mobile Web forms page is a specialized ASP.NET Web forms page. In addition, similar to other Web forms pages, a mobile Web forms page has an .ASPX extension.

You can use the Mobile Internet Toolkit to create mobile Web forms pages and controls that are device independent. This means that when a supported device requests a mobile Web forms page, the page automatically identifies the device and displays the Web page in a format suitable for the specific device type.

To build a mobile Web forms page, you need to place a Form control on the mobile Web forms page. A Form control is like a container that holds the other controls placed on the mobile Web forms page. Though you can place several Form controls on a mobile Web forms page, a Form control cannot contain another Form control within itself.

Next I'll discuss how to create a mobile Web application.

Creating a Mobile Web Application

If you are a Visual Basic developer, you have experienced how easy it is to create applications. All you need to create a Visual Basic application is to add a mobile Web form to the project, drag controls onto the form, set properties, and then double-click the controls to write the code. Mobile Web forms bring the same simplicity and ease to creating mobile Web applications.

To create a mobile Web application using mobile Web forms, you simply need to drag the Forms control to the mobile Web forms page, add content and controls to the mobile Web form, and then double-click the mobile Web controls to add the code.

As discussed in the previous chapter, the mobile Web application will consist of a series of questions on which the users will be evaluated. The user's name and score will be stored in two session variables that will hold values until the user logs out. The application will also check to see whether the score attained by the user is higher than the highest score currently stored in the database. If the session score is higher than the highest score, the application will update the UserRecord table with the name and score of the session user.

Now let's create the mobile Web application. First you will learn how to design the forms for the application. The main form, as shown in Figure 34-3, will accept the user's name; as previously mentioned, it will be stored in a session variable that will be valid until the user does not log out of the session.

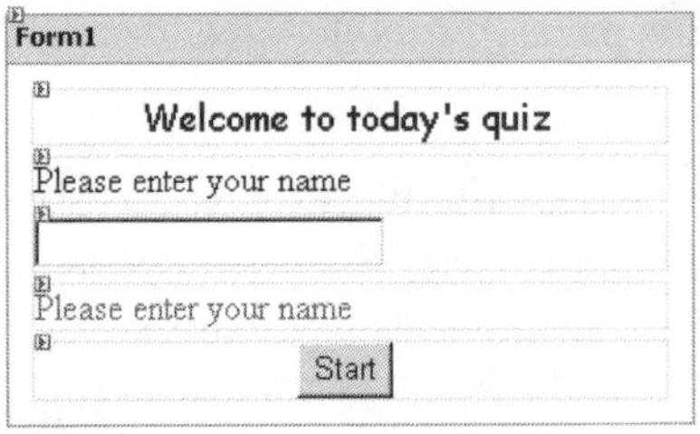

FIGURE 34-3 *The design of the main form for the application*

When the user clicks on the Start button, the next form (shown in Figure 34-4) is displayed. The form contains the first question of the quiz. After the user attempts the question and clicks on the Next button, the next question is displayed in the next form.

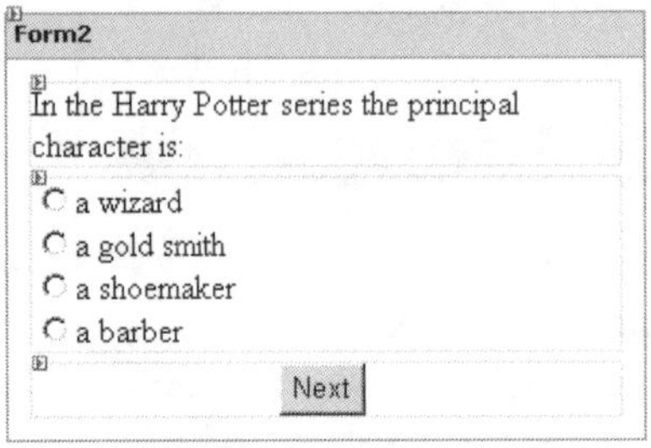

FIGURE 34-4 *The design of the second form for the application*

The subsequent forms contain the rest of the questions for the quiz. The last form (shown in Figure 34-5) displays the user's score and the highest score attained by a user in the quiz.

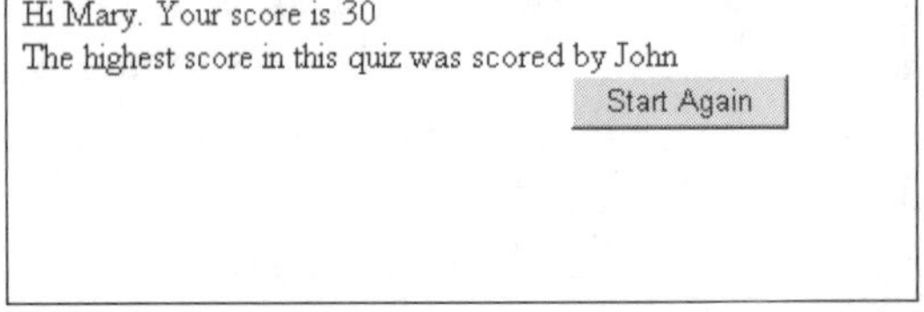

FIGURE 34-5 *The seventh form for the application in the browser window*

Though Visual Basic.NET automatically generates a lot of code, you'll add and modify the code to customize the application to your requirements. In addition, you'll also write the code to connect to the database and retrieve data from it.

Designing the Forms for the MobileQuiz Application

As discussed in Chapter 33, the high-level design for the application involves designing mobile Web forms. The main form of the mobile Web application enables the user to accept the username. Refer to Figure 34-3, which displays the design of the main form.

Before designing a mobile Web application, you first need to create it. To create a mobile Web application, you need to follow these steps:

1. In the Visual Studio.NET window, choose File, New, Project to open the New Project dialog box, as shown in Figurer 34-6.

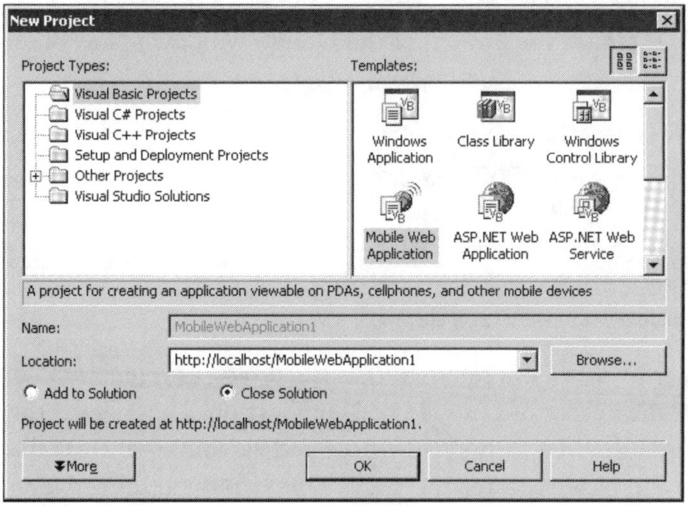

FIGURE 34-6 *The New Project dialog box*

2. In the Project Types pane, choose Visual Basic Projects. You can also select Visual C# Projects to select an application that uses Visual C#, but you'll create this application using Visual Basic Projects.
3. In the Templates pane, select Mobile Web Application.
4. Specify the name and location for the application.
5. Click on OK to create the mobile Web application.

Note that, by default, Form1 is present on the mobile Web page. Recall that a form is like a container that holds other controls. In this example, when you browse the mobile Web application, each form will be displayed on a new page. In addition, the display of the form will automatically adapt based on the device you are using to access the mobile Web application.

You can add controls to the mobile Web form by dragging them from the Toolbox to the mobile Web form. Note that you can place controls only on a Form control or on a Panel control. A Panel control, like a Form control, acts as a container for other controls. The only difference between a Form control and a Panel control is that a Form control cannot be placed within another Form control, whereas a Panel control can hold another Panel control.

When you follow the preceding steps, Visual Basic.NET automatically generates some code. To view the HTML code, switch to the HTML view for the page by clicking the HTML tab (at the bottom of the Design window.) Now observe the following code:

```
<%@ Register TagPrefix="mobile" Namespace="System.Web.UI.MobileControls"
 Assembly="System.Web.Mobile, Version=1.0.3300.0, Culture=neutral,
 PublicKeyToken=b03f5f7f11d50a3a" %>
<%@ Page Language="vb" AutoEventWireup="false"
Codebehind="MobileWebForm1.aspx.vb"
Inherits="MobileWebApplication4.MobileWebForm1" %>
```

The preceding lines of code, also referred to as the prolog of a mobile Web form, must be present in the header of a mobile Web application. The @ Register directive specifies the mobile Web form's namespace and assembly, whereas the @Page directive specifies the base class for the page. The TagPrefix directive instructs mobile Web forms to add Web form controls to the mobile Web form. The Language attribute varies depending on the application you use for creating the mobile Web application.

Also note the following code:

```
<mobile:Form id="Form1" runat="server"></mobile:Form>
```

This code indicates that the form with ID Form1 is a mobile Web control. The attribute runat="server" should be present for each mobile Web control that you add to the form.

Now that a form has been added to your mobile Web page, you can add controls to the form. As previously mentioned, you add controls to a form by dragging controls from the Toolbox to the mobile Web form. Now you will add controls to the main form of the application. The main Web form, as shown in Figure 34-3, is a simple form that accepts the user's name and displays a welcome message. The form contains two labels, a text box, and a button. When the user clicks the Start button, the next form (Form2) becomes the active form.

The top two controls on the form are the labels. You will set two properties for the labels: Text and ID. The Text property specifies the text that will appear on the form, and the ID property specifies the object name that is assigned to the label to easily identify and refer to it in the code. Table 34-1 describes the properties for the labels on the main form.

> **TIP**
>
> While specifying the ID for a control, it is good practice to follow a naming convention. This will help other developers in your team to easily identify the controls.

Table 34-1 Properties Assigned to the Labels on the Main Form

Control	Property	Value
Label 1	ID	LblWelcomeMsg
Label 1	Text	Welcome to today's quiz
Label 2	ID	LblName
Label 2	Text	Please enter your name

To easily identify the welcome text, you can change the font and color of the text. You will now do just that to the text in the LblWelcomeMsg control. To change the font, set the Font property in the Properties window. To specify the Font Style, set the Name property. For this example, use the Font Style, Comic Sans MS. Next you can change the color and alignment of the text. To change the color, click on the ForeColor property. From the Color palette that appears, you can choose the color of your choice. For this example, use Navy. However, you can choose any color you want. To change the alignment of the text, use the Alignment property under the group Appearance. For this example, center the text. Now that you have specified the properties for the labels, let's move on the text box and the button.

As shown in Figure 34-3, under the Label controls on the main form is a text box. The text box will accept the user's name. You should also add a validation to this control to ensure that the user does not leave this field blank. However, before you add validations to the text box, you will change the ID property of the text box. For this example, specify the ID property of the text box as TxtEnterName. Let's now add validations for the text box.

You can add validations on a control to restrict the type of data entered into that control. To add a validation to a control:

1. Drag the RequiredFieldValidator control to the bottom of the form.
2. In the Properties window, click the Control to Validate property. All controls on the form appear in a drop-down menu. Because you need to add the validation for the text box, select TxtEnterName.
3. For the Error Message property, enter the error message to be displayed when the user does not enter data in the field. For this example, enter the error message Please enter your name.

After changing the properties for validating text in a form, you need to add a small amount of code to ensure that the user does not move to the next form until he or she has entered the required information. Before you add the code, however, you need to add another control to the form—the button. The properties you need to change for the button are described in Table 34-2.

Table 34-2 Properties Assigned to the Button on the Main Form

Control	Property	Value
Button	ID	BtnStart
Button	Text	Start
Button	Alignment	Center

To insert a button on the form, drag the button to the form. Change the ID, Text, and Alignment properties as you did for the other controls on the form. Now you need to specify the task to be performed when the user clicks the Start button. When the user clicks on the Start button, Form2 should be displayed. However, before you specify the code, you need to first create Form2.

To create Form2, drag the Form control from the Toolbox to the mobile Web forms page. You will now write the code for moving to Form2 when the user clicks the Start button control.

To do this, you first need to open the Code window. To open the Code window, either press the F7 key or double-click on the control for which you want to write the code. In the Code window, write the following code for the Click event of the Start button.

```
Private Sub BtnStart_Click(ByVal sender As System.Object, ByVal e As
System.EventArgs) Handles BtnStart.Click
If Page.IsValid Then
        Session("UserName") = TxtEnterName.Text
        ActiveForm = Form2
    End If
End Sub
```

In the preceding code, note the first line. The Page.IsValid property checks to see whether the page is in the valid format. In other words, it checks to make sure the data entered on the form follows the validation specified for the controls. Recall that in the previous step you had added validations on the TxtEnterName control. If the user does not enter the name in the text box, Page.IsValid will return false, and further code will not be executed.

The code ActiveForm=Form2 makes Form2 the active form.

Now that you have written the code for the Start button, navigate to the Declarations section of the mobile Web form. Visual Basic.NET generates the following code by default when you add various Form controls to the mobile Web form:

```
Public Class MobileWebForm1
    Inherits System.Web.UI.MobileControls.MobilePage
    Protected WithEvents LblWelcomeMsg As System.Web.UI.MobileControls.Label
    Protected WithEvents LblName As System.Web.UI.MobileControls.Label
    Protected WithEvents TxtEnterName As System.Web.UI.MobileControls.TextBox
    Protected WithEvents RequiredFieldValidator1 As
System.Web.UI.MobileControls.RequiredFieldValidator
    Protected WithEvents BtnStart As System.Web.UI.MobileControls.Command
    Protected WithEvents Form2 As System.Web.UI.MobileControls.Form
    Protected WithEvents Form1 As System.Web.UI.MobileControls.Form
```

Let's go ahead and create the next form. Before you do so, however, take a look at its design (refer back to Figure 34-4). The next form consists of a label that contains the question, four radio buttons for the options, and a button to move to the next form. The tricky part when creating this form is adding the radio buttons. This is because the Toolbox does not contain a separate control for adding radio buttons. To add a radio button to the mobile Web form, you need to use the SelectionList control. (This will be explained a little later.)

First, add a label on the mobile Web form and set properties for the label as shown in Table 34-3.

Table 34-3 Properties Assigned to the Label on the Second Form

Control	Property	Value
Label	ID	LblQuestion1Stem
Label	Text	In the Harry Potter series the principal character is:

Below the label, you need to add a radio button. To add a radio button to the mobile Web form, drag a SelectionList control to the mobile Web form. Then, in the Properties window, change the ID for the control to RdForm2. Next click the SelectType property. A drop-down menu appears, as shown in Figure 34-7.

Because you need to create a radio button, select Radio. Now you need to add the text for the radio buttons. To do so, click the Items property. The RdForm2 dialog box appears. Click the Create New Item button. Next you need to add the value for the items. In the Item Text box, enter the text a wizard. This will be the text for the first option. Next click on the Selected box. This will ensure that the first option is selected when the page is loaded in the mobile browser. To add another option, click the Create New Item button again. In the Item Text box, enter the text a gold smith. The text for the other two radio buttons is given in Table 34-4.

Table 34-4 Properties Assigned to the Labels on the Main Form

Option	Value
Option3	a shoemaker
Option4	a barber

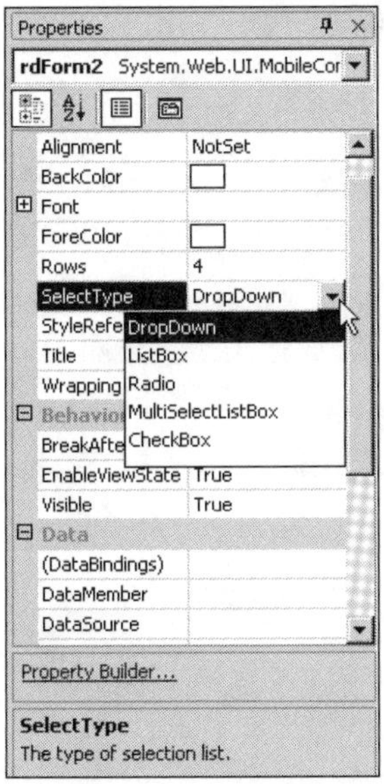

FIGURE 34-7 *The* SelectType *property drop-down menu*

Finally, click on OK to create the options for the radio buttons. The second form is almost ready. All you now need to do is add a button to move to the next form. The properties you need to assign to the controls are listed in Table 34-5.

Table 34-5 Properties Assigned to the Button on the Second Form

Control	Property	Value
Button	ID	CmdForm2
Button	Text	Next
Button	Alignment	Center

In addition to these properties, you also need to add the code for moving to the next form. And because you need to calculate the user's score, you need to write the code to do so. However, before you write the code for checking which option the user has selected and accordingly increasing the score, you need to define two session variables that will store the user's name and score for a particular session. To declare the session variables, in the Solution Explorer, right-click Global.asax and then choose View Code. Type the following code for the Start event of the session:

```
Sub Session_Start(ByVal sender As Object, ByVal e As EventArgs)
        ' Fires when the session is started
        Dim UserName As String
        Dim Score As Integer
End Sub
```

The preceding code declares two session variables, UserName and Score, of data types String and Integer, respectively. Close the file and then open the Code window for the mobile Web page. Enter the following code for the Click event of the CmdForm2 button:

```
Private Sub CmdForm2_Click(ByVal sender As System.Object, ByVal e As
System.EventArgs) Handles
CmdForm2.Click
'Code to calculate the score and move to the next form
        If RdForm2.SelectedIndex = 0 Then
            Session("Score") = 10
        Else
            Session("Score") = 0
        End If
        ActiveForm = Form3
End Sub
```

In the preceding code, the first option is the right answer. Hence, the Selected-Index property is checked for the control. The SelectedIndex property stores the value of the option selected by the user. The first radio button has the index value 0, the second option 1, and so on. In the code, if the user selects the first option (at index 0), the score is incremented by 10.

Also note that the ToString method has been used while displaying the text in the Label control. This is because to display the score in the Label control, it should be of the String data type. By using the ToString method, you can convert values stored as Integer to the String data type.

The other forms are similar to the second form. The properties you need to add for the third Form control are listed in Table 34-6.

Table 34-6 Properties Assigned to the Controls on the Third Form

Control	Property	Value
Label	ID	LblQuestion2Stem
Label	Text	Tenzing Norgay and __ were the first people to climb Mt.Everest
SelectionList	SelectType	Radio
SelectionList	ID	RdForm3
SelectionList	Collection	John Hillary
SelectionList	Collection	Edmund Hillary
SelectionList	Collection	Tim Smith
SelectionList	Collection	Aldrin Alwyn
Button	ID	CmdForm3
Button	Text	Next
Button	Alignment	Center

Now compare your form with Figure 34-8.

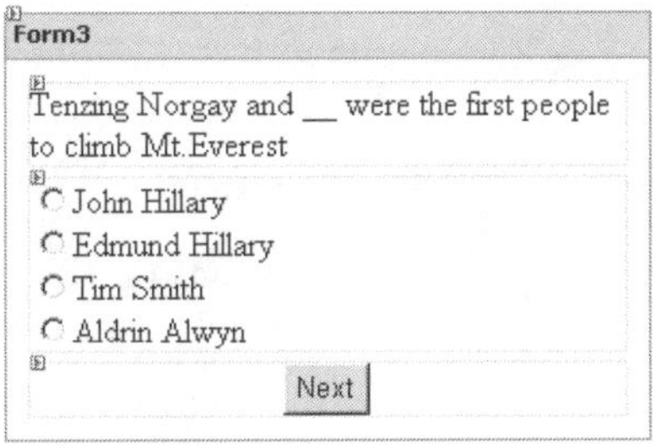

FIGURE 34-8 *The design of the third form for the application*

Now that the form is ready, you will add the code for the button. Before the next form is made the active form, you need to increment the score by 10 points if the answer is correct. To do so, enter the following code for the Click event of the CmdForm3 control:

```
Private Sub CmdForm3_Click(ByVal sender As System.Object, ByVal e As
System.EventArgs) Handles
CmdForm3.Click
        If RdForm3.SelectedIndex = 1 Then
                Session("Score") = Session("Score") + 10
        End If
        ActiveForm = form4
    End Sub
```

Now that you have created Form3, let's create the next form. The controls and properties that you need to define for Form4 are shown in Table 34-7.

Table 34-7 Properties Assigned to the Controls on the Fourth Form

Control	Property	Value
Label	ID	LblQuestion3stem
Label	Text	Margaret Thatcher was the Prime Minister of which country?
SelectionList	SelectType	Radio
SelectionList	ID	RdForm4
SelectionList	Collection	Britain
SelectionList	Collection	Sri Lanka
SelectionList	Collection	India
SelectionList	Collection	Australia
Button	ID	CmdForm4
Button	Text	Next
Button	Alignment	Center

Compare your form with Figure 34-9.

Next add the following code for the Click event of the CmdForm4 button:

```
Private Sub CmdForm4_Click(ByVal sender As System.Object, ByVal e As
System.EventArgs) Handles
CmdForm4.Click
```

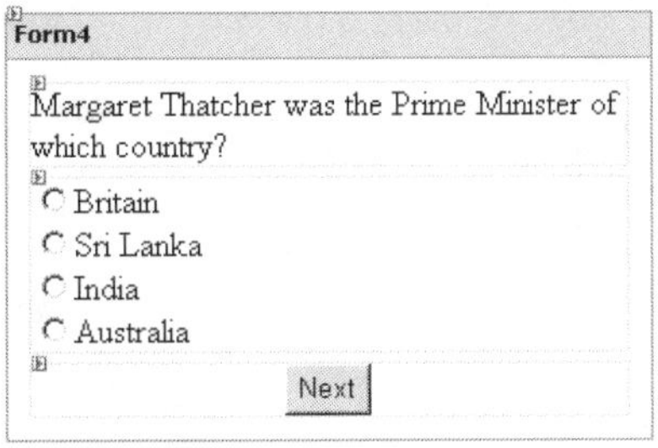

FIGURE 34-9 *The design of the fourth form for the application*

```
    If RdForm4.SelectedIndex = 0 Then
        Session("Score") = Session("Score") + 10
    End If
        ActiveForm = form5
End Sub
```

In the preceding code, the SelectedIndex property has been checked with the value 0. This is because the third option is the correct answer. You now need to add two more questions to complete the application. Create the next form based on the properties specified in Table 34-8.

Table 34-8 Properties Assigned to the Controls on the Fifth Form

Control	Property	Value
Label1	ID	LblQuestion4Stem
Label1	Text	Who created the cartoon character Goofy?
SelectionList	SelectType	Radio
SelectionList	ID	RdForm5
SelectionList	Collection	Walt Disney
SelectionList	Collection	Mickey Mouse
SelectionList	Collection	Tim Matthew
Button	ID	CmdForm5
Button	Text	Next
Button	Alignment	Center

Compare your form with Figure 34-10.

FIGURE 34-10 *The design of the fifth form for the application*

Next add the following code for the Click event of the CmdForm5 button:

```
Private Sub CmdForm5_Click(ByVal sender As System.Object, ByVal e As
System.EventArgs) Handles
CmdForm5.Click
        If RdForm5.SelectedIndex = 0 Then
            Session("Score") = Session("Score") + 10
        End If
        ActiveForm = Form6
End Sub
```

Because the management of Markup Toys wants you to post five questions, you need to add one more form. The controls you need to add to the mobile Web form are given in Table 34-9.

Table 34-9 Properties Assigned to the Controls on the Sixth Form

Control	Property	Value
Label1	ID	LblQuestion5Stem
Label1	Text	The largest ocean in the world is:
SelectionList	SelectType	Radio
SelectionList	ID	RdForm6
SelectionList	Collection	Pacific
SelectionList	Collection	Atlantic
SelectionList	Collection	Indian

Control	Property	Value
SelectionList	Collection	Arctic
Button	ID	CmdForm6
Button	Text	Submit
Button	Alignment	Center

Compare your form with Figure 34-11.

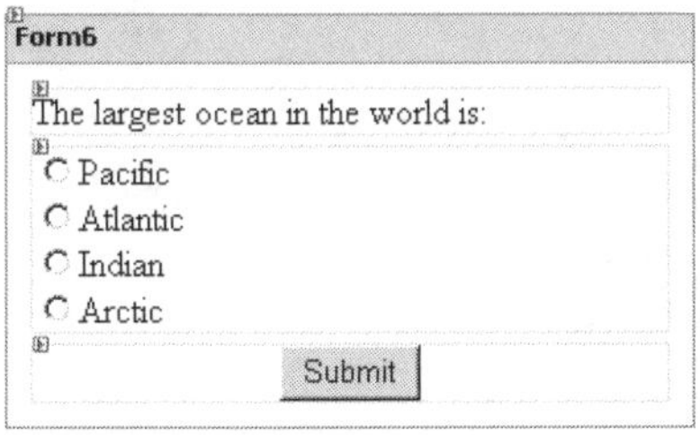

FIGURE 34-11 *The design of the sixth form for the application*

Next add the following code for the `Click` event of the `CmdForm6` button:

```
Private Sub CmdForm6_Click(ByVal sender As System.Object, ByVal e As
System.EventArgs) Handles
CmdForm6.Click
    If RdForm6.SelectedIndex = 1 Then
            Session("Score") = Session("Score") + 10
    End If
End Sub
```

To complete the application, you now need to create a form that displays the user's name and score as well as the highest score attained for the quiz. To do so, create a new form and drag two labels and a button to the mobile Web form. Change the ID of the labels to `LblDisplay`, `LblDisplay1` and the ID of the button to `CmdStartAgain`. Change the `Text` property of the button to `Start Again`.

Compare your form with Figure 34-12.

Now let's add the code to check whether the score of the current user is higher than the score of the user with the current highest score. If the score is more than

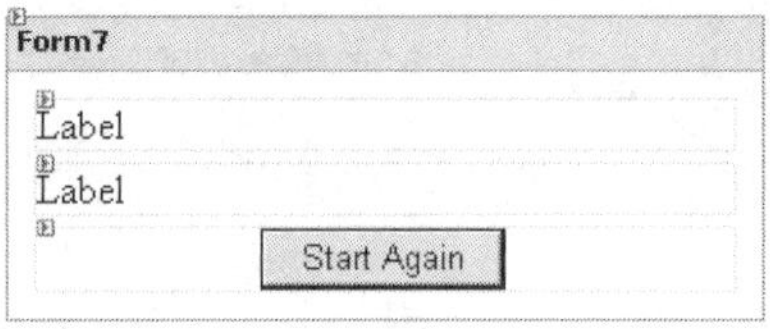

FIGURE 34-12 *The design of the seventh form for the application*

the current highest score, you'll update the score and the name in the UserRecord table. To connect to the database, drag a SQL Connection control to the mobile Web form and then, in the Properties window, specify the connection string. Test the connection to make sure the connection is established with the database that stores the UserRecord table.

The code to retrieve the highest score and the name of the user with the highest score is given below. Add the following code in the Click event of the button of the sixth form. Note, however, that you need to add this code beneath the code you added in the previous section.

```
Dim Score As Integer
Dim sqlAdapter As SqlClient.SqlDataAdapter
Dim lstrSql As String
Dim Dataset As New DataSet()
Dim MaxScore As Integer
Dim UserName  As String
lstrSql = "Select UserName , MaxScore from Userrecord where MaxScore = (select
max(MaxScore) from UserRecord)"
sqlAdapter = New SqlClient.SqlDataAdapter(lstrSql, SqlConnection1)
sqlAdapter.Fill(DataSet)
MaxScore = DataSet.Tables(0).Rows(0).Item(0)
UserName  = DataSet.Tables(0).Rows(0).Item(1)
If Score > MaxScore Then
        Dim commandbld As New SqlClient.SqlCommandBuilder(sqlAdapter)
        DataSet.Tables(0).Rows(0).Item(0) = Score
        DataSet.Tables(0).Rows(0).Item(1) = Session("UserName ")
        sqlAdapter.Update(DataSet)
        UserName  = Session("UserName ")
        commandbld.Dispose()
End If
```

```
        LblDisplay.Text = "Hi  " + Session("UserName").ToString + "your score is " +
Session("Score").ToString
        LblDisplay1.Text = "The highest score in this quiz was scored by " +
UserName .ToString
        SqlConnection1.Close()
        sqlAdapter.Dispose()
        ActiveForm = Form7
End Sub
```

All you need to do now is add the code for the button of Form7. In the `Click` event of the `Start Again` button, add the following code:

```
Private Sub StartAgainButton_Click(ByVal sender As Object, ByVal e As
System.EventArgs) Handles
StartAgainButton.Click
        ActiveForm = Form1
End Sub
```

Your application is now ready. Let's test it to make sure it functions the way you want it to. While creating a mobile Web application, viewing the output in a browser window is helpful in debugging. However, you probably would also like to test the application on a mobile device. Fortunately, you do not require a mobile phone or a handheld PC to test your application. Instead, you can test your mobile Web application in a mobile-like environment by using a WAP device emulator. In this book, the Microsoft Mobile Explorer 3.0 Emulator (MME Emulator) is used. This emulator acts like a mobile phone that runs the Microsoft Mobile Explorer microbrowser.

Testing a Mobile Web Application

When you build and run the application, the output is displayed by default in Internet Explorer. To test the application in MME Emulator, do the following:

1. Choose View, Mobile Explorer Browser, Show Browser.
2. Type the address in the Address box of the emulator and then press Enter.

The output of the page appears as shown in Figure 34-13.

FIGURE 34-13 *The main form in the MME Emulator*

When you navigate to the next page, it is displayed as shown in Figure 34-14.

Now that you have learned about the code that enables the mobile Web application to function, I'll provide the complete code of the MobileWeb.aspx and MobileWeb.aspx.vb pages of the application. Listing 34-1 provides the code of the MobileWeb.aspx page.

Listing 34-1 MobileWeb.aspx

```
Public Class MobileWebForm1
    Inherits System.Web.UI.MobileControls.MobilePage
    Protected WithEvents LblWelcomeMsg As System.Web.UI.MobileControls.Label
    Protected WithEvents LblName As System.Web.UI.MobileControls.Label
    Protected WithEvents TxtEnterName As System.Web.UI.MobileControls.TextBox
    Protected WithEvents RequiredFieldValidator1 As
System.Web.UI.MobileControls.RequiredFieldValidator
    Protected WithEvents BtnStart As System.Web.UI.MobileControls.Command
    Protected WithEvents Form2 As System.Web.UI.MobileControls.Form
```

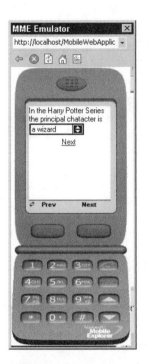

FIGURE 34-14 *The second form in the MME Emulator*

```
Protected WithEvents LblQuestion1Stem As System.Web.UI.MobileControls.Label
Protected WithEvents RdForm2 As System.Web.UI.MobileControls.SelectionList
Protected WithEvents CmdForm2 As System.Web.UI.MobileControls.Command
Protected WithEvents Form3 As System.Web.UI.MobileControls.Form
Protected WithEvents LblQuestion2Stem As System.Web.UI.MobileControls.Label
Protected WithEvents RdForm3 As System.Web.UI.MobileControls.SelectionList
Protected WithEvents CmdForm3 As System.Web.UI.MobileControls.Command
Protected WithEvents Form4 As System.Web.UI.MobileControls.Form
Protected WithEvents LblQuestion3stem As System.Web.UI.MobileControls.Label
Protected WithEvents RdForm4 As System.Web.UI.MobileControls.SelectionList
Protected WithEvents CmdForm4 As System.Web.UI.MobileControls.Command
Protected WithEvents Form5 As System.Web.UI.MobileControls.Form
Protected WithEvents LblQuestion4Stem As System.Web.UI.MobileControls.Label
Protected WithEvents RdForm5 As System.Web.UI.MobileControls.SelectionList
Protected WithEvents CmdForm5 As System.Web.UI.MobileControls.Command
Protected WithEvents Form6 As System.Web.UI.MobileControls.Form
Protected WithEvents LblQuestion5Stem As System.Web.UI.MobileControls.Label
```

```
        Protected WithEvents RdForm6 As System.Web.UI.MobileControls.SelectionList
        Protected WithEvents CmdForm6 As System.Web.UI.MobileControls.Command
        Protected WithEvents Form7 As System.Web.UI.MobileControls.Form
        Protected WithEvents LblDisplay As System.Web.UI.MobileControls.Label
        Protected WithEvents LblDisplay1 As System.Web.UI.MobileControls.Label
        Protected WithEvents CmdStartAgain As System.Web.UI.MobileControls.Command
        Protected WithEvents SqlConnection1 As System.Data.SqlClient.SqlConnection
        Protected WithEvents Form1 As System.Web.UI.MobileControls.Form
#Region " Web Form Designer Generated Code "
    'This call is required by the Web Form Designer.
    <System.Diagnostics.DebuggerStepThrough()> Private Sub InitializeComponent()
        Me.SqlConnection1 = New System.Data.SqlClient.SqlConnection()
        'SqlConnection1
        Me.SqlConnection1.ConnectionString = "data source=VEERABH-D190;initial
        catalog=master;integrated security=SSPI;persist " & _
        "security info=False;workstation id=VEERABH-D190;packet size=4096"
    End Sub
    Private Sub Page_Init(ByVal sender As System.Object, ByVal e As
System.EventArgs) Handles
    MyBase.Init
        'CODEGEN: This method call is required by the Web Form Designer
        'Do not modify it using the code editor.
        InitializeComponent()
    End Sub
#End Region
    Private Sub Page_Load(ByVal sender As System.Object, ByVal e As
System.EventArgs) Handles
    MyBase.Load
        'Put user code to initialize the page here
    End Sub
    Private Sub BtnStart_Click(ByVal sender As System.Object, ByVal e As
System.EventArgs) Handles
    BtnStart.Click
        If Page.IsValid Then
            Session("UserName") = TxtEnterName.Text
            ActiveForm = Form2
        End If
    End Sub
```

```
    Private Sub CmdForm2_Click(ByVal sender As System.Object, ByVal e As
System.EventArgs) Handles
    CmdForm2.Click
        'code to calculate the score and move to the next form
        If RdForm2.SelectedIndex = 0  Then
            Session("Score") = 10
        Else
            Session("Score") = 0
        End If
        ActiveForm = Form3
    End Sub
    Private Sub CmdForm3_Click(ByVal sender As System.Object, ByVal e As
System.EventArgs) Handles
    CmdForm3.Click
        If RdForm3.SelectedIndex = 1 Then
            Session("Score") = Session("Score") + 10
        End If
        ActiveForm = form4
    End Sub
    Private Sub CmdForm4_Click(ByVal sender As System.Object, ByVal e As
System.EventArgs) Handles
  CmdForm4.Click
        If RdForm4.SelectedIndex = 0 Then
            Session("Score") = Session("Score") + 10
        End If
        ActiveForm = form5
    End Sub
    Private Sub CmdForm5_Click(ByVal sender As System.Object, ByVal e As
System.EventArgs) Handles
    CmdForm5.Click
        If RdForm5.SelectedIndex = 0 Then
            Session("Score") = Session("Score") + 10
        End If
        ActiveForm = Form6
    End Sub
    Private Sub CmdForm6_Click(ByVal sender As System.Object, ByVal e As
System.EventArgs) Handles CmdForm6.Click
        If RdForm6.SelectedIndex = 1 Then
```

```
            Session("Score") = Session("Score") + 10
        End If
        Dim Score As Integer
        Dim sqlAdapter As SqlClient.SqlDataAdapter
        Dim lstrSql As String
        Dim Dataset As New DataSet()
        Dim MaxScore As Integer
        Dim UserName As String
        lstrSql = "Select UserName, MaxScore from UserRecord where MaxScore =
(select max(MaxScore)
        from UserRecord)"
        sqlAdapter = New SqlClient.SqlDataAdapter(lstrSql, SqlConnection1)
        sqlAdapter.Fill(Dataset)
        MaxScore = Dataset.Tables(0).Rows(0).Item(0)
        UserName = Dataset.Tables(0).Rows(0).Item(1)
        If Score > MaxScore Then
            Dim commandbld As New SqlClient.SqlCommandBuilder(sqlAdapter)
            Dataset.Tables(0).Rows(0).Item(0) = Score
            Dataset.Tables(0).Rows(0).Item(1) = Session("UserName")
            sqlAdapter.Update(Dataset)
            UserName = Session("UserName")
            commandbld.Dispose()
        End If
        LblDisplay.Text = "Hi  " + Session ("UserName").ToString + "your score is " +
        Session("Score").ToString
        LblDisplay1.Text = "The highest score in this quiz was scored by " +
UserName .ToString
        SqlConnection1.Close()
        sqlAdapter.Dispose()
        ActiveForm = Form7
    End Sub
End Class
```

Listing 34-2 provides the code of the MobileWeb.aspx.vb page.

Listing 34-2 MobileWeb.aspx.vb

```
<%@ Register TagPrefix="mobile" Namespace="System.Web.UI.MobileControls"
Assembly="System.Web.Mobile, Version=1.0.3300.0, Culture=neutral,
PublicKeyToken=b03f5f7f11d50a3a" %>
<%@ Page Language="vb" AutoEventWireup="false" Codebehind="MobileWebForm1.aspx.vb"
Inherits="Mobile_Web_Application.MobileWebForm1" %>
<meta name="GENERATOR" content="Microsoft Visual Studio.NET 7.0">
<meta name="CODE_LANGUAGE" content="Visual Basic 7.0">
<meta name="vs_targetSchema" content="http://schemas.microsoft.com/Mobile/Page">
<body Xmlns:mobile="http://schemas.microsoft.com/Mobile/WebForm">
                <mobile:Form id="Form1" runat="server">
                <mobile:Label id="LblWelcomeMsg" runat="server" Font-Name="Comic
Sans MS"
                Alignment="Center" ForeColor="Navy">Welcome to today's
quiz</mobile:Label>
                <mobile:Label id="LblName" runat="server">Please enter your
name</mobile:Label>
                <mobile:TextBox id="TxtEnterName" runat="server"></mobile:TextBox>
                <mobile:RequiredFieldValidator id="RequiredFieldValidator1"
runat="server"
                ErrorMessage="Please
                enter your name"
ControlToValidate="TxtEnterName"></mobile:RequiredFieldValidator>
                <mobile:Command id="BtnStart" runat="server"
Alignment="Center">Start</mobile:Command>
                </mobile:Form>
                <mobile:Form id="Form2" runat="server">
                <mobile:Label id="LblQuestion1Stem" runat="server">In the Harry
Potter series the principal
                character is:</mobile:Label>
                <mobile:SelectionList id="RdForm2" runat="server" SelectType="Radio">
                <Item Value="a wizard" Text="a wizard"></Item>
                <Item Value="a gold smith" Text="a gold smith"></Item>
                <Item Value="a shoemaker" Text="a shoemaker" </Item>
                <Item Value="a barber" Text=" a barber "></Item>
                </mobile:SelectionList>
```

```
<mobile:Command id="CmdForm2" runat="server"
Alignment="Center">Next</mobile:Command>
</mobile:Form>
<mobile:Form id="Form3" runat="server">
<mobile:Label id="LblQuestion2Stem" runat="server">Tenzing Norgay and
__ were the first
people to climb Mt.Everest</mobile:Label>
<mobile:SelectionList id="RdForm3" runat="server" SelectType="Radio">
<Item Value="John Hillary" Text="John Hillary"></Item>
<Item Value="Edmund Hillary" Text="Edmund Hillary"></Item>
<Item Value="Tim Smith" Text="Tim Smith"></Item>
<Item Value="Aldrin Alwyn" Text="Aldrin Alwyn"></Item>
</mobile:SelectionList>
<mobile:Command id="CmdForm3" runat="server"
Alignment="Center">Next</mobile:Command>
</mobile:Form>
<mobile:Form id="Form4" runat="server">
<mobile:Label id="LblQuestion3stem" runat="server">Margaret
Thatcher was the Prime Minister of
which country?</mobile:Label>
<mobile:SelectionList id="RdForm4" runat="server"
SelectType="Radio">
<Item Value="Britain" Text="Britain"></Item>
<Item Value="Sri Lanka" Text="Sri Lanka"></Item>
<Item Value="India" Text="India"></Item>
<Item Value="Australia" Text="Australia"></Item>
</mobile:SelectionList>
<mobile:Command id="CmdForm4" runat="server"
Alignment="Center">Next</mobile:Command>
</mobile:Form>
<mobile:Form id="Form5" runat="server">
<mobile:Label id="LblQuestion4Stem" runat="server">Who created the
cartoon character
Goofy?</mobile:Label>
<mobile:SelectionList id="RdForm5" runat="server" SelectType="Radio">
<Item Value="Walt Disney" Text="Walt Disney"></Item>
```

```
                <Item Value="Mickey Mouse" Text="Mickey Mouse"></Item>
                <Item Value="Tim Matthew" Text="Tim Matthew"></Item>
                </mobile:SelectionList>
                <mobile:Command id="CmdForm5" runat="server"
                Alignment="Center">Next</mobile:Command>
                </mobile:Form>
                <mobile:Form id="Form6" runat="server">
                <mobile:Label id="LblQuestion5Stem" runat="server">The largest
ocean in the world
                is:</mobile:Label>
                <mobile:SelectionList id="RdForm6" runat="server" SelectType="Radio">
                <Item Value="Pacific" Text="Pacific"></Item>
                <Item Value="Atlantic" Text="Atlantic"></Item>
                <Item Value="Indian" Text="Indian"></Item>
                <Item Value="Arctic" Text="Arctic"></Item>
                </mobile:SelectionList>
                <mobile:Command id="CmdForm6" runat="server"
                Alignment="Center">Submit</mobile:Command>
                </mobile:Form>
                <mobile:Form id="Form7" runat="server">
                <mobile:Label id="LblDisplay" runat="server">Label</mobile:Label>
                <mobile:Label id="LblDisplay1" runat="server">Label</mobile:Label>
                <mobile:Command id="CmdStartAgain" runat="server"
Alignment="Center">Start
                Again</mobile:Command>
                </mobile:Form>
</body>
```

These sample files (MobileWeb.aspx and MobileWeb.aspx.vb) are included at the Web site **www.premierpressbooks.com/downloads.asp**.

Summary

In this chapter, you learned how to design the forms used by the mobile Web application. You also learned about the working of the application. Then you learned about the code attached to the various controls on the forms. Next you learned how the connection to the database is established and how the data retrieved from the database is displayed to the users. Finally, you learned how to use the MME Emulator to test your mobile Web application.

PART VII

Appendixes

Appendix A

**.NET Vision
and Goals**

The world of computing is moving fast toward the Web. Businesses today operate on varied technologies and platforms. The need of the hour is a uniform base on which businesses can operate and developers can develop. The uniform base will enable developers to work on independent platforms and, at the same time, not bother about compatibility with other systems. Also, platforms that fully integrate with the Internet will provide businesses with an opportunity they never had before. Microsoft kept in mind these growing needs for the computer community when designing the .NET framework. This appendix will discuss the vision of the .NET framework and the design goals for developing effective business solutions using the .NET platform.

The .NET Vision

The .NET initiative aims to address the challenge facing organizations by combining an architectural vision with a complete set of Microsoft technologies. Application architects use these technologies to develop, deploy, and support multitier, distributed applications. The vision of the .NET initiative is to provide a highly integrated but flexible platform to enable developers to build end-to-end business solutions that can leverage existing architectures and applications.

The Windows DNA architecture aimed at building tightly coupled, distributed Web applications. However, as the requirements for distributed applications moved toward more loosely coupled principles, the Microsoft .NET architecture evolved.

The Philosophy of .NET

The .NET philosophy is aimed at providing a logical approach for developing successful business solutions. This philosophy intends to provide developers with the ability to develop flexible and scalable applications. The key principle of creating distributed applications with the .NET framework is to logically partition an application into three fundamental tiers or layers:

- ◆ The presentation layer
- ◆ The business logic layer
- ◆ The data access and storage layer

By partitioning applications along these lines, using component-based programming techniques, and fully utilizing the features of the .NET framework, developers can now build highly scalable and flexible applications and thus create successful business solutions.

A simple application model consists of a client (the presentation layer) that communicates with the middle tier. The middle tier (the business logic layer) consists of the application server and an application containing the business logic. The application, in turn, communicates with a database that supplies and stores data (the data access and storage layer).

The next few sections discuss these elements in more detail, starting with the presentation layer.

The Presentation Layer

The presentation layer consists of either a rich-client or thin-client interface to an application. The rich-client interface provides a full programming interface to the operating system's capabilities and uses components extensively, either directly by using the Microsoft Win32 API or indirectly through Windows forms. Using a thin-client interface (such as a Web browser), a developer can build business logic that can be executed on any of the three application tiers. With the features that the .NET framework provides, the thin client is able to provide a visually rich, flexible, and interactive user interface to applications. Thin clients are also more portable across platforms.

The Business Logic/Application Layer

The business logic layer, also called the application layer, is divided into application servers and services that support clients. Web applications can be written to take advantage of COM+ services, directory services, and security services using the .NET framework. Application services, in turn, can interact with several data services on the data access layer.

The Data Access and Storage

This layer consists of data services that support data access and storage. The common data access services include:

- *ADO.NET.* Provides a simplified programmatic access to data by using either scripting or programming languages
- *OLE DB.* An established universal data provider
- *XML.* A markup standard for specifying data structures.

Advantages of the .NET Framework

By adopting the .NET framework's distributed application model, developers can derive many advantages. The .NET framework offers a lot more than the ancestral programming languages and platforms. The .NET framework provides developers with the following:

- A rich programming framework for building Win32 client applications
- A unified Web development platform that provides the services necessary for developers to build enterprise-class Web applications
- A URL-addressable resource that programmatically returns information to clients who have requested it
- The ability to build components that efficiently manage data from multiple data sources and that support disconnected scenarios
- Standards-based support for processing XML
- The ability to interact with COM components, .NET framework services, external type libraries, and many operating system services
- Control access to operations and resources based on policy and a set of configurable rules to determine which permissions to grant to code, based on the code's domain, user, and assembly
- The ability to pass objects by value or by reference between distributed applications.
- A programming interface to many of the protocols found on the network, such as HTTP, DNS, TCP, and UDP.
- The ability to use the COM+ Services, including transactions, object pooling, and queued components

- ◆ Access to the Active Directory from managed code
- ◆ Lower total cost of ownership by enabling powerful enterprise-class management of systems, applications, and devices
- ◆ Support for globalization and localization of resources

Let's now discuss the shift in the .NET framework architecture, its causes, and its impact on the computer community.

The Architectural Shift in .NET

Ever since the computing mainstream moved toward Internet technologies, business-computing models changed dramatically. This change was based on a complex, costly, and often-proprietary model called the client/server computing model. This was the revolutionary Web model.

You can characterize the Web model as a collection of diverse information and applications that reside on varied hardware platforms. Since the inception of the Internet, constantly occupying the minds of the developer community has been the desire to provide a common information-delivery platform that is scalable, extensible, and highly available. The Web platform is flexible and limited by only the computer capacity and the imagination of the application designer.

As the Web browser rapidly became omnipresent and Web servers proliferated throughout companies, it was clear—despite the best efforts of client/server software producers to Web-enable their products—that developers needed a radically different way of thinking about the application model. Obviously, new techniques and tools were required to meet the technology shifts and challenges facing developers. The next section discusses these technology shifts and the developer challenges.

Technology Shifts and Developer Challenges

Once the Internet revolution took hold and new technologies appeared, developers faced several challenges that existing design models and tools could not adequately address. The following issues were central to the developers' dilemma:

◆ *Heterogeneous environments.* One of the earliest, and perhaps biggest, challenges was the need to build applications that could easily integrate heterogeneous environments. Most large organizations had a diverse range of terminals, rich clients, and thin (Web) clients. In addition to accommodating the large client base, new applications had to interact with legacy data and applications hosted on mainframe and midrange computers, often from different hardware vendors.

◆ *Scalability.* Before Internet technologies overwhelmed the computer community, the computing environment was a closed system due to the limitations in resources and access requirements. Scalability was, therefore, an issue that was easy to manage because strategists had ample historical data on which to base their projections for scaling the computing environment to match consumer demand. Also, the application development life cycle typically spanned several years, thus providing planners with ample time to plan for system and application scaling. However, the influx of the Internet altered the corporate mindset significantly. Organizations viewed this new technology as an ideal, low-cost method for sharing information throughout the organization. Along with these advantages, organizations realized the challenges. The new design paradigm required system designs to accommodate a user-base size from less than one hundred to more than one million. The traditional foundation for scalability planning crumbled when companies opened their doors to the outside world.

◆ *Rapid application development and deployment.* The intranet and Internet phenomena highlighted the possibility of, and need for, rapid application deployment. As a result, the viability of the traditional development platform and processes were questioned. Organizations were not prepared to wait for years to be able to use an application. From an investment perspective, the business community questioned any investment in applications that would be legacy systems by the time they were completed. The concept of rapid application development changed even further as organizations expanded their application horizon from the intranet to the Internet. To be competitive, developers needed to create applications virtually on demand for immediate use—just-in-time (JIT) development. To achieve this, they needed to completely revamp and revitalize their approach to application development.

◆ *Platform administration and management.* It did not take long for professionals to realize that the Internet world was far from perfect. Professionals soon discovered that the freedom and flexibility brought a completely new set of administration and management issues that revolved around clients, applications, and hosts. The browser, for one, did not have an industry standard, and from a development perspective, the lack of standardization meant that application designers had to accommodate the HTML-rendering capabilities of each browser version separately. Application deployment was even more difficult to manage because system administrators had to contend with large numbers of content providers rather than a single developer group. Dynamic and data-driven content on the Web sites made management even more difficult due to the existence of diverse data stores and different scripting languages, and so did the users' expectations of 24-hour/7-day-a-week uninterrupted access.

◆ *Network-aware applications.* Advances in portable computing technology and the decline in cost for portable computers—such as laptops, notebooks, and palmtops—put the final nail in the coffin for Web application developers. Mobile computing evolved at an unprecedented rate. Developers no longer had the liberty to distinguish between offline and online usage because the user community expected to be able to use applications and services at all times.

All these challenges posed problems that the developer community needed solutions to. The .NET framework guided application developers to be able to create well-designed applications to overcome the challenges posed by the traditional development platforms. Precise goals for the design phase of the application development life cycle were defined to provide a direction to developers. The following section will talk about the design goals of the .NET framework.

.NET Framework Design Goals

During the design phase of an application, design goals are established. The following aspects of application development were kept in mind to meet the design goals:

- ◆ *Availability:* Is the application to be present and ready for use?
- ◆ *Manageability:* Can the application be administered?
- ◆ *Performance:* What is the measure of an application's operation under load?
- ◆ *Reliability:* Is the application able to perform in a predictable manner?
- ◆ *Scalability:* Can the application match increasing demand with an increase in resources?
- ◆ *Securability:* Is the application ready to protect its resources?

The following sections discuss each of these aspects in detail and discuss how the .NET framework supports application development with these design goals in mind.

Availability

All applications must be available at least some of the time, but Web-based applications and mission-critical enterprise applications typically must provide round-the-clock services. If your enterprise application needs to work round-the-clock, you need to design your application for high availability. Availability refers to the uptime for your applications and the amount of time your applications are available for use. Advances in hardware and software have dramatically increased the quality of high-availability applications. However, availability is not easy to implement and requires a considerably more complex architectural infrastructure than the previous generations of client/server applications.

Companies that increasingly rely on Web-based, distributed applications for important business activity need a range of availability engineering options to meet service-level requirements in a cost-effective manner. Web-based applications usually depend on multiple servers, perhaps hundreds or thousands of client workstations, internal and external network communications, database services, operational processes, and a host of other infrastructure services that must work uniformly together. Where the business ideal is a continuous flow of information, creating high-availability applications becomes an important business strategy.

Realistically, not all applications require 100% uptime. However, some applications must provide very high availability with virtually no perceivable downtime. Application failures occur for many reasons, including the following:

- Lack of stable software engineering processes
- Weak code
- Inadequate testing
- Change management problems
- Lack of constant monitoring and analysis
- Interaction with external services or applications
- Different operating conditions such as usage-level changes and peak overloads
- Unusual events such as security failures and broadcast storms
- Hardware failures such as disks, controllers, network devices, servers, power supplies, memory, and CPU failures
- Natural disasters

If applications fail as a result of natural disasters, there's not much you can do. However, such causes for application failures are pretty rare as compared to the causes you can prevent—they account for just about 10% of the total application downtime. The other 90% of application downtime is a combined result of inadequate testing, change management problems, lack of ongoing failure monitoring and rigorous procedures, and backup/restoration errors.

The application downtime obviously includes the amount of time necessary for repairs because applications being repaired are not available for use. Availability is commonly expressed as a percentage, such as 99% availability.

What might surprise you is the fact that 99% availability is not too great by industry standards. In fact, if your application is 99% available, it is actually down for 88 hours in a year. Similar calculations disclose that 99.9% availability means 8.5 hours of downtime per year, and 99.99% availability means a downtime of 1 hour per year. As per industry standards, it is common for enterprise applications to have 99.9% availability.

As you move towards greater availability, however, you face greater challenges in the form of the following:

- Increasing hardware costs for the application due to server, network, and disk redundancy
- Greater difficulty in identifying and eliminating complex failures

◆ Growing requirements for comprehensive testing of every automatic and people-based procedure that might affect your application

Choosing the right hardware and software technology infrastructure certainly helps the high-availability cause. Also, high levels of availability are not possible without a serious commitment to skilled personnel, quality life-cycle processes, and operational excellence.

Planning Availability Levels

Determining the satisfactory availability levels for your requirements is never easy. Not only is it difficult to estimate the actual required availability that satisfies your anticipated business requirements and also meets budget and schedule expectations, the usage pattern and running environment of software can change over time. The original availability assumptions might change and, as a result, require reconsideration of the original availability plans.

In deciding what level of availability is appropriate for your application, you need to answer a few questions:

◆ Who are the customers, and what are their expectations?

◆ How much downtime is acceptable?

◆ Do internal company processes depend on the service?

◆ What is the schedule and budget?

A project's schedules and budget should not conflict with a requirement for business- or mission-critical availability. Although it is tempting to build and deploy a less-than-perfect version of your application, don't do it. The cost of round-the-clock maintenance hassles and lost customers isn't worth it. If you must implement a high-availability application and the budget and schedules aren't viable, the right thing to is to retarget the scope of the project and get the appropriate funding.

Designing for availability poses difficult challenges. Because of the wide variety of application architectures, no single availability solution works for every situation. The decision to deploy a comprehensive, fault-tolerant, fully redundant, load-balanced solution may be appropriate for high-volume, online-transaction processing. On the other hand, some applications can accept modest downtime with little consequence to the customers. Ultimately, such design decisions depend on a combination of business requirements, application-specific data, and the available budget.

The main technique for increasing availability is redundancy. For example, you might take a close look at your application's architecture and decide to implement full redundancy including cloned front-end servers, redundant network infrastructure, and cloned backend servers.

Designing for Availability

Engineering your applications for availability is all about doing your best to create reliable applications. You must also be ready to accept the fact that your application will probably fail sometimes. So you must design quick-recovery mechanisms to minimize downtime.

Some design ideas for generating highly available applications are listed here. However, you must not forget the basic requirements of having tested and proven life-cycle processes, trained staff, and a rigorous commitment to availability.

◆ Avoid older, traditional approaches to availability, such as multiple CPUs and a duplicated system with fully replicated components. These approaches have several drawbacks.

◆ Reduce unplanned downtime with clustering. Cluster service with a shared disk avoids most downtime and provides automatic recovery from hardware or software failures.

◆ Use network load balancing to redefine clusters and redirect traffic to other servers when there are failures.

◆ Use RAID for data stores to use multiple hard disks so that data is stored in multiple places.

◆ Reduce planned downtime by using rolling upgrades available with Windows 2000 Advanced Server.

◆ Isolate mission-critical applications. Eliminate data and system dependencies by using separate physical backbones for each in the case of mission-critical applications.

◆ Use queuing to enable your application to communicate with other applications by sending and receiving asynchronous messages.

◆ Use the distributed file system (DFS) to resolve drive letters to UNC names to provide real file nomenclatures.

Testing for Availability

Testing for availability means running an application for a planned period of time, collecting failure events and repair times, and comparing the availability percentage to the original estimate.

Some testing concepts that can help you create long-term applications are as follows:

- Test the change control process.
- Test catastrophic failure and recover technologies.
- Test the failover technologies.
- Test the monitoring technology.
- Test the help desk procedures.
- Test for resource conflicts.

Best Practices for Availability

The following best practices are recommended for creating applications with high-availability:

- Use clustering.
- Use network load balancing.
- Use service-level agreements.
- Provide vigilant monitoring.
- Establish a help desk to reduce downtime.
- Test the recovery plan.
- Choose good infrastructure.
- Synchronize all clocks.
- Use data backups.
- Review all security plans.
- Advocate training and certification.
- Pay attention to the budget.

Manageability

Managing distributed applications can be a whole new experience as compared to managing traditional, standalone applications because distributed Web-based applications pose an interesting problem. Managing an enterprise application contributes highly to the total cost of ownership, but to minimize operation and management costs, you want the cost of ongoing application administration to decrease. This is a dilemma that emerging technologies have brought with them. As a solution, you need an efficient way to deploy, configure, upgrade, and monitor all local and remote components and services of your distributed application.

Managing a modern .NET application requires an efficient way to handle local and remote application support processes, including the following:

◆ Initial deployment

◆ Configuration tuning

◆ Scheduled and unscheduled maintenance

◆ Frequent health checks

◆ Occasional troubleshooting

Designing for Manageability

Manageability for an enterprise-scale application should include some efficient way to handle common administrative tasks such as local and remote installation, configuration changes, and maintenance updates over the lifetime of the application. Generally, designing manageable distributed applications requires three design features:

◆ *Management agents.* Each hardware device, operating system service, and application service requires a management agent. Management agents monitor the local resource, publish data about the resource's current state and performance, and provide local configuration services as a way to make remote management possible.

◆ *The collection process.* The information collection process collects, filters, correlates, and stores information from all of the management agents.

◆ *The management console.* The management console workstation aggregates and reports on application-management information. From this central console, an administrator can monitor all devices, analyze operational profiles, automate certain recurring activities, receive notifications from managed elements, and initiate remote configuration changes.

In addition to a sound design, you also need to collate application information over the application's lifetime to ensure constant manageability.

Testing for Manageability

Testing for manageability is about making sure the deployment, maintenance, and monitoring technologies you have designed into your application are working as expected. The following are some important testing recommendations for verifying that you have created a manageable application:

◆ Test cluster configuration.

◆ Test network load balancing.

◆ Test application synchronization.

◆ Test change control procedures.

Performance

Common application metrics, such as transaction throughput and resource utilization, define application performance. Network throughput and disk access are common application-performance bottlenecks. From a user's perspective, application response time defines performance. You'll often find yourself at a crossroad, however, where one path leads you to high-performing applications, and the other leads to cost control. You must take your pick intelligently.

Performance problems typically do not become apparent until testers place an application under an increased load. However, the responsibility for application performance is important both at design time and at runtime.

At design time, developers must avoid using code that could hinder the application's performance. Developers can follow accepted programming practices and take advantage of the inherent performance-enhancing capabilities of the programming language.

At runtime, the application should undergo extensive performance testing to identify application bottlenecks such as contention for resources or slow-running code. However, before conducting extensive performance tests, make sure the application is functionally sound.

Designing for Performance

It is imperative that you define performance requirements before you start development and debugging. You must do the following before you start developing your application:

- Identify project constraints such as schedules or the choice of tools and technologies you can use.
- Determine services that the application will perform, including performance scenarios, database access, and other services.
- Specify the load on the application, such as the number of clients that will use this application and how much time elapses between the response and request chain.

You can then use this information to select appropriate metrics and determine specific performance goals.

Testing for Performance

After you've identified specific performance requirements and have developed your application, you can begin testing to determine whether the application meets those requirements. Performance monitoring is primarily a collection of the following related activities:

- Measuring performance
- Defining performance tests
- Determining baseline performance
- Stress testing
- Solving performance problems

Reliability

Reliability is all about an application's ability to operate failure free. As distributed Web-based applications continue to influence everything from your customer's experience to your relationship with vendors, there is an increasing need to improve the reliability and operating quality of software, primarily for the following reasons:

- The cost of application failure is high.
- The expense of repairing corrupted data is high.

◆ Users bypass unreliable Web sites, resulting in lost revenue and reduced future sales.

◆ Unreliable systems are difficult to maintain and improve because the failure points typically are hidden throughout the system.

◆ Modern software technology makes it easy to create reliable applications.

Designing for Reliability

The process of designing applications for reliability involves estimating the application's expected usage pattern, specifying the required reliability profile, and engineering the software architecture with the intention of meeting the profile. Good reliability designs typically do the following:

◆ Put reliability requirements in the design specification

◆ Use good architectural infrastructure

◆ Build management information into the application

◆ Use redundancy for reliability

◆ Use quality development tools

◆ Use built-in application health checks

◆ Use consistent error handling

Testing for Reliability

Testing for reliability is about exercising an application so that failures are discovered and removed before the system is deployed. It is no doubt difficult to identify all potential problems, but you should aim at identifying as many as you can by estimating various usage scenarios.

The following are important testing strategies:

◆ Component stress testing

◆ Integration stress testing

◆ Real-world testing

◆ Random destruction testing

Best Practices for Reliability

For creating and deploying reliable applications, it is important for you to keep reliability as a foremost concern throughout the application-development life cycle. The following are some best practices for reliable application development:

◆ Invest in people.

◆ Use a robust operating system.

◆ Remove failure points from your application design.

◆ Provide ongoing reliability monitoring.

◆ Invest in quality software-engineering processes.

◆ Use smart testing.

◆ Deploy changes very carefully.

Scalability

Scalability is the capability to add resources to an application to produce an equivalent increase in service capacity. Scalability must be part of the design process because it is not a discrete feature you can add later.

Designing for Scalability

The design of an application has the greatest impact on its scalability. Smart designs can greatly improve the scalability of applications. Other factors that influence scalability, though on a lesser scale, include hardware, software, and code. The primary goal when designing for scalability is to ensure efficient resource management.

To design applications for high scalability, keep the following design aspects in mind:

◆ The application must not have to wait any more than is absolutely necessary for using vital resources.

◆ The application must not have to contend for resources—such as memory, processor, and bandwidth—with other applications.

◆ The application must be designed for commutability; operations should be able to be applied in any order to achieve the same results.

◆ The application must be designed for interchangeability by using resource pooling with technologies such as COM+ and ODBC connections.

◆ The relationship between resources and activities must be minimized to avoid bottlenecks.

Testing for Scalability

To make a truly scalable application, it is critical that you rigorously and regularly test it for scalability problems. The purpose of scalability testing is to identify major workloads and mitigate bottlenecks that can impede the scalability of the application.

If your application does not meet performance requirements, you should analyze data from the test results to identify bottlenecks in the system and to determine a cause. You can also identify bottlenecks using tools such as Windows Task Manager, Windows Performance Monitor, and the Component Services administrative tool. You can often alleviate bottlenecks through performance tuning.

Securability

Securability is the ability to provide security to an application and its data. Security is about controlling access to a variety of resources such as application components, data, and hardware. The securability of an application is impacted by numerous design choices such as the selection of communication protocols and the method of user authentication.

Designing for Securability

Security is an issue that can affect your application—and consequently you—every day. New security threats emerge daily. The following are some guidelines to help you design secure applications:

◆ Analyze the impending threats. Threats could include spoofing identity, tampering with data, repudiability, information disclosure, denial of service, and elevation of privilege.

◆ Prioritize threats based on the criticality, the effort involved in eliminating the threat, and the potential damage to your application.

◆ Apply available security policies to your application.

- Select appropriate and applicable security technologies based on the type of threats.
- Design security services that your application must support.

Testing for Securability

Security testing is about validating your application's security services and identifying potential security flaws. There are no standard methods for conducting security testing, however, because attackers have no standard method of breaking into things. The following are some methods you can use to test the securability of your applications:

- Test for buffer overflows.
- Conduct source-code security reviews.
- Validate contingency plans.
- Attack your application.

Best Practices for Securability

The following are some best practices for developing secure applications:

- Exercise constant vigilance.
- Conduct periodic reviews.
- Establish and follow security policies.
- Secure data.
- Use access-control mechanisms.
- Use the least-access approach.
- Enable strong authentication.
- Encourage the use of strong passwords.
- Use system-integrated authorization.
- Avoid buffer overflows.
- Require minimal privileges.
- Layer your application.
- Validate user input.
- Develop contingency plans

- ◆ Conduct scheduled backups.
- ◆ Monitor not-found errors.
- ◆ Use a perimeter network to protect your internal network.
- ◆ Develop applications using the .NET framework.

Appendix B

**Developing
Console
Applications in
Visual Basic .NET**

You've probably created console applications using Visual Basic, and now you will use the new features provided by .NET to create them. You use the Console Application project template provided in Visual Studio.NET to create a Visual Basic.NET console application. This template automates the work of adding the necessary files and folders to the project. The files and folder that are automatically added to the application are as follows:

- *AssemblyInfo.vb*. This file consists of all the information about the assembly of the application.
- *Module1.vb*. This file contains the `Sub Main()` method, which acts as an entry point for the application.
- *References*. This folder consists of references to the .NET framework namespaces, such as `System`, `System.Data`, and `System.XML`.

The `Console` class is a part of the .NET framework class library, which provides basic support for applications that read characters from and write characters to the console. Data from the console is read from the standard input stream, whereas the normal data and the error data are written to the standard output stream. These streams get automatically associated with the console when you run your application. The method and the property members of the stream objects represented by `In`, `Out`, and `Error` properties can be explicitly invoked.

Coding a Visual Basic .NET Console Application

Consider a scenario in which you are creating an application that accepts the name and working experience of an employee. The steps for generating a simple Visual Basic.NET console application for this scenario are as follows:

1. In Visual Studio.NET, choose New from File menu and choose Project from the New submenu.
2. In the New Project dialog box, select Visual Basic Projects from the Project Types window. Select Console Application from the Templates win-

dow. Name the application `ConsoleApplication2` and click OK. Visual Studio.NET creates a module named `Module1` containing `Sub Main()` by default.

3. Add the following code within the `Sub Main()` and `End Sub` block:

```
Dim strName As String
Dim iExp As Integer
Console.Write("Please Enter Your Name: ")
strName = Console.ReadLine()
Console.Write("Please Enter Your Work Experience in Years : ")
iExp = CInt(Console.ReadLine())
Console.WriteLine("Your Name is " & strName)
Console.WriteLine("Your work experience is: " & iExp)
```

4. Press the Ctrl and F5 keys to execute the application. Enter the name and work experience and press the Enter key. The output for the console application is shown in Figure B-1.

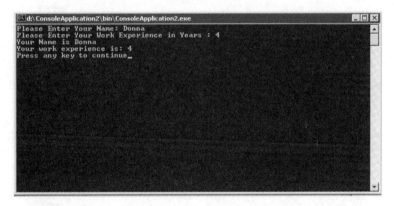

FIGURE B-1 *The output of the console application*

Appendix C

*The Graphical
Device Interface
(GDI)*

Each type of object is followed by a set of routines used to create that object. The graphical component of the Windows environment is referred to as the graphical device interface (GDI). It is a subsystem of the Windows operating system that enables an application to communicate with device drivers. Let's say you are drawing a triangle on the screen. You need to consider where the triangle should start, the color of the border, the color to be used to fill the triangle, and the size of the triangle so as to specify this in your application. The GDI acts as a buffer between applications and output devices, thus presenting a device-independent view of the application.

You need to call the methods of GDI classes, which in turn call specific device drivers to write an application that needs to draw on screens or printers. An enhanced version of the GDI, called GDI+, comes with the latest version of the Windows operating system, codenamed Whistler. GDI+ provides two sets of classes; the first set is written using C++, and another set is written using managed code.

The two distinct features of GDI+ are as follows:

◆ GDI+ provides new capabilities such as gradient brushes and alpha blending.

◆ GDI+ has a revised programming model. This has been devised to make graphics programming easier and flexible.

GDI Categories

Three types of drawing categories are supported by GDI: two-dimensional vector graphics, bitmaps, and texts. Let's now discuss them in detail.

Two-Dimensional Vector Graphics

An image with a width and a height is referred to as a two-dimensional vector image, so you can assume that all two-dimensional images have a width and a height. You can represent these 2-D images as arrays of points on a plane. For example, to represent a rectangle, you can specify the endpoints of the line by using upper-left and lower-right corners. Vector graphics use this mechanism to draw images. 2-D vector graphics are suitable to draw simple images.

Bitmaps

You can store images as bitmaps (defined as an array of bits), which specify the color of each pixel in a rectangular array of pixels. Images that cannot be represented using vector graphics are stored as bitmaps. For example, a photograph cannot be stored as a 2-D vector graphic because this might involve an endless number of coordinates. To solve this problem, you use bitmaps instead. The `Bitmap` class inherited from the `Image` class represents bitmaps in GDI.

Text

Unlike images, you can also draw text by using GDI. This text can be drawn in a variety of fonts, styles, and sizes.

Implementing GDI

All the classes of GDI are contained in the `System.Drawing` namespace class. The methods to draw lines, rectangles, ellipses, arcs, and text are defined in the `System.Drawing.Graphics` class. Some of the important methods used in the `Graphics` class are as follows:

◆ `DrawArc()`. To draw an arc that spans part of an ellipse

◆ `DrawEllipse()`. To draw an ellipse

◆ `DrawLine()`. To draw a line

◆ `DrawRectangle()`. To draw a rectangle

◆ `DrawString()`. To draw text

All of these methods use a `System.Drawing.Pen` object to draw on the screen. You use the pen object to draw lines and curves, but the `Pen` class cannot be inherited. You can use any of the colors defined in the `System.Drawing.Color` class to specify colors while specifying a `Pen` object. Alternatively, you can also use an overloaded constructor that accepts a `System.Drawing.Brush` object. To specify the coordinates and the bounding rectangle, you can use the System.Drawing.Rec-tangleF structure. All the coordinate points are specified as Single.

Consider an example in which you are required to draw on a form. To try this example, you need to first create a Windows application project. A form window is displayed. Double-click on the form to view the code window. In the Form Paint event, change the procedure in the following manner and then execute the project by pressing the F5 key.

```
Private Sub Form1_Paint(ByVal sender As Object, ByVal ev As
System.Windows.Forms.PaintEventArgs) Handles MyBase.Paint
        Dim Pen1 As Pen = New Pen(Color.Blue)
        Dim Brush1 As SolidBrush = New SolidBrush(Color.Black)
        Dim Rect1 As RectangleF = New RectangleF(50, 50, 200, 200)
        ev.Graphics.DrawEllipse(Pen1, Rect1)
End Sub
```

> **NOTE**
>
> The Paint event is called every time a form is redrawn. When the form is maximized, minimized, or resized, for example, it is redrawn and the Paint event is called.

In the preceding sample code, the Form1_Paint() event handler takes an object of the PaintEventArgs class, which is used to provide data about the Paint event. It is this data that includes the area that needs to be redrawn. The Graphics class is a member of the PaintEventArgs class, which specifies the Graphics object to be used to paint the form. You can use this member of the PaintEventArgs class to draw graphics on the form.

In the preceding code, you declared a Pen object and a SolidBrush object as shown here. The Pen object, Pen1, is created with blue color, and the SolidBrush object, Brush1, is created with black color.

```
Dim Pen1 As Pen = New Pen(Color.Blue)
Dim Brush1 As SolidBrush = New SolidBrush(Color.Black)
```

A RectangleF structure, Rect1, is then created with the upper-left corner at (50,50) and the lower-right corner at (200,200).

```
Dim Rect1 As RectangleF = New RectangleF(50, 50, 200, 200)
```

A rectangle is then drawn on the screen, and the text "Hello" is written.

```
ev.Graphics.DrawEllipse(Pen1, Rect)
```

Figure C-1 shows the output displayed when you run the preceding code:

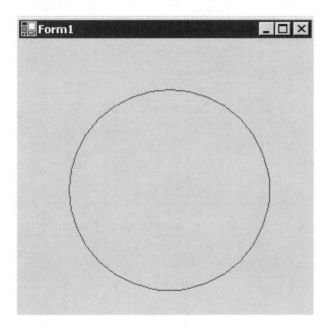

FIGURE C-1 *The output of the GDI application code*

Appendix D

Localization

People all over the world speak different languages and follow different conventions and cultures. In addition, there are people in different regions that speak the same language, but their conventions and cultures vary. Take the European countries, for example, where people speak different languages but use the same currency. Also, there are countries where people living in the same region speak multiple languages. Therefore, you cannot identify a locale specifically on the basis of region or language. A *locale* is specifically defined as a combination of a language and region.

You can create international-ready applications using ASP.NET. These applications can be used globally without specifying, modifying, or recompiling. The process of creating international applications is defined as *internationalization*. When creating an international application, you must know the language to be used to design the user interface and the locale-specific settings such as currency formats and number formats.

Internationalization can be further classified as globalization, localizability, and localization. *Globalization* is defined as the process of designing and implementing applications that include generic coding and design considerations so that they can adapt themselves according to the locale in which they are used.

An intermediate phase between globalization and localization is defined as *localizability*—a quality-assurance phase that verifies that a globalized application is ready for localization by separating the resources that require localization from the rest of the application.

Localization is defined as the process of working with resources such as string and image representations for specific locales. Localization primarily relates to the translation of the user interface.

Conceptually, a globalized application consists of two parts: a data block and a code block. The *data block* has all user-interface resources and is locale dependent. The *code block* has the application code that can work with the data blocks irrespective of locales.

You can represent data in a number of ways identified as character sets. You will use these character sets for localization later in this appendix.

Understanding Character Sets

A set of characters grouped together from different languages is defined as a *character set*. Any character/text that you input from your keyboard has a code associated with it, and this code is referred to as a *character code*. Thus, a character code is an internal representation of a character. Some of the commonly used character sets are American National Standards Institute (ANSI), Double Byte Character Set (DBCS), and Unicode. Table D-1 gives a description of these commonly used character sets.

Table D-1 Character Sets and Their Descriptions

Character Sets	Description
American National Standards Institute (ANSI)	Consists of 256 characters and punctuation codes. Each character is represented as a single byte.
Double Byte Character Set (DBCS)	Consists of a combination of the standard ASCII character set and alphabets from East Asian languages. East Asian characters are represented as 2 bytes.
Unicode	Consists of characters from almost all major languages spoken today. It enables you to easily transfer data between different locales.

Configuration Settings

Configuration settings enable you to access locale-specific properties for the entire application. This feature is provided by ASP.NET. These settings are included in the <globalization> tag of the Web.config configuration file of each ASP.NET application. The following code illustrates the configuration settings used in globalization:

```
<globalization
    requestEncoding="any valid encoding string"
    responseEncoding="any valid encoding string"
    fileEncoding="any valid encoding string"
```

```
culture="any valid culture string"
uiCulture="any valid culture string"
/>
```

In the preceding code:

◆ `requestEncoding` specifies the way the request data is encoded.

◆ `responseEncoding` specifies the way the response data is encoded.

◆ `fileEncoding` specifies the way the ASPX, ASMX, and ASAX files are encoded.

◆ `culture` specifies the default culture used to process the Web requests.

◆ `uiCulture` specifies the default culture used to search for resources.

You can control the settings of the entire globalization application by specifying the configuration settings in the `<globalization>` tag. However, you can also specify the page-level configuration settings for a specific page. The page-level settings override the settings specified in the Web.config file. It is always advisable to specify page-level setting because if the ASPX file is moved to a server that does not use the same settings as your application, the page-level settings will ensure that the correct encoding is done.

You will now learn to make region and culture settings in ASP.NET applications.

Culture and Region

In addition to configuration settings, you will use the classes provided by the .NET framework to create international applications. These classes are a part of the `System.Globalization` namespace. In addition, you will also use the `Thread` class of the `System.Threading` namespace to control the locale-specific settings for each executing instance of an application.

Consider this example: You want to create an application that displays text based on the language used in a specific region. For this purpose, you can use a localized application provided by the .NET framework. You will use the localization classes contained within the `System.Globalization` namespace. These classes enable an application to determine the locale at runtime, thus giving the flexibility of creating applications that can automatically adapt themselves to the locale in which they run. The following sections describe the `CultureInfo` and `RegionInfo` classes of this namespace.

NOTE

Combination of a language and a region is defined as a *locale*. For example, English-US is the locale that represents the culture specific to the English language spoken in the United States.

The CultureInfo *Class*

The CultureInfo class represents country-, region-, language-, or culture-specific information. The culture names have prefixes or suffixes to specify the scripts for the culture. For example, the prefix "ar-" represents the Arabic script, and the suffix "In-" represents the International sort. The culture name "ar-AE" represents Arabic-U.A.E. Table D-2 lists some of the specific culture names.

Table D-2 Some Specific Culture Names with Their Descriptions

Culture Name	Description
ar–AE	Arabic–U.A.E.
ar–EG	Arabic–Egypt
ar–KW	Arabic–Kuwait
bg–BG	Bulgarian–Bulgaria
cs–CZ	Czech–Czech Republic
de–DE	German–Germany
el–GR	Greek–Greece
en–US	English–United States
en–NZ	English–New Zealand
es–ES	Spanish–Spain
fa–IR	Farsi–Iran
fr–FR	French–France
fr–BE	French–Belgium
hi–IN	Hindi–India

continues

Table D-2 (continued)

Culture Name	Description
hu-HU	Hungarian-Hungary
id-ID	Indonesian-Indonesia
ja-JP	Japanese-Japan
ru-RU	Russian-Russia
sa-IN	Sanskrit-India
th-TH	Thai-Thailand
ur-PK	Urdu-Islamic Republic of Pakistan
zh-CHT or zh-CHS	Chinese (Traditional) or Chinese (Simplified)

A specific identifier identifies each culture. For example, the culture "en-US" has a unique identifier value, 0x0409. You can access the complete list of culture names from the .NET documentation.

Now you will learn to create an object of the CultureInfo class. When you create an object, the constructor of the CultureInfo is automatically called. You will use the following Visual Basic syntax to create a CultureInfo object:

```
Dim CuInfo as CultureInfo
CuInfo = new CultureInfo (culture name/culture identifier)
```

The culture name or the culture identifier is represented in the following format:

```
langcode-country/region
```

To specify the CultureInfo object to a "German-Germany" culture, you will use the following code:

```
Dim CuInfo as CultureInfo
CuInfo = new CultureInfo ("ru-RU")
```

or

```
Dim CultIdentifier As Integer
cultIdentifier = &H407
Dim Cult As New CultureInfo(CultIdentifier)
```

"ru-RU" is the culture name, and 0x0419 is the culture identifier for the "Russian-Russia" culture.

You can also access the culture-specific information directly from the `CultureInfo` class without creating an object of the `CultureInfo` class. The `CultureInfo` class is used to represent the information specific to the culture used by the system. Table D-3 describes the properties of the `CultureInfo` class that can be used to access the culture-specific information.

Table D-3 The *CultureInfo* Class: Properties and Their Uses

Property	Uses
`Name`	Used to return the name of the culture in the `<language-code2>-<country/regioncode2>` format.
`DisplayName`	Used to return the full name of the culture in .NET framework language in the `<language>-<country/region>` format.
`NativeName`	Used to return the full name of the culture in the user interface language in the `<language>-<country/region>` format.
`EnglishName`	Used to return the full name of the culture in English in the `<language>-<country/region>` format.
`CurrentCulture`	Used to return the `CultureInfo` instance, which represents the current culture for the current thread.
`CurrentUICulture`	Used to return the `CultureInfo` instance, which represents the current culture for the culture-specific resources.
`LCID`	Used to return the culture identifier of the `CultureInfo` instance.

The RegionInfo *Class*

The `RegionInfo` class represents country-specific or region-specific information. The `RegionInfo` class information does not depend on the user's language or culture. Unlike `CultureInfo` names, the `RegionInfo` names are not case sensitive. Table D-4 lists the two-letter codes supported by the `RegionInfo` class to represent countries or regions. You can refer the complete list of region names in the .NET documentation.

Table D-4 Two-Letter Codes and Their Region Names

Two-Letter Code	Country/Region
AE	United Arab Emirates
AU	Australia
AT	Austria
BG	Bulgaria
BR	Brazil
CA	Canada
CH	Switzerland
CZ	Czech Republic
DE	Germany
EG	Egypt
ES	Spain
GB	United Kingdom
GR	Greece
HU	Hungary
IN	India
JP	Japan
LB	Lebanon
MX	Mexico
NZ	New Zealand
PK	Pakistan
RU	Russia
SG	Singapore
TR	Turkey
US	United States
ZA	South Africa

When creating an object of the `RegionInfo` class for a specific region, you must pass the region name or culture identifier as an argument to the `RegionInfo` constructor. Table D-5 shows some of the properties of the `RegionInfo` class.

Table D-5 The *RegionInfo* Class: Properties and Their Uses

Property	Uses
CurrentRegion	Used to return the `RegionInfo` instance, which represents the country/region for the current thread.
Name	Used to return the two-letter code for the country/region of the `RegionInfo` instance.
EnglishName	Used to return the complete name of the country/region in English.
DisplayName	Used to return the complete name of the country/region in the .NET framework.
CurrencySymbol	Used to return the currency symbol associated with the country/region.
IsMetric	Used to indicate whether or not the country/region uses the metric system of measurement.

Resource Files

As previously discussed, a global ASP.NET application can be divided into two parts: data block and code block. These separate parts help create localized versions of the applications without modifying the executable content. To develop localized versions of a global ASP.NET application, you need to create localized versions of the data files. These data files are called resource files and must be created in a binary resource file format at runtime. The appropriate resources are loaded depending on the culture settings provided by the browser at runtime.

When you create an application, it is a part of an assembly called the *main assembly*. You need to recompile the application if any change is made to this main assembly. This is because you need to add the resources to provide support for more cultures; it is therefore always advisable to keep only the default set of resources in the main assembly. The other sets of resources can be kept in separate assemblies called *satellite assemblies*.

The first step in creating a resource file is to identify the resources specific to different cultures and include them in files. You need to include resources in a separate file for each culture. To do so, you need to create a text file. This text file stores a key/value pair for each resource. For example, you need to write the following code to store a value Name as a resource:

```
;A key/value pair
NameMessage = "Name"
```

The text A key/value pair preceded by a semicolon represents a comment. NameMessage is a key, and the value assigned to the key is Name. These key names are case sensitive.

You can also use XML format to include the identified resources in ResX format, and you can include an embedded object in addition to the string resources. The following is a typical ResX format:

```
[Header]
[Entries: Strings]
key=value
[Entries: Objects]
```

A specific naming convention should be followed for resource entries files so that the resource files are traceable during runtime. You should name these file as Strings.txt or Strings.ResX for the default culture. For any other culture, the file name must be of the form Strings.culture-name.txt or Strings.culture-name.ResX. For example, if the culture is "fr-FR," the file should be named as Strings.fr-FR.txt or Strings.fr-FR.ResX.

After including all the resources in a file (in text or ResX format), you need to convert it to a format that the .NET runtime can understand. To do so, you use the Resource File Generator (ResGen.exe) utility. The following is the syntax for the Resource File Generator:

```
resgen [/compile] filename.extension
[outputFilename.extension]
```

Here, filename.extension is a file that includes all the resource entries. The extension can be one of the following:

- ◆ *TXT.* Denotes a text file to be converted to a RESOURCES or RESX file. This file can consist of only string resources.
- ◆ *RESX.* Denotes an XML-based resource file to be converted to a RESOURCES or TXT file.
- ◆ *RESOURCES.* Denotes a resource file to be converted to a RESX or TXT file. `outputFilename.extension` is the RESOURCES file that is generated after conversion, and `/compile` specifies multiple RESX or TXT files to convert to a RESOURCES file in a single bulk operation, which is optional.

Creating a Localized Application Using VB.NET

You can create a localized version of an application without modifying the application code. As previously discussed, all the text and localizable resources are kept in resource files.

Visual Basic.NET provides the `Localizable` property for Windows forms to create localized applications. The Visual Studio.NET project system automatically adds a neutral resource file to the project when the `Localizable` property is set to `True`. The file name is the same as that of the form and the extension RESX. This file contains the strings and resources in the language in which the application is developed. For each localized version of the form, additional resource files are created. The resource file's name contains the name of the culture. For example, to create a localized version of a form named Form1 for the language French (France), the name of the resource file will be Form1.fr-FR.resx.

You will now learn to create an application that accepts the culture preference from a user and displays the form's text in the language specific to that culture. To create the application, you need to perform the following steps:

1. Choose File, New, Project. Select Visual Basic Project templates from the Project Types pane in the New Project dialog box. From the Templates pane, select Windows Application. Enter the name of the project as `Localization`. Click on the OK button to close the New Project dialog box. This adds the form Form1 to the project automatically.
2. Create a label and set its `Text` property as `Select Language`.

3. Create a combo box and set its `Name` property as `Combo1`.

4. Create a button and set its `Text` property as `OK`. Change the `Name` property of the control to `btnOK`. Compare your form with Figure D-1.

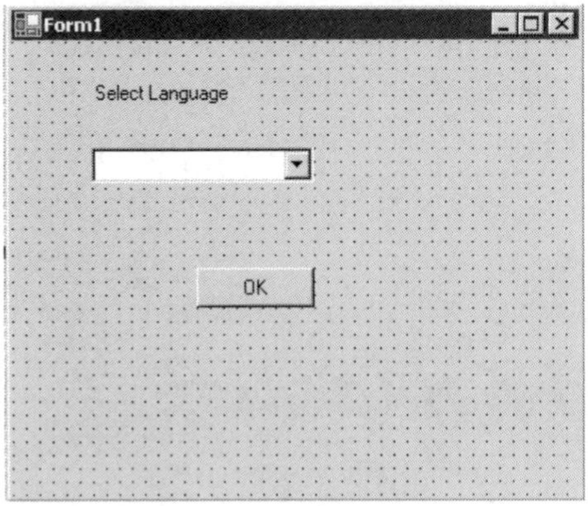

FIGURE D-1 *The design of Form1*

5. Type the following code in the `Form1_Load()` event handler to populate the combo box:

```
combo1.Items.Add("English (US)")
combo1.Items.Add("French (France)")
```

6. Type the following code in the `Click` event of the `btnOK` button.

```
Dim Culture As String
Select Case CmbLanguage.SelectedIndex
    Case 0
        Culture = "en-US"
    Case 1
        Culture = "fr-FR"
End Select
Dim NextForm As New Form2(Culture)
NextForm.Show()
```

The preceding code assigns the value `en-US` or `fr-FR` to the string, based on the user selection after declaring a string variable. Then an instance of Form2 is created. The constructor of Form2 takes the `Culture` string as a parameter.

You need to perform the following steps to create a localized form based on the user selection:

1. From the Project menu, choose the Add Windows Form command. In the Add New Item dialog box, ensure that Windows Form is selected in the Templates pane. Type the name of the new form as Form2.vb. Click on the OK button to close the Add New Item dialog box.

2. To switch to the Properties window, press the F4 key. The Localizable property of Form2 is set to True. Set the Language property of the form to Default.

3. Add two labels and set their Text properties to Enter Your Name? and Enter Your Age?.

4. Add two text boxes.

5. Add a button. Set the Text property of the button to OK.

6. Press the F4 key to switch to the Properties window of the selected form. Set the Language property of the form to French (France). Click the Show All Files button to display the Form2.vb file. Expand the Form2.vb node to display the RESX file for different languages.

7. Select Label 1 to set its Text property to Comment vous appellez vous?. Select Label 2 and set its Text property to Quel age avez-vous?. Figure D-2 shows the design of this form.

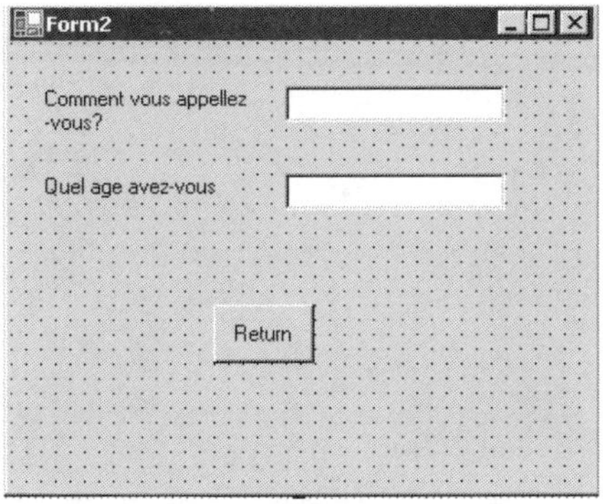

FIGURE D-2 *The design of Form2*

8. Open the Code View window by choosing Code from the View menu. Use the following statements to import the System.Globalization and System.Threading namespaces:

```
Imports System.Globalization
Imports System.Threading
```

9. Expand the Windows Forms Designer generated code node to specify the following string parameter:

```
Public Sub New(ByVal culturestr As String)
```

10. Add the following code before the `InitializeComponent()` statement:

```
Thread.CurrentThread.CurrentUICulture = New
CultureInfo(CultureStr)
```

In the preceding statement, a new instance of the `CultureInfo` class is created. This instance is assigned to the `CurrentUICulture` property of the current thread. The `CurrentUICulture` property is used to look up culture-specific resources and load them. Therefore, when you specify `fr-FR` as the culture name, the Form2.fr-FR.resx file is loaded for the current instance of an application, and strings from the resource file are displayed at runtime.

11. Type the following code in the `Button1_Click()` event handler:

```
Close()
```

12. Choose Start from the Select menu. Select a language from the drop-down list and click on the OK button. Note that in Figures D-3 and D-4 the text in Form2 is displayed in the specified language.

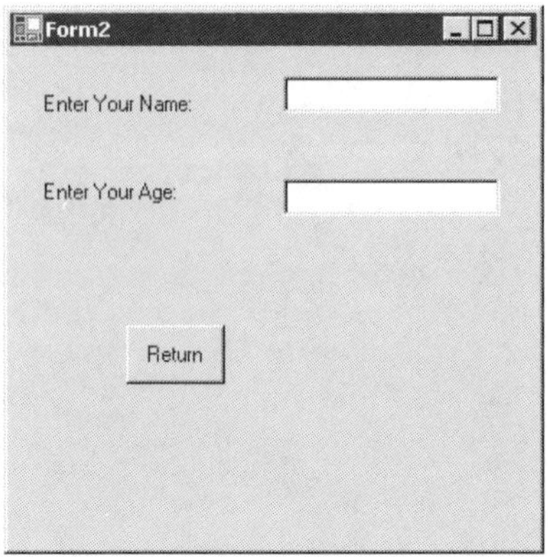

FIGURE D-3 *Form2 when en-US is selected in Form1's combo box*

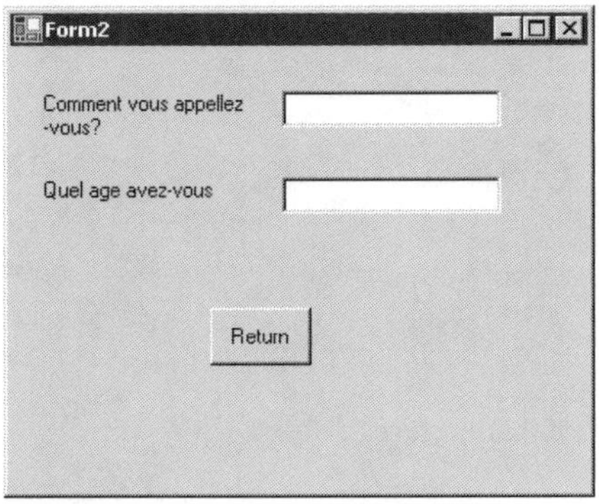

FIGURE D-4 *Form2 when* fr-FR *is selected in Form1's combo box*

Appendix E

It is not necessary for an application created using Visual Studio.NET to be confined to the system on which it was created. You can distribute the application as an installation (or deployment) program so that a user can install your application. Installation of an application involves the creation of a folder structure on the end user's computer, and then some modifications to the registry are made by the application so that the application runs successfully. In Visual Studio.NET applications, the common language runtime (CLR) files are made available by the installation program for successful execution of an application.

In this section, you will learn to deploy Windows applications by using an installation program.

Unlike other projects provided by Visual Studio.NET you can also create an installation program for your application by using a deployment project. In this section, you will be introduced to different types of installation programs available in Visual Studio.NET. Visual Studio.NET provides the following three types of installation programs:

◆ Microsoft Windows Installer files
◆ Merge modules
◆ Cabinet files

The following sections discuss these three installation programs.

Microsoft Windows Installer Files

Microsoft Windows Installer files, also known as MSI (Microsoft Installer) files, help you install applications by using the Microsoft Installer service introduced with Microsoft Windows 2000.

This service was introduced by Microsoft to optimize project deployment, enabling you to reinstall application files that may have been accidentally deleted *without* adversely affecting the application. Some of the Microsoft products installed using the Microsoft Installer service are Microsoft Office 2000 and Microsoft Commerce Server 2000.

When compiling a deployment project for a Windows application, Visual Studio.NET creates an MSI file that includes the .NET runtime files required to execute your application.

Merge Modules

Merge modules are created for packaging components that need to be shared across applications. Consider an example in which you have a set of dynamic link library (DLL) files that are to be used in three applications. Instead of individually adding the DLL files in the deployment project for all three applications, you can create a merge module for the DLL files and then add it to the deployment project for the three applications. This is one of the important benefits provided by merge modules. The MSI file, generated by compiling the deployment project to which the merge module is added, stores information about the version of the module. When installing the application, the information related to the version is added to a Windows Installer database, thus ensuring that the component is not uninstalled when a component is used by multiple applications and you uninstall one of the applications.

Cabinet (CAB) Files

Cabinet files are used to package ActiveX controls that a user can download and install from a Web site. You can create a CAB file with the help of the basic support provided by Visual Studio.NET. You will learn about these features later in this appendix.

Saving Installation Program Files

You can store installation programs for your application in the following locations:

◆ *Shared folders.* You can store your installation program in shared folders on a network so that other users can access the program and install your application. Corporate organizations usually employ this method of saving installation programs when computers are connected over a network.

◆ *Installation media.* As previously discussed, you can also distribute your application by using storage-media devices such as CD-ROMs, DVDs, and floppy disks.

◆ *Web sites.* The easiest way to reach the masses is to host your application on Web sites from which the users can download the installation files. You can commercialize your installation program or make your installation program freely downloadable.

Deploying a Project

The first step in deploying an application is to create a deployment project. Next, you need to add this project to another existing deployed project. Then you need to perform the following steps:

1. Open any project for which the installation program is to be created. Preferably, use an application that involves the use of .NET runtime files.

2. From the File menu, select Add Project, New Project to open the Add New Project dialog box.

3. In the Add New Project dialog box, select Setup and Deployment Projects from the Project Types list, as shown in Figure E-1.

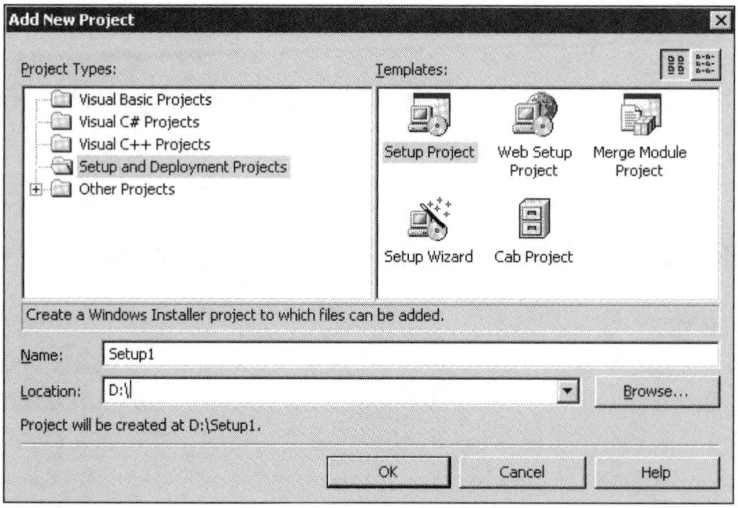

FIGURE E-1 *The Add New Project dialog box*

4. Click the Setup Project icon in the Templates pane. This is used to create an MSI file for deploying a Windows application.

5. Enter Setup1 in the Name text box as the name of the project and then click on OK. You have added a new deployment project.

A deployment project consists of a number of editors. Visual Studio.NET opens the File System editor (see Figure E-2) by default when you add a new deployment project to your solution. The following sections discuss some of the editors provided in .NET framework.

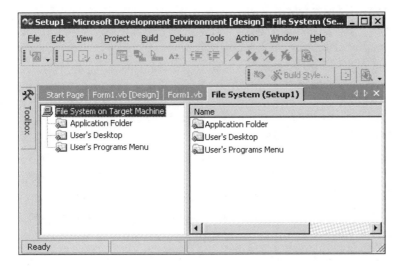

FIGURE E-2 *The File System editor*

The File System Editor

The File System editor is used to design the folder structure of your application as it should appear on a user computer. In addition, you can add the final output of an application to your project and create shortcuts for the output file.

The Registry Editor

The system registry is defined as a complex structure that consists of a number of nodes and subnodes. You often need to add data to the system registry when creating an application.

The Registry editor displays the nodes and subnodes of the registry in a hierarchy, thus simplifying your task of specifying a subnode.

The File Types Editor

You use the File Types editor to associate file extensions with your application. For example, the EXE file extension is associated with installation files.

The User Interface Editor

A user interface enables you to select a destination directory and specify user information before installing an application. The Setup Project template is used to provide a set of standard screens that can be added to a deployment project. You can fine-tune your installation program by using the User Interface editor.

The Custom Actions Editor

At times, you might need to configure an application after installing it on a user computer. For example, you might need to register a set of DLL files after your application is installed. Such tasks aren't part of the standard setup process but are essential for the functioning of your application. These tasks are defined as custom actions.

To do this, you can create custom actions in batch files or DLL files, and then you can include the files into your deployment project by using the Custom Actions editor.

The Launch Conditions Editor

You use the Launch Conditions editor to check a user's computer for software or hardware that is required to install your application. For example, a user should be able to install Windows XP only if the user has 128MB of random access memory (RAM).

Adding Files

After adding a deployment project to your application, you need to add the output of your application to the deployment project. Then you need to specify the location of application shortcuts so that your application is easily assessable by users.

After you read through this section, you should be able to configure the template-generated deployment project to deploy your application successfully.

Adding an Executable File

The executable file used to run the application is the output of a Windows application. Visual Studio.NET automatically determines the dependencies for your project and adds the required assemblies and DLL files to your application when you add the executable file of your application to a deployment project.

You need to perform the following steps to add your application's output to the deployment project:

1. From the Project menu, select Add, Project Output to open the Add Project Output Group dialog box shown in Figure E-3.

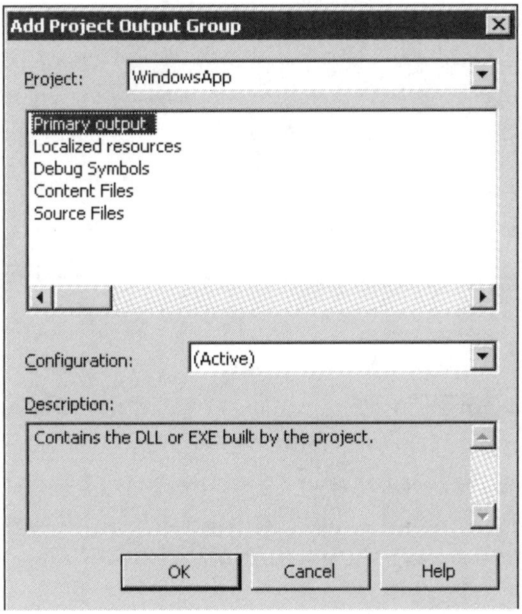

FIGURE E-3 *The Add Project Output Group dialog box*

2. Retain the default options for all settings in the Add Project Output Group dialog box and click OK to return to the File System editor. These default options denote that you're adding the primary output of your application to the deployment project.

3. In the File System on Target Machine node, click the Application Folder. The right pane of the File System editor displays the contents of the Application Folder.

All folders in the File System on Target Machine node represent the folders on a user's computer, including the Application Folder. Therefore, you can store the shortcuts in the User's Desktop folder.

To enable end users to access your application conveniently, you will include shortcuts to the primary output of your application on the user's computer desktop or in the Programs menu. To add these shortcuts, you need to perform the following steps:

1. Right-click on the file for the primary output of your application and then select the Create Shortcut to the <file name> menu option (where <file name> is the name of the file for the primary output).

2. Type a name for the shortcut so that it helps end users identify your application.

3. Drag the shortcut to the User's Desktop folder in the File System on Target Machine node so that the shortcut is stored on the user's computer.

Enhancing a Deployment Project

You will now learn to enhance your deployment projects by adding icons for your application and by optimizing project performance. You will also change deployment project properties to ensure that users without the latest version of Windows Installer can also install your application. Finally, you will learn to add screens to the deployment project to optimize it for the application. The following section shows you how to add icons to your application.

Adding Icons

Standard Windows executable file icons represent shortcuts to the primary output of your application. Imagine the plight of a user who has to routinely use these hard-to-identify icons to launch your application. To solve this problem, you should use an icon that easily, if not uniquely, identifies your application. Follow these steps to change the icons for the sample application's shortcuts to things that a user might relate the application to:

1. Select the Application Folder from the File System editor.

2. From the Project menu, choose Add, File to open the Add Files dialog box.

3. Navigate to the location of the icon file (an icon file is followed by the extension ICO) and click Open.

4. Right-click an application shortcut and select Properties Window from the shortcut menu.

5. In the Properties window, select the (Browse) option from the Icon list to open the Icon dialog box (see Figure E-4).

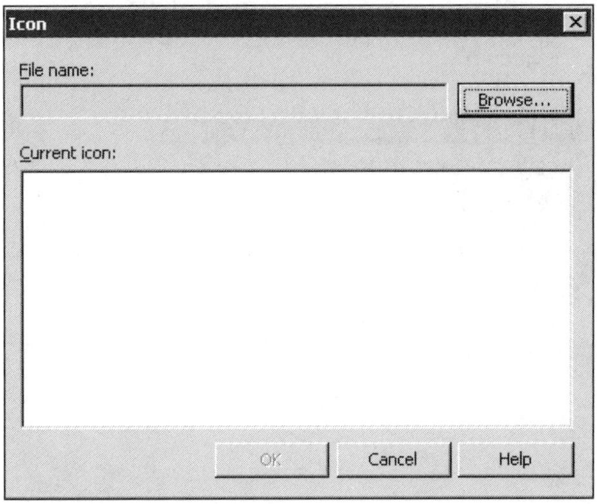

FIGURE E-4 *The Icon dialog box*

6. Double-click the Application Folder in the Select Item in Project dialog box. You will observe that the name of the icon appears in the folder.

7. Click on OK to move the selected icon to the Icon dialog box. The icon selected in step 3 appears in the Current Icon list of the Icon dialog box.

8. Click on the Close button to close the Icon dialog box.

Follow these steps to add icons to all the shortcuts created for the application.

Adding Screens to the Deployment Project

You will use the Setup Project template provided by Visual Studio.NET to add a set of standard screens for creating a setup project or application. In addition to the default screens, you can customize your application by adding more screens as per your project requirement. For example, you might include a license-agreement screen in your application as per the corporate world's requirement. To add this screen to your deployment project, you need to use the User Interface editor provided by Visual Studio.NET. To open this editor, choose Editor, User Interface from View menu. The User Interface editor is opened. Notice that there are two types installations: Install and Administrative Install. Figure E-5 displays the User Interface editor.

You use the Install installation type for installing an application to the local computer. The system administrator uses the Administrative Install installation type to install an application on a network.

FIGURE E-5 *The User Interface editor*

Visual Studio.NET allows you to add only selected screens for each stage of deployment. The scheme followed by Visual Studio.NET is as follows:

◆ *Start stage.* This stage refers to adding the Splash, Welcome, License Agreement, Radio Buttons, Checkboxes, Textboxes, Installation Folder, and Confirm Installation screens. It is always advisable that you add the required screens as listed here.

◆ *Progress stage.* When your application is being installed and there is no user interaction, you can add only the Progress screen. This is done in the progress stage.

◆ *End stage.* In the end stage, which is the final stage of a setup application, you can add only the Register User and Finished screens.

In the running example, you will add the License Agreement screen to your project. For this, you need to add the License Agreement file to your application. This process is similar to the process of adding icons, which was discussed earlier. The only difference is that you need to import rich text format (RTF) files with the license agreement.

After you add the license agreement file to your application, you need to follow these steps to add the License Agreement screen to your application:

1. Click the Start stage in the User Interface editor. (To open the User Interface editor, choose Editor, User Interface from the View menu.)

2. Select Add Dialog from the Action menu.

3. Select License Agreement from the Add Dialog box and then click OK.

4. Move the License Agreement screen to the Welcome screen.

5. To associate the License Agreement screen with the text file you imported for the license agreement, right-click the License Agreement screen and then select Properties Window from the shortcut menu that appears.

6. Select the (Browse) option in the LicenseFile list to open the Select Item in Project dialog box. Figure E-6 displays the Select Item in Project dialog box.

7. Double-click on the Application Folder.

NOTE

If you use a text file as the file for the license agreement, select All Files (*.*) from the Files of type list.

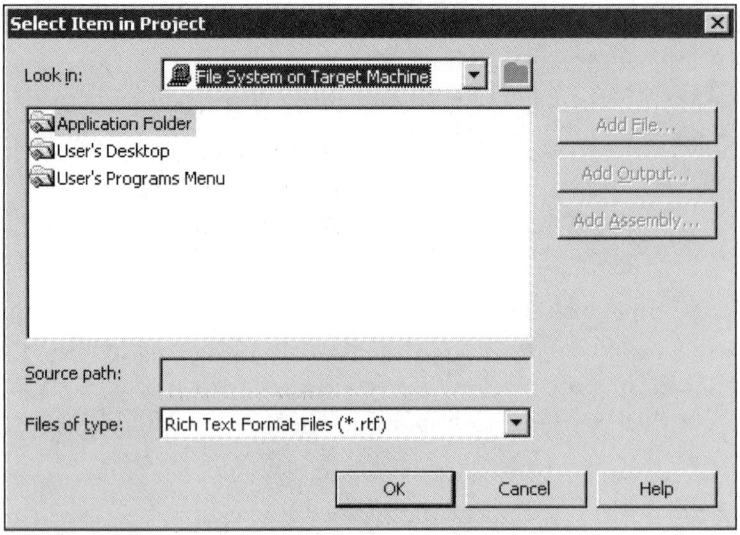

FIGURE E-6 *The Select Item in Project dialog box*

8. Select the License Agreement file and then click on OK.

Repeat these steps to include the License Agreement screen in Administrative Install as well so that this is displayed in both the Install and the Administrative Install installation types.

Adding the Windows Installer Bootstrapper

You should include the latest version of Windows Installer with your application to enable users with earlier versions of Windows to install your application. This is done by including the Windows Installer bootstrapper with your application by changing the project properties. To include the Windows Installer bootstrapper, you need to perform the following steps:

1. Choose View, Solution Explorer to open the Solution Explorer dialog box.

2. Right-click the name of the deployment project, Setup1, and then select Properties from the shortcut menu.

3. Select the Windows Installer Bootstrapper option from the Bootstrapper list, as shown in Figure E-7.

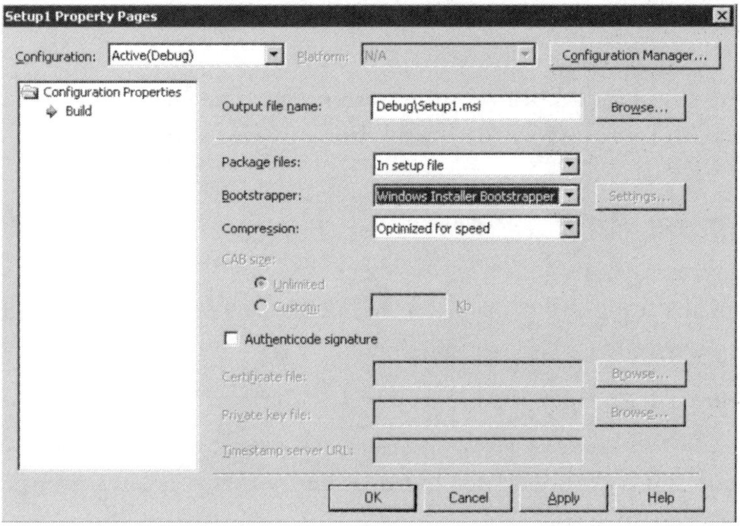

FIGURE E-7   *The property page of the Setup1 deployment project*

4. Click on the Apply button and then click on OK to close the Setup1 Property Pages dialog box.

The deployment project is now ready for compiling and testing.

Verifying the Deployment Project

In this section, you will learn the procedure for compiling and testing your deployment project on a test platform.

Compiling the Application

You develop your application in the Debug configuration during the development stage. After finalizing your application, compile it in the Release configuration so that your application is optimized for speed and performance. Create an installation program. Perform the following steps to compile your application in the Release configuration:

1. Choose Build, Configuration Manager to open the Configuration Manager dialog box.

2. Select Release from the Active Solution Configuration list.

3. Close the Configuration Manager dialog box by clicking on the Close button.

4. Choose Build Solution from the Build menu. The MSI file for your application is created by the Visual Studio.NET compiler.

Launching the Application

You must make sure your application has been packaged correctly. To do so, you need to install the application on a test computer by performing the following steps:

1. Double-click on the MSI file to start installation. Verify that the Welcome screen appears.

2. Click on the Next button to continue. Verify that the License Agreement screen appears.

3. Select the I Agree option to accept the license agreement and then click on the Next button. Also make sure the Next option is disabled when the I Agree option to accept the license agreement is not selected. Verify that the Select Installation Folder screen appears.

4. To install your application in the Default folder, click on the Next button. Verify that the Confirm Installation screen appears.

5. Click on the Next button to install your application. Verify that the Progress screen appears. When your application is installed, the installation program moves to the next screen and the Installation Complete screen appears.

6. Click on the Close button to complete the installation of your application.

Developing Merge Module Projects

Merge modules are used to deploy components that are shared across applications. You can package a component in a merge module by using Visual Studio.NET. To do so, perform the following steps:

1. In Visual Studio.NET, select File, New, Project.

2. From the Project Types pane, select Setup and Deployment Projects.

3. From the Templates pane, select Merge Module Project.

4. Specify the name of the merge module project (as shown in Figure E-8) and click on the OK button.

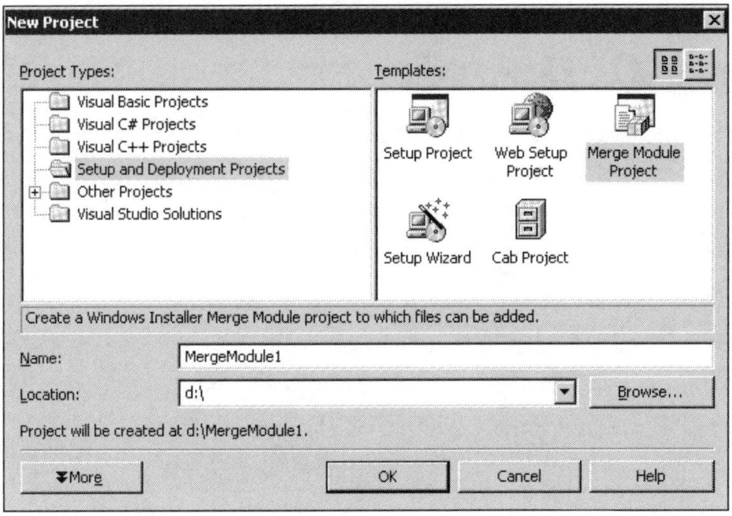

FIGURE E-8 *The New Project dialog box*

5. You have created a merge module project. As in Microsoft Windows Installer, you can use various deployment editors to add assemblies and files to the merge module. However, a merge module project provides only four deployment editors: File System, Registry, File Types, and Custom Actions.

The files contained in a merge module are installed at the location set by the merge model's author. However, you can provide flexibility to the end users of the merge module by specifying the location of files. To do this, you need to set the Module Retargetable Folder property exposed by the merge module.

After performing these steps, build the project. When creating a merge module project, a file with the MSM extension is created. You can now merge this file into a Windows Installer package. To add a merge module to a setup project, perform the following steps:

1. Open an existing setup project or create a new setup project.

2. In the Solution Explorer window, select the setup project.

3. Select Project, Add, Merge Module.

4. In the Add Modules dialog box, click to select the MSM files to be included in the setup project and then click on Open.

Developing CAB Projects

As discussed earlier in this appendix, CAB projects are used to package components that can be downloaded from a Web server to a Web browser. This type of project is used when you want a component to execute on a client computer instead of a Web server. To create a CAB project, you need to perform the following steps:

1. In Visual Studio.NET, select File, New, Project.

2. From the Project Types pane, select Setup and Deployment Projects.

3. From the Templates pane, select CAB Project.

4. Specify the name of the CAB project and click on OK.

NOTE

CAB projects do not provide deployment editors for including files and registry entries.

Appendix F

The .NET Family

With the current emphasis on the .NET framework and its benefits to e-commerce, Microsoft has introduced a set of products and services you can use to implement business solutions using the .NET framework. These products and services essentially form the .NET family and consist of .NET Enterprise Servers, .NET Server, Windows XP, and the .NET Passport service. In addition, Visual Studio.NET forms an integral part of this set by helping you create applications using the .NET framework.

In this appendix, you will be introduced to .NET Enterprise Servers, .NET Server, Windows XP, and their roles in the .NET framework. You will also look at how the .NET Passport service works as well as its benefits.

.NET Enterprise Servers

An important requirement in business is to constantly find better and easier ways to enhance business opportunity and get an edge over competitors. This constant endeavor requires companies to look for and implement solutions to build an integrated and scalable business infrastructure. .NET Enterprise Servers provide the solution to such a quest.

An enterprise can use .NET Enterprise Servers to implement and manage solutions to Web-enable businesses. With this view, .NET Enterprise Servers have been designed keeping two considerations in mind. The first is to provide accessibility to all Web users. To facilitate this, the servers have been built using open Web standards such as XML. The second consideration is the interoperability and scalability of the servers, which have been created to ensure interoperability with the existing infrastructure.

The .NET Enterprise Servers include the following:

- ◆ Application Center 2000
- ◆ BizTalk Server 2000
- ◆ Commerce Server 2000
- ◆ Content Management Server 2001

- ◆ Exchange 2000
- ◆ Host Integration Server 2000
- ◆ Internet Security and Acceleration (ISA) Server
- ◆ Mobile Information 2001 Server
- ◆ SharePoint Portal Server 2001
- ◆ SQL Server 2000

The following sections discuss the role of each .NET Enterprise Server in the .NET framework.

Application Center 2000

Companies often host high-availability Web applications. As a developer or a Web site administrator, you can deploy and manage such applications built on Windows 2000 by using Application Center 2000. Application Center 2000 is a server that facilitates the deployment and management of Web applications by implementing clustering.

Application Center 2000 enables you to create groups that include elements of an application, such as Web sites and COM+ components, which can be managed through an Application Center cluster. Further, cluster management is simplified by enabling you to manage an entire cluster of servers as a single server. Application Center 2000 also supports the automation of application deployment from one cluster to another. The changes resulting from a deployment are synchronized across all the members in a cluster. Therefore, an Application Center cluster offers the same content to users independent of the cluster member catering to client requests.

Additionally, Application Center clusters are scalable, thereby enabling you to add or remove members to or from the cluster based on requirements.

In its effort to ensure the continued availability of a Web site, Application Center 2000 also offers monitoring capabilities. It can be used for performance checks on either an entire cluster or individual members of a cluster. You can also use Application Center 2000 to automate responses to specific events or conditions. For instance, when the processor usage of a cluster member exceeds the threshold limit, all subsequent user requests for similar resources will be redirected to an alternate cluster member.

As an additional feature to manage clusters and maintain Web site availability, Application Center 2000 supports the distribution of workloads among members of a cluster. Application Center 2000 supports Network Load Balancing (NLB) to balance IP requests and Component Load Balancing (CLB) to balance the activation of COM+ components across cluster members.

BizTalk Server 2000

You can create applications in different formats based on ease of use or the functionality required. This poses compatibility- and interoperability-related problems across platforms. You can integrate applications created in different formats by using BizTalk Server 2000. BizTalk Server 2000 provides a suite of tools and services you can use to create and deploy integrated business processes within an organization or across organizations. These graphical tools, such as BizTalk Orchestration Designer and BizTalk Messaging Manager, empower you to integrate, manage, and automate dynamic business processes.

BizTalk Server 2000 not only ensures the integrity of all communication and data exchange between transacting parties, it also ensures the security of the communication and data transfer. To facilitate a secure document exchange, BizTalk Server 2000 implements secure and reliable connections irrespective of the operating system, programming language, or programming model. For this purpose, BizTalk Server 2000 uses technologies such as public key encryption and digital signatures. In addition to the security risks, the electronic exchange of documents is also marred with problems related to exchange across different platforms. BizTalk Server 2000 resolves the exchange of documents across platforms by managing data translation, encryption, and data tracking services. For instance, BizTalk Server 2000 tools such as BizTalk Mapper ensure transformation of documents into a commonly accepted format. BizTalk Server 2000 uses an open industry framework called BizTalk Framework 2.0 to facilitate routing and analysis of data and documents exchanged across electronic or organizational barriers. Another important tool in BizTalk Server 2000 that enables you to manage document exchange between applications and trading partners is the BizTalk Messaging Manager. BizTalk Server 2000 also offers tools such as BizTalk Orchestration Designer that allow the use of XLANG, an XML-based language.

Commerce Server 2000

Generally, organizations are in search of a scalable platform that they can readily customize to create e-commerce Web sites in a cost effective and less cumbersome way. This is exactly what Commerce Server 2000 has to offer. Commerce Server 2000 is a server that provides you with the ability to create e-commerce sites quickly and with ease.

To facilitate the creation of e-commerce sites, Commerce Server 2000 provides Solution Sites that you can readily use as templates to create your own Web sites. You can build on Solution Sites by adding new functionalities and enhancements as per customer and organizational requirements.

Commerce Server 2000 also empowers business managers to manage Web sites in a real-time environment. This, in turn, means that whenever the content on a Web site is updated to meet customer requirements, the changes take effect immediately. As a result, this gives the managers a chance to provide highly personalized and relevant content on their sites at all times. Additionally, with Commerce Server 2000, you can provide business managers with essential decision-support mechanisms such as data warehousing and data mining. The server also incorporates analytical capabilities that can be used to analyze business scenarios and to update sites in real time based on the results of the analysis.

You can integrate Commerce Server 2000 with other .NET Enterprise Servers to provide enhanced functionalities.

Content Management Server 2001

Not only is the maintenance of content-driven Web sites difficult, the creation of such sites is also time consuming. As the name of the server suggests, Content Management Server 2001 enables content providers to effectively manage Web content. You can readily develop, publish, and maintain highly dynamic, content-driven Web sites for the Internet and intranet by using Content Management Server 2001.

Content Management Server 2001 offers a novel way to archive all the updated documents automatically. You can also track versions of a particular document. In addition, Content Management Server 2001 permits multiple levels of review and approval of a document before it is published on a Web site. It is also possible for users to schedule the publication and archival of content by using scheduling tools.

As with other .NET Enterprise Servers, Content Management Server 2001 permits scalability to meet the growing demands of an ever-changing online market. You can create clusters of servers running Content Management Server 2001 and ensure workload balancing.

Content Management Server 2001 also supports integration with Windows 2000 Advanced Server, SQL Server 2000, Commerce Server 2000, and FrontPage 2000.

Exchange 2000

Communication forms the backbone for any business establishment. With most commercial transactions shifting to the Internet, it becomes essential to supply the right information to the right person at the right time. Therefore, there is an emphasis and a requirement for a reliable and scalable messaging service. Exchange 2000 is a messaging infrastructure that can provide the necessary solutions to the communication-related problems of an enterprise.

To meet the growing demands of an organization in terms of communication, Exchange 2000 supports a range of collaborative activities, including discussion groups and scheduling capabilities. To facilitate access to information across geographic and organizational barriers, Exchange 2000 supports features such as instant messaging and video conferencing. With Exchange 2000, you can set up conferences by using MS NetMeeting with any T.120 client. The Conference Management Service of Exchange 2000 enables you to control access to conferences. Additionally, Exchange 2000 provides services such as contact and task management.

Exchange 2000 provides a single platform that you can use for e-mail, voice mail, fax, and page messages. Additionally, Exchange 2000 provides chat services based on the IRC protocol for text-based chat. Users can also access e-mail and contacts remotely from the Internet.

In addition to supporting such data exchange, Exchange 2000 also enables you to conduct discussions through data conferencing. In an online business, it becomes imperative to allow remote access to information and data. Users can also access the data stored in Exchange 2000 from a Web browser. For interoperability's sake, Exchange 2000 supports Internet standards such as XML and HTTP.

You can also create Web forms in Exchange 2000. Additionally, Outlook Web Access forms an integral component of Exchange 2000. Outlook Web Access has been updated in scalability and functionality from its earlier version. It also supports the addition of audio and video clips to a message.

Exchange 2000 also supports clustering. This allows high availability and scalability. The Enterprise Edition of Exchange 2000 supports multiple storage groups and databases. Exchange 2000 also provides features to ensure secured communication. For instance, you can set permissions for items or documents and can achieve new levels of security for workflow applications.

Host Integration Server 2000

You can handle interoperability with non-Windows systems by using Host Integration Server 2000. This means you can utilize existing AS/400 and mainframe systems' data or applications by using Host Integration Server 2000 while retaining them in their original form. To achieve this, Host Integration Server 2000 enables you to develop applications that integrate host system to Internet or host system to intranet.

Host Integration Server 2000 allows three-fold interoperability: It enables you to interact with host systems through data integration, network integration, and application integration.

Using Host Integration Server 2000, you can also reap the benefits of a comprehensive security system that incorporates the Windows 2000 Active Directory and Windows NT 4.0 domain security model as well as host-based security. This security system ensures that all client-to-server and network-to-network VPN connections are secure and tunneled by using Host Integration Server 2000. Host Integration Server 2000 offers an invaluable tool to integrate the best that Internet, intranet, and client/server technologies have to offer.

As with other .NET Enterprise Servers, Host Integration Server 2000 supports clustering and workload balancing. It is also possible to integrate host systems with .NET-based applications. For instance, you can integrate Host Integration Server 2000 with BizTalk and Commerce Server.

Internet Security and Acceleration (ISA) Server

As more and more organizations turn to the Internet for business opportunities, there is an increasing need for fast and secure connections to the Internet. With this in mind, Microsoft developed the Internet Security and Acceleration (ISA)

Server 2000. ISA Server 2000 implements a Web cache to facilitate fast Internet access. Additionally, to secure the connection to the Internet without compromising network performance, ISA Server implements a firewall. You can therefore use this server to enhance Internet access and to implement organizational security policies.

It is also possible to scale the Web cache by adding additional ISA servers. Alternatively, you can increase the capacity of an ISA Server Web cache by adding multiple processors, implementing symmetric multiprocessing (SMP), increasing disk space, or increasing RAM.

Additionally, ISA Server implements multiple caching technologies, which are discussed in the following sections.

Forward Caching

In forward caching, clients from within the network of an organization access servers on the Internet. The frequently accessed Web content is cached on the ISA Server.

Distributed Caching

An ISA Server implements distributed caching when multiple ISA Server computers are used. In such a case, ISA Server uses the Cache Array Routing Protocol (CARP), which creates a single logical cache by using ISA Server computers.

Hierarchical Caching

In a hierarchy of interconnected ISA Server computers, you can ensure that users access caches that are located in geographic proximity. To do so, you can place ISA Server Web caches in a hierarchy depending on geographical location and link client nodes to the nearest leaf node of the hierarchy. Whenever the client requests a resource, it goes to the nearest (leaf) node and then travels up the hierarchy until the requested object is found.

Scheduled Caching

You can update the ISA Web cache by scheduling the automatic update of the cache content. Such a caching mechanism is called scheduled caching.

Reverse Caching

In reverse caching, an ISA Server is placed as a layer over an organization's Web server. In this case, all incoming requests from clients are provided from the ISA cache. If the requested object is not available in the ISA cache, the request is forwarded to the underlying Web server that it sheaths. This secures the communication between clients on the Internet and the publishing Web servers located within an organization.

Mobile Information 2001 Server

Mobile Information 2001 Server provides the capability to develop mobile applications by using standard Web and WAP applications' authoring tools. The server also provides .NET Mobile Web SDK to design and render Web applications. You can also create applications with a common interface regardless of the mobile device used to access the application. This is possible because Mobile Information 2001 Server enables you to use mobile controls and Web forms, which ensure that the content and interface you create remain compatible with various mobile devices.

With mobile access to information arises the question of security and privacy of the data accessed. Mobile Information 2001 Server ensures end-to-end security of the information accessed and communications across mobile devices. To prevent unauthorized interception of data and communications, all notifications from enterprise applications are sent to mobile devices securely through technologies such as Secure Socket Layer (SSL), IP Security Protocol (IPSec), and VPN solutions. Additionally, the server application allows the use of the .NET Passport service, PKI, and smartcards.

Mobile Information 2001 Server supports Web standards such as HTTP, HTTP Distributed Authoring and Versioning (DAV), SMTP, and the like to provide interoperability with mobile devices and integration with the existing applications and infrastructure. In addition, Mobile Information 2001 Server supports mobile devices with the WAP 1.1 browser. Mobile Information 2001 Server also is capable of sending notifications to mobile devices capable of receiving SMS or to an SMTP addressable device such as a pager.

The Mobile Information Server 2002 Enterprise Edition includes the new features discussed in the following sections.

Microsoft Server ActiveSync

The Microsoft Server ActiveSync feature has been added to synchronize information from Microsoft Exchange 2000 Server, such as e-mail and a calendar sent to a Pocket PC 2002–based device. This feature securely synchronizes the required information over a wireless link.

Enhanced Security

The Mobile Information Server Enterprise Edition enables you to use either SSL or IPSec to secure the link between Mobile Information Server Enterprise Edition and Mobile Information Server Carrier Edition.

SharePoint Portal Server 2001

SharePoint Portal Server includes document-management features such as document locking and versioning. To ensure that the correct version of the document is published, there is a need to monitor the creation of the document and to coordinate the work being done on the document by different users, maybe simultaneously. With each user contributing to the document in a specific way, it becomes essential to retain the latest changes to the document and prevent simultaneous access to the document. SharePoint Portal Server enables a user to address this by providing features such as document locking and versioning. These features make it easier to control and track a document that passes through different phases in its life cycle before it finally sees the light of the day or is published. The approval-routing feature enables you to track changes as a document passes through different phases in its life cycle. To further ease the life of the user, SharePoint Portal Server integrates these features with the applications you use to create and manage documents, such as Microsoft Word.

SharePoint Portal Server also provides the capability to store documents and keep a track of the metadata related with business documents in Document Profile forms. Additionally, SharePoint Portal Server provides features that help you work with documents with ease, such as Document Collaboration, Profiling, and Lifecycle Management.

To ensure interoperability, the server supports all the Internet standards, such as XML and HTTP, and ActiveX Data Objects (ADO) and OLE DB for data access. Therefore, it becomes possible for you to integrate Active Server Pages

(ASP) functionality into the Web portal. SharePoint Portal Server 2001 also consists of built-in services you can use to create Web-based applications.

For users to benefit from the features of the SharePoint Portal Server, a user interface needs to be created for SharePoint Portal Server. To create a user interface for SharePoint Portal Server, you use the Microsoft Digital Dashboard technology. Digital dashboards are Web applications that run on Windows 2000 IIS and can be accessed by using Web browsers such as Internet Explorer. Digital dashboards make extensive use of Web Part technology.

> **NOTE**
>
> Each digital dashboard is composed of individual sections known as Web Parts. A Web Part is a customizable section that encapsulates a script fragment with a custom property schema that Microsoft defines. You can either use third-party Web Parts or create customized Web Parts by using HTML, XML, and JavaScript.

SQL Server 2000

The need to store and maintain information in a systematic manner that can be queried with ease can never be overlooked by an organization. To meet this requirement, organizations can use SQL Server 2000. SQL Server 2000 is a server that enables you to create databases and analyze and query the data in these databases.

Some of the features of SQL Server 2000 are as follows:

◆ Comprehensive data store

◆ Enhanced analytical capabilities

◆ Full-text search

◆ Indexed views

◆ Support for Web-enabled database applications

◆ Enhanced application development features

◆ Scalability

Comprehensive Data Store

SQL Server 2000 is fully integrated with the Web and enables you to access the data and query databases from the Web itself.

Enhanced Analytical Capabilities

The Analysis Services feature introduces data mining to locate information in online analytical processing (OLAP) cubes and relational databases. These features can help you analyze and predict useful information by using the data stored in SQL Server 2000 databases.

Full-Text Search

You can use the full-text search feature of SQL Server 2000 to query the data stored in SQL Server 2000 databases.

Indexed Views

A new feature called indexed views simplifies data access, resulting in application performance boost.

Support for Web-Enabled Database Applications

SQL Server 2000 supports XML data exchange with client applications and data access through ADO, OLE DB, and ODBC. Therefore, in SQL Server 2000, it is possible to create and maintain Web-enabled database applications.

Enhanced Application Development Features

It is possible to ensure high availability of business applications by using the SQL Server 2000 features such as online backups, clustering, and log shipping. You can also import data from heterogeneous systems (such as flat files and legacy databases) by using routines that can extract, transform, and load the data automatically.

The most important feature provided by SQL Server 2000 is Meta Data Services, which enables you to store, view, and retrieve descriptions of objects in your applications and system.

Scalability

To meet the needs of an ever-expanding business scenario, it is possible to scale SQL Server 2000 by adding multiple processors and additional RAM. You can also create clusters of SQL Server 2000 and distribute the database and data across servers. Additionally, you can interactively tune and debug queries and quickly move and transform data to and from any source.

So far, this appendix has discussed the .NET Enterprise Servers that enable you to create and deploy solutions to use the .NET framework. The Whistler group of products is an additional set of Microsoft products designed as a foundation for the .NET platform.

The Whistler family of products incorporates enhancements to enable businesses to implement the .NET framework with ease. For instance, the Whistler products support real-time communications such as instant messaging and exchanging voice and video. Additionally, built-in support for enhanced Windows Media Services also enables these products to meet the .NET vision.

The Whistler family of Microsoft products includes the Windows .NET Server family of server applications and client-side Windows XP.

Let's now look at the .NET Passport service provided by Windows XP.

.NET Passport Service

Microsoft provides a solution to such problems with the .NET Passport service. .NET Passport is an Internet-based authentication service that allows users to sign in to multiple participating Web sites by using a single e-mail address and password. This means that Web sites need not maintain separate authentication mechanisms. In addition, .NET Passport eliminates the need to type personal information repeatedly for each site visited during a Web browsing session. This makes the entire process of Web site personalization based on user profiles a simple and fast task. Users can also store credit card–related information in .NET Passport. Therefore, not only is the time necessary for online transactions reduced, the entire process is simplified.

For a user to benefit from .NET Passport, he or she needs to create a .NET Passport account. An account is created when a user registers for .NET Passport. A user can choose to register for .NET Passport by using any of the following methods:

NOTE

A participating Web site is a site that has registered with .NET Passport.

◆ Signing up for an e-mail account on **www.hotmail.com** or **www.msn.com**

◆ Registering at the .NET Passport site, **www.passport.com**

◆ Registering at a participating Web site such as **www.mcafee.com**

◆ Using the Windows XP Registration Wizard

A user with an e-mail account on **www.hotmail.com** or **www.msn.com** is automatically registered as a .NET Passport user.

Although the home page of .NET Passport enables you to register directly by using the .NET Passport registration page, a participating Web site will redirect all potential .NET Passport users to a .NET Passport registration page. Additionally, although .NET Passport's home page only requires an e-mail address and password to create a .NET Passport account, a participating site might require additional information. For instance, a participating site might require the user's address. Such additional information is stored in the user's .NET Passport account (if indicated by the site by the presence of an icon).

When creating a .NET Passport account, a user can specify which information can be shared with the participating sites during a Web browsing session. For instance, users can specify whether a participating Web site can have access to their e-mail address or first and last name only. Optionally, users can share all the remaining information in addition to the their e-mail address and first and last name. Therefore, in .NET Passport service, users exercise complete control over their information. Regardless of the information that a user has shared while registering for .NET Passport, all participating sites (besides the site used for registration) receive only the information that the user has chosen to share. In any case, the password of a user is never communicated to a participating Web site.

A .NET Passport account stores credentials pertaining to the user. These credentials are unique and are used to validate the user whenever he or she visits a participating Web site.

A .NET Passport account consists of the following information:

◆ *.NET Passport Unique Identifier.* This identifier, also called a PUID, is a 64-bit numeric value assigned by .NET Passport.

◆ *.NET Passport User Profile.* This profile stores all the information specified while registering for .NET Passport, such as first name, last name, e-mail address, phone number, city, state and postal code.

◆ *.NET Passport Credential.* This component of the .NET Passport account consists of two components: the Standard .NET Passport Credential and the Security key. The Standard .NET Passport Credential stores the basic inputs required to create a .NET Passport account. These inputs are the e-mail address or phone number of the user along with a password or PIN. The security key is a four-digit key that is required to sign in to the strong-credential security level. When creating the key, the user selects three questions and specifies the answers for these questions. These questions will help the user restore the key if the server disables the account as a precautionary measure.

◆ *.NET Passport wallet.* A user can create a .NET Passport wallet to store credit card–related information and billing and shipping addresses. This can be done when registering at the .NET Passport site or by accessing the member services page.

After a .NET Passport account has been created for a user, he or she can implement the services offered by .NET Passport. .NET Passport provides a set of services to implement user authenticity, security, and privacy. These services are as follows:

◆ .NET Passport Single Sign-In

◆ .NET Passport Express Purchase

◆ Kids .NET Passport

Each of these services enhances the Web experience for users in its own way. Let's look at each of the .NET Passport services in detail.

.NET Passport Single Sign-In

The .NET Passport Single Sign-In service enables users to use a single .NET Passport account across Web sites. Therefore, during a single Web browsing session, a user can navigate across participating sites by supplying his or her sign-in name and password only once. This eliminates the need to authenticate the user at all the sites visited. .NET Passport prevents unauthorized access to Web sites (and services offered by the sites) by using powerful Internet security technologies. Some of the security-based implementations in .NET Passport are as follows:

◆ Use of standard Web technologies and techniques such as SSL, HTTP redirects, cookies, and JavaScript

◆ No sharing of the password used by users to sign in to .NET Passport

◆ Encryption of all authentication- and profile-related information when sent to a participating site

◆ User control of information to be shared between participating sites

◆ Implementation of security levels

Three different security levels can be implemented depending on the sensitivity of the content or the service offered by the site. These three levels of authentication are as follows:

◆ *Standard sign-in.* Participating Web sites implement the Standard sign-in if the content or service offered by the site is not sensitive enough to merit high security.

◆ *Secure Channel sign-in.* Secure Channel sign-in shares most features of the Standard sign-in. The essential difference lies in the implementation of an end-to-end secure channel for authentication. In this security level, the .NET Passport ticket is written in a secure format to avoid any manipulation of the ticket. Even the .NET Passport sign-in page is displayed using SSL with up to 128-bit encryption.

◆ *Strong Credential sign-in.* Strong Credentials sign-in is designed to ensure security and privacy for the most sensitive data. This level involves a two-stage sign-in. Although the first stage is similar to the Secure Channel sign-in, the second stage requires the user to enter a four-digit security key on a sign-in page. To ensure end-to-end security, the second sign-in page is displayed using SSL. Further, the key is disabled after five consecutive unsuccessful attempts to type the correct key. To enable the key, the user needs to reset the security key to regain access to the .NET Passport account. This key-resetting process requires the user to answer three secret questions that the user decided on while selecting the secret key.

.NET Passport Express Purchase

The information stored in the .NET Passport wallet is used when a user uses the .NET Passport express purchase service. To implement this service, participating sites need to accept labels for e-commerce POST data complying with the Electronic Commerce Modeling Language (ECML). Additionally, the site needs to add the .NET Passport express purchase link or button. This button is used to redirect a .NET Passport user to his or her respective .NET Passport wallet. This initiates a .NET Passport express purchase.

When a user initiates a .NET Passport express purchase, the following sequence of activities occurs:

> **NOTE**
>
> ECML is an XML-based standard that allows the automation of information exchange between users and merchants through digital wallets.

1. The site ID of the participating site is authenticated by the .NET Passport wallet server.

2. A user who is already signed in to .NET Passport is required to reenter his or her password. Users who have not signed in are required to sign in to .NET Passport.

3. The user selects the credit card and the billing and shipping addresses from his or her .NET Passport wallet.

4. Credit card details and the billing and shipping addresses are encrypted using an encryption key and are sent back to the participating site.

5. The participating site decrypts the information by using the .NET Passport Manager.

Similarly, with a special emphasis on the online security and privacy of children, .NET Passport provides the Kids .NET Passport service.

> **NOTE**
>
> When a site registers as a .NET Passport participating site, .NET Passport grants a unique ID and encryption key to the site. The ID granted to the site is known as its site ID. The site ID is used to authenticate the site whenever it redirects a user to the .NET Passport Login server.
>
> The encryption key is used to retrieve the user-related information sent by the .NET Passport Login server.

Kids .NET Passport Service

The Kids .NET Passport service is implemented by using .NET Passport Single Sign-In. The service essentially requires that all registered participating sites comply with the Children's Online Privacy Protection Act (COPPA). The Kids .NET Passport service allows parents or guardians of children under age 13 to control the information and its subsequent use by Web sites.

HASHING

COPPA is an Internet law that seeks to ensure the online privacy of children. The law ensures that the collection, use, and disclosure of all personal information related to children by online services and Web sites are done following parental consent.

To use the service, .NET Passport users register their children to create Kids .NET Passport accounts. When a child signs in to a participating site, .NET Passport follows a two-stage authentication process. In the first stage, .NET Passport verifies the child's date of birth by using the profile information. In the second stage, if the child is younger than 13, the Kids .NET Passport account is checked to determine whether a consent level has been granted to the site for the child. The Kids .NET Passport account is used to store information such as name, date of birth, and e-mail address. In addition, the account stores information about the sites that can be accessed by children and the associated level of consent for each site.

Kids .NET Passport allows parents and guardians to specify one of three levels of consent for each participating site. Based on the level of consent, the collection and use of personal information related to children is restricted. The consent levels that a parent or guardian can grant to a site are as follows:

◆ *Deny.* The Deny consent level is used to prevent a site from collecting any information from the child. Additionally, this consent might also disable the use of the services offered by a site or the site itself.

NOTE

To implement .NET Passport Single Sign-In (SSI) and the Kids .NET Passport service, each participating site needs to install .NET Passport Manager. .NET Passport Manager is a Component Object Model (COM) object located on the server side that manages the authentication and profile information of the users as they navigate from or within a participating Web site.

One reason why .NET Passport Manager is a COM object is so that not every participating site would be required to have .NET framework components. Besides, the .NET Passport service can easily interoperate with COM components.

◆ *Limited.* The Limited consent level allows participating sites to only collect, store, and use the information collected from the child. This consent level prevents disclosure of the information to other companies or individuals except if necessary for the working of the site or services.

◆ *Full.* The Full consent level allows a site or service to collect, store, use, and disclose the information collected from children.

To use either of these .NET Passport services, a user needs to sign in to a .NET

Passport participating site. A user can do this by clicking on the .NET Passport sign-in link located on the site. When a user clicks the sign-in link, the site redirects the user to the .NET Passport Login server.

When redirecting the user to the .NET Passport Login server, the site sends its site ID. The .NET Passport Login server uses this site ID to verify the site from the list of registered participating Web sites. (See Figure F-1 for this sequence.)

If a matching entry is found, the .NET Passport Login server displays a sign-in page. The participating site can either cobrand the .NET Passport sign-in page or embed a small sign-in module within a page. The user enters .NET Passport credentials on the page. The .NET Passport Login server then authenticates these credentials by using the .NET Passport data-

TIP

When a user authenticated by .NET Passport visits a site where he or she has not signed in, the user needs to click on the .NET Passport sign-in link. The participating site initiates the .NET Passport authentication process. Henceforth, the user can visit any other participating site simply by clicking the sign-in link on the site.

Some users owning a private computer might prefer to be signed in automatically to .NET Passport. To facilitate this, users can store their .NET Passport sign-in name and password on a computer. This option enables users to remain signed in to .NET Passport at all times on the computer where the .NET Passport credentials are stored. However, users with access to a public computer only may choose not to do so.

base. The .NET Passport database stores the credentials and authentication- and profile-related information (such as the PUID) for all the users who have registered for .NET Passport.

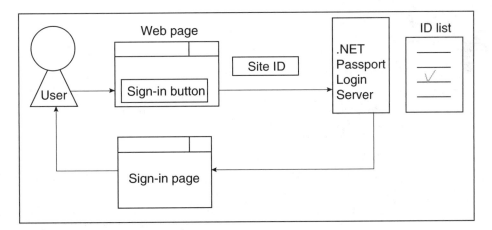

FIGURE F-1 *Stage 1 of the .NET Password authentication process*

Upon locating a matching record in the database, the .NET Passport Login server retrieves the .NET Passport Unique ID (PUID) and the sharable user profile information for the respective user from the database. Figure F-2 shows Stage 2 of the process. This entire process is known as the .NET Passport authentication process.

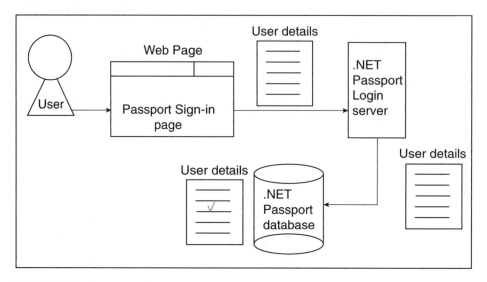

FIGURE F-2 *Stage 2 of the .NET Password authentication process*

Using the information retrieved from the database, the .NET Passport Login server creates three .NET Passport cookies as follows:

◆ Ticket cookie

◆ Profile cookie

◆ Visited Sites cookie

The Ticket cookie stores the PUID and the time stamp when the user was authenticated. All the information related to the user profile is stored in the Profile cookie. The Visited Sites cookie is constantly updated with the names of the sites to which a user signs in.

Next, the data stored in the Ticket and Profile cookies is encrypted by the .NET Passport Login server and sent to the user's browser. From the browser, the information is forwarded to the respective participating site. The participating site sends this information to .NET Passport Manager. At .NET Passport Manager, the information is decrypted to obtain the user's PUID and the profile information. .NET Passport Manager uses the profile information to personalize the content on the Web site based on the user's preferences, as shown in Figure F-3.

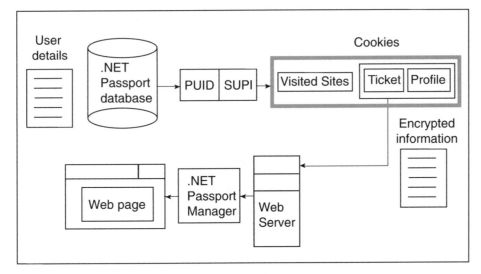

FIGURE F-3 *Stage 3 of the .NET Password authentication process*

The user can now navigate within the site or to other participating sites. When the time specified in the Ticket cookie expires, however, the user is unable to access the participating site. In this case, to resume access to the site, the user needs to sign in to the participating site again. To do so, the user is required to reenter the password. Failure to do so denies .NET Passport services to the user. Additionally, if a user types an incorrect password several times, .NET Passport blocks access to the .NET Passport account.

NOTE

The use of the information related to a .NET Passport user is bound by the privacy policy of the site. The participating site can also store the PUID and the profile information of a user in its own database. In addition, the information can also be written by the site to cookies and stored on the user's computer. Hashing transforms the strings contained in a message into a string of lesser value of a fixed length. This string represents the original string.

To sign out of .NET Passport, the user needs to click the sign-out link placed on the participating Web site. The participating site replaces the sign-in link with a sign-out link after a user has been authenticated. When a user clicks the .NET Passport sign-out link, the .NET Passport server ensures that each participating site visited by the user during the browsing session deletes the cookies placed on the user's computer during sign-in. As such, the cookies placed on the user's computer are deleted when the user ends a Web browsing session. This is not the case, however, when the user signs in automatically to .NET Passport. The cookies can also be set for expiration by .NET Passport or the participating site.

With the widespread and ever-increasing dependence on wireless devices, .NET Passport has been enhanced for use on wireless cell phones and Pocket PC devices. However, not all the features related to .NET Passport are supported on mobile devices. For instance, features such as strong credential sign-in and inline sign-in are not supported on mobile devices because the processing and network capabilities of such devices currently pose a bottleneck to accomplish this.

So far, you've looked at the .NET Passport service and its benefits. You will now look at Visual Studio.NET, the integrated environment for creating applications by using .NET languages.

Visual Studio .NET

Visual Studio.NET provides an integrated development environment that enables you to create solutions for the .NET framework. Visual Studio.NET integrates the best of programming languages in a single interface you can use to develop enterprise-scale Web applications and high-performance desktop applications.

Visual Studio.NET enables you to create a myriad of applications. Some of the applications commonly developed using Visual Studio.NET are as follows:

◆ Console applications
◆ Windows applications
◆ ASP.NET applications
◆ Web services

You can create Web services and applications by using the languages offered by Visual Studio.NET. Visual Studio.NET provides the following programming languages:

◆ Visual Basic.NET
◆ Visual C#

◆ Visual Foxpro

◆ Visual C++.NET

With so many languages to choose from, you might be wondering which language to use for developing applications in Visual Studio.NET. You can use any language from the suite made available by Visual Studio.NET. It is likely that familiarity with a previous version of the language will guide your selection.

In addition to the incorporated feature of the programming languages, Visual Studio.NET includes certain enhanced features of its own. Some of these features are as follows:

◆ Implementation of Web forms

◆ Implementation of Web services

◆ Implementation of Windows forms

◆ Implementation of the project-independent object model

◆ Enhanced debugging

◆ Support for ASP.NET programming

◆ Enhanced IDE

The following sections will elaborate each of these features.

Implementation of Web Forms

Visual Studio.NET provides Web forms to enable you to create Web applications. The applications created using Web forms can be implemented on any browser or mobile device. To ensure compliance across devices, Web forms implement controls that render HTML compliant to the specific browser.

Web forms are implemented as classes that are compiled into DLL(s), thereby ensuring server-side code security.

Implementation of Web Services

Another important feature of Visual Studio.NET is the creation, deployment, and debugging of Web services. The support for Internet standards such as HTTP and XML allows use of Web services across platforms.

Implementation of Windows Forms

Visual Studio.NET supports Windows forms that you can use to create Windows applications for the .NET framework. Windows forms are object oriented and consist of an extensible set of classes. You can implement Windows forms and Windows forms controls to create the presentation tier.

Implementation of Project-Independent Object Model

Visual Studio.NET as a Rapid Application Development tool has various ways to represent IDE tools, the components of a solution, and the information exchange with the developer. Visual Studio.NET implements a project-independent object model to access the components and events of the Visual Studio.NET IDE. This model includes components that represent solutions, projects, tools, code editors, debuggers, code objects, documents, and events. You can use this model through macros, add-ins, wizards, and the Visual Studio.NET Integration Program (VSIP). VSIP is a program that can be used to extend the Visual Studio.NET IDE. This program provides you with additional objects and interfaces to create customized tools, file types, and designers.

Enhanced Debugging

Visual Studio.NET provides an integrated debugger that can be used to debug solutions written in different languages. In addition, you can associate the debugger to a currently executing program. This enables you to debug multiple programs simultaneously. You can also debug multithreaded programs or programs executing on a remote computer.

Support for ASP.NET Programming

An important feature of Visual Studio.NET is support for ASP.NET programming. This support incorporates technologies such as ASP.NET that simplify the design, development, and deployment of business solutions. You can create Web applications by using Visual Studio.NET. You can also use the Visual Studio.NET tools such as Visual Designer for Web pages and code-aware text editors for writing code.

Enhanced IDE

The Visual Studio.NET IDE extends across the programming languages supported by Visual Studio.NET. You can even create customized tools to enhance the capabilities of Visual Studio by creating macros and using the customization features of the IDE. Visual Studio also now enables you to simultaneously debug and troubleshoot a Web application such as an ASP .NET page, along with its corresponding DLLs.

The projects created using Visual Studio.NET are stored in containers for easy manageability and accessibility. Containers are used to store components of applications, such as files and folders. Visual Studio.NET provides two types of containers:

◆ *Project.* A project consists of all the interrelated components of an application.

◆ *Solution.* A solution consists of one or more related projects. A solution container can be used to store projects. You can also implement solutions to apply specific settings and options to multiple projects. To create a project, you can select the New Project button on the Start Page.

When you begin creating a Windows application project from the Start Page, the following components are displayed:

◆ *Windows Forms Designer.* You use the Windows Forms Designer to design the user interface for the application.

◆ *Solution Explorer.* Solution Explorer provides a hierarchical view of application-related information such as project name, solution name, references, and the various files that are a part of the solution.

◆ *The Properties window.* You use the Properties window to view the characteristics associated with an object, such as a text box control on a form.

◆ *Toolbox.* The Toolbox includes multiple tabs. Each tab has a list of items providing functionalities to aid in the creation of applications.

◆ *The Output window.* You use the Output window to view the status of the activities performed by Visual Studio.NET, such as updating references and building satellite assemblies.

◆ *Task List.* You use the Task List to identify the errors detected when applying enterprise template policies, editing code, or compiling code. Other features include user notes for the solution.

◆ *Server Explorer.* You use the Server Explorer to view information related to the servers available on the network. In addition, Server Explorer enables you to perform administrative tasks.

◆ *The Dynamic Help window.* You use the Dynamic Help window to view a context-specific list of help topics.

◆ *The Component tray.* You use the Component tray to view the invisible controls (such as OleDbDataAdapter) in an application and to modify these while creating the application.

◆ *The Class View window.* You use the Class View window to view the classes, methods, and properties associated with a solution.

◆ *Code and Text Editor.* The Code and Text Editor provides you with word-processing capabilities that enable you to enter and edit code and text.

Index

A